Guide on the Convention on the Recognition and Enforcement of Foreign Arbitral Awards

United Nations
UNCITRAL

Guide on the Convention on the Recognition and Enforcement of Foreign Arbitral Awards

New York, 1958

UNCITRAL Secretariat

Emmanuel Gaillard and George A. Bermann, Editors

TUTA SUB AEGIDE PALLAS · 1683 ·

BRILL
NIJHOFF

LEIDEN | BOSTON

This book may be cited as: THE UNCITRAL SECRETARIAT GUIDE ON THE NEW YORK CONVENTION (E. Gaillard and G. Bermann eds., Spec. ed., Brill Nijhoff, 2017).

This English language hard cover volume is based on the UNCITRAL Secretariat Guide on the Convention on the Recognition and Enforcement of Foreign Arbitral Awards (New York, 1958) (the "UNCITRAL Guide").

The publication of the UNCITRAL Guide was requested by UNCITRAL in 2014, on the understanding that "The Guide" is a product of the work of the Secretariat based on expert input, and was not substantively discussed by the United Nations Commission on International Trade Law (UNCITRAL). Accordingly, the Guide does not purport to reflect the views or opinions of UNCITRAL member States and does not constitute an official interpretation of the New York Convention.

Nothing in this volume alters the rights of UNCITRAL in relation to the publication, distribution and editing of the UNCITRAL Guide, or in relation to any subsequent amendments to or translations of the UNCITRAL Guide published by UNCITRAL in any language.

Library of Congress Control Number: 2017941100

ISBN 978-90-04-35193-6 (hardback)
ISBN 978-90-04-35194-3 (e-book)

This book is printed on acid-free paper and produced in a sustainable manner.

Contents

United Nations
UNCITRAL

UNCITRAL Secretary Foreword

The New York Convention is rightly celebrated as the most significant international instrument for the recognition and enforcement of arbitral awards. For the past fifty years, UNCITRAL, whose origin and mandate partly result from the diplomatic process that culminated in the adoption of the New York Convention, has adopted several important legal standards that offer a comprehensive substantive-law framework for out-of-court settlement of business and investment disputes. UNCITRAL has also crafted a number of tools to facilitate a thorough understanding of the legal standards it develops and promotes, and to assist with their uniform interpretation and application. The project of preparing such a tool in relation to the New York Convention has been on the agenda of UNCITRAL since 2007, when the General Assembly requested the Secretary-General to increase efforts to promote wider adherence to the Convention, its uniform interpretation and effective implementation. The UNCITRAL Secretariat Guide on the New York Convention has been prepared to fulfil that request.

I would like to express my deep gratitude to the experts, Professors Emmanuel Gaillard and George Bermann for their essential contributions to the UNCITRAL Secretariat Guide on the New York Convention, and to their research teams, who assembled and reviewed a wealth of materials, including the vast bibliography and numerous court decisions available on the Convention. A special word of thanks is also well deserved by Ms. Yas Banifatemi for developing an online platform in support of the Guide.

This ambitious project would not have been brought to fruition without the participation of large numbers of contributors in many parts of the world, who keep us abreast of developments in their region. Our Secretariat is grateful for their continued support to the work of UNCITRAL, and to that project in particular. It is anticipated that the online platform associated with the Guide will be regularly updated through the addition of new materials, and the coverage of new jurisdictions in the project.

May the launch of this edition of the Guide at a time when UNCITRAL celebrates its 50th anniversary contribute to increased awareness of the New York Convention, and better understanding of the benefits which modern trade law, including means for the peaceful settlement of disputes, may yield as tools for development, peace and security, in line with the sustainable development agenda pursued by the United Nations.

Renaud Sorieul, The Secretary of UNCITRAL

1958 NEW YORK CONVENTION GUIDE

Experts' Foreword

We are delighted to see the publication of the UNCITRAL Secretariat Guide on the New York Convention, which is the culmination of years of dedicated research on the Convention's interpretation and application in its Contracting States. The New York Convention has served as the cornerstone of the international arbitration system from its signature in 1958 until the present day and continues to structure international arbitration on a worldwide basis.

This Guide was conceived with no particular views on how courts of the Contracting States should apply the New York Convention. The goal of the Guide was instead to canvass the richness of national case law on the Convention in an objective manner. To lay the groundwork for the Guide, research teams at Shearman & Sterling and Columbia University gathered, analyzed and translated Convention case law in order to identify the key trends in how each of its articles has been interpreted and applied in practice. The materials gathered from an initial 15 civil law and common law jurisdictions grew as contributors to the project provided case law and information on the implementation of the Convention from a further 30 jurisdictions.

The final version of the Guide provides a detailed analysis of the judicial interpretation and application of the New York Convention by reference to case law from 45 Contracting States. The Guide, and the newyorkconvention1958.org website which supplements it, will become an essential tool that benefits all those involved in the interpretation and application of the New York Convention, including judges, arbitrators, practitioners, academics and Government officials.

The following pages of the Guide give clear expression to the principal finding of our research, namely, that the Contracting States have interpreted and applied the New York Convention in an overwhelmingly consistent manner and that courts have diverged from the general trends in the case law in only isolated instances. As such, the Convention continues to fulfill its purpose of facilitating the worldwide recognition and enforcement of arbitral awards to the greatest extent possible.

Emmanuel Gaillard, Head of International Arbitration, Shearman & Sterling;
Visiting Professor of Law, Yale Law School

George Bermann, Professor of Law, Columbia Law School

The NewYorkConvention1958.org website

In 2012, Shearman & Sterling and Columbia Law School launched, in cooperation with UNCITRAL, the newyorkconvention1958.org website. It is the product of a coordinated effort to create an interactive online platform that makes information gathered during the preparation of the Guide on the New York Convention publicly available.

The new version of the website, launched on 8 July 2016, complements the Guide through its sophisticated global legal database. Today, this website goes beyond its initial objective and endeavors to collect and share new data published worldwide on the application and interpretation of the New York Convention.

Thanks to our numerous and dedicated contributors, the website makes accessible more than 1200 cases from a wide number of common law and civil law jurisdictions. It offers free access to those decisions in their original language, as well as more than a hundred English translations.

The 23 chapters of the Guide are available in all official languages of the United Nations and include direct links from the Guide to the original case law and *travaux préparatoires* discussed therein.

The website also offers access to the largest bibliography ever consolidated on the New York Convention. The bibliography has more than 800 references, over 200 of which have links to publicly accessible online versions.

Additionally, the website includes jurisdiction briefs providing essential information relating to the implementation of the New York Convention in its Contracting States. It also provides an interactive signatories' map and the latest news on the New York Convention.

The website's design has been upgraded into an intuitive user-friendly interface. It allows better compatibility with search engines and devices, including tablets and smartphones.

The newyorkconvention1958.org website is a unique tool that puts technology at the service of scientific research and legal analysis to the benefit of its users. The search engine allows users to tailor their research to any parameters they wish. By making all of the above material fully searchable by key words run through the entirety of the platform's data, users can conduct a variety of searches by jurisdiction(s) and by New York Convention article(s) through its case law, *travaux préparatoires*, bibliography and chapters of the Guide.

In the months to come, the website will offer information on the application of the New York Convention in additional jurisdictions in order to offer users as wide and representative a view of judicial practice in this field as possible and increase opportunities to perform personal tailored research on that basis.

The newyorkconvention1958.org website strives to become an essential efficient tool to every judge, arbitrator, practitioner, academic, student and Government official interested in the interpretation and application of the New York Convention.

We encourage each and every one to participate in this universal Project. Documents, decisions, or any other relevant information on signatory States to the New York Convention can be shared with our research assistants' team through the "Contribute" page of the website, for the benefit of all.

Dr. Yas Banifatemi, Executive Director and Coordinator
Head of Public International Law, Shearman & Sterling

Preface

From the Final Act of the United Nations Conference on International Commercial Arbitration of 10 June 1958 to General Assembly resolution 62/65 of 6 December 2007

1. The New York Convention on the Recognition and Enforcement of Foreign Arbitral Awards (the "New York Convention" or the "Convention") is one of the most important and successful United Nations treaties in the area of international trade law. Although the Convention, adopted by diplomatic conference on 10 June 1958, was prepared by the United Nations prior to the establishment of the United Nations Commission on International Trade Law (UNCITRAL), promotion of the Convention is an integral part of the work programme of UNCITRAL. The Convention is widely recognized as a foundational instrument of international arbitration and requires courts of Contracting States to give effect to an agreement to arbitrate when seized of an action in a matter covered by an arbitration agreement and also to recognize and enforce awards made in other States, subject to specific limited exceptions. The Convention entered into force on 7 June 1959, and there are to date 156 States parties to the Convention.

2. The General Assembly adopted on 6 December 2007 resolution 62/65 in which it recognized the value of arbitration as a method of settling disputes in international commercial relations in a manner that contributes to harmonious commercial relations, stimulates international trade and development, and promotes the rule of law at the international and national levels. The General Assembly expressed its conviction that the New York Convention strengthens respect for binding commitments, inspires confidence in the rule of law and ensures fair treatment in the resolution of disputes arising over contractual rights and obligations. It emphasized the necessity for further national efforts to achieve universal adherence to the Convention, together with its uniform interpretation and effective implementation. The General Assembly expressed its hope that States that are not yet parties to the Convention would soon become parties to it, which would ensure that the legal certainty afforded by the Convention is universally enjoyed, and would decrease the level of risk and transactional costs associated with doing business, thus promoting international trade.

3. The General Assembly requested the Secretary-General to increase efforts to promote wider adherence to the Convention and its uniform interpretation and effective implementation. The UNCITRAL Secretariat Guide on the New York Convention (the "Guide on the New York

Convention" or the "Guide") has been prepared with the aim to fulfil that request.

Promoting uniform interpretation of UNCITRAL instruments

4. UNCITRAL, in accordance with its mandate, has undertaken the preparation of the tools necessary for a thorough understanding of the instruments it develops and for their uniform interpretation.

5. One of these instruments, the website www.newyorkconvention1958.org, has been established by Shearman & Sterling LLP, The Columbia Law School and UNCITRAL in order to make the information gathered in preparation of the Guide on the New York Convention publicly available. The site contains an electronic version of the Guide in all official languages of the United Nations, a significant corpus of judicial interpretation of the New York Convention by States Parties, information on the ratification of the Convention, the *travaux préparatoires*, as well as a bibliography, that is a comprehensive directory of publications relating to the application and interpretation of the Convention. This website provides legislators, judges, practitioners, parties and academics with a wealth of information that is dynamic and ever-growing. It offers an interactivity between contents and an indexing that enables the various elements of the site to link to one another, in a unique canvas. The search engine of the website allows a thorough search among the decisions, and enables searching the Guide, the *travaux préparatoires*, the case law and the bibliography. In relation to each case, it contains the full text of the decision, a translation of the decision in English where relevant, as well as a summary of the cases. It supplements the cases collected in the CLOUT (Case Law on UNCITRAL Texts) database and serves as a primary reference tool underlying the Guide on the New York Convention.

6. The Guide on the New York Convention presents the information on the Convention by article. Each section contains a synopsis of the relevant case law for the relevant article, highlighting common views and reporting any divergent approach. The Guide was prepared using the decisions cited in the website www.newyorkconvention1958.org as well as other decisions, fully cited in the footnotes.

7. The Guide on the New York Convention does not constitute an independent authority indicating the interpretation to be given to individual provisions but rather serves as a reference tool collating a wide range of decisions from a number of jurisdictions. The purpose of the Guide is to assist in the dissemination of information on the New York Convention and further promote its adoption as well as its uniform interpretation and

effective implementation. In addition, the Guide is meant to help judges, arbitrators, practitioners, academics and Government officials use more efficiently the case law relating to the Convention.

Introduction

1. The Convention on the Recognition and Enforcement of Foreign Arbitral Awards was adopted by the United Nations following a diplomatic conference held in May and June 1958 at the United Nations Headquarters in New York.[1] The New York Convention entered into force on 7 June 1959.[2] At the date of this Guide, the Convention has 156 Contracting States.[3]

2. UNCITRAL considers the New York Convention to be one of the most important United Nations treaties in the area of international trade law and the cornerstone of the international arbitration system.[4] Since its inception, the Convention's regime for recognition and enforcement has become deeply rooted in the legal systems of its Contracting States and has contributed to the status of international arbitration as today's normal means of resolving commercial disputes.

3. States adhering to the New York Convention undertake to give effect to an agreement to arbitrate when seized of an action in a matter covered by an arbitration agreement, and to recognize and enforce awards made in other States, subject to specific limited exceptions.

4. By imposing stricter rules on recognition and enforcement of foreign arbitral awards, a Contracting State will breach its obligations under the Convention. This principle is reflected in article III, which grants Contracting States the discretion to determine the applicable rules for recognition and enforcement so long as, in doing so, they do not impose "substantially more onerous conditions or higher fees or charges on the recognition or enforcement of arbitral awards [...] than are imposed on the recognition or enforcement of domestic arbitral awards."

The New York Convention sets a maximum level of control at the recognition and enforcement stage

5. The conditions for recognition and enforcement in the Convention establish a "ceiling", or maximum level of control, which Contracting States may exert over arbitral awards and arbitration agreements. On the other hand, Contracting States are free to apply more liberal rules than those set

[1] United Nations, Treaty Series, vol. 330, No. 4739; UN DOC E/CONF.26/SR. 1-25, Summary Records of the United Nations Conference on International Commercial Arbitration, New York, 20 May - 10 June 1958.

[2] New York Convention, article XII.

[3] The current status of the New York Convention is available on the UNCITRAL website.

[4] See Renaud Sorieul, The Secretary of UNCITRAL, on the 1958 New York Convention Guide website [available at http://newyorkconvention1958.org].

forth in the Convention. The Convention's aim is not to limit the pre-existing freedom of the Contracting States to treat foreign arbitral awards or arbitration agreements as favourably as they please, but rather to facilitate their recognition and enforcement to the greatest extent possible.

6. The New York Convention's pro-enforcement policy is enshrined at article VII (1), which is considered to be one of its cornerstones.[5] Known as the "more-favourable-right" provision, article VII (1) provides that, in addition to the Convention, a party seeking recognition and enforcement shall not be deprived of the right to rely on a more favourable domestic law or treaty. In accordance with article VII (1), a Contracting State will not be in breach of the Convention by enforcing arbitral awards and arbitration agreements pursuant to more liberal regimes than the Convention itself.

7. The New York Convention therefore exists as a safeguard which guarantees a minimum standard of liberalism in its Contracting States, but which does not need to be applied. Today, in some of the most pro-arbitration jurisdictions, the number of cases referring to Convention is scarce precisely because the ordinary rules governing the recognition and enforcement of awards are more liberal and, in accordance with article VII (1), routinely applied without any need to refer to the Convention.[6]

The New York Convention contains its own mechanism for adapting to the development of international arbitration

8. While the New York Convention is undoubtedly the most significant international instrument for the recognition and enforcement of arbitral awards, it does not operate in isolation. In some circumstances, other international treaties, or the domestic law of the country where enforcement is sought, will also apply to the question of whether a foreign arbitral award should be recognized and enforced.

9. The genius of the New York Convention is to have foreseen, and made provision for, the progressive liberalization of the law of international arbitration. Article VII (1), which governs the relationship between the Convention and other applicable treaties and laws, derogates from the rules that normally govern the application of conflicting provisions of treaties, and provides that in the event that more than one regime might apply, the rule

---

[5] One commentator has described this provision as the "treasure, the ingenious idea" of the New York Convention. See Philippe Fouchard, *Suggestions pour accroître l'efficacité internationale des sentences arbitrales*, 1998 REV. ARB. 653, 663.

[6] See Dominique Hascher, *Les perspectives françaises sur le contrôle de la sentence internationale ou étrangère*, I (2) MCGILL JOURNAL OF DISPUTE RESOLUTION 1 (2015).

which shall prevail is neither the more recent nor the more specific, but instead that which is more favourable to the recognition and enforcement.[7]

10. While in recent years, some important scholars have suggested that the time has come to initiate a revision of the New York Convention,[8] there is no danger in leaving the Convention in its current form.[9] Article VII (1), which will grow in importance with the continued modernization of national arbitration laws, ensures that the Convention cannot freeze the development of international arbitration. It is this provision which has allowed courts in the Contracting States to advance many of the most important innovations underpinning the modern system of international arbitration. The Convention therefore possesses the necessary tools to ensure its durability while permitting the courts of Contracting States to continually improve upon it.

The New York Convention has been applied in a consistent manner

11. This Guide serves as a reference tool that collates a wide range of decisions on the New York Convention and analyses extensively how courts of Contracting States interpret and apply its provisions.

12. The practices highlighted in the following chapters demonstrate that, despite the diversity of the Contracting States' legal systems, the interpretation and application of the Convention has been rather consistent and in conformity with the Convention's policy of favouring recognition and enforcement. Many Contracting States which first adhered to a more interventionist approach to international arbitration have, in accordance with obligations undertaken under the Convention, moved towards a liberal regime that limits court control over the arbitral process.

13. Almost 60 years after its creation, the New York Convention continues to fulfil its objective of facilitating the recognition and enforcement of foreign arbitral awards, and in the years to come, will

---

[7] See the comments of the Swiss Federal Supreme Court in *Denysiana S.A. v. Jassica S.A.*, March 14, 1984, Arrêts du Tribunal Fédéral 110 Ib 191, 194, describing that article VII (1) enshrines the principle of maximum effectiveness ("*règle d'efficacité maximale*").

[8] See, in particular, Pieter Sanders, *A Twenty Years' Review of the Convention on the Recognition and Enforcement of Foreign Arbitral Awards*, 13 INT'L LAW 269 (1979); Jan Paulsson, *Towards Minimum Standards of Enforcement: Feasibility of a Model Law*, in IMPROVING YHE EFFICIENCY OF ARBITRATION AGREEMENTS AND AWARDS: 40 YEARS OF APPLICATION OF THE NEW YORK CONVENTION 574 (A.J. van den Berg ed., 1998); Albert Jan van den Berg, *Hypothetical Draft Convention on the International Enforcement of Arbitration Agreements and Awards*, AJB Rev 06 (May 2008).

[9] See Emmanuel Gaillard, *The Urgency of Not Revising the New York Convention*, in 50 YEARS OF THE NEW YORK CONVENTION: ICCA INTERNATIONAL ARBITRATION CONFERENCE 689 (A.J. van den Berg ed., 2009); see also V.V. Veeder, *Is There a Need to Revise the New York Convention?*, in THE REVIEW OF INTERNATIONAL ARBITRAL AWARDS, IAI SERIES ON INTERNATIONAL ARBITRATION NO. 6, 183 (2010).

guarantee the continued growth of international arbitration and create conditions in which cross-border economic exchanges can flourish.

Article I

1. This Convention shall apply to the recognition and enforcement of arbitral awards made in the territory of a State other than the State where the recognition and enforcement of such awards are sought, and arising out of differences between persons, whether physical or legal. It shall also apply to arbitral awards not considered as domestic awards in the State where their recognition and enforcement are sought.

2. The term "arbitral awards" shall include not only awards made by arbitrators appointed for each case but also those made by permanent arbitral bodies to which the parties have submitted.

3. When signing, ratifying or acceding to this Convention, or notifying extension under article X hereof, any State may on the basis of reciprocity declare that it will apply the Convention to the recognition and enforcement of awards made only in the territory of another Contracting State. It may also declare that it will apply the Convention only to differences arising out of legal relationships, whether contractual or not, which are considered as commercial under the national law of the State making such declaration.

Travaux préparatoires

The *travaux préparatoires* on article I as adopted in 1958 are contained in the following documents:

Draft Convention on the Recognition and Enforcement of Foreign Arbitral Awards and comments by Governments and Organizations:

Report of the Committee on the Enforcement of International Arbitral Awards: E/2704 and annex.

Comments by Governments and Organizations on the Draft Convention on the Recognition and Enforcement of Foreign Arbitral Awards: E/2822, annexes I-II; E/2822/Add.1, annex I; E/2822/Add.2, annex I; E/2822/ Add.4, annex I; E/2822/Add.5, annex I; E/2822/Add.6, annex I; E/CONF. 26/3; E/CONF.26/3/Add.1.

Activities of Inter-Governmental and Non-Governmental Organizations in the Field of International Commercial Arbitration: Consolidated Report by the Secretary-General: E/CONF.26/4.

Comments on the Draft Convention on the Recognition and Enforcement of Foreign Arbitral Awards: Note by the Secretary-General: E/CONF. 26/2.

United Nations Conference on International Commercial Arbitration:

Amendments to the Draft Convention Submitted by Governmental Delegations: E/CONF.26/7; E/CONF.26/L.6; E/CONF.26/L.7; E/CONF.26/L.8/Corr.1; E/CONF.26/L.9; E/CONF.26/L.9/Rev.1; E/CONF.26/L.10; E/CONF.26/L.10/Rev.1; E/CONF.26/L.12; E/CONF.26/L.13; E/CONF.26/L.14; E/CONF.26/L.16; E/CONF.26/C.1/L.1; E/CONF.26/C.1/L.2; E/CONF.26/L.26; E/CONF.26/L.27; E/CONF.26/L.28; E/CONF. 26/L.29; E/CONF.26/L. 29/Corr. 1; E/CONF.26/C.1/L.6.

Further Amendments to the Draft Convention Submitted by Governmental Delegations: E/CONF.26/L.41.

Report of Working Party I: E/CONF.26/L.42; E/CONF.26/L.49.

Text of Articles Adopted by the Conference: E/CONF.26/L.46; E/CONF.26/L.58.

Text of the Convention on the Recognition and Enforcement of Foreign Arbitral Awards as Provisionally Approved by Drafting Committee: E/CONF.26/L.61; E/CONF.26/8.

New Text of Articles I (3), V(1)*(a), (b)*, and *(e)* Adopted by the Conference at its 23rd Meeting: E/CONF.26/L.63.

Summary records:

Summary Records of the Fifth, Sixth, Seventh, Eighth, Ninth, Fifteenth, Sixteenth, Twenty-first, Twenty-third and Twenty-fourth Meetings of the United Nations Conference on International Commercial Arbitration: E/CONF.26/SR.5; E/CONF.26/SR.6; E/CONF.26/SR.7; E/CONF.26/SR.8; E/CONF.26/SR.9; E/CONF.26/SR.15; E/CONF.26/SR.16; E/CONF.26/SR.21; E/CONF.26/SR.23; E/CONF.26/SR.24.

Summary Record of the Second Meeting of the Committee on the Enforcement of International Arbitral Awards: E/AC.42/SR.2.

Summary Record of the Third Meeting of the Committee on the Enforcement of International Arbitral Awards: E/AC.42/SR.3.

(Available on the Internet at http://www.uncitral.org)
(For the *travaux préparatoires*, case law and bibliographical references, see also on the Internet at http://newyorkconvention1958.org)

Introduction

1. Article I sets out in broad terms the scope of the New York Convention.[10] Article I (1) provides that the New York Convention applies to the recognition and enforcement of arbitral awards "made in the territory of a State other than the State where the recognition and enforcement of such awards are sought, and arising out of differences between persons, whether physical or legal". It also states that the New York Convention applies to awards that are "not considered as domestic awards in the State where their recognition and enforcement are sought". Article I (2) provides that the term "arbitral awards" shall include not only awards made by arbitrators appointed for each case but also those made by permanent arbitral bodies to which the parties have submitted". Finally, article I (3) allows each Contracting State, when signing, ratifying or acceding to the Convention, to restrict the scope of application of the Convention by making the reservations allowed by the Convention. The first reservation, known as the "reciprocity reservation", allows a State to apply the Convention only to awards made in the territory of another Contracting State. The second reservation, known as the "commercial reservation", allows a State to apply the Convention only to "differences arising out of legal relationships, whether contractual or not, which are considered as commercial under the national law of the State making such declaration".

---

[10] Although article I does not refer to arbitration agreements, such agreements fall within the scope of the Convention. Because article II was a late addition, neither article I nor the other provisions of the Convention were modified to reflect this addition. See the chapter of the Guide on article II, paras. 2-3.

2. Article I of the New York Convention "marks a clear departure" from the Geneva Convention on the Execution of Foreign Arbitral Awards of 1927 (the "1927 Geneva Convention") in two respects.[11]

3. First, article I gives the New York Convention a broader scope than the 1927 Geneva Convention. Pursuant to article I (1), the New York Convention applies to awards made in any foreign State, irrespective of whether that State is a Contracting State.[12] During the United Nations Conference on International Commercial Arbitration convened for the preparation and adoption of the Convention ("the Conference"), it was noted that maintaining the wording of the 1927 Geneva Convention, which provided for enforcement of only those awards that were made in a Contracting State, could give rise to the "paradoxical" situation where the award creditor and award debtor are both nationals of Contracting States, but the award cannot be enforced under the Convention because the State in which the award was made is not a party to the Convention.[13] To avoid such a situation, the drafters of the New York Convention discarded the mandatory reciprocity requirement contained in the 1927 Geneva Convention and replaced it with an opt-in reciprocity reservation at article I (3).

4. Second, the 1927 Geneva Convention applied only to arbitral awards that were rendered in proceedings "between persons who are subject to the jurisdiction of one of the High Contracting Parties".[14] Considering this requirement to be "vague and ambiguous", [15] the *ad hoc* Committee established by the United Nations Economic and Social Council (the "ECOSOC *ad hoc* Committee") removed it from the 1955 draft Convention. The Yugoslav delegate then suggested that the requirement be reinstated,[16] but this proposal was expressly rejected by the other delegates, thereby

---

[11] *Gas Authority of India Ltd. v. Spie Capag SA and others*, High Court of Delhi, India, 15 October 1993, Suit No. 1440, IA No. 5206.

[12] Javier Rubinstein, Georgina Fabian, *The Territorial Scope of the New York Convention and Its Implementation in Common and Civil Law Countries*, in ENFORCEMENT OF ARBITRATION AGREEMENTS AND INTERNATIONAL ARBITRAL AWARDS: THE NEW YORK CONVENTION IN PRACTICE 91, 95 (E. Gaillard, D. Di Pietro eds., 2008).

[13] *Travaux préparatoires*, Recognition and Enforcement of Foreign Arbitral Awards, Report by the Secretary-General, Annex II, Comments by Non-Governmental Organizations, E/2822, p. 8.

[14] See article 1 of the 1927 Geneva Convention. See also *Travaux préparatoires*, United Nations Conference on International Commercial Arbitration, Comments on the Draft Convention on the Recognition and Enforcement of Foreign Arbitral Awards, Note by the Secretary-General, E/CONF.26/2, p. 2.

[15] *Travaux préparatoires*, Report of the Committee on the Enforcement of International Arbitral Awards, E/2704, E/AC.42/4/Rev.1., p. 7.

[16] *Travaux préparatoires*, United Nations Conference on International Commercial Arbitration, Consideration of the Draft Convention on the Recognition and Enforcement of Foreign Arbitral Awards, E/CONF.26/L.12. See also *Travaux préparatoires*, United Nations Conference on International Commercial Arbitration, Summary Record of the Sixteenth Meeting, E/CONF.26/SR.16, p. 6.

indicating that, unlike in the case of the 1927 Geneva Convention, the scope of application of the New York Convention does not depend on the nationality or residence of the parties to the arbitration proceedings.[17]

5. Article I, like the rest of the Convention, was drafted with the aim of "going further than the Geneva Convention in facilitating the enforcement of foreign arbitral awards".[18] By making the reciprocity requirement optional and doing away with the nationality or residence requirement, article I ensures that the New York Convention has a broad scope of application.

Analysis

Article I (1)

A. Meaning of "recognition and enforcement"

6. Pursuant to article I (1), the New York Convention applies to the "recognition and enforcement" of awards which fall within its scope. The Convention does not apply to court actions seeking to set aside awards or to stay ongoing arbitration proceedings.

a. Defining and distinguishing "recognition" and "enforcement"

7. The New York Convention does not define the terms "recognition" and "enforcement" and case law interpreting these terms is scarce. Of the few reported cases, a Colombian court has held that, while "recognition" concerns recognizing the legal force and effect of an award, "enforcement" concerns the forced execution of an award previously recognized by the same State.[19]

8. Commentators are in broad agreement that "recognition" refers to the process of considering an arbitral award as binding but not necessarily

---

[17] The nationality or residence may, however, play a role in the context of "non-domestic awards". An enforcing court may deem an award rendered in its territory "non-domestic" if one or both parties to arbitration are foreign or reside abroad. It should be noted that, in this regard, the nationality is used to enlarge the scope of the Convention, rather than to restrict it. See below paras. 53-55. See also ALBERT JAN VAN DEN BERG, THE NEW YORK ARBITRATION CONVENTION OF 1958: TOWARDS A UNIFORM JUDICIAL INTERPRETATION 15 (1981); GEORGIOS PETROCHILOS, PROCEDURAL LAW IN INTERNATIONAL ARBITRATION 360, para. 8.54 (2004).

[18] *Travaux préparatoires*, Report of the Committee on the Enforcement of International Arbitral Awards, E/2704, E/AC.42/4/Rev.1., p. 5.

[19] *Drummond Ltd. v. Ferrovias en Liquidación, Ferrocariles Nacionales de Colombia S.A.* (FENOCO), Supreme Court of Justice, Colombia, 19 December 2011, 11001-0203-000-2008-01760-00. As regards the meaning of "enforcement", see also *Pavan s.r.l. v. Leng d'Or, S.A.*, Court of First Instance, Spain, 11 June 2007, 584/06, XXXV Y.B. COM. ARB. 444 (2010).

enforceable, while "enforcement" refers to the process of giving effect to an award.[20]

9. A closely related issue to that of the definition of the terms "recognition" and "enforcement" is whether a party must seek recognition and enforcement together or whether it can independently seek the recognition of an award.

10. In a 1981 decision, the German Supreme Court construed "recognition and enforcement" to mean that the two actions were interrelated and could not be sought separately.[21]

11. Courts from other jurisdictions have considered that recognition can be requested on its own. For example, the Indian Supreme Court held that recognition may be requested "as a shield against re-agitation of issues with which the award deals".[22] The same court found that the successful party to an award could rely on the award where proceedings were brought against it in respect of a matter which had already been dealt with in the award.

12. Similarly, courts from other jurisdictions, including Portugal[23] and the United States,[24] have held that recognition can be sought separately from enforcement.

13. This approach finds support in the *travaux préparatoires* to the Convention[25] and in commentary.[26]

---

[20] Javier Rubinstein, Georgina Fabian, *The Territorial Scope of the New York Convention and Its Implementation in Common and Civil Law Countries*, in ENFORCEMENT OF ARBITRATION AGREEMENTS AND INTERNATIONAL ARBITRAL AWARDS: THE NEW YORK CONVENTION IN PRACTICE 91, 93 (E. Gaillard, D. Di Pietro eds., 2008); Bernd Ehle, *Commentary on Article I*, in NEW YORK ARBITRATION CONVENTION ON THE RECOGNITION AND ENFORCEMENT OF FOREIGN ARBITRAL AWARDS OF 10 JUNE 1958 – COMMENTARY 26, 77 (R. Wolff ed., 2012).

[21] *Compagnia Italiana di Assicurazioni (COMITAS) S.p.A., Società di Assicurazioni Gia Mutua Marittima Nazionale (MUTUAMAR) S.p.A. and others v. Schwartzmeer und Ostsee Versicherungsaktiengesellschaft* (SOVAG), Bundesgerichtshof [BGH], Germany, 8 October 1981, VIII Y.B. COM. ARB. 366 (1983).

[22] *Brace Transport Corporation* of *Monrovia, Bermuda v. Orient Middle East Lines Ltd. and others*, Supreme Court, India, 12 October 1993, Civil Appeals Nos 5438-39 of 1993.

[23] Évora Court of Appeal, Portugal, 31 January 2008, 1141/06-2.

[24] *Yusuf Ahmed Alghanim & Sons, W.L.L. v. Toys "R" Us, Inc.*, Court of Appeals, Second Circuit, United States of America, 10 September 1997, 126 F.3d 15.

[25] *Travaux préparatoires*, Committee on the Enforcement of International Arbitral Awards, Summary Record of the First Meeting, E/AC.42/SR.1, p.7. Commenting on the title of an early draft proposed by the ICC, the delegate of Belgium remarked that the purpose of the Convention "would be made clearer" if the title of the ICC draft was amended to refer to "recognition and enforcement of arbitral awards", rather than referring to the enforcement of awards only.

b. *Non-applicability of the Convention to setting aside proceedings*

14. The Convention does not apply to setting aside proceedings. This has been confirmed by national courts. For instance, a Hong Kong court has held *obiter* that "various decisions have made clear that the Convention is not applicable for setting aside awards".[27] Similarly, numerous United States decisions have noted that while a petitioner's request for recognition of an award was properly brought under the New York Convention, a respondent's cross-motion to set aside the award was governed by domestic law on arbitration and not the New York Convention.[28]

15. In the same vein, French courts[29] and Indian courts[30] have held that the New York Convention does not apply to setting aside applications.

16. Commentators are in agreement that the New York Convention does not apply to an application to set aside an award.[31]

---

[26] FOUCHARD GAILLARD GOLDMAN ON INTERNATIONAL COMMERCIAL ARBITRATION 966, para. 1667 (E. Gaillard, J. Savage eds., 1999). See also Javier Rubinstein, Georgina Fabian, *The Territorial Scope of the New York Convention and Its Implementation in Common and Civil Law Countries*, in ENFORCEMENT OF ARBITRATION AGREEMENTS AND INTERNATIONAL ARBITRAL AWARDS: THE NEW YORK CONVENTION IN PRACTICE 91, 93 (E. Gaillard, D. Di Pietro eds., 2008); ALBERT JAN VAN DEN BERG, THE NEW YORK ARBITRATION CONVENTION OF 1958: TOWARDS A UNIFORM JUDICIAL INTERPRETATION 243-45 (1981).

[27] *Shenzhen Nan Da Industrial and Trade United Co. Ltd. v. FM International Ltd.* [HK], High Court, Supreme Court of Hong Kong, Hong Kong, 2 March 1992, 1991 No. MP 1249.

[28] *Yusuf Ahmed Alghanim & Sons, W.L.L. v. Toys "R" Us, Inc.*, Court of Appeals, Second Circuit, United States of America, 10 September 1997, 126 F.3d 15. See also *Federal Insurance Company, as subrogee* of *Transammonia, Inc. v. Bergesen D.Y. ASA OSLO, as agents of the Norwegian Flag LP G/C "Hugo N" and its owner, General Gas Carrier Corporation, Limited*, District Court, Southern District of New York, United States of America, 7 September 2012, 12 Civ. 3851 (PAE); *ESCO Corporation v. Bradken Resources PTY Ltd.*, District Court, District of Oregon, Portland Division, United States of America, 31 January 2011, 10-788-AC.

[29] *SNC Facciano Giuseppe v.* Société *Coopérative Agricole Nouricia*, Court of Appeal of Paris, France, 9 June 2011, 10/11062. See also *Commandement des Forces Aériennes de la République Islamique d'Iran v. Société Bendone Derossi International Limited Partnership*, Court of Cassation, France, 5 May 1987, 85-13.162; *Société Maatschappij Voor Industriele Research en Ontwikkeling v. M. Lievremont et autres*, Court of Cassation, France, 25 May 1983, 82-11.699; *General National Maritime Transport Company v. Société Götaverken Arendal A.B.*, Court of Appeal of Paris, France, 21 February 1980.

[30] See, e.g., *Compagnie Saint Gobain Pont-à-Mousson v. Fertilizer Corporation* of *India Ltd.*, High Court of Delhi, India, 28 August 1970, ILR 1970 Delhi 927.

[31] ALBERT JAN VAN DEN BERG, THE NEW YORK ARBITRATION CONVENTION OF 1958: TOWARDS A UNIFORM JUDICIAL INTERPRETATION 20 (1981); Javier Rubinstein, Georgina Fabian, *The Territorial Scope of the New York Convention and Its Implementation in Common and Civil Law Countries*, in ENFORCEMENT OF ARBITRATION AGREEMENTS AND INTERNATIONAL ARBITRAL AWARDS: THE NEW YORK CONVENTION IN PRACTICE 91, 94 (E. Gaillard, D. Di Pietro eds., 2008).

c. *Non-applicability of the Convention to actions to stay arbitration proceedings*

17. The Convention does not apply to actions to stay arbitration proceedings. This has been confirmed by the scarce case law that exists on this issue. A United States court has held that the New York Convention makes "no mention of actions to restrain a pending or ongoing arbitration" and that, on that basis, the Convention does not apply to actions to stay arbitration proceedings.[32]

B. Meaning of "arbitral awards"

18. The Convention does not define "arbitral awards". During the negotiation of article I, the Austrian delegate noted that "it will depend on the law of the State in which an award is to be enforced whether a particular decision is to be regarded as an arbitral award".[33] This suggests that it is up to the courts of the Contracting States where recognition and enforcement is sought to determine when a decision can be characterized as an "arbitral award" under the New York Convention.

19. Several courts have held that, in determining what is meant by the term "arbitral award", consideration must be given to the object and purpose of the New York Convention.[34] For example, a Colombian court has held that the term "arbitral award" is to be construed in accordance with the spirit of the New York Convention.[35]

20. Courts have generally accepted that the determination whether a decision is an award depends on its nature and content, not on the label given to it by the arbitrators.[36] For example, a United States court has held that a

---

32 *Firooz Ghassabian v. Fatollah Hematian et al.*, District Court, Southern District of New York, United States of America, 27 August 2008, 08 Civ. 4400 SAS.

33 *Travaux préparatoires*, Recognition and Enforcement of Foreign Arbitral Awards, Report by the Secretary-General, Annex I, Comments by Governments, E/2822, p. 10.

34 *Compania Italiana di Assicurazioni (COMITAS) S.p.A., Società di Assicurazioni Gia Mutua Marittima Nazionale (MUTUAMAR) S.p.A. and others v. Schwartzmeer und Ostsee Versicherungsaktiengesellschaft (SOVAG), Bundesgerichtshof* [BGH], Germany, 8 October 1981, VIII Y.B. COM. ARB. 366 (1983); *Merck & Co. Inc., Merck Frosst Canada Inc., Frosst Laboratories Inc. v. Tecnoquimicas S.A.*, Supreme Court of Justice, Colombia, 26 January 1999, E-7474.

35 *Merck & Co. Inc., Merck Frosst Canada Inc., Frosst Laboratories Inc. v. Tecnoquimicas S.A.*, Supreme Court of Justice, Colombia, 26 January 1999, E-7474.

36 *Blackwater Security Consulting LLC et al. v. Richard P. Nordan*, District Court, Eastern District of North Carolina, Northern Division, United States of America, 21 January 2011, 2:06-CV-49-F; *Merck & Co. Inc., Merck Frosst Canada Inc., Frosst Laboratories Inc. v. Tecnoquimicas S.A.*, Supreme Court of Justice, Colombia, 26 January 1999, E-7474; *Publicis Communication v. Publicis S.A., True North Communications Inc.*, Court of Appeals, Seventh Circuit, United States of America, 14 March 2000, 206 F.3d 725; Bundesgerichtshof [BGH], Germany, 18 January 2007, III ZB 35/06.

decision need not be titled "award" for it to be enforceable under the New York Convention.[37] Similarly, it would not suffice for arbitrators to label a decision "award" to make it an award within the meaning of the New York Convention.[38]

21. Courts have found that only those decisions made by arbitrators that determine all or some aspects of the dispute, including jurisdiction,[39] in a final and binding manner, can be considered "arbitral awards" within the meaning of the New York Convention.[40] Accordingly, courts have found that in order for a decision to be considered an "arbitral award" under the New York Convention it needs to (i) be made by arbitrators, (ii) resolve a dispute or part thereof in a final manner, and (iii) be binding.[41]

22. First, reported case law shows that only decisions made by arbitrators are to be considered "awards" within the meaning of the New York Convention. For example, a United States court has held that a decision by the Permanent Court of Arbitration ("PCA") denying a request for arbitration on the basis of a *prima facie* screening of the documentation submitted by the parties did not constitute an award within the meaning of the New York Convention. The court added that the decision of the PCA could not be regarded as an "award" because "no arbitrators were ever appointed to adjudicate the parties' dispute".[42] Similarly, a United States court has held that a decision made by a third party determining a company's share price was not an award made by arbitrators and the New York Convention was therefore inapplicable.[43] Commentators are in broad agreement that decisions rendered in valuation and expert determination

---

[37] *Blackwater Security Consulting LLC et al. v. Richard P. Nordan*, District Court, Eastern District of North Carolina, Northern Division, United States of America, 21 January 2011, 2:06-CV-49-F.

[38] See in the context of setting aside proceedings, *Braspetro Oil Services Company - Brasoil v. The Management and Implementation Authority* of *the Great Man-Made River Project,* Court of Appeal of Paris, France, 1 July 1999, XXIV Y.B. COM. ARB. 296 (1999). In this case, the court held that the "qualification of [a decision as an] award does not depend on the terms used by the arbitrators or by the parties." As a result, the court held that a decision by which the tribunal resolved in a final manner the dispute between the parties was an award, notwithstanding the fact that the tribunal characterized its decision as an "order".

[39] See the chapter of the Guide on article I, paras. 28-32.

[40] For a discussion of the effect of article I (2) and the notion of arbitral award within the meaning of the New York Convention, see the chapter of the Guide on article I, paras. 65-68.

[41] See the chapter of the Guide on article V (1)*(e)*, paras. 5-19.

[42] *Marks 3- Zet-Ernst Marks GmbH & Co. KG v. Presstek, Inc.*, District Court, District of New Hampshire, United States of America, 9 August 2005, Civ.05-CV-121-JD, XXXI Y.B. COM. ARB. 1256 (2006). See also in the context of setting aside of an award, *Société Opinter France v. Société Dacomex*, Court of Appeal of Paris, France, 15 January 1985, 1986 REV. ARB. 87.

[43] *Frydman v. Cosmair Inc.*, District Court, Southern District of New York, United States of America, 25 July 1996, 94 Civ. 3772 LAP.

proceedings are not "awards made by arbitrators" and cannot be recognized and enforced under the New York Convention.[44]

23. Second, reported case law shows that decisions that finally resolve a dispute, either in whole or in part, are considered to be "awards" within the meaning of the Convention.[45] For example, an Australian court held that for a decision to be an "arbitral award" within the meaning of the New York Convention, it needs to finally determine all or at least some of the matters submitted to the arbitral tribunal.[46] Similarly, a United States court held that for a decision to be regarded as an "award", it needs to finally and definitely dispose of a separate independent claim.[47] In construing the "finality" requirement, a Colombian court held that awards are final "not because they put an end to the arbitration or to the tribunal's function, but because they settle in a final manner some of the disputes that have been submitted to arbitration".[48]

24. Third, reported case law shows that only a decision that is binding on the parties can be regarded as an "arbitral award" within the meaning of the New York Convention.[49] For example, a German court has held that an award was binding because it was not subject to appeal either before another arbitral tribunal or a national court.[50] Applying a similar approach, the French Court of Cassation refused to enforce an award on the ground that it

---

[44] FOUCHARD GAILLARD GOLDMAN ON INTERNATIONAL COMMERCIAL ARBITRATION 19, para. 25 (E. Gaillard, J. Savage eds., 1999); Bernd Ehle, *Commentary on Article I*, in NEW YORK CONVENTION ON THE RECOGNITION AND ENFORCEMENT OF FOREIGN ARBITRAL AWARDS—COMMENTARY 26, 37 (R. Wolff ed., 2012); Domenico Di Pietro, *What Constitutes an Arbitral Award Under the New York Convention*, in ENFORCEMENT OF ARBITRATION AGREEMENTS AND INTERNATIONAL ARBITRAL AWARDS: THE NEW YORK CONVENTION IN PRACTICE 139, 145 (E. Gaillard, D. Di Pietro eds., 2008); CHARLES JARROSSON, LA NOTION D'ARBITRAGE 123, 158, 162 (1987).

[45] See the chapter of the Guide on article I, paras. 26-40.

[46] *Resort Condominiums International Inc. v. Ray Bolwell and Resort Condominiums, Pty. Ltd.*, Supreme Court of Queensland, Australia, 29 October 1993, XX Y.B. COM. ARB. 628 (1995).

[47] *Hall Steel Company v. Metalloyd Ltd.*, District Court, Eastern District of Michigan, Southern Division, United States of America, 7 June 2007, 492 F. Supp. 2d 715, XXXIII Y.B. COM. ARB. 978 (2008).

[48] *Drummond Ltd. v. Instituto Nacional de Concesiones—INCO et al.*, Supreme Court of Justice, Colombia, 19 December 2011 and 3 May 2012, XXXVII Y.B. COM. ARB. 205 (2012) (with English translation). See also *Resort Condominiums International Inc. v. Ray Bolwell and Resort Condominiums, Pty. Ltd.*, Supreme Court of Queensland, Australia, 29 October 1993, XX Y.B. COM. ARB. 628 (1995).

[49] See the chapters of the Guide on article IV, paras. 68-72, and article V (1)(*e*), paras 13-14. The burden of proving that an award has not become binding is on the party opposing enforcement.

[50] See Bundesgerichtshof [BGH], Germany, 18 January 1990, III ZR 269/88.

was not binding because one of the parties was seeking review of the award before another arbitral tribunal.[51]

25. Courts have applied the above two criteria—namely, the finality and the binding effect of an award—to decisions made by arbitrators when determining whether particular decisions qualify as "arbitral awards" under the Convention.

a. Procedural orders

26. Courts have held that if a procedural order resolves an issue between the parties in a final manner, such order can be characterized as an "award" capable of being enforced under the New York Convention. For instance, the United States Court of Appeals for the Seventh Circuit held that a procedural order by which a tribunal directed one party to turn over certain tax records to the other was "final" and thus subject to recognition under the New York Convention.[52] Another United States court has decided that a "Termination Order" ending arbitration proceedings for failure of the parties to pay the arbitration fees was a final award and enforceable under the Convention.[53]

27. An Australian court has refused enforcement of an "Interim Arbitration Order and Award" by which the tribunal enjoined—until the final conclusion of the arbitration—a party from carrying out certain activities relating to a licence contract, such as, *inter alia*, entering into a similar contract with another party or falling to carry out provisions of the licence contract. The court found that the "Interim Arbitration Order and Award" did not amount to an enforceable award as it was of an "interlocutory and procedural nature" and did not attempt to finally solve the dispute between the parties.[54]

b. Awards on jurisdiction

28. An issue that has arisen before courts is whether awards on jurisdiction are enforceable under the Convention. Reported case law on this issue is scarce and concerns the recognition and enforcement of awards that

---

[51] *La Société Diag v. The Czech Republic,* Court of Cassation, France, 5 March 2014, 12-29.112.

[52] *Publicis Communication v. Publicis S.A., True North Communications Inc*., Court of Appeals, Seventh Circuit, United States of America, 14 March 2000, 206 F.3d 725.

[53] *Blackwater Security Consulting LLC et al. v. Richard P. Nordan*, District Court, Eastern District of North Carolina, Northern Division, United States of America, 21 January 2011, 2:06-CV-49-F.

[54] *Resort Condominiums International Inc. v. Ray Bolwell and Resort Condominiums, Pty. Ltd.,* Supreme Court of Queensland, Australia, 29 October 1993, XX Y.B. COM. ARB. 628 (1995).

deal with both jurisdiction and the allocation of costs incurred during the jurisdictional phase of the proceedings.

29. Of the few reported cases, a United States court has held that an "Interim Final Arbitration Award" affirming jurisdiction and containing an assessment of costs was not enforceable under the New York Convention on the ground that arbitration proceedings were still ongoing and that the party seeking confirmation did not show that the enforcement of the award on jurisdiction was necessary to "preserve the status quo".[55] However, relying on previous case law, the court noted that an award need not conclusively resolve all matters in dispute for it to be eligible for recognition under the Convention, provided that the party seeking recognition and enforcement is able to identify an immediate need for relief.

30. The Supreme Court of Queensland, Australia, has held that an interim award refusing jurisdiction and containing a decision on costs is enforceable under the New York Convention. The court noted that the fact that "there was no determination [...] on the merits can have no relevance to the ability of the Respondent [...] to enforce the interim award [...] with respect to the costs".[56]

31. In one case, a Colombian court refused to grant enforcement of an "Interlocutory Award on Jurisdiction" on the ground that an award affirming the jurisdiction of a tribunal does not "substantially put an end to the arbitral proceedings and settle the dispute" and thus cannot be considered as falling under the New York Convention.[57]

32. Commentators have taken the view that awards on jurisdiction can be considered as genuine "awards" capable of recognition and enforcement under the New York Convention.[58]

---

55 *Hall Steel Company v. Metalloyd Ltd.*, District Court, Eastern District of Michigan, Southern Division, United States of America, 7 June 2007, 492 F. Supp. 2d 715, XXXIII Y.B. COM. ARB. 978 (2008).

56 *Austin John Montague v. Commonwealth Development Corporation*, Supreme Court of Queensland, Australia, 27 June 2000, Appeal No. 8159 of 1999, DC No. 29 of 1999, XXVI Y.B. COM. ARB. 744 (2001). See also Bundesgerichtshof [BGH], Germany, 18 January 2007, III ZB 35/06; Hanseatisches Oberlandesgericht [OLG] Hamburg, Germany, 14 March 2006, 6 Sch 11/05.

57 *Merck & Co. Inc., Merck Frosst Canada Inc. & Frosst Laboratories Inc. v. Tecnoquimicas S.A.*, Supreme Court of Justice, Colombia, 1 March 1999, E-7474 (unofficial translation).

58 FOUCHARD GAILLARD GOLDMAN ON INTERNATIONAL COMMERCIAL ARBITRATION 739, para. 1357 (E. Gaillard, J. Savage eds., 1999); Domenico Di Pietro, *What Constitutes an Arbitral Award Under the New York Convention*, in ENFORCEMENT OF ARBITRATION AGREEMENTS AND INTERNATIONAL ARBITRAL AWARDS: THE NEW YORK CONVENTION IN PRACTICE 139, 153 (E. Gaillard, D. Di Pietro eds., 2008); GARY B. BORN, INTERNATIONAL COMMERCIAL ARBITRATION 2935-36 (2014).

c. *Interim or partial awards*

33. Courts have considered whether interim or partial awards are enforceable under the Convention. For example, a Bulgarian court has held that a partial award requiring one party to pay certain sums to the other was not enforceable under the Convention because it did not finally settle the dispute between the parties. The court added that the lack of finality was further demonstrated by the fact that the arbitration proceedings were still pending.[59]

34. Other courts have held that an interim or partial award amounts to an "award" within the meaning of the Convention, if it finally determines at least part of the dispute referred to arbitration.[60] For example, a German court held that an interim award containing a binding decision on some of the claims advanced is capable of recognition and enforcement under the New York Convention.[61] Similarly, the Supreme Court of Justice of Colombia held that a "Partial Award" amounted to an "award" within the meaning of the New York Convention. In so doing, the court noted that the award settled in a final manner "several of the (counter-) claims".[62] Similarly, a United States court held that "an interim award that finally and definitely disposes of a separate, independent claim may be confirmed notwithstanding the absence of an award that finally disposes of all claims that were submitted to arbitration".[63] Noting that a partial award decided claims that were severable from the rest of the claims in the pending arbitration proceedings, the court granted recognition of the partial award under the New York Convention.

35. In an *obiter dictum*, the Italian Court of Cassation noted that a partial award on liability could be enforced in Italy under the New York Convention.[64] The Court of Cassation added that a final award on the level of damages can be considered separately from an interim award on liability for the purposes of enforcement.

---

[59] *ECONERG Ltd. v. National Electricity Company AD*, Supreme Court of Appeal, Civil Collegium, Fifth Civil Department, Bulgaria, 23 February 1999, 356/99, XXV Y.B. COM. ARB. 678 (2000).

[60] *Resort Condominiums International Inc. v. Ray Bolwell and Resort Condominiums, Pty.* Ltd., Supreme Court of Queensland, Australia, 29 October 1993, XX Y.B. COM. ARB. 628 (1995).

[61] Oberlandesgericht [OLG] Thüringen, Germany, 8 August 2007, 4 Sch 03/06.

[62] *Drummond Ltd. v. Instituto Nacional de Concesiones—INCO et al.*, Supreme Court of Justice, Colombia, 19 December 2011 and 3 May 2012, XXXVII Y.B. COM. ARB. 205 (2012) (with English translation).

[63] *Alcatel Space, S.A. v. Alcatel Space Industries, S.A. and others*, District Court, Southern District of New York, United States of America, 25 June 2002, 02 Civ.2674 SAS, XXVIII Y.B. COM. ARB. 990 (2003).

[64] *Walter Thosti Boswau Bauaktiengesellschaft v. Costruire Coop. srl.*, Court of Cassation, Italy, 7 June 1995, 6426, XXII Y.B. COM. ARB. 727 (1997).

d. *Consent awards*

36. The Convention is silent on the question of its applicability to decisions that record the terms of a settlement between parties. During the Conference, the issue of the application of the Convention to such decisions was raised, but not decided upon.[65] Reported case law does not address this issue.

e. *Lodi Irrituali*

37. The question of whether an award rendered in an *arbitrato irrituale* (informal arbitration) falls within the scope of the New York Convention has also arisen. An *arbitrato irrituale* is based on the parties' intentions and results in an award which is essentially a contract. Awards rendered in such proceedings bind the parties as soon as they are rendered, but can only be enforced after being confirmed by a competent court.[66]

38. The German Supreme Court held that the Convention applies neither to the recognition nor the enforcement of a *lodo irrituale*, i.e., an award rendered in an *arbitrato irrituale*. The court noted that a *lodo irrituale* can be compared to an interlocutory decision "because it offers the possibility of obtaining a judgment thereon by which it becomes a final judgment".[67] A similar view has been taken by another German court that has held that an award which has the effect of a contract and not a judgment cannot be enforced under the New York Convention.[68]

39. On the other hand, in the context of proceedings in which one party sought a referral to arbitration pursuant to article II of the Convention, the Italian Court of Cassation noted *obiter* that a *lodo irrituale* falls within the

---

[65] *Travaux préparatoires*, Recognition and Enforcement of Foreign Arbitral Awards, Report by the Secretary-General, Annex I, Comments by Governments, E/2822, pp. 7, 10; *Travaux préparatoires*, United Nations Conference on International Commercial Arbitration, Consideration of the Draft Convention on the Recognition and Enforcement of Foreign Arbitral Awards, E/CONF.26/L.26. See also *Travaux préparatoires*, United Nations Conference on International Commercial Arbitration, Activities of Inter-Governmental and Non-Governmental Organizations in the Field of International Commercial Arbitration, Consolidated Report by the Secretary-General, E/CONF.26/4, p. 26.

[66] Bayerisches Oberstes Landesgericht [BayObLG], Germany, 22 November 2002, 4 Z Sch 13/02, XXIX Y.B. COM. ARB. 754 (2004).

[67] *Compagnia Italiana di Assicurazioni (COMITAS) S.p.A., Società di Assicurazioni Gia Mutua Marittima Nazionale (MUTUAMAR) S.p.A. and others v. Schwartzmeer und Ostsee Versicherungsaktiengesellschaft (SOVAG)*, Bundesgerichtshof [BGH], Germany, 8 October 1981, VIII Y.B. COM. ARB. 366 (1983) (with English translation).

[68] Bayerisches Oberstes Landesgericht [BayObLG], Germany, 22 November 2002, 4 Z Sch 13/02, XXIX Y.B. COM. ARB. 754 (2004).

scope of the Convention.[69] The court reasoned that the fact that the New York Convention refers to "an arbitral award which has a binding force between the parties, [...] does not signify as such that the binding force must necessarily operate on the judicial level".[70] The court added that the New York Convention has eliminated the *double exequatur* requirement, and that therefore there is no need to obtain an exequatur decision in the State where a *lodo irrituale* was rendered in order for it to be enforceable under the Convention.[71] In a further decision, also in the context of referral proceedings, the Italian Court of Cassation stated *obiter* that the New York Convention should be interpreted "as broadly as possible", by taking into account "the difference in law and mentality in the various Contracting States".[72] The court reasoned that differences between a regular arbitration (i.e., *arbitrato rituale*) and an informal arbitration (i.e., *arbitrato irrituale*) should be irrelevant for the purposes of enforcement under the New York Convention.

40. Commentators are generally of the view that a *lodo irrituale* does not amount to an "arbitral award" under the New York Convention.[73]

C. Arbitral awards falling within the scope of the Convention

41. In the 1955 draft of the Convention, article I provided that the Convention applied to the "recognition and enforcement of arbitral awards made in the territory of a State other than the State in which such awards are relied upon". The 1955 draft of the Convention adopted a "territorial criterion" for determining the application of the Convention, focusing on the place where the award was rendered. The application of this territorial criterion excluded from the scope of the Convention awards that were rendered in the State where recognition and enforcement was sought. This

---

69 *Gaetano Butera v. Pietro e Romano Pagnan*, Court of Cassation, Italy, 18 September 1978, 4167, IV Y.B. COM. ARB. 296 (1979); *Colella Legnami S.p.A. v. Carey Hirsch Lumber Company*, Court of Cassation, Italy, 6 July 1982, 4039, IX Y.B. COM. ARB. 429 (1984).

70 *Gaetano Butera v. Pietro e Romano Pagnan*, Court of Cassation, Italy, 18 September 1978, 4167, IV Y.B. COM. ARB. 296 (1979) (with English translation).

71 *Id.*

72 *Colella Legnami S.p.A. v. Carey Hirsch Lumber Company*, Court of Cassation, Italy, 6 July 1982, 4039, IX Y.B.COM. ARB. 429 (1984) (with English translation).

73 See Bernd Ehle, *Commentary on Article I*, in NEW YORK CONVENTION ON THE RECOGNITION AND ENFORCEMENT OF FOREIGN ARBITRAL AWARDS OF 10 JUNE 1958—COMMENTARY 26, 40 (R. Wolff ed., 2012); ALBERT JAN VAN DEN BERG, THE NEW YORK ARBITRATION CONVENTION OF 1958: TOWARDS A UNIFORM JUDICIAL INTERPRETATION 47 (1981); Domenico Di Pietro, *What Constitutes an Arbitral Award Under the New York Convention*, in ENFORCEMENT OF ARBITRATION AGREEMENTS AND INTERNATIONAL ARBITRAL AWARDS: THE NEW YORK CONVENTION IN PRACTICE 139, 148 (E. Gaillard, D. Di Pietro eds., 2008); *contra* GARY B. BORN, INTERNATIONAL COMMERCIAL ARBITRATION 2925 (2014).

made the 1955 draft of the Convention more restrictive than the 1927 Geneva Convention.[74]

42. Delegates from several countries considered that the narrow territorial approach taken by the ECOSOC *ad hoc* Committee placed undue emphasis on the seat of arbitration, which was often chosen "as a matter of convenience"[75] and could be "fortuitous and artificial".[76] For these reasons, delegates from Austria, Belgium, Germany, France, Italy, Netherlands, Sweden and Switzerland jointly proposed a draft amendment to article I (1), pursuant to which the Convention would apply to awards "other than those considered as domestic in the country in which they are relied upon".[77]

43. The matter was referred to a working party composed of representatives of ten States, which was tasked with reconciling the views of those "favouring the principle of the place of arbitration and those favouring the principle of the nationality of the arbitral award".[78] The working party proposed a text of article I, which was later adopted by the Conference that included both the "territorial" and the "non-domestic" criteria.[79] The Convention thereby recognizes that Contracting States may want to consider factors other than the seat of the arbitration when determining whether an award falls within the scope of the Convention.[80]

---

[74] Pursuant to article 1, the 1927 Geneva Convention applied to awards rendered "in the territory of one of the High Contracting Parties". This wording did not exclude from the scope of the 1927 Geneva Convention awards rendered in the States where enforcement was sought, provided that they were made between persons "subject to the jurisdiction of the Contracting States". See also *Travaux préparatoires*, United Nations Conference on International Commercial Arbitration, Comments on the Recognition and Enforcement of Foreign Arbitral Awards, Note by the Secretary-General, E/CONF. 26/2, p. 2.

[75] *Travaux préparatoires*, United Nations Conference on International Commercial Arbitration, Comments on Draft Convention on the Recognition and Enforcement of Foreign Arbitral Awards, Note by the Secretary-General, E/CONF.26/2, p. 3.

[76] *Travaux préparatoires*, United Nations Conference on International Commercial Arbitration, Summary Record of the Fifth Meeting, E/CONF.26/SR.5, p. 8.

[77] *Travaux préparatoires*, United Nations Conference on International Commercial Arbitration, Consideration of the Draft Convention on the Recognition and Enforcement of Foreign Arbitral Awards - Austria, Belgium, Federal Republic of Germany, France, Italy, Netherlands, Sweden, Switzerland: amendment to article I, paragraph 1, of the draft Convention, E/CONF.26/L.6.

[78] *Travaux préparatoires*, United Nations Conference on International Commercial Arbitration, Consideration of the Draft Convention on the Recognition and Enforcement of Foreign Arbitral Awards , Report of Working Party No. 1 on article I, paragraph 1 and article II of the draft Convention (E/2704 and Corr.1), E/CONF.26/L.42. The Working Group was composed of: Colombia, Czechoslovakia, the Federal Republic of Germany, France, India, Israel, Italy, Turkey, the Union of Soviet Socialist Republics and the United Kingdom.

[79] See also *Travaux préparatoires*, United Nations Conference on International Commercial Arbitration, Summary Record of the Sixth Meeting, E/CONF.26/SR.6, p. 8.

[80] Phillipe Fouchard, *Quand un arbitrage est-il international?*, 1970 REV. ARB. 59, 65. For the approach adopted under chapter 8 of the UNCITRAL Model Law on International

a. *Awards "made in the territory of a State other than the State where the recognition and enforcement of such awards are sought"*

44. Pursuant to the first sentence of article I (1), the New York Convention applies to awards "made in the territory of a State other than the State where the recognition and enforcement of such awards are sought". Unless a State has made a reciprocity reservation pursuant to article I (3),[81] the Convention applies to awards made in any State, whether or not a Contracting State.[82]

45. In certain jurisdictions, the criterion expressed in the first sentence of article I (1) is the only one used to determine whether or not an award falls within the scope of the Convention. Thus, in several jurisdictions—including Australia,[83] Brazil,[84] Cameroon,[85] England,[86] Germany,[87] Luxembourg,[88]

Commercial Arbitration, see paragraph 50 of the Explanatory Note by the UNCITRAL secretariat on the Model Law, available on the Internet at www.unictral.org.

[81] See the chapter of the Guide on article I, paras. 70-82.

[82] *Black Sea Shipping Co. v. Italturist SpA*, Court of Appeal of Milan, Italy, 4 October 1991, 1618, XVIII Y.B. COM. ARB. 415 (1993); Oberlandesgericht [OLG] Stuttgart, Germany, 18 October 1999, 5 U 89/98, XXIX Y.B. COM. ARB. 700 (2004); *R S.A. v. A Ltd.*, Court of Justice of Geneva, Switzerland, 15 April 1999; *Cadena de Tiendas Venezolanas S.A. - Cativen v. GMR Asesores SL Inmomercado and others*, Court of Appeal of Madrid, Spain, 1 April 2009, 63/2009 (Section 10), XXXV Y.B. COM. ARB. 448 (2010). See also Bernd Ehle, *Commentary on Article I*, in NEW YORK CONVENTION ON THE RECOGNITION AND ENFORCEMENT OF FOREIGN ARBITRAL AWARDS OF 10 JUNE 1958—COMMENTARY 26, 56 (R. Wolff ed., 2012); Javier Rubinstein, Georgina Fabian, *The Territorial Scope of the New York Convention and Its Implementation in Common and Civil Law Countries*, in ENFORCEMENT OF ARBITRATION AGREEMENTS AND INTERNATIONAL ARBITRAL AWARDS: THE NEW YORK CONVENTION IN PRACTICE 91, 95 (E. Gaillard, D. Di Pietro eds., 2008); ALBERT JAN VAN DEN BERG, THE NEW YORK ARBITRATION CONVENTION OF 1958: TOWARDS A UNIFORM JUDICIAL INTERPRETATION 12 (1981).

[83] *FG Hemisphere Associates LLC v. Democratic Republic* of *Congo*, Supreme Court of New South Wales, Australia, 1 November 2010, [2010] NSWSC; *Uganda Telecom Ltd. v. Hi-Tech Telecom Pty Ltd.*, Federal Court, Australia, 22 February 2011, NSD 171 of 2010. See also Section 3 of the 1974 Australian International Arbitration Act, amended in 2011 ("Foreign award means an arbitral award made, in pursuance of an arbitration agreement, in a country other than Australia, being an arbitral award in relation to which the Convention applies").

[84] *Nuovo Pignone SPA and others v. Petromec Inc. and Marítima Petróleo e Engenharia Ltda*, Superior Court of Justice, Brazil, 24 May 2011, Special Appeal 1.231.554. See Article 34 of the 1996 Brazilian Arbitration Act ("A foreign arbitral award is an award made outside of the national territory").

[85] *African Petroleum Consultants (APC) v. Société Nationale de Raffinage*, High Court of Fako Division, Cameroon, 15 May 2002, Suit No. HCF/91/M/2001-2002.

[86] *Yukos Oil Co. v. Dardana Ltd.*, Court of Appeal, England and Wales, 18 April 2002, [2002] EWCA Civ 543; *IPCO v. Nigerian National Petroleum Corp.*, High Court of Justice, England and Wales, 17 April 2008, [2008] EWHC 797 (Comm). See also Section 100(1) of the 1996 English Arbitration Act ("'[a] New York Convention award' means an award made, in pursuance of an arbitration agreement, in the territory of a state (other than the United Kingdom) which is a party to the New York Convention").

[87] German courts initially held that an award falls within the scope of the Convention when a foreign procedural law governs the arbitration proceedings, irrespective of the place

the Netherlands[89] and Spain[90]—an award falls within the scope of the New York Convention only when it is made in a State other than the State where recognition and enforcement is sought.

46. The Indian Supreme Court initially held that awards rendered in the territory of another State under Indian procedural law were domestic awards and did not fall within the scope of the New York Convention.[91] More recently, the Indian Supreme Court has reversed this approach and held that awards rendered in the territory of another State "would only be subject to jurisdiction of Indian courts when [they] are sought to be enforced in India" in accordance with the legislative provisions implementing the New York Convention. The Court added that this holding would be applicable *ex nunc* "to all arbitration agreements executed [after 6 September 2012]".[92]

47. In China, courts have held that an award falls within the scope of the Convention when it is rendered under the auspices of a foreign arbitral institution. In one case, a court held that an award rendered in Paris fell within the scope of the New York Convention because it was rendered by "the arbitral tribunal of the International Chamber of Commerce" ("ICC").[93] In another case, a court held that an award rendered in Mongolia was subject to enforcement under the Convention, because it "was made by a Mongolian institution".[94] Chinese courts have further held that awards rendered in *ad*

---

where the award is made. After the adoption of the 1998 German Arbitration Act, German courts have held that the only relevant criterion to be taken into account when determining whether an award is domestic or falls within the scope of the Convention, is the geographical location where the award was rendered. See Oberlandesgericht [OLG] München, Germany, 28 November 2005, 34 Sch 019/05; Kammergericht [KG] Berlin, Germany, 17 April 2008, 20 Sch 02/08, XXXIV Y.B. COM. ARB. 510 (2009).

88 *Kersa Holding Company Luxembourg v. Infancourtage, Famajuk Investment and Isny*, Court of Appeal, Luxembourg, 24 November 1993, XXI Y.B. COM. ARB. 617 (1996).

89 *LoJack Equipment Ireland Ltd. v. A, Voorzieningenrechter*, Court of First Instance of Amsterdam, Netherlands, 18 June 2009, 411230/KG RK 08-3652, XXXIV Y.B. COM. ARB. 715 (2009). See also article 1075 of the 2004 Netherlands Arbitration Act ("An arbitral award made in a foreign State to which a treaty concerning recognition and enforcement is applicable may be recognized and enforced in the Netherlands").

90 *Cadena de Tiendas Venezolanas S.A. - Cativen v. GMR Asesores SL Inmomercado and others, Audiencia Provincial*, Court of Appeal of Madrid, Spain, 1 April 2009, 63/2009 (Section 10), XXXV Y.B. COM. ARB. 448 (2010). See also article 46 (1) of the 2003 Spanish Arbitration Act as amended in 2011 ("A foreign award is an award which has been issued outside of Spanish territory").

91 *National Thermal Power Corp v. Singer Company and others*, Supreme Court, India, 7 May 1992, 1993 AIR 998; 1992 SCR (3) 106; 1992 SCC (3) 551; JT 1992 (3) 198; 1992 SCALE (1) 1034.

92 *Bharat Aluminium Co. v. Kaiser Aluminium Technical Service Inc.*, Supreme Court, India, 6 September 2012, Civil Appeal No.7019 of 2005.

93 *Hemofarm DD, MAG International Trade Holding DD, Suram Media Ltd. v. Jinan Yongning Pharmaceutical Co. Ltd.*, Supreme People's Court, China, 2 June 2008, [2008] Min Si Ta Zi No. 11 (unofficial translation).

94 *Aiduoladuo Co., Ltd. v. Zhejiang Zhancheng Construction Group Co., Ltd.*, Supreme People's Court, China, 8 December 2009, [2009] Min Si Ta Zi No. 46 (unofficial translation).

hoc arbitration proceedings are enforceable under the New York Convention provided that the seat of the arbitration is in a country other than China.[95]

48. With respect to jurisdictions—including Belgium, France, Panama, Peru, Sweden, Switzerland, and Tunisia—that allow parties, in certain circumstances, to opt out of setting aside actions altogether,[96] the question has arisen whether an award would still be enforceable under the New York Convention if the parties had availed themselves of this possibility. Although there is no reported case law on this issue, commentators have generally taken the view that the waiver does not have any bearing on the enforceability of the award under the Convention,[97] and that a party may nevertheless seek the enforcement of such award, pursuant to the first sentence of article I (1) of the New York Convention.[98] Indeed, the Convention applies to awards made in the territory of another Contracting State, without requiring that a certain level of control be exercised in the territory of that State.[99]

---

95 *Guangzhou Ocean Shipping Co., Ltd. v. Marships* of *Connecticut Company, Guangzhou Maritime Court*, China, 17 October 1990.

96 See, e.g., article 1718 of the 2013 Belgian Judicial Code, article 1522 of the 2011 French Civil Code of Procedure; article 36 of the 2006 Panama Legislative Decree; article 63(8) of the Peruvian 2008 Legislative Arbitration Decree; article 51 of the 1999 Swedish Arbitration Act; article 192 of the 1987 Swiss Private International Law Act; article 78(6) of the 1993 Tunisian Arbitration Code.

97 ADAM SAMUEL, JURISDICTIONAL PROBLEMS IN INTERNATIONAL COMMERCIAL ARBITRATION: A STUDY OF BELGIAN, DUTCH, ENGLISH, FRENCH, SWEDISH, SWISS, UNITED STATES AND WEST GERMAN LAW 296 (1989).

98 See, e.g., Markus Wirth, Chapter 12 PILA—*Is it Time for Reform? If Yes, What Shall be Its Scope,* in NEW DEVELOPMENTS IN INTERNATIONAL COMMERCIAL ARBITRATION 51, 72 (C. Muller, A. Rigozzi eds., 2011); Bernard Hanotiau, Olivier Caprasse, *Introductory Report,* in THE REVIEW OF INTERNATIONAL ARBITRAL AWARDS, IAI SERIES ON INTERNATIONAL ARBITRATION NO. 6, 7, 84 (E. Gaillard ed., 2010); Jan Paulsson, *Arbitration Unbound in Belgium*, 2(1) ARB. INT'L 72-73 (1986); Emmanuel Gaillard, *The Enforcement of Awards Set Aside in the Country* of *Origin*, 14 ICSID REV. 16, 34 (1999); Domitille Baizeau, *Commentary on Chapter 12 PILS, Article 192: Waiver of annulment*, in ARBITRATION IN SWITZERLAND: THE PRACTITIONER'S GUIDE 283, 291 (M. Arroyo ed., 2013); Elliott Geisinger, Alexandre Mazuranic, *Challenge and Revision of the Award,* in INTERNATIONAL ARBITRATION IN SWITZERLAND: A HANDBOOK FOR PRACTITIONERS 223, 258 (E. Geisinger, N. Voser eds., 2nd ed. 2013).

99 The same conclusion applies with respect to the "non-domestic criterion" set out in the second sentence of article I (1) of the Convention. See, e.g., Federal Tribunal, Switzerland, 31 October 2005, 4P/198/2005/sza. Article 192(2) of the Swiss Private International Law Act provides that "if the awards are to be enforced in Switzerland, the New York Convention of June 10, 1958 on the Recognition and Enforcement of Foreign Arbitral Awards applies by analogy". See also article 78(6) of the 1993 Tunisian Arbitration Code, article 51 of the 1999 Swedish Arbitration Act and article 1522 (2) of the 2011 French Civil Code of Procedure.

b. *Awards "not considered as domestic awards in the State where their recognition and enforcement are sought"*

49. Pursuant to the second sentence of article I (1), the New York Convention also applies to awards "not considered as domestic" in the State where recognition and enforcement is sought. This "non-domestic" criterion is in addition to the "territorial criterion" set out in the first sentence of article I (1) of the Convention. Accordingly, courts in the United States have applied, in addition to the "territorial criterion",[100] the "non-domestic criterion" to determine whether an award falls within the scope of the New York Convention.[101] Similarly, relying on the "non-domestic" criterion, a Chinese court held that an award rendered in Beijing pursuant to the ICC Arbitration Rules was not considered as domestic in China.[102]

50. The New York Convention does not define the term "domestic". As a result, Contracting States have discretion to decide, in accordance with their own law, what constitutes a non-domestic award.[103] A United States court has held that "the definition appears to have been left out deliberately in order to cover as wide a variety of eligible awards as possible [...]."[104]

51. National courts have considered whether an award could be deemed a "non-domestic award" under article I in a number of situations.

52. First, courts have held an award to be non-domestic, within the meaning of article I, when it is made in the State where recognition and enforcement is sought under the procedural law of another State. For example, a United States court has held that an award rendered in the United States was non-domestic, *inter alia*, because it was made pursuant to a

[100] See *Gulf Petro Trading Company Inc., et al. v. Nigerian National Petroleum Corporation, et al.*, Court of Appeals, Fifth Circuit, United States of America, 7 January 2008, 512 F.3d 742; *GSS Group Ltd. (Global Security Seals Group Ltd) v. National Port Authority*, District Court, District of Columbia, United States of America, 25 May 2012, 680 F.3d 805.

[101] See, e.g., *Jacada Ltd. v. International Marketing Strategies, Inc.*, Court of Appeals, Sixth Circuit, United States of America, 18 March 2005, 03-2521; *Yusuf Ahmed Alghanim & Sons, W.L.L. v. Toys "R" Us, Inc.*, Court of Appeals, Second Circuit, United States of America, 10 September 1997, 126 F. 3d 15.

[102] *Duferco S.A. v. Ningbo Arts & Crafts Import & Export Co., Ltd.*, Ningbo Intermediate People's Court, China, 22 April 2009, [2008] Yong Zhong Jian Zi No. 4.

[103] *Republic of Argentina v. BG Group PLC*, District Court, District of Columbia, United States of America, 7 June 2010, 715 F. Supp. 2d 108. The court held that the second sentence of article I (1) refers to awards "that are issued within the borders of the nation where enforcement is sought, yet are sufficiently foreign in character as to not be considered "domestic awards" in that country".

[104] *Sigval Bergesen, as Owners of the M/T Sydfonn and others v. Joseph Müller Corporation*, Court of Appeals, Second Circuit, United States of America, 17 June 1983, 710 F.2d 928.

foreign procedural law and the ICC Arbitration Rules.[105] This application of the non-domestic criterion finds support in the *travaux préparatoires*.[106]

53. Second, courts have held an award to be non-domestic when it is made in the State where recognition and enforcement is sought but concerns a dispute involving one or more international elements. For example, pursuant to Section 202 of the United States Federal Arbitration Act ("FAA"), which broadly defines what constitutes a "non-domestic" award in the United States,[107] courts have held that "the citizenship of the parties, the location of property involved in the dispute, where the agreement was to be performed or enforced, or whether the award contains another reasonable relation with a foreign country [...]", all impact whether or not an award is to be considered "non-domestic".[108]

54. Some United States courts have held that an award is non-domestic when one[109] or both[110] parties to the arbitration are non-United States

---

105 *RZS Holdings AVV (United States) v. PDVSA Petroleos S.A. et al.*, District Court, Eastern District of Virginia, Alexandria Division, United States of America, 5 February 2009, 598 F. Supp. 2d 762.

106 *Travaux préparatoires*, Recognition and Enforcement of Foreign Arbitral Awards, Report by the Secretary-General, Annex I, Comments by Governments, E/2822, pp. 5, 6. The German delegate stated that "the nature of the arbitral award is determined by reference to the rules of procedure which are applicable, *in toto* or else as subsidiary rules, to the award". See also *Travaux préparatoires*, United Nations Conference on International Commercial Arbitration, Summary Record of the Fifth Meeting, E/CONF.26/SR.5, p. 10. In support of the German delegate's observations, the Turkish delegate proposed that the "criterion for determining the nationality of an award should be the municipal procedural law under which the award was made".

107 See *Sigval Bergesen, as Owners of the M/T Sydfonn and others v. Joseph Müller Corporation*, Court of Appeals, Second Circuit, United States of America, 17 June 1983, 710 F.2d 928 ("Inasmuch as it was apparently left to each state to define which awards were to be considered nondomestic, [...] Congress spelled out its definition of that concept in section 202"). Section 202 provides for the Convention to govern recognition and enforcement of awards arising out of a relationship, whether contractual or not, that involves a party that is not a citizen of the United States or that "involves property located abroad, envisages performance or enforcement abroad, or has some other reasonable relation with one or more foreign States". See 9 United States Code Chapter II—Convention on the Recognition and Enforcement of Foreign Arbitral Awards, Section 202

108 *Jacada Ltd. v. International Marketing Strategies, Inc.*, Court of Appeals, Sixth Circuit, United States of America, 18 March 2005, 03-2521.

109 *Ocean Partners Holdings LIMITED and Ocean Partners USA, Inc. v. Doe Run Resources CORP.*, District Court, Eastern District of Missouri, Eastern Division, United States of America, 12 March 2012, 4:11-CV-173 (CEJ); *Anthony N. LaPine v. Kyocera Corporation*, District Court, Northern District of California, United States of America, 22 May 2008, C 07-06132 MHP; *Trevino Hernandez, S. de R.L. de C.V. v. Smart & Final Inc.*, District Court, Southern District of California, United States of America, 17 June 2010, 09-cv-2266 BEN (NLS); *Liberty Re Ltd. v. Transamerica Occidental Life Insurance Company*, District Court, Southern District of New York, United States of America, 20 May 2005, 04 Civ 5044 (NRB); *Industrial Risk Insurers v. M.A.N. Gutehoffnungshutte*, Court of Appeals, Eleventh Circuit, United States of America, 22 May 1998, 141 F.3d 1434.

nationals or have their principal place of business outside of the United States. For example, the United States Court of Appeals for the Second Circuit held that an award rendered in the United States pursuant to New York law was a foreign award, because the arbitration involved two parties that both had their principal place of business outside the enforcing jurisdiction.[111] Similarly, the United States District Court for the Northern District of California held that, despite the fact that the arbitral award was made in the United States under California law, the award fell under the New York Convention because one of the parties had its principle place of business in Japan.[112]

55. Other United States courts have used a combination of factors set out in Section 202 of the FAA to determine whether or not an award is "non-domestic".[113] In one case, a United States court held that an award was "non-domestic" on the grounds that the assets and property in dispute were located abroad, one of the parties was incorporated outside the United States and the contract envisaged performance exclusively overseas.[114] In another case, a United States court held that an award was non-domestic on the grounds that two of the three disputing parties were non-domestic and the contract was performed in the Middle East.[115]

56. In a situation where the award creditor's action for recognition and enforcement and the award debtor's action for setting aside are brought before the same court—a scenario that may occur when the award creditor brings its action for recognition and enforcement under the second sentence of article I (1)—courts are in broad agreement that the New York Convention

---

[110] *Sigval Bergesen, as Owners of the M/T Sydfonn and others v. Joseph Müller Corporation*, Court of Appeals, Second Circuit, United States of America, 17 June 1983, 710 F.2d 928; *Trans Chemical Limited v. China National Machinery Import and Export Corporation*, District Court, Southern District of Texas, Houston Division, United States of America, 7 July 1997, 978 F. Supp. 266; *Continental Grain Company, et al. v. Foremost Farms Incorporated, et al.*, District Court, Southern District of New York, United States of America, 23 March 1998, 98 Civ. 0848 (DC).

[111] *Sigval Bergesen, as Owners of the M/T Sydfonn and others v. Joseph Müller Corporation*, Court of Appeals, Second Circuit, United States of America, 17 June 1983, 710 F.2d 928.

[112] *Anthony N. LaPine v. Kyocera Corporation*, District Court, Northern District of California, United States of America, 22 May 2008, C 07-06132 MHP.

[113] *Yusuf Ahmed Alghanim & Sons, W.L.L. v. Toys "R" Us, Inc.*, Court of Appeals, Second Circuit, United States of America, 10 September 1997, 126 F. 3d 15; *Republic of Argentina v. BG Group PLC*, District Court, District of Columbia, United States of America, 7 June 2010, 715 F. Supp. 2d 108; *Jacada Ltd. v. International Marketing Strategies, Inc.*, Court of Appeals, Sixth Circuit, United States of America, 18 March 2005, 03-2521; *Mayer Zeiler v. Joseph Deitsch*, Court of Appeals, Second Circuit, United States of America, 23 August 2007, 500 F.3d 157.

[114] *Jacada Ltd. v. International Marketing Strategies, Inc.*, Court of Appeals, Sixth Circuit, United States of America, 18 March 2005, 03-2521.

[115] *Yusuf Ahmed Alghanim & Sons, W.L.L. v. Toys "R" Us, Inc.*, Court of Appeals, Second Circuit, United States of America, 10 September 1997, 126 F.3d 15.

only applies to the action for recognition and enforcement, while domestic law on arbitration applies to the setting aside proceedings.[116] Commentators support the view that an award rendered in the State where recognition and enforcement is sought is capable of being regarded as a non-domestic award for the purposes of enforcement and as domestic award for the purposes of setting aside.[117]

57. The issue of whether or not awards rendered in proceedings that are considered not to be governed by any national law—sometimes referred to as "a-national" or "non-national" awards—fall within the scope of New York Convention has arisen before national courts.

58. An early draft of the Convention prepared by the ICC, in which the term "international awards" was used, arguably included "a-national" awards within the scope of the Convention.[118] This draft was not adopted by the ECOSOC *ad hoc* Committee which was "reluctant to accept the idea put forward by the ICC that 'international awards' should be 'completely independent of national law'."[119] However, similar language to the one employed in the ICC draft appears in article V (1)*(d)* of the Convention as adopted.[120] Although dealing with one of the grounds on which recognition and enforcement may be refused, article V (1)*(d)* can be deemed to imply that an award need not be rendered pursuant to a domestic procedural law to be enforceable under the Convention.

59. Courts have often relied both on the text of article I and the text of article V (1)*(d)* of the Convention to hold that "a-national awards" fall within the scope of the New York Convention. For example, the Dutch Supreme Court found that the "intention of the Convention [was] to recognize as arbitral awards also those [awards] which [...] cannot be deemed to be

---

116 *Id.* See also *Federal Insurance Company, as subrogee* of *Transammonia, Inc.v. Bergesen D.Y. ASA OSLO, as agents of the Norwegian Flag LP G/C "Hugo N" and its owner, General Gas Carrier Corporation, Limited*, District Court, Southern District of New York, United States of America, 7 September 2012, 12 Civ. 3851(PAE); *ESCO Corporation v. Bradken Resources PTY Ltd.*, District Court, District of Oregon, Portland Division, United States of America, 31 January 2011, 10-788-AC.

117 Michael Pryles, *Foreign Awards and the New York Convention*, 9(3) ARB. INT'L 259, 264 (1993). See also V.S. Deshpande, *Jurisdiction Over 'Foreign' and 'Domestic' Awards in the New York Convention*, 7(2) ARB. INT'L 123, 127 (1991).

118 See *Travaux préparatoires*, Enforcement of International Arbitral Awards, Statement Submitted by the International Chamber of Commerce, E/C.2/373, p. 13.

119 See *Travaux préparatoires*, Report of the Committee on the Enforcement of International Arbitral Awards, E/2704, E/AC.42/4/Rev.1., p. 11.

120 Article V (1)(*d*) provides that recognition and enforcement may be refused if "the composition of the arbitral authority or the arbitral procedure was not in accordance with the agreement of the parties, or, failing such agreement, was not in accordance with the law of the country where the arbitration took place". For a detailed analysis of this provision, see the chapter of the Guide on article V (1)(*d*).

connected with the law of any specific country".[121] In finding that "a-national" awards fall within the scope of the Convention, the court overruled The Hague Court of Appeal's decision, which had previously held that an award must be based on "some national law".[122]

60. Similarly, the United States Court of Appeals for the Ninth Circuit, referring to the Dutch Supreme Court decision above, held that "the fairest reading of the Convention itself appears to be that it applies to the enforcement of non-national awards".[123] Noting that article V (1)*(d)* of the New York Convention allows a party to resist enforcement if "the arbitral procedure was not in accordance with the agreement of the parties", the court ruled that an award need not be made under national law to be enforced under the New York Convention. On this basis, the court found an award made by the Iran-United States Claims Tribunal to fall within the scope of the Convention.

61. French courts have also held that the New York Convention applies to "a-national" awards. For example, the Court of Appeal of Rouen found that an award rendered on the basis of an arbitration clause that expressly excluded the application of any national procedural law and regulated the procedure itself, fell within the scope of the New York Convention.[124]

62. Although the issue has been debated for some time,[125] the position that "a-national" awards fall within the scope of the Convention finds support in commentary.[126]

---

121 *Société Européenne d'Etudes et d'Entreprises (S.E.E.E.) v. Federal Republic of Yugoslavia*, Supreme Court, Netherlands, 7 November 1975, I Y.B. COM. ARB. 195 (1976).

122 *Société Européenne d'Etudes et d'Entreprises (S.E.E.E.) v. Federal Republic of Yugoslavia,* Court of Appeal of The Hague, Netherlands, 8 September 1972, I Y.B. COM. ARB. 195 (1976).

123 *Ministry* of *Defense of the Islamic Republic of Iran v. Gould Inc., Gould Marketing, Inc., Hoffman Export Corporation, and Gould International, Inc.*, Court of Appeals, Ninth Circuit, United States of America, 23 October 1989, 887 F.2d 1357.

124 *Société Européenne d'Etudes et d'Entreprises (S.E.E.E.) v. République Socialiste Fédérale de Yougoslavie,* Court of Appeal of Rouen, France, 13 November 1984, 982/82. See also *Société Aksa v. Société Norsolor*, Court of Appeal of Paris, France, 9 December 1980,1981 REV. ARB. 306.

125 ALBERT JAN VAN DEN BERG, THE NEW YORK ARBITRATION CONVENTION OF 1958: TOWARDS A UNIFORM JUDICIAL INTERPRETATION 34-40 (1981); Pieter Sanders, *Commentary*, I Y.B. COM. ARB. 207 (1976); Bernd Ehle, *Commentary on Article I*, in NEW YORK CONVENTION ON THE RECOGNITION AND ENFORCEMENT OF FOREIGN ARBITRAL AWARDS OF 10 JUNE 1958—COMMENTARY 26, 61 (R. Wolff ed., 2012).

126 Philippe Fouchard, *Commentary of General National Maritime Transport Co. v. Götaverken Arendal A.B.*, 107 J.D.I. 660, 669 and 673 (1980); Javier Rubinstein, Georgina Fabian, *The Territorial Scope of the New York Convention and Its Implementation in Common and Civil Law Countries*, in ENFORCEMENT OF ARBITRATION AGREEMENTS AND INTERNATIONAL ARBITRAL AWARDS: THE NEW YORK CONVENTION IN PRACTICE 91, 137 (E. Gaillard, D. Di Pietro eds., 2008); Tihilo Rensmann, *Anational Arbitral Awards: Legal*

63. The importance of the issue should however not be overestimated. The plain language of article I suggests that all awards which comply with either of the two criteria set out therein fall within the scope of the Convention irrespective of whether the law applicable to the arbitration proceedings was national or not.[127] Relying on the language of article I, the United States Court of Appeals for the Ninth Circuit held that article I does not "[c]ontain a separate jurisdictional requirement that the award be rendered subject to a 'national law'."[128]

D. Meaning of "arising out of differences"

64. Article I (1) provides that the New York Convention applies to the recognition and enforcement of arbitral awards "arising out of differences" between persons, whether physical or legal. Very few reported cases have addressed the meaning of the term "differences". Of those that have, the Supreme Court of Queensland, Australia, held that the term "differences" has a "clear meaning when used in connection with arbitration proceedings" and that it refers to a dispute.[129]

Article I (2)

65. Article I (2) provides that the term "arbitral awards" includes both "awards made by arbitrators appointed for each case" and awards "made by permanent arbitral bodies to which the parties have submitted."

66. Although the importance of a specific reference to awards made by permanent arbitral bodies was questioned during the Conference,[130] it was

---

Phenomenon or Academic Phantom, 15(2) J. INT'L ARB. 37, 64 (1998); Aida B. Avanessian, *The New York Convention and Denationalised Arbitral Awards (With Emphasis on the Iran-United States Claims Tribunal)*, 8(1) J. INT'L ARB. 5, 22 (1991); ICCA'S GUIDE TO THE INTERPRETATION OF THE 1958 NEW YORK CONVENTION: A HANDBOOK FOR JUDGES 23 (P. Sanders ed., 2011).

127 SEE ADAM SAMUEL, JURISDICTIONAL PROBLEMS IN INTERNATIONAL COMMERCIAL ARBITRATION: A STUDY OF BELGIAN, DUTCH, ENGLISH, FRENCH, SWEDISH, SWISS, UNITED STATES AND WEST GERMAN LAW 294 (1989); Hans van Houtte, *La loi belge du 27 mars 1985 sur l'arbitrage international*, 1986 REV. ARB. 29.

128 *Ministry of Defense of the Islamic Republic of Iran v. Gould Inc., Gould Marketing, Inc., Hoffman Export Corporation, and Gould International, Inc.*, Court of Appeals, Ninth Circuit, United States of America, 23 October 1989, 887 F.2d 1357.

129 *Resort Condominiums International Inc. v. Ray Bolwell and Resort Condominiums, Pty. Ltd.*, Supreme Court of Queensland, Australia, 29 October 1993, XX Y.B. COM. ARB. 628 (1995).

130 The delegate of France noted that "during all the years of the application of the 1923 Geneva Protocol and the 1927 Convention, no suggestion had ever been made that the term 'arbitral award' did not include an award made by a private permanent arbitral body". See *Travaux préparatoires*, United Nations Conference on International Commercial Arbitration, Summary Record of the Eight Meeting, E/CONF.26/SR.8, p. 4. The Chairman of the Conference similarly stated that there was "no need to state that the convention would apply to

eventually inserted at the behest of the Soviet and Czechoslovak delegates, who considered that the inclusion of the provision would "strengthen the Convention" and avoid certain difficulties "which had been encountered in the past and might arise again in the future".[131]

67. In this respect, the Italian Court of Cassation held that, pursuant to article I (2), the Convention applies not only to awards rendered by arbitrators appointed for a specific case, but also to awards rendered by permanent arbitral tribunals, such as, in the instant case, an arbitration panel sitting under the auspices of the Court of Arbitration at the Chamber of Commerce in Sofia.[132]

68. As an illustration, courts in reported cases have found that the term "permanent arbitral bodies" includes the following institutions: the Iran-United States Claims Tribunal,[133] the ICC International Court of Arbitration,[134] the Singapore International Arbitral Centre,[135] the Commercial Arbitration Centre in Sweden,[136] the Court of International Commercial Arbitration at the Chamber of Commerce and Industry of Ukraine,[137] the Arbitration Institute of the Central Chamber of Commerce of Finland,[138] and the Vienna Commodity Exchange Arbitration Board.[139]

Article I (3)

69. During the drafting of article I, the delegates of Israel and Bulgaria considered that a general reservation clause, "permitting any State to make such reservations as it saw fit", should be included in the text of the Convention in order to facilitate the accession of as large a number of States

---

awards made by permanent arbitral bodies, for their awards were no different from those made by specially appointed arbitrators." See *Travaux préparatoires*, Committee on the Enforcement of International Arbitral Awards, Summary Record of the Third Meeting, E/AC.42/SR.3, p. 4.

131 *Travaux préparatoires*, United Nations Conference on International Commercial Arbitration, Summary Record of the Eight Meeting, E/CONF.26/SR.8, pp. 6-8.

132 *Eugenio Menaguale v. Intercommerce (as legal successor* of *State Enterprise Balet*), Court of Cassation, Italy, 17 April 1978, 1842, IV Y.B. COM. ARB. 282 (1979).

133 *Ministry of Defense of the Islamic Republic of Iran v. Gould Inc., Gould Marketing, Inc., Hoffman Export Corporation, and Gould International, Inc.*, Court of Appeals, Ninth Circuit, United States of America, 23 October 1989, 887 F.2d 1357.

134 *FG Hemisphere Associates LLC v. Democratic Republic of Congo*, Supreme Court of New South Wales, Australia, 1 November 2010, [2010] NSWSC.

135 *Transpac Capital Pte Ltd. v. Buntoro*, Supreme Court of New South Wales, Australia, 7 July 2008, 11373 of 2008.

136 *Egyptian Concrete Company & Hashem Ali Maher v. STC Finance & Ismail Ibrahim Mahmoud Thabet & Sabishi Trading and Contracting Company*, Court of Cassation, Egypt, 27 March 1996, 2660/59.

137 Oberlandesgericht [OLG] Brandenburg, Germany, 2 September 1999, 8 Sch 01/99.

138 Oberlandesgericht [OLG] Brandenburg, Germany, 13 June 2002, 8 Sch 02/01.

139 *Holzindustrie Schweighofer GmbH v. Industria Legnami Trentina - ILET srl.*, Court of Appeal of Florence, Italy, 3 June 1988, XV Y.B. COM. ARB. 498 (1990).

as possible.[140] Other delegates were of the opinion that the greatest possible number of accessions should not be obtained "at the price of the Convention's usefulness".[141] In this context, the Turkish delegate noted that a significant number of reservations "would lessen the practical value of the Convention".[142] The matter was referred to a working group which reported that most of its members were opposed to including any reservation.[143] Nevertheless, the final text of article I (3) allows Contracting States to restrict the application of the Convention to awards made in the territory of another Contracting State and/or awards arising out of legal relationships considered to be commercial under the law of the State where recognition and enforcement is sought.

A. Reciprocity reservation

a. The territorial criterion and the reciprocity reservation

70. Pursuant to article I (3), Contracting States may declare that they will apply the Convention to the "recognition and enforcement of awards made only in the territory of another Contracting State".

71. Courts have held that when a Contracting State makes the reciprocity reservation, it will apply the New York Convention only to awards rendered in the territory of a State which is a party to the Convention.[144]

72. In those cases, courts have consistently held that the nationality of the parties is irrelevant for the purposes of establishing reciprocity.[145] What

---

[140] *Travaux préparatoires*, United Nations Conference on International Commercial Arbitration, Summary Record of the Twenty-first Meeting, E/CONF.26/SR.21, pp. 10-11.

[141] *Travaux préparatoires*, United Nations Conference on International Commercial Arbitration, Summary Record of the Twenty-first Meeting, E/CONF.26/SR.21, p. 11.

[142] *Travaux préparatoires*, United Nations Conference on International Commercial Arbitration, Summary Record of the Fifteenth Meeting, E/CONF.26/SR.15, p. 3.

[143] *Travaux préparatoires*, United Nations Conference on International Commercial Arbitration, Summary Record of the Fifteenth Meeting, E/CONF.26/SR.15, p. 3.

[144] *Norsolor S.A. v. Pabalk Ticaret Limited Sirketi*, Court of Appeal of Paris, France, 19 November 1982, I I0I92; Bundesgerichtshof [BGH], Germany, 14 April 1988, III ZR 12/87; *GSS Group Ltd. (Global Security Seals Group Ltd) v. National Port Authority*, District Court, District of Columbia, United States of America, 25 May 2012, 680 F.3d 805; Oberlandesgericht [OLG] Hamburg, Germany, 15 April 1964, II Y.B. COM. ARB. 232 (1977); *Yukos Oil Co. v. Dardana Ltd.*, Court of Appeal, England and Wales, 18 April 2002, [2002] EWCA Civ 543.

[145] *Gas Authority of India Ltd. v. Spie Capag S.A. and others*, High Court of Delhi, India, 15 October 1993, Suit No. 1440, IA No. 5206; *La Société Nationale Pour La Recherche, La Production, Le Transport, La Transformation et la Commercialisation Des Hydrocarbures v. Shaneen Natural Resources Company, Inc.*, District Court, Southern District of New York, United States of America, 15 November 1983, 585 F. Supp. 57; *Société Européenne d'Etudes*

matters is that reciprocity exists between the State where the award was rendered and the State where recognition and enforcement is sought.[146] For example, the Luxembourg Court of Appeal held that the fact that the two claimants had the nationality of a State that was not a party to the New York Convention was irrelevant, as the State where the award was rendered was a Contracting State.[147]

73. In certain States that have made the reciprocity reservation, the legislation implementing the Convention provides that, if the Official Gazette of that State does not indicate a given State's ratification of or accession to the Convention, the latter State cannot be considered to have acceded to the Convention. Therefore, as a result of the reciprocity reservation, an award rendered in such State will be unenforceable.[148] In one case, a court in India—where reciprocity is required—refused to refer the parties to arbitration in South Africa on the ground that the Indian Official Gazette did not mention South Africa's accession to the Convention, despite the fact that South Africa had acceded at that time.[149]

74. In Malaysia, a court initially held that a foreign award may only be enforced under the Convention if it appears from an order in the Malaysian Official Gazette that the State where the award was made is a Contracting Party to the Convention.[150] The Federal Court of Malaysia subsequently reversed this position, holding that an Order in the Official Gazette had only evidentiary value and that "the issue whether a State is a party to the New York Convention can be proved by adducing such other evidence as may be appropriate".[151]

---

et d'Entreprises (S.E.E.E.) v. République Socialiste Fédérale de Yougoslavie, Court of Appeals of Rouen, France, 13 November 1984, 982/82.

146 *Kersa Holding Company Luxembourg v. Infancourtage, Famajuk Investment and Isny*, Court of Appeal of Luxembourg, Luxembourg, 24 November 1993, XXI Y.B. COM. ARB. 617 (1996); Oberlandesgericht [OLG] Hamm, Germany, 6 July 1994, XXII Y.B. COM. ARB. 702 (1997).

147 *Kersa Holding Company Luxembourg v. Infancourtage, Famajuk Investment and Isny*, Court of Appeal of Luxembourg, Luxembourg, 24 November 1993, XXI Y.B. COM. ARB. 617 (1996).

148 *Gas Authority of India Ltd. v. Spie Capag S.A. and others*, High Court of Delhi, India, 15 October 1993, Suit No. 1440, IA No. 5206; *Brace Transport Corporation of Monrovia, Bermuda v. Orient Middle East Lines Ltd. and ors.*, Supreme Court, India, 12 October 1993, Civil Appeals Nos 5438-39 of 1993.

149 *Swiss Singapore Overseas Enterprises Pvt. Ltd. v. M/V African Trader*, High Court of Gujarat, India, 7 February 2005, Civil Application No. 23 of 2005.

150 *Sri Lanka Cricket v. World Sport Nimbus Pte Ltd.*, Court of Appeal of Putrajaya, Malaysia, 14 March 2006, W-04-964- 2004, XXXIII Y.B. COM. ARB. 607 (2008).

151 *Lombard Commodities Limited v. Alami Vegetable Oil Products SDN BHD*, Federal Court, Malaysia, 3 November 2009, Civil Appeal No. 02(f)-37-2008(W), XXXV Y.B. COM. ARB. 420 (2010). In so holding, the court relied on the relevant provision of the 1996 English Arbitration Act which provides that: "If Her Majesty by Order in Council declares that a state

75. There are only a handful of cases in which the enforcement of an award was refused on the basis of the reciprocity reservation. For example, in a decision rendered before Switzerland withdrew its reciprocity reservation in 1989, the Swiss Federal Tribunal held that an award rendered in London could not be enforced under the Convention as, at the time the award was rendered, the United Kingdom was not a party to the Convention.[152]

b. The non-domestic criterion and the reciprocity reservation

76. An argument has been made before United States courts that the reciprocity reservation excludes not only awards made in non-Contracting States from the scope of the New York Convention, but, also awards made in the enforcing State.[153] This argument is based on the expression "another Contracting State" in article I (3). United States courts have rejected this interpretation of article I (3). In so doing, they have held that the reciprocity reservation is distinct from the non-domestic provision contained in article I (1) and that it only concerns the inapplicability of the Convention to awards rendered in States that are not a party to the Convention.[154]

c. Meaning of "Contracting State"

77. When a State has made the reciprocity reservation under article I (3), that State will apply the Convention to the recognition and enforcement of awards made only in the territory of another "Contracting State".[155]

78. A question that has arisen with respect to the temporal application of the Convention is whether the State where the award is made must be a party

---

specified in the Order is a party to the New York Convention, or is a party in respect of any territory so specified, the Order shall, while in force, be conclusive evidence of that fact." See also *IPCO v. Nigerian National Petroleum Corp.*, High Court of Justice, England and Wales, 17 April 2008, [2008] EWHC 797 (Comm).

152 *Provenda S.A. v. Alimenta S.A. Switzerland*, Federal Tribunal, Switzerland, 12 December 1975, 101 Ia 521.

153 *Republic of Argentina v. BG Group PLC*, District Court, District of Columbia, United States of America, 7 June 2010, 715 F. Supp. 2d 108.

154 See *Republic of Argentina v. BG Group PLC*, District Court, District of Columbia, United States of America, 7 June 2010, 715 F. Supp. 2d 108. See also *Trans Chemical Limited v. China National Machinery Import and Export Corporation*, District Court, Southern District of Texas, Houston Division, United States of America, 7 July 1997, 978 F. Supp. 266.

155 *GSS Group Ltd. (Global Security Seals Group Ltd) v. National Port Authority*, District Court, District of Columbia, United States of America, 25 May 2012, 680 F.3d 805; *JCD (Japan) v. Zhongshan Gangyuan Industry Company Ltd.*, Zhongshan Intermediate People's Court, China, 22 October 2008, [2005] Zhong Zhong Fa Min Si Chu Zi No. 111; Court of Justice of Geneva, Switzerland, 14 April 1983, 187. The question of when a State becomes a party to the Convention has arisen in certain jurisdictions. For instance, the Supreme Court of Austria held that the Convention enters into force when a country has deposited its instruments in accordance with article IX. See Supreme Court, Austria, 17 November 1965, I Y.B. COM. ARB. 182 (1976).

to the Convention at the time the award is rendered and/or at the time recognition and enforcement is sought.

79. A Belgian court has refused to apply the Convention to an award rendered in a State that was not a party to the Convention at the time the award was made.[156]

80. Other courts have held that the question of whether a State is a party to the New York Convention is to be determined at the time recognition and enforcement is sought rather than at the time the award is rendered. For example, the House of Lords held that "an arbitration award made in the territory of a foreign state is enforceable in the United Kingdom [...] if the State in which the award was made is a party to the Convention at the date when proceedings to enforce the award begin, even if it was not a party at the date when the award was made".[157] Similarly, the Supreme Court of Austria granted enforcement of an award that was made in a State that was not a party to the Convention at the time the award was rendered, but had become a party by the time the enforcement proceedings were initiated.[158]

81. Courts in other jurisdictions including, Germany[159] and Hong Kong,[160] have adopted the same approach.

82. While the 1927 Geneva Convention provided that it was only applicable to arbitral awards made "after the coming into force of the [1923] Protocol on Arbitration Clauses", the New York Convention is silent on the question of its temporal application. Although not containing a specific reference as to the time at which a State becomes a Contracting State, the *travaux préparatoires* of the Convention indicate that the application of the New York Convention is not subject to any temporal limitation.[161]

---

[156] *Société Nationale pour la Recherche, le Transport et la Commercialisation des Hydrocarbures (Sonatrach) v. Ford, Bacon and Davis Inc.*, Court of First Instance of Brussels, Belgium, 6 December 1988, XV Y.B. COM. ARB. 370 (1990).

[157] *Minister of Public Works of the Government of the State* of *Kuwait v. Sir Frederick Snow & Partners,* House of Lords, England and Wales, 1 March 1984, [1984] A.C. 426.

[158] Supreme Court, Austria, 17 November 1965, I Y.B. COM. ARB. 182 (1976).

[159] Oberlandesgericht [OLG] Köln, Germany, 10 June 1976, IV Y.B. COM. ARB. 258 (1979); Hanseatisches Oberlandesgericht [OLG] Hamburg, Germany, 27 July 1978, IV Y.B. COM. ARB. 266 (1979).

[160] *Polytek Engineering Company Limited v. Hebei Import & Export Corporation,* High Court of the Hong Kong Special Administrative Region, Hong Kong, 16 January 1998, 116 of 1997, XXIII Y.B. COM. ARB. 666 (1998).

[161] *Travaux préparatoires*, United Nations Conference on International Commercial Arbitration, Summary Record of the Twenty-first Meeting, E/CONF.26/SR.21, p. 4.

B. Commercial reservation

83. The second reservation available to States under article I (3) is the commercial reservation. A Contracting State may declare that it will apply the Convention "only to differences arising out of legal relationships, whether contractual or not, which are considered as commercial under the national law of the State making such declaration".[162]

84. In the course of the drafting of article I, the ECOSOC *ad hoc* Committee considered whether the Convention should be limited to arbitral awards arising out of commercial disputes, as was envisaged in the early draft of the Convention prepared by the ICC.[163] After noting that certain countries do not differentiate between civil and commercial matters, the Committee decided not to limit the applicability of the New York Convention to commercial disputes. However, at the suggestion of the Dutch delegate on the penultimate day of the Conference, the commercial reservation was added.[164]

a. Meaning of "legal relationships considered as commercial under the national law of the State making such declaration"

85. When a State has made a commercial reservation, that State applies the New York Convention only to disputes arising out of "legal relationships considered as commercial under the national law of the State making such declaration". Courts have interpreted the scope of this phrase to be broad.[165] For example, a court in India has construed the phrase as being of the "largest import" encompassing "all the business and trade transactions in any of their forms".[166] A United States court has similarly held that the notion of "commercial relationship" is broad, noting that its purpose is only "to

[162] If an award did not arise out of a legal relationship considered as commercial, such award will not benefit from the regime established by the New York Convention, but the enforcement of such award will be governed by domestic law. See Philippe Fouchard, *La levée par la France de sa réserve de commercialité pour l'application de la Convention de New York,* 1990 REV. ARB. 571, 574, 579.

[163] *Travaux préparatoires*, Report of the Committee on the Enforcement of International Arbitral Awards, E/2704, E/AC.42/4/Rev.1., p. 8.

[164] The Dutch delegate argued that the text of the Convention which prevented States from limiting the application of the Convention to commercial disputes, would cause great difficulties to countries in which commercial law was distinct from civil law, such as France, Belgium and Turkey. See *Travaux préparatoires*, United Nations Conference on International Commercial Arbitration, Summary Record of the Twenty-third Meeting, E/CONF.26/SR.23, pp. 7, 12.

[165] Michael Pryles, *Reservations Available to Member States: The Reciprocal and Commercial Reservations*, in ENFORCEMENT OF ARBITRATION AGREEMENTS AND INTERNATIONAL ARBITRAL AWARDS: THE NEW YORK CONVENTION IN PRACTICE 161, 178-79 (E. Gaillard, D. Di Pietro eds., 2008).

[166] *Union of India and ors v. Lief Hoegh & Co. and ors.*, High Court of Gujarat, India, 4 May 1982.

exclude matrimonial and other domestic relations awards, political awards, and the like".[167]

86. By way of example, the following legal relationships have been deemed to be commercial: a cereal purchase contract,[168] a charter-party,[169] a contract for provision of consulting services,[170] a contract for the shipment of goods,[171] an agreement for the division of property and businesses,[172] a joint venture agreement to establish and operate a chain of stores,[173] a seamen's employment contract,[174] a contract for the reorganization of a company and buyout of shareholders,[175] a contract for the construction of a nitrophosphate plant,[176] and a dispute between corporate shareholders regarding the proceeds of a stock transaction.[177]

87. Conversely, in one case, an Indian court held that a contract for the supply of technical know-how in return for a fee was not a commercial contract.[178] In another case, a Tunisian court held that a contract for an

---

167 *Island Territory of Curacao v. Solitron Devices, Inc.*, Court of Appeals, Second Circuit, United States of America, 14 February 1973, 356 F. Supp. 1.

168 *West Plains Company v. Northwest Organic Community Mills Co-operative Ltd.*, Queen's Bench for Saskatchewan, Canada, 5 May 2009, 2009 SKQB 162.

169 *Swiss Singapore Overseas Enterprises Pvt Ltd. v. M/V African Trader*, High Court of Gujarat, India, 7 February 2005, Civil Application No. 23 of 2005.

170 *R.M. Investments & Trading Co. v. Boeing Co.*, Supreme Court, India, 10 February 1994, 1994 AIR 1136.

171 *European Grain and Shipping Ltd. v. Bombay Extractions Ltd.*, High Court of Bombay, India, 5 November 1981, AIR 1983 Bom 36.

172 *Harendra H. Mehta, et al. v. Mukesh H. Mehta, et al.*, Supreme Court, India, 13 May 1999, 1999(3) SCR 562.

173 *Trevino Hernandez, S. de R.L. de C.V. v. Smart & Final Inc.*, District Court, Southern District of California, United States of America, 17 June 2010, 09-cv-2266 BEN (NLS).

174 *Nurettin Mayakan v. Carnival Corporation*, District Court, Middle District of Florida, Orlando Division, United States of America, 8 April 2010, 6:09-cv-2099-Orl-31DAB; *Aggarao v. MOL Ship Management Company Ltd., Nissan Motor Car Carrier Company, Ltd., trading as Nissan Carrier Fleet World Car Careers*, Court of Appeals, Fourth Circuit, United States of America, 16 March 2012, 675 F.3d 355; *Bautista v. Star Cruises and Norwegian Cruise Line, Ltd.*, District Court, Southern District of Florida, United States of America, 14 October 2003, 286 F. Supp. 2d 1352; *Ernesto Francisco v. Stolt Achievement MT*, Court of Appeals, Fifth Circuit, United States of America, 4 June 2002, 293 F.3d 270; *contra Wilfredo Jaranilla v. Megasea Maritime Ltd., Prankar Maritime S.A., Greece and Kouros Maritime Enterprises*, District Court, Eastern District of Louisiana, United States of America, 12 October 2001,171 F. Supp. 2d 644.

175 *Anthony N. LaPine v. Kyocera Corporation*, District Court, Northern District of California, United States of America, 22 May 2008, C 07-06132 MHP.

176 *Fertilizer Corp. of India v. IDI Mgmt. Inc.*, District Court, Southern District of Ohio, United States of America, 9 June 1981, 517 F. Supp. 948.

177 *Louise Henry v. Patrick J. Murphy*, District Court, Southern District of New York, United States of America, 8 January 2002, M-82 (PART I JFK), XXVII Y.B. COM. ARB. 863 (2002).

178 *Kanoria Chemicals & Industries v. Josef Meissner GmbH & Co. and anor.*, High Court of Calcutta, India, 1 January 1986, Suit No. 93 of 1984.

architectural plan for a resort was not commercial under Tunisian law.[179] In yet a further case, a United States court held that a dispute arising out of proceedings to disqualify counsel was non-commercial.[180]

b. Meaning of "whether contractual or not"

88. An issue that has arisen before courts is whether the expression "whether contractual or not" includes claims in tort.

89. Courts have found that the expression "whether contractual or not" does cover torts. For example, the Court of Appeal of Alberta, Canada, held that the Convention "extend[s] [its] scope to liability in tort so long as the relationship that creates liability is one that can fairly be described as commercial". The Court found that the claim that a corporation had conspired with its subsidiaries to cause harm to a person concerned a dispute "arising out of a commercial legal relationship, whether contractual or not".[181]

90. Similarly, the High Court of Delhi held that the Convention applies to "disputes arising out of legal relationships whether *stricto sensu* contractual or not provided they are considered as commercial under the domestic law of the State making such a declaration".[182]

91. The case law is fully consistent with the *travaux préparatoires*.[183]

---

179 *Taieb Haddad v. Hans Barett, Société d'Investissement Kal*, Supreme Court, Tunisia, 10 November 1993, XXIII Y.B. COM. ARB. 770 (1998).

180 *R3 Aerospace v. Marshall of Cambridge Aerospace Ltd.*, District Court, Southern District of New York, United States of America, 29 May 1996, 927 F. Supp. 121.

181 *Raverit Steel v. Kone Corp.*, Court of Appeal of Alberta, Canada, 16 January 1992, ABCA 7.

182 *Gas Authority of India Ltd. v. Spie Capag SA and others*, High Court of Delhi, India, 15 October 1993, Suit No. 1440, IA No. 5206. See also *European Grain and Shipping Ltd. v. Bombay Extractions Ltd.*, High Court of Bombay, India, 5 November 1981, AIR 1983 Bom 36.

183 In the course of the drafting of the commerciality reservation, the Greek delegate proposed to include, "in addition to disputes arising out of commercial contracts, disputes arising out of commercial obligations ex delictu and quasi ex delictu". See *Travaux préparatoires*, Recognition and Enforcement of Foreign Arbitral Awards, Comments by Governments on the draft Convention on the Recognition and Enforcement of Foreign Arbitral Awards, E/2822/Add.2, Annex I, p. 1. The Italian delegate proposed to use the term "relations" instead of the term "contract" so as to "cover both contractual and non-contractual disputes". See *Travaux préparatoires*, United Nations Conference on International Commercial Arbitration, Summary Record of the Twenty-first Meeting, E/CONF.26/SR.21, p. 16. The delegate from the United Kingdom proposed a further amendment to include the wording "whether contractual or not" after the wording "legal relationship", which was accepted by the Conference. See *Travaux préparatoires*, United Nations Conference on International Commercial Arbitration, Summary Record of the Twenty-third Meeting, E/CONF.26/SR.23, p. 11.

Article II

1. Each Contracting State shall recognize an agreement in writing under which the parties undertake to submit to arbitration all or any differences which have arisen or which may arise between them in respect of a defined legal relationship, whether contractual or not, concerning a subject matter capable of settlement by arbitration.

2. The term "agreement in writing" shall include an arbitral clause in a contract or an arbitration agreement, signed by the parties or contained in an exchange of letters or telegrams.

3. The court of a Contracting State, when seized of an action in a matter in respect of which the parties have made an agreement within the meaning of this article, shall, at the request of one of the parties, refer the parties to arbitration, unless it finds that the said agreement is null and void, inoperative or incapable of being performed.

Travaux préparatoires

The *travaux préparatoires* on article II as adopted in 1958 are contained in the following documents:

Draft Convention on the Recognition and Enforcement of Foreign Arbitral Awards and comments by Governments and Organizations:

Report of the Committee on the Enforcement of International Arbitral Awards: E/2704 and annex.

Comments by Governments and Organizations on the Draft Convention on the Recognition and Enforcement of Foreign Arbitral Awards: E/2822, annexes I-II; E/2822/Add.1, annex I; E/2822/Add.2, annex I; E/2822/Add.4, annex I; E/2822/Add.5, annex I; E/CONF.26/3/Add.1.

United Nations Conference on International Commercial Arbitration:

Amendments to the Draft Convention Submitted by Governmental Delegations: E/CONF.26/7; E/CONF.26/L.8; E/CONF.26/L.17; E/CONF.26/L.18; E/CONF.26/L.18; E/CONF.26/L.20; E/CONF.26/L.22; E/CONF.26/L.31; E/CONF.26/C.3/L.1; E/CONF.26/L.34.

Comparison of Drafts Relating to Articles III, IV and V of the Draft Convention: E/CONF.26/L.33.

Statement submitted by the Observer of the Hague Conference on Private International Law: E/CONF.26/L.36.

Further Amendments to the Draft Convention Submitted by Governmental Delegations: E/CONF.26/L.40.

Text of Additional Protocol on the Validity of Arbitral Agreements Submitted by Working Party No. 2: E/CONF.26/L.52.

Amendments by Governmental Delegations to the Drafts Submitted by the Working Parties and Further Suggested Drafts: E/CONF.26/L.45; E/CONF.26/C.3/L.3; E/CONF.26/L.53; E/CONF.26/L.54.

Text of New Articles to be Included in the Convention Adopted by the Conference: E/CONF.26/L.59.

Text of the Convention on the Recognition and Enforcement of Foreign Arbitral Awards as Provisionally Approved by the Drafting Committee: E/CONF.26/L.61; E/CONF.26/8.

Summary records:

Summary Records of the Seventh, Ninth, Eleventh, Twelfth, Thirteenth, Fourteenth, Seventeenth, Twenty-first, Twenty-third and Twenty-fourth Meetings of the United Nations Conference on International Commercial Arbitration: E/CONF.26/SR.7; E/CONF.26/SR.9; E/CONF.26/SR.11; E/CONF.26/SR.12; E/CONF.26/SR.13; E/CONF.26/SR.14; E/CONF.26/SR.17; E/CONF.26/SR.21; E/CONF.26/SR.23; E/CONF.26/SR.24.

Summary Record of the Fourth Meeting of the Committee on the Enforcement of International Arbitral Awards: E/AC.42/SR.4.

(Available on the Internet at http://www.uncitral.org)

(For the *travaux préparatoires*, case law and bibliographical references, see also on the Internet at http://newyorkconvention1958.org)

Introduction

1. Article II governs the recognition and enforcement of arbitration agreements. Provided that certain conditions are satisfied, article II mandates Contracting States to recognize an agreement in writing to submit disputes to arbitration and to enforce such an agreement by referring the parties to arbitration.

2. The scope of the New York Convention was initially meant to be limited to the recognition and enforcement of arbitral awards to the exclusion of arbitration agreements.[184] While issues pertaining to the validity of arbitration agreements had arisen in the context of discussions about the recognition and enforcement of arbitral awards in connection with articles IV (1)*(b)* and V (1)*(a)* of the Convention[185], it was only during the United Nations Conference on International Commercial Arbitration convened for the preparation and adoption of the Convention, less than three weeks before the Convention was adopted, that the drafters decided to include a specific provision on the recognition and enforcement of arbitration agreements.[186] By that time, most of the other provisions had already been adopted and they were not modified to reflect this late addition.[187] This explains why the recognition and enforcement of arbitration agreements is not mentioned in the Convention's title or in any other provisions, including articles I and VII.

3. For example, article I (1) which defines the scope of application of the Convention does not deal with arbitration agreements. However, the commercial reservation in article I (3) which applies to "differences arising out of legal relationships" encompasses, by its own terms, arbitration agreements set out in article II. By contrast, the Convention does not explicitly settle the issue whether the reciprocity reservation in article I (3)

---

[184] *Travaux préparatoires*, Report of the Committee on the Enforcement of International Arbitral Awards, E/2704, E/AC.42/4/Rev.1, p. 6, paras. 18-19. The Polish (E/CONF.26/7) and Swedish (E/CONF.26/L.8) proposals to add a provision on the validity of arbitration clauses were discussed during the Seventh and Ninth Meeting of the Conference but were ultimately rejected.

[185] *Travaux préparatoires*, United Nations Conference on International Commercial Arbitration, Summary Records of the Eleventh (E/CONF.26/SR.11, pp. 7-12), Twelfth (E/CONF.26/SR.12, pp. 3-6), Thirteenth (E/CONF.26/SR.13, pp. 4-7 and 9-11), Fourteenth (E/CONF.26/SR.14, pp. 4-5 and 7-9), Seventeenth (E/CONF.26/SR.17, pp. 4-6) Meetings.

[186] *Travaux préparatoires*, United Nations Conference on International Commercial Arbitration, Summary Records of the Twenty-first Meeting, E/CONF.26/SR.21, p. 17. See E/2822 Annexes I and II.

[187] *Ibid.*

which deals with "the recognition and enforcement of awards made [...] in the territory of another Contracting State" applies *mutadis mutandis* to arbitration agreements.

4. Certain courts have reasoned by analogy to article I (1) that the Convention applies only to arbitration agreements providing for a seat in a State other than the State of the court seized with the dispute.[188] This interpretation has been endorsed by certain commentators.[189]

5. Other commentators have suggested that article II was meant to apply to the recognition and enforcement of all arbitration agreements irrespective of the seat. A commentator, for example, points out that the proposal by Israel (which was further modified by Italy) to introduce a general reservation clause enabling States not to apply article II in certain situations had been rejected during the Conference. Accordingly, this would leave no doubt as to the intention of the drafters of the New York Convention that article II should cover both domestic and international situations without any limitations.[190] Another early commentator of the Convention also took the view that article II, unlike the 1923 Geneva Protocol on Arbitration Clauses, does not require the parties to be subject to the jurisdiction of different Contracting States, thereby giving the provision a general application.[191] Other commentators have suggested that the New York Convention did not intend to incorporate any territorial limitations on the

---

188 *Kaverit Steel and Crane v. Kone Corp.*, Alberta Court of Queen's Bench, Canada, 14 May 1991; *Compagnie de Navigation et Transports S.A. v. MSC Mediterranean Shipping Company S.A.*, Federal Tribunal, Switzerland, 16 January 1995; Federal Tribunal, Switzerland, 21 March 1995, 5C.215/1994/lit; Federal Tribunal, Switzerland, 25 October 2010, 4 A 279/2010; *X v. Y*, Federal Tribunal, Switzerland, 9 January 2008, 4A_436/2007.

189 Reinmar Wolff, *Commentary on Article II*, in NEW YORK CONVENTION ON THE RECOGNITION AND ENFORCEMENT OF FOREIGN ARBITRAL AWARDS OF 10 JUNE 1958—COMMENTARY 85, 99-104 (R. Wolff ed., 2012); ICCA'S GUIDE TO THE INTERPRETATION OF THE 1958 NEW YORK CONVENTION: A HANDBOOK FOR JUDGES 19 (P. Sanders ed., 2011); Jean-François Poudret, Gabriel Cottier, *Remarques sur l'application de l'Article II de la Convention de New York*, 1995 ASA BULL. 383, 384.

190 Eugenio Minoli, *L'Italie et la Convention de New York pour la reconnaissance et l'exécution des sentences arbitrales étrangères*, in INTERNATIONAL ARBITRATION LIBER AMICORUM FOR MARTIN DOMKE 199, 203 (P. Sanders ed., 1967). See also the *Travaux préparatoires*, United Nations Conference on International Commercial Arbitration, Summary Records of the Twenty-First Meeting, E/CONF.26/SR.21, p. 14, the comments by the representative of Norway that "a reservation to the effect that the Convention would apply to disputes of an international character was essential" and by the representative of Italy that "his proposal was designed to ensure that the Convention would not apply to disputes which were not international."

191 Frédéric-Edouard Klein, *Autonomie de la volonté et arbitrage (suite et fin)*, 1958 R.C.D.I.P. 479, 491.

scope of application on arbitration agreements falling within the scope of article II.[192]

6. In that spirit, the High Court of Delhi held that, on the face of article II, there is no "express or implied limitation or fetter which calls for recognition and enforcement of only those arbitration agreements which will result in foreign awards. Such a construction cannot be placed upon the said article as this would go against the spirit and grain of the convention". The court concluded that "the New York Convention will apply to an arbitration agreement if it has a foreign element or flavour involving international trade and commerce even though such an agreement does not lead to a foreign award [...]."[193] The same approach has been adopted by United States courts pursuant to the Federal Arbitration Act and the New York Convention.[194] French courts have similarly taken the view that the Convention should apply to a challenge to the existence or validity of an arbitration agreement, and that this was not restricted in any way by the language of article I.[195]

7. Article II governs the form and effects of arbitration agreements. Article II (1) requires each Contracting State to recognize an "agreement in writing" under which the parties undertake to submit their disputes to arbitration. This provision has been interpreted as establishing a presumption that arbitration agreements are valid.[196] Article II (2), which governs the form of "agreements in writing", covers agreements that have been "signed by the parties or contained in an exchange of letters or telegrams."

8. To ensure that arbitration agreements are complied with, article II (3) requires national courts seized of a matter covered by an arbitration agreement to refer the parties to arbitration, "unless it finds that the said agreement is null and void, inoperative or incapable of being performed." The underlying principle that the parties to an arbitration agreement are required to honour their undertaking to submit to arbitration any dispute

---

[192] See, e.g., Philippe Fouchard, *La levée par la France de sa réserve de commercialité pour l'application de la Convention de New York*, 1990 REV. ARB. 571, reasoning that given France's withdrawal of the commercial reservation, article II applies to all arbitration agreements.

[193] *Gas Authority of India Ltd. v. SPIE-CAPAG SA and ors*, High Court of Delhi, India, 15 October 1993, Suit No. 1440; IA No. 5206.

[194] *Fred Freudensprung v. Offshore Technical Services, Inc., et al.*, Court of Appeals, Fifth Circuit, United States of America, 9 August 2004, 03-20226.

[195] *Société Bomar Oil N.V. v. Entreprise tunisienne d'activités pétrolières (ETAP)*, Court of Appeal of Versailles, France, 23 January 1991, upheld by *Société Bomar Oil N.V. v. Entreprise tunisienne d'activités pétrolières (ETAP)*, Court of Cassation, France, 9 November 1993, 91-15.194.

[196] ALBERT JAN VAN DEN BERG, THE NEW YORK ARBITRATION CONVENTION OF 1958: TOWARDS A UNIFORM JUDICIAL INTERPRETATION 156 (1981); ICCA'S GUIDE TO THE INTERPRETATION OF THE 1958 NEW YORK CONVENTION: A HANDBOOK FOR JUDGES 37 (P. SANDERS ED., 2011).

covered by their arbitration agreement is given effect by the mandatory requirement on national courts to refer the parties to arbitration when presented with a valid arbitration agreement. It follows that national courts are prohibited from hearing the merits of such disputes. In accordance with the principle of competence-competence, which empowers arbitrators to rule on their own jurisdiction, a challenge to the existence or validity of an arbitration agreement will not prevent an arbitral tribunal from proceeding with the arbitration.[197]

9. By accepting the principle of competence-competence, national courts do not relinquish their power to review the existence and validity of an arbitration agreement as they recover their power of full scrutiny of the arbitration agreement at the end of the arbitral process, once the award is rendered by the arbitral tribunal. The question arises whether, at the pre-award stage, in complying with their obligation to refer the parties to arbitration pursuant to article II (3), national courts could conduct a full or a limited review of the arbitration agreement to determine whether a valid arbitration agreement exists. In some jurisdictions, courts have limited their scrutiny to a *prima facie* review, thereby leaving the arbitrators to be the first to fully decide the issue of their jurisdiction. This principle, sometimes referred to as the "negative effect of competence-competence", gives arbitrators priority in determining their jurisdiction, while the courts keep the power to conduct a full review of the existence, validity and scope of the arbitration agreement at the end of the arbitral process.[198] In other jurisdictions, courts conduct a full review of the existence, validity and scope of the arbitration agreement in order to determine whether to refer the parties to arbitration.

10. The standard to be applied by the courts in determining whether the agreement is "null and void, inoperative or incapable of being performed" when deciding whether to refer the parties to arbitration therefore remains debated.[199]

---

[197] PHILIPPE FOUCHARD, L'ARBITRAGE COMMERCIAL INTERNATIONAL, para. 203 (1965); Antonias Dimolitsa, *Separability and Kompetenz-Kompetenz*, in IMPROVING THE EFFICIENCY OF ARBITRATION AND AWARDS: 40 YEARS OF APPLICATION OF THE NEW YORK CONVENTION, ICCA CONGRESS SERIES NO. 9, 217 (A.J. van den Berg ed., 1999).

[198] Emmanuel Gaillard, Yas Banifatemi, *Prima facie Review of Existence, Validity of Arbitration Agreement*, N.Y.L.J., (December 2005); Dorothee Schramm, Elliott Geisinger,Philippe Pinsolle, *Article II*, in RECOGNITION AND ENFORCEMENT OF FOREIGN ARBITRAL AWARDS: A GLOBAL COMMENTARY ON THE NEW YORK CONVENTION 37, 95-96 (H. Kronke, P. Nacimiento et al. eds., 2010).

[199] See the chapter of the Guide on article II, paras. 79-99.

Analysis

Article II (1)

A. The obligation to recognize an agreement in writing

11. Article II (1) provides that, when certain conditions are met, Contracting States "shall" recognize an agreement in writing to arbitrate.

12. The obligation to recognize an "agreement in writing" is widely accepted by national courts. The Supreme Court of the United States has held that the compulsory language "shall" in article II (1) leaves courts with no discretion as they must recognize the arbitration agreement in accordance with the clear provisions of the Federal Arbitration Act and the New York Convention.[200] Similarly, the Swiss Federal Tribunal has interpreted article II as obliging Contracting States to recognize the validity and effect of an arbitration agreement.[201] The mandatory nature of the requirement to recognize and enforce arbitration agreements has been confirmed by decisions in most jurisdictions.[202]

B. Meaning of "agreement"

13. Article II (1) deals with the agreement to arbitrate. When deciding whether to enforce an arbitration agreement, courts rely on the consent of the parties to establish whether they have agreed to submit the underlying dispute to arbitration.

14. The task of a court in determining an agreement to arbitration has been defined as follows by the Supreme Court of the United States under both the Federal Arbitration Act and the New York Convention: "the first

---

[200] *Scherk v. Alberto-Culver Company*, Supreme Court, United States of America, 17 June 1974, 73-781. See also *Lindo (Nicaragua) v. NCL (Bahamas), Ltd.*, Court of Appeals, Eleventh Circuit, United States of America, 29 August 2011, 10-10367; *Ernesto Francisco v. Stolt Achievement MT*, Court of Appeals, Fifth Circuit, United States of America, 4 June 2002, 01-30694.

[201] *Tradax Export S.A. v. Amoco Iran Oil Company*, Federal Tribunal, Switzerland, 7 February 1984.

[202] *Seeley International Pty Ltd. v. Electra Air*, Federal Court, Australia, 29 January 2008, SAD 157 of 2007; *Sunward Overseas SA v. Servicios Maritimos Limitada Semar*, Supreme Court of Justice, Colombia, 20 November 1992, 472; *SA C.F.T.E. v. Jacques Dechavanne*, Court of Appeal of Grenoble, France, 13 September 1993; *Westco Airconditioning Ltd. v. Sui Chong Construction & Engineering Co. Ltd.*, Court of First Instance, High Court of the Hong Kong Special Administrative Region, Hong Kong, 3 February 1998, A12848; *Renusagar Power Co. Ltd. v. General Electric Company and anor.*, Supreme Court, India, 16 August 1984; *Louis Dreyfus Corporation of New York v. Oriana Soc. di Navigazione S.p.a*, Court of Cassation, Italy, 27 February 1970, 470, I Y.B. COM. ARB. 189 (1976).

task of a court asked to compel arbitration of a dispute is to determine whether the parties agreed to arbitrate" the dispute.[203] As confirmed by an Australian court, consent falls to be assessed on a case-by-case basis.[204]

15. Reported case law in various jurisdictions applying the Convention shows that parties were referred to arbitration pursuant to article II (3) when courts have found that the parties had consented to arbitration. Consent to arbitration has been found in a variety of situations, including when the parties (i) participated in the negotiation of the contract, (ii) participated in the performance of the contract, (iii) participated in both the negotiation and performance of the contract, (iv) had knowledge of the arbitration agreement, or (v) participated in the arbitral proceedings without raising any objection to the arbitral tribunal's jurisdiction.

16. First, a United States court held that participation in the negotiation of the contract containing the arbitration clause through an exchange of documents evidences the parties' consent to arbitrate any dispute arising out of that contract, thereby satisfying the requirements of article II.[205] In so ruling, the court noted that the party had affixed its stamp to the broker's slip as further evidence of consent.

17. Second, evidence of consent has been found in the parties' conduct in performing the contract. In situations where a party does not sign the contract or return a written confirmation, but nevertheless performs its obligations, many courts have held that such conduct amounts to a tacit acceptance of the terms of the contract, including the arbitration agreement.[206] For example, the Indian Supreme Court has enforced an arbitral award notwithstanding the fact that the arbitration agreement was

---

203 *Mitsubishi Motors Corp v. Soler Chrysler-Plymouth*, Supreme Court, United States of America, 2 July 1985, 3-1569.

204 *ACD Tridon v. Tridon Australia*, Supreme Court of New South Wales, Australia, 4 October 2002, 5738 of 2001. See also *Moscow Dynamo v. Alexander M. Ovechkin*, District Court, District of Columbia, United States of America, 18 January 2006, 05-2245 (EGS) where the United States District Court of Colombia denied enforcement of the alleged arbitration clause as it was unable to find "factual predicate or legal authority to support [the] argument that a written agreement to arbitrate can be found absent a written exchange demonstrating both parties' agreement to arbitrate with one another."

205 *Chloe Z Fishing Co. Inc., et al. v. Odyssey Re (London) Ltd., formerly known as Sphere Drake Insurance, P.L.C., et al.*, District Court, Southern District of California, United States of America, 26 April 2000, 109 F. Supp. 2d 1236 (2000).

206 *Metropolitan Steel Corporation Ltd. v. Macsteel International U.K. Ltd.*, High Court of Karachi, Pakistan, 7 March 2006, XXXII Y.B. COM. ARB. 449 (2007); *Standard Bent Glass Corp. v. Glassrobots OY [Fin.]*, Court of Appeals, Third Circuit, United States of America, 20 June 2003, 02-2169; *Compagnie de Navigation et Transports S.A. v. MSC Mediterranean Shipping Company S.A.*, Federal Tribunal, Switzerland, 16 January 1995; *Smita Conductors Ltd. v. Euro Alloys Ltd.*, Supreme Court, India, 31 August 2001, Civil Appeal No. 12930 of 1996. *Contra, Concordia Trading BV. v. Nantong Gangde Oil Co., Ltd.*, Supreme People's Court, China, 3 August 2009, [2009] MinSiTaZi No. 22.

neither signed nor contained in an exchange of documents. It held that the party, in particular by opening letters of credit in reliance on the contract and invoking the contract's force majeure clause, accepted the terms of the written contract, including the arbitration clause.[207] Following the same reasoning, but applying French law on the basis of the "more-favourable-right" provision at article VII (1),[208] a French court upheld an arbitration agreement contained in a booking note on the ground that the parties had performed the booking note. The court held that since the parties had knowledge of the booking note, which constituted the parties' sole "meeting of minds", they were bound by the arbitration agreement contained therein.[209]

18. Third, when a party that did not sign the contract containing the arbitration agreement had nevertheless participated in the negotiation of, and performed obligations under, that contract, certain courts have referred that non-signatory to arbitration. In a case concerning an action to set aside an award, but dealing with the issue of the binding character of an arbitration agreement on a non-signatory, the Paris Court of Appeal confirmed that the parent company that participated in the negotiation of and assumed obligations under the main contract was bound by the arbitration agreement, despite not being a party to the main contract.[210] However, this approach is not universally accepted. For instance, in the *Dallah* case, the Supreme Court of the United Kingdom, relying on the New York Convention, refused to grant leave to a party seeking to enforce an award rendered against the Islamic Republic of Pakistan on the grounds that there was no evidence that the common intention of the parties was to add the Government of Pakistan as a party to the main contract, despite its participating in negotiations and in the performance of certain obligations under that contract.[211]

---

[207] *Smita Conductors Ltd. v. Euro Alloys Ltd.*, Supreme Court, India, 31 August 2001, Civil Appeal No. 12930 of 1996.

[208] ALBERT JAN VAN DEN BERG, THE NEW YORK ARBITRATION CONVENTION OF 1958: TOWARDS A UNIFORM JUDICIAL INTERPRETATION 81 (1981); Emmanuel Gaillard, *The Relationship of the New York Convention with other Treaties and with Domestic Law*, in ENFORCEMENT OF ARBITRATION AGREEMENTS AND INTERNATIONAL ARBITRAL AWARDS: THE NEW YORK CONVENTION IN PRACTICE 69, 70 (E. Gaillard, D. Di Pietro eds., 2008).

[209] *SA Groupama transports v. Société MS Régine Hans und Klaus Heinrich KG*, Court of Appeal of Basse Terre, France, 18 April 2005.

[210] *Société Kis France et autres v. Société Générale et autres*, Court of Appeal of Paris, France, 31 October 1989, 1992 REV. ARB. 90. For a similar reasoning, finding that the Government of Turkmenistan "acted as the alter ego of [a State owned entity] in regard to this Joint Venture with [the claimant in the arbitration]": *Bridas S.A.P.I.C., Bridas Energy International, Ltd., Intercontinental Oil and Gas Ventures, Ltd., and Bridas Corp v. Government of Turkmenistan*, Court of Appeals, Fifth Circuit, United States of America, 21 April 2006, 04-20842.

[211] *Dallah Real Estate and Tourism Holding Company v. Ministry of Religious Affairs, Government of Pakistan*, Supreme Court, England and Wales, 3 November 2010, UKSC 2009/0165. See also the contrary decision by the French Paris Court of Appeal in the same

19. Fourth, consent has also been found in situations where a party had knowledge of the arbitration agreement. For instance, when the arbitration agreement is printed on the back of the contract (or contained in general terms and conditions printed on the back of the contract), parties have been deemed to have knowledge of the agreement to arbitrate as they had the opportunity to review the arbitration agreement.[212] In this vein, in a dispute where the arbitration agreement was contained in a document other than the main contract, the Italian Court of Cassation noted that, in order to establish the parties' consent to an arbitration agreement, the parties had to have knowledge of the arbitration agreement through a specific reference to it in the main contract ("*per relationem perfecta*").[213]

20. In some jurisdictions, parties are deemed to have knowledge of the arbitration agreement when, irrespective of whether they had actual knowledge of the arbitration agreement, they should reasonably have known about it. In such cases, courts will enforce arbitration agreements when parties are aware of the arbitration agreement or should have been aware of the arbitration agreement. For instance, the Italian Court of Cassation now recognizes that, when the parties are professional businessmen who should be aware of the content of general terms and conditions in their field, a generic reference to such terms and conditions ("*per relationem imperfecta*") satisfies the requirement of article II of the Convention.[214] German courts also admit that consent can be implied from relevant international trade usages when the contract is typical of the industry and the parties are active in the relevant field of business.[215]

21. Some courts have also ruled that parties are bound by an arbitration agreement incorporated by reference on the grounds that they should have been aware of its terms. It is indeed very common in international trade for parties not to set out the terms of their contract in detail, but instead to refer to separate documents, such as general conditions and standard-form agreements produced by professional bodies, which may contain arbitration agreements.[216] Some courts have accepted that, by referring to general terms

matter: *Gouvernement du Pakistan—Ministère des affaires religieuses v. société Dallah Real Estate and Tourism Holding Company*, Court of Appeal of Paris, France, 17 February 2011, 09/28533, 09/28535 and 09/28541, 2011 REV. ARB. 286.

212 Court of Appeal of the Canton of Basel-Landschaft, Switzerland, 5 July 1994, 30-94/261; *Bobbie Brooks Inc. v. Lanificio Walter Banci s.a.s.*, Court of Appeal of Firenze, Italy, 8 October 1977, IV Y.B. COM. ARB. 289 (1979).

213 *Louis Dreyfus S.p.A. v. Cereal Mangimi S.r.l.*, Court of Cassation, Italy, 19 May 2009, 11529.

214 *Del Medico & C. SAS v. Iberprotein Sl*, Court of Cassation, Italy, 16 June 2011, 13231.

215 Bundesgerichtshof [BGH], Germany, 3 December 1992, III ZR 30/91.

216 Domenico Di Pietro, *Validity of Arbitration Clauses Incorporated by Reference*, in ENFORCEMENT OF ARBITRATION AGREEMENTS AND INTERNATIONAL ARBITRAL AWARDS: THE NEW YORK CONVENTION 1958 IN PRACTICE 355 (E. Gaillard, D. Di Pietro eds., 2008).

and conditions in their contract, the parties have consented to the arbitration agreement therein because they should reasonably have known about the arbitration agreement.[217] Indeed, as noted by an Indian court, article II does not specify that the agreement to arbitrate must be contained in a single document.[218] Hence, in a case where the Convention applied, a United States court upheld an arbitration agreement contained in general terms and conditions on the grounds that the parties had tacitly consented to the general terms and conditions to which the contract referred, notwithstanding the fact that the plaintiff had never been in possession of those general terms and conditions. The court reasoned that failure to request the terms and conditions referred to in a contract implied tacit acceptance of its terms, including the arbitration agreement.[219] In the same vein, in *Bomar*, relying on both the Convention and French law, a French court held that an arbitration agreement contained in a document referred to in the main contract should be enforced insofar as it could be demonstrated that the parties were aware or should have been aware of it.[220] A number of courts have thus upheld arbitration agreements contained in general conditions referred to in the main contract.[221] In the same vein, in a dispute arising out of a bill of lading expressly referring to a charter party agreement,[222] the Indian Supreme Court upheld an arbitration agreement contained in the charter party agreement. As confirmation of this approach, article 7(6) (Option I) of the UNCITRAL Model Law on International Commercial

217 *Owners & Parties Interested in the Vessel M.V. Baltic Confidence, et al. v. State Trading Corp. of India, et al. (India)*, Supreme Court, India, 20 August 2001, Special Leave Petition (civil) 17183 of 2001; *Tradax Export S.A. v. Amoco Iran Oil Company*, Federal Tribunal, Switzerland, 7 February 1984; *X S.A. v. Y Ltd.*, Federal Tribunal, Switzerland, 12 January 1989, 5P.249/1988.

218 *Gas Authority of India Ltd. v. SPIE-CAPAG SA and ors*, High Court of Delhi, India, 15 October 1993, Suit No. 1440; IA No. 5206.

219 *Copape Produtos de Pétroleo LTDA. v. Glencore LTD.*, District Court, Southern District of New York, United States of America, 8 February 2012, 11 Civ. 5744 LAK.

220 *Société Bomar Oil N.V. v. Entreprise tunisienne d'activités pétrolières (ETAP)*, Court of Appeal of Versailles, France, 23 January 1991, upheld by *Société Bomar Oil N.V. v. Entreprise tunisienne d'activités pétrolières (ETAP)*, Court of Cassation, France, 9 November 1993, 91-15.194. See also *SA Groupama transports v. Société MS Régine Hans und Klaus Heinrich KG*, Court of Appeal of Basse Terre, France, 18 April 2005.

221 *Del Medico & C. SAS v. Iberprotein Sl*, Court of Cassation, Italy, 16 June 2011, 13231; *Copape Produtos de Pétroleo LTDA. v. Glencore LTD.*, District Court, Southern District of New York, United States of America, 8 February 2012, 11 Civ. 5744 LAK; *Standard Bent Glass Corp. v. Glassrobots OY [Fin.]*, Court of Appeals, Third Circuit, United States of America, 20 June 2003, 02-2169; *SA Groupama transports v. Société MS Régine Hans und Klaus Heinrich KG*, Court of Cassation, France, 21 November 2006, 05-21.818; Court of Appeal of the Canton of Basel-Landschaft, Switzerland, 5 July 1994, 30-94/261; Oberlandesgericht [OLG] Cologne, Germany, 16 December 1992, XXI Y.B. COM. ARB. 535 (1996).

222 *Owners & Parties Interested in the Vessel M.V. Baltic Confidence, et al. v. State Trading Corp. of India, et al. (India)*, Supreme Court, India, 20 August 2001, Special Leave Petition (civil) 17183 of 2001. See also *Tradax Export SA v. Amoco Iran Oil Company*, Federal Tribunal, Switzerland, 7 February 1984; *Welex A.G. v. Rosa Maritime Ltd.*, Court of Appeal, England and Wales, 3 July 2003, A3/02/2230 A3/02/2231.

Arbitration expressly provides that a reference in a contract to any document containing an arbitration clause qualifies as an arbitration agreement in writing.[223]

22. Fifth, courts have relied on the procedural behaviour of the parties to infer their consent to arbitrate their disputes. Hence, participation in the arbitral proceedings without any objection to the jurisdiction of the arbitral tribunal has been held to establish the parties' agreement to arbitrate.[224] For instance, having found that an unsigned arbitration agreement did not comply with the requirements of article II (2), the Brazilian Superior Court of Justice nevertheless enforced an award rendered under that arbitration agreement on the grounds that the parties had consented to the arbitral tribunal's jurisdiction by participating in the arbitral proceedings without raising any objections to the arbitral tribunal's jurisdiction.[225] Likewise, an Australian court enforced an arbitral award on costs rendered under the auspices of the ICC in Paris where the arbitral tribunal found that it did not have jurisdiction as the arbitration agreement was invalid. The Australian court held that, by signing the Terms of Reference, the parties had consented to submit their dispute to arbitration.[226]

23. The reliance placed by courts on the parties' consent to arbitration is consistent with the Convention's philosophy of providing "satisfactory evidence of the agreement".[227] Commentators have emphasized the importance of the intention of the parties and whether there is a "meeting of minds".[228]

---

[223] Article 7(6) (Option I) of the UNCITRAL Model Law on International Commercial Arbitration.

[224] *CTA Lind & Co. Scandinavia AB in Liquidation's bankruptcy Estate v. Erik Lind*, District Court, Middle District of Florida, Tampa Division, United States of America, 7 April 2009, 8:08-cv-1380-T-30TGW; *China Nanhai Oil Joint Service Corporation Shenzhen Branch v. Gee Tai Holdings Co. Ltd.*, High Court, Supreme Court of Hong Kong, Hong Kong, 13 July 1994, 1992 No. MP 2411; Oberlandesgericht [OLG] Schleswig, Germany, 30 March 2000, 16 SchH 05/99.

[225] *L'Aiglon S/A v. Têxtil União S/A*, Superior Court of Justice, Brazil, 18 May 2005, SEC 856.

[226] *Commonwealth Development Corp v. Montague*, Supreme Court of Queensland, Australia, 27 June 2000, Appeal No. 8159 of 1999; DC No. 29 of 1999.

[227] *Travaux préparatoires*, United Nations Conference on International Commercial Arbitration, Comments by Governments and Organizations on the Draft Convention on the Recognition and Enforcement of Foreign Arbitral Awards, Comments by the United Kingdom, E/2822/Add.4, Annex I, p. 5.

[228] Reinmar Wolff, *Commentary on Article II*, in NEW YORK CONVENTION ON THE RECOGNITION AND ENFORCEMENT OF FOREIGN ARBITRAL AWARDS OF 10 JUNE 1958—COMMENTARY 85, 128-132 (R. WOLFF ED., 2012); ICCA'S GUIDE TO THE INTERPRETATION OF THE 1958 NEW YORK CONVENTION: A HANDBOOK FOR JUDGES 45 (P. Sanders ed., 2011).

C. Scope of the "agreement in writing"

24. Article II (1) requires national courts to recognize an agreement in writing under which the parties have undertaken to submit to arbitration all "differences" in respect of a legal relationship which is capable of settlement by arbitration.

a. Meaning of "differences"

25. Article II (1) refers to the parties' undertaking to submit to arbitration "all or any differences" which have arisen or which may arise between them, and which are covered by their agreement.

26. Very few reported cases have addressed this issue and all of them have adopted a broad interpretation of "differences" in line with the pro-arbitration bias of the Convention.

27. In interpreting the word "differences", the High Court of Hong Kong has held that the parties should be referred to arbitration even when there is a dispute as to the existence of a dispute.[229] The court concluded that whether or not a dispute existed was a matter for the arbitral tribunal to determine. The Australian Supreme Court relied on the words "all or any" in article II (1) to confirm that article II (1) should be construed broadly.[230] Similarly, the Court of Appeal of England and Wales in *Fiona Trust* held that, in the absence of clear language to the contrary, arbitration clauses are to be given the broadest interpretation possible, since the parties, as rational businessmen, were likely to have intended any dispute arising out of the relationship into which they had entered to be decided by the same tribunal.[231]

b. "Defined legal relationship"

28. Article II (1)'s requirement that the dispute must have arisen "in respect of a defined legal relationship, whether contractual or not", is very broad and seldom disputed in case law.

---

[229] *Guangdong Agriculture Ltd. v. Conagra International Far East Company Ltd.*, High Court, Supreme Court of Hong Kong, Hong Kong, 24 September 1992, HCA003032/1992.

[230] *Seeley International Pty Ltd. v. Electra Air*, Federal Court, Australia, 29 January 2008, SAD 157 of 2007.

[231] *Fiona Trust & Holding Corp. v. Privalov*, Court of Appeal, England and Wales, 24 January 2007, 2006 2353 A3 QBCMF, upheld by *Fili Shipping Co. Ltd. and others v. Premium Nafta Products Ltd. and others*, House of Lords, England and Wales, 17 October 2007.

29. Relying on the text of article II, the Canadian Supreme Court has held that extra-contractual claims could fall within the scope of an arbitration agreement when the claims relate to contractual obligations.[232]

c. *"Subject matter capable of settlement by arbitration"*

30. The requirement that the dispute concerns a "subject matter capable of settlement by arbitration" refers to the arbitrability of the dispute.[233] Given the New York Convention's lack of guidance on this topic, national courts have determined whether a specific subject matter can be settled by arbitration either by referring to the law applicable to the arbitration agreement or by referring to their own law.

31. Some courts have determined that this issue should be resolved according to the law applicable to the arbitration agreement. In making this determination, they have referred to the conflict of laws rule in article V (1)*(a)* of the Convention, i.e., "the law to which the parties have subjected [the arbitration agreement] or, failing any indication thereon, under the law of the country where the award was made."[234] By analogy, courts have interpreted the expression "where the award was made" to mean "where the award shall be made", i.e., by reference to the seat of arbitration. Swiss and Austrian courts have followed this approach.[235]

32. Other courts have assessed whether a dispute was capable of settlement by arbitration pursuant to their own system of law. In so doing, courts have followed three different approaches to conclude that the *lex fori* should apply to determine whether a dispute is capable of settlement by arbitration.

33. First, a number of courts have relied on article V (2)*(a)* of the Convention which provides that whether the subject matter of a dispute is capable of settlement by arbitration is to be assessed pursuant to the law of

---

[232] *Kaverit Steel and Crane v. Kone Corp.*, Alberta Court of Queen's Bench, Canada, 14 May 1991, AJN°450 and *Kaverit Steel v. Kone Corp.*, Court of Appeal of Alberta, Canada, 16 January 1992, ABCA 7.

[233] Dorothee Schramm, Elliott Geisinger, Philippe Pinsolle, *Article II*, in RECOGNITION AND ENFORCEMENT OF FOREIGN ARBITRAL AWARDS: A GLOBAL COMMENTARY ON THE NEW YORK CONVENTION 37, 69-73 (H. Kronke, P. Nacimiento et al. eds., 2010); Albert Jan van den Berg, *The New York Convention of 1958: An Overview*, in ENFORCEMENT OF ARBITRATION AGREEMENTS AND INTERNATIONAL ARBITRAL AWARDS: THE NEW YORK CONVENTION 1958 IN PRACTICE 39, 53 (E. Gaillard, D. Di Pietro eds., 2008); Jan Paulsson, *Arbitrability, Still Through a Glass Darkly*, in ARBITRATION IN THE NEXT DECADE 95, 96 (ICC Pub. No. 612E, 1999).

[234] *Misr Insurance Company v. Alexandria Shipping Agencies Company*, Court of Cassation, Egypt, 23 December 1991, 547/51 (unofficial translation).

[235] Federal Tribunal, Switzerland, 21 March 1995, 5C.215/1994/lit; Supreme Court, Austria, 17 November 1971, I Y.B. COM. ARB. 183 (1976).

the country where recognition and enforcement is sought. By analogy, the Italian Court of Cassation determined that the *lex fori*, that is, the law of the State of the court seized, should be applied to determine whether a dispute is capable of settlement by arbitration.[236] Belgian courts have followed the same approach.[237]

34. Second, in assessing whether a dispute is capable of settlement by arbitration and consequently deciding whether to refer the parties to arbitration pursuant to article II (3), courts in the United States have applied the Federal Arbitration Act, that is the *lex fori*, but without any reference to article V (2)*(a)*.[238] Hence, United States courts have recognized that disputes arising out of a Statute are capable of settlement by arbitration under the Convention. By way of example, disputes arising out of the Sherman Antitrust Act,[239] the Securities Act and Exchange Act,[240] the Jones Act on employment,[241] and bankruptcy legislation[242] were held to be capable of settlement by arbitration. United States courts have also accepted that disputes arising out of employment[243] and distributorship contracts[244] are capable of settlement by arbitration.[245]

35. Third, French courts have rejected the application of a particular national law to assess whether or not a dispute is capable of settlement by arbitration. Relying on article VII of the Convention, the Paris Court of

---

236 *Compagnia Generale Construzioni "COGECO" S.p.A. v. Piersanti*, Court of Cassation, Italy, 27 April 1979, XVI Y.B. COM. ARB. 229 (1996).

237 *Colvi NV. v. Interdica*, Supreme Court, Belgium, 15 October 2004, C.02.0216.N.

238 *Scherk v. Alberto-Culver Company*, Supreme Court, United States of America, 17 June 1974, 73-781; *Rhone Mediterranee Compagnia Francese v. Lauro*, Court of Appeals, Third Circuit, United States of America, 6 July 1983, 82-3523.

239 *Mitsubishi Motors Corp v. Soler Chrysler-Plymouth*, Supreme Court, United States of America, 2 July 1985, 3-1569.

240 *Scherk v. Alberto-Culver Company*, Supreme Court, United States of America, 17 June 1974, 73-781.

241 *Lindo v. NCL, Ltd.*, Court of Appeals, Eleventh Circuit, United States of America, 29 August 2011, 10-10367.

242 *Société Nationale Algérienne Pour La Recherche, La Production and others v. Distrigas Corp.*, District Court, District of Massachusetts, United States of America, 17 March 1987, 86-2014-Y.

243 *Lindo v. NCL, Ltd.*, Court of Appeals, Eleventh Circuit, United States of America, 29 August 2011, 10-10367; *Jane Doe v. Princess Cruise Lines, LTD., a foreign corporation, d.b.a. Princess Cruises*, Court of Appeals, Eleventh Circuit, United States of America, 23 September 2011, 10-10809.

244 *Becker Autoradio U.S.A., Inc. v. Becker Autoradiowerk GmbH*, Court of Appeals, Third Circuit, United States of America, 17 July 1978, 77-2566, 77-2567; *Travelport Global Distribution Systems B.V. v. Bellview Airlines Limited*, District Court, Southern District of New York, United States of America, 10 September 2012, 12 Civ. 3483(DLC).

245 In so doing, courts have assessed whether, for each Statute, it was the congressional intent to have a specific category of disputes capable of settlement by arbitration: *Mitsubishi Motors Corp v. Soler Chrysler-Plymouth*, Supreme Court, United States of America, 2 July 1985, 437 United States 614. More generally, see GARY B. BORN, INTERNATIONAL COMMERCIAL ARBITRATION 769, 778 (2009).

Appeal held that French law should apply because it was more favourable than article II, and that the principle of the validity of international arbitration agreements, which is a "substantive rule of French international arbitration law", establishes the validity of any arbitration clause "irrespective of any reference to national law".[246] The Paris Court of Appeal expressly distinguished this principle from articles II and V of the Convention "which call, in particular, for the application of national laws to render the clause valid."[247] By way of example, a French court referred the parties to arbitration on the basis of an arbitration agreement contained in an employment contract notwithstanding the petitioner's argument that employment disputes were not capable of settlement by arbitration. The court noted that the Convention applied since the employment contract was international and France had withdrawn its commercial reservation.[248]

Article II (2)

36. Article II (2) defines the "in writing" requirement. An "agreement in writing" includes "an arbitral clause in a contract, or an arbitration agreement, signed by the parties or contained in an exchange of letters or telegrams."

37. Prior to UNCITRAL addressing the issue, national courts had diverged on whether the more-favourable-rule principle embodied in article VII (1) of the Convention applied to the requirement that an arbitration agreement be "in writing" within the meaning of article II. In 2006, UNCITRAL confirmed that article VII (1) "should be applied to allow any interested party to avail itself of rights it may have, under the law or treaties of the country where an arbitration agreement is sought to be relied upon, to seek recognition of the validity of such an arbitration agreement."[249] Since

---

[246] *Ste A.B.S. American Bureau* of *Shipping v. Copropriété Maritime Jules Verne et autres*, Court of Appeal of Paris, France, 4 December 2002, 2001/17293, upheld by *Copropriété Maritime Jules Verne et autres v. Société A.B.S. American bureau* of *shipping*, Court of Cassation, France, 7 June 2006, 03-12.034

[247] *Ste A.B.S. American Bureau* of *Shipping v. Copropriété Maritime Jules Verne et autres*, Court of Appeal of Paris, France, 4 December 2002, 2001/17293.

[248] *SA C.F.T.E. v. Jacques Dechavanne*, Court of Appeal of Grenoble, France, 13 September 1993.

[249] Recommendation regarding the interpretation of article II, paragraph 2, and article VII, paragraph 1, of the Convention on the Recognition and Enforcement of Foreign Arbitral Awards, done in New York, 10 June 1958 (2006), *Official Records of the General Assembly*, Sixty-first Session, Supplement No. 17 (A/61/17), paras. 177-81 and Annex II, available at www.uncitral.org/pdf/english/texts/arbitration/NY-conv/A2E.pdf. The *Travaux préparatoires* to the Recommendation are contained in *Official Records of the General Assembly*, Fifty-sixth Session, Supplement No. 17 (A/56/17), para. 313; *Ibid.*, Fifty-seventh Session, Supplement No. 17 (A/57/17), para. 183; and in United Nations documents A/CN.9/468, paras. 88-106; A/CN.9/485, paras. 60-77; A/CN.9/487, paras. 42-63; A/CN.9/508, paras. 40-50; A/CN.9/592, paras. 82-88; A/CN.9/WG.II/WP.118, paras. 25-33; A/CN.9/607; and A/CN.9/609, and its addenda 1 to 6.

then, national courts have more consistently enforced arbitration agreements pursuant to the less stringent formal requirements available under their national laws or treaties as provided for by article VII with respect to arbitral awards.[250]

A. "Arbitral clause in a contract" versus "arbitration agreement"

38. The Convention provides that an "agreement in writing" may be either an "arbitral clause in a contract" or an "arbitration agreement".

39. Examples of "arbitral clauses in a contract" within the meaning of article II (2) have been found when the arbitration agreement is printed on the back of the contract.[251]

40. Regarding the "arbitration agreement", an Australian court has confirmed that the Terms of Reference signed in arbitration proceedings under the auspices of the ICC International Court of Arbitration qualified as an "arbitration agreement" and an "agreement in writing" within the meaning of article II (2).[252] In that case, one of the respondents in the arbitral proceedings had successfully objected to the jurisdiction of the arbitral tribunal. The arbitral tribunal then issued an award on costs in favour of that respondent who then sought to enforce the award. The appellant opposed enforcement on the grounds that the arbitral tribunal had found that there was no valid arbitration agreement binding the respondent. The Supreme Court of Queensland enforced the award, finding that the Terms of Reference signed by the parties to the arbitration proceedings constituted an "agreement in writing" within the meaning of article II.

41. The distinction between an arbitration clause in a contract and a "submission agreement"[253] has lost most of its relevance in contemporary arbitral practice. In a 1994 decision, the United States Court of Appeals for the Fifth Circuit distinguished between an arbitral clause in a contract and an arbitration agreement. It ruled that, within the meaning of article II (2), while the former needed to be signed by the parties, no such requirement applied to

---

[250] For a more detailed analysis on the interaction between articles II and VII, see the chapter of the Guide on article VII, paras. 31-35.

[251] See the chapter of the Guide on article II, para. 19. See also Bayerisches Oberstes Landesgericht [BayObLG], Germany, 17 September 1998, BayObLG 4 Z Sch 1/98; Bundesgerichtshof [BGH], Germany, 25 May 1970, VII ZR 157/68; Oberlandesgericht [OLG] Schleswig, Germany, 30 March 2000, 16 SchH 05/99; Bundesgerichtshof [BGH], Germany, 12 February 1976, III ZR 42/74.

[252] *Commonwealth Development Corp v. Montague*, Supreme Court of Queensland, Australia, 27 June 2000, Appeal No. 8159 of 1999; DC No. 29 of 1999.

[253] The expression "arbitration agreement" is generally used to include both arbitration clauses and submission agreements. See FOUCHARD GAILLARD GOLDMAN ON INTERNATIONAL COMMERCIAL ARBITRATION 193-96 (E. Gaillard, J. Savage eds., 1999).

the latter.[254] This position was subsequently rejected by the United States Court of Appeals for the Second Circuit. It held that the signature requirement in article II (2) of the Convention applies to both contracts containing an arbitral clause and arbitration agreements, unless they are contained in an exchange of letters or telegrams.[255]

B. The signature requirement

42. Pursuant to article II (2), the requirement of an agreement in writing is met when an arbitral clause or an arbitration agreement is signed by the parties.

43. When the parties to the contract or instrument containing the arbitration agreement have signed such contract or instrument, the signature requirement of article II (2) is to be regarded as satisfied. This has been generally followed by courts.[256]

44. Conversely, certain courts have refused to enforce arbitration agreements against parties that have not signed it.[257] For example, the Chinese Supreme Court denied enforcement of an award on the ground that only one party had signed the contract containing the arbitration clause.[258] Similarly, the Brazilian Superior Court of Justice refused to enforce an

---

[254] *Sphere Drake Insurance PLC v. Marine Towing*, Court of Appeals, Fifth Circuit, United States of America, 23 March 1994, 93-3200. See also *Borsack v. Chalk & Vermilion Fine Arts, Ltd.*, District Court, South District of New York, United States of America, 7 August 1997, 96 CV 6587 (BDP).

[255] *Kahn Lucas Lancaster, Inc. v. Lark International Ltd.*, Court of Appeals, Second Circuit, United States of America, 9 July 1999, 97-9436. See also *Czarina, L.L.C. v. W.F. Poe Syndicate*, Court of Appeals, Eleventh Circuit, United States of America, 4 February 2004, 03-10518; *Moscow Dynamo v. Alexander M. Ovechkin*, District Court, District of Columbia, United States of America, 18 January 2006, 05-2245 (EGS).

[256] *Sunward Overseas S.A. v. Servicios Maritimos Limitada Semar*, Supreme Court of Justice, Colombia, 20 November 1992, 472; *Krauss Maffei Verfahrenstechnik GmbH et al. v. Bristol Myers Squibb S.p.A.*, Court of Cassation, Italy, 10 March 2000, 58; *Steve Didmon v. Frontier Drilling (United States), INC., et al.*, District Court, Southern District of Texas, Houston Division, United States of America, 19 March 2012, H-11-2051; *Kahn Lucas Lancaster, Inc. v. Lark International Ltd.*, Court of Appeals, Second Circuit, United States of America, 29 July 1999, 97-9436; *Smita Conductors Ltd. v. Euro Alloys Ltd.*, Supreme Court, India, 31 August 2001, Civil Appeal No. 12930 of 1996; Bundesgerichtshof [BGH], Germany, 8 June 2010, XI ZR 349/08; Bundesgerichtshof [BGH], Germany, 25 January 2011, XI ZR 350/08.

[257] Court of Appeal of the Republic and Canton of Ticino, Second civil Chamber, Switzerland, 2 April 2003, 14.2002.81.

[258] *Concordia Trading B.V. v. Nantong Gangde Oil Co., Ltd.*, Supreme People's Court, China, 3 August 2009, [2009] MinSiTaZi No. 22.

arbitration agreement because the parties had not signed the contract containing the arbitration agreement.[259]

45. In the same vein, in *Javor v. Francoeur*, the Canadian Supreme Court of British Columbia refused to enforce an award rendered against the respondent because it had not signed the arbitration agreement. During the arbitral proceedings, the tribunal found that the respondent was the alter-ego of the corporate party which had signed the arbitration agreement and consequently ordered the respondent to participate in the arbitral proceedings. The court relied on the text of article II (2) of the British Columbia Foreign Arbitral Awards Act (which incorporates article II (2) of the Convention) and ruled that the purpose of the Act was to limit enforcement of awards to "part[ies] signatory to the [arbitration] agreement." It held that since the respondent was not a named party or a signatory to the arbitration agreement, the award could not be enforced against it.[260]

46. By contrast, a number of courts have enforced arbitration agreements against parties that had not signed the arbitration agreement. For instance, United States courts have held that non-signatories can be bound by an arbitration agreement to the extent that the arbitration agreement is not null and void under the Convention and that a contract law theory—such as agency, estoppel, or principles relating to alter-egos and third party beneficiaries—applies to the case at hand.[261] In France, entities that had not signed the arbitration agreement have been referred to arbitration pursuant to the group of companies doctrine.[262]

---

[259] *Plexus Cotton Limited v. Santana Têxtil S/A*, Superior Court of Justice, Brazil, 15 February 2006, SEC 967; *Indutech SpA v. Algocentro Armazéns Gerais Ltda.*, Superior Court of Justice, Brazil, 17 December 2008, SEC 978; *Kanematsu USA Inc. v. ATS—Advanced Telecommunications Systems do Brasil Ltda.*, Superior Court of Justice, Brazil, 18 April 2012, SEC 885.

[260] *Javor v. Francoeur*, Supreme Court of British Columbia, Canada, 6 March 2003. See also *Dallah Real Estate and Tourism Holding Company v. Ministry of Religious Affairs, Government of Pakistan*, Supreme Court, England and Wales, 3 November 2010, UKSC 2009/0165.

[261] *Formostar, LLC, et al. v. Henry Florentius, et al.*, District Court, District of Nevada, United States of America, 13 July 2012, 2:11-cv-01166-GMN-CWH; *Flexi-Van Leasing, Inc. v. Through Transport Mutual Insurance Association, Ltd., et al.*, Court of Appeals, Third Circuit, United States of America, 18 August 2004, 03-3383; *Sarhank Group v. Oracle Corporation*, Court of Appeals, Second Circuit, United States of America, 14 April 2005, 02-9383; *Milton Escobal v. Celebration Cruise Operator Inc., Celebration Cruise Line LLC*, Court of Appeals, Eleventh Circuit, United States of America, 20 July 2012, 11-14022. See also for a case where none of the contract law theories were found applicable: *Bel-Ray Co., Inc. (United States) v. Chemrite (Pty) Ltd. (South Africa)*, Court of Appeals, Third Circuit, United States of America, 28 June 1999, 98-6297; *Sarhank Group v. Oracle Corporation*, Court of Appeals, Second Circuit, United States of America, 14 April 2005, 02-9383.

[262] *Société Kis France et autres v. Société Générale et autres*, Court of Appeal of Paris, France, 31 October 1989, 1992 REV. ARB. 90.

C. An arbitral clause or an arbitration agreement included in an exchange of documents

a. An exchange

47. Under article II (2), an agreement will also meet the "in-writing" requirement if it is contained in an exchange of letters or telegrams. As noted by a German court, the essential factor in the exchange of documents requirement under the New York Convention is mutuality; that is, reciprocal transmission of documents.[263]

48. The United States District Court for the District of Colombia has confirmed that one party's unilateral conduct is insufficient to establish an "agreement in writing" within the meaning of article II (2) of the Convention.[264] In that case, the counter-party never responded either explicitly or implicitly to the letters containing the arbitration agreements.

49. In the context of an investment arbitration dispute, the United States Court of Appeals for the Second Circuit has confirmed that the requirement of an exchange of documents within the meaning of article II of the Convention is fulfilled by an offer to arbitrate contained in a bilateral investment treaty and its subsequent acceptance by an investor in the Request for Arbitration.[265]

b. Non-exhaustive list of documents

50. Even though article II (2) only makes express reference to "an exchange of letters or telegrams", it is widely accepted that article II (2) covers any exchange of documents and is not limited to letters and telegrams. Most courts recognize that an arbitration agreement contained in an exchange of documents or other written communications, whether physical or electronic, satisfies the requirement of article II (2).[266]

---

263 Oberlandesgericht [OLG] Frankfurt, Germany, 26 June 2006, 26 Sch 28/05; Bayerisches Oberstes Landesgericht [BayObLG], Germany, 12 December 2002, 4 Z Sch 16/02.

264 *Moscow Dynamo v. Alexander M. Ovechkin*, District Court, District of Columbia, United States of America, 18 January 2006, 05-2245 (EGS).

265 *Republic of Ecuador v. Chevron Corp. (United States)*, Court of Appeals, Second Circuit, United States of America, 17 March 2011, 10-1020-cv (L), 10-1026 (Con). See also *Ministry of Defense of the Islamic Republic of Iran v. Gould Inc., Gould Marketing, Inc., Hoffman Export Corporation, and Gould International, Inc.*, Court of Appeals, Ninth Circuit, United States of America, 23 October 1989, 88-5879/88-5881 for the Iran-US Claims Tribunal Statutes qualifying as an "agreement in writing".

266 For an exchange of telexes and faxes, see *Compagnie de Navigation et Transports S.A. v. MSC Mediterranean Shipping Company S.A.*, Federal Tribunal, Switzerland, 16 January 1995; *C S.A. v. E. Corporation*, Court of Justice of Geneva, Switzerland, 14 April 1983, 187. For an exchange by e-mails with a confirmation by fax, see *Great Offshore Ltd. v. Iranian*

51. By way of example, a Canadian court ruling upon the validity of an arbitration agreement under article V (1)*(a)* has confirmed that an "agreement in writing" under article II (2) can take various forms and should be given a functional and pragmatic interpretation.[267]

52. Indeed, at its thirty-ninth session, in July 2006, UNCITRAL expressly recommended that article II (2) be applied "recognizing that the circumstances described therein are not exhaustive".[268] As further confirmation, at the same session, UNCITRAL amended the Model Law on International Commercial Arbitration to clarify that "the requirement that an arbitration agreement be in writing is met by an electronic communication [...]".[269] In accordance with the UNCITRAL Recommendation, a recent Spanish decision has held that the list of documents set out in article II is not exhaustive and therefore an arbitration agreement concluded by electronic means of communications fulfils the "in-writing" requirement.[270]

53. Relying on the wording "include" in article II (2), certain commentators have also considered that the circumstances described in article II (2) are not exhaustive.[271]

Offshore Engineering & Construction Co., Supreme Court, Civil Appellate Jurisdiction, India, 25 August 2008, Arbitration Petition No. 10 of 2006.

[267] *Sheldon Proctor v. Leon Schellenberg*, Court of Appeal of Manitoba, Canada, 11 December 2002.

[268] Recommendation regarding the interpretation of article II, paragraph 2, and article VII, paragraph 1, of the Convention on the Recognition and Enforcement of Foreign Arbitral Awards, done in New York, 10 June 1958 (2006), para. 1. *Official Records of the General Assembly, Sixty-first Session, Supplement No. 17* (A/61/17), paras. 177-81 and Annex II, available at www.uncitral.org/pdf/english/texts/arbitration/NY-conv/A2E.pdf. As early as 2005, the United Nations Convention on the Use of Electronic Communications in International Contracts prepared by UNCITRAL provided that it applies, pursuant to its article 20, to the use of electronic communications in connection with the formation or performance of an agreement falling under the New York Convention. See the Resolution 60/21 adopted by the General Assembly on 23 November 2005 on the United Nations Convention on the Use of Electronic Communications in International Contracts, available at www.uncitral.org/pdf/english/ texts/electcom/06-57452_Ebook.pdf.

[269] Article 7(4) (Option I) of the UNCITRAL Model Law on International Commercial Arbitration.

[270] High Court of Justice of Cataluña, Spain, 15 March 2012, RJ 2012/6120.

[271] See, e.g., Toby Landau, Salim Moollan, *Article II and the Requirement* of *the Form*, in ENFORCEMENT OF ARBITRATION AGREEMENTS AND INTERNATIONAL ARBITRAL AWARDS—THE NEW YORK CONVENTION 1958 IN PRACTICE 189, 244-47 (E. Gaillard, D. Di Pietro eds., 2008); Gabrielle Kaufmann-Kohler, *Arbitration Agreements in Online Business to Business Transactions*, in LIBER AMICORUM K.-H. BOCKSTIEGEL 355, 358-62 (2001). In fairness, taken in isolation, this argument is not determinative as it is not supported by the Convention's other official languages. For instance, the French uses the expression "*On entend par "convention écrite"* [...]" which does not suggest a non-exhaustive list but rather a definition of the "agreement in writing".

c. *Whether the signature requirement applies to an exchange of documents*

54. Where the arbitration agreement is contained in an exchange of documents, the text of article II (2) does not, on its face, require the parties' signature on the agreement to arbitrate.

55. The Swiss Federal Tribunal has confirmed that when the arbitration agreement is contained in an exchange of documents, the signature requirement does not apply.[272] Similarly, ruling upon Section 7 of the Indian Arbitration Act of 1996 (which mirrors article II (2) of the Convention), the Supreme Court of India has upheld an arbitration agreement contained in an unsigned contract exchanged between parties.[273] This approach has been followed in many jurisdictions.[274]

56. By contrast, a limited number of decisions have refused to enforce an unsigned arbitration agreement that had been exchanged via telexes.[275]

57. The *travaux préparatoires* and the wording of article II (2) support the approach that the signature requirement does not apply to an exchange of documents. The drafters of the New York Convention sought to adopt a flexible "in-writing" requirement in order to reflect business reality.[276] For this reason, a distinction was drawn between "an arbitral clause [...] or an arbitration agreement, signed by the parties" "or" "contained in an exchange of letters or telegrams."

---

[272] *Compagnie de Navigation et Transports S.A. v. MSC Mediterranean Shipping Company S.A.*, Federal Tribunal, Switzerland, 16 January 1995; *Tradax Export SA v. Amoco Iran Oil Company*, Federal Tribunal, Switzerland,7 February 1984.

[273] *M/S Unissi (India) Pvt Ltd. v. Post Graduate Institute of Medical Education and Research*, Supreme Court, India, 1 October 2008, Civil Appeal No. 6039 of 2008.

[274] *Not Indicated v. Not Indicated*, Supreme Court, Austria, 21 February 1978, X Y.B. COM. ARB. 418 (1985); *Standard Bent Glass Corp. v. Glassrobots OY*, Court of Appeals, Third Circuit, United States of America, 20 June 2003, 02-2169. See also at the award enforcement stage: Landgericht [LG] Zweibrücken, Germany, 11 January 1978, 6.0 H 1/77; Oberlandesgericht [OLG] Schleswig, Germany, 30 March 2000, 16 SchH 05/99.

[275] See, e.g., *Oleaginosa Moreno Hermanos Sociedad Anonima Comercial Industrial Financeira Imobiliaria y Agropecuaria v. Moinho Paulista Ltd*, Superior Court of Justice, Brazil, 17 May 2006, SEC 866, upheld by *Oleaginosa Moreno Hermanos Sociedad Anónima Comercial Industrial Financeira Imobiliaria y Agropecuaria v. Moinho Paulista Ltda.*, Superior Court of Justice, Brazil, 7 March 2007, Motion for Clarification on SEC 866.

[276] *Travaux préparatoires*, United Nations Conference on International Commercial Arbitration, Comments by Governments and Organizations on the Draft Convention on the Recognition and Enforcement of Foreign Arbitral Awards, E/2822/Add. 4 (United Kingdom); *Travaux préparatoires*, United Nations Conference on International Commercial Arbitration, Summary Records of the Thirteenth Meeting, E/CONF.26/SR.13 (Representative of the Hague Conference on Private International Law); *Travaux préparatoires*, Report of the Committee on the Enforcement of International Arbitral Awards, E/AC.42/SR.7 (Sweden, India); *Travaux préparatoires*, United Nations Conference on International Commercial Arbitration, Summary Records of the Ninth Meeting E/CONF.26/SR.9 (Representative of Germany), p. 3.

Article II (3)

58. Where there is an agreement in writing as defined under article II (1) and (2), article II (3) requires national courts to refer the parties to arbitration, if requested to do so by at least one party, unless the court finds that the agreement is null and void, inoperative or incapable of being performed.

A. General principles

a. Obligation to refer the parties to arbitration

59. Article II (3) provides that a "court of a Contracting State, when seized of an action in a matter in respect of which the parties have made an agreement in writing within the meaning of this article, shall [...] refer the parties to arbitration [...]." As noted by the Supreme Court of Canada, the object and purpose of article II (3) is to strengthen the obligation to enforce arbitration agreements.[277]

60. The *travaux préparatoires* are silent on the scope of the obligation of courts to refer parties to arbitration. The expression "refer the parties to arbitration" has its origin in the 1923 Geneva Protocol on Arbitration Clauses, which provides, in relevant part, that the "tribunals of the Contracting Parties [...] shall refer the parties on the application of either of them to the decision of the arbitrators."[278] The expression was proposed by the Swedish delegation at the Conference and adopted after further modification by the drafting committee.[279]

61. Courts interpret the word "shall" in article II (3) to indicate that referral to arbitration is mandatory and cannot be left to the courts' discretion.[280] In practice, courts have fulfilled their obligation to refer the parties to arbitration in two different manners.

---

277 *GreCon Dimter Inc. v. J.R. Normand Inc. and Scierie Thomas-Louis Tremblay Inc.*, Supreme Court, Canada,22 July 2005, 30217.

278 1923 Geneva Protocol on Arbitration Clauses, Article 4.

279 *Travaux préparatoires*, United Nations Conference on International Commercial Arbitration, Summary Record of the Twenty-First Meeting, E/CONF.26/SR.21, pp. 17-23; *Travaux préparatoires*, United Nations Conference on International Commercial Arbitration, Consideration on the Draft Convention on the Recognition and Enforcement of Foreign Arbitral Awards, E/CONF.26/L.59.

280 See, e.g., *Renusagar Power Co. Ltd. v. General Electric Company and anor*, Supreme Court, India, 16 August 1984; *Shin-Etsu Chemical Co. Ltd. v. Aksh Optifibre Ltd. and anor*, Supreme Court, India, 12 August 2005; *Ishwar D. Jain v. Henri Courier de Mere*, Court of Appeals, Seventh Circuit, United States of America, 3 April 1995, 94-3314; *Aasma et al. v. American Steamship Owners Mutual Protection and Indemnity Association Inc. (USA)*, Court of Appeals, Sixth Circuit, United States of America, 29 August 1996, 94-3881, 94-3883;

62. The first approach, endorsed in civil law jurisdictions, consists in declining jurisdiction in the presence of an arbitration agreement. For instance, in a number of decisions, French and Swiss courts have held that, pursuant to article II of the Convention, the presence of an arbitration agreement rendered national courts incompetent and have thus referred the parties to arbitration.[281]

63. The second approach, endorsed in most common law jurisdictions, consists in staying judicial proceedings, thereby giving effect to the courts' obligation to enforce arbitration agreements. By way of example, the Australian Federal Court, in interpreting Section 7(2) of the Australian International Arbitration Act in light of article II (3) of the Convention, has held that the expression "shall refer the parties to arbitration [...] should not be taken as to having the meaning of obliging the parties to arbitrate."[282] Rather, the court explained that courts should stay judicial proceedings, but cannot compel the parties to arbitrate if they do not wish to do so.

64. Both approaches are consistent with the obligation of the courts of Contracting Parties to the Convention to refer the parties to arbitration.

65. Courts in certain jurisdictions go as far as issuing anti-suit injunctions in favour of arbitration. In particular, the Court of Appeal of England and Wales has held that such anti-suit injunctions designed to compel parties to comply with an arbitration agreement were not in violation of the New York Convention.[283]

InterGen N.V. (Netherlands) v. Grina (Switzerland), Court of Appeals, First Circuit, United States of America, 22 September 2003, 03-1056; *Ingosstrakh v. Aabis Rederi Sovfrakht*, City Court of Moscow, Former USSR, 6 May 1968, I Y.B. COM. ARB. 206 (1976); *Louis Dreyfus Corporation of New York v. Oriana Soc. di Navigazione S.p.a*, Court of Cassation, Italy, 27 February 1970, 470, I Y.B. COM. ARB. 189 (1976); *Nile Cotton Ginning Company v. Cargill Limited*, Court of Appeal of Cairo, Egypt, 29 June 2003, 92-7876.

[281] *Société Sysmode S.A.R.L. et Société Sysmode France v. Société Metra HOS et Société SEMA*, Court of Appeal of Paris, 8 December 1988; *Les Trefileries & Ateliers de Commercy v. Société Philipp Brothers France et Société Derby & Co. Limited*, Court of Appeal of Nancy, 5 December 1980. See also *Fondation M v. Banque X*, Federal Tribunal, Switzerland, 29 April 1996.

[282] *Hi-Fert Pty Ltd. v. Kuikiang Maritime Carriers Inc.*, Federal Court, Australia, 26 May 1998, NG 1100 & 1101 of 1997. See also *Westco Airconditioning Ltd. v. Sui Chong Construction and Engineering Ltd*, Court of First Instance, High Court of the Hong Kong Special Administrative Region, Hong Kong, 3 February 1998, No. A12848.

[283] *Aggeliki Charis Compania Maritima SA v. Pagnan SpA*, Court of Appeal, England and Wales, 17 May 1994; *Midgulf International Ltd. v. Groupe Chimiche Tunisien*, Court of Appeal, England and Wales, 10 February 2010, A3/2009/1664; A3/2009/1664(A); A3/2009/1664(B); A3/2009/1664(C).

b. Party request necessary

66. Pursuant to article II (3), the courts' obligation to refer the parties to arbitration is triggered by the "request of one of the parties".

67. Whether or not a court can refer the parties to arbitration *ex officio* is not expressly settled by article II (3). However, as arbitration, by definition, is premised on consent, the parties are always at liberty to waive their prior agreement to arbitrate. If neither party alleges the existence of an arbitration agreement, the court will not *ex officio* refer the parties to arbitration but rather will, as a result, uphold its own jurisdiction.[284] In such situations, courts often consider that the parties have waived their right to arbitrate.

68. For instance, United States courts generally find that parties waive their right to arbitrate when they "substantially" participate in litigation, or when they seek to invalidate the arbitration agreement before the courts of another country.[285] In assessing whether the conduct of the parties amounted to a waiver of their right to arbitrate, a Brazilian court held that such waiver must be clearly established; i.e., all the parties had to act in a manner that unequivocally demonstrated their wish to waive the arbitration agreement.[286]

69. The *travaux préparatoires* to the Convention reflect the drafters' contemplation that parties would fail to raise the existence of an arbitration agreement in proceedings before national courts. Indeed, the drafters specifically deleted the expression "of its own motion" from an earlier draft of article II (3) in order to leave greater freedom to the parties and to preserve the possibility for the parties to waive their right to have a particular dispute resolved through arbitration.[287]

c. Matters in respect of which there is an agreement

70. Article II (3) limits the obligation to refer the parties to arbitration to "matter[s] in respect of which" there is an agreement in writing, as defined in article II (1) and (2).

---

[284] See, e.g., *British Telecommunications Plc v. SAE Group Inc*, High Court of Justice, England and Wales, 18 February 2009, HT-08-336, [2009] EWHC 252 (TCC).

[285] *Anna Dockeray v. Carnival Corporation*, District Court, Southern District of Florida, Miami Division, United States of America, 11 May 2010, 10-20799; *Apple & Eve LLC v. Yantai North Andre Juice Co. Ltd*, District Court, Eastern District of New York, United States of America, 27 April 2009, 07-CV-745 (JFB)(WDW).

[286] *Companhia Nacional de Cimento Portland—CNCP v. CP Cimento e Participações S/A*, Court of Justice of Rio de Janeiro, Brazil, 18 September 2007, Civil Appeal 24.798/2007. Compare with *L'Aiglon S/A v. Têxtil União S/A*, Superior Court of Justice, Brazil, 18 May 2005, SEC 856 (chapter of the Guide on article II, para. 22) where the Superior Court of Justice held that participation in arbitral proceedings amounts to consent to arbitration.

[287] *Travaux préparatoires*, United Nations Conference on International Commercial Arbitration, Summary Records of the Twenty-fourth Meeting, E/CONF.26/SR.24.

71. The Court of Appeal of England and Wales has indicated that, under both the English Arbitration Act of 1975 and the New York Convention, courts "are bound to send a dispute to arbitration if it is a dispute with regard to any matter to be referred."[288] To interpret the word "matter", the Australian Federal Court relied on the pro-arbitration policy of the Convention and held that the term was of "wide import" and was not limited, for the purposes of Section 7(2)*(b)* of the Australian Arbitration Act (which is similar to article II (3) of the Convention), to issues arising out of the parties' pleadings.[289]

72. In determining whether a dispute or a particular claim falls under the obligation to refer the parties to arbitration, national courts assess the scope of the agreement to arbitrate.[290] For instance, an Australian Court stayed proceedings pursuant to Section 7(2) of the Arbitration Act (implementing article II (3) of the New York Convention) by construing the broad language of the arbitration agreement which covered "all dispute arising in connection with this agreement or execution thereof [...]". The court concluded that claims related to the performance of the agreement were within the scope of the arbitration agreement.[291] Conversely, when parties have voluntarily excluded certain issues from the scope of their arbitration agreement, courts will refer them to arbitration to the extent that the dispute does not fall within the exclusion.[292]

73. Similarly, in determining whether or not to refer the dispute to arbitration under both the Federal Arbitration Act and the Convention, the United States Court of Appeals for the Eleventh Circuit assessed whether the dispute related to, arose from, or was connected with the employment agreements at stake. The court determined that claims of false imprisonment, intentional infliction of emotional distress, spoliation of evidence, invasion of privacy, and fraudulent misrepresentation were not dependent on the

---

[288] *Kammgarn Spinnerei GmbH v. Nova (Jersey) Knit Ltd*, Court of Appeal, England, 2 April 1976.

[289] *Casaceli v. Natuzzi S.p.A. (formerly known as Industrie Natuzzi S.p.A.)*, Federal Court, Australia, 29 June 2012, NSD 396 of 2012. See also *CTA International Pty Ltd. v. Sichuan Changhong Electric Co.*, Supreme Court of Victoria, Australia, 6 September 2002, 4278 of 2001.

[290] *Nicola v. Ideal Image Development Corporation Inc.*, Federal Court, Australia, 16 October, NSD 1738 of 2008; *Commonwealth Development, Corp v. Montague*, Supreme Court of Queensland, Australia, 27 June 2000, Appeal No 8159 of 1999, DC No 29 of 1999.

[291] *CTA International Pty Ltd. v. Sichuan Changhong Electric Co.*, Supreme Court of Victoria, Australia, 6 September 2002, 4278 of 2001.

[292] *Société Générale Assurance Méditerranéenne— G.A.M. v. Société FSA-RE et S.A. Garantie Assistance*, Court of Appeal of Paris, France, 14 March 2008, 07/16773.

parties' employment relationship and therefore did not fall within the scope of the arbitration clause.[293]

d. Provisional and conservatory measures

74. The duty to refer the parties to arbitration does not extend to provisional and conservatory measures, except if the arbitration agreement itself refers to such measures. Most courts exercise jurisdiction to order interim or provisional relief in support of arbitration upon application by a party notwithstanding the presence of an arbitration agreement.[294]

75. For example, a French court has confirmed that the presence of an arbitration agreement does not prevent one of the parties from obtaining urgent provisional measures which do not require a ruling on the merits of the dispute.[295] The Australian Federal Court has similarly held that the existence of an otherwise applicable arbitration clause did not prevent a party from seeking injunctive or declaratory relief.[296]

76. Commentators have confirmed that national courts' jurisdiction to order provisional measures does not breach the New York Convention as it does not prejudice the merits of the dispute.[297]

B. Enforcement of arbitration agreements under article II (3)

77. Article II (3) requires national courts to refer the parties to arbitration unless they find that the relevant agreement is "null and void, inoperative or incapable of being performed."

---

[293] *Jane Doe v. Princess Cruise Lines, LTD., a foreign corporation, d.b.a. Princess Cruises*, Court of Appeals, Eleventh Circuit, United States of America, 23 September 2011, 10-10809.

[294] *Hi-Fert Pty Ltd. v. Kuikiang Maritime Carriers Inc.*, Federal Court, Australia, 26 May 1998, NG 1100 & 1101 of 1997; *Société Fieldworks-INC v. Société Erim, S.A. Logic Instrument et Société ADD-on Computer Distribution (A.C.D.)*, Court of Appeal of Versailles, France, 4 July 1996, 3603/96, 3703/96, 3998/96; *Toyota Services Afrique (TSA) v. Société Promotion de Représentation Automobiles (PREMOTO)*, Supreme Court, Côte d'Ivoire, OHADA, 4 December 1997, Arrêt n°317/97.

[295] *Société Fieldworks-INC v. Société Erim, S.A. Logic Instrument et Société ADD-on Computer Distribution (A.C.D.)*, Court of Appeal of Versailles, France, 4 July 1996. The new 2011 French arbitration law limits the jurisdiction of the French courts' to order interim relief to the period prior to the constitution of the arbitral tribunal: see article 1449 of the French Code of civil procedure.

[296] *Electra Air Conditioning BV v. Seeley International Pty Ltd*, Federal Court, Australia, 8 October 2008, SAD 16 of 2008.

[297] Dorothee Schramm, Elliott Geisinger, Philippe Pinsolle, *Article II*, in RECOGNITION AND ENFORCEMENT OF FOREIGN ARBITRAL AWARDS: A GLOBAL COMMENTARY ON THE NEW YORK CONVENTION 37, 139-144 (H. Kronke, P. Nacimiento et al. eds., 2010).

78. Neither the *travaux préparatoires* nor the text of the Convention provides any indication of the standard of review that should be applied by national courts in this exercise, or any further elucidation of the terms "null and void, inoperative or incapable of being performed."

a. Standard of review

79. The New York Convention does not address the issue of the standard of review of arbitration agreements under article II (3).[298]

80. Two trends are discernible in the case law. Some courts perform a full review of the agreement to arbitrate to assess whether it is "null and void, inoperative or incapable of being performed", while others confine themselves to a limited or *prima facie* inquiry, which itself can take on various forms and distinctions.

81. As the Convention does not prohibit courts from conducting either a *prima facie* review of the arbitration agreement[299] or a full review of its existence and validity, none of the two approaches can be held to breach the New York Convention.

82. The full review standard has been endorsed by certain jurisdictions, notably Italy and Germany.

83. The Italian Court of Cassation held that article II (3) allows national courts to assess the validity and efficacy of the arbitration agreement, noting that it is an inherent part of the power of the domestic court to review the validity of the arbitration agreement.[300]

84. While not expressly referring to the Convention, German courts also conduct a full review of the arbitration agreement in assessing whether to refer the parties to arbitration. In so doing, courts rely on the German Code of Civil Procedure that expressly provides that prior to the constitution of the arbitral tribunal, a party may apply to a court to establish the admissibility or inadmissibility of arbitration proceedings.[301] By way of example, relying on

---

[298] The same conclusion may be drawn from case law regarding article 8 of the UNCITRAL Model Law on International Commercial Arbitration, see UNCITRAL, 2012 DIGEST OF CASE LAW ON THE MODEL LAW ON INTERNATIONAL COMMERCIAL ARBITRATION, Article 16 (2012), 75-76, para. 3, available at www.uncitral.org/pdf/english/clout/MAL-digest-2012-e.pdf.

[299] This view is mirrored under the UNCITRAL Model Law on International Commercial Arbitration where article 8(1) in fine exactly reflects the text of article II (3) of the Convention: Frédéric Bachand, *Does Article 8 of the Model Law Call for Full or Prima Facie Review of the Arbitral Tribunal's Jurisdiction?*, 22 ARB. INT'L 463 (2006).

[300] *Heraeus Kulzer GmbH v. Dellatorre Vera SpA*, Court of Cassation, Italy, 5 January 2007, 35.

[301] See Section 1032 of the Code of Civil Procedure (ZPO).

Section 1032 of the Code of Civil Procedure, the German Federal Supreme Court conducted a full review of the arbitration agreement contained in a standard form consumer contract. It held that, notwithstanding the principle of competence-competence, the lower court had erred in limiting its scrutiny of the arbitration agreement, as the court's competence may not be curtailed by agreement of the parties. Having confirmed that the arbitration agreement complied with the formal and substantive requirements of German law, the court referred the parties to arbitration.[302] German commentators confirm that German courts follow the same approach under the New York Convention.[303]

85. Other jurisdictions have restricted their review of the arbitration agreement to a limited analysis to confirm *prima facie* that it is not "null and void, inoperative or incapable of being performed".[304]

86. For instance, in France, courts apply a *prima facie* standard of review of the arbitration agreement. They hold that courts are precluded from performing an in-depth analysis of the arbitration agreement and must refer the parties to arbitration unless the arbitration agreement is manifestly null and void.[305]

---

[302] Bundesgerichtshof [BGH], Germany, 13 January 2005, III ZR 265/03.

[303] Dorothee Schramm, Elliott Geisinger, Philippe Pinsolle, *Article II*, in RECOGNITION AND ENFORCEMENT OF FOREIGN ARBITRAL AWARDS: A GLOBAL COMMENTARY ON THE NEW YORK CONVENTION 37, 99-100 (H. Kronke, P. Nacimiento et al. eds., 2010); Peter Huber, *Arbitration Agreement and Substantive Claim Before Court*, in ARBITRATION IN GERMANY: THE MODEL LAW IN PRACTICE 139, 143-44, para. 15 (K. H. Böckstiegel, S. Kröll and P. Nacimiento eds., 2007).

[304] For an argument in favour of a *prima facie* standard, see R. Doak Bishop, Wade M. Coriell, Marcelo Medina, *The 'Null and Void' Provision* of *the New York Convention*, in ENFORCEMENT OF ARBITRATION AGREEMENTS AND INTERNATIONAL ARBITRAL AWARDS: THE NEW YORK CONVENTION 1958 IN PRACTICE 275, 280-86 (E. Gaillard, D. Di Pietro eds., 2008); Yas Banifatemi, Emmanuel Gaillard, *Negative Effect of Competence-Competence—The Rule of Priority in Favour of the Arbitrators*, in ENFORCEMENT OF ARBITRATION AGREEMENTS AND INTERNATIONAL ARBITRAL AWARDS: THE NEW YORK CONVENTION 1958 IN PRACTICE 257 (E. Gaillard, D. Di Pietro eds., 2008); FOUCHARD GAILLARD GOLDMAN ON INTERNATIONAL COMMERCIAL ARBITRATION 407-08 (E. Gaillard, J. Savage eds., 1996). *Contra*, see Jean-François Poudret, Gabriel Cottier, *Remarques sur l'application de l'article II de la Convention de New York (Arrêt du Tribunal Fédéral du 16 janvier 1995),* 13 ASA BULL. 383, 388-89 (1995).

[305] *Legal Department du Ministère de la Justice de la République d'Irak v. Société Fincantieri Cantieri Navali Italiani, Société Finmeccanica et Société Armamenti E Aerospazio*, Court of Appeal of Paris, France, 15 June 2006; *SA Groupama transports v. Société MS Régine Hans und Klaus Heinrich KG*, Court of Cassation, France, 21 November 2006, 05-21.818; *Ste A.B.S. American Bureau of Shipping v. Copropriété Maritime Jules Verne et autres*, Court of Appeal of Paris, France, 4 December 2002; *Société Generali France Assurances et al. v. Société Universal Legend et al.*, Court of Cassation, France, 11 July 2006, 05-18.681. The new 2011 French arbitration law confirmed that even *prima facie* review by courts of an arbitration agreement is time-barred after the arbitral tribunal is seized (see article 1448 of the French Code of civil procedure).

87. Similarly, in India, the Supreme Court has relied on the spirit and the pro-enforcement bias of the New York Convention in order to determine the standard of review of arbitration agreements. In *Sin-Etsu*, the Supreme Court held that, although nothing in the language of article II (3) itself "indicated whether a finding as to the nature of the arbitral agreement has to be *ex facie* or *prima facie*, requiring only a *prima facie* showing better served the purpose of the New York Convention, which was to enable expeditious arbitration without avoidable intervention by judicial authorities".[306] The court emphasized that a *prima facie* review of the arbitration agreement at the pre-award stage would allow an expedited arbitral process while ensuring a fair opportunity to contest the award after full trial.

88. In Venezuela, the Supreme Court of Justice relied on the competence-competence principle and article II (3) of the Convention to conclude that it could not conduct a full analysis of the arbitration agreement, but should instead limit itself to a *prima facie* analysis of whether the arbitration agreement was "null and void, inoperative or incapable of being performed." The Supreme Court of Justice further held that, in applying the *prima facie* standard, Venezuelan courts should limit themselves to an assessment of whether there is an arbitration agreement in writing and should not enter into an analysis of whether a party had consented to arbitrate.[307]

89. The *prima facie* standard has also been embraced in the Philippines by adopting the Special Rules of Court on Alternative Dispute Resolution ("Special ADR Rules") which constitute guidelines by the Supreme Court binding on lower courts. Rule 2.4 of the Special ADR Rules explicitly provides for a *prima facie* test in order to determine whether the arbitration agreement is "null and void, inoperative or incapable of being performed".[308] The same approach has been followed in Singapore.[309]

90. In a number of jurisdictions, courts have adopted a *prima facie* standard of review, but have confined its scope to certain situations or issues.

---

[306] *Shin-Etsu Chemical Co. Ltd. (Japan) v. Aksh Optifibre Ltd. & Anr. (Ind)*, Supreme Court, India, 12 August 2005, Appeal (civil) 5048 of 2005; Emmanuel Gaillard, Yas Banifatemi, *Prima Facie Review of Existence, Validity* of *Arbitration Agreement*, N.Y.L.J., 1 December 2005, 3. See also *JS Ocean Liner LLC v. MV Golden Progress, Abhoul Marine LLC*, High Court of Bombay, India, 25 January 2007.

[307] *Astivenca Astilleros de Venezuela, C.A. v. Oceanlink Offshore A.S.*, Supreme Court of Justice, Venezuela, 10 November 2011, Exp. No. 09-0573, XXXVI Y.B. COM. ARB. 496 (2011).

[308] Rule 2.4 of the Special ADR Rules. See ARBITRATION IN THE PHILIPPINES UNDER THE ALTERNATIVE DISPUTE RESOLUTION ACT OF 2004 R.A. 9285 (E. Lizares ed., 2011), 200-212, paras. 11.01-11.02.

[309] *Tomolugen Holdings v. Silica Investors Ltd. and other appeals*, Singapore Court of Appeal, 26 October 2015.

91. For instance, Swiss courts apply a *prima facie* standard of review to the extent that the arbitration agreement provides for Switzerland as the seat of arbitration.[310] Under such a scenario, the Swiss Federal Tribunal held that the court's review was limited to a *prima facie* verification of the existence and validity of the arbitration clause.[311] On the other hand, where the arbitration agreement provides for a seat outside Switzerland, the Swiss Federal Tribunal has held that it was entitled to conduct a full review of the existence and validity of the arbitration agreement.[312]

92. In Canada, courts have adopted a *prima facie* standard of review of the arbitration agreement, but have limited its scope to questions of facts. As a result, Canadian courts are entitled to conduct a full review of the arbitration agreement to the extent that the challenge to the arbitrators' jurisdiction pertains to "question[s] of law". This principle was established by the Supreme Court of Canada in *Dell*. Having set out the two schools of thought on the standard of review, the court held that article II (3) of the Convention did not provide that a court is required to rule on whether the arbitration agreement is null and void, inoperative or incapable of being performed before the arbitrators do. The court continued and held that, as a general rule, "any challenge to the arbitrator's jurisdiction must be resolved first by the arbitrator" in accordance with the competence-competence principle.[313] While the Canadian Supreme Court has clearly adopted a *prima facie* standard of review as a general rule, it then limited the arbitrators' power to rule on their jurisdiction to the sole facts of the case, thus upholding the courts' competence to rule on the arbitrators' jurisdiction in relation to questions of law and to assessing whether the challenge to the arbitrators' jurisdiction constituted a dilatory tactic.

93. In England, courts have endorsed the principle that arbitrators should be the first tribunal to rule on their jurisdiction, but have limited this principle in a number of ways. In the seminal *Fiona Trust* decision,[314] the

---

310 On the issue whether this solution should be extended to all arbitration agreements, see in favour: Emmanuel Gaillard, *La reconnaissance, en droit suisse, de la seconde moitié du principe d'effet négatif de la compétence-compétence*, in GLOBAL REFLECTIONS ON INTERNATIONAL LAW, COMMERCE AND DISPUTE RESOLUTION—LIBER AMICORUM IN HONOUR OF ROBERT BRINER 311 (G. Aksen et al. eds., 2005); *contra* Jean-François Poudret, Gabriel Cottier, *Remarques sur l'application de l'Article II de la Convention de New York*, 13 ASA BULL. 383 (1995).

311 *Fondation M v. Banque X*, Federal Tribunal, Switzerland, 29 April 1996.

312 *Compagnie de Navigation et Transports S.A. v. MSC Mediterranean Shipping Company S.A.*, Federal Tribunal, Switzerland, 16 January 1995; Federal Tribunal, Switzerland, 25 October 2010, 4 A 279 / 2010.

313 *Dell Computer Corporation v. Union des consommateurs and Olivier Dumoulin*, Supreme Court of Canada, 13 July 2007.

314 *Fiona Trust & Holding Corp. v. Privalov*, Court of Appeal, England and Wales, 24 January 2007, 2006 2353 A3 QBCMF, upheld by *Fili Shipping Co. Ltd. and others v. Premium Nafta Products Ltd. and others*, House of Lords, England and Wales, 17 October 2007.

Court of Appeal of England and Wales established that "it will, in general, be right for the arbitrators to be the first tribunal to consider whether they have jurisdiction to determine the dispute." However, the court further held that courts maintain within their jurisdiction the right to determine whether an arbitration agreement had come into existence at all. Relying on *Fiona Trust*, the High Court of Justice in *Albon* explained that, despite the fact that the arbitral tribunal had jurisdiction to determine whether the arbitration agreement was ever concluded in accordance with the principle of competence-competence, such principle "does not preclude the court itself from determining that question."[315] It held that, prior to staying judicial proceedings and referring the parties to arbitration under Section 9(1) of the 1996 Arbitration Act,[316] it should be satisfied that (i) there existed a valid arbitration agreement and (ii) the dispute fell within its scope. In reviewing this two-step process in *Berezovsky*, the Court of Appeal held that a stay would be granted when the applicant had proven, on the balance of probabilities, that the arbitration agreement existed and apparently covered the matters in dispute.[317]

94. In practice, once a court is satisfied that an arbitration agreement exists and that the dispute falls within its terms pursuant to Section 9(1) of the 1996 Arbitration Act, it will grant a stay pursuant to Section 9(4) of the 1996 Arbitration Act (giving effect to article II (3) of the Convention) unless it finds that the arbitration agreement is null and void, inoperative or incapable of being performed.[318] As ruled by the High Court of Justice in *A v. B.*, courts should conduct a cost analysis to determine whether the issue of whether the arbitration agreement is "null and void, inoperative or incapable of being performed" should be dealt with by the arbitral tribunal or by the courts.[319] The court held that it will "depend heavily on the extent to which the resolution of that issue will involve findings of fact which impact on substantive rights and obligations of the parties which are already in issue and whether in general the trial can be confined to a relatively circumscribed

---

315 *Albon (t/a NA Carriage Co) v. Naza Motor Trading Sdn Bhd*, High Court of Justice, England and Wales, 29 March 2007, HC05C02150, [2007] EWHC 665 (Ch).

316 Section 9(1) of the English 1996 Arbitration Act gives effect to article II of the Convention. It provides: "A party to an arbitration agreement against whom legal proceedings are brought (whether by way of claim or counterclaim) in respect of a matter which under the agreement is to be referred to arbitration may (upon notice to the other parties to the proceedings) apply to the court in which the proceedings have been brought to stay the proceedings so far as they concern that matter."

317 *Joint Stock Company "Aeroflot-Russian Airlines" v. Berezovsky & Ors*, Court of Appeal, England and Wales, 2 July 2013, [2013] EWCA Civ 784.

318 *Golden Ocean Group Ltd. v. Humpuss Intermoda Transportasi TBK Ltd. & anr*, High Court of Justice, England and Wales, 16 May 2013, [2013] EWHC 1240; *Joint Stock Company "Aeroflot-Russian Airlines" v. Berezovsky & Ors*, Court of Appeal, England and Wales, 2 July 2013, [2013] EWCA Civ 784.

319 *A v. B.*, High Court of Justice, England and Wales, 28 July 2006, 2005 FOLIO 683, [2006] EWHC 2006 (Comm).

area of investigation or is likely to extend widely over the substantive matters in dispute between the parties. If the latter is the case the appropriate tribunal to resolve the jurisdictional issues is more likely to be the arbitration tribunal, provided it has *Kompetenz-Kompetenz*" English courts have consistently followed this approach.[320]

95. In the United States, courts have approached the standard of review issue in terms of whether the court or the arbitral tribunal has "primary power" to determine the validity of an arbitration agreement. The leading case in this regard, although it does not cite the New York Convention, was rendered by the Supreme Court in *First Options*.[321]

96. In *First Options*, the Supreme Court held that there is a presumption in favour of courts deciding whether the arbitral tribunal has jurisdiction, unless the parties have agreed explicitly to submit this issue to the arbitral tribunal in their arbitration agreement. However, once the court is satisfied that a valid arbitration agreement exists, and that it complies with the requirements of both the Federal Arbitration Act and the Convention, the Supreme Court held that the presumption reverses in favour of the arbitral tribunal.[322]

97. United States courts have found that parties agreed to empower the arbitrators to determine the existence and validity of the arbitration agreement when the arbitration rules explicitly allowed the arbitrators to do so. For instance, the Court of Appeals for the Second Circuit held that a reference to the UNCITRAL Arbitration Rules constituted "clear and unmistakable evidence of the parties' intent" to have arbitrators decide on their jurisdiction.[323] Such "clear and unmistakable evidence" has also been inferred from arbitration agreements stating that "any and all" disputes are to be resolved by arbitration.[324]

---

[320] *Joint Stock Company "Aeroflot-Russian Airlines" v. Berezovsky & Ors*, Court of Appeal, England and Wales, 2 July 2013, [2013] EWCA Civ 784; *Golden Ocean Group Ltd. v. Humpuss Intermoda Transportasi TBK Ltd. & anr*, High Court of Justice, England and Wales, 16 May 2013, [2013] EWHC 1240.

[321] *First Options of Chicago Inc. v. Kaplan*, Supreme Court, United States of America, 22 May 1995, 514 United States 938 (1995). See also William Park, *The Arbitrability Dicta in First Options v. Kaplan: What Sort* of *Kompetenz-Kompetenz Has Crossed the Atlantic?*, 12 ARB. INT'L 137 (1996), reprinted in 11 INT'L ARB. Rep. 28 (1996).

[322] *First Options of Chicago Inc. v. Kaplan*, Supreme Court, United States of America, 22 May 1995, 514 United States 938 (1995).

[323] *Republic of Ecuador v. Chevron Corp. (United States)*, Court of Appeals, Second Circuit, United States of America, 17 March 2011, 10-1020-cv (L), 10-1026 (Con). For a similar reasoning regarding the AAA Arbitration Rules, see also *JSC Surgutneftegaz v. President and fellows of Harvard College*, District Court, Southern District of New York, United States of America, 3 August 2005, 04 Civ. 6069 (RCC).

[324] *Oriental Republic of Uruguay, et al. v. Chemical Overseas Holdings, Inc., Chemical Overseas Holdings, Inc. and others v. Republica Oriental del Uruguay, et al.*, District Court,

98. In the absence of clear and unmistakable evidence of the parties' intention, the Supreme Court in *Prima Paint* held that, if a claim goes to the "making" of the arbitration agreement, courts have jurisdiction.[325] Subsequent decisions applying the New York Convention have followed the same reasoning.[326] In so doing, courts have determined that both challenges to the existence of the contract containing the arbitration agreement and to the validity of the arbitration agreement go to the "making" of the arbitration agreement, and thus should be adjudicated by the courts.[327] For instance, in *Sphere Drake*, the Court of Appeals of the Second Circuit held that if "a party alleges that a contract is void and provide some evidence in support, then the party need not specifically allege that the arbitration clause in that contract is void and the party is entitled to trial [this issue before the court]."[328] Similarly, in *Nanosolutions*, the District Court of Columbia, relying on the decision of the Supreme Court in *Buckeye*, held that "challenges [specific to] the validity of the agreement to arbitrate may be adjudicated by this Court."[329] However, when assessing the validity of the arbitration agreement, courts have performed a "very limited inquiry" in line with the "strong federal policy favouring arbitration" stemming from the Federal Arbitration Act implementing the New York Convention.[330]

99. On the other hand, when United States courts face a challenge which goes to the validity of the contract as a whole, they have referred the parties

Southern District of New York, United States of America, 24 January 2006, 05 Civ. 6151 (WHP) and 05 Civ. 6154 (WHP), XXXI Y.B. COM. ARB. 1406 (2006).

325 *Prima Paint Corporation v. Flood & Conklin MFG*, Supreme Court, United States of America, 12 June 1967, 388 United States 395 (87 S.Ct. 1801, 18 L.Ed.2d 1270).

326 See, e.g., *Phoenix Bulk Carriers Ltd. v. Oldendorff Carriers GmbH & Co., KG*, District Court, Southern District of New York, United States of America, 6 November 2002, 2002 United States Dust. LEXIS 21421, XXVIII Y.B. COM. ARB. 1088 (2003).

327 *The Canada Life Assurance Company v. The Guardian Life Insurance Company of America*, District Court, Southern District of New York, United States of America, 22 January 2003, 242 F. Supp. 2d 344; *Guang Dong Light Headgear Factory v. ACI International, Inc.*, District Court, District of Kansas, United States of America, 10 May 2005, 03-4165-JAR; *Dedon GMBH and Dedon Inc. v. Janus et CIE*, Court of Appeals, Second Circuit, United States of America, 6 January 2011, 10-4331.

328 *Sphere Drake Insurance Limited v. Clarendon America Insurance Company*, Court of Appeals, Second Circuit, United States of America, 28 August 2001, 00-9464, XXVII Y.B. COM. ARB. 700 (2002).

329 *Nanosolutions, LLC et al. v. Rudy Prajza, et al.*, District Court, District of Columbia, United States of America, 2 June 2011, 10-1741.

330 *Bautista v. Star Cruises and Norwegian Cruise Line, Ltd.*, District Court, Southern District of Florida, United States of America, 14 October 2003, 03-21642-CIV. See also *Agnelo Cardoso v. Carnival Corporation*, District Court, Southern District of Florida, United States of America, 15 March 2010, 09-23442-CIV-GOLD/ MCALILEY; *Boston Telecommunications Group, Inc. et al. v. Deloitte Touche Tohmatsu, et al.*, District Court, Northern District of California, United States of America, 7 August 2003, C 02-5971 JSW.

to arbitration pursuant to both the New York Convention and the Federal Arbitration Act.[331]

b. Courts' review of the existence and validity of an "agreement in writing"

100. Article II (3) requires national courts to refer the parties to arbitration "unless [they find] that the said agreement is null and void, inoperative or incapable of being performed."

101. United States courts have held that the grounds for refusing to refer parties to arbitration listed under article II (3) are exhaustive.[332] Similarly, an Indian court has held that there are only three grounds under article II (3) for refusing enforcement of an arbitration agreement: (i) the agreement is null and void; (ii) the agreement is inoperative; and (iii) the agreement is incapable for being performed.[333]

102. On the other hand, the United States Court of Appeals for the Second Circuit determined that it had jurisdiction to establish whether an arbitration agreement existed before referring the dispute to the arbitrators.[334] In so ruling, the Court did not refer to any exceptions provided for under article II (3).

(i) "Null and void"

103. Article II (3) of the Convention is silent with regards to the legal standard for determining whether an arbitration agreement is null and void. Some courts consider that the issue is to be determined under the applicable

---

[331] *Prima Paint Corporation v. Flood & Conklin MFG*, Supreme Court, United States of America, 12 June 1967, 388 United States 395 (87 S.Ct 1801, 18 L.Ed.2d 1270); *Sphere Drake Insurance Limited v. Clarendon America Insurance Company*, Court of Appeals, Second Circuit, United States of America, 28 August 2001, 00-9464, XXVII Y.B. COM. ARB. 700 (2002); *Nanosolutions, LLC et al. v. Rudy Prajza, et al.*, District Court, District of Columbia, United States of America, 2 June 2011, 10-1741; *Ascension Orthopedics, Inc. v. Curasan AG*, District Court, Western District of Texas, Austin Division, United States of America, 20 September 2006, A-06-CA-424 LY.

[332] *Lindo (Nicaragua) v. NCL (Bahamas), Ltd. (Bahamas)*, Court of Appeals, Eleventh Circuit, United States of America, 29 August 2011, 10-10367; *Aggarao (Philippines) v. MOL Ship Management Company Ltd. (Japan), Nissan Motor Car Carrier Company, Ltd., trading as Nissan Carrier Fleet (Japan), World Car Careers (Lebanon)*, Court of Appeals, Fourth Circuit, United States of America, 16 March 2012, 10-2211.

[333] *Gas Authority of India Ltd. v. SPIE-CAPAG SA and ors*, High Court of Delhi, India, 15 October 1993, Suit No. 1440, IA No. 5206. See also in Canada: *Automatic Systems Inc. v. Bracknell Corporation*, Court of Appeal of Ontario, Canada, 17 February 1994.

[334] *Dedon GMBH and Dedon Inc. v. Janus et CIE*, Court of Appeals, Second Circuit, United States of America, 6 January 2011, 10-4331.

municipal law, either the *lex fori*[335] or the law applicable pursuant to the conflict-of-laws rule contained in article V (1)*(a)* of the Convention.[336]

104. United States courts and English courts have defined the expression "null and void" to mean "devoid of legal effect".[337] In practice, they have applied an international standard of contract law defences. In accordance with longstanding case law, United States courts have ruled upon the "null and void" ground pursuant to "standard breach-of-contract defences that can be applied neutrally on an international scale, such as fraud, mistake, duress, and waiver."[338] In applying such international standards, United States courts have adopted a narrow interpretation in light of "a general policy of enforceability of agreements to arbitrate".[339] For instance, courts have dismissed the argument that the arbitration agreement was void and unenforceable as contrary to public policy of the United States, reasoning that this defence "could not be applied neutrally on an international scale and, moreover, does not outweigh the policy favouring arbitration."[340]

105. In addition, parties have sought to invalidate arbitration agreements and escape their obligation to arbitrate by arguing that the main contract containing the agreement was null and void. The vast majority of courts

---

[335] Piero Bernardini, *Arbitration Clauses: Achieving Effectiveness in the Law Applicable to the Arbitration Clause*, in IMPROVING THE EFFICIENCY OF ARBITRATION AGREEMENTS AND AWARDS: 40 YEARS OF APPLICATION OF THE NEW YORK CONVENTION 197, 200 (A.J. van den Berg ed., 1998).

[336] Federal Supreme Court, Switzerland, 21 March 1995, 5C.215/1994/lit.

[337] *Rhone Mediterranee Compagnia Francese v. Lauro*, Court of Appeals, Third Circuit, United States of America, 6 July 1983, 82-3523. See also *Albon (t/a NA Carriage Co) v. Naza Motor Trading Sdn Bhd*, High Court of Justice, England and Wales, 29 March 2007, HC05C02150, [2007] EWHC 665 (Ch); *Golden Ocean Group Ltd. v. Humpuss Intermoda Transportasi TBK Ltd. & anr*, High Court of Justice, England and Wales, 16 May 2013, [2013] EWHC 1240.

[338] *St. Hugh Williams v. NCL (Bahamas) LTD., d.b.a. NCL.*, Court of Appeals, Eleventh Circuit, United States of America, 9 July 2012, 11-12150; *Allen v. Royal Caribbean Cruise, Ltd.*, District Court, Southern District of Florida, United States of America, 29 September 2008, 08-22014.

[339] *Rhone Mediterranee Compagnia Francese v. Lauro*, Court of Appeals, *Third* Circuit, United States of America, 6 July 1983, 82-3523; *Anna Dockeray v. Carnival Corporation*, District Court, Southern District of Florida, Miami Division, United States of America, 11 May 2010, 10-20799; *Oriental Commercial and Shipping (UK) v. Rosseel, NV. (Belgium)*, District Court, Southern District of New York, United States of America, 4 March 1985, 84 Civ. 7173 (PKL).

[340] *Allen v. Royal Caribbean Cruise, Ltd.*, District Court, Southern District of Florida, United States of America, 29 September 2008, 08-22014. See also *Aggarao (Philippines) v. MOL Ship Management Company Ltd. (Japan), Nissan Motor Car Carrier Company, Ltd., trading as Nissan Carrier Fleet (Japan), World Car Careers (Lebanon)*, Court of Appeals, Fourth Circuit, United States of America, 16 March 2012, 10-2211; *Ledee (Puerto Rico) v. Ceramiche Ragno (Italy)*, Court of Appeals, First Circuit, United States of America, 4 August 1982, 684 F.2d 184, 82-1057. Concerning the unconscionability defence, see *Rizalyn Bautista, et al. v. Star Cruises, et al.*, Court of Appeals, Eleventh Circuit, United States of America, 15 July 2005, 03-15884.

distinguish between the invalidity of the contract and the invalidity of the arbitration agreement in accordance with the principle of the severability of the arbitration agreement—sometimes referred to as the principle of autonomy.

106. In *Fiona Trust*, the Court of Appeal of England and Wales stayed the judicial proceedings before it pursuant to Section 9(1) of the 1996 Arbitration Act (giving effect to article II (1) of the New York Convention) as the applicant alleged the invalidity of the overall contract, but did not challenge the validity of the arbitration agreement itself.[341] Relying heavily on the severability principle, the Court of Appeal held that a dispute regarding the invalidity of the overall contract, but not specifically directed at the arbitration agreement, should be addressed by the arbitrators. In the same manner, a Dutch court held that "the validity of the arbitration agreement is ascertained separately, independent of the validity of the main contract in respect of which arbitration has been agreed, even if both are contained in the same document."[342] The Madras High Court similarly made express reference to the "doctrine of separability", and referred the parties to arbitration on the basis that "[t]he plaintiffs cannot ignore the Arbitration Clause and invoke the jurisdiction of a Civil Court, just on the basis that even according to the defendants the underlying agreement was void."[343]

107. The severability doctrine has been endorsed by most countries,[344] arbitral institutions,[345] UNCITRAL instruments on arbitration,[346] and

---

[341] *Fiona Trust & Holding Corp. v. Privalov*, Court of Appeal, England and Wales, 24 January 2007, 2006 2353 A3 QBCMF, upheld by *Fili Shipping Co. Ltd. and others v. Premium Nafta Products Ltd. and others*, House of Lords, England and Wales, 17 October 2007.

[342] *Claimant v. Ocean International Marketing B.V., et al.*, Court of First Instance of Rotterdam, Netherlands, 29 July 2009, 194816/HA ZA 03-925.

[343] *Ramasamy Athappan and Nandakumar Athappan v. Secretariat of Court, International Chamber of Commerce*, High Court of Madras, India, 29 October 2008. See also Oberlandesgericht [OLG] Celle, Germany, 8 Sch 3/01, 2 October 2001.

[344] See, e.g., Swiss Private International Law, Chapter 12, article 178(3), Colombian Arbitration Act, article 5; French arbitration law, article 1447; English Arbitration Act, article 7; Australian Arbitration Act, Chapter VI, article 16; Brazilian Arbitration Act, article 8; Chinese Arbitration Act, article 19.

[345] ICC Arbitration Rules, article 6(4); LCIA Arbitration Rules, article 23(1).

[346] Article 16(1) of the UNCITRAL Model Law on International Commercial Arbitration provides that "an arbitration clause which forms part of a contract shall be treated as an agreement independent of the other terms of the contract. A decision by the arbitral tribunal that the contract is null and void shall not entail *ipso jure* the invalidity of the arbitration clause." A list of countries that have enacted legislation based on the UNCITRAL Model Law on International Commercial Arbitration is available on the Internet at www.uncitral.org. See also UNCITRAL Arbitration Rules, article 23(1).

leading commentators who consider that an arbitration agreement constitutes an agreement within an agreement.[347]

(ii) "Inoperative"

108. Courts generally assess the standard of "inoperability" under the broader expression "null and void, inoperative or incapable of being performed" without any further distinction. However, the relevant case law suggests that the word "inoperative" covers situations where the arbitration agreement has become inapplicable to the parties or their dispute.[348]

109. For instance, in circumstances where the parties had waived their right to arbitrate by initiating judicial proceedings, an Indian court has held that the arbitration agreement was inoperative under Section 45 of the Indian Arbitration Act of 1996, which mirrors article II (3) of the Convention.[349] Accordingly, it refused to refer to arbitration the parties which had submitted numerous civil and criminal suits before Indian courts.

110. A French court has found that it had jurisdiction as the timeframe specified for the constitution of the arbitral tribunal had expired, thereby dismissing the argument that there was no manifest inapplicability of the arbitration agreement pursuant to article II of the Convention. The court ruled that the arbitration agreement was "*caduc*" and concluded that it had jurisdiction over the dispute without any reference to the Convention.[350]

111. Another situation of the alleged inoperability of an arbitration agreement can be found in the *Westco* decision rendered by the High Court of Hong Kong. A party alleged that non-compliance with procedural conditions prior to the commencement of the arbitral proceedings rendered the agreement to arbitrate inoperative. The High Court dismissed the argument and referred the parties to arbitration.[351]

---

[347] R. Doak Bishop, Wade M. Coriell, Marcelo Medina, *The 'Null and Void' Provision of the New York Convention*, in ENFORCEMENT OF ARBITRATION AGREEMENTS AND INTERNATIONAL ARBITRAL AWARDS: THE NEW YORK CONVENTION IN PRACTICE 275, 278 (E. Gaillard, D. Di Pietro eds., 2008).

[348] See, e.g., *Golden Ocean Group Ltd. v. Humpuss Intermoda Transportasi TBK Ltd. & anr*, High Court of Justice, England and Wales, 16 May 2013, [2013] EWHC 1240.

[349] *Ramasamy Athappan and Nandakumar Athappan v. Secretariat of Court, International Chamber of Commerce*, High Court of Madras, India, 29 October 2008. See also the citations para. 67.

[350] *Société Gefu Kuchenboss GmbH & CO.KG et Société Gefu Geschafts-Und Verwaltungs GmbH v. Société Coréma*, Court of Appeal of Toulouse, France, 9 April 2008.

[351] *Westco Airconditioning Ltd. v. Sui Chong Construction & Engineering Co. Ltd*, Court of First Instance, High Court of the Hong Kong Special Administrative Region, Hong Kong, 3 February 1998, A12848.

(iii) "Incapable of being performed"

112. The "incapable of being performed" provision is generally understood as relating to situations where the arbitration cannot effectively be set in motion.[352] As explained by an Indian court relying on Section 45 of the Indian Arbitration Act of 1996 (which mirrors article II (3) of the Convention) "the phrase incapable of being performed signifies, in effect, frustration and the consequent discharge. If, after the making of the contract, the promise becomes incapable of being fulfilled or performed, due to unforeseen contingencies, the contract is frustrated."[353]

113. It emerges from case law that an arbitration agreement has been held incapable of being performed when the arbitration agreement was pathological, i.e., in two main situations: (i) when the arbitration agreement is unclear and does not provide sufficient indication to allow the arbitration to proceed, and (ii) when the arbitration agreement designates an inexistent arbitral institution.

114. For instance, ruling upon Section 44 of the Indian Arbitration Act of 1996 (implementing articles I and II of the Convention), an Indian court denied enforcement of an arbitral clause providing for "Durban Arbitration and English Law to apply."[354] The court held that the alleged arbitration agreement was "absolutely vague, ambiguous and self-contradictory". Similarly, the Swiss Federal Tribunal refused to enforce an arbitral clause providing for arbitration "through the American Arbitration Association or to any other American court" on the ground that the arbitration agreement was not sufficiently clear so as to exclude beyond doubt the jurisdiction of the state courts under both article II (3) and Swiss law.[355]

115. In a case where the arbitration agreement designated a non-existent arbitral institution, a United States court nevertheless compelled the parties to arbitration pursuant to article II (3) of the Convention and the Federal Arbitration Act. The court reasoned that the UNCITRAL Arbitration Rules referred to in the arbitration agreement provided for a method for

---

[352] Stefan Kröll, *The 'Incapable of Being Performed' Exception in Article II (3) of the New York Convention*, in ENFORCEMENT OF ARBITRATION AGREEMENTS AND INTERNATIONAL ARBITRAL AWARDS—THE NEW YORK CONVENTION 1958 IN PRACTICE 323, 326 (E. Gaillard, D. Di Pietro eds., 2008).

[353] *Ramasamy Athappan and Nandakumar Athappan v. Secretariat of Court, International Chamber of Commerce*, High Court of Madras, India, 29 October 2008. See also the references cited in para. 67.

[354] *Swiss Singapore Overseas Enterprises Pvt Ltd. v. M/V African Trader*, High Court of Gujarat, India, 7 February 2005, Civil Application No. 23 of 2005.

[355] Federal Tribunal, Switzerland, 25 October 2010, 4A279/2010. It is unclear from that case whether the Federal Tribunal analysed the arbitration agreement under the "incapable of being performed" ground as the decision concluded that the arbitration agreement was invalid under the "null and void, inoperative or incapable of being performed" provision.

constituting an arbitral tribunal in the absence of a prior agreement by the parties and dismissed the plaintiff's claims that the agreement was incapable of being performed.[356]

116. In Russian Federation, the Highest Arbitrazh Court of the Russian Federation held that, in order for the arbitration agreement to be enforceable under the Convention, the agreement had to contain clear language from which the true intentions of the parties to refer the dispute to an arbitration body could be ascertained.[357] Another Russian court held an arbitration agreement to be "incapable of being performed" within the meaning of article II (3) of the Convention because it was not a standard arbitration clause pursuant to the UNCITRAL Rules and it was therefore impossible to conclude that the parties had agreed on those Rules.[358] It further added that the appointing authority, the "President of the International Chamber of Commerce", did not exist.

117. Other courts have adopted a pro-arbitration stance and interpreted vague or inconsistent arbitration agreements so as to uphold such agreements. For instance, French courts have enforced an arbitral award rendered under the auspices of the Arbitration Court of the Chamber of Commerce of Yugoslavia notwithstanding that the wording of the arbitration agreement provided for arbitration under the auspices of a non-existent institution, the "Belgrade Chamber of Commerce". The court held that the parties intended to refer to the Arbitration Court of the Chamber of Commerce of Yugoslavia, which has its headquarters in Belgrade.[359] Similar reasoning has been adopted in Switzerland,[360] Germany,[361] and Hong Kong[362] where the courts have held that the intention of the parties to have their dispute resolved by arbitration should prevail.

---

[356] *Travelport Global Distribution Systems B.V. v. Bellview Airlines Limited*, District Court, Southern District of New York, United States of America, 10 September 2012, 12 Civ. 3483(DLC).

[357] *Tula Ammunition Factory (Russian Federation) v. Sporting Supplies International (United States)*, Highest Arbitrazh Court, Russian Federation, 27 July 2011, VAS-7301/11.

[358] *ZAO UralEnergoGaz (Russian Federation) v. OOO ABB Electroengineering (Russian Federation)*, Ninth Arbitrazh Court of Appeal, Russian Federation, 24 June 2009, No. A40-27854/09-61-247.

[359] *Epoux Convert v. Société Droga*, Court of Appeal of Paris, France, 14 December 1983, 1994 REV. ARB. 483.

[360] Federal Tribunal, Switzerland, 8 July 2003, 129 III 675.

[361] Kammergericht [KT] Berlin, 15 October 1999, XXVI Y.B. COM. ARB. 328 (2001).

[362] *Lucky Goldstar International Limited v. Ng Moo Kee Engineering Limited*, High Court, Supreme Court of Hong Kong, Hong Kong, 5 May 1993, XX Y.B. COM. ARB. 280 (1995).

Article III

Each Contracting State shall recognize arbitral awards as binding and enforce them in accordance with the rules of procedure of the territory where the award is relied upon, under the conditions laid down in the following articles. There shall not be imposed substantially more onerous conditions or higher fees or charges on the recognition or enforcement of arbitral awards to which this Convention applies than are imposed on the recognition or enforcement of domestic arbitral awards.

Travaux préparatoires

The *travaux préparatoires* on article III as adopted in 1958 are contained in the following documents:

Committee on the Enforcement of International Arbitral Awards:

Enforcement of international arbitral awards: statement submitted by the International Chamber of Commerce, a non-governmental organization having consultative status in category A: E/C.2/373.

Summary Records of the Committee on the Enforcement of International Arbitral Awards, 3rd meeting: E/AC.42/SR.3.

Report of the Committee on the Enforcement of International Arbitral Awards: E/AC.42/4.

Report of the Committee on the Enforcement of International Arbitral Awards (Resolution of the Economic and Social Council establishing the Committee, Composition and Organisation of the Committee, General Considerations, Draft Convention): E/2704 : E/AC.42/4/Rev.1.

Draft Convention on the Recognition and Enforcement of Foreign Arbitral Awards and comments by Governments and Organizations:

Comments on the Draft Convention on the Recognition and Enforcement of Foreign Arbitral Awards: E/CONF.26/2.

Report by the Secretary-General, Recognition and Enforcement of Foreign Arbitral Awards, 31 Jan 1956: E/2822.

United Nations Conference on International Commercial Arbitration:

Amendments to the Draft Convention Submitted by Governmental Delegations: E/CONF.26/L.11.

Amendments to the Draft Convention Submitted by Governmental Delegations: E/CONF.26/L.15.

Amendments to the Draft Convention Submitted by Governmental Delegations: E/CONF.26/L.21.

Text of the Convention on the Recognition and Enforcement of Foreign Arbitral Awards as Provisionally Approved by the Drafting Committee on 6 June 1958: E/CONF.26/L.61.

Report on article I, paragraph 1 and article II of the draft Convention (E/2704 and Corr.1): E/CONF.26/L.42/Corr.1.

Text of article 2 as adopted by the Conference at its 16th meeting: E/CONF.26/L.47.

Text of the Convention as provisionally approved by the Drafting Committee on 9 June 1958: E/CONF.26/8.

Final Act and Convention on the Recognition and Enforcement of Foreign Arbitral Awards: E/CONF.26/8/Rev.1.

Summary records:

Report of Working Party No. 1 on Art. I, para. 1, and Art. II of the draft Convention: E/CONF.26/L.42.

Summary Records of the Second, Tenth, Eleventh, Sixteenth and Twenty-third Meetings of the United Nations Conference on International Commercial Arbitration: E/CONF.26/SR.2; E/CONF.26/SR.10; E/CONF.26/SR.11; E/CONF.26/SR.16; E/CONF.26/SR.23.

(Available on the Internet at http://www.uncitral.org)
(For the *travaux préparatoires*, case law and bibliographical references, see also on the Internet at http://newyorkconvention1958.org)

Introduction

1. Article III embodies the pro-enforcement policy of the New York Convention, and sets forth the general principle that "each Contracting State shall recognize arbitral awards as binding and enforce them". As a result of article III, foreign arbitral awards are entitled to a *prima facie* right to recognition and enforcement in the Contracting States.

2. The text of article III follows the wording of the 1927 Geneva Convention, which provided that an "arbitral award [...] shall be recognized as binding and shall be enforced in accordance with the rules of procedure of the territory where the award is relied upon".[363] However, the 1927 Geneva Convention did not include any safeguards that would prevent national courts from imposing unduly complicated or onerous procedural hurdles at the recognition and enforcement stage.

3. Following lengthy discussions between the drafters to the Convention, the final text of article III achieved a balanced solution that permits each Contracting State to apply its own national rules of procedure to the recognition and enforcement of foreign arbitral awards, while guaranteeing that such recognition and enforcement will comply with a number of fundamental principles.[364]

4. The first principle is that, while the recognition and enforcement of foreign arbitral awards under the Convention shall be conducted "in accordance with the rules of procedure of the territory where the award is relied upon", the "conditions" under which recognition and enforcement of foreign awards can be granted are exclusively governed by the Convention.

---

363 Article 1 of the 1927 Geneva Convention.

364 The Conference's delegates initially envisaged a uniform set of rules that would govern the recognition and enforcement of foreign arbitral awards in all Contracting States. See *Travaux préparatoires*, United Nations Conference on International Commercial Arbitration, Comments on the Draft Convention on the Recognition and Enforcement of Foreign Arbitral Awards, E/CONF.26/2, para.7, p. 4. They eventually decided to refer to "the rules of procedure of the country where the award is relied upon". See *Travaux préparatoires*, United Nations Conference on International Commercial Arbitration, Comments on the Draft Convention on the Recognition and Enforcement of Foreign Arbitral Awards, E/CONF.26/2, p. 4. Various alternative texts were also proposed. See *Travaux préparatoires*, United Nations Conference on International Commercial Arbitration, Report on article I, paragraph 1 and article II of the draft Convention (E/2704 and Corr.1), E/CONF.26/L.42/Corr.1; *Travaux préparatoires*, United Nations Conference on International Commercial Arbitration, Summary Records of the Twenty-Third Meeting, E/CONF.26/SR.23, p. 14. The principle set by the drafters of article III nevertheless remained similar to that previously provided for by articles 1 and 5 of the 1927 Geneva Convention.

5. The second principle is that the national rules of procedure governing the recognition and enforcement of foreign arbitral awards in each Contracting State shall not impose "substantially more onerous conditions or higher fees or charges on the recognition or enforcement of arbitral awards to which this Convention applies than are imposed on the recognition or enforcement of domestic arbitral awards."

6. While article III grants Contracting States the freedom to apply their own national rules of procedure at the recognition and enforcement stage, courts have applied article III in accordance with the Convention's policy of promoting recognition and enforcement to the greatest extent possible.

Analysis

A. General principle

a. Obligation to recognize arbitral awards as binding and enforce them

7. The first sentence of article III provides that "[e]ach Contracting State shall recognize arbitral awards as binding and enforce them".[365]

8. The general principle set forth by article III has been referred to by a number of courts as embodying Convention's "pro-enforcement bias". For example, a United States court stated that "[t]he Convention and its implementing legislation have a pro-enforcement bias [...]", of which "[a]rt. III of the Convention is illustrative."[366] The Court of Appeal of England and Wales also held that, pursuant to this principle, foreign arbitral awards are entitled to a "*prima facie*" right to recognition and enforcement.[367] A number of other courts have expressed the same view.[368]

---

365 The obligation to recognize and enforce arbitral awards under the Convention is not binding on States that are not parties to the Convention. See *The Attorney General of Belize v. BCB Holdings Limited and The Belize Bank Limited*, Supreme Court, Belize, 8 August 2012, XXXVIII Y.B. COM. ARB. 324 (2013), in which the Belize Supreme Court ruled that it had no legal obligation to recognize and enforce arbitral awards in accordance with Article III because Belize was not a Contracting State.

366 *Glencore Grain Rotterdam BV. v. Shivnath Rai Harnarain Company*, Court of Appeals, Ninth Circuit, United States of America, 26 March 2002, 01-15539.

367 See, e.g., *Yukos Oil Co. v. Dardana Ltd.*, Court of Appeal, England and Wales, 18 April 2002, A3/2001/102.

368 See, e.g., *Gouvernement de la région de Kaliningrad (Fédération de Russie) v. République de Lituanie*, Court of Appeal of Paris, France, 18 November 2010, 09/19535; *Sojuznefteexport (SNE) (Russian Federation) v. Joc Oil Ltd. (Bermuda)*, Court of Appeal of Bermuda, Bermuda, 7 July 1989, XV Y.B. COM. ARB. 384 (1990); *AO Techsnabexport (Russian Federation) v. Globe Nuclear Services and Supply, Limited (United States of America)*, District Court, District of Maryland, United States of America, 28 August 2009,

9. Courts of the Contracting States have frequently pointed to the mandatory nature of the obligation under article III, which results from the word "shall".[369] For example, a court in Cameroon noted that "the meaning of article I and article III [...] is that Cameroon having signed the New York Convention of 1958 is bound to recognize and enforce arbitral awards made in another Contracting State".[370] A Bulgarian court similarly found that "by virtue of Art. III [...], each signatory country [to the Convention] shall recognize the validity of the final arbitration award and shall allow its enforcement".[371] An Italian court ruled that "article III of the Convention obliges sic et simpli[ci]ter a Contracting State to recognize and enforce an arbitral award".[372] Courts in England[373] and in Germany[374] have also recognized the mandatory nature of article III.

10. Leading commentators similarly describe article III of the Convention as the source of the Contracting States' obligation to recognize and enforce foreign arbitral awards.[375] A number of these commentators also

---

AW-08-1521, XXXIV Y.B. COM. ARB. 1174 (2009); *WTB—Walter Thosti Boswau Bauaktiengesellschaft (Germany) v. Costruire Coop. srl (Italy)*, Court of Cassation, Italy, 7 June 1995, 6426.

[369] See, e.g., *Altain Khuder LLC v. IMC Mining Inc., et al. and IMC Aviation Solutions Pty. Ltd. v. Altain Khuder LLC*, Supreme Court of Victoria, Commercial and Equity Division, Commercial Court, Australia, 28 January 2011 and Supreme Court of Victoria, Court of Appeal, Australia, 22 August 2011, XXXVI Y.B. COM. ARB. 242 (2011); *Merck & Co. Inc. (United States), Merck Frosst Canada Inc. (Canada), Frosst Laboratories Inc. (Colombia) v. Tecnoquimicas SA (Colombia)*, Supreme Court of Justice, Colombia, 24 March 1999, XXVI Y.B. COM. ARB. 755 (2001); *Brace Transport Corp.* of *Monrovia, Bermuda v. Orient Middle East Lines Ltd.*, Supreme Court, India, 12 October 1993, 5438-39 of 1993; *Guarantor (Russian Federation) v. Borrower (Swedish Company)*, Supreme Court, Judicial Collegium, Russian Federation, 22 May 1997, XXV Y.B. COM. ARB. 641 (2000); *Jorf Lasfar Energy Company S.C.A. v. AMCI Export Corporation*, District Court, Western District of Pennsylvania, United States of America, 5 May 2006, 05-0423.

[370] *African Petroleum Consultants (APC) v. Société Nationale de Raffinage*, High Court of Fako Division, OHADA, Cameroon, 15 May 2002, HCF/91/M/2001-2002.

[371] *ECONERG Ltd. (Croatia) v. National Electricity Company AD (Bulgaria)*, Supreme Court of Appeal, Civil Collegium, Fifth Civil Department, Bulgaria, 23 February 1999, XXV Y.B. COM. ARB. 641 (2000).

[372] *S.a.S. Wieland K. G. (Austria) v. Società Industriale Meridionale (S.I.M.) (Italy)*, Court of Appeal of Messina, Italy, 19 May 1976, V Y.B. COM. ARB. 266 (1980).

[373] *Gater Assets Ltd. v. Nak Naftogaz Ukrainiy*, Court of Appeal, England and Wales, 17 October 2007, A3/2007/0738, para. 11.

[374] *Claimant (UK) v. Defendant (Germany)*, Oberlandesgericht, Rostock, Germany, 22 November 2001, 1 Sch 03/00, XXIX Y.B. COM. ARB. 732 (2004).

[375] See, e.g., ICCA'S GUIDE TO THE INTERPRETATION OF THE 1958 NEW YORK CONVENTION: A HANDBOOK FOR JUDGES 69 (P. Sanders ed., 2011); Ramona Martinez, *Recognition and Enforcement of International Arbitral Awards Under the United Nations Convention* of *1958: The "Refusal" Provisions*, 24 INT'L LAW 487, 495-96 (1990); Emilia Onyema, *Formalities of the Enforcement Procedure (Articles III and IV)*, in ENFORCEMENT OF ARBITRATION AGREEMENTS AND INTERNATIONAL ARBITRAL AWARDS: THE NEW YORK CONVENTION IN PRACTICE 597 (E. Gaillard, D. Di Pietro eds., 2008); Loukas A. Mistelis, Domenico D. Pietro, *New York Convention, Article III [Obligation to Recognise and Enforce Arbitral Awards]*, in CONCISE INTERNATIONAL ARBITRATION 10 (L.A. Mistelis ed., 2010).

characterize this obligation as a "presumptive" one, or have referred to it as embodying the "pro-enforcement bias" of the Convention.[376]

11. While parties seeking recognition and enforcement of foreign arbitral awards have often seized the courts of Contracting States where the award-debtor had assets, or where they believed the collection of a monetary award was more likely,[377] neither article III nor any other provision of the Convention requires the presence of assets in the jurisdiction where recognition and enforcement is sought. With the exception of a German decision that refused enforcement of a foreign arbitral award in a case where the award-debtor had no assets in Germany,[378] the courts of the Contracting States have not conditioned recognition and enforcement under the Convention to the presence of assets. Leading commentators confirm that the presence of assets in the jurisdiction in which recognition and enforcement is sought is not a condition of the recognition and enforcement of an award under the Convention.[379]

12. Although article III does not expressly provide that arbitral awards have *res judicata* effect, a number of national courts have ruled that it has such a consequence in practice. For example, a United States court ruled that "[t]hough the convention does not expressly speak to the res judicata effect of an international arbitral award [...] it reflects the principle that until it is

---

376 See, e.g., Maxi Scherer, *Article III (Recognition and Enforcement of Arbitral Awards; General Rule)*, in NEW YORK CONVENTION ON THE RECOGNITION AND ENFORCEMENT OF FOREIGN ARBITRAL AWARDS OF 10 JUNE 1958 OF 10 JUNE 1958—COMMENTARY 193, 196 (R. Wolff ed., 2012);Emilia Onyema, *Formalities of the Enforcement Procedure (Articles III and IV)*, in ENFORCEMENT OF ARBITRATION AGREEMENTS AND INTERNATIONAL ARBITRAL AWARDS: THE NEW YORK CONVENTION IN PRACTICE 597 (E. Gaillard, D. Di Pietro eds., 2008); Andreas Börner, *Article III*, in RECOGNITION AND ENFORCEMENT OF FOREIGN ARBITRAL AWARDS: A GLOBAL COMMENTARY ON THE NEW YORK CONVENTION 115 (H. Kronke, P. Nacimiento et al. eds., 2010). See also GARY B. BORN, INTERNATIONAL COMMERCIAL ARBITRATION 3394 (2014).

377 See, e.g., *Gulf Petro Trading Company Inc., et al. v. Nigerian National Petroleum Corporation, et al.*, Court of Appeals, Fifth Circuit, United States of America, 7 January 2008, 06-40713; *Far Eastern Shipping Company v. AKP Sovocomflot (United Kingdom* of *Great Britain and Northern Ireland)*, Queen's Bench Division, 14 November 1994, XXI Y.B. COM. ARB. 699 (1996); *Brace Transport Corp.* of *Monrovia v. Orient Middle East Lines Ltd. and ors*, Supreme Court, India, 12 October 1993, 5438-39 of 1993, in which the Supreme Court of India observed that "[w]hen it becomes necessary to enforce an international award [...] [t]he first step is to determine the country or countries in which enforcement is to be sought. In order to reach this decision, the party seeking enforcement needs to locate the State or States in which the losing party has (or is likely to have) assets available to meet the award".

378 Kammergericht [KG], Berlin, Germany, 10 August 2006, 20 Sch 07/04.

379 See, e.g., Loukas A. Mistelis, Domenico D. Pietro, *New York Convention, Article III [Obligation to Recognise and Enforce Arbitral Awards]*, in CONCISE INTERNATIONAL ARBITRATION 10 (L.A. Mistelis ed., 2010); Emilia Onyema, *Formalities of the Enforcement Procedure Procedure (Articles III and IV)*, in ENFORCEMENT OF ARBITRATION AGREEMENTS AND INTERNATIONAL ARBITRAL AWARDS: THE NEW YORK CONVENTION IN PRACTICE 597, 603 (E. Gaillard, D. Di Pietro eds., 2008).

successfully challenged, an arbitral award presumptively establishes the rights and liabilities of the parties to the arbitration."[380] This view is equally shared in commentary on the New York Convention.[381]

b. Conditions laid down in the Convention

13. Article III provides that Contracting States shall recognize and enforce arbitral awards "under the conditions laid down in the following articles [of the Convention]."

14. Various courts have held that these "conditions" refer to the conditions set out in articles IV, V, VI and VII of the Convention.[382]

15. National courts have applied these conditions in reported case law on article III.[383] For example, the Italian Court of Cassation overturned the

---

[380] *American Express Bank Ltd. v. Banco Español de Crédito S.A.*, Southern District Court of New York, United States of America, 13 February 2009, 1:06-cv-03484-RJH. See also *Gulf Petro Trading Company Inc., et al. v. Nigerian National Petroleum Corporation, et al.*, Court of Appeals, Fifth Circuit, United States of America, 7 January 2008, 06-40713.

[381] See, e.g., Andreas Börner, *Article III*, in RECOGNITION AND ENFORCEMENT OF FOREIGN ARBITRAL AWARDS: A GLOBAL COMMENTARY ON THE NEW YORK CONVENTION 115 (H. Kronke, P. Nacimiento et al. eds., 2010); Maxi Scherer, *Article III (Recognition and Enforcement of Arbitral Awards; General Rule)*, in NEW YORK CONVENTION ON THE RECOGNITION AND ENFORCEMENT OF FOREIGN ARBITRAL AWARDS OF 10 JUNE 1958—COMMENTARY 193, 196-97 (R. Wolff ed., 2012); GARY B. BORN, INTERNATIONAL COMMERCIAL ARBITRATION 3741 (2014).

[382] For a detailed discussion of these provisions, see the chapters of the Guide on articles IV, V VI and VII. For example, a Swiss court stated that: "According to Art. III first sentence [...], foreign arbitral decisions are recognized and enforced in Switzerland if the requirements in Arts. IV et seq. Convention are met," *Italian party v. Swiss company*, Bezirksgericht of Zurich, Switzerland, 14 February 2003, XXIX Y.B. COM. ARB. 819 (2004); See also *D. S.A. (Spain) v. W. G.m.b.H.. (Austria)*, Oberster Gerichtshof, Austria, 26 April 2006, XXXII Y.B. COM. ARB. 259 (2007). An English court referred to "article III's requirement that enforcement be accorded 'under the conditions laid down in the following articles' (viz articles IV/VI)"; *Gater Assets Ltd. v. Nak Naftogaz Ukrainiy*, Court of Appeals, England and Wales, 17 October 2007, A3/2007/0738.

[383] See, e.g., *Czarina, L.L.C. v. W.F. Poe Syndicate*, Court of Appeals, Eleventh Circuit, United States of America, 4 February 2004, 03-10518; *Greek Buyer v. Ukrainian Seller*, Administrative Court of Appeal of Athens, Greece, 18 July 2011, XXXVII Y.B. COM. ARB. 234 (2012); *Daihatsu Motor Co., Inc. (Japan) v. Terrain Vehicles, Inc. (United States)*, District Court, Northern District of Illinois, Eastern Division, United States of America, 29 May 1992, XVIII Y.B. COM. ARB. 575 (1993); *WTB—Walter Thosti Boswau Bauaktiengesellschaft v. Costruire Coop. srl*, Court of Cassation, Italy, 7 June 1995, 6426; *Zeevi Holdings Ltd. (in receivership) (Israel) v. The Republic* of *Bulgaria*, District Court of Jerusalem, Israel, 13 January 2009, XXXIV Y.B. COM. ARB. 632 (2009); *Adamas Management & Services Inc. v. Aurado Energy Inc.*, Court of Queen's Bench of New Brunswick, Canada, 28 July 2004, S/M/57/04, XXX Y.B. COM. ARB. 479 (2005); *Brothers for Import, Export and Supply Company (Egypt) v. Hano Acorporish (Republic of Korea)*, Court of Appeal of Cairo, Egypt, 2 July 2008, 23/125; *Egyptian British Company for General Development (GALINA) v. Danish Agriculture Seelizer Company*, Court of Appeal of Cairo, Egypt, 26 May 2004, 7/121; *Engineering Industries Company & Sobhi A. Farid Institute v. Roadstar Management &*

decision of an appeals court granting recognition and enforcement of an arbitral award where the applicant had not produced an authenticated copy of the award as required by article IV, holding that this was an application condition of the Convention pursuant to article III.[384] The Supreme Court of Georgia held that arbitral awards "shall be recognized as binding and enforceable" pursuant to article III and thus upheld an award after observing that there were no grounds to refuse recognition under article V of the Convention.[385]

16. Courts of the Contracting States have confirmed that the "conditions" referred to in article III are those exclusively listed in the Convention and that no other condition contained in the Contracting States' national laws shall apply at the recognition and enforcement stage. For instance, in a case where a party argued that enforcement should be refused because the award was rendered by an even number of arbitrators, which Italian law prohibits, the Italian Court of Cassation observed that none of the Convention's exhaustive grounds included such a condition, and that the conditions under Italian law were irrelevant in this respect.[386]

17. Leading commentators confirm that the "conditions" governing the recognition and enforcement of foreign arbitral awards are those exclusively listed by the Convention.[387]

Roadstar International, Court of Appeal of Cairo, Egypt, 29 September 2003, 22/119; *Nile Cotton Ginning Company v. Cargill Limited*, Court of Appeal of Cairo, Egypt, 29 June 2003, 129/118; *Hamdy Mohamed Abdel-Al v. Faj Henwa Berenger Corporation*, Court of Appeal of Cairo, Egypt, 26 March 2003, 10/119; *Cairo for Real Estate Company v. Abdel Rahman Hassan Sharbatly*, Court of Appeal of Cairo, Egypt, 26 February 2003, 23/119.

[384] *Globtrade Italiana srl v. East Point Trading Ltd*, Court of Cassation, Italy, 8 October 2008, 24856.

[385] *"S.F.M." LLC v. Batumi City Hall*, Supreme Court, Georgia, 15 May 2009, a-471-sh-21-09. See also *Ltd. "R.L." v. JSC "Z. Factory"* Supreme Court, Georgia, 2 April 2004, a-204-sh-43-03.

[386] *Nigi Agricoltura srl v. Inter Eltra Kommerz und Produktion GmbH*, Supreme Court, Italy, 23 July 2009, 17312. See also *Privilegiata Fabbrica Maraschino Excelsior Girolamo Luxardo SpA v. Agrarcommerz AG*, Supreme Court of Cassation, Italy, 15 January 1992, XVIII Y.B. COM. ARB. 427 (1993).

[387] See, e.g., ALBERT JAN VAN DEN BERG, THE NEW YORK ARBITRATION CONVENTION OF 1958: TOWARDS A UNIFORM JUDICIAL INTERPRETATION 239 (1981); Andreas Börner, *Article III*, in RECOGNITION AND ENFORCEMENT OF FOREIGN ARBITRAL AWARDS: A GLOBAL COMMENTARY ON THE NEW YORK CONVENTION 115, 116 (H. Kronke, P. Nacimiento et al. eds., 2010); Maxi Scherer, *Article III (Recognition and Enforcement* of *Arbitral Awards; General Rule*), in NEW YORK CONVENTION ON THE RECOGNITION AND ENFORCEMENT OF FOREIGN ARBITRAL AWARDS OF 10 JUNE 1958—COMMENTARY 193, 202 (R. Wolff ed., 2012).

B. Rules of procedure of the territory where the award is relied upon

18. Article III provides that the recognition and enforcement of foreign arbitral awards shall be granted "in accordance with the rules of procedure of the territory where the award is relied upon."

19. As the *travaux préparatoires* make clear, the drafters of the New York Convention refrained from devising a harmonized set of procedural rules applicable to the recognition and enforcement of foreign arbitral awards in each Contracting State.[388] As a result, the Convention does not refer to any specific set of rules, leaving it to each Contracting State to define the rules of procedure applicable to the recognition and enforcement of arbitral awards in its territory.[389]

a. Meaning of the rules of procedure of the territory where the award is relied upon

20. Reported case law shows that the "rules of procedure of the territory where the award is relied upon" refer to the national procedural rules applicable in each Contracting State where recognition and enforcement is sought.

21. In accordance with the wording of article III, courts of the Contracting States have applied the procedural rules of their national laws to the recognition and enforcement of arbitral awards, and not the laws of the country where the arbitration took place or any other law.[390] For example, a

---

[388] See *Travaux préparatoires*, United Nations Conference on International Commercial Arbitration, Comments on Draft Convention on the Recognition and Enforcement of Foreign Arbitral Awards, E/CONF.26/2, p. 4; *Travaux préparatoires*, United Nations Conference on International Commercial Arbitration, Consideration of other measures for increasing the effectiveness of arbitration in the settlement of private law disputes, E/CONF.26/6, p. 12; *Travaux préparatoires*, United Nations Conference on International Commercial Arbitration, Consideration of the draft convention on the recognition and enforcement of foreign arbitral awards, Text of Article II as adopted by the Conference at its 16th meeting, E/CONF.26/L.47.

[389] The Spanish Supreme Court observed that Spanish procedural rules shall be applied to the recognition and enforcement of foreign arbitral awards pursuant to article III of the New York Convention because that article "does not itself provide for a particular recognition and enforcement mechanism". *Saroc, S.p.A. (Italy) v. Sahece, S.A. (Spain)*, Supreme Court, Spain, 4 March 2003, XXXII Y.B. COM. ARB. 571 (2007). See also *Zeevi Holdings Ltd. v. The Republic of Bulgaria*, Southern District of New York, United States of America, 29 March 2011, 09 Civ. 8856 (RJS), XXXVI Y.B. COM. ARB. 464 (2011).

[390] *Kuwait No. 1, contract party v. contract party*, Supreme Appeal Court, Cassation Circuit, (Kuwait), 21 November 1988, XXII Y.B. COM. ARB. 748 (1997). See also *TermoRio S.A. E.S.P. (Colombia), LeaseCo Group and others v. Electranta S.P. (Colombia), et al.*, Court of Appeals, District of Columbia Circuit, United States of America, 25 May 2007, 06-7058, XXXIII Y.B. COM. ARB. 955 (2008); *China National Building Material Investment Co., Ltd. (PR China) v. BNK International LLC (United States)*, District Court, Western District of Texas, United States of America, 4 December 2009, A-09-CA-488-SS, XXXV Y.B. COM. ARB. 507 (2010).

United States court rejected the application of English procedural rules to the recognition and enforcement of an arbitral award in the United States, on the ground that enforcement was sought in the United States.[391] The Supreme Court of Canada held that the word "territory" in article III referred to the relevant provincial unit where enforcement was sought (in the case at hand, the province of Alberta), instead of the Contracting State in its entirety.[392] The courts of Cameroon,[393] Bulgaria,[394] the Czech Republic,[395] Colombia,[396] Egypt,[397] England and Wales,[398] France,[399] Germany,[400] Greece,[401] India,[402] Italy,[403] Japan,[404] the Netherlands,[405] Portugal[406], and

---

391 *Artemis Shipping & Navigation Co. S.A. v. Tormar Shipping AS*, District Court, Eastern District of Louisiana, United States of America, 9 December 2003, 03-217.

392 *Yugraneft Corporation v. Rexx Management Corporation*, Supreme Court, Canada, 20 May 2010, 2010 SCC 19.

393 *African Petroleum Consultants (APC) v. Société Nationale de Raffinage*, High Court of Fako Division, OHADA, Cameroon, 15 May 2002, HCF/91/M/2001-2002.

394 See, e.g., *ECONERG Ltd. (Croatia) v. National Electricity Company AD (Bulgaria)*, Supreme Court of Appeal, Civil Collegium, Fifth Civil Department, Bulgaria, 23 February 1999, XXV Y.B. COM. ARB. 641 (2000).

395 See, e.g., *F&G A.S.R. v. K, s.p.*, Supreme Administrative Court, Czech Republic, 29 March 2001, XXXVIII Y.B. COM. ARB. 363 (2013).

396 See, e.g., *Merck & Co. Inc. (United States), Merck Frosst Canada Inc. (Canada), Frosst Laboratories Inc. (Colombia) v. Tecnoquimicas S.A. (Colombia)*, Supreme Court of Justice, Colombia, 24 March 1999, XXVI Y.B. COM. ARB. 755 (2001); *Merck & Co. Inc. (United States), Merck Frosst Canada Ind. & Frosst Laboratories Inc. (Colombia) v. Tecnoquimicas S.A. (Colombia)*, Supreme Court of Justice, Colombia, 1 March 1999, E-7474; *Sunward Overseas S.A. v. Servicios Maritimos Limitada Semar (Ltda.) (Colombia)*, Supreme Court of Justice, Colombia, 20 November 1992, XX Y.B. COM. ARB. 651 (1995); *Petrotesting Colombia S.A. et al. v. Ross Energy S.A.*, Supreme Court of Justice, Colombia, 27 July 2011, XXXVII Y.B. COM. ARB. 200 (2012).

397 See, e.g., *Omnipol v. Samiram*, Court of Appeal of Cairo, Egypt, 30 May 2005, 10/122.

398 See, e.g., *Gater Assets Ltd. v. Nak Naftogaz Ukrainiy*, Court of Appeal, England and Wales, 17 October 2007, A3/2007/0738.

399 See, e.g., *S.A. Recam Sonofadex v. S.N.C. Cantieri Rizzardi de Gianfranco Rizzardi*, Court of Appeal of Orleans, France, 5 October 2000; *Société I.A.I.G.C.—Inter-Arab Investment Guarantee Corporation v. Société B.A.I.I.—Banque arabe et internationale d'investissement SA (BAII)*, Court of Appeal of Paris, France, 23 October 1997, 96/80232; *Société Acteurs Auteurs Associés (A.A.A.) v. Société Hemdale Film Corporation*, Court of First Instance of Paris, France, 22 November 1989, 10247/89.

400 See, e.g., Bundesgerichtshof [BGH], Germany, 4 October 2005, VII ZB 09/05; Bundesgerichtshof [BGH], Germany, 4 October 2005, VII ZB 8/05.

401 See, e.g., *Not indicated v. Not indicated*, Court of First Instance of Piraeus, Greece, 1968, I Y.B. COM. ARB. 185 (1976); *Greek Buyer v. Ukrainian Seller*, Court of Appeal of Athens, Greece, 18 July 2011, XXXVII Y.B. COM. ARB. 234 (2012).

402 See, e.g., *Orient Middle East Lines Ltd., Bombay and others (India) v. M/s Brace Transport Corporation of Monrovia and another (Liberia)*, High Court of Gujarat, India, 19 April 1985, XIV Y.B. COM. ARB. 648 (1989).

403 See, e.g., *WTB—Walter Thosti Boswau Bauaktiengesellschaft (Germany) v. Costruire Coop. srl (Italy)*, Court of Cassation, Italy, 7 June 1995, 6426.

404 See, e.g., *Zhe-jiang Provincial Light Industrial Products Import & Export Corp. (China) v. Takeyari K. K. (Japan)*, District Court of Okayama, Civil Section II, Japan, 14 July 1993, XXII Y.B. COM. ARB. 744 (1997).

Spain[407] have followed the same approach. Leading commentators also confirm that article III requires courts to apply the national rules of procedure of their own country.[408]

22. In a number of reported cases on article III, courts have considered whether certain rules should be characterized as "conditions" governing the recognition and enforcement of foreign arbitral awards (which are exclusively listed in the Convention) or "rules of procedure" applicable to the recognition and enforcement of these awards (which are contained in national laws).

23. Courts have considered that the "rules of procedure" that may be applied under article III should be interpreted narrowly, and should be determined independently of the categories observed under national laws. For instance, the Italian Court of Cassation held that "rules of procedure" should be interpreted restrictively and that the principle of *lis pendens*,

---

[405] See, e.g., *Société d'Etudes et de Commerce SA (France) v. Weyl Beef Products BV*, Court of First Instance of Amelo, Netherlands, 19 July 2000, XXVI Y.B. COM. ARB. 827 (2001).

[406] *T. S.A. v. S. S.A.*, Court of Appeal of Lisbon, Portugal, 8 June 2010, XXXVIII Y.B. COM. ARB. 438 (2013).

[407] See, e.g., *Unión Naval de Levante S.A. (Spain) v. Bisba Comercial Inc. (Panama)*, Supreme Court, Spain, 9 October 2003, XXX Y.B. COM. ARB. 623 (2005); *Saroc, S.p.A. (Italy) v. Sahece, S.A. (Spain)*, Supreme Court, Plenary Session, Spain, 4 March 2003, XXXII Y.B. COM. ARB. 571 (2007); *Unión Naval de Levante S.A. (Spain) v. Bisba Comercial Inc. (Panama)*, Supreme Court, Spain, 9 October 2003, XXX Y.B. COM. ARB. 623 (2005); *Mr. Genaro (Spain), Mr. Carmelo (Spain) and Agraria del Tormes S.A. (Spain) v. Majeriforeningen Danish Dairy Board (Denmark)*, Court of Appeal of Zamora, Spain, 27 November 2009, XXXV Y.B. COM. ARB. 454 (2010).

[408] See, e.g., William W. Park, *Respecting the New York Convention*, 18(2) ICC BULL. 65, 70 (2007); ALBERT JAN VAN DEN BERG, THE NEW YORK ARBITRATION CONVENTION OF 1958: TOWARDS A UNIFORM JUDICIAL INTERPRETATION 236 (1981); FOUCHARD GAILLARD GOLDMAN ON INTERNATIONAL COMMERCIAL ARBITRATION 982, para. 1671 (E. Gaillard, J. Savage eds., 1999); Andreas Börner, *Article III*, in RECOGNITION AND ENFORCEMENT OF FOREIGN ARBITRAL AWARDS: A GLOBAL COMMENTARY ON THE NEW YORK CONVENTION 115, 117 (H. Kronke, P. Nacimiento et al. eds., 2010); Maxi Scherer, *Article III (Recognition and Enforcement of Arbitral Awards; General Rule)*, in NEW YORK CONVENTION ON THE RECOGNITION AND ENFORCEMENT OF FOREIGN ARBITRAL AWARDS OF 10 JUNE 1958—COMMENTARY 193, 197 (R. Wolff ed., 2012); Emilia Onyema, *Formalities of the Enforcement Procedure (Articles III and IV)*, in ENFORCEMENT OF ARBITRATION AGREEMENTS AND INTERNATIONAL ARBITRAL AWARDS: THE NEW YORK CONVENTION IN PRACTICE 597, 603 (E. Gaillard, D. Di Pietro eds., 2008); Ramona Martinez, *Recognition and Enforcement of International Arbitral Awards Under the United Nations Convention* of *1958: The "Refusal" Provisions*, 24 INT'L LAW 487, 496 (1990); ICCA'S GUIDE TO THE INTERPRETATION OF THE 1958 NEW YORK CONVENTION: A HANDBOOK FOR JUDGES 69 (P. Sanders ed., 2011).

despite being part of the Italian Code of Civil Procedure, could not be applied by the court by virtue of article III.[409]

24. In the absence of any guidance in the text of the Convention, Contracting States are free to determine the content of the rules of procedure applicable to the recognition and enforcement of arbitral awards. For instance, the Supreme Court of Canada stated that the text of the Convention, including article III, must "be construed in a manner that takes into account the fact that it was intended to interface with a variety of legal traditions".[410] The English High Court, when applying article III, also noted that "the court is not directly concerned to ensure that the English approach is the same as that adopted in other Convention states".[411]

25. The flexibility afforded under article III to Contracting States to apply their national rules of procedure gives rise to the possibility that an award could be granted recognition and enforcement in one Contracting State and denied recognition and enforcement in another based on a rule of procedure that exists in the former but not the latter. However, reported case law provides very few examples of such situations.[412]

---

409 *Privilegiata Fabbrica Maraschino Excelsior Girolamo Luxardo SpA v. Agrarcommerz AG*, Court of Cassation, Italy, 15 January 1992, XVIII Y.B. COM. ARB. 427 (1993). See also *Società La Naviera Grancebaco S.A. (Panama) v. Ditta Italgrani (Italy)*, Court of First Instance of Naples, Italy, 30 June 1976, IV Y.B. COM. ARB. 277 (1979).

410 *Yugraneft Corporation. v. Rexx Management Corporation*, Supreme Court, Canada, 20 May 2010, 2010 SCC 19.

411 *IPCO v. Nigerian National Petroleum Corp.*, High Court of Justice Queen's Bench Division, England and Wales, 17 April 2008, 2004 Folio 1031. Courts of the United States have also recognized that the wording of article III entails that different procedural rules would be applied in the courts of various Contracting States. See *Zeevi Holdings Ltd. v. The Republic of Bulgaria*, District Court, Southern District of New York, United States of America, 29 March 2011, 09 Civ. 8856 (RJS), XXXVI Y.B. COM. ARB. 464 (2011); *Monegasque de Reassurances S.A.M. (Monde Re) v. Nak Naftogaz* of *Ukraine and State of Ukraine*, Court of Appeals, Second Circuit, United States of America, 15 November 2002, 017947, 01-9153; *TermoRio S.A. E.S.P. (Colombia), LeaseCo Group and others v. Electranta S.P. (Colombia), et al.*, Court of Appeals, District of Columbia Circuit, United States of America, 25 May 2007, 06-7058, XXXIII Y.B. COM. ARB. 955 (2008).

412 For example, both an Israeli court and a United States court were faced with the same award in which the underlying agreement to arbitrate provided that the award could only be enforced in Bulgaria. The United States Court, applying article III, enforced the forum selection clause pursuant to the doctrine of *forum non conveniens* and dismissed the case. Conversely, an Israel court granted enforcement, holding that the award could only be refused based on the grounds under article V of the Convention, which did not include the *forum non conveniens* doctrine. See *Zeevi Holdings Ltd. (in receivership) (Israel) v. The Republic of Bulgaria*, District Court of Jerusalem, Israel, 13 January 2009, XXXIV Y.B. COM. ARB. 632 (2009) and *Zeevi Holdings Ltd. v. The Republic of Bulgaria*, District Court, Southern District of New York, United States of America, 29 March 2011, 09 Civ. 8856 (RJS), XXXVI Y.B. COM. ARB. 464 (2011). On the issue of the applicability of the *forum non conveniens* doctrine under article III, see the chapter of the Guide on article III para. 32 and fn. 427.

b. *Application by national courts*

26. In many of the reported cases on article III, courts have applied specific rules of procedure from their national legislation that govern the recognition and enforcement of foreign arbitral awards.[413]

27. Only a few reported cases have addressed the situation where the national law of a Contracting State does not contain any rules of procedure specifically applicable to the recognition and enforcement of foreign arbitral awards. Indian courts have held that, in the absence of such rules, procedural rules applicable to the recognition and enforcement of domestic arbitral awards should be transposed to foreign arbitral awards.[414] The Cairo Court of Appeal confirmed that Contracting States are not obliged to enact specific rules of procedure to govern the recognition and enforcement of foreign arbitral awards.[415] Commentators on the New York Convention equally consider that where a Contracting State's national law does not contain specific procedural rules applicable to the recognition and enforcement of

---

[413] See, e.g., *Privilegiata Fabbrica Maraschino Excelsior Girolamo Luxardo SpA v. Agrarcommerz AG*, Court of Cassation, Italy, 15 January 1992, XVIII Y.B. COM. ARB. 427 (1993); *ECONERG Ltd. (Croatia) v. National Electricity Company AD (Bulgaria)*, Supreme Court of Appeal, Civil Collegium, Fifth Civil Department, Bulgaria, 23 February 1999, XXV Y.B. COM. ARB. 641 (2000); *F&G A.S.R. v. K, s.p.*, Supreme Administrative Court, Czech Republic, 29 March 2001, XXXVIII Y.B. COM. ARB. 363 (2013); *Société d'Etudes et de Commerce SA (France) v. Weyl Beef Products BV*, Court of First Instance of Amelo, Netherlands, 19 July 2000, XXVI Y.B. COM. ARB. 827 (2001); *Unión Naval de Levante S.A. v. Bisba Comercial Inc.*, Supreme Court, Spain, 9 October 2003, XXX Y.B. COM. ARB. 623 (2005); *Brace Transport Corporation* of *Monrovia, Bermuda v. Orient Middle East Lines Ltd. and ors*, High Court of Gujarat, India, 19 April 1985, AIR 1986 Guj 62; *Romanian Company v. Panamanian Company*, Supreme Court, Romania, 3 June 1984, XIV Y.B. COM. ARB. 691 (1989); *WTB—Walter Thosti Boswau Bauaktiengesellschaft (Germany) v. Costruire Coop. srl (Italy)*, Court of Cassation, Italy, 7 June 1995, 6426; *Contract party v. Contract party*, Supreme Appeal Court, Cassation Circuit, Kuwait, 21 November 1988, XXII Y.B. COM. ARB. 748 (1997); *Al Ahram Beverages Company v. Société Française d'Etudes et de Construction*, Court of Appeal of Tanta, Egypt, 17 November 2009, 42/42; *Abdel Wahed Hassan Suleiman v. Danish Dairy and Agriculture Seelizer Company*, Court of Appeal of Cairo, Egypt, 25 September 2005; *Omnipol v. Samiram*, Court of Appeal of Cairo, Egypt, 30 May 2005, 10/122; *El Nasr Company for Fertilizers & Chemical Industries (SEMADCO) v. John Brown Deutsche Engineering*, Court of Cassation, Egypt, 10 January 2005, 966/73; *Orient Middle East Lines Ltd., Bombay and others (India) v. M/s Brace Transport Corporation of Monrovia and another (Liberia)*, High Court of Gujarat, India, 19 April 1985, XIV Y.B. COM. ARB. 648 (1989).

[414] *Orient Middle East Lines Ltd., Bombay and others (India) v. M/s Brace Transport Corporation of Monrovia and another (Liberia)*, High Court of Gujarat, India, 19 April 1985, XIV Y.B. COM. ARB. 648 (1989). The Indian court held that "if the said [domestic] Act is silent with regard to any procedural aspect [...], then [the Code of Civil Procedure and other procedural statutes] of this country where the award is relied upon have to be followed".

[415] *Ahmed Mostapha Shawky v. Andersen Worldwide & Wahid El Din Abdel Ghaffar Megahed & Emad Hafez Ragheb & Nabil Istanboly Akram Istanboly*, Court of Appeal of Cairo, Egypt, 23 May 2001, 25/116.

foreign arbitral awards, the procedural rules governing domestic arbitral awards should be applied.[416]

28. Different types of domestic procedural rules have been applied in reported case law on article III.

29. In a number of cases, courts have applied national rules that determine the competent authority to hear applications for recognition and enforcement of foreign arbitral awards. For example, the Supreme Court of Romania held that, in accordance with article III, the court having jurisdiction to hear applications for recognition and enforcement of foreign arbitral awards was to be determined in accordance with rules of procedure of Romanian law.[417] Similarly, a court in Cameroon observed that the determination of the specific court having jurisdiction to hear a request for recognition and enforcement of a foreign arbitral award should be a matter of Cameroon law.[418]

30. In other reported cases on article III, courts have held that the limitation period applicable to an application for recognition and enforcement of a foreign arbitral awards is a procedural rule governed by national law. For instance, the Supreme Court of Canada, after interpreting the text of the Convention and its *travaux préparatoires*, held that the Convention "was intended to allow Contracting States to impose time limits on the recognition and enforcement of foreign arbitral awards if they so wished".[419] Courts in Russian Federation,[420] India[421] and the United

---

[416] See, e.g., FOUCHARD GAILLARD GOLDMAN ON INTERNATIONAL COMMERCIAL ARBITRATION 982, para. 1671 (E. Gaillard, J. Savage eds., 1999); Emilia Onyema, *Formalities of the Enforcement Procedure (Articles III and IV)*, in ENFORCEMENT OF ARBITRATION AGREEMENTS AND INTERNATIONAL ARBITRAL AWARDS—THE NEW YORK CONVENTION IN PRACTICE 597, 603 (E. Gaillard, D. Di Pietro eds., 2008); ALBERT JAN VAN DEN BERG, THE NEW YORK ARBITRATION CONVENTION OF 1958: TOWARDS A UNIFORM JUDICIAL INTERPRETATION 238 (1981).

[417] *Romanian Company v. Panamanian Company*, Supreme Court, Romania, 3 June 1984, XIV Y.B. COM. ARB. 691 (1989).

[418] *African Petroleum Consultants (APC) v. Société Nationale de Raffinage*, High Court of Fako Division, OHADA, Cameroon, 15 May 2002, HCF/91/M/2001-2002. For other examples, see, e.g., Court of Appeal of Porto, Portugal, 21 June 2005, 0427126; *Brace Transport Corporation* of *Monrovia, Bermuda v. Orient Middle East Lines Ltd. and ors*, High Court of Gujarat, India, 19 April 1985, AIR 1986 Guj 62; *Centrotex, S.A. (Czech Republic) v. Agencia Gestora de Negocios, S.A. (Agensa) (Spain)*, Supreme Court, Spain, 13 November 2001, XXXI Y.B. COM. ARB. 834 (2006).

[419] *Yugraneft Corporation. v. Rexx Management Corporation*, Supreme Court, Canada, 20 May 2010, 2010 SCC 19.

[420] *OAO Ryazan Metal Ceramics Instrumentation Plant (Russian Federation)*, Constitutional Court, Russian Federation, 2 November 2011, 1479-O-O/2011.

[421] *Brace Transport Corporation* of *Monrovia, Bermuda v. Orient Middle East Lines Ltd. and ors*, High Court of Gujarat, India, 19 April 1985, AIR 1986 Guj 62.

Kingdom[422] have equally applied limitation periods found in their national procedural rules pursuant to article III of the Convention.

31. Leading commentators confirm that the determination of the court having jurisdiction to hear requests for recognition and enforcement of foreign arbitral awards, or of the limitation periods applicable to recognition and enforcement, constitute procedural issues that should be governed by the Contracting States' national laws.[423]

32. Reported case law provides other isolated examples where courts have applied national rules of procedure to the recognition and enforcement of foreign arbitral awards, some of which have been criticized by commentators. These include rules concerning the ranking of creditors' claims,[424] the setting-off of claims,[425] the enforcement of a forum selection clause,[426] the doctrine of *forum non conveniens*[427] and issues of diplomatic protection.[428]

---

[422] *The Government of Kuwait v. Sir Frederick Snow & Partners and Others (United Kingdom of Great Britain and Northern Ireland)*, Court of Appeal, United Kingdom, 17 March 1983, IX Y.B. COM. ARB. 451 (1984).

[423] See Maxi Scherer, *Article III (Recognition and Enforcement of Arbitral Awards; General Rule)*, in NEW YORK CONVENTION ON THE RECOGNITION AND ENFORCEMENT OF FOREIGN ARBITRAL AWARDS OF 10 JUNE 1958— COMMENTARY 193, 199-202 (R. Wolff ed., 2012); Andreas Börner, *Article III*, in RECOGNITION AND ENFORCEMENT OF FOREIGN ARBITRAL AWARDS: A GLOBAL COMMENTARY ON THE NEW YORK CONVENTION 115, 122-27 (H. Kronke, P. Nacimiento et al. eds., 2010); ALBERT JAN VAN DEN BERG, THE NEW YORK ARBITRATION CONVENTION OF 1958: TOWARDS A UNIFORM JUDICIAL INTERPRETATION 240 (1981). See also United Nation Commission on International Trade Law, Report on the survey relating to the legislative implementation of the Convention on the Recognition and Enforcement of Foreign Arbitral Awards (New York, 1958), A/CN.9/656/ Add.1, at 2/3.

[424] See, e.g., *Artemis Shipping & Navigation Co. SA v. Tormar Shipping AS*, District Court, Eastern District of Louisiana, United States of America, 9 December 2003, 03-217.

[425] See *Rumanian Firm C. v. German (F.R.) party* Landgericht [LG] Hamburg, Oberlandesgericht [OLG] Hamburg, Germany, 27 March 1974, 27 March 1975, II Y.B. COM. ARB. 240 (1977). This decision has been criticized in the doctrine. See, e.g., Andreas Börner, *Article III*, in RECOGNITION AND ENFORCEMENT OF FOREIGN ARBITRAL AWARDS: A GLOBAL COMMENTARY ON THE NEW YORK CONVENTION 115, 130-31 (H. Kronke, P. Nacimiento et al. eds., 2010); Maxi Scherer, *Article III (Recognition and Enforcement of Arbitral Awards; General Rule)*, in NEW YORK CONVENTION ON THE RECOGNITION AND ENFORCEMENT OF FOREIGN ARBITRAL AWARDS: COMMENTARY 193, 203-04 (R. Wolff ed., 2012), who considers that "permitting counter-claims or set-off defenses during recognition or enforcement proceedings is contrary to Articles III and V."

[426] *Zeevi Holdings Ltd. v. The Republic of Bulgaria*, District Court, Southern District of New York, United States of America, 29 March 2011, 09 Civ. 8856 (RJS), XXXVI Y.B. COM. ARB. 464 (2011).

[427] *Monegasque de Reassurances S.A.M. (Monde Re) v. Nak Naftogaz of Ukraine and State of Ukraine, Court of Appeals*, Second Circuit, United States of America, 15 November 2002, 01-7947, 01-9153. Such an interpretation has been widely criticized by commentators. See, e.g., American Law Institute, Restatement of the Law—The United States Law of International Commercial Arbitration, Tentative Draft No. 4 (April 17, 2015); George A. Bermann, *'Domesticating' the New York Convention: the Impact of the Federal Arbitration*

C. There should not be imposed substantially more onerous conditions or higher fees or charges than are imposed on the recognition or enforcement of domestic arbitral awards

33. The second sentence of article III provides that "[t]here shall not be imposed substantially more onerous conditions or higher fees or charges on the recognition or enforcement of arbitral awards to which this Convention applies than are imposed on the recognition or enforcement of domestic arbitral awards". This rule limits the Contracting States' discretion to determine the rules of procedure applicable to the recognition and enforcement of foreign arbitral awards in their territories. As the *travaux préparatoires* show, the purpose of this limitation, which has been referred to as the "national treatment" or "non-discrimination" rule,[429] is to prevent national courts from imposing "unduly complicated enforcement procedures" and insurmountable procedural hurdles at the recognition and enforcement stage.[430]

Act, 2(2) J. INT. DISP. SETTLEMENT 317, 326 (2011); Maxi Scherer, *Article III (Recognition and Enforcement of Arbitral Awards; General Rule)*, in NEW YORK CONVENTION ON THE RECOGNITION AND ENFORCEMENT OF FOREIGN ARBITRAL AWARDS OF 10 JUNE 1958—COMMENTARY 193, 203 (R. Wolff ed., 2012); William W. Park, *Respecting the New York Convention*, 18(2) ICC BULL. 65, 68-72 (2007); Dimitri Santoro, *Forum Non Conveniens: A Valid Defense under the New York Convention?*, 21 ASA BULL. 713, 723 (2003).

[428] See, e.g., Bundesgerichtshof[BGH], Germany, 4 October 2005, VII ZB 09/05; Bundesgerichtshof, Germany, 4 October 2005, VII ZB 8/05.

[429] See *Travaux préparatoires*, United Nations Conference on International Commercial Arbitration, Summary Records of the Tenth Meeting, E/CONF.26/SR.10, pp. 3 and 7. Other expressions have been used by national courts, such as "the non-discrimination provision", "the discrimination prohibition in article III" or the "principle of equivalence". *OAO Rosneft (Russian Federation) v. Yukos Capital s.a.r.l. (Luxembourg)*, Supreme Court, Netherlands, 25 June 2010, XXXV Y.B. COM. ARB. 423 (2010); *Catz International BV. v. Gilan Trading KFT, Provisions Judge of the District Court of Rotterdam* and Court of Appeal of The Hague, Netherlands, 28 February 2011 and 20 December 2011, XXXVII Y.B. COM. ARB. 271 (2012); Supreme Court of Justice, Portugal, 19 March 2009, 299/09; Supreme Court of Justice, Portugal, 22 April 2004, 04B705; *Gater Assets Ltd. v. Nak Naftogaz Ukrainiy*, Court of Appeal, England and Wales, 17 October 2007, A3/2007/0738; *Monegasque de Reassurances S.A.M. (Monde Re) v. Nak Naftogaz of Ukraine and State of Ukraine*, Court of Appeals, Second Circuit, United States of America, 15 November 2002, 01-7947, 01-9153.

[430] *Travaux préparatoires*, United Nations Conference on International Commercial Arbitration, Comments on the Draft Convention on the Recognition and Enforcement of Foreign Arbitral Awards, E/CONF.26/2, p. 4; *Travaux préparatoires*, United Nations Conference on International Commercial Arbitration, Consideration of the Draft Convention on the Recognition and Enforcement of Foreign Arbitral Awards—Amendment to article II of the Draft Convention (United Kingdom), E/CONF.26/L.11; *Travaux préparatoires*, United Nations Conference on International Commercial Arbitration, Summary Records of the Tenth Meeting, E/CONF.26/SR.10, p. 3; *Travaux préparatoires*, United Nations Conference on International Commercial Arbitration, Consideration of the Draft Convention on the Recognition and Enforcement of Foreign Arbitral Awards—Proposed amendment to the United Kingdom amendment to Article II of the draft Convention (Israel), E/CONF.26/L.21.

34. While the second sentence of article III prevents Contracting States from discriminating against foreign arbitral awards, nothing prevents Contracting States from imposing conditions to the recognition and enforcement of foreign arbitral awards that are less onerous than those imposed on domestic awards. The *travaux préparatoires* confirm that the drafters of the New York Convention intentionally rejected the idea that the rules of procedure applicable to the recognition and enforcement of foreign and domestic awards should be identical.[431]

35. This view is also confirmed in reported case law. For example, an Italian Court of Appeal held that Article 825 of the Italian Code of Civil Procedure, which requires a deposit of a domestic award within five days after it has been signed by the arbitrators and an order for enforcement of the award by the court, should not apply to foreign arbitral awards.[432]

36. Leading commentators confirm that the second sentence of article III does not entail that the rules of procedure applicable to the recognition and enforcement of foreign arbitral awards should necessarily be identical to the ones applicable to domestic awards.[433]

a. Meaning of "conditions or fees or charges"

37. The Convention does not define the terms "conditions", "fees" or "charges" The specific meaning of these terms has been considered in very few reported cases.

38. In one reported case where a party objected to the enforcement of an award on the ground that the costs of the arbitration awarded by the arbitral tribunal were "extravagant", a Greek court held that the notion of "fees or charges" under the Convention refers to "the expenses of the proceedings for the declaration of enforcement of the foreign arbitral award", and not to the procedural costs awarded by the foreign arbitral tribunal.[434]

---

[431] See *Travaux préparatoires*, United Nations Conference on International Commercial Arbitration, Summary Records of the Tenth Meeting, E/CONF.26/SR.10, p. 5; *Travaux préparatoires*, United Nations Conference on International Commercial Arbitration, Summary Records of the Eleventh Meeting, E/CONF.26/SR.11, p. 5.

[432] *Ditte Frey Milota and Seitelberger v. Ditte F. Cuccaro e figli*, Court of Appeal of Naples, Italy, 13 December 1974, I Y.B. COM. ARB. 193 (1976).

[433] See, e.g., FOUCHARD GAILLARD GOLDMAN ON INTERNATIONAL COMMERCIAL ARBITRATION 982, para. 1671 (E. Gaillard, J. Savage eds., 1999); Andreas Börner, *Article III*, in RECOGNITION AND ENFORCEMENT OF FOREIGN ARBITRAL AWARDS: A GLOBAL COMMENTARY ON THE NEW YORK CONVENTION 115, 119 (H. Kronke, P. Nacimiento et al. eds., 2010).

[434] *Shipowner (Malta) v. Contractor*, Supreme Court, Greece, 2007, XXXIII Y.B. COM. ARB. 565 (2008).

39. The term "conditions" has been interpreted as referring to the procedural rules and conditions for recognition and enforcement under a Contracting State's national law, and not the substantive grounds for refusal to recognize and enforce under article V of the Convention.[435]

b. Application by national courts

40. The second sentence of article III has been applied in a number of reported cases.[436]

41. In some cases, courts have declined to impose certain conditions on the recognition and enforcement of foreign arbitral awards which they held did not apply to domestic awards. For example, the Portuguese Supreme Court ruled that a party seeking enforcement of a foreign arbitral award did not need to obtain prior recognition of that award, because such a requirement did not apply to domestic awards.[437] The Dutch Supreme Court held that imposing a rule that allowed parties to appeal in cassation a decision granting enforcement to foreign arbitral awards would violate article III, because the same possibility was not available for domestic awards rendered in the Netherlands.[438] In a similar vein, an Egyptian court considered that the provisions of the Egyptian Code of Civil and Commercial Procedure governing the enforcement of foreign arbitral awards imposed conditions that were more onerous than the conditions imposed by the Egyptian Arbitration Law to the recognition and enforcement of domestic awards and, on that basis, decided to apply the latter provisions to the recognition and enforcement of a foreign arbitral award.[439] A Hong Kong

---

[435] See Maxi Scherer, *Article III (Recognition and Enforcement of Arbitral Awards; General Rule)*, in NEW YORK CONVENTION ON THE RECOGNITION AND ENFORCEMENT OF FOREIGN ARBITRAL AWARDS OF 10 JUNE 1958— COMMENTARY 193, 205 (R. Wolff ed., 2012).

[436] See, e.g., *Glencore Grain Rotterdam B.V. v. Shivnath Rai Harnarain Company*, Court of Appeals, Ninth Circuit, United States of America, 26 March 2002, 01-15539; *Company Y v. State X and Company Z*, Court of Appeal, Berlin, Germany, 10 August 2006, XXXII Y.B. COM. ARB. 363 (2007); *B. v. A.*, Court of Appeal of Lisbon, Portugal, 12 July 2012, XXXVIII Y.B. COM. ARB. 443 (2013); *Xilam Films v. Lnk-Video S.A*, Court of Appeal of Lisbon, Portugal, 12 July 2012, 7328/10.0TBOER.L1-1; Court of Appeal of Coimbra, Portugal, 19 January 2010, 70/09.6TBCBR.C1; Court of Appeal of Evora, Portugal, 31 January 2008, 1141/06-2; Court of Appeal of Porto, Portugal, 26 October 2004, 0325170; Court of Appeal of Porto, Portugal, 2 October 2001, 0120965; *OAO Rosneft (Russian Federation) v. Yukos Capital s.a.r.l. (Luxembourg)*, Supreme Court, First Chamber, Netherlands, 25 June 2010, XXXV Y.B. COM. ARB. 423 (2010); *S.A. (Belgium) v. B Sociedade Nacional, S.A*, Supreme Court of Justice, Portugal, 19 March 2009, 299/09, XXXVI Y.B. COM. ARB. 313 (2011).

[437] *S.A. (Belgium) v. B Sociedade Nacional, S.A.*, Supreme Court of Justice, Portugal, 19 March 2009, XXXVI Y.B. COM. ARB. 313 (2011).

[438] *OAO Rosneft (Russian Federation) v. Yukos Capital s.a.r.l. (Luxembourg)*, Supreme Court, Netherlands, 25 June 2010, XXXV Y.B. COM. ARB. 423 (2010).

[439] *Al Ahram Beverages Company v. Société Française d'Etudes et de Construction*, Court of Appeal of Tanta, Egypt, 17 November 2009, 42/42; *Omnipol v. Samiram*, Court of

court similarly held that requiring a creditor to provide security to enforce a foreign award would impose more onerous conditions than the ones faced by a creditor seeking to enforce a domestic award because "a creditor seeking to enforce a domestic award [...] would have no such liability".[440]

42. In other cases, courts have rejected arguments that the conditions applicable to the recognition and enforcement of foreign arbitral awards were more onerous than those applicable to domestic ones.[441] For instance, a Swiss court considered that the use of oral proceedings in the context of the enforcement of a foreign award was not contrary to article III on the ground that oral proceedings could also be used for the enforcement of domestic awards.[442] Likewise, a United States court held that the fact that the legislation applicable to domestic awards which automatically designated the venue in the district where the arbitral award was rendered, but not for foreign awards, was "not so onerous [to the recognition or enforcement of foreign arbitral awards] that [the court] should disregard the plain meaning of [its national law] in an effort to honor the spirit of Article III".[443] The court observed that, in such a situation, parties could achieve the same result by providing for a place of arbitration in their agreement.

Appeal of Cairo, Egypt, 30 May 2005, 10/122; *Abdel Wahed Hassan Suleiman v. Danish Dairy and Agriculture Seelizer Company*, Court of Appeal of Cairo, Egypt, 25 September 2005; *El Nasr Company for Fertilizers & Chemical Industries (SEMADCO) v. John Brown Deutsche Engineering*, Court of Cassation, Egypt, 10 January 2005, 966/73; *John Brown Deutsche Engineering v. El Nasr Company for Fertilizers & Chemical Industries (SEMADCO)*, 32/119, Court of Appeal of Cairo, Egypt, 6 August 2003, 32/119; *United Engineering Industrial v. Mirco Trading SI*, Court of Appeal of Cairo, Egypt, 27 July 2003, 7/120.

[440] *T.K. Bulkhandling GmbH v. Meridian Success International Ltd.*, Court of First Instance, High Court of Hong Kong Special Administrative Division, 28 November 1990, 1998 No. MP 4765. See also *Shandong Hongri Acron Chemical Joint Stock Company Limited v. PetroChina International (Hong Kong) Corporation Limited*, Court of Appeal, Hong Kong, 13 June 2011, 25 July 2011 and 11 August 2011, XXXVI Y.B. COM. ARB. 287 (2011).

[441] See, e.g., *Monegasque de Reassurances S.A.M. (Monde Re) v. Nak Naftogaz of Ukraine and State of Ukraine*, Court of Appeals, Second Circuit, United States of America, 15 November 2002, 01-7947, 01-9153, where a United States court held that the doctrine of *forum non conveniens* did not create more onerous conditions on foreign arbitral awards since this doctrine also applies to domestic arbitrations.

[442] *N. Z. v. I. (Romania)*, Court of Appeal of Basel-Stadt, Switzerland, 27 February 1989, XVII Y.B. COM. ARB. 581 (1992). For other examples, see also *Gouvernement de la Fédération de Russie v. Compagnie Noga d'importation et d'exportation*, Court of Appeal of Paris, France, 22 March 2001, 2001/208101.

[443] *Canada Inc. (f/k/a Nora Beverages, Inc.) v. North Country Natural Spring Water Ltd.*, District Court, Eastern District Pennsylvania, United States of America, 21 October 2002, 02-1416.

Article IV

1. To obtain the recognition and enforcement mentioned in the preceding article, the party applying for recognition and enforcement shall, at the time of the application, supply:

a) The duly authenticated original award or a duly certified copy thereof;

b) The original agreement referred to in article II or a duly certified copy thereof.

2. If the said award or agreement is not made in an official language of the country in which the award is relied upon, the party applying for recognition and enforcement of the award shall produce a translation of these documents into such language. The translation shall be certified by an official or sworn translator or by a diplomatic or consular agent.

Travaux préparatoires

The *travaux préparatoires* on article IV as adopted in 1958 are contained in the following documents:

Draft Convention on the Recognition and Enforcement of Foreign Arbitral Awards and comments by Governments and Organizations:

Report of the Committee on the Enforcement of International Arbitral Awards: E/2704 and Annex.

Comments by Governments and Organizations on the Draft Convention on the Recognition and Enforcement of Foreign Arbitral Awards: Annexes I-II of E/2822; E/CONF.26/3; E/CONF.26/3/Add.1.

Activities of Inter-Governmental and Non-Governmental Organizations in the Field of International Commercial Arbitration: Consolidated Report by the Secretary-General: E/CONF.26/4.

United Nations Conference on International Commercial Arbitration:

Amendments to the Draft Convention Submitted by Governmental Delegations: E/CONF.26/L.17; E/CONF.26/L31; E/CONF.26/L.34.

Comparison of Drafts Relating to Articles III, IV and V of the Draft Convention: E/CONF.26/L.33/Rev.1.

Further Amendments to the Draft Convention Submitted by Governmental Delegations: E/CONF.26/L.40.

Text of Articles III, IV and V of the Draft Convention Proposed by Working Party III: E/CONF.26/L.43.

Text of Articles Adopted by the Conference: E/CONF.26/L.48.

Text of the Convention on the Recognition and Enforcement of Foreign Arbitral Awards as Provisionally Approved by Drafting Committee: E/CONF.26/L.61; E/CONF.26/8.

Summary records:

Summary Records of the Eleventh, Twelfth, Thirteenth, Fourteenth, Seventeenth and Twenty-third Meetings of the United Nations Conference on International Commercial Arbitration: E/CONF.26/SR.11; E/CONF.26/SR.12: E/CONF.26/SR.13; E/CONF.26/SR.14; E/CONF.26/SR.17; E/CONF.26/SR.23.

Summary Record of the Seventh Meeting of the Committee on the Enforcement of International Arbitral Awards: E/AC.42/SR.7.

(Available on the Internet at http://www.uncitral.org)
(For the *travaux préparatoires*, case law and bibliographical references, see also on the Internet at http://newyorkconvention1958.org).

Introduction

1. Article IV of the Convention governs the formal conditions which an applicant must meet in order to obtain recognition and enforcement of an award in accordance with article III. Its purpose is to ensure that the enforcing court has before it the necessary evidence that the applicant's

request for recognition and enforcement "represents the true state of affairs".[444]

2. In line with the overall goals of the Convention, article IV aims to overcome the drawbacks of the formal requirements that an applicant had to meet under the previous regimes for obtaining recognition and enforcement of awards.

3. As discussed elsewhere in this Guide,[445] one of the principal barriers to recognition and enforcement prior to the adoption of the Convention was the requirement of *double exequatur*.[446] The 1927 Geneva Convention required that the party relying upon an award or seeking its enforcement supply, *inter alia*, "[d]ocumentary or other evidence to prove that the award ha[d] become final [...] in the country in which it was made".[447] In practice, in most countries, proof of finality could only be obtained by seeking leave for recognition and enforcement before the national courts and, thus, applicants seeking enforcement of an award had to provide proof of *exequatur* of the award in the country of the seat of the arbitration.[448] In addition to proof of finality of the award, the 1927 Geneva Convention required that the applicant produce a variety of other documentation.[449] As a result, an important burden was placed on the party seeking to obtain recognition and enforcement of an award.

4. The New York Convention eliminated the requirement that the applicant provide proof of finality of the award. While the first draft of article IV set out very similar requirements to those of the 1927 Geneva

---

444 Emilia Onyema, *Formalities of the Enforcement Procedure (Articles III and IV)*, in ENFORCEMENT OF ARBITRATION AGREEMENTS AND INTERNATIONAL ARBITRAL AWARDS: THE NEW YORK CONVENTION IN PRACTICE 597, 605 (E. Gaillard, D. Di Pietro eds., 2008).

445 See the chapter of the Guide on article V (1)*(e)*, paras. 2-4.

446 See Jan Kleinheisterkamp, *Recognition and Enforcement of Foreign Arbitral Awards*, in MAX PLANCK ENCYCLOPEDIA OF PUBLIC INTERNATIONAL LAW paras. 9-12 (www.mpepil.com/, last updated 2008); Dirk Otto, *Article IV*, in RECOGNITION AND ENFORCEMENT OF FOREIGN ARBITRAL AWARDS: A GLOBAL COMMENTARY ON THE NEW YORK CONVENTION 143, 145 (H. Kronke, P. Nacimiento et al. eds., 2010).

447 Article 4 of the 1927 Geneva Convention.

448 Dirk Otto, *Article IV*, in RECOGNITION AND ENFORCEMENT OF FOREIGN ARBITRAL AWARDS: A GLOBAL COMMENTARY ON THE NEW YORK CONVENTION 143, 145 (H. Kronke, P. Nacimiento et al. eds., 2010); Reinmar Wolff, *Commentary on Article IV*, in NEW YORK CONVENTION ON THE RECOGNITION AND ENFORCEMENT OF FOREIGN ARBITRAL AWARDS OF 10 JUNE 1958—COMMENTARY 207, 209 (R. Wolff ed., 2012).

449 See article 4(3) of the 1927 Geneva Convention (obligating the applicant to provide documentation showing, *inter alia*, that the prerequisites of article 1*(a)* and *(c)* were met, which in turn required that "the award ha[d] been made in pursuance of a submission to arbitration which [was] valid under the law applicable thereto" and that "the award ha[d] been made by the Arbitral Tribunal provided for in the submission to arbitration or constituted in the manner agreed upon by the parties and in conformity with the law governing the arbitration procedure").

Convention,[450] in the course of the negotiations, this idea was abandoned. The initiative first came from the delegate of the Netherlands who noted that demanding that the applicant prove that the award had become final or that its enforcement had not been suspended by a court in the country where it was made meant requiring proof of negative facts and thus placing a significant onus on the applicant.[451] The Dutch delegate proposed that the applicant be required to provide only the arbitral award and the arbitration agreement (and, where relevant, a translation thereof) and that the burden of proving that the award was not final in the country of the seat be shifted onto the party opposing recognition and enforcement. In the course of the negotiations, other delegations supported the Dutch proposal,[452] and the final version of article IV ultimately abolished the requirement that proof of finality be furnished by the applicant.[453]

5. Pursuant to article IV (1), an applicant seeking recognition and enforcement of an award is required to supply the enforcing court with two documents: the duly authenticated original award (or a duly certified copy) and the original agreement referred to in article II (or a duly certified copy). Pursuant to article IV (2), if these two documents are not made in an official language of the country in which recognition or enforcement is sought, the applicant is required to produce a translation thereof.

6. Thus, article IV of the Convention imposes significantly fewer requirements compared to the 1927 Geneva Convention. In this way, the Convention eliminates unnecessary formalities and ensures that foreign arbitral awards are recognized and enforced as early as possible.[454]

---

450 *Travaux préparatoires*, United Nations Conference on International Commercial Arbitration, Report of the Committee on the Enforcement of International Arbitral Awards, E/2704, E/AC.42/4/Rev.1, Annex, p. 3.

451 *Travaux préparatoires*, United Nations Conference on International Commercial Arbitration, Recognition and Enforcement of Foreign Arbitral Awards, Comments by Governments on the draft Convention on the Recognition and Enforcement of Foreign Arbitral Awards, E/CONF.26/3/Add.1, para. 7.

452 *Travaux préparatoires*, United Nations Conference on International Commercial Arbitration, Summary Record of the Twelfth Meeting, E/CONF.26/SR.12, p. 4; *Travaux préparatoires*, United Nations Conference on International Commercial Arbitration, Summary Record of the Seventeenth Meeting, E/CONF.26/SR.17, p. 2.

453 This has been hailed as a "revolution" and "one of the principal achievements of the New York Convention" See ALBERT JAN VAN DEN BERG, THE NEW YORK ARBITRATION CONVENTION OF 1958: TOWARDS A UNIFORM JUDICIAL INTERPRETATION (1981), 247; Emmanuel Gaillard, *The Relationship of the New York Convention with Other Treaties and with Domestic Law*, in ENFORCEMENT OF ARBITRATION AGREEMENTS AND INTERNATIONAL ARBITRAL AWARDS: THE NEW YORK CONVENTION IN PRACTICE 69, 87 (E. Gaillard, D. Di Pietro eds., 2008).

454 It should be noted that article 35 (2) of the UNCITRAL Model Law on International Commercial Arbitration, which mirrors article IV of the Convention, has been amended in 2006 to liberalize formal requirements: no "duly authenticated" or "certified copies" of the

Analysis

General principles

A. *Prima facie* right to recognition and enforcement

7. National courts have held that, once the applicant has supplied the documents referred to in article IV, it is deemed that it has obtained a *prima facie* right to recognition and enforcement of the award.

8. For example, the Court of Appeal of England and Wales has held that, once a party seeking recognition or enforcement has, under section 102(1) of the 1996 Arbitration Act (which gives effect to article IV of the Convention), produced the duly authenticated award or a duly certified copy and the original arbitration agreement or a duly certified copy, it attains a *prima facie* right to recognition and enforcement.[455] Thereafter, according to that court, recognition and enforcement may be refused only if the party opposing recognition and enforcement proves that the situation falls within the scope of section 103(2) of the Arbitration Act (which directly incorporates and whose wording is equivalent to article V (1) of the Convention).[456] The Italian Court of Cassation has similarly held that the burden on the party requesting enforcement is limited to the production of the documents required under article IV, whereupon there is a presumption of enforceability of the award.[457] Courts from other jurisdictions, including Japan, Spain and the United States, have adopted the same approach.[458]

B. An exhaustive set of requirements

9. Article IV (1) lists two items that the applicant should supply to the enforcing court in order to have the award recognized and enforced: the duly authenticated original award (or a duly certified copy) and the original

award are required and presentation of a copy of the arbitration agreement is also no longer required.

[455] *Yukos Oil Co. v. Dardana Ltd.*, Court of Appeal, England and Wales, 18 April 2002, [2002] EWCA Civ 543.

[456] *Id.*

[457] *WTB—Walter Thosti Boswau Bauaktiengesellschaft v. Costruire Coop. srl*, Court of Cassation, Italy, 7 June 1995, 6426.

[458] See, e.g., *Buyer v. Seller*, High Court of Tokyo, Japan, 27 January 1994, XX Y.B. COM. ARB. 742 (1995); *Cominco France S. A. v. Soquiber S. L.*, High Court of Justice, Spain, 24 March 1982, VIII Y.B. COM. ARB. 408 (1983); *Czarina, L.L.C. v. W.F. Poe Syndicate*, Court of Appeals, Eleventh Circuit, United States of America, 4 February 2004, 358 F.3d 1286. See also ALBERT JAN VAN DEN BERG, THE NEW YORK ARBITRATION CONVENTION OF 1958: TOWARDS A UNIFORM JUDICIAL INTERPRETATION 247-48; Emilia Onyema, *Formalities of the Enforcement Procedure (Articles III and IV)*, in ENFORCEMENT OF ARBITRATION AGREEMENTS AND INTERNATIONAL ARBITRAL AWARDS: THE NEW YORK CONVENTION IN PRACTICE 597, 605 (E. Gaillard, D. Di Pietro eds., 2008).

agreement referred to in article II (or a duly certified copy). A handful of cases have addressed the issue of whether the documents referred to under article IV (1) and, if applicable, a translation thereof, are the only documents that an applicant must supply in order to obtain recognition or enforcement.

10. The majority of courts have ruled that the documents required under article IV are the only documents an applicant should provide to obtain recognition and enforcement of an award. For example, the Italian Court of Cassation has held that, pursuant to article IV, the party seeking enforcement has to submit only the original award and the arbitration agreement.[459] In the same vein, the Spanish Supreme Court has ruled that article IV requires the party seeking enforcement to supply only the award and arbitration agreement when filing its application. According to the Spanish Supreme Court, further documentation may be filed in response to any defences raised by the party opposing enforcement, but only after these have been raised.[460] The Supreme Court of Greece has also held that, in order to obtain enforcement, an applicant has only to provide the documents referred to under article IV.[461] Courts from other jurisdictions—including Austria, Mexico and the Netherlands—have followed the same path.[462]

11. During the drafting of article IV, a proposal was made that the applicant be required—as under the 1927 Geneva Convention—to supply additional "documentary and other evidence" in order to obtain the right to recognition and enforcement of an award.[463] This proposal was rejected. It is thus clear that the drafters of the Convention considered the possibility of

---

[459] *Tortora Amedeo v. Tolimar S.A.*, Court of Cassation, Italy, 27 June 1983, 4399, X Y.B. COM. ARB. 470 (1985).

[460] *Kil Management A/S (Denmark) v. J. García Carrión, S.A. (Spain)*, Supreme Court, Civil Chamber, Spain, 28 March 2000, 1724 of 1998, XXXII Y.B. COM. ARB. 518 (2007).

[461] See Supreme Court, Greece, 1973, Case No. 926, I Y.B. COM. ARB. 186 (1976). See also Court of Appeal of Athens, Greece, 1972, Case No. 2768, I Y.B. COM. ARB. 186 (1976).

[462] See Supreme Court, Austria, 21 February 1978, X Y.B. COM. ARB. 418 (1985); *Presse Office S.A. v. Centro Editorial Hoy S.A.*, High Court of Justice, Eighteenth Civil Court of First Instance for the Federal District of Mexico, Mexico, 24 February 1977, IV Y.B. COM. ARB. 301 (1979); *Palm and Vegetable Oils SDN. BHD. v. Algemene Oliehandel International B.V.*, President of the Court of Utrecht, Netherlands, 22 November 1984, XI Y.B. COM. ARB. 521 (1986). For a minority view pursuant to which denial of recognition and enforcement could be based on the failure to provide additional documents such as a certificate that the award had entered into force or the applicable arbitration rules, see, respectively, *ECONERG Ltd. v. National Electricity Company AD*, Supreme Court of Appeal, Civil Collegium, Fifth Civil Department, Bulgaria, 23 February 1999, 356/99, XXV Y.B. COM. ARB. 641 (2000); *Glencore Grain Ltd. v. TSS Grain Millers Ltd.*, High Court of Mombasa, Kenya, 5 July 2002, Civil Suit No. 388 of 2000, XXXIV Y.B. COM. ARB. 666 (2009).

[463] See *Travaux préparatoires*, United Nations Conference on International Commercial Arbitration, Summary Record of the Seventeenth Meeting, E/CONF.26/SR.17, pp. 6-7 (the proposal was that the applicant be required to supply "documentary and other evidence to prove that the conditions laid down in the following articles have been fulfilled").

requiring additional documents to be provided by applicants and squarely dismissed it.

12. Commentators have confirmed the understanding that, in order to have an award recognized and enforced, an applicant is only required to supply the documents listed under article IV.[464]

C. Whether applicants can supply some, but not all, article IV documents

13. Article IV requires that the applicant "shall [...] supply" the documents specified therein. The issue has arisen before courts whether an applicant must strictly comply with article IV or whether a more flexible approach could be applied.

a. Documents specified under article IV (1)

14. Reported case law shows that some courts have insisted that the applicant provide all documents in the form prescribed by article IV (1), whereas others have granted recognition and enforcement of an award despite the fact that the applicant had not provided the duly authenticated award or the original arbitration agreement (or duly certified copies thereof).

15. In some cases, courts have denied enforcement due to the applicant's failure to provide one or both of the documents as required under article IV (1). For example, Italian courts have denied requests for recognition and enforcement on the ground that the applicant had not submitted a duly authenticated award or a certified arbitration agreement.[465] Similarly, the Spanish Supreme Court has denied enforcement where the applicant failed to provide the documents listed under article IV. In one case, enforcement was not granted because the applicant had failed to provide the arbitration agreement referred to under article IV (1)*(b)* of the Convention.[466]

---

464 See Emilia Onyema, *Formalities on the Enforcement Procedure (Articles III and IV)*, in ENFORCEMENT OF ARBITRATION AGREEMENTS AND INTERNATIONAL ARBITRAL AWARDS: THE NEW YORK CONVENTION IN PRACTICE 597, 605 (E. Gaillard, D. Di Pietro eds., 2008); Dirk Otto, *Article IV*, in RECOGNITION AND ENFORCEMENT OF FOREIGN ARBITRAL AWARDS: A GLOBAL COMMENTARY ON THE NEW YORK CONVENTION 143, 148 (H. Kronke, P. Nacimiento et al. eds., 2010); ALBERT JAN VAN DEN BERG, THE NEW YORK ARBITRATION CONVENTION OF 1958: TOWARDS A UNIFORM JUDICIAL INTERPRETATION 248 (1981).

465 *Jassica S.A. v. Ditta Polojaz*, Court of Cassation, Italy, 12 February 1987, 1526, XVII Y.B. COM. ARB. 525 (1992). See also *Israel Portland Cement Works (Nesher) Ltd. v. Moccia Irme SpA*, Court of Cassation, Italy, 19 December 1991, 13665, XVIII Y.B. COM. ARB. 419 (1993); *Globtrade Italiana srl v. East Point Trading Ltd.*, Court of Cassation, Italy, 8 October 2008, 24856.

466 *Glencore Grain Limited (United Kingdom) v. Sociedad Ibérica de Molturación, S.A. (Spain)*, Supreme Court, Spain, 14 January 2003, 16508/2003, XXX Y.B. COM. ARB. 605 (2005).

In another, the court denied enforcement because, contrary to the requirements of article IV, the applicant supplied uncertified and non-authenticated copies of the awards and also failed to provide the arbitration agreement.[467] Both Chinese[468] and United States[469] courts have also denied enforcement in circumstances where a party had failed to provide a document as required under article IV.

16. Swiss courts have adopted a more flexible approach and, in cases where the applicant had failed to show that the relevant document was duly authenticated or duly certified, have held that enforcement should be granted if the party opposing recognition and enforcement does not dispute the authenticity of that document.[470] In a different case before the Commercial Court in Zurich, the court granted enforcement, despite the fact that the applicant had submitted a non-certified photocopy of the award.[471] The court held that too strict a standard should not be applied to the formal requirement for the submission of documents when the conditions for recognition are undisputed and are beyond doubt.

17. Other courts have granted enforcement despite the fact that the applicant had not provided the original arbitration agreement (or a duly certified copy thereof). To do so, German courts have often relied on the more-favourable-right principle set out in article VII (1),[472] holding that it is not necessary that the applicant supply the arbitration agreement under article IV (1)*(b)*, because domestic German law does not so require.

---

[467] *Satico Shipping Company Limited (Cyprus) v. Maderas Iglesias (Spain)*, Supreme Court, Civil Chamber, Spain, 1 April 2003, 2009 of 2001, XXXII Y.B. COM. ARB. 582 (2007).

[468] *Hanjin Shipping Co., Ltd. v. Guangdong Fuhong Oil Co., Ltd.*, Supreme People's Court, China, 2 June 2006, [2005] Min Si Ta Zi No. 53; *Concordia Trading B.V. v. Nantong Gangde Oil Co., Ltd.*, Supreme Peoples Court, China, 3 August 2009, [2009] Min Si Ta Zi No. 22.

[469] See *Czarina, L.L.C. v. W.F. Poe Syndicate*, Court of Appeals, Eleventh Circuit, United States of America, 4 February 2004, 358 F.3d 1286; *Guang Dong Light Headgear Factory Co. v. ACI Int'l, Inc*, District Court, District of Kansas, United States of America, 10 May 2005, 03-4165-JAR.

[470] Commercial Court of Zurich, Switzerland, 20 April 1990, 21, XVII Y.B. COM. ARB. 584 (1992); *Inter Maritime Management S.A. v. Russin & Vecchi*, Federal Tribunal, Switzerland, 9 January 1995, XXII Y.B. COM. ARB. 789 (1997); Federal Tribunal, Switzerland, 4 October 2010, 4A_124/2010; Federal Tribunal, Switzerland, 10 October 2011, 5A 427/2011.

[471] Commercial Court of Zurich, Switzerland, 20 April 1990, 21, XVII Y.B. COM. ARB. 584 (1992).

[472] See Bayerisches Oberstes Landesgericht [BayObLG], Germany, 11 August 2000, 4 Z Sch 05/00; Oberlandesgericht [OLG] München, Germany, 15 March 2006, 34 Sch 06/05; Kammergericht [KG], Germany, 10 August 2006, 20 Sch 07/04; Oberlandesgericht [OLG] Celle, Germany, 14 December 2006, 8 Sch 14/05; Oberlandesgericht [OLG] München, Germany, 23 February 2007, 34 Sch 31/06. For a more detailed discussion on the interaction of articles IV and VII, see the chapter of the Guide on article VII, paras. 36-38.

b. Documents specified under article IV (2)

18. Courts have sometimes taken a flexible approach in relation to the article IV (2) requirement that the applicant provide a translation of the documents referred to under article IV (1). For example, Dutch courts have deemed translations to be unnecessary where the relevant documents were drawn up in languages that they understand.[473] In a case before the District Court of Amsterdam, the applicant provided certified copies of the award and the arbitral agreement, both of which were in English, but failed to supply Dutch translations.[474] Noting that it mastered the English language sufficiently, the court did not require translations to be submitted and concluded that the article IV requirements were met.[475]

19. A Norwegian court also held that, in light of the fact that it had sufficient command of the language in which the award was drafted, there was no need for a translation thereof to be submitted.[476]

20. As in the case of documents required under article IV (1), German courts have relied on article VII (1) of the Convention and held that an applicant need not provide a translation for its request to be deemed admissible.[477] Similarly, they have held that when translations are provided, they are not subject to the certification requirements of article IV (2).[478]

D. "[A]t the time of the application"

21. Article IV expressly provides that the applicant shall supply the documents listed thereunder "at the time of the application". The question has arisen whether, where an applicant has failed to submit the requisite documents at the time of application, it can do so at a later stage in the enforcement proceedings.

---

473 *China Packaging Design Corporation v. SCA Recycling Reukema Trading B.V.*, Court of First Instance of Zutphen, Netherlands, 11 November 1998, XXIV Y.B. COM. ARB. 724 (1999). See also *LoJack Equipment Ireland Ltd. (Ireland) v. A*, Commercial Court of Amsterdam, Netherlands, 18 June 2009, 411230/KG RK 08-3652, XXXIV Y.B. COM. ARB. 715 (2009).

474 *China Packaging Design Corporation v. SCA Recycling Reukema Trading B.V.*, Court of First Instance of Zutphen, Netherlands, 11 November 1998, XXIV Y.B. COM. ARB. 724 (1999).

475 *SPP (Middle East) Ltd. v. The Arab Republic of Egypt*, President of the District Court of Amsterdam, Netherlands, 12 July 1984, X Y.B. COM. ARB. 487 (1985).

476 *Pulsarr Industrial Research B.V. (Netherlands) v. Nils H. Nilsen A.S. (Norway)*, Enforcement Court of Vardø, Norway, 10 July 2002, XXVIII Y.B. COM. ARB. 821 (2003).

477 Bayerisches Oberstes Landesgericht [BayObLG], Germany, 11 August 2000, 4 Z Sch 05/00; *K Trading Company (Syria) v. Bayerischen Motoren Werke AG (Germany)*, Bayerisches Oberstes Landesgericht [BayObLG], Germany, 23 September 2004, 4Z Sch 005-04; Kammergericht [KG], Germany, 10 August 2006, 20 Sch 07/04.

478 Oberlandesgericht [OLG] Schleswig, Germany, 15 July 2003, 16 Sch 01/03; Bundesgerichtshof [BGH], Germany, 25 September 2003, III ZB 68/02.

22. Italian courts have held that failure to provide the requisite documents listed under article IV at the very moment when the application is made would lead to a rejection of the application for recognition and enforcement.[479] The approach of Italian courts appears to stem from their consideration of the production of the arbitral award and the arbitration agreement as a procedural prerequisite for the commencement of the enforcement proceedings.[480] At the same time, the Italian Court of Cassation has clarified that the rejection of an application for failure to produce the requisite documents does not affect the merits of the enforcement request and, therefore, does not prevent a subsequent application to be made *de novo*.[481]

23. Most other courts have held that an applicant could provide the requisite documents in the course of the enforcement proceedings. For example, in a case before the Chinese courts, the Supreme People's Court reversed a ruling of the Shanxi Province High Court denying enforcement because the applicant had failed to provide a certified copy of the arbitration agreement.[482] The Supreme People's Court found that the application should not be rejected on the sole ground that the submitted materials were incomplete and that such incompleteness should not be a basis for refusal to recognize and enforce the arbitral award. It held that, rather, in such circumstances, the applicant should be ordered to supplement the outstanding materials within a reasonable period.

24. Courts in Switzerland,[483] the United States[484] and India[485] have also taken this approach and have generally granted enforcement of an award

---

[479] See *Lezina Shipping Co. S.A. v. Casillo Grani snc*, Court of Appeal of Bari, Italy, 19 March 1991, XXI Y.B. COM. ARB. 585 (1996); *Israel Portland Cement Works (Nesher) Ltd. v. Moccia Irme SpA*, Court of Cassation, Italy, 19 December 1991, 13665, XVIII Y.B. COM. ARB. 419 (1993); *s.r.l. Ditta Michele Tavella v. Palmco Oil Mill L.D.N. B.M.D.*, Court of Cassation, Italy, 12 November 1992, 12187, XIX Y.B. COM. ARB. 692 (1994); *srl Campomarzio Impianti v. Lampart Vegypary Gepgyar*, Court of Cassation, Italy, 20 September 1995, 9980, XXIV Y.B. COM. ARB. 698 (1999); *Microware s.r.l. in liquidation v. Indicia Diagnostics S.A.*, Court of Cassation, Italy, 23 July 2009, 17291.

[480] *Lezina Shipping Co. S.A. v. Casillo Grani snc, Court* of *Appeal* of *Bari*, Italy, 19 March 1991, XXI Y.B. COM. ARB. 585 (1996).

[481] *s.r.l. Campomarzio Impianti v. Lampart Vegypary Gepgyar*, Court of Cassation, 20 September 1995, Italy, 9980, XXIV Y.B. COM. ARB. 698 (1999) (overruling *Israel Portland Cement Works (Nesher) Ltd. v. Moccia Irme SpA*, Court of Cassation, Italy, 19 December 1991, 13665, XVIII Y.B. COM. ARB. 419 (1993)).

[482] *Wei Mao International (Hong Kong) Co. Ltd. (Hong Kong SAR) v. Shanxi Tianli Industrial Co. Ltd. (China PR)*, Supreme People's Court, China, 5 July 2004.

[483] Federal Tribunal, Switzerland, 8 December 2003, 4P.173/2003/ech.

[484] *China National Building Material Investment Co. Ltd. v. BNK International*, District Court, Western District of Texas, Austin Division, United States of America, 3 December 2009, A-09-CA-488-SS.

[485] *Renusagar Power Company v. General Electric Company*, High Court of Bombay, India, 12 October 1989.

where the relevant document had not been supplied with the application, but was ultimately produced in the course of the proceedings.

Article IV (1)*(a)*

25. Article IV (1)*(a)* requires the applicant to produce "[t]he duly authenticated original award or a duly certified copy thereof" in order to obtain recognition and enforcement of an award.

26. Reported case law on article IV (1)*(a)* addresses principally issues related to the form and content in which the award[486] is supplied by the applicant and the processes of authentication and certification.

A. The requirement that the applicant provide the "award"

a. The content of the award

27. Article IV does not set out any specific requirements as to what must be contained in an award in order for it to be deemed appropriate for recognition and enforcement. Several elements of this kind have been considered by courts.

28. The entirety of the award. In an *obiter dictum*, an Austrian court has stated that the term "award" under article IV refers to the entirety of the award, including the introduction, *dictum* and reasons for the decision.[487]

29. *The names of the parties.* In one case, the Supreme Court of New South Wales held that the names of the parties must appear on the award. In that case, the party opposing enforcement argued that the name used for the respondent in the award was not its name. The court examined the award and ascertained that the award did refer to the party opposing enforcement, albeit using an incorrect name.[488]

30. One commentator has argued that the names of the parties should be present in the award supplied by the applicant in order for the award to be enforceable.[489]

---

[486] The question of what constitutes an award is dealt with above, and will not be discussed here.

[487] *D S.A. (Spain) v. W GmbH (Austria)*, Supreme Court, Austria, 26 April 2006, 3Ob211/05h, XXXII Y.B. COM. ARB. 259 (2007).

[488] *LKT Industrial Berhad (Malaysia) v. Chun*, Supreme Court of New South Wales, Australia, 13 September 2004, 50174.

[489] Dirk Otto, *Article IV*, in RECOGNITION AND ENFORCEMENT OF FOREIGN ARBITRAL AWARDS: A GLOBAL COMMENTARY ON THE NEW YORK CONVENTION 143, 154 (H. Kronke, P. Nacimiento et al. eds., 2010).

31. *The names and signatures of the arbitrators.* There has been more debate among courts as to whether the award supplied by an applicant must contain the names and signatures of all arbitrators and whether the signatures of all arbitrators must be authenticated.

32. In past decisions, two courts—in two different contexts—have required that the award produced bear the (authenticated) signatures of the three arbitrators. Thus, in the first case, an Italian court had held that the signatures of all arbitrators must be authenticated on the copy provided by the applicant.[490] In that case, the applicant sought enforcement of an award rendered in London. The court denied enforcement of the award, having found that only two of the three arbitrators' signatures were authenticated. The court noted that, while under English law the authentication of two signatures would have sufficed for the award to be considered authentic, under Italian law—which the enforcing court deemed to govern the authentication—all signatures needed to be authenticated. Thus, the court's ruling is not founded on article IV, but rather stems from its application of Italian law.

33. In the second case, a German court denied an application for the enforcement of an award rendered pursuant to the Copenhagen Arbitration Committee for Grain and Feedstuff Trade, *inter alia*, on the ground that the copy of the award presented by the applicant did not contain the names of the arbitrators.[491] The court noted that, under the Rules of the Copenhagen Arbitration Committee for Grain and Feedstuff Trade in force at the time, the parties to an arbitration are provided an extract of the award which does not contain the names of the arbitrators other than the president of the Committee. The court held that this did not alter the fact that, under article IV, a copy of an award must fully reflect the original award, including the names and signatures of the arbitrators.

34. On the other hand, in a 2010 decision, the Swiss Federal Tribunal granted enforcement despite the fact that one or more signatures were not present on the award provided by the applicant. The court rejected the argument of the party opposing enforcement that the applicant had failed to satisfy the conditions of article IV because it had produced an award signed only by the chairman of the arbitral tribunal. The court held that the form requirements under article IV were not to be interpreted restrictively since

490 *SODIME—Società Distillerie Meridionali v. Schuurmans & Van Ginneken BV*, Court of Cassation, Italy, 14 March 1995, 2919, XXI Y.B. COM. ARB. 607 (1996).

491 Oberlandesgericht [OLG] Köln, Germany, 10 June 1976, IV Y.B. COM. ARB. 258 (1979).

the purpose of the Convention was to facilitate the enforcement of arbitral awards.[492]

b. The form of the award

(i) Partial awards

35. In two cases before the Italian courts, an issue arose whether, in addition to supplying the final award on damages, the applicant should have provided the partial award on liability in order to obtain recognition and enforcement.

36. In the first, the Court of Appeal of Bologna denied enforcement after finding that, in the circumstances of that case, the final award was inseparable from the partial award. The court reasoned that the latter was necessary as the former did not ascertain liability nor did it order the party against whom enforcement was sought to make any payment.[493]

37. In the second, the Court of Cassation reversed the decision of the lower court rejecting a request for enforcement on the ground that the applicant had failed to provide a copy of the partial award together with the final award.[494] The Court of Cassation held that once the applicant supplied the final award, it satisfied the requirements of article IV, and that the lower court should rather have analysed whether the enforcement of the final award separately from the partial award could fall within one of the exhaustively listed grounds for refusing enforcement under article V (1) or article V (2).

(ii) Dissenting opinions

38. Courts have consistently held that the applicant satisfies the requirements of article IV even if it has not provided the dissenting opinion in cases where such dissenting opinion exists.[495]

39. The Austrian Supreme Court considered an argument from the party opposing enforcement that, in order to obtain recognition and enforcement of

---

[492] Federal Tribunal, Switzerland, 4 October 2010, 4A_124/2010. The Austrian Supreme Court has held that an award signed by a majority of arbitrators can be recognized as long as there is an explanation as to why an arbitrator has not signed the award. See Supreme Court, Austria, 13 April 2011, 3 Ob 154/10h.

[493] Court of Appeal of Bologna, Italy, 4 February 1993, XIX Y.B. COM. ARB. 700 (1994).

[494] *WTB—Walter Thosti Boswau Bauaktiengesellschaft v. Costruire Coop. srl*, Court of Cassation, Italy, 7 June 1995, 6426.

[495] Unless the applicable arbitration rules provide otherwise, a dissenting opinion does not form part of the award. See FOUCHARD GAILLARD GOLDMAN ON INTERNATIONAL COMMERCIAL ARBITRATION 768, para. 1404 (E. Gaillard, J. Savage eds., 1999).

an award under the auspices of the ICC International Court of Arbitration, the applicant was obligated to also supply the dissenting opinion of one of the arbitrators. In dismissing the argument, the court held that a dissenting opinion was a separate document from the award, which is not approved by the International Court of Arbitration of the ICC and that there was no obligation to supply the dissenting opinion, since it was not part of the arbitral award.[496]

40. The High Court of Bombay has also held that the applicant need not provide the "minority opinion".[497] The party opposing enforcement argued that the applicant had failed to comply with section 8(1)*(a)* of the Indian Foreign Awards Act of 1961 (like article IV, requiring that the petitioner produce the original award or a copy thereof) because it had failed to supply the minority opinion prepared by one of the arbitrators. The court rejected the submission, noting that, in accordance with the ICC arbitration rules in force at the time, the award was to be declared by a majority opinion and, therefore, what was enforceable was solely the majority award.[498]

(iii) Merger of a judgment and an award

41. A Swiss court has considered whether a judgment of a United States court confirming an award could be sufficient basis for enforcement.[499] The Camera di Esecuzione e Fallimenti del Tribunale d'Appello (Debt Collection and Bankruptcy Chamber of the Court of Appeal) held that an enforcement decision could not be issued based on the judgment of the United States court. It acknowledged that under the "doctrine of merger" applicable in the United States, a court could confirm an award rendered in the United States with the effect that the judgment of the United States court and the award become one and the same. It then held that Swiss law did not have the doctrine of merger and under Swiss law, enforcement had to be based on an enforceable award. The Court of Appeal also observed that the award creditor had not complied with the requirements of article IV as it had not provided the original arbitration agreement and a duly certified copy of the award.

---

[496] *D S.A. (Spain) v. W GmbH (Austria)*, Supreme Court, Austria, 26 April 2006, 3Ob211/05h, XXXII Y.B. COM. ARB. 259 (2007).

[497] The High Court of Bombay appears to have used the terms "minority opinion" and "minority award" interchangeably, whereas it did not use the term "dissenting opinion".

[498] *General Electric Company v. Renusagar Power Company*, High Court of Bombay, India, 21 October 1988.

[499] Debt Collection and Bankruptcy Chamber of the Court of Appeal of the Republic and Canton of Ticino, Switzerland, 27 November 2008, 14.2008.78.

B. Authentication and certification

42. Neither the text of article IV nor the *travaux préparatoires* of the provision provide a definition of the terms "authenticated" and "certified".

43. There is very little case law in which an express definition of the terms "authenticated" and "certified" is discussed. An Austrian court has held that authentication means confirmation that the signatures of the arbitrators are authentic.[500] The same court has held that certification is the process by which a copy of a document is attested to be a true copy of the original document.[501]

44. Commentators are in agreement that the process of authentication entails a confirmation of the authenticity of the arbitrators' signatures and that certification is a confirmation that the document provided is a true copy of the original.[502]

45. Under the rubric of article IV (1)*(a)*, courts have dealt with a number of issues, including, principally, the law governing the process of authentication and/ or certification, the authority competent to perform the authentication and/or certification, and whether certification must be done of an authenticated award.

a. Governing law

46. While the 1927 Geneva Convention required that the authentication of an award be done in accordance with the law of the country in which the award was made,[503] article IV (1)*(a)* does not provide the law governing authentication and certification. During the drafting of the New York Convention, the ECOSOC *ad hoc* Committee considered that a different

---

[500] *O Limited (Cyprus) v. M Corp. (formerly A, Inc.) (United States) and others*, Supreme Court, Austria, 3 September 2008, 3Ob35/08f, XXXIV Y.B. COM. ARB. 409 (2009).

[501] *Ibid.*, See also *Glencore Grain Ltd. v. TSS Grain Millers Ltd.*, High Court of Mombasa, Kenya, 5 July 2002, Civil Suit No. 388 of 2000, XXXIV Y.B. COM. ARB. 666 (2009); Federal Tribunal, Switzerland, 4 October 2010, 4A_124/2010.

[502] See FOUCHARD GAILLARD GOLDMAN ON INTERNATIONAL COMMERCIAL ARBITRATION 970, para. 1675 (E. Gaillard, J. Savage eds., 1999); ALBERT JAN VAN DEN BERG, THE NEW YORK ARBITRATION CONVENTION OF 1958: TOWARDS A UNIFORM JUDICIAL INTERPRETATION 251 (1981); Dirk Otto, *Article IV*, in RECOGNITION AND ENFORCEMENT OF FOREIGN ARBITRAL AWARDS: A GLOBAL COMMENTARY ON THE NEW YORK CONVENTION 143, 177 (H. Kronke, P. Nacimiento et al. eds., 2010); ICCA'S GUIDE TO THE INTERPRETATION OF THE 1958 NEW YORK CONVENTION: A HANDBOOK FOR JUDGES 72, 74 (P. Sanders ed., 2011); Maxi Scherer, *Article IV (Formal Requirements for the Recognition and Enforcement of Arbitral Awards)*, in NEW YORK CONVENTION ON THE RECOGNITION AND ENFORCEMENT OF FOREIGN ARBITRAL AWARDS OF 10 JUNE 1958—COMMENTARY 207, 210 (R. Wolff ed., 2012).

[503] See article 4(1) of the 1927 Geneva Convention.

approach should be taken in the New York Convention. The Committee explained that "it was preferable to allow greater latitude with regard to this question to the tribunal of the country in which the recognition or enforcement was being requested".[504] It considered that the term "duly authenticated" allows such an approach.[505] At the same time, some delegates did not consider that the terms "duly authenticated" and "duly certified" made it sufficiently clear that the enforcing court was given wide discretion.[506] The final text of the Convention maintained the wording "duly authenticated" and "duly certified" and no applicable law was specified.

47. The lack of a stipulated governing law on authentication and certification has enabled courts to adopt varying approaches. Some courts have considered that the law of the State in which the award was made ought to be applied to the process of authentication, whereas others have emphasized the fact that authentications carried out in accordance with either the law of the enforcing State or the law of the State in which the award was made would be compliant with article IV (1).

48. One German court has considered that, for the sake of practicality, authentication should be governed by the law of the country where enforcement is sought.[507] Similarly, Italian courts have taken the position that the applicable rules ought to be those of the enforcing State.[508]

49. Another court reasoned that the New York Convention does not specify the governing law and held that a party seeking enforcement is free to submit an award authenticated pursuant to either the law in which the

---

504 *Travaux préparatoires*, United Nations Conference on International Commercial Arbitration, Report of the Committee on the Enforcement of International Arbitral Awards, E/2704, E/AC.42/4/Rev.1, p. 14.

505 *Ibid.*

506 *Travaux préparatoires*, United Nations Conference on International Commercial Arbitration, Recognition and Enforcement of Foreign Arbitral Awards, Comments by Governments on the draft Convention on the Recognition and Enforcement of Foreign Arbitral Awards, E/CONF.26/3, p. 3; *Travaux préparatoires*, United Nations Conference on International Commercial Arbitration, Activities of Inter-Governmental and Non-Governmental Organizations in the Field of International Commercial Arbitration, Consolidated Report by the Secretary-General, E/CONF.26/4, p. 29.

507 Oberlandesgericht [OLG] Schleswig, Germany, 15 July 2003, 16 Sch 01/03.

508 See *Globtrade Italiana srl v. East Point Trading Ltd.*, Court of Cassation, Italy, 8 October 2008, 24856. See *SODIME—Società Distillerie Meridionali v. Schuurmans & Van Ginneken BV*, Court of Cassation, Italy, 14 March 1995, 2919, XXI Y.B. COM. ARB. 607 (1996). Previously, an Italian court had taken the position that the law governing authentication should be the law of the State in which the award was made, see *Renato Marino Navegacio s.a. v. Chim-Metal s.r.l*, Court of Appeal of Milan, Italy, 21 December 1979, VII Y.B. COM. ARB. 338 (1982). See also *ECONERG Ltd. v. National Electricity Company AD*, Case No. 356/99, Supreme Court of Appeal, Civil Collegium, Fifth Civil Department, Bulgaria, 23 February 1999, 356/99, XXV Y.B. COM. ARB. 641 (2000); *Renusagar Power Company v. General Electric Company*, High Court of Bombay, India, 12 October 1989.

award was made or the law of the country where enforcement was sought.[509] The court added that authentication by the diplomatic or consular agents of the enforcing State might help avoiding difficulties on the practical level.

50. A number of authors have taken the view that, under article IV, and consistent with the *travaux préparatoires*,[510] an applicant can comply with the authentication requirements under either the law of the country in which the award was made or the law of the country in which enforcement is sought.[511]

b. Competent authority

51. Article IV (1)*(a)* does not specify the competent authority that should perform the authentication or certification. During the drafting, a proposal that the authority competent to authenticate an award should be the consulate of the country where the award is relied upon was not adopted.[512]

52. Accordingly, courts have found various authorities to be competent to authenticate an award or certify a copy of an award.

53. In different contexts, consular officers,[513] notaries public,[514] the chairperson of the tribunal,[515] and domestic courts[516] have all been considered as authorities competent to perform an authentication.

---

[509] Supreme Court, Austria, 11 June 1969, 3, II Y.B. COM. ARB. 232 (1977).

[510] Dirk Otto, *Article IV*, in RECOGNITION AND ENFORCEMENT OF FOREIGN ARBITRAL AWARDS: A GLOBAL COMMENTARY ON THE NEW YORK CONVENTION 143, 145 (H. Kronke, P. Nacimiento et al. eds., 2010).

[511] See FOUCHARD GAILLARD GOLDMAN ON INTERNATIONAL COMMERCIAL ARBITRATION 970, para. 1675 (E. Gaillard, J. Savage eds., 1999); ALBERT JAN VAN DEN BERG, THE NEW YORK ARBITRATION CONVENTION OF 1958: TOWARDS A UNIFORM JUDICIAL INTERPRETATION 252-54 (1981); Dirk Otto, *Article IV*, in RECOGNITION AND ENFORCEMENT OF FOREIGN ARBITRAL AWARDS: A GLOBAL COMMENTARY ON THE NEW YORK CONVENTION 143, 178-79 (H. Kronke, P. Nacimiento et al. eds., 2010);Maxi Scherer, *Article IV (Formal Requirements for the Recognition and Enforcement of Arbitral Awards)*, in NEW YORK CONVENTION ON THE RECOGNITION AND ENFORCEMENT OF FOREIGN ARBITRAL AWARDS OF 10 JUNE 1958—COMMENTARY 207, 212 (R. Wolff ed., 2012).

[512] *Travaux préparatoires*, United Nations Conference on International Commercial Arbitration, Summary Record of the Seventeenth Meeting, E/CONF.26/SR.17, p. 7.

[513] *Guang Dong Light Headgear Factory Co. v. ACI Int'l, Inc*, District Court, District of Kansas, United States of America, 10 May 2005, 03-4165-JAR; Bundesgerichtshof [BGH], Germany, 16 December 2010, III ZB 100/09.

[514] Oberlandesgericht [OLG] Rostock, Germany, 28 October 1999; Bundesgerichtshof [BGH], Germany, 16 December 2010, III ZB 100/09.

[515] *Inter-Arab Investment Guarantee Corporation v. Banque Arabe et Internationale d'Investissements*, Court of Appeal of Brussels, Belgium, 24 January 1997, XXII Y.B. COM. ARB. 643 (1997).

54. Similarly, consular representatives[517] or notaries public[518] have also been considered to be authorities competent to certify a copy of an award. Some courts have found the arbitral institution under the rules of which the award was made to be competent to certify awards.[519] Members of the arbitral tribunal[520] or its chairperson,[521] as well as attorneys[522] have also been considered as authorities competent to perform a certification of an award.

55. A Canadian court has held that, in the circumstances of that case, a private individual was competent to certify the copy of the award.[523] The holder of the original award—a private individual—had provided an affidavit that the copy provided to the court was an accurate one. Having noted that the party opposing enforcement did not challenge the accuracy or authenticity of the copy but rather merely objected to the attestation, the court accepted the affidavit as sufficient proof that the copy of the award was an accurate copy.

---

516 *ECONERG Ltd. v. National Electricity Company AD*, Case No. 356/99, Supreme Court of Appeal, Civil Collegium, Fifth Civil Department, Bulgaria, 23 February 1999, 356/99, XXV Y.B. COM. ARB. 641 (2000).

517 *Guang Dong Light Headgear Factory Co. v. ACI Int'l, Inc*, District Court, District of Kansas, United States of America, 10 May 2005, 03-4165-JAR; *Presse Office S.A. v. Centro Editorial*, Supreme Court of Justice, Mexico, 24 February 1977, IV Y.B. COM. ARB. 301 (1979); Bayerisches Oberstes Landesgericht [BayObLG], Germany, 23 September 2004, 4Z Sch 005-04.

518 *Transpac Capital Pte Limited v. Buntoro*, Supreme Court of New South Wales, Common Law Division, Australia, 7 July 2008, 2008/11373; Oberlandesgericht [OLG] Rostock, Germany, 28 October 1999; *Trans-Pacific Shipping Co. v. Atlantic & Orient Shipping Corporation (BVI)*, Federal Court, Canada, 27 April 2005, XXXI Y.B. COM. ARB. 601 (2006).

519 *Continental Grain Company, et al. v. Foremost Farms Incorporated, et al.*, District Court, Southern District of New York, United States of America, 23 March 1998, 98 Civ. 0848 (DC), XXV Y.B. COM. ARB. 641 (2000); Hanseatisches Oberlandesgericht [OLG] Hamburg, Germany, 27 July 1978, IV Y.B. COM. ARB. 266 (1979); Bundesgerichtshof [BGH], Germany, 16 December 2010, III ZB 100/09.

520 See, e.g., *Bergesen v. Joseph Müller Corp*, Court of Appeals, Second Circuit, United States of America, 17 June 1983, 710 F.2d 928, IX Y.B. COM. ARB. 487 (1984) (even though here the chairman of the tribunal certified the award, the decision does not exclude the possibility that the other members of the tribunal could do the same: "copies of award and the agreement which have been certified by a member of the arbitration panel provide a sufficient basis upon which to enforce the award").

521 *Bergesen v. Joseph Müller Corp*, Court of Appeals, Second Circuit, United States of America, 17 June 1983, 710 F.2d 928, IX Y.B. COM. ARB. 487 (1984); *Inter-Arab Investment Guarantee Corporation v. Banque Arabe et Internationale d'Investissements*, Court of Appeal of Brussels, Belgium, 24 January 1997, XXII Y.B. COM. ARB. 643 (1997).

522 *Overseas Cosmos, Inc. v. NR Vessel Corp.*, District Court, Southern District of New York, United States of America, 8 December 1997, 97 Civ. 5898 (DC), XXIII Y.B. COM. ARB. 1096 (1998). The Court previously noted that the genuineness of the arbitration award was not in dispute. See also *Guangdong v. Chiu Shing Trading*, High Court, Supreme Court of Hong Kong, Hong Kong, 23 August 1991, Miscellaneous proceedings No. 1625 of 1991.

523 *Trans-Pacific Shipping Co. v. Atlantic & Orient Shipping Corporation (BVI)*, Federal Court, Canada, 27 April 2005, XXXI Y.B. COM. ARB. 601 (2006).

56. Other courts have found that the applicant had not shown that the person who authenticated or certified the copy of the award could, under the circumstances, be deemed competent to do so under the relevant applicable law.[524]

c. Whether certification must be of an authenticated original award

57. Article IV (1)*(a)* requires the applicant to provide either "the duly authenticated original award" or "a duly certified copy thereof". The question has arisen whether, when supplying a certified copy of an award, that copy must be of a previously authenticated copy or whether a certified copy of the award, without authentication of the signatures of the arbitrators, would suffice. The drafting history of article IV shows that, for a large part of the negotiations, the text of article IV (1)*(a)* required the applicant to provide either the original award or a certified copy thereof, without there being any requirement for authentication.[525] The authentication prerequisite was added at a later stage.[526] In other words, the certification requirement had been inserted by the drafters independently from the authentication requirement.

58. Reported case law on this point is scarce, with two courts having taken different approaches.

59. One court has held that when an applicant supplies certified copies of the award, the arbitrators' signatures on the award must be previously authenticated.[527]

60. Conversely, another court has held that in cases where the authenticity of the original award is not disputed, a certified copy of an

---

[524] *Glencore Grain Ltd. v. TSS Grain Millers Ltd.*, High Court of Mombasa, Kenya 5 July 2002, Civil Suit No. 388 of 2000, XXXIV Y.B. COM. ARB. 666 (2009) (finding that the applicant had not proven that the Director General of the institution that rendered the award had the authority to authenticate awards); *O Limited (Cyprus) v. M Corp. (formerly A, Inc.) (United States) and others*, Supreme Court, Austria, 3 September 2008, 3Ob35/08f XXXIV Y.B. COM. ARB. 409 (2009) (finding that "it cannot be deduced from the LCIA Arbitration Rules that [they] provide that certifications are to be issued by a secretary"); *ECONERG Ltd. v. National Electricity Company AD*, Supreme Court of Appeal, Civil Collegium, Fifth Civil Department, Bulgaria, 23 February 1999, 356/99, XXV Y.B. COM. ARB. 641 (2000) (finding that the award was authenticated neither by the competent authority under the law applicable to the arbitration agreement nor under the law of the enforcing court).

[525] *Travaux préparatoires*, United Nations Conference on International Commercial Arbitration, Working Party No. 3, Consideration of the Draft Convention on the Recognition and Enforcement of Foreign Arbitral Awards (Item 4 of the Agenda), E/CONF.26/L.43, p. 1.

[526] *Travaux préparatoires*, Summary Records of the Seventeenth Meeting of the United Nations Conference on International Commercial Arbitration, E/CONF.26/SR.17, p. 7.

[527] *O Limited (Cyprus) v. M Corp. (formerly A, Inc.) (United States) and others*, Supreme Court, Austria, 3 September 2008, 3Ob35/08f, XXXIV Y.B. COM. ARB. 409 (2009).

award which was not previously authenticated would meet the requirements of article IV (1)*(a)*.[528]

61. Commentators have argued that requiring certification to be done on an authenticated award would not accord with the spirit of article IV which, they contend, is to eliminate unnecessary formalism.[529]

Article IV (1)*(b)*

62. Article IV (1)*(b)* provides that, in order to obtain recognition and enforcement, an applicant must also submit to the enforcing court "the original agreement referred to in article II or a duly certified copy thereof". In this context, courts have often considered whether an arbitration agreement provided by the applicant is in conformity with the requirements of article II. This has been examined in detail in the chapter of the Guide on article II and will not be discussed here anew.

A. The requirement that the applicant provide the arbitration agreement "referred to in article II"

63. Article IV (1)*(b)* requires the applicant to supply "the original agreement referred to in article II". Accordingly, courts have often considered issues arising out of article II in conjunction with article IV (1)*(b)*, in particular, issues of proof required to meet the requirements of "the original agreement referred to in article II".

64. Courts have found that the applicant bears the burden of supplying documentary evidence that constitutes an "agreement in writing" under article II (2). For example, the Swiss Federal Tribunal has held that, under article IV (1)*(b)*, the burden is upon the applicant to provide an arbitration agreement which meets the requirements of form under article II of the Convention.[530] Likewise, the Spanish courts have held that the applicant bears the burden of proving that the conditions of article IV (1)*(b)* are met, *inter alia*, by supplying an arbitration agreement "in the form established by Art. IV (1)*(b)* together with Art. II".[531] The United States Court of Appeals

[528] Bundesgerichtshof [BGH], Germany, 22 February 2001, III ZB 71/99; Oberlandesgericht [OLG] Rostock, Germany, 28 October 1999.

[529] ALBERT JAN VAN DEN BERG, THE NEW YORK ARBITRATION CONVENTION OF 1958: TOWARDS A UNIFORM JUDICIAL INTERPRETATION 256-57 (1981); Maxi Scherer, *Article IV (Formal Requirements for the Recognition and Enforcement of Arbitral Awards)*, in NEW YORK CONVENTION ON THE RECOGNITION AND ENFORCEMENT OF FOREIGN ARBITRAL AWARDS OF 10 JUNE 1958—COMMENTARY 207, 215 (R. Wolff ed., 2012).

[530] Federal Tribunal, Switzerland, 31 May 2002, 4P.102/2001.

[531] *Glencore Grain Limited (United Kingdom) v. Sociedad Ibérica de Molturación, S.A. (Spain)*, Supreme Court, Spain, 14 January 2003, 16508/2003, XXX Y.B. COM. ARB. 605 (2005). See also *Shaanxi Provincial Medical Health Products I/E Corporation (PR China) v. Olpesa, S.A. (Spain)*, Supreme Court, Spain, 7 October 2003, 112/2002, XXX Y.B. COM.

for the Eleventh Circuit has also held that the applicant is required to "meet Article II's agreement-in-writing requirement".[532]

65. Courts have further clarified that, for the purposes of article IV (1)*(b)*, the applicant need only provide *prima facie* proof of an arbitration agreement.[533] For instance, the Court of Appeal of England and Wales has held that an applicant can produce "terms in writing, containing an arbitration clause" or a "record" of an arbitration agreement made in writing, explaining that "all that is probably required at the first stage [...] is apparently valid documentation containing an arbitration claus[e]".[534] Similarly, the High Court in Singapore ruled that "a document produced to a court in accordance with [the Section of the Singaporean International Arbitration Act transposing article IV (1)*(b)* of the Convention] shall, upon mere production be received by the court as *prima facie* evidence of the matters to which it relates".[535]

66. As discussed above and elsewhere in this Guide,[536] German courts have often relied on the more-favourable-right principle under article VII (1) to hold that it is not necessary for an applicant to supply the arbitration agreement at all.[537]

ARB. 617 (2005); *Satico Shipping Company Limited (Cyprus) v. Maderas Iglesias (Spain)*, Supreme Court, Civil Chamber, Plenary Session, Spain, 1 April 2003, 2009 of 2001, XXXII Y.B. COM. ARB. 582 (2007).

[532] *Czarina, L.L.C. v. W.F. Poe Syndicate*, Court of Appeals, Eleventh Circuit, United States of America, 4 February 2004, 358 F.3d 1286. See also *Guang Dong Light Headgear Factory Co. v. ACI Int'l, Inc*, District Court, District of Kansas, United States of America, 10 May 2005, 03-4165-JAR.

[533] *Aloe Vera of America, Inc (United States) v. Asianic Food (S) Pte Ltd. (Singapore) and Another*, Supreme Court of Singapore, High Court, Singapore, 10 May 2006, OS 762/2004, RA 327/2005, XXXII Y.B. COM. ARB. 489 (2007) (the Court held that at this stage the "examination [...] is a formalistic one and not a substantive one"); *Seller v. Buyer*, Supreme Court, Austria, 22 May 1991, XXI Y.B. COM. ARB. 521 (1996); *Denmark Skibstekniske Konsulenter A/S I Likvidation (formerly known as Knud E Hansen A/S) v. Ultrapolis 3000 Investments Ltd. (formerly known as Ultrapolis 3000 Theme Park Investments Ltd.)*, High Court, Singapore, 9 April 2010, 108, 2010 S.L.R. 661.

[534] *Yukos Oil Co. v. Dardana Ltd.*, Court of Appeal, England and Wales, 18 April 2002, [2002] EWCA Civ 543.

[535] *Denmark Skibstekniske Konsulenter A/S I Likvidation (formerly known as Knud E Hansen A/S) v. Ultrapolis 3000 Investments Ltd. (formerly known as Ultrapolis 3000 Theme Park Investments Ltd.)*, High Court, Singapore, 9 April 2010, 108, 2010 S.L.R. 661.

[536] See the chapter of the Guide on article IV para. 17, and the chapter on article VII, paras. 36-38.

[537] See also Bayerisches Oberstes Landesgericht [BayObLG], Germany, 11 August 2000, 4 Z Sch 05/00; Ober-landesgericht [OLG] München, Germany, 15 March 2006, 34 Sch 06/05; Kammergericht [KG], Germany, 10 August 2006, 20 Sch 07/04; Oberlandesgericht [OLG] Celle, Germany, 14 December 2006, 8 Sch 14/05; Oberlandesgericht [OLG] München, Germany, 23 February 2007, 34 Sch 31/06.

67. Commentators have also taken the view that, under article IV (1)*(b)*, an applicant need only provide *prima facie* proof that the arbitration agreement conforms to the formal requirements of article II.[538]

B. No requirement to prove the validity of the arbitration agreement

68. Closely related to the issue of whether or not an applicant must establish that the arbitration agreement which it has supplied meets the requirements of an "agreement in writing" is the question of whether, under article IV, an applicant must show that the arbitration agreement is valid.

69. Enforcing courts are in agreement that, under article IV (1)*(b)*, an applicant need not prove the validity of an arbitration agreement and that it is for the party opposing enforcement to raise this issue under article V.[539]

70. For example, the Court of Appeal of England and Wales held that, once an applicant provides an arbitration agreement that meets the requirements of article IV (1)*(b)*, the burden shifts onto the defendant to prove that the arbitration agreement is not valid under article V (1)*(a)*.[540] The Court of Appeal of Bermuda also held that an applicant is required to only provide the arbitration agreement, with the party opposing enforcement bearing the burden of making out a case with respect to the validity of the agreement.[541]

71. The same approach has been applied by courts in other jurisdictions, including Italy,[542] Spain[543] and Austria.[544]

---

[538] ICCA'S GUIDE TO THE INTERPRETATION OF THE 1958 NEW YORK CONVENTION: A HANDBOOK FOR JUDGES 75 (P. Sanders ed., 2011).

[539] For a more detailed discussion on the burden of proof under article V see the chapter of the Guide on the introduction to article V paras. 13-16 and the chapter on article V (1)*(a)*, paras. 43-47.

[540] *Yukos Oil Co. v. Dardana Ltd*, Court of Appeal, England and Wales, 18 April 2002, [2002] EWCA Civ 543. The approach in *Dardana* was followed by the High Court of Justice of England and Wales in *Dallah v. Pakistan* and by the High Court of Singapore in *Ultrapolis*. See *Dallah Real Estate and Tourism Holding Company v. Ministry of Religious Affairs, Government of Pakistan*, High Court of Justice, England and Wales, 1 August 2008, [2008] EWHC 1901, Annex 6; *Denmark Skibstekniske Konsulenter A/S I Likvidation (formerly known as Knud E Hansen A/S) v. Ultrapolis 3000 Investments Ltd. (formerly known as Ultrapolis 3000 Theme Park Investments Ltd.)*, High Court, Singapore, 9 April 2010, 108, 2010 S.L.R. 661.

[541] *Sojuznefteexport (SNE) v. Joc Oil Ltd.*, Court of Appeal of Bermuda, Bermuda, 7 July 1989, XV Y.B. COM. ARB. 384 (1990).

[542] *Jassica S.A. v. Ditta Polojaz*, Court of Cassation, Italy, 12 February 1987, 1526, XVII Y.B. COM. ARB. 525 (1992).

[543] *Union Générale de Cinéma, SA (France) v. X Y Z Desarrollos, S.A. (Spain)*, Supreme Court, Civil Chamber, Spain, 11 April 2000, 3536 of 1998, XXXII Y.B. COM. ARB. 525 (2007); *Strategic Bulk Carriers Inc. (Liberia) v. Sociedad Ibérica de Molturación,*

72. The above approach finds support in the *travaux préparatoires* of article IV (1)*(b)*[545] and in commentary.[546]

C. No requirement to authenticate the arbitration agreement

73. While article IV (1)*(a)* requires the applicant to supply an authenticated copy of the award (or a certified copy), article IV (1)*(b)* does not mandate authentication of the arbitration agreement.

74. During the drafting of article IV, the Belgian delegate proposed that the arbitration agreement be authenticated as well.[547] This was opposed by the French delegate who considered that the production of the arbitration agreement should not be subject to excessive requirements, particularly in light of the fact that many arbitrations were based on arbitral clauses agreed to in an exchange of correspondence.[548] The final text of article IV (1)*(b)* does not include an authentication requirement.

75. None of the court decisions reviewed contain any discussion on this point.

Article IV (2)

76. Article IV (2) requires the applicant to supply a translation of the award or the arbitration agreement if these are not made in an official language of the country in which recognition and enforcement is sought. The translations are to be provided in addition to the original documents and not

---

S.A. (Spain), Supreme Court, Civil Chamber, Spain, 26 February 2002, 153 of 2001, XXXII Y.B. COM. ARB. 550 (2007).

544 *Seller v. Buyer*, Supreme Court, Austria, 22 May 1991, XXI Y.B. COM. ARB. 521 (1996).

545 The delegate of the ICC at the Conference stated that "when there was a prima facie proof that the parties had agreed to submit their dispute to arbitration, it should be for the defendant to prove that the contrary was the case". *Travaux préparatoires*, United Nations Conference on International Commercial Arbitration, Summary Record of the Eleventh Meeting, E/CONF.26/SR.11, p. 12.

546 FOUCHARD GAILLARD GOLDMAN ON INTERNATIONAL COMMERCIAL ARBITRATION 968, para. 1673 (E. Gaillard, J. Savage eds., 1999); ICCA'S GUIDE TO THE INTERPRETATION OF THE 1958 NEW YORK CONVENTION: A HANDBOOK FOR JUDGES 75 (P. Sanders ed., 2011); Dirk Otto, *Article IV*, in RECOGNITION AND ENFORCEMENT OF FOREIGN ARBITRAL AWARDS: A GLOBAL COMMENTARY ON THE NEW YORK CONVENTION 143, 167 (H. Kronke, P. Nacimiento et al. eds., 2010).

547 *Travaux préparatoires*, United Nations Conference on International Commercial Arbitration, Summary Records of the Seventeenth meeting of the United Nations Conference on International Commercial Arbitration, United Nations document E/CONF.26/SR.17, pp. 6-7.

548 *Travaux préparatoires*, United Nations Conference on International Commercial Arbitration, Summary Records of the Seventeenth meeting of the United Nations Conference on International Commercial Arbitration, United Nations document E/CONF.26/SR.17, p. 7.

in lieu thereof.[549] Article IV (2) further provides that such translations are to be certified by an official or sworn translator or a diplomatic or consular agent.

77. Under the rubric of article IV (2), enforcing courts have examined issues related to the law governing translation, the authorities competent to perform the translation, and the object of translation.

A. Governing law

78. Like article IV (1) which does not provide for an applicable law in relation to authentication and certification, article IV (2) does not provide for a law governing translations.

79. Very little case law exists on the issue of governing law. In one case, a Swiss court stated that the certification of the translation by a translator or a consular or diplomatic agent needed to comply with the law of the seat of the arbitration and that this law could impose less stringent certification requirements or even dispose of such requirements entirely.[550]

80. The Austrian Supreme Court has held that the applicant is free to choose from either the law of the State in which the award was made or the law of the State in which enforcement is sought.[551]

B. Certification "by an official or sworn translator or by a diplomatic or consular agent"

81. Unlike article IV (1), article IV (2) does specify the authority competent to perform the certification of the translation: an official or sworn translator or a diplomatic or consular agent.

82. Applying this requirement, a Swiss court has denied enforcement in a case where the translation was certified not by an official translator or a diplomatic or consular agent, but rather by a notary public. However, it noted that the notary had certified only the authenticity of the copy of the arbitral award used for the translation.[552] The same court also added that, generally, a translation made by a third party and certified by a notary public who is capable of understanding the language of the translation could meet the criteria of article IV (2).

---

[549] *Inter Maritime Management S.A. v. Russin & Vecchi*, Federal Tribunal, Switzerland, 9 January 1995, XXII Y.B. COM. ARB. 789 (1997).

[550] Court of Appeal of the Canton of Zug, Switzerland, 27 February 1998, JZ 1997/104.161.

[551] Supreme Court, Austria, 11 June 1969, 3, II Y.B. COM. ARB. 232 (1977).

[552] Court of Appeal of the Canton of Zug, Switzerland, 27 February 1998, JZ 1997/104.161.

83. Article IV (2) does not indicate whether the official or sworn translator or the diplomatic or consular agent must be of the State in which the award was made or of the State in which enforcement is sought. Reported case law on this point is scarce. In line with its ruling on the law governing translation,[553] the Austrian Supreme Court has noted that the applicant is free to choose from translators either from the enforcing State or from the State in which the award was made.[554] Similarly, French courts have held that applicants do not need to submit a translation from a translator featuring on the list of experts of the enforcing court.[555]

C. The object of translation

84. Article IV (2) specifies that the object of the translation is the award and the arbitration agreement. In this context, courts have dealt with the issue of whether or not an applicant would meet the requirements of article IV if it provided translations of excerpts of these documents.

85. An Austrian court held that the applicant should provide a full translation of the relevant document.[556] However, the court did not deny enforcement to the applicant, but rather, returned the case to the lower court and instructed it to afford the applicant an opportunity to provide a full translation.[557]

86. Swiss courts have taken a pragmatic approach in this regard. For example, a Zurich court accepted that the party supplying a translation of the arbitral agreement met the requirements of article IV by supplying a translation of the arbitration clause and not the entire contract.[558]

87. Moreover, the Swiss Federal Tribunal has ruled that a partial translation of an award met the requirements of article IV (2).[559] The court stated that based on a flexible, pragmatic and non-formalistic interpretation of article IV (2), the provision of only a partial translation of the arbitral award was sufficient, and that a more restrictive interpretation would run counter to the recognition and enforcement friendly spirit and objective of

---

[553] Supreme Court, Austria, 13 April 2011, 3 Ob 154/10h.

[554] Supreme Court, Austria, 11 June 1969, 3, II Y.B. COM. ARB. 232 (1977).

[555] *S.A.R.L. Synergie v. Société SC Conect S.A.*, Court of Appeal of Paris, France, 18 March 2004, 2001/18372, 2001/18379, 2001/18382; *Société GFI Informatique S.A. v. Société Engineering Ingegneria Informatica S.P.A. et Société Engineering Sanita Enti Locali S.PA. (ex GFI SANITÀ S.P.A.)*, Court of Appeal of Paris, France, 27 November 2008, 07/11672.

[556] *D S.A. (Spain) v. W GmbH (Austria)*, Supreme Court, Austria, 26 April 2006, 3Ob211/05h, XXXII Y.B. COM. ARB. 259 (2007).

[557] *Ibid.* The same court has also explained that there is no requirement that dissenting opinions be translated given that dissenting opinions are not normally a part of the award.

[558] Court of Appeal of Zurich, Switzerland, 17 July 2003, XXIX Y.B. COM. ARB. 819 (2004). See also *R S.A. v. A Ltd*, Court of Justice of Geneva, Switzerland, 15 April 1999.

[559] Federal Tribunal, Switzerland, 2 July 2012, 5A_754/2011.

the Convention. It concluded that it would be too formalistic to require a translation of the full award in light of the fact that the applicant had presented the court with a translation that covered the dispositif of the award and the section on costs which was in dispute between the parties.

Article V

1. Recognition and enforcement of the award may be refused, at the request of the party against whom it is invoked, only if that party furnishes to the competent authority where the recognition and enforcement is sought, proof that:

a) The parties to the agreement referred to in article II were, under the law applicable to them, under some incapacity, or the said agreement is not valid under the law to which the parties have subjected it or, failing any indication thereon, under the law of the country where the award was made; or

b) The party against whom the award is invoked was not given proper notice of the appointment of the arbitrator or of the arbitration proceedings or was otherwise unable to present his case; or

c) The award deals with a difference not contemplated by or not falling within the terms of the submission to arbitration, or it contains decisions on matters beyond the scope of the submission to arbitration, provided that, if the decisions on matters submitted to arbitration can be separated from those not so submitted, that part of the award which contains decisions on matters submitted to arbitration may be recognized and enforced; or

d) The composition of the arbitral authority or the arbitral procedure was not in accordance with the agreement of the parties, or, failing such agreement, was not in accordance with the law of the country where the arbitration took place; or

e) The award has not yet become binding on the parties, or has been set aside or suspended by a competent authority of the country in which, or under the law of which, that award was made.

2. Recognition and enforcement of an arbitral award may also be refused if the competent authority in the

country where recognition and enforcement is sought finds that:

a) The subject matter of the difference is not capable of settlement by arbitration under the law of that country; or

b) The recognition or enforcement of the award would be contrary to the public policy of that country.

Travaux préparatoires

The *travaux préparatoires* on article V as adopted in 1958 are contained in the following documents:

Draft Convention on the Recognition and Enforcement of Foreign Arbitral Awards and comments by Governments and Organizations:

Report of the Committee on the Enforcement of International Arbitral Awards: E/2704 and Annex.

Comments by Governments and Organizations on the Draft Convention on the Recognition and Enforcement of Foreign Arbitral Awards: E/2822, Annexes I-II; E/2822/Add.1; E/2822/Add.2; E/2822/Add.4; E/2822/Add.5; E/2822/Corr.1; E/2840; E/CONF.26/3; E/CONF.26/3/Add.1.

Activities of Inter-Governmental and Non-Governmental Organizations in the Field of Intertional Commercial Arbitration: Consolidated Report by the Secretary-General: E/CONF.26/4.

Comments on the Draft Convention on the Recognition and Enforcement of Foreign Arbitral Awards: Note by the Secretary General: E/CONF.26/2. United Nations Conference on International Commercial Arbitration:

Amendments to the Draft Convention Submitted by Governmental Delegations: E/CONF.26/L.8; E/CONF.26/L.15; E/CONF.26/L.15/Rev.1; E/CONF.26/L.16; E/CONF.26/L.17; E/CONF.26/L.23; E/CONF.26/L.24; E/CONF.26/L.30; E/CONF.26/L.31; E/CONF.26/L.32; E/CONF.26/L.34; E/CONF.26/L.35.

Comparison of Drafts Relating to Articles III, IV and V of the Draft Convention: E/CONF.26/L.33; E/CONF.26/L.33/Rev.1.

Further Amendments to the Draft Convention Submitted by Governmental Delegations: E/CONF.26/L.37/Rev.1; E/CONF.26/L.38; E/CONF.26/L.39; E/CONF.26/L.40.

Text of Articles III, IV and V of the Draft Convention Proposed by Working Party III: E/CONF.26/L.43.

Amendments by Governmental Delegations to the Drafts Submitted by the Working Parties and Further Suggested Drafts: E/CONF.26/L.45.

Text of Articles Adopted by the Conference: E/CONF.26/L.48.

Text of the Convention on the Recognition and Enforcement of Foreign Arbitral Awards as Provisionally Approved by the Drafting Committee: E/CONF.26/L.61; E/CONF.26/8.

New text of Articles I (3), V (1)*(a), (b),* and *(e)* Adopted by the Conference at its 23rd meeting: E/CONF.26/L.63.

Final Act and Convention on the Recognition and Enforcement of Foreign Arbitral Awards: E/CONF.26/8/Rev.1.Summary records:

Summary Records of the Second, Third, Fourth, Fifth, Sixth, Seventh, Ninth, Tenth, Eleventh, Twelfth, Thirteenth, Fourteenth, Sixteenth, Seventeenth, Twentieth, Twenty-First; Twenty-Third and Twenty-Fourth Meetings of the United Nations Conference on International Commercial Arbitration: E/CONF.26/SR.2; E/CONF.26/SR.3; E/CONF.26/SR.4; E/CONF.26/SR.5; E/CONF.26/SR.6; E/CONF.26/SR.7; E/CONF.26/SR.9; E/CONF.26/SR.10; E/CONF.26/SR.11; E/CONF.26/SR.12; E/CONF.26/SR.13; E/CONF.26/SR.14;E/CONF.26/SR.16; E/CONF.26/SR.17; E/CONF.26/SR.20; E/CONF.26/SR.21; E/CONF.26/SR.23; E/CONF.26/SR.24. Summary Records of the First, Second, Fourth, Fifth, Sixth, Seventh and Eighth Meetings of the Committee on Enforcement of International Arbitral Awards: E/AC.42/SR.1; E/AC.42/SR.2; E/AC.42/SR.4; E/AC.42/ SR.5; E/AC.42/SR.6; E/AC.42/SR.7; E/AC.42/SR.8.

Committee on the Enforcement of International Arbitral Awards:

Enforcement of International Arbitral Awards: statement submitted by the International Chamber of Commerce, a non-governmental organization having consultative status in category A: E/C.2/373.

Comments received from Governments regarding the Draft Convention on the Enforcement of International Arbitral Awards: E/AC.42/1.

(Available on the Internet at http://www.uncitral.org)
(For the *travaux préparatoires*, case law and bibliographical references, see also on the Internet at http://newyorkconvention1958.org)

Introduction

1. Article V of the New York Convention sets forth the limited and exhaustive grounds on which recognition and enforcement of an arbitral award may be refused by a competent authority in the Contracting State where recognition and enforcement is sought. Article V (1) lists the grounds for refusal that must be raised "at the request of the party against whom [the award] is invoked". Article V (2) lists the grounds on which a court may refuse enforcement of its own motion.

2. The drafters of the New York Convention sought to overcome the hurdles that an applicant had to meet under the previous regime for recognition and enforcement of foreign arbitral awards. The 1927 Geneva Convention placed the burden on the party relying on an arbitral award to prove five cumulative conditions in order to obtain recognition and enforcement, including that the award was "final", which in practice required the party to effectively obtain two decisions of exequatur, one at the country where the award was issued, and one at the place of enforcement.[560] As a further obstacle, under the 1927 Geneva Convention a court was required to refuse recognition and enforcement if the award had been annulled in its country of origin, if the respondent had not been given proper notice or was under a legal incapacity, or if the award dealt with differences not contemplated in the parties' arbitration agreement.[561] The 1927 Geneva Convention also allowed a party opposing recognition and enforcement to raise any additional grounds for refusal available under the law governing the arbitration.[562]

---

[560] Article 1 of the 1927 Geneva Convention. See the chapter of the Guide on article V (1)(e) of the New York Convention, paras. 2-4.
[561] Article 2 of the 1927 Geneva Convention.
[562] Article 3 of the 1927 Geneva Convention.

3. While the first draft of article V of the New York Convention closely followed the wording of the 1927 Geneva Convention,[563] significant changes were introduced during the drafting process. The final text of article V reflects the recommendation of the Dutch delegation to eliminate the requirement of *double exequatur*, to restrict the grounds for refusal of recognition and enforcement as much as possible and to place the burden of proving such grounds on the party opposing recognition and enforcement.[564] Furthermore, while the 1927 Geneva Convention provided that recognition and enforcement "shall be refused" if one of the grounds for non-enforcement in its article II were present, the final text of article V omits any language that makes refusal to recognize and enforce mandatory.

4. As discussed in the following chapters on article V of the Guide, courts in the Contracting States have generally construed the grounds for refusal under the Convention narrowly, and have exercised their discretion to refuse recognition and enforcement of foreign arbitral awards under the New York Convention in exceptional cases only.[565]

A. Court discretion under article V

5. The objective of the New York Convention is to facilitate the recognition and enforcement of arbitral awards to the greatest extent possible and to provide a maximum level of control which Contracting States may exert over arbitral awards. In accordance with this objective, the Convention grants courts of the Contracting States the discretion to refuse to recognize and enforce an award on the grounds listed in article V, without obligating them to do so.[566]

6. In some Contracting States, courts have exercised this discretion by reference to the permissive language of the English version of the Convention (or equivalent phrasing in legislation implementing the

---

[563] *Travaux préparatoires*, Draft Convention on the Recognition and Enforcement of Foreign Arbitral Awards, Report of the Committee on the Enforcement of International Arbitral Awards, E/2704, E/AC.42/4/Rev. 1, Annex, p. 2.

[564] *Travaux préparatoires*, United Nations Conference on International Commercial Arbitration, Recognition and Enforcement of Foreign Arbitral Awards, Comments by Governments on the draft Convention on the Recognition and Enforcement of Foreign Arbitral Awards, E/CONF.26/3/Add.1, para. 7. See also Pieter Sanders, *The Making of the Convention*, in ENFORCING ARBITRATION AWARDS UNDER THE NEW YORK CONVENTION: EXPERIENCE AND PROSPECTS (United Nations, 1999).

[565] See, e.g., the chapters of the Guide on articles V (1)(*a*), V (1)(*b*), V (1)(*c*), V (1)(*d*), V (2)(*a*) and V (2)(*b*).

[566] ALBERT JAN VAN DEN BERG, THE NEW YORK ARBITRATION CONVENTION OF 1958: TOWARDS A UNIFORM JUDICIAL INTERPRETATION 265 (1981); GARY B. BORN, INTERNATIONAL COMMERCIAL ARBITRATION 3428-33 (2014); Teresa Cheng, *Celebrating the Fiftieth Anniversary of the New York Convention*, in 50 YEARS OF THE NEW YORK CONVENTION: ICCA INTERNATIONAL ARBITRATION CONFERENCE 679, 680 (A.J. van den Berg, ed., 2009).

Convention in their territory), which provides that recognition and enforcement "may be refused" if one of the grounds for refusal under article V is present.[567] Certain commentators similarly note that the wording of the official versions of the Convention, with the exception of the French version which uses the present tense, permits a court to exercise its discretion to recognize and enforce.[568]

7. As other commentators point out, the French version of the Convention is equally permissive, as reflected by the more-favourable-right provision at article VII (1), which confirms the intention of the Convention's drafters to establish a "ceiling", or maximum level of control for the enforcement of arbitral awards, leaving each State free to act less restrictively.[569] Courts in France have recognized and enforced arbitral awards based on a narrower range of grounds for refusal under French law than under article V in accordance with article VII (1).[570]

B. Exhaustive character of grounds under article V

8. The New York Convention contains an exhaustive list of the grounds upon which courts in the Contracting States may refuse recognition and enforcement. Article V (1) states that recognition and enforcement may be refused "only if" the requesting party furnishes proof that one of the enumerated grounds in that paragraph is present. Article V (2) states that recognition and enforcement "may also be refused" if the enforcing court finds that one of the two grounds listed in that paragraph is present.

9. The grounds for refusal under article V do not include an erroneous decision in law or in fact by the arbitral tribunal. A court seized with an application for recognition and enforcement under the Convention may not

---

567 *China Agribusiness Development Corporation v. Balli Trading,* High Court of Justice, England and Wales, 20 January 1997, XXIV Y.B. COM. ARB. 732 (1999); *Nigerian National Petroleum Corporation v. IPCO (Nigeria) Ltd.*, Court of Appeal, England and Wales, 21 October 2008,[2008] EWCA Civ 1157; *Chromalloy Aeroservices v. Arab Republic of Egypt,* District Court, District of Columbia, United States of America, 31 July 1996, 94-2339; *China Nanhai Oil Joint Service Corporation Shenzhen Branch v. Gee Tai Holdings Co. Ltd.*, High Court, Supreme Court of Hong Kong, Hong Kong, 13 July 1994, 1992 No. MP 2411.

568 Jan Paulsson, *May or Must Under the New York Convention: An Exercise in Syntax and Linguistics,* 14 ARB. INT'L 227 (1998); Gary H. Sampliner, *Enforcement of Foreign Arbitral Awards After Annulment in their Country of Origin,* 11(9) INT'L ARB. Rep. 22, 23 (1996); Fifi Junita, *Public Policy Exception in International Commercial Arbitration—Promoting Uniform Model Norms,* 5 CONTEM. ASIA ARB. J. 45, 59-60 (2012).

569 Emmanuel Gaillard, *Enforcement of Awards Set Aside in the Country* of *Origin: The French Experience,* in IMPROVING THE EFFICIENCY OF ARBITRATION AGREEMENTS AND AWARDS: 40 YEARS OF APPLICATION OF THE NEW YORK CONVENTION, ICCA CONGRESS SERIES NO. 9, 505, 517 (1998); Thomas Clay, *La Convention de New York vue par la doctrine française,* 27 ASA Bull. 50, 54-56 (2009).

570 See the chapters of the Guide on article V (1)*(e)*, para. 29, fn. 992 and article VII, paras. 42-44.

review the merits of the arbitral tribunal's decision. This principle is unanimously confirmed in the case law[571] and commentary[572] on the New York Convention.

10. Courts of the Contracting States have also consistently found that the Convention does not allow refusal to recognize and enforce based on procedural grounds other than those listed in article V. For instance, a Swiss appeals court rejected a challenge to recognition and enforcement on the ground that one party was invited to participate in the arbitration in a language it did not understand shortly before the commencement of the arbitration, holding that this did not constitute one of the enumerated grounds under article V.[573] Courts in Belgium,[574] the United Kingdom,[575] Colombia,[576] Luxembourg,[577] Israel,[578] Canada,[579] Germany,[580] Hong

---

571 See, e.g., *Trading company (Israel) v. Buyer (Germany),* Oberlandesgericht, Cologne, Germany, 23 April 2004, XXX Y.B. COM. ARB. 557 (2005); *Kotraco, Inc. v. V/O Rosvneshtorg,* Moscow District Court, Russian Federation, 31 October 1995, XXIII Y.B. COM. ARB. 735 (1998); *AB Götaverken (Sweden) v. General National Maritime Transport Company (Libya),* Supreme Court, Sweden, 13 August 1979, VI Y.B. COM. ARB. 237 (1981); *Generica Ltd. v. Pharmaceutical Basics, Inc. et al.,* District Court, Northern District of Illinois, Illinois, United States of America, 18 September 1996, 95 C 5935, XXII Y.B. COM. ARB. 1029 (1997); *Xiamen Xinjindi Group Ltd. v. Eton Properties Ltd.,* High Court, Hong Kong, 14 June 2012, HCLL 13/2011.

572 See, e.g., FOUCHARD GAILLARD GOLDMAN ON INTERNATIONAL COMMERCIAL ARBITRATION 983, para. 1693 (E. Gaillard, J. Savage eds., 1999); GARY B. BORN, INTERNATIONAL COMMERCIAL ARBITRATION 3707 (2014); ALBERT JAN VAN DEN BERG, THE NEW YORK ARBITRATION CONVENTION OF 1958: TOWARDS A UNIFORM JUDICIAL INTERPRETATION 269-73 (1981); JULIAN D.M.LEW, LOUKAS A. MISTELIS, STEFAN M. KRÖLL, COMPARATIVE INTERNATIONAL COMMERCIAL ARBITRATION paras. 26-66 (2003); NIGEL BLACKABY ET AL., REDFERN AND HUNTER ON INTERNATIONAL ARBITRATION para. 11.56 (2015); Pieter Sanders, *A Twenty Years' Review* of *the Convention on the Recognition and Enforcement of Foreign Arbitral Awards,* 13 INT'L LAW 269 (1979); Michael Hwang and Amy Lai, *Do Egregious Errors Amount to a Breach* of *Public Policy?,* 71 ARBITRATION 1 (2005).

573 *N.Z. v. I,* Appellationsgericht, Basel-Stadt, Switzerland, 27 February 1989, XVII Y.B. COM. ARB. 581 (1992).

574 *Inter-Arab Investment Guarantee Corp. v. Banque Arabe et Internationale d'Investissements,* Cour d'Appel, Brussels, Belgium, 25 January 1996, XXII Y.B. COM. ARB. 643 (1997).

575 *Rosseel NV v. Oriental Commercial Shipping,* High Court of Justice, England and Wales, 16 November 1990, XVI Y.B. COM. ARB. 615 (1991).

576 *Petrotesting Colombia S.A. v. Southeast Investment Corporation,* Corte Suprema de Justicia, Colombia, 27 July 2011; *Drummond Ltd. v. Instiuto Nacional de Concesiones,* Corte Suprema de Justicia, Colombia, 3 May 2012, XXXVII Y.B. COM. ARB. 205 (2012).

577 *Sovereign Participations International S.A. v. Chadmore Developments Ltd.,* Cour d'Appel, Luxembourg, 28 January 1999, XXIV Y.B. COM. ARB. 714 (1999).

578 *Zeevi Holdings Ltd. (in receivership) (Israel) v. The Republic* of *Bulgaria,* District Court, Jerusalem, Israel, 13 January 2009, XXXIV Y.B. COM. ARB. 632 (2009).

579 *Abener Energia, S.A. and Sunopta Inc. v. Suopta Inc. and Abener Energia, S.A.,* Ontario Superior Court of Justice, Canada, 15 June 2009, 2009 CanLII 30678.

580 *Parties not indicated,* Oberlandesgericht, Hamm, Germany, 2 November 1983, XIV Y.B. COM. ARB. 629 (1989).

Kong,[581] the Netherlands,[582] Italy[583] and Bermuda[584] have advanced the same position. Leading commentators on the New York Convention equally confirm that the grounds for refusal under article V are exhaustive.[585]

11. In certain early cases, courts of the United States considered that an arbitrator's manifest disregard of the law, which constitutes a ground for vacating domestic arbitral awards under the United States Federal Arbitration Act, could also constitute a ground for refusing to enforce a foreign arbitral award under the Convention.[586] In more recent cases, however, United States courts have held that the exhaustive nature of the grounds for refusal under article V bars the application of this doctrine to awards falling under the Convention. In the words of one United States appeals court, "[t]here is now considerable caselaw holding that, in an action to confirm an award rendered in, or under the law of, a foreign jurisdiction, the grounds for relief enumerated in Art. V of the Convention are the only grounds available for setting aside an arbitral awards [sic]".[587] Commentators confirm this view.[588]

---

581 *Karaha Bodas Company LLC v. Perusahaan Pertambangan Minyak Dan Gas Bumi Negara,* Court of Final Appeal, Hong Kong, 5 December 2008, FACV 6/2008.

582 *German Party v. Dutch Party,* President of Rechtbank, The Hague, The Netherlands, 26 April 1973, IV Y.B. COM. ARB. 305 (1979).

583 C.G. *Impianti SpA (Italy) v. B.M.A.A.B. and Sons International Contracting Company WLL (Kuwait),* Corte di Appello, Milan, Italy, 29 April 2009, XXXV Y.B. COM. ARB. 415 (2010).

584 *Sojuznefteexport v. Joc Oil Ltd.,* Court of Appeal, Bermuda, 7 July 1989, XV Y.B. COM. ARB. 384 (1990).

585 GARY B. BORN, INTERNATIONAL COMMERCIAL ARBITRATION 3426-27 (2014); Roy Goode, *The Role* of *the Lex Loci Arbitri in International Commercial Arbitration,* 17 ARB. INT'L 19, 22 (2001); ALBERT JAN VAN DEN BERG, THE NEW YORK ARBITRATION CONVENTION OF 1958: TOWARDS A UNIFORM JUDICIAL INTERPRETATION 265 (1981); JULIAN LEW AND LOUKAS MISTELIS, COMPARATIVE INTERNATIONAL COMMERCIAL ARBITRATION, PARA. 26-70 (2003); NIGEL BLACKABY ET AL., REDFERN AND HUNTER ON INTERNATIONAL ARBITRATION para. 11.57 (2015); MARIKE R.P. PAULSSON, THE 1958 NEW YORK CONVENTION IN ACTION 166 (2016).

586 *Wilko v. Swan,* Court of Appeals, Second Circuit, United Stated of America, 7 December 1953, 346 United States 427; *Office of Supply, Government of the Republic* of *Korea v. New York Navigation Company, Inc.,* Court of Appeals, Second Circuit, United States of America, 8 November 1972, 469 F.2d 377 (1972); *American Construction Machinery & Equipment Corp. Ltd. v. Mechanised Construction of Pakistan Ltd.,* District Court, Southern District of New York, United States of America, 23 March 1987, 659 F. Supp. 426 (S.D.N.Y. 1987).

587 *Yusuf Ahmed Alghanim & Sons, W.LL v. Toys "R" Us, Inc.,* Court of Appeals, Second Circuit, United States of America, 10 September 1997, XXIII Y.B. COM. ARB. 1058 (1998). See also *Brandeis Intsel Ltd. v. Calabrian Chemicals,* District Court, Southern District of New York, United States of America, 5 January 1987, 656 F. Supp. 160 (S.D.N.Y. 1987).

588 GARY B. BORN, INTERNATIONAL COMMERCIAL ARBITRATION 3711 (2014); Kenneth R. Davis, *Unconventional Wisdom: A New Look at Articles V and VII of the Convention on the Recognition and Enforcement* of *Foreign Arbitral Awards,* 37 TEX. INT'L L.J. 43 (2002), 70-71; Ray Y. Chan, *The Enforceability* of *Annulled Foreign Arbitral Awards in the United States: A Critique* of *Chromalloy,* 17 BOSTON U. INT'L L.J. 141, 160 (1999); Eric

12. An Australian court interpreted the legislation originally implementing the Convention in Australia, which omitted the words "only" in the chapeau to article V,[589] as granting it residual discretion to refuse recognition and enforcement for reasons not enumerated in the Convention.[590] In 2010, the legislation was amended to provide that "[t]he court may only refuse to enforce the foreign award in the circumstances" listed in article V.[591]

C. Burden of proof under article V

13. Article 1 of the 1927 Geneva Convention expressly required the party seeking to rely on an award to prove a number of positive conditions before recognition and enforcement was granted. However, it provided no guidance on whether the court where recognition and enforcement was sought should examine the grounds for non-enforcement under article 2 *ex officio*, or only at the request of the party opposing recognition and enforcement. It was also silent on which party had the ultimate burden of proving these grounds for refusal.

14. Following a proposal made by the German delegation during the drafting of the New York Convention,[592] article V sets forth a clear rule with respect to the burden of proving the grounds for refusing to recognize and enforce an arbitral award.

15. The introductory sentence of article V (1) provides that recognition and enforcement may only be refused "at the request of the party against whom [the award] is invoked", and if that party "furnishes proof" of the grounds listed in that paragraph. In accordance with this wording, courts in the Contracting States have consistently recognized that the party opposing

---

A. Schwartz, *A Comment on Chromalloy: Hilmarton, à l'américaine,* 14(2) J. INT'L ARB. 126, 132 (1997); Stephen T. Ostrowski and Yuval Shany, *Chromalloy: United States Law and International Arbitration at the Crossroads,* 73 N.Y.U. L. REV. 1650, 1675 (1998).

[589] See Section 8(5) of the International Arbitration Act 1974 (Cth), which, prior to enumerating the grounds on which recognition and enforcement could be refused, stated that "the court may, at the request of the party against whom it is invoked, refuse to enforce the award if that party proves to the satisfaction of the court that [...]".

[590] *Resort Condominiums International Inc. v. Ray Bowell,* Supreme Court of Queensland, Australia, 29 October 1993, XX Y.B. COM. ARB. 628 (1995).

[591] See International Arbitration Act 1974 (Cth), section 8(3A), as amended by International Arbitration Amendment Act 2010 (Cth), section 7.

[592] *Travaux préparatoires*, United Nations Conference on International Commercial Arbitration, Recognition and Enforcement of Foreign Arbitral Awards, Comparison of Drafts Relating to Articles III, IV and V of the draft Convention on the Recognition and Enforcement of Foreign Arbitral Awards, E/CONF.26/L.33/Rev.1, p. 3.

recognition and enforcement has the burden of raising and proving the grounds for non-enforcement under article V (1).[593]

16. Article V (2) provides that the grounds under the second paragraph may be observed by a court *ex officio*. Courts of the Contracting States have confirmed that the grounds for refusal under article V (2) do not have to be pleaded by the party opposing recognition and enforcement.[594] While article V (2) does not specifically allocate the burden of proof to either party, courts of the Contracting States have considered that the party opposing recognition and enforcement has the ultimate burden of proving such grounds.[595] Leading commentators on the Convention express the same view.[596]

---

[593] See, e.g., *Dutch Shipowner v. German Cattle and Meat Dealer*, Bundesgerichtshof, Germany, 1 February 2001, XXIX Y.B. COM. ARB. 700 (2004); *Trans World Film SpA v. Film Polski Import and Export* of *Films*, Corte di Cassazione, Italy, 22 February 1992, XVIII Y.B. COM. ARB. 433 (1993); *Europcar Italia SpA v. Maiellano Tours Inc*., Court of Appeals, Second Circuit, United States of America, 2 September 1998, 97-7224, XXIV Y.B. COM. ARB. 860 (1999); *Encyclopedia Universalis S.A. v. Encyclopedia Britannica Inc*., Court of Appeals, Second Circuit, United States of America, 31 March 2005, 04-0288-cv, XXX Y.B. COM. ARB. 1136 (2005).

[594] See, e.g., *Efxinos Shipping Co. Ltd. v. Rawi Shipping Lines Ltd*., Corte Di Appello Genova, Italy, 2 May 1980, VIII Y.B. COM. ARB. 381 (1983); *Rosseel NV v. Oriental Commercial Shipping*, High Court of Justice, England and Wales, 16 November 1990, XVI COM. ARB. 615 (1991); *Sovereign Participations International S.A. v. Chadmore Developments Ltd.*, Cour d'Appel, Luxembourg, 28 January 1999, XXIV Y.B. COM. ARB. 714 (1999).

[595] See, e.g., *Licensee v. Licensor,* Oberlandesgericht, Düsseldorf, Germany, 21 July 2004, XXXII Y.B. COM. ARB. 315 (2007); *Gater Assets Ltd. v. Nak Naftogaz Ukrainiy*, Court of Appeal, England and Wales, 17 October 2007, [2007] EWCA Civ 988; *Hebei Import & Export Corp. v. Polytek Engineering Co. Ltd*., Court of Final Appeal, Hong Kong, 9 February 1999, [1999] 2 HKC 205; *NTT Docomo Inc. v. Ultra D.O.O.*, District Court, Southern District of New York, United States of America, 12 October 2010, 10 Civ. 3823 (RMB)(JCF). See also the chapter of Guide on article V (2)*(b)*, para. 57.

[596] See, e.g., GARY B. BORN, INTERNATIONAL COMMERCIAL ARBITRATION 3418-19 (2014); Dirk Otto, Omaia Elwan, *Article V (2),* in RECOGNITION AND ENFORCEMENT OF FOREIGN ARBITRAL AWARDS: A GLOBAL COMMENTARY ON THE NEW YORK CONVENTION 345, 348 (H. Kronke, P. Nacimiento et al. eds., 2010).

Article V (1)*(a)*

1. Recognition and enforcement of the award may be refused, at the request of the party against whom it is invoked, only if that party furnishes to the competent authority where the recognition and enforcement is sought, proof that:

a) The parties to the agreement referred to in article II were, under the law applicable to them, under some incapacity, or the said agreement is not valid under the law to which the parties have subjected it or, failing any indication thereon, under the law of the country where the award was made; or [...]

Travaux préparatoires

The *travaux préparatoires* on article V (1)*(a)* as adopted in 1958 are contained in the following documents:

Draft Convention on the Recognition and Enforcement of Foreign Arbitral Awards and comments by Governments and Organizations:

Report of the Committee on the Enforcement of International Arbitral Awards: E/2704 and Annex.

Comments by Governments and Organizations on the Draft Convention on the Recognition and Enforcement of Foreign Arbitral Awards: E/2822, Annexes I-II; E/CONF.26/3; E/CONF.26/3/Add.1.

Comments on the Draft Convention on the Recognition and Enforcement of Foreign Arbitral Awards: Note by the Secretary General: E/CONF.26/2.

United Nations Conference on International Commercial Arbitration:

Amendments to the Draft Convention Submitted by Governmental Delegations: E/CONF.26/L.17; E/CO.26/L.34.

Comparison of Drafts Relating to Articles III, IV and V of the Draft Convention: E/CONF.26/L.33/Rev.1.

Further Amendments to the Draft Convention Submitted by Governmental Delegations: E/CONF.26/L.40.

Text of Articles III, IV and V of the Draft Convention Proposed by Working Party III: E/CONF.26/L.43.

Text of Articles Adopted by the Conference: E/CONF.26/L.48.

Text of the Convention on the Recognition and Enforcement of Foreign Arbitral Awards as Provisionally Approved by the Drafting Committee: E/CONF.26/L.61; E/CONF.26/8.

New text of Articles I (3), V (1)*(a), (b)*, and *(e)* Adopted by the Conference at its 23rd meeting: E/CONF.26/L.63.

Final Act and Convention on the Recognition and Enforcement of Foreign Arbitral Awards: E/CONF.26/8/Rev.1.

Summary records:

Summary Records of the Eleventh, Thirteenth, Fourteenth, Seventeenth, Twenty-Third and Twenty-Fourth Meetings of the United Nations Conference on International Commercial Arbitration: E/CONF.26/SR.11; E/CONF.26/SR.13; E/CONF.26/SR.14; E/CONF.26/SR.17; E/CONF.26/SR.23; E/CONF.26/SR.24.

Summary Records of the Sixth Meeting of the Committee on Enforcement of International Arbitral Awards: E/AC.42/SR.6.

Committee on the Enforcement of International Arbitral Awards:

Enforcement of International Arbitral Awards: statement submitted by the International Chamber of Commerce, a non-governmental organization having consultative status in category A: E/C.2/373.

Report of the Committee on the Enforcement of International Arbitral Awards: E/AC.42/4.

(Available on the Internet at http://www.uncitral.org)
(For the *travaux préparatoires*, case law and bibliographical references, see also on the Internet at http://newyorkconvention1958.org)

Introduction

1. Article V (1)*(a)* sets forth the first enumerated defence to the recognition and enforcement of a foreign arbitral award. It enables the courts of a Contracting State to refuse recognition and enforcement in two situations: first, if "[t]he parties to the [arbitration] agreement [...] were, under the law applicable to them, under some incapacity" and, second, if the "[arbitration] agreement is not valid under the law to which the parties have subjected it or, failing any indication thereon, under the law of the country where the award was made."

2. The 1927 Geneva Convention addressed these defences to recognition and enforcement in a different manner. Pursuant to article 1*(a)* of the 1927 Geneva Convention, it was for the party seeking recognition and enforcement of an award to prove the validity of an arbitration agreement under the law applicable to it. In accordance with article 2*(b)*, the enforcing court was required to refuse recognition and enforcement of an arbitral award if it was satisfied that "the party against whom it is sought to use the award [...], being under a legal incapacity, [...] was not properly represented [...]".

3. Initially, the draft of the ECOSOC *ad hoc* Committee reiterated only the provision related to the legal incapacity of a party but not that related to the validity of the arbitration agreement.[597] However, during the United Nations Conference on International Commercial Arbitration convened for the preparation and adoption of the Convention, State delegates decided to abandon this provision on the ground that, as reported by the Norwegian delegate, it would be rare in practice for a party to be improperly represented during arbitral proceedings.[598] Furthermore, during the Conference, the drafters of the Convention introduced a provision related to the validity of the arbitration agreement. It was, at first, added as an independent ground for obtaining recognition and enforcement, but then modified to become a ground for refusing to recognize and enforce an arbitral award.[599] This provision was revised to clarify that the "law applicable" to the arbitration

---

[597] See *Travaux préparatoires*, Draft Convention on the Recognition and Enforcement of Foreign Arbitral Awards, Report of the Committee on the Enforcement of International Arbitral Awards, E/2704, E/AC.42/4/ Rev.1, Annex, p. 2. Article IV (*c*) of the ECOSOC draft provided that recognition and enforcement may be refused if "the competent authority in the country where recognition of enforcement is sought, is satisfied: [...] that the party against whom the award is invoked, being under a legal incapacity, was not properly represented."

[598] See *Travaux préparatoires*, Text of the Convention as provisionally approved by the Drafting Committee on 6 June 1958, E/CONF.26/L.61, p. 3; *Travaux préparatoires*, United Nations Conference on International Commercial Arbitration, Summary Records of the Seventeenth Meeting, E/CONF.26/SR.17, p. 9.

[599] See *Travaux préparatoires*, United Nations Conference on International Commercial Arbitration, Summary Records of the Seventeenth Meeting, E/CONF.26/SR.17, p. 3; *Travaux préparatoires*, Text of Articles III, IV and V of the draft Convention proposed by the Working Party for adoption of the Conference, E/CONF.26/L.43, p. 1.

agreement should mean the "national law to which the parties have subjected their agreement, or, failing any indication thereon, under the law of the country where the award was made".[600]

4. It was on the very last day of the Conference that article V (1)*(a)* surfaced in its current form at the recommendation of the Dutch delegate, who proposed to reintroduce a defence based on party incapacity.[601]

5. Article V (1)*(a)* extends the principles enriched in article II to the recognition and enforcement stage. Just as parties cannot be referred to arbitration under article II if they are not bound by a valid arbitration agreement,[602] national courts may deny recognition and enforcement of an award pursuant to article V (1)*(a)* if the consent of the parties is not valid either because the parties lacked the capacity to agree to arbitrate or because the arbitration agreement is invalid under the law applicable to it.

6. While the incapacity defence under article V (1)*(a)* has been of limited relevance in practice, the invalidity of the arbitration agreement defence is often invoked by parties opposing recognition and enforcement of an arbitral award.[603] However, in the majority of reported cases, courts have rejected challenges to recognition and enforcement of an arbitral award based on article V (1)*(a)*.

Analysis

Incapacity of the parties

7. Article V (1)*(a)* provides in its first limb that recognition and enforcement may be refused if "[t]he parties to the agreement referred to in article II were, under the law applicable to them, under some incapacity [...]".

A. Meaning of "the parties to the agreement referred to in article II"

8. Article V (1)*(a)* refers to "the parties to the agreement referred to in article II". This departs from the language of the 1927 Geneva Convention,

---

[600] *Travaux préparatoires,* United Nations Conference on International Commercial Arbitration, Summary Records of the Twenty-third Meeting, E/CONF.26/SR.23, p. 14.

[601] *Travaux préparatoires,* United Nations Conference on International Commercial Arbitration, Summary Records of the Twenty-fourth Meeting, E/CONF.26/SR.24, p. 7.

[602] For a more detailed discussion, see the chapter of the Guide on article II, paras. 13-23.

[603] See. e.g., Stefan Kröll, *Recognition and Enforcement* of *Awards,* in ARBITRATION IN GERMANY: THE MODEL LAW IN PRACTICE 506, 530 (K. H. Böckstiegel, S. Kröll and P. Nacimiento eds., 2007).

which referred to "the party against whom it is sought to use the award".[604] This change in the wording suggests that the incapacity defence may be raised with respect to the party opposing enforcement or the party seeking enforcement.[605] The Italian Court of Cassation confirmed that the party opposing enforcement could raise the incapacity defence with respect to the parties seeking enforcement.[606]

9. Although article V (1)*(a)* refers to the incapacity of "the parties" in the plural, courts have interpreted this provision as meaning that the lack of capacity of one party is sufficient for the enforcing court to deny recognition and enforcement.[607] Commentators have generally supported the reading of article V (1)*(a)* that proof of the incapacity of one, and not necessarily both, of the parties suffices to deny recognition and enforcement of an arbitral award.[608]

B. Concept of incapacity

10. Neither the Convention nor the *travaux préparatoires* define "incapacity".

11. "Capacity" is traditionally defined as the legal ability of a person to act and enter into an agreement in its own name and on its own behalf.[609]

---

[604] See article 2(*b*) of the 1927 Geneva Convention. See also Ignacio Suarez Anzorena, *The Incapacity Defence Under the New York Convention*, in ENFORCEMENT OF ARBITRATION AGREEMENTS AND INTERNATIONAL ARBITRAL AWARDS: THE NEW YORK CONVENTION IN PRACTICE 615, 616-18 (E. Gaillard, D. Di Pietro eds. 2008).

[605] See Patricia Nacimiento, *Article V (1)(a)*, in RECOGNITION AND ENFORCEMENT OF FOREIGN ARBITRAL AWARDS: A GLOBAL COMMENTARY ON THE NEW YORK CONVENTION 205, 218 (H. Kronke, P. Nacimiento et al. eds., 2010); Todd J. Fox, Stephan Wilske, *Commentary* of *Article V (1)(a)*, in NEW YORK CONVENTION ON THE RECOGNITION AND ENFORCEMENT OF FOREIGN ARBITRAL AWARDS OF 10 JUNE 1958—COMMENTARY 267, 271 (R. Wolff ed., 2012).

[606] *Société Arabe des Engrais Phosphates et Azotes—SAEPA and Société Industrielle d'Acide Phosphorique et d'Engrais—SIAPE v. Gemanco srl*, Court of Cassation, Italy, 9 May 1996, XXII Y.B. COM. ARB. 737 (1997).

[607] See, e.g., *Sokofl Star Shipping Co. Inc. v. GPVO Technopromexport*, District Court of Moscow (Civil Department), Russian Federation, 11 April 1997, XXIII Y.B. COM. ARB. 742 (1998); *Agrimpex S.A. v. J.F. Braun & Sons, Inc.*, Supreme Court, Greece, 14 January 1977, IV Y.B. COM. ARB. 269 (1979).

[608] See ALBERT JAN VAN DEN BERG, THE NEW YORK ARBITRATION CONVENTION OF 1958: TOWARDS A UNIFORM JUDICIAL INTERPRETATION 275 (1981) who gives the section on incapacity the title "Incapacity of a party"; Patricia Nacimiento, *Article V (1)(a)*, in RECOGNITION AND ENFORCEMENT OF FOREIGN ARBITRAL AWARDS: A GLOBAL COMMENTARY ON THE NEW YORK CONVENTION 205, 218 (H. Kronke, P. Nacimiento et al. eds., 2010); Todd J. Fox, Stephan Wilske, *Commentary* of *Article V (1)(a)*, in NEW YORK CONVENTION ON THE RECOGNITION AND ENFORCEMENT OF FOREIGN ARBITRAL AWARDS OF 10 JUNE 1958—COMMENTARY 267, 271-72 (R. Wolff ed., 2012).

[609] FOUCHARD GAILLARD GOLDMAN ON INTERNATIONAL COMMERCIAL ARBITRATION 242, para. 453 (E. Gaillard, J. Savage eds., 1999). See also Ignacio Suarez Anzorena, *The Incapacity Defence Under the New York Convention*, in ENFORCEMENT OF ARBITRATION

The text of article V (1)*(a)* confirms that incapacity refers to the legal restriction preventing a party from entering into a legal and binding relationship, here an arbitration agreement, in its own name and on its own account.[610] In the few reported cases, parties have alleged the incapacity of individuals and of legal entities.

12. With respect to the incapacity of individuals, in one Canadian reported case, a party opposed recognition and enforcement on grounds that that party did not have the opportunity to obtain independent legal advice during the negotiation and conclusion of the contract at issue, which contained the arbitration agreement.[611] In interpreting the Canadian law incorporating the UNCITRAL Model Law on International Commercial Arbitration which contains a similar provision to that of article V (1)*(a)*, the court did not object that the incapacity defence could apply in this situation. It, however, ultimately rejected it on the facts as the defendant had failed to show evidence of "oppression, high pressure tactics or misrepresentation."

13. There are no reported cases where recognition has been challenged pursuant to article V (1)*(a)* on the grounds that an arbitration agreement was entered into by a minor or a disabled person. However, commentators generally agree that the incapacity defence should cover the situation in which an individual is unable to judge where its own interest lies.[612]

14. With respect to incapacity of legal entities, national courts have entertained the incapacity defence in relation to both public and private legal entities. The text of the Convention confirms this approach. Indeed, article V (1)*(a)* refers only to a "party" and draws no distinction between public and private entities. Furthermore, article I, which defines the scope of application

---

AGREEMENTS AND INTERNATIONAL ARBITRAL AWARDS: THE NEW YORK CONVENTION IN PRACTICE 615, 621 (E. Gaillard, D. Di Pietro eds., 2008).

[610] Ignacio Suarez Anzorena, *The Incapacity Defence Under the New York Convention*, in ENFORCEMENT OF ARBITRATION AGREEMENTS AND INTERNATIONAL ARBITRAL AWARDS: THE NEW YORK CONVENTION IN PRACTICE 615, 621 (E. Gaillard, D. Di Pietro eds., 2008).

[611] *Grow Biz International Inc. v. D.L.T. Holdings Inc.*, Supreme Court, Province of Prince Edward Island, Canada, 23 March 2001, XXX Y.B. COM. ARB. 450 (2005). See also in a case where the court denied recognition and enforcement because the party was not given proper notice pursuant to Section 103(2) (*c*) of the English 1996 Arbitration Act (implementing article V (1)(*b*) of the Convention) as a result of his serious and life-threatening cancer: *Ajay Kanoria, Esols Worldwide Limited, Indekka Software PVT Ltd. v. Tony Francis Guinness*, Court of Appeal, England and Wales, 21 February 2006, [2006] EWCA Civ 222.

[612] ICCA'S GUIDE TO THE INTERPRETATION OF THE 1958 NEW YORK CONVENTION: A HANDBOOK FOR JUDGES 84 (P. Sanders ed., 2011); FOUCHARD GAILLARD GOLDMAN ON INTERNATIONAL COMMERCIAL ARBITRATION 317, para. 539 (E. Gaillard, J. Savage eds., 1999); also Ignacio Suarez Anzorena, *The Incapacity Defence Under the New York Convention*, in ENFORCEMENT OF ARBITRATION AGREEMENTS AND INTERNATIONAL ARBITRAL AWARDS: THE NEW YORK CONVENTION IN PRACTICE 615, 621, 625, 628 (E. Gaillard, D. Di Pietro eds., 2008).

of the Convention, refers to "persons, whether physical or legal".[613] In this context, parties have, in a number of situations, opposed recognition and enforcement on the grounds of a legal entity's incapacity, although courts have often rejected this defence.

15. First, the District Court of Moscow accepted a challenge to enforcement based on article V (1)*(a)* where an award was rendered in favour of a company which did not exist, as it had never been registered at its purported seat of incorporation.[614]

16. Second, legal entities have challenged enforcement pursuant to article V (1)*(a)* on the grounds that one party was under some legal restriction. For instance, relying on the New York Convention generally, a Syrian court refused to enforce an award rendered against the Syrian Ministry of Defence because the arbitration agreement had been entered into in breach of a Syrian public policy provision requiring the preliminary advice of the Syrian Council of State for the referral of the dispute to arbitration.[615] Conversely, a Russian court confirmed the recognition and enforcement of an award pursuant to the Convention on the ground that no legal restriction prohibited a company's general director from signing the arbitration agreement and binding the company.[616]

17. Third, in a few early cases, courts have confirmed that issues of alleged lack of representative power fall under the incapacity defence of

---

[613] See, e.g., ALBERT JAN VAN DEN BERG, THE NEW YORK ARBITRATION CONVENTION OF 1958: TOWARDS A UNIFORM JUDICIAL INTERPRETATION 276-79 (1981); DOMENICO DI PIETRO, MARTIN PLATTE, ENFORCEMENT OF INTERNATIONAL ARBITRATION AWARDS—THE NEW YORK CONVENTION OF 1958, 138 (Cameron May 2001); FOUCHARD GAILLARD GOLDMAN ON INTERNATIONAL COMMERCIAL ARBITRATION 984, para. 1695 (E. Gaillard, J. Savage eds., 1999); Ignacio Suarez Anzorena, *The Incapacity Defence Under the New York Convention,* in ENFORCEMENT OF ARBITRATION AGREEMENTS AND INTERNATIONAL ARBITRAL AWARDS: THE NEW YORK CONVENTION IN PRACTICE 615, 622 (E. Gaillard, D. Di Pietro eds., 2008); Todd J. Fox, Stephan Wilske, *Commentary* of *Article V (1)(a),* in NEW YORK CONVENTION ON THE RECOGNITION AND ENFORCEMENT OF FOREIGN ARBITRAL AWARDS OF 10 JUNE 1958—COMMENTARY 267, 271 (R. Wolff ed., 2012).

[614] *Sokofl Star Shipping Co. Inc v. GPVO Technopromexport,* District Court of Moscow (Civil Department), Russian Federation, 11 April 1997, XXIII Y.B. COM. ARB. 742 (1998). See also *Sojuznefteexport v. Joc Oil Ltd.,* Court of Appeal, Bermuda, 7 July 1989, XV Y.B. COM. ARB. 384 (1990).

[615] *Fougerollem S.A. v. Ministry* of *Defence* of *the Syrian Arab Republic,* Administrative Tribunal of Damascus, Syria, 31 March 1988, XV Y.B. COM. ARB. 515 (1990). See also *Société Arabe des Engrais Phosphates et Azotes— SAEPA and Société Industrielle d'Acide Phosphorique et d'Engrais—SIAPE v. Gemanco srl,* Court of Appeal of Bari, Italy, 2 November 1993, XXII Y.B. COM. ARB. 737 (1997).

[616] *Dana Feed A/S v. OOO Arctic Salmon,* Federal Arbitrazh Court, Northwestern District, Russian Federation, 9 December 2004, XXXII Y.B. COM. ARB. 658 (2008).

article V (1)*(a)*.[617] The Spanish Supreme Court, for instance, confirmed that issues of alleged powers conferred by a company's board of directors and issues of alleged contractual representative powers, such as those given under a power of attorney, fall under the incapacity defence of article V (1)*(a)*. In this case, the court found that the party opposing recognition and enforcement had not proven that the power of attorney was not valid under the applicable law.[618] In *Dalmine*, the Italian Court of Cassation held that the incapacity defence under article V (1)*(a)* encompasses whether a natural person has the authority to act on behalf of a company pursuant to its constitutional documents, but ultimately rejected the article V (1)*(a)* defence as individuals that had signed the arbitration agreement had the necessary power to conclude it.[619] In another situation, the Austrian Supreme Court held that lack of proper representation could be found where the power of attorney to sign the contract containing the arbitration agreement was invalid. However, in that case, the court found that the party opposing enforcement had failed to show that the party who signed the agreement on its behalf lacked the required authority.[620]

18. Although issues of proper representation and authority differ from that of capacity *stricto sensu*,[621] commentators support the idea that the incapacity defence should extend to situations where legal entities allegedly act *ultra vires* their constitutional documents, or where the representative power is alleged to be invalid.[622]

C. Meaning of the "law applicable to them"

19. Pursuant to article V (1)*(a)*, the incapacity of the parties is to be assessed under "the law applicable to them".[623] It is clear however from the

---

[617] See, e.g., *Ltd. "R.L." v. JSC "Z. Factory"*, Supreme Court, Georgia, 2 April 2004, a-204-sh-43-03; *Agrimpex S.A. v. J.F. Braun & Sons, Inc.*, Supreme Court, Greece, 14 January 1977, IV Y.B. COM. ARB. 269 (1979).

[618] *Unión de Cooperativas Agrícolas Epis-Centre v. La Palentina S.A.*, Supreme Court, Spain, 17 February 1998, XXXVII Y.B. COM. ARB. 533 (2002).

[619] *Dalmine S.p.A. v. M.& M. Sheet Metal Forming Machinery A.G.*, Court of Cassation, Italy, 23 April 1997, XXIV Y.B. COM. ARB. 709 (1999). See also Bundesgerichtshof [BGH], Germany, 23 April 1998, III ZR 194/96.

[620] *K v. F AG*, Oberster Gerichtshof, Austria, 23 October 2007, XXXIII Y.B. COM. ARB. 354 (2008). See also *O Limited v. S GmbH*, Oberster Gerichtshof, Austria, 24 August 2005, XXXII Y.B. COM. ARB. 254 (2007).

[621] EMMANUEL GAILLARD, LE POUVOIR EN DROIT PRIVE 48, para. 64 (Economica 1985).

[622] Ignacio Suarez Anzorena, *The Incapacity Defence Under the New York Convention*, in ENFORCEMENT OF ARBITRATION AGREEMENTS AND INTERNATIONAL ARBITRAL AWARDS: THE NEW YORK CONVENTION IN PRACTICE 615, 623-24 (E. Gaillard, D. Di Pietro eds., 2008); RUSSELL ON ARBITRATION 463 (D. Sutton, J. Gill, M. Gearing eds., 2007).

[623] The expression "under the law applicable to them" was deleted from articles 34 and 36 of the UNCITRAL Model Law on International Commercial Arbitration, because, as explained by the UNCITRAL Secretariat, this expression "was viewed as containing [...]

text of article V (1)*(a)* that the law applicable to the capacity of a party is different from the law governing the validity of an arbitration agreement, as stated in the second part of the provision.[624]

20. As reflected in the *travaux préparatoires* to the Convention, the expression "law applicable to them" was meant to be determined "according to the law governing [a party's] personal status".[625] The Convention is however silent on how to determine the applicable law.

21. Courts applying article V (1)*(a)* have followed different approaches in choosing the law applicable to determine a party's capacity, depending on what is being alleged by the party opposing recognition and enforcement: (i) the incapacity of a party *stricto sensu*, or (ii) the lack of authority of the party to enter into an agreement on behalf of another party.

22. In the few cases addressing the issue of incapacity of a natural or legal person *stricto sensu*, courts have generally determined the law applicable to that party's capacity pursuant to their own system of law. For instance, when deciding on a challenge to enforcement under article V (1)*(a)*, the Spanish Supreme Court applied Spanish conflict of laws rule to determine that the capacity of a party should be assessed pursuant to its personal law, i.e., the law of the nationality of that party.[626] With respect to the capacity of an individual, commentators have distinguished between civil law jurisdictions, where such capacity is generally governed by the law of the person's nationality, and common law jurisdictions, where it is generally governed by the law of the person's domicile or habitual residence.[627] As regards the capacity *stricto sensu* of legal persons, in many jurisdictions, the

---

potentially misleading conflict-of-law rule": Explanatory Note by the UNCITRAL Secretariat on the Model Law on International Commercial Arbitration, para. 54. See also Summary Records of the 317th meeting of the United Nations Commission on International Trade Law for meetings devoted to the preparation of the UNCITRAL Model Law on International Commercial Arbitration, A/CN.9/246, Annex, Yearbook of the United Nations Commission on International Trade Law, 1985, Vol. XVI, 446.

[624] See, e.g., FOUCHARD GAILLARD GOLDMAN ON INTERNATIONAL COMMERCIAL ARBITRATION 984, para. 1695 (E. Gaillard, J. Savage eds., 1999); ALBERT JAN VAN DEN BERG, THE NEW YORK ARBITRATION CONVENTION OF 1958: TOWARDS A UNIFORM JUDICIAL INTERPRETATION 277 (1981).

[625] *Travaux préparatoires,* United Nations Conference on International Commercial Arbitration, Summary Records of the Twenty-fourth Meeting, E/CONF.26/SR.24, p. 7.

[626] *Unión de Cooperativas Agrícolas Epis-Centre v. La Palentina S.A.,* Supreme Court, Spain, 17 February 1998, XXVII Y.B. COM. ARB. 533 (2002).

[627] ALBERT JAN VAN DEN BERG, THE NEW YORK ARBITRATION CONVENTION OF 1958: TOWARDS A UNIFORM JUDICIAL INTERPRETATION 276 (1981); Patricia Nacimiento, *Article V (1)(a),* in RECOGNITION AND ENFORCEMENT OF FOREIGN ARBITRAL AWARDS: A GLOBAL COMMENTARY ON THE NEW YORK CONVENTION 205, 219 (H. Kronke, P. Nacimiento et al. eds., 2010); Stefan Kröll, *Recognition and Enforcement* of *Awards,* in ARBITRATION IN GERMANY: THE MODEL LAW IN PRACTICE 506, 528-29 (K. H. Böckstiegel, S. Kröll, P. Nacimiento eds., 2007).

applicable law will be the law of the place of incorporation or the place of business of the entity at issue.[628]

23. In cases that concern challenging the authority of a party to conclude an arbitration agreement on behalf of another party, some courts have assessed the validity of a party's power to conclude an arbitration agreement on behalf of another party pursuant to the personal law of the party that was purportedly bound by the arbitration agreement.[629] For instance, in *La Palentina*, the Spanish Supreme Court held that when the act of representation is carried out by a company's organs, the national law of that entity will apply.[630] When the authority of a party to conclude an arbitration agreement on behalf of another party is based on a power of attorney, a German court held that its validity should be assessed pursuant to the law of the State where the power of attorney was to be exercised.[631]

D. Relevant time for incapacity

24. Article V (1)*(a)* of the Convention does not specify the point in time at which a party must be under an incapacity. However, the use of the past tense in article V (1)*(a)* "[...] that the parties were [...] under some incapacity" indicates that incapacity should be assessed at the time of conclusion of [the contract containing] the arbitration agreement.[632] The drafters of the New York Convention sought to abandon the approach

---

628 ALBERT JAN VAN DEN BERG, THE NEW YORK ARBITRATION CONVENTION OF 1958: TOWARDS A UNIFORM JUDICIAL INTERPRETATION 276 (1981); Patricia Nacimiento, *Article V (1)(a),* in RECOGNITION AND ENFORCEMENT OF FOREIGN ARBITRAL AWARDS: A GLOBAL COMMENTARY ON THE NEW YORK CONVENTION 205, 220 (H. Kronke, P. Nacimiento et al. eds., 2010); Stefan Kröll, *Recognition and Enforcement* of *Awards,* in ARBITRATION IN GERMANY: THE MODEL LAW IN PRACTICE 528-29 (K. H. Böckstiegel, S. Kröll, P. Nacimiento eds., 2007) for the position in Germany.

629 See, e.g., *Dana Feed A/S v. OOO Artic Salmon*, Federal Arbitrazh Court, Northwestern District, Russian Federation, 9 December 2004, XXXIII Y.B. COM. ARB. 658 (2008).

630 *Unión de Cooperativas Agrícolas Epis-Centre v. La Palentina S.A.*, Supreme Court, Spain, 17 February 1998, XXXVII Y.B. COM. ARB. 533 (2002). See also *Dalmine S.p.A. v. M.&M. Sheet Metal Forming Machinery A.G.,* Court of Cassation, Italy, 23 April 1997, XXIV Y.B. COM. ARB. 709 (1999).

631 Oberlandesgericht [OLG] Celle, Germany, 4 September 2003, XXX Y.B. COM. ARB. 528 (2005).

632 See Ignacio Suarez Anzorena, *The Incapacity Defence Under the New York Convention*, in ENFORCEMENT OF ARBITRATION AGREEMENTS AND INTERNATIONAL ARBITRAL AWARDS: THE NEW YORK CONVENTION IN PRACTICE 615, 631 (E. Gaillard, D. Di Pietro eds., 2008); Patricia Nacimiento, *Article V (1)(a),* in RECOGNITION AND ENFORCEMENT OF FOREIGN ARBITRAL AWARDS: A GLOBAL COMMENTARY ON THE NEW YORK CONVENTION 205, 218 (H. Kronke, P. Nacimiento et al. eds., 2010); Todd J. Fox, Stephan Wilske, *Commentary* of *Article V (1)(a)*, in NEW YORK CONVENTION ON THE RECOGNITION AND ENFORCEMENT OF FOREIGN ARBITRAL AWARDS OF 10 JUNE 1958—COMMENTARY 267, 272 (R. Wolff ed., 2012).

followed under the 1927 Geneva Convention, which focused on improper representation during the arbitral proceedings.[633]

25. With very few exceptions,[634] courts have assessed the capacity of a party at the time of conclusion of the arbitration agreement. For example, the Italian Court of Cassation accepted that the point in time at which representative capacity should be examined under article V (1)*(a)* was the time of conclusion of the arbitration agreement.[635] In more recent decisions, courts in the United States,[636] Russian Federation[637] and Canada[638] have followed the same approach.

Invalidity of the arbitration agreement

26. The second limb of article V (1)*(a)* provides that recognition and enforcement may be refused on the ground that the arbitration agreement "is not valid under the law to which the parties have subjected it or, failing any indication thereon, under the law of the country where the award was made."

27. Courts have generally determined the validity of an arbitration agreement within the meaning of article V (1)*(a)* by following the conflict of laws rule set out in that provision. Certain courts have however considered that the reference to article II in article V (1)*(a)* requires the validity of the arbitration agreement to be determined pursuant to the form requirements set by article II.

A. The choice of law rule under article V (1)*(a)*

28. Article V (1)*(a)* provides that validity of an arbitration agreement is to be determined "under the law to which the parties have subjected it", or "failing any indication thereon", "under the law of the country where the award was made".

---

633 See *Travaux préparatoires*: United Nations Conference on International Commercial Arbitration, Summary Records of Seventeenth Meeting, E/CONF.26/SR.17, p. 9.

634 See *James P. Corcoran, Superintendent of Insurance of the State of New York et al. v. Ardra Insurance Co. Ltd., Richard A. and Jeanne S. DiLoreto*, Supreme Court of New York County, United States of America, 10 April 1990, XVI Y.B. COM. ARB. 663 (1991).

635 *Dalmine S.p.A. v. M.& M. Sheet Metal Forming Machinery A.G.*, Court of Cassation, Italy, 23 April 1997, XXIV Y.B. COM. ARB. 709 (1999).

636 *Seung Woo Lee, as Co-Receiver for Medison Co. Ltd. a Korean corporation and others v. Imaging3, Inc. and others*, Court of Appeals, Ninth Circuit, United States of America, 19 June 2008, 06-55993, XXXIII Y.B. COM. ARB. 1180 (2008); *China National Building Material Investment Co. Ltd. v. BNK International LLC*, District Court, Western District of Texas, Austin Division, United States of America, 3 December 2009, A-09-CA-488-SS.

637 *Dana Feed A/S v. OOO Arctic Salmon*, Federal Arbitrazh Court, Northwestern District, Russian Federation, 9 December 2004, XXXIII Y.B. COM. ARB. 658 (2008).

638 *Grow Biz International Inc. v. D.L.T. Holdings Inc.*, Supreme Court, Province of Prince Edward Island, Canada, 23 March 2001, XXX Y.B. COM. ARB. 450 (2005).

a. *The primacy of the parties' choice of law*

29. Pursuant to article V (1)*(a)*, the invalidity of an arbitration agreement shall, in the first instance, be assessed pursuant to the law chosen by the parties.[639] Accordingly, courts have often applied the law chosen by the parties to govern the main agreement, or the law chosen by the parties governing the arbitral procedure, as an implicit choice of law governing the arbitration agreement.

30. In practice, parties seldom expressly choose the law to govern their arbitration agreement. In reported case law, courts have looked to other factors to find that the parties have implicitly chosen the law to govern the arbitration agreement. For instance, a United States court held that the choice of the parties with respect to the law governing the arbitral proceedings amounted to an implicit choice of law regarding the validity of the arbitration agreement.[640] In another case, the Egyptian Court of Cassation ruled that the law governing the parties' main agreement should also govern the validity of the arbitration agreement.[641] The Egyptian Court of Cassation found that because the parties chose Swedish law to govern their contract, that law should apply to the arbitration agreement in order to determine its validity within the meaning of article V (1)*(a)*.

b. *The applicable law in the absence of the parties' choice*

31. Where the parties have not expressly or implicitly selected a law to govern their arbitration agreement, courts have turned to the subsidiary rule and have assessed the validity of an arbitration agreement under the "law of the country where the award was made" pursuant to article V (1)*(a)*.[642]

---

[639] See, e.g., *Mabofi Holdings Limited v. RosGas A.G.*, Federal Arbitrazh Court for the Moscow District, Russian Federation, 24 January 2012, A40-65888/11-8/553; Supreme Court, Spain, 10 February 1984, X Y.B. COM. ARB. 493 (1985). See also Patricia Nacimiento, *Article V (1)(a)*, in RECOGNITION AND ENFORCEMENT OF FOREIGN ARBITRAL AWARDS: A GLOBAL COMMENTARY ON THE NEW YORK CONVENTION 205, 227 (H. Kronke, P. Nacimiento et al. eds., 2010); ALBERT JAN VAN DEN BERG, THE NEW YORK ARBITRATION CONVENTION OF 1958: TOWARDS A UNIFORM JUDICIAL INTERPRETATION 282 (1981); Todd J. Fox, Stephan Wilske, *Commentary* of *Article V (1)(a)*, in NEW YORK CONVENTION ON THE RECOGNITION AND ENFORCEMENT OF FOREIGN ARBITRAL AWARDS OF 10 JUNE 1958—COMMENTARY 267, 275 (R. Wolff ed., 2012).

[640] *Telenor Mobile Communications AS v. Storm LLC*, District Court, Southern District of New York, United States of America, 2 November 2007, 524 F. Supp. 2d 332.

[641] *Egyptian Company for Concrete & Hashem Ali Maher v. STC Finance & Ismail Ibrahim Mahmoud Thabet & Sabishi Trading and Contracting Company*, Court of Cassation, Egypt, 27 March 1996, 2660/59. See also *Stena RoRo AB v. OAO Baltiysky Zavod*, Highest Arbitrazh Court, Russian Federation, 13 September 2011, A56-60007/2008; *Ltd. "R.L." v. JSC "Z. Factory"*, Supreme Court, Georgia, 2 April 2004, a-204-sh-43-03.

[642] See, e.g., *Rocco Giuseppe e Figli s.n.c. v. Federal Commerce and Navigation Ltd.*, Court of Cassation, Italy, 15 December 1982, X Y.B. COM. ARB. 464 (1985); *Official Receiver*

32. For instance, the Supreme Court of Austria, in assessing the validity of an arbitration agreement under article V (1)*(a)* held that, since neither party had contended that the arbitration agreement was governed by a particular law, its validity would be assessed according to the law of the country where the arbitral award was made.[643]

33. In a few reported cases, courts have looked directly to the law of the country where the award was made without expressly examining whether the parties had chosen a law applicable to the arbitration agreement.[644] In these cases, the challenging parties have not expressly relied on any law chosen by the parties to govern the validity of the arbitration agreement. For example, the Svea Court of Appeal, in assessing the validity of an arbitration agreement, applied the law of the country where the award was made, without first expressly considering whether the parties had explicitly or implicitly selected a governing law for the arbitration agreement.[645]

34. The Convention is silent on how to determine where the award "was made." Courts have, with the exception of one reported case,[646] determined that the seat of arbitration as determined in the arbitration agreement was the place where the award was "made".[647] For example, the English High Court in *Dallah* noted that the validity of the arbitration agreement was to be assessed according to the law of the country where the award was made, i.e., the law of the country of the seat of arbitration.[648] The court concluded that

---

in the bankruptcy of *Lanificio Walter Banci S.a.s. v. Bobbie Brooks Inc.,* Court of Cassation, Italy, 15 April 1980, VI Y.B. COM. ARB. 233 (1981); Supreme Court, Spain, 10 February 1984, X Y.B. COM. ARB. 493 (1985).

643 *K v. F AG,* Oberster Gerichtshof, Austria, 23 October 2007, XXXIII Y.B. COM. ARB. 354 (2008).

644 *G. A. Pap-KG Holzgrosshandlung v. Ditta Giovanni G. Pecoraro,* Court of Appeal of Naples (Salerno Section), Italy, 13 February 1978, VI Y.B. COM. ARB. 228 (1981). See also where the decision does not make any reference to the parties' agreement: *United States VOEST ALPINE International Trade Company v. Jiangsu Provincial Foreign Trade Corporation,* Nanjing Intermediate People's Court, China, 13 April 2009, (2008) Ning Min Wu Chu Zi No. 43.

645 *Planavergne S.A., Fontanes v. Kalle Bergander i Stockholm AB,* Svea Court of Appeal, Sweden, 7 September 2001, T 4645-99.

646 *Richard Henry Moffit Outhwaite v. Robert Ralph Scrymegeour Hiscox,* House of Lord, England and Wales, 24 July 1991, XVII Y.B. COM. ARB. 599 (1992). In this case, the House of Lords determined that the award is "made" at the place where it is signed and not at the seat of arbitration designated by the parties.

647 See, e.g., *K v. F AG,* Oberster Gerichtshof, Austria, 23 October 2007, XXXIII Y.B. COM. ARB. 354 (2008); Supreme Court, Spain, 10 February 1984, X Y.B. COM. ARB. 493 (1985); *Shandong Textiles Import and Export Corporation v. Da Hua Non-ferous Metals Company Limited,* Court of First Instance, High Court of the Hong Kong Special Administrative Region, Hong Kong, 6 March 2002, HCCT 80/1997.

648 *Dallah Real Estate and Tourism Holding Company v. Ministry* of *Religious Affairs,* Government of Pakistan, High Court of Justice, England and Wales, 1 August 2008, [2008] EWHC 1901, upheld by *Dallah Real Estate and Tourism Holding Company v. Ministry* of *Religious Affairs,* Government of Pakistan, Court of Appeal, England and Wales, 20 July 2009,

the seat of arbitration being in France, the validity of the arbitration agreement ought to be assessed pursuant to French law. Similarly, a Dutch court reasoned that, given the absence of a determination as to the law governing the arbitration agreement and the fact that the arbitration clause designated England as the seat of arbitration, English law would apply to determine the validity of the arbitration agreement.[649]

35. It is well established in arbitral practice, as well as reflected in institutions' arbitral rules and in arbitration laws, that an award is made at the seat of the arbitration.[650]

B. Meaning of "invalidity"

36. Reported case law shows that parties have seldom been successful in opposing recognition and enforcement of an arbitral award pursuant to article V (1)*(a)* on the ground that the arbitration agreement was invalid.

37. In a number of cases, the party opposing recognition and enforcement argued that a defect in the main agreement rendered the arbitration agreement invalid. Courts have generally dismissed this argument pursuant to the principle of severability, which holds that an arbitration agreement is legally independent from the underlying contract which contains it, and the nullity of a contract does not imply that the arbitration agreement therein is invalid.[651]

2008/2613; *Dallah Real Estate and Tourism Holding Company v. Ministry* of *Religious Affairs,* Government of Pakistan, Supreme Court, United Kingdom, 3 November 2010, UKSC 2009/0165.

[649] *Société d'Etudes et de Commerce SA v. Weyl Beef Products BV, Arrondissementsrechtbank,* Court of First Instance of Almelo, Netherlands, 19 July 2000, XXVI Y.B. COM. ARB. 827 (2001).

[650] See, e.g., Article 31(3) of the ICC Rules (2012) ("The award shall be deemed to be made at the place of the arbitration and on the date stated therein"); Article 31(3) of the UNCITRAL Model Law on International Commercial Arbitration ("The award shall state its date and the place of arbitration as determined in accordance with article 20(1). The award shall be deemed to have been made at that place"); Section 53 of the English Arbitration Act 1996 ("Unless otherwise agreed by the parties, where the seat of the arbitration is in England and Wales, or Northern Ireland, any award in the proceedings shall be treated as made there, regardless of where it was signed, despatched or delivered to any of the parties").

[651] See, e.g., *Altain Khuder LLC v. IMC Mining Inc and IMC Mining Solutions Pty Ltd,* Supreme Court of Victoria, Australia, 28 January 2011; *China Minmetals Materials Import & Export Co. v. Chi Mei Corp.,* Court of Appeals, Third Circuit, United States of America, 26 June 2003, 02-2897 and 02-3542; *International Investor Kcsc v. Sanghi Polyesters Ltd.,* High Court of Andhra, India, 9 September 2002, Civil Revision Petition Nos 331 and 1441 of 2002; Oberlandesgericht [OLG] Koblenz, Germany, 28 July 2005, 2 Sch 4/05; Oberlandesgericht [OLG] Hamburg, Germany, 12 March 1998, XXIX Y.B. COM. ARB. 663 (2004); Oberlandesgericht [OLG] Saarbrücken, Germany, 30 May 2011, 4 Sch 03/10. For a more detailed analysis on the issue of severability, see the chapter of the Guide on article II, paras. 105-07.

38. In some cases, parties have argued that the arbitration agreement was invalid pursuant to article V (1)*(a)* on the ground that one of the parties had not signed the arbitration agreement. For instance, in *Dallah*, the Supreme Court of the United Kingdom denied enforcement of an award on the ground that one party to the award was not validly bound by the arbitration agreement.[652] Conversely, the Supreme Court of Victoria in *IMC Mining Solutions*, in assessing a challenge based on Section 8(5)*(a)* of the Australian International Arbitration Act of 1974 (implementing article V (1)*(a)* of the Convention), held that the party which had allegedly not signed the arbitration agreement was validly bound by it in accordance with the law applicable to the arbitration agreement, which was different from the law applicable to the main agreement.[653] Similarly, a Swiss court enforced an arbitral award rendered on the basis of an arbitration agreement by reference despite it not being signed by one of the parties.[654] In some jurisdictions, courts have ruled that, despite not having signed the arbitration agreement, a party's behaviour in the arbitral proceedings, including its participation therein, could constitute a valid arbitration agreement within the meaning of article V (1)*(a)*.[655]

C. Formal validity of an arbitration agreement

39. Although article V (1)*(a)* sets outs the choice of law rules for assessing the validity of the arbitration agreement, parties opposing enforcement have often argued that enforcement should be denied on the basis that the arbitration agreement fails to comply with the form requirements of article II.[656]

40. In one reported case, the Italian Court of Cassation held that the requirements of article II do not apply in the context of assessing the validity of the arbitration agreement pursuant to article V (1)*(a)*.[657] The court

---

[652] *Dallah Real Estate and Tourism Holding Company v. Ministry of Religious Affairs,* Government of Pakistan, Supreme Court, United Kingdom, 3 November 2010, UKSC 2009/0165.

[653] *Altain Khuder LLC v. IMC Mining Inc and IMC Mining Solutions Pty Ltd,* Supreme Court of Victoria, Australia, 28 January 2011.

[654] Camera di esecuzione e fallimenti del Tribunale d'appello, Repubblica e Cantone Ticino, Switzerland, 22 February 2010, 14.2009.104.

[655] *Comverse Inc. v. American Telecommunications do Brazil Ltda,* Superior Court of Justice, Brazil, 14 June 2012, SEC 3.709; *China National Building Material Investment Co. Ltd. v. BNK International LLC,* District Court, Western District of Texas, Austin Division, United States of America, 3 December 2009, A-09-CA-488-SS. See also the cases referenced in the chapter of the Guide on article II, para. 22.

[656] For a more detailed discussion on the form requirements in article II (2), see the chapter of the Guide on article II, paras. 36-57.

[657] *Official Receiver in the bankruptcy of Lanificio Walter Banci S.a.s. v. Bobbie Brooks Inc.,* Court of Cassation, Italy, 15 April 1980, VI Y.B. COM. ARB. 233 (1981). See also G. HAIGHT, CONVENTION ON THE RECOGNITION AND ENFORCEMENT OF FOREIGN ARBITRAL AWARDS: SUMMARY ANALYSIS OF RECORD OF UNITED NATIONS CONFERENCE 51 (1958).

reasoned that an arbitration agreement that fails to comply with the form requirement of article II could be held valid under article V (1)*(a)*, as article V deals with recognition and enforcement of arbitral awards whereas article II deals with recognition and enforcement of arbitration agreements.

41. In a number of reported cases, however, courts have assessed the validity of the arbitration agreement pursuant to the form requirements of article II.[658] As explained by a United States appeals court in China Minmetals, articles II, IV (1)*(b)* and V (1)*(a)* of the Convention contemplate as a whole that an enforcing court should enforce only valid agreements to arbitrate and only awards based on those agreements.[659]

42. In this context, courts have generally accepted that, if the arbitration agreement fails to comply with the form requirements of article II, enforcement will still be ordered if, on the basis of the more-favourable-right provision at article VII (1), the agreement complies with the more liberal rules of the jurisdiction where enforcement is sought.[660] In a series of decisions, German courts have applied the more favourable provisions of the German Code of Civil Procedure at the award enforcement stage to assess the validity of an arbitration agreement under article V (1)*(a)*.[661]

---

[658] See, e.g., *Concordia Trading B.V. v. Nantong Gangde Oil Co., Ltd,* Supreme People's Court, China, 3 August 2009, [2009] MinSiTaZi No. 22; *Misr Foreign Trade Co. v. R.D Harboties (Mercantile),* Court of Cassation, Egypt, 22 January 2008, 2010/64; Oberlandesgericht [OLG] Celle, Germany, 18 September 2003, 8 Scg 12/02; *C S.A. v. E. Corporation,* Court of Justice of Geneva, Switzerland, 14 April 1983, 187; *Agrimpex S.A. v. J.F. Braun & Sons, Inc.,* Supreme Court, Greece, 14 January 1977, IV Y.B. COM. ARB. 269 (1979); Landgericht [LG] Bremen, Germany, 8 June 1967, 11-OH 11/1966. See also a decision rendered in Russian Federation applying the same reasoning without mentioning article II: *Lugana Handelsgesellschaft mbH (Germany) v. OAO Ryazan Metal Ceramics Instrumentation Plant (Russian Federation),* Presidium of the Highest Arbitrazh Court, Russian Federation, 2 February 2010, A54-3028/2008-S10. For a more detailed discussion on the forms requirement in article II (2), see the chapter of the Guide on article II, paras. 36-57.

[659] *China Minmetals Materials Import & Export Co. v. Chi Mei Corp.,* Court of Appeals, Third Circuit, United States of America, 26 June 2003, 02-2897 and 02-3542.

[660] See, e.g., *Société Bomar Oil N.V. v. Entreprise tunisienne d'activités pétrolières (ETAP),* Court of Appeal of Versailles, France, 23 January 1991, 1994 REV. ARB. 108; *Ste A.B.S. American Bureau* of *Shipping v. Copropriété Maritime Jules Verne et autres,* Court of Appeal of Paris, France, 4 December 2002, 2001/17293, 2006 REV. ARB. 945.

[661] Oberlandesgericht [OLG] Celle, Germany, 14 December 2006, 8 Sch 14/05. See also Oberlandesgericht [OLG] Celle, Germany, 18 September 2003, 8 Sch 12/02; Oberlandesgericht [OLG] Frankfurt, Germany, 18 October 2007, 26 Sch 1/07; Bundesgerichtshof [BGH] Germany, 30 September 2010, III ZB 69/09; Bundesgerichtshof [BGH] Germany, 21 September 2005, XXXI Y.B. COM. ARB. 679 (2006). See *contra* Oberlandesgericht [OLG] Schleswig, Germany, 30 March 2000, 16 SchH 05/99. For a more detailed discussion on the relationship between article II and article VII, see the chapter of the Guide on article VII, paras. 31-35.

Procedural issues arising in connection with article V (1)*(a)*

A. Burden of proof

43. Article V (1) provides that the party against whom the award is invoked must furnish proof of the ground for denying recognition and enforcement of an arbitral award.

44. With respect to article V (1)*(a)*, courts have typically ruled that it is for the party opposing recognition and enforcement to prove either that one of the parties was under some legal incapacity at the time of the conclusion of the arbitration agreement or that the arbitration agreement was invalid under the applicable law.[662] The party seeking recognition and enforcement only bears the burden of supplying documentary evidence of the arbitration agreement pursuant to article IV (1)*(b)*, which provides that the party applying for recognition and enforcement shall supply the original arbitration agreement or a copy thereof.[663]

45. For example, the Court of Appeal of England and Wales in *Yukos Oil Company v. Dardana Ltd.* held that, once the party seeking enforcement has provided *prima facie* evidence of the existence of the arbitration agreement, the burden shifts to the party opposing enforcement to prove any of the grounds for refusal under article V (1), including that the parties never entered into a valid arbitration agreement under article V (1)*(a)*.[664] Courts in other jurisdictions including those in Italy,[665] Spain,[666] Austria,[667] Australia,[668] and Bermuda[669] have followed the same approach.

---

662 See generally: *O Limited v. S GmbH,* Oberster Gerichtshof, Austria, 24 August 2005, XXXII Y.B. COM. ARB. 254 (2007). For cases concerning the incapacity defence, see, e.g, *Dalmine S.p.A. v. M.& M. Sheet Metal Forming Machinery A.G.,* Court of Cassation, Italy, 23 April 1997, XXIV Y.B. COM. ARB. 709 (1999); *Grow Biz International Inc. v. D.L.T. Holdings Inc.,* Supreme Court, Province of Prince Edward Island, Canada, 23 March 2001, XXX Y.B. COM. ARB. 450 (2005); *China National Building Material Investment Co. Ltd. v. BNK International LLC,* District Court for the Western District of Texas, Austin Division, United States of America, 3 December 2009, A-09-CA-488-SS. For cases concerning the invalidity of the arbitration agreement, see, e.g., *Dallah Real Estate and Tourism Holding Company v. Ministry of Religious Affairs, Government of Pakistan,* Supreme Court, United Kingdom, 3 November 2010, UKSC 2009/0165; *Altain Khuder LLC v. IMC mining Inc and IMC Mining Solutions Pty Ltd,* Supreme Court of Victoria, Australia, 28 January 2011.

663 For a more detailed analysis on article IV (1)(*b*), see the chapter of the Guide on article IV, paras. 62-75.

664 *Yukos Oil Company v. Dardana Ltd,* Court of Appeal, England and Wales, 18 April 2002, A3/2001/1029. See also *Dallah Real Estate and Tourism Holding Company v. Ministry of Religious Affairs,* Government of Pakistan, Supreme Court, United Kingdom, 3 November 2010, UKSC 2009/0165.

665 *Jassica S.A. v. Ditta Gioacchino Polojaz,* Court of Cassation, Italy, 12 February 1987, XVII Y.B. COM. ARB. 525 (1992).

46. However, certain courts have required the party seeking enforcement to prove that the arbitration agreement was valid in order to rely on it. Certain German courts, on the basis of the reference in article V (1)*(a)* to the "agreement referred to in Article II", have ruled that the party relying on the arbitration agreement has the onus of proving its conformity with the requirements of article II.[670]

47. The text and the drafting history of the Convention suggest that the applicant should only prove *prima facie* the existence of the arbitration agreement while the party opposing recognition and enforcement has the onus of proving its invalidity.[671] Commentators have generally favoured this approach.[672]

B. Relevance of the findings of arbitral tribunals or courts

48. Article V (1)*(a)* is silent with respect to the standard of judicial review by enforcing courts.

49. In assessing challenges to recognition and enforcement under article V (1)*(a)*, certain courts have decided matters related to the jurisdiction of the arbitral tribunal and the validity of the arbitration agreement *de novo*. For instance, in *China Minmetals*, a United States appeals court held that it "must make an independent determination of the agreement's validity [...] at least in

---

666 *Union Générale de Cinéma, S.A. (France) v. X Y Z Desarrollos, S.A. (Spain)*, Supreme Court, Spain, 11 April 2000, 3536 of 1998, XXXII Y.B. COM. ARB. 525 (2007); *Strategic Bulk Carriers Inc. (Liberia) v. Sociedad Ibérica de Molturación, S.A. (Spain)*, Supreme Court, Spain, 26 February 2002, 153 of 2001, XXXII Y.B. COM. ARB. 550 (2007).

667 *Seller v. Buyer*, Supreme Court, Austria, 22 May 1991, XXI Y.B. COM. ARB. 521 (1996).

668 See also *Altain Khuder LLC v. IMC mining Inc and IMC Mining Solutions Pty Ltd*, Supreme Court of Victoria, Australia, 28 January 2011.

669 *Sojuznefteexport (SNE) v. Joc Oil Ltd.*, Court of Appeal of Bermuda, Bermuda, 7 July 1989, XV Y.B. COM. ARB. 384 (1990).

670 Oberlandesgericht [OLG] München, Germany, 12 October 2009, XXXV Y.B. COM. ARB. 383 (2010); Oberlandesgericht [OLG] Celle, Germany, 4 September 2003, XXX Y.B. COM. ARB. 528 (2005). See also with respect to Switzerland: Federal Tribunal, Switzerland, 31 May 2002, 4P.102/2001; *C S.A. v. E. Corporation*, Court of Justice of Geneva, Switzerland, 14 April 1983, 187.

671 See *Travaux préparatoires*, United Nations Conference on International Commercial Arbitration, Summary Record of the Eleventh Meeting, E/CONF.26/SR.11, p. 12.

672 FOUCHARD GAILLARD GOLDMAN ON INTERNATIONAL COMMERCIAL ARBITRATION 968, para. 1673 (E. Gaillard, J. Savage eds., 1999); Todd J. Fox, Stephan Wilske, *Commentary of Article V (1)(a)*, in NEW YORK CONVENTION ON THE RECOGNITION AND ENFORCEMENT OF FOREIGN ARBITRAL AWARDS OF 10 JUNE 1958— COMMENTARY 267, 278, para. 126 (R. Wolff ed., 2012); Patricia Nacimiento, *Article V (1)(a)*, in RECOGNITION AND ENFORCEMENT OF FOREIGN ARBITRAL AWARDS: A GLOBAL COMMENTARY ON THE NEW YORK CONVENTION 205, 211 (H. Kronke, P. Nacimiento et al. eds., 2010).

the absence of a waiver precluding the defence."[673] In *Dallah*, the Supreme Court of the United Kingdom referred to *China Minmetals* and noted that article V (1)*(a)* does not restrict the nature of the review to be carried out by the court asked to enforce the award.[674] Similarly, in Germany, some courts have found that they were not bound by the arbitral tribunal's findings on jurisdiction, including issues relating to the incapacity of a party and the invalidity of the arbitration agreement.[675]

50. In the United States, certain courts have held that, under article V (1)*(a)*, a court could not or should not review *de novo* the findings of the arbitral tribunal with respect to its own jurisdiction.[676] Other courts on the contrary have considered that they have jurisdiction to review factual and legal questions to determine jurisdiction unless there is "clear and unmistakable evidence" that the parties intended to submit this issue to the arbitrators.[677] They have been lenient in finding such "clear and unmistakable evidence" and have accepted that evidence of the parties' consent to submit the issue of jurisdiction to the arbitral tribunal may be found in the arbitral rules selected by the parties. For instance, in the context of an award rendered on the basis of a bilateral investment treaty, a United States Court of Appeals held that the parties' choice of the UNCITRAL Arbitration Rules (providing that the tribunal has the power to rule on objections that it has no jurisdiction) constituted "clear and unmistakable evidence" of their intent to arbitrate issues going to the jurisdiction of the arbitral tribunal.[678]

---

[673] *China Minmetals Materials Import & Export Co. v. Chi Mei Corp.,* Court of Appeals, Third Circuit, United States of America, 26 June 2003, 02-2897 and 02-3542.

[674] *Dallah Real Estate and Tourism Holding Company v. Ministry of Religious Affairs,* Government of Pakistan, Supreme Court, United Kingdom, 3 November 2010, UKSC 2009/0165.

[675] Oberlandesgericht [OLG] Schleswig, Germany, 30 March 2000, 16 SchH 5/99; Oberlandesgericht [OLG] Celle, Germany, 18 September 2003, 8 Sch 12/02. See also Oberlandesgericht [OLG] Celle, Germany, 4 September 2003, 8 Sch 11/02, XXX Y.B. COM. ARB. 528 (2005) (although the Court did not relied on article V (1)(a) of the Convention), and with respect to the second limb of article V (1)(*a*), see Oberlandesgericht [OLG] Celle, Germany, 14 December 2006, 8 Sch 14/05.

[676] *Thai-Lao Lignite Co. Ltd. et al. v. Government of the Lao People's Democratic Republic,* District Court, Southern District of New York, United States of America, 3 August 2011, 10 Civ. 5256 (KMW); *Joseph Walker and Company, LLC. v. Oceanic Fats and Oil(s) Pte, Ltd.,* District Court, District of Columbia, United States of America, 11 September 2002, 01-2693.

[677] *Sarhank Group v. Oracle Corporation,* Court of Appeals, Second Circuit, United States of America, 14 April 2005, 02-9383.

[678] *Werner Schneider, acting in his capacity as insolvency administrator of Walter Bau AG (In Liquidation) v. the Kingdom* of *Thailand,* Court of Appeals, Second Circuit, United States of America, 8 August 2012, 11-1458-cv. See also *Republic* of *Ecuador v. Chevron Corp.,* Court of Appeals, Second Circuit, United States of America, 17 March 2011, 10-1020-cv (L), 10-1026 (Con).

51. Other courts have directly relied on the findings of the arbitral tribunal in assessing its jurisdiction under an arbitration agreement.[679] For example, the Svea Court of Appeal relied on the findings of the arbitral tribunal to hold the arbitration agreement valid within the meaning of article V (1)*(a)*. In so ruling, it reviewed neither the legal nor the factual arguments presented by the party opposing recognition and enforcement.[680]

52. Going one step further, certain courts have refrained from examining factual or legal issues as they are prohibited from reviewing the merits of an award. For example, the Highest Arbitrazh Court in Russian Federation ruled that under article V (1) of the Convention, it "[did] not have the right to re-examine a foreign arbitral award on the merits". It therefore relied on the findings of the arbitral tribunal regarding the issue whether the party applying for recognition and enforcement was properly bound by the arbitration agreement pursuant to the applicable law.[681] Similarly, the High Court of Singapore, relying on Section 31(2)*(a)* and *(b)* of the Singapore International Arbitration Act (implementing article V (1)*(a)* of the Convention), held that a court could not review the arbitral tribunal's findings with respect to jurisdiction unless extraordinary circumstances exist. Therefore, the court found that the party opposing recognition and enforcement had not brought new evidence and rejected the challenge.[682]

53. Some courts have even considered themselves to be bound by the arbitrator's findings on their jurisdiction and the validity of the arbitration agreement.[683]

C. Preclusion

54. The Convention is silent on whether a party's actions or inactions during the course of arbitration or court-related proceedings may preclude it from later raising a defence under article V in general, and more specifically under article V (1)*(a)*.

55. Certain courts have held that a party is precluded from relying on any defence it failed to raise during the course of arbitration proceedings, including on the grounds that a party was under some incapacity or that the

---

[679] See, e.g., *Four Seasons Hotels and Resorts, B.V., et al. v. Consorcio Barr, S.A.*, United States District Court, Southern District of Florida, Miami Division, United States of America, 4 June 2003, 02-23249.

[680] *Planavergne S.A., Fontanes v. Kalle Bergander i Stockholm AB*, Svea Court of Appeal, Sweden, 7 September 2001, T 4645-99.

[681] *Stena RoRo AB v. OAO Baltiysky Zavod*, Highest Arbitrazh Court, Russian Federation, 13 September 2011, A56-60007/2008.

[682] *Aloe Vera of America, Inc v. Asianic Food (S) Pte Ltd. and another*, High Court, Singapore, 10 May 2006, [2006] SGHC 78.

[683] Oberlandesgericht [OLG] Schleswig, Germany, 24 June 1999, 16 SchH 01/99.

arbitration agreement was invalid. For instance, the Greek Supreme Court ruled that a party opposing enforcement is precluded from relying on any defects of the arbitration agreement if it failed to raise those during the course of the arbitral proceedings.[684] The same principle has been applied in many other jurisdictions, including Germany,[685] Australia,[686] and the United States.[687] In France, the Arbitration Act expressly provides that a party who fails to object to an irregularity before the arbitral tribunal shall be deemed to have waived the right to invoke it before the enforcing court.[688]

56. On the other hand, certain courts have held that a party would not be precluded from raising a defence under article V (1)*(a)* on the ground that it had not participated in the arbitral proceedings[689] or had not raised those grounds in setting aside proceedings.[690]

57. In a different context, certain courts have upheld arbitration agreements that, although initially defective, had been cured during the course of an arbitration. For instance, an Italian court held that the signature of the Terms of Reference in an arbitration proceeding under the auspices of the ICC International Court of Arbitration cured the otherwise defective arbitration agreement.[691] In the same vein, courts have relied on the procedural behaviour of the parties to infer the existence of a valid arbitration

---

684 *Agrimpex S.A. v. J.F. Braun & Sons, Inc.*, Supreme Court, Greece, 14 January 1977, IV Y.B. COM. ARB. 269 (1979).

685 Oberlandesgericht [OLG] München, Germany, 11 July 2011, 34 Sch 15/10; Oberlandesgericht [OLG] Frankfurt, Germany, 18 October 2007, 26 Sch 1/07; Oberlandesgericht [OLG] Hamm, Germany, 27 September 2005, 29 Sch 01/05; Oberlandesgericht [OLG] Koblenz, Germany, 28 July 2005, 2 Sch 4/05; Oberlandesgericht [OLG] Schleswig, Germany, 30 March 2000, 16 SchH 05/99.

686 *Altain Khuder LLC v. IMC mining Inc. and IMC Mining Solutions Pty Ltd,* Supreme Court of Victoria, Australia, 28 January 2011.

687 *China National Building Material Investment Co. Ltd. v. BNK International LLC,* District Court, Western District of Texas, Austin Division, United States of America, 3 December 2009, A-09-CA-488-SS; *China Minmetals Materials Import & Export Co. v. Chi Mei Corp.*, Court of Appeals, Third Circuit, United States of America, 26 June 2003, 02-2897 and 02-3542; *Joseph Walker and Company LLC v. Oceanic Fats and Oil(s) Ptd, Ltd.*, District Court, District of Columbia, United States of America, 11 September 2002, 01-2693.

688 Article 1466 of the French Code of Civil Procedure, applicable to international arbitration as per article 1506 of the French Code of Civil Procedure.

689 *Dallah Real Estate and Tourism Holding Company v. Ministry of Religious Affairs,* Government of Pakistan, Supreme Court, United Kingdom, 3 November 2010, UKSC 2009/0165

690 See, e.g., Bundesgerichtshof, [BGH], Germany, 16 December 2010, III ZB 100/09.

691 *Société Arabe des Engrais Phosphates et Azotes—SAEPA and Société Industrielle d'Acide Phosphorique et d'Engrais—SIAPE v. Gemanco srl,* Court of Appeal of Bari, Italy, 2 November 1993, XXII Y.B. COM. ARB. 737 (1997). The Italian Court of Cassation has subsequently reversed the decision of the Court of Appeal of Bari on grounds unrelated to the New York Convention. See also *Commonwealth Development Corp v. Montague,* Supreme Court of Queensland, Australia, 27 June 2000, Appeal No 8159 of 1999; DC No 29 of 1999.

agreement within the meaning of article V (1)*(a)*.[692] For example, the Presidium of the Highest Arbitrazh Court in Russian Federation held that the participation of the parties in the arbitral proceedings was deemed to be a confirmation of the written arbitration agreement pursuant to article V (1)*(a)* of the Convention, notwithstanding the lack of a proper arbitration agreement between the parties.[693]

[692] CTA *Lind & Co. Scandinavia AB in Liquidation's bankruptcy Estate v. Erik Lind,* District Court, Middle District of Florida, Tampa Division, United States of America, 7 April 2009, 8:08-cv-1380-T-30TGW; *China Nanhai Oil Joint Service Corporation Shenzhen Branch v. Gee Tai Holdings Co. Ltd,* High Court, Supreme Court of Hong Kong, Hong Kong, 13 July 1994, 1992 No. MP 2411; Oberlandesgericht [OLG] Schleswig, Germany, 30 March 2000, 16 SchH 05/99; Landgericht [LG] Bremen, Germany, 8 June 1967, 11-OH 11/1966; Oberlandesgericht [OLG] Hamburg, Germany, 30 July 1998, XXV Y.B. COM. ARB. 641 (2000); *L'Aiglon S/A v. Têxtil União S/A,* Superior Court of Justice, Brazil, 18 May 2005, SEC 856 (relying on the practice of international contracts in the matter of cotton-trade to assess to validity of the arbitration agreement).

[693] *Lugana Handelsgesellschaft mbH v. OAO Ryazan Metal Ceramics Instrumentation Plant,* Presidium of the Highest Arbitrazh Court, Russian Federation, 2 February 2010, A54-3028/2008-S10.

Article V (1)*(b)*

1. Recognition and enforcement of the award may be refused, at the request of the party against whom it is invoked, only if that party furnishes to the competent authority where the recognition and enforcement is sought, proof that:

[…]

b) The party against whom the award is invoked was not given proper notice of the appointment of the arbitrator or of the arbitration proceedings or was otherwise unable to present his case;

[…]

Travaux préparatoires

The *travaux préparatoires* on article V (1)*(b)* as adopted in 1958 are contained in the following documents:

Draft Convention on the Recognition and Enforcement of Foreign Arbitral Awards and comments by Governments and Organizations:

Report of the Committee on the Enforcement of International Arbitral Awards: E/2704 and Annex.

Comments by Governments and Organizations on the Draft Convention on the Recognition and Enforcement of Foreign Arbitral Awards: E/2822, Annexes I-II; E/CONF.26/3; E/CONF.26/3/Add.1.

Comments on the Draft Convention on the Recognition and Enforcement of Foreign Arbitral Awards: Note by the Secretary General: E/CONF.26/2.

United Nations Conference on International Commercial Arbitration:

Amendments to the Draft Convention Submitted by Governmental Delegations: E/CONF.26/L.17; E/CONF.26/L.34.

Comparison of Drafts Relating to Articles III, IV and V of the Draft Convention: E/CONF.26/L.33/Rev.1.

Further Amendments to the Draft Convention Submitted by Governmental Delegations: E/CONF.26/L.40.

Text of Articles III, IV and V of the Draft Convention Proposed by Working Party III: E/CONF.26/L.43.

Text of Articles Adopted by the Conference: E/CONF.26/L.48.

Text of the Convention on the Recognition and Enforcement of Foreign Arbitral Awards as Provisionally Approved by the Drafting Committee: E/CONF.26/L.61; E/CONF.26/8.

New text of Articles I (3), V (1)*(a), (b),* and *(e)* Adopted by the Conference at its 23rd meeting: E/CONF.26/L.63.

Final Act and Convention on the Recognition and Enforcement of Foreign Arbitral Awards: E/CONF.26/8/Rev.1.

Summary records:

Summary Records of the Eleventh, Thirteenth, Fourteenth, Seventeenth, and Twenty-Third Meetings of the United Nations Conference on International Commercial Arbitration: E/CONF.26/SR.11; E/CONF.26/SR.13; E/CONF.26/SR.14; E/CONF.26/SR.17; E/CONF.26/SR.23.

Summary Records of the Sixth Meeting of the Committee on Enforcement of International Arbitral Awards: E/AC.42/SR.6.

Committee on the Enforcement of International Arbitral Awards:

Enforcement of International Arbitral Awards: statement submitted by the International Chamber of Commerce, a non-governmental organization having consultative status in category A: E/C.2/373.

Report of the Committee on the Enforcement of International Arbitral Awards: E/AC.42/4.

(Available on the Internet at http://www.uncitral.org)
(For the *travaux préparatoires*, case law and bibliographical references, see also on the Internet at http://newyorkconvention1958.org)

Introduction

1. Article V (1)*(b)* addresses due process in arbitral proceedings. Specifically, it provides that parties must have had proper notice of the appointment of the arbitrators and of the arbitration proceedings as well as, more broadly, an opportunity to present their case.

2. Procedural irregularities under article V (1)*(b)* have to be raised and proven by the party opposing recognition and enforcement of an award, and cannot be raised by a court on its own motion.[694]

3. The drafters of the New York Convention followed the language of the 1927 Geneva Convention[695] but went further to enhance and facilitate enforcement.[696] In furtherance of this goal, although article V (1)*(b)* is modelled after article 2*(b)* of the 1927 Geneva Convention, it is more limited and is interpreted more narrowly.[697]

4. Article V (1)*(b)* also includes different requirements than its predecessor. As indicated in the *travaux préparatoires*, an early draft of what became article V (1)*(b)*, mirroring article 2*(b)* of the 1927 Geneva Convention, stated that there were grounds for refusal of enforcement of an

---

[694] *Travaux préparatoires*, Comments by Governments and Organisations on the Draft Convention on the Recognition and Enforcement of Foreign Arbitral Awards, Annex I of E/2822/ADD.1, p. 2. See also *Travaux préparatoires*, Amendments to Articles 3, 4 and Suggestion of Additional Articles (Sweden), E/CONF.26/L.8.

[695] Article 2(*b*) of the 1927 Geneva Convention states that "[...] recognition and enforcement of the award shall be refused if the Court is satisfied: That the party against whom it is sought to use the award was not given notice of the arbitration proceedings in sufficient time to enable him to present his case; or that, being under a legal incapacity, he was not properly represented".

[696] See, e.g., *Travaux préparatoires*, Memorandum by the Secretary General, E/2840, p. 2, para. 4. See also Albert Jan van den Berg, *Summary of Court Decisions on the N.Y. Convention*, in THE NEW YORK CONVENTION OF 1958, ASA SPECIAL SERIES NO. 9, para. 508 (M. Blessing ed., 1996); *Consorcio Rive S.A. de C.V. (Mexico) v. Briggs* of *Cancun, Inc. (United States)*, Court of Appeals, Fifth Circuit, United States of America, 26 November 2003, 01-30553, (citing *Parsons & Whittemore Overseas Co. v. Société Générale de L'Industrie du Papier (RAKTA)*, Court of Appeals, Second Circuit, United States of America, 23 December 1974, 508 F.2d 969, 975).

[697] See Maxi Scherer, *Violation of Due Process, Article V (1)(b)*, in NEW YORK CONVENTION ON THE RECOGNITION AND ENFORCEMENT OF FOREIGN ARBITRAL AWARDS OF 10 JUNE 1958—COMMENTARY 279, paras. 132-35 (R. Wolff ed., 2012).

award where a party "was not given notice [...] of the arbitration proceedings in due form or in sufficient time to enable him to present his case".[698] The drafters of the New York Convention retained the notice requirements of due process as they appeared in article 2*(b)* of the 1927 Geneva Convention. However, they wished to also cover other serious breaches of due process and thus included the inability of a party to present its own case as a separate requirement. The proposal of the delegate of the Netherlands to the Conference to draft article V (1)*(b)*, as it now stands, was ultimately adopted.[699]

5. Article V (1)*(b)* is often raised by parties opposing recognition and enforcement of an award despite the fact that the vast majority are unsuccessful in proving a breach.[700]

6. Courts are usually not formalistic in their approach to article V (1)*(b)*, but focus on the actual facts and conduct of the parties, which leads to a restrictive application of article V (1)*(b)*.[701]

---

698 *Travaux préparatoires*, Draft Convention on the Recognition and Enforcement of Foreign Arbitral Awards and Comments by Governments and Organizations, Report of the Committee on the Enforcement of International Arbitral Awards, E/2704 and Annex, p. 2.

699 *Travaux préparatoires*, Summary Records of the United Nations Conference on International Commercial Arbitration, Twenty-third Meeting, E/CONF.26/SR.23, p. 15.

700 See FOUCHARD GAILLARD GOLDMAN ON INTERNATIONAL COMMERCIAL ARBITRATION 1001-03, para. 1698 (E. Gaillard, J. Savage eds., 1999); ALBERT JAN VAN DEN BERG, THE NEW YORK ARBITRATION CONVENTION OF 1958: TOWARDS A UNIFORM JUDICIAL INTERPRETATION 297 (1981); Andrés Jana, Angie Armer et al., *Article V (1)(b)*, in RECOGNITION AND ENFORCEMENT OF FOREIGN ARBITRAL AWARDS: A GLOBAL COMMENTARY ON THE NEW YORK CONVENTION 231, 233 (H. Kronke, P. Nacimiento et al. eds., 2010); Pierre A. Karrer, *Must an Arbitral Tribunal Really Ensure that its Award is Enforceable?*, in GLOBAL REFLECTIONS ON INTERNATIONAL LAW, COMMERCE AND DISPUTE RESOLUTION, LIBER AMICORUM IN HONOUR OF ROBERT BRINER 431 (G. Asken et al. eds., 2005).

701 See, e.g., *X v. Y*, Bundesgericht [BLG], Switzerland, 4 October 2010, 4A_124/2010; *OOO Sandora (Ukraine) v.OOO Euro-Import Group (Russian Federation)*, Federal Arbitrazh Court, Moscow District, Russian Federation, 12 November 2010, A40-51459/10-63-440; Camera di esecuzione e fallimenti del Tribunale d'appello, Repubblica e Cantone Ticino, Switzerland, 22 February 2010, 14.2009.104; *OAO Byerezastroymaterialy (Belarus) v. Individual Entrepreneur D.V. Goryelov (Russian Federation)*, Federal Arbitrazh Court, North Caucasus District, Russian Federation, 14 September 2009, No. A01-342/2009; *Consorcio Rive S.A. de C.V. (Mexico) v. Briggs of Cancun, Inc. (United States)*, Court of Appeals, Fifth Circuit, United States of America, 26 November 2003, 01-30553; *Geotech Lizenz A.G. v. Evergreen Systems, Inc.*, District Court, Eastern District of New York, United States of America, 27 October 1988, CV 88-1406 (697 F. Supp 1248 (E.D.N.Y. 1988); *Union Générale de Cinéma SA (France) v. XYZ Desarrollos, S.A. (Spain)*, Supreme Court, Spain, 11 April 2000, XXXII Y.B. COM. ARB. 525 (2007); *M.F. Global Inc., et al. v. Elio D. Cattan, et al.*, District Court, Western District of Pennsylvania, United States of America, 6 March 2006, 04cv0593; *Karaha Bodas Co. (Cayman Islands) v. Perusahaan Pertambangan Minyak Dan Gas Bumi Negara (Indonesia)*, Court of Appeals, Fifth Circuit, United States of America, 23 March 2004, 02-20042, 03-20602.

7. Article V (1)*(b)* has some interaction and overlap with article V (2)*(b)*, the latter of which provides that a court may refuse to recognize or enforce an award if the award "would be contrary to the public policy of that country." In many respects, due process is closely connected to public policy.[702] It is therefore not unusual for parties to raise both provisions in their attempt to resist enforcement of an award. However, courts may not *sua sponte* raise possible breaches of article V (1)*(b)* whereas they may do so with respect to public policy under article V (2)*(b)*.[703]

Analysis

A. The requirement that the parties be given "proper notice"

8. Article V (1)*(b)* provides that parties against whom the award is invoked must have been given proper notice, failing which recognition and enforcement of the award may be refused.

a. Courts consider the parties' knowledge and conduct in assessing "proper notice"

9. Proper notice has been interpreted narrowly by courts, which usually apply more liberal standards than would be required for giving notice under domestic law. For example, a Mexican court held that parties waived Mexican procedural formalities on notice when they decided to submit their case to arbitration. Therefore, the fact that the notice did not comply with those formalities did not make the notice insufficient and did not prevent recognition and enforcement of the award.[704]

10. Some courts have been reluctant to graft external notice requirements onto article V (1)*(b)*. For example, in two cases, Chinese courts refused to apply the additional treaty requirements on notice contained in the mutual legal assistance treaties between China and Korea. The courts found that notice was adequate for the purposes of the New York Convention even though it did not conform to the treaty's definition of notice.[705] In assessing notice, an Egyptian court found that notice was sufficient on the basis that it

---

[702] See the chapter of the Guide on article V (2)(*b*), para 42.

[703] *X SA v. Y. Ltd.*, Federal Tribunal, Switzerland, 8 February 1978, P. 217/76. See also Andrés Jana, Angie Armer et al., *Article V (1)(b)*, in RECOGNITION AND ENFORCEMENT OF FOREIGN ARBITRAL AWARDS: A GLOBAL COMMENTARY ON THE NEW YORK CONVENTION 231, 235 (H. Kronke, P. Nacimiento et al. eds., 2010).

[704] *Presse Office S.A. v. Centro Editorial Hoy S.A.*, High Court of Justice, Eighteenth Civil Court of First Instance, Federal District of Mexico, Mexico, 24 February 1977, IV Y.B. COM. ARB. 301 (1979).

[705] TS *Haimalu Co., Ltd. v. Daqing PoPeyes Food Co., Ltd.*, Supreme People's Court, China, 3 March 2006, Min Si Ta Zi No. 46; *Boertong Corp. (Group) v. Beijing Liantaichang Trade Co. Ltd.*, Supreme People's Court, China, 14 December 2006, Min Si Ta Zi No. 36.

was adequate under Swedish law, which was the law governing the arbitration.[706] A German court took a similar approach and applied the law of the arbitration, in that case Ukrainian law, in assessing whether proper notice had been given.[707]

11. The burden to prove that notice was not properly given is on the party opposing recognition and enforcement and the evidence must be provided[708] and be clear.[709]

12. Courts have applied high standards regarding the burden of proof that notice was improperly given. For example, an Australian court rejected a party's insistence that it had never received notice of the arbitration when the carrier's records showed that someone signed for the papers even when the addressee himself was overseas at the time of delivery.[710] Additionally, where a claimant asserted that notice was sent and received and the party opposing recognition and enforcement could not provide evidence to the contrary, an Australian court and an Egyptian court both refused to find a breach of due process.[711]

13. Courts have upheld recognition and enforcement of awards in the face of notice challenges by looking beyond the notice itself to evaluate the parties' access to, and involvement in, the arbitration. This has been the case where parties were aware of a proceeding or hearing and thus able to participate in the arbitral proceedings.[712] For example, a Russian court

---

[706] *Egyptian Concrete Company & Hashem Ali Maher v. STC Finance & Ismail Ibrahim Mahmoud Thabet & Sabishi Trading and Contracting Company,* Court of Cassation, Egypt, 27 March 1996, 2660/59.

[707] Kammergericht [KG], Berlin, Germany, 17 April 2008, 20 Sch 02/08.

[708] *Egyptian Saudi Hotels Company v. Kurt & Daves Corporation,* Court of Cassation, Egypt, 16 July 1990, 2994/57.

[709] Oberlandesgericht [OLG], Celle, Higher Regional Court, of Celle, Germany, 14 December 2006, 8 Sch 14/05; *A v. B,* Federal Tribunal, Switzerland, 16 December 2011, 5A_441/2011.

[710] *LKT Industrial Berhad (Malaysia) v. Chun,* Supreme Court of New South Wales, Australia, 13 September 2004, 50174 of 2003.

[711] *Egyptian Saudi Hotels Company v. Kurt & Daves Corporation,* Court of Cassation, Egypt, 16 July 1990, 2994/57; *Uganda Telecom Ltd. v. Hi-Tech Telecom Pty Ltd.,* Federal Court, Australia, 22 February 2011, NSD 171 of 2010.

[712] *OOO Sandora (Ukraine) v. OOO Euro-Import Group (Russian Federation),* Federal Arbitrazh Court, District of Moscow, Russian Federation, 12 November 2010, A40-51459/10-63-440; Camera di esecuzione e fallimenti del Tribunale d'appello, Repubblica e Cantone Ticino, Switzerland, 22 February 2010, 14.2009.104; *Consorcio Rive S.A. de C.V. (Mexico) v. Briggs of Cancun, Inc. (United States),* Court of Appeals, Fifth Circuit, United States of America, 26 November 2003, 01-30553; *Geotech Lizenz A.G. v. Evergreen Systems, Inc.,* District Court, Eastern District of New York, United States of America, 27 October 1988, CV 88-1406 (697 F. Supp 1248 (E.D.N.Y. 1988)); *Union Générale de Cinéma S.A. (France) v. XYZ Desarrollos, S.A. (Spain),* Supreme Court, Spain, 11 April 2000, XXXII Y.B. COM. ARB. 525 (2007); *R.M.F. Global Inc., et al. v. Elio D. Cattan, et al.,* District Court, Western District of Pennsylvania, United States of America, 6 March 2006, 04cv0593.

rejected a party's argument that notice was insufficient when the party's representative attended the proceedings.[713] A Swiss court also refused to deny recognition and enforcement of an award when a party alleged insufficient notice because the court reasoned that the party had been able to present its case.[714] The Spanish Supreme Court likewise upheld the recognition and enforcement of an award in the face of a claim that notice was insufficient because there was proof in the record, including receipts for the delivery of registered letters, that notice was adequate.[715]

14. As a further illustration, an Italian court found that there was no breach where a party's actions demonstrated that it was aware of the proceedings.[716] A United States court similarly refused to find a breach where the party claiming it had not received notice had in fact been referred to arbitration by a court. Under the circumstances, the form and technicality of the notice itself did not matter.[717]

15. Recognition and enforcement has been refused under article V (1)*(b)* where there was clear proof that no notice had been given. For example, a Chinese court refused recognition and enforcement of an award on the basis that there was clearly no notice.[718] A Georgian court also refused recognition and enforcement when there was no evidence before the Georgian court that any notice was ever sent.[719] Similarly, a German court refused recognition and enforcement of an award when there was evidence that no effort had been made to find the defendant's current address to notify it of the arbitration.[720] Likewise, a Russian court denied recognition and enforcement of an award where there was no evidence that a party had received notice. In the absence of proof of delivery of the notice, combined

[713] *OOO Sandora (Ukraine) v. OOO Euro-Import Group (Russian Federation)*, Federal Arbitrazh Court, District of Moscow, Russian Federation, 12 November 2010, A40-51459/10-63-440

[714] Camera di esecuzione e fallimenti del Tribunale d'appello, Repubblica e Cantone Ticino, Switzerland, 22 February 2010, 14.2009.104.

[715] *Union Générale de Cinéma SA (France) v. XYZ Desarollos, S.A. (Spain),* Supreme Court, Spain, 11 April 2000, XXXII Y.B. COM. ARB. 525 (2007).

[716] *Bobbie Brooks Inc. v. Lanificio Walter Bucci s.a.s.*, Court of Appeal, Florence, Italy, 8 October 1977, IV Y.B. COM. ARB. 289 (1979).

[717] *R.M.F. Global Inc., et al. v. Elio D. Cattan et al.,* District Court, Western District of Pennsylvania, United States, 6 March 2006, 04cv0593.

[718] *Aiduoladuo (Mongolia) Co., Ltd. v. Zhejiang Zhancheng Construction Group Co., Ltd.,* Supreme People's Court, China, 8 December 2009, Min Si Ta Zi No. 46; *Cosmos Marine Managements S.A. v. Tianjin Kaiqiang Trading Ltd.,* Supreme People's Court, China, 10 January 2007, Min Si Ta Zi No. 34.

[719] *The Kiev [...] Institute v. "M", Scientific-Industrial Technological Institute* of *Tbilisi*, Supreme Court, Georgia, 17 March 2003, 3a-17-02.

[720] Bayerisches Oberstes Landesgericht [BayObLG], Germany, 16 March 2000, 4 Z Sch 50/99.

with the fact that the party was not present at the proceedings, the court concluded that notice was insufficient.[721]

b. Content of the notice

16. Article V (1)*(b)* requires that the parties be given proper notice of the appointment of the arbitrator and of the arbitration proceedings.

(i) Proper notice of the appointment of the arbitrator

17. Article V (1)*(b)* is silent as to what the notice of an appointment of the arbitrator must include. What is clear from the plain language of the text is that parties must receive some notice of the appointment of an arbitrator. In the absence of any notice, a court may refuse to enforce an award.[722] Courts have therefore been left to draw the contours of this notice requirement.

18. For instance, a Spanish court found that notification of the request to appoint an arbitrator, of the appointment, and confirmation thereof was sufficient notice.[723] Certain courts have confirmed that parties should receive a request to nominate an arbitrator.[724]

19. Courts have considered whether the notice of the appointment of the arbitrators must necessarily include the names of the arbitrators. A German court held that notice of the appointment of the arbitrators was insufficient where the notice did not include the names of the arbitrators, even if, in that case, the applicable arbitral rules did not provide for disclosure of the arbitrators' names.[725]

(ii) Proper notice of the arbitration proceedings

20. Article V (1)*(b)* requires that a party be given notice of the arbitration proceedings. Notice of the arbitration proceedings requires that all

---

[721] *OAO Byerezastroymaterialy (Belarus) v. Individual Entrepreneur D.V. Gorelov (Russian Federation),* Federal Arbitrazh Court, North Caucasus District, Russian Federation, 14 September 2009, No. A01-342/2009.

[722] *Cosmos Marine Managements S.A. v. Tianjin Kaiqiang Trading Ltd.,* Supreme People's Court, China, 10 January 2007, Min Si Ta Zi No. 34.

[723] *English Company X v. Spanish Company Y,* Supreme Court, Spain, 10 February 1984, X Y.B. COM. ARB. 493 (1985).

[724] Oberlandesgericht, Celle, Germany, 14 December 2006, 8 Sch 14/05; *Guang Dong Light Headgear Factory Co. v. ACI International Inc.,* District Court, District of Kansas, United States of America, 10 May 2005, 03-4165-JAR.

[725] *Danish Buyer v. German (F.R.) Seller,* Oberlandesgericht [OLG], Köln, Germany, 10 June 1976, IV Y.B. COM. ARB. 258 (1979).

respondents are notified of an arbitration so that they are aware of the proceedings.[726]

21. Some courts have held that this notice requirement continues as the arbitration progresses requiring that all parties be informed of the arbitration procedures, including the dates, times and locations of any hearings so that parties can participate in the arbitration proceedings.[727] However, as noted by the Supreme Court of Colombia, if a party chooses not to participate in the proceedings, it cannot then avail itself of the defence under article V (1)*(b)*.[728]

c. Mechanics of the "notice" requirement

(i) Form of notice

22. Article V (1)*(b)* is silent as to the form of notice. As a result, no specific form is required for notice.

23. The *travaux préparatoires* reveal that the drafters of the New York Convention contemplated the possibility of specifying the form of notice. One of the early drafts of the clause included the term "due form." The delegates to the Conference discussed the notion of "due form" and ultimately rejected it. The German delegation questioned the criteria that would be applied to determine "due form" and suggested its deletion because it would be difficult to determine in practice what constitutes "due form."[729] The delegates of the United Kingdom and of the former Union of Soviet Socialist Republics suggested that "notified in [...] due form" be replaced with "notified [...] in writing."[730] Furthermore, it was highlighted that "due form" did not appear in article 2*(b)* of the 1927 Geneva Convention, and

---

[726] *Cosmos Marine Managements S.A. v. Tianjin Kaiqiang Trading Ltd.,* Supreme People's Court, China, 10 January 2007, Min Si Ta Zi No. 34; *Petrotesting Colombia S.A. & Southeast Investment Corporation v. Ross Energy S.A.,* Supreme Court of Justice, Colombia, 27 July 2011, 11001-0203-000-2007-01956-00; *Guang Dong Light Headgear Factory Co. v. ACI International Inc.,* District Court, District of Kansas, United States of America, 10 May 2005, 03-4165-JAR.

[727] *Loral Space & Communications Holdings Corporation (United States) v. ZAO Globalstar—Space Telecommunications (Russian Federation),* Presidium of the Highest Court of the Russian Federation, Russian Federation, 20 January 2009, A40-31732/07-30-319; *Consorcio Rive S.A. de C.V. (Mexico) v. Briggs* of *Cancun, Inc. (United States),* Court of Appeals, Fifth Circuit, United States of America, 26 November 2003, 01-30553.

[728] *Petrotesting Colombia S.A. & Southeast Investment Corporation v. Ross Energy S.A.,* Supreme Court of Justice, Colombia, 27 July 2011, 11001-0203-000-2007-01956-00.

[729] *Travaux préparatoires,* Report by the Secretary-General, Recognition and Enforcement of Foreign Arbitral Awards, 31 January 1956, E/2822, Annex I, p. 23.

[730] *Travaux préparatoires,* Committee on the Enforcement of International Arbitral Awards, Sixth Meeting, E/AC.42/SR.6, p. 4.

therefore should be deleted.[731] "Due form" was ultimately removed and the drafters of the New York Convention did not add a requirement that notice be in writing or in any other specific form.

24. Courts are thus left to interpret what is acceptable notice and what constitutes a breach.[732] For example, the Swiss Federal Tribunal stated that a simple letter would constitute adequate notice and thus did not require any particular form.[733]

(ii) Service of notice

25. Article V (1)*(b)* is also silent on the service of notice. Thus there are no formal requirements under the Convention for service of notice either.[734]

26. The delivery and receipt of notice have been interpreted practically and flexibly, the courts having generally considered the conduct of the parties, not the technicalities of service, to evaluate whether or not the parties knew or ought to have known of the existence of the arbitration.[735] In that vein, the reasonable attempt by a claimant to notify a respondent is relevant even if a respondent does not receive the notice. For example, notice delivered by registered mail was held to be sufficient despite the fact that the addressee never picked it up.[736]

27. The majority of courts have not been formalistic with regards to who receives notice. Arguments that the party who received the notice was not the legal representative, authorized agent or precise legal entity have generally failed.[737]

---

[731] *Travaux préparatoires,* Comments by Governments and Organisations on the Draft Convention on the Recognition and Enforcement of Foreign Arbitral Awards, Annex I of E/2822, p. 23.

[732] Albert Jan van den Berg, *Summary of Court Decisions on the N.Y. Convention,* in THE NEW YORK CONVENTION OF 1958, ASA SPECIAL SERIES NO. 9, para. 509 (M. Blessing ed., 1996).

[733] *Y v. X,* Federal Tribunal, Switzerland, 3 January 2006, 5P.292/2005.

[734] *Petrotesting Colombia S.A. & Southeast Investment Corporation v. Ross Energy S.A.,* Supreme Court of Justice, Colombia, 27 July 2011, 11001-0203-000-2007-01956-00; *Drummond Ltd. v. Ferrovias en Liquidación, Ferrocariles Nacionales de Colombia S.A. (FENOCO),* Supreme Court of Justice, Colombia, 19 December 2011, 11001-0203-000-2008-01760-00; *Y v. X,* Federal Tribunal, Switzerland, 3 January 2006, 5P.292/2005.

[735] *Project XJ220 Ltd. v. Mohamed Yassin D. (Spain),* Supreme Court, Spain, 1 February 2000, XXXII Y.B. COM. ARB. 507 (2007).

[736] Kammergericht [KG], Germany, 17 April 2008, 20 Sch 02/08.

[737] *Uganda Telecom Ltd. v. Hi-Tech Telecom Pty Ltd.,* Federal Court, Australia, 22 February 2011, NSD 171 of 2010; *Consortium Codest Engineering (Italy) v. OOO Gruppa Most (Russian Federation),* Highest Arbitrazh Court, Russian Federation, 22 February 2005, A40-47341/03-25-179; *TH&T International Corp. v. Chengdu Hualong Auto Parts Co., Ltd.,*

(iii) Whether the notice should be served in a timely manner

28. Article V (1)*(b)* does not provide that notice of the appointment of the arbitrator or of the arbitration proceedings should be served in a timely manner. The language "in sufficient time", contained in article 2*(b)* of the 1927 Geneva Convention and in the early drafts of the article,[738] was later deleted.

29. Generally, timeliness of notice has been interpreted narrowly and with a focus on substance rather than form. As noted by the Supreme Court of Lithuania, late notice is not necessarily improper if the party was still able to participate in the proceedings.[739] Similarly, a Russian court held that late notice of a hearing, which prevented a party from obtaining visas to attend the hearing, was not a violation of the obligation to give proper notice because the party was otherwise aware several months in advance that the hearings would be held in London.[740]

B. Evidence that a party was "unable to present his case"

30. Article V (1)*(b)* also provides that a court may refuse to recognize or enforce an award if the party against whom the award is invoked successfully proves that it was unable to present its case.

a. Meaning of "unable to present his case"

31. This second protection in article V (1)*(b)* means that parties should have been provided with an opportunity to present their case;[741] that they should have had an opportunity to be heard regarding their claims, evidence and defences.

32. Some courts in the United States have interpreted this provision to mean that parties must have an opportunity to be heard at a "meaningful time and in a meaningful manner".[742] As stated by the Swiss Federal Tribunal,

---

Sichuan Higher People's Court, China, 12 December 2003, Cheng Min Chu Zi No. 531; *Altain Khuder LLC v. IMC Mining Inc.*, Supreme Court of Victoria, Australia, 28 January 2011, 3827 of 2010; *A v. B*, Federal Tribunal, Switzerland, 16 December 2011, 5A_441/2011.

738 *Travaux préparatoires,* Report by the Secretary General, Recognition and Enforcement of Foreign Arbitral Awards, 31 January 1956, Annex II of E/2822, p. 19.

739 *Jusimi Corporation v. UAB "Cygnus",* Supreme Court, Lithuania, 8 September 2003, 3K-3-782/2003.

740 *Loral Space & Communications Holdings Corporation (United States) v. ZAO Globalstar—Space Telecommunications (Russian Federation),* Presidium of the Highest Arbitrazh Court, Russian Federation, 20 January 2009, A40-31732/07-30-319.

741 See FOUCHARD GAILLARD GOLDMAN ON INTERNATIONAL COMMERCIAL ARBITRATION para. 1698 (E. Gaillard, J. Savage eds., 1999).

742 *Iran Aircraft Indus. v. Avco Corp.*, Courts of Appeals, Second Circuit, United States of America, 24 November 1992, 92-7217, 980 F.2d 141, 146; *Karaha Bodas Co. (Cayman*

"[b]y its general wording, this provision covers any restriction, whatever its nature, of the parties' rights. It appears to contemplate, amongst others, the violation of the right to be heard".[743]

33. In practice, courts have refused recognition and enforcement of awards on the grounds in article V (1)*(b)* where the process has been particularly egregious or where the arbitration radically strayed from standards of due process, such as when a party was prevented from submitting crucial evidence[744] or from receiving or commenting on evidence from an opposing party.[745] For example, a court found a breach of due process when an arbitral tribunal declared inadmissible the submission filed by a party after the closing of the proceedings while relying on a subsequent submission filed thereafter by the other party.[746] Similarly, a Dutch court found a breach of due process when a party was denied the right to comment on or respond to evidence and arguments from the opposing party.[747]

34. Exceptional circumstances may also lead to a finding of a breach of due process. For example, an Italian court found that a month had not been enough time for a party to prepare and present its case in light of the fact that there had been a recent earthquake.[748]

35. The onus is on the parties to present their cases and there will not be a breach where a party could have presented its case but did not.[749] Courts have usually considered that there is no breach of due process where a party has impeded its own ability to present its case, such as by failing to demand

---

Islands) v. Perusahaan Pertambangan Minyak Dan Gas Bumi Negara (Indonesia), Court of Appeals, Fifth Circuit, United States of America, 23 March 2004, 02-20042, 03-20602.

743 *Chrome Resources S.A. v. Leopold Lazarus Ltd.*, Federal Tribunal, Switzerland, 8 February 1978, XI Y.B. COM. ARB. 538 (1986).

744 *Iran Aircraft Indus v. Avco Corp.*, Court of Appeals, Second Circuit, United States of America, 24 November 1992, 92-7217.

745 *M. Adeossi v. Sonapra*, Court of First Instance, Cotonou, Benin, 25 January 1994, Ordonnance No. 19/94; Landgericht [LG] Regional Court, Bremen, Germany, 20 January 1983, 12-O-184/1981.

746 *M. Adeossi v. Sonapra*, Court of First Instance, Cotonou, Benin, 25 January 1994, Ordonnance No. 19/94.

747 *Rice Trading (Guyana) Ltd. v. Nidera Handelscompagnie BV*, Court of Appeal, The Hague, Netherlands, 28 April 1998, XXIII Y.B. COM. ARB. 731 (1998).

748 *Bauer & Grobmann OHG v. Fratelli Cerrone Alfredo e Raffaele*, Court of Appeal, Naples, Salerno Section, Italy, 18 May 1982, X Y.B. COM. ARB, (1985).

749 *First State Ins. Co. (United States) v. Banco de Seguros Del Estado (Uruguay)*, Court of Appeals, First Circuit, United States of America, 27 June 2001, 00-2454 (254 F.3d 354); *Standard Elec. Corp. v. Bridas Sociedad Anonima Petrolera, Indus. Y Commercial*, District Court, Southern District of New York, United States of America, 24 August 1990, 90 Civ. 0720 (KC); *D v. Franz J*, Supreme Court, Austria, 1 September 2010, 3 Ob 122/10b. See also FOUCHARD GAILLARD GOLDMAN ON INTERNATIONAL COMMERCIAL ARBITRATION 1001-03, para. 1698 (E. Gaillard, J. Savage eds., 1999).

an extension of time or by otherwise failing to participate in the arbitral proceedings.[750]

36. In the same vein, most courts have been strict in refusing to find breaches where parties did not remedy their own defaults. The United States Court of Appeals for the First Circuit rejected an alleged breach of due process when a party claimed that its counsel was not representing it meaningfully. The Court reasoned that it was the fault of its own representatives.[751] Another United States Court held that there was no breach of due process when a party complained about a tribunal-appointed expert because that party never objected to the expert or requested a copy of the report.[752] An Italian court held that article V (1)*(b)* "concerns the impossibility rather than the difficulty of presenting one's case."[753] Similarly, a Swiss court found that a party had ample opportunity to present its case when its counsel resigned and it failed to appoint new counsel. The Court reasoned that the party had the time to appoint new counsel but failed to do so.[754]

b. Tribunals' discretion to organize and control the arbitral proceedings

37. Courts have uniformly emphasized that parties who had the opportunity to correct an issue or procedural flaw but did not, will not benefit from the protections of article V (1)*(b)*. In addition to respecting the spirit and the pro-enforcement bias of the New York Convention, the majority of courts have taken into account the wide discretion vested in arbitral tribunals to organize and control the arbitral proceedings.

38. Courts allow arbitral tribunals significant discretion to establish procedural rules and control their implementation.[755] For instance, a German

---

750 *Dutch Seller v. German (F.R.) Buyer*, Regional Court, Zweibrucken, Germany, 11 January 1978; *Bobbie Brooks Inc. v. Lanificio Walter Bucci s.a.s.*, Court of Appeal, Florence, Italy, 8 October 1977, IV Y.B. COM. ARB. 289 (1979).

751 *First State Ins. Co. (United States) v. Banco de Seguros Del Estado (Uruguay)*, Court of Appeals, First Circuit, United States of America, 27 June 2001, 00-2454 (254 F.3d 354).

752 *Standard Elec. Corp. v. Bridas Sociedad Anonima Petrolera, Indus. Y Comercial*, District Court, Southern District of New York, United States of America, 24 August 1990, 90 Civ. 0720 (KC).

753 *De Maio Giuseppe e Fratelli snc v. Interskins Ltd.*, Court of Cassation, Italy, 21 January 2000, 671, XXVII Y.B. COM. ARB. 492 (2002).

754 *X v. Y*, Camera di esecuzione e fallimenti del Tribunale d'appello, Repubblica e Cantone Ticino, Switzerland, 7 August 1995, 14.9400021.

755 Oberlandesgericht [OLG], Celle, Germany, 31 May 2007, 8 Sch 06/06; *Century Indemnity Company, et al. v. Axa Belgium (f/k/a Royale Belge Incendie Reassurance)*, District Court, Southern District of New York, United States of America, 24 September 2012, 11 Civ. 7263 (JMF); *Compagnie des Bauxites de Guinee v. Hammermills, Inc.*, District Court, District of Columbia, United States of America, 29 May 1992, 90-0169.

court found no breach of due process when an arbitral tribunal refused applications to submit evidence.[756] The United States District Court for the Southern District of New York similarly found no breach of due process when an arbitral tribunal imposed the United States Federal Rules of Civil Procedure on an arbitration at the last minute. The Court held that arbitrators have broad discretion to determine arbitral procedure and noted that they had, in that case, referred to the Federal Rules of Civil Procedure for guidance.[757]

39. Courts have considered that the rules imposed by arbitral tribunals do not need to conform to domestic standards of due process.[758] A German court found that there was no breach of due process when a tribunal did not hold oral hearings because that was within its discretion and the arbitral rules so permitted.[759] A Swiss court likewise found that an arbitral tribunal had the discretion to consult an industry expert ex parte and thus upheld the recognition and enforcement of the award.[760] The United States District Court for the Northern District of California held that discovery was not guaranteed in arbitration and that its absence does not interfere with the ability of a party to present its case.[761] The United States Court of Appeals for the Fifth Circuit also upheld the recognition and enforcement of an award where an arbitral tribunal refused additional discovery because the parties already had sufficient opportunity to present their cases.[762]

40. Courts have held that arbitral tribunals are not obliged to consider every issue raised by a party,[763] nor are they required to divulge every detail

---

756 Oberlandesgericht [OLG], Celle, Germany, 31 May 2007, 8 Sch 06/06.

757 *Century Indemnity Company, et al. v. Axa Belgium (f/k/a Royale Belge Incendie Reassurance),* District Court, Southern District of New York, United States of America, 24 September 2012, 11 Civ. 7263 (JMF).

758 Hanseatisches Oberlandesgericht [OLG], Hamburg, Germany, 30 July 1998, 6 Sch 3/98; *X S.A. v. Y Ltd.,* Federal Tribunal, Switzerland, 8 February 1978, P.217/76; *L Ltd. v. C S.A. (GE),* Court of Justice, Geneva, Switzerland, 17 September 1976, 549.

759 Hanseatisches Oberlandesgericht [OLG], Hamburg, Germany, 30 July 1998, 6 Sch 3/98.

760 *X S.A. v. Y Ltd.,* Federal Tribunal, Switzerland, 8 February 1978, P.217/76; *L Ltd. v. C S.A. (GE),* Court of Justice, Geneva, Switzerland, 17 September 1976, 549.

761 *Anthony N. LaPine v. Kyosera Corporation,* District Court, Northern District of California, United States of America, 22 May 2008, C 07-06132 MHP.

762 *Karaha Bodas Co. (Cayman Islands) v. Perusahaan Pertambangan Minyak Dan Gas Bumi Negara (Indonesia),* Court of Appeals, Fifth Circuit, United States of America, 23 March 2004, 02-20042, 03-20602.

763 *Budejovicky Budvar, N.P. v. Czech Beer Importers, Inc.,* District Court, District of Connecticut, United States of America, 10 July 2006, 1246 (JBA); Oberlandesgericht [OLG] Frankfurt, Germany, 27 August 2009, 26 SchH 03/09.

of their reasoning.[764] Arbitral tribunals similarly have the power to reformulate the issues presented by the parties.[765]

41. Arbitral tribunals can exercise their discretion to determine what is necessary for a party to present its case and most courts have demonstrated that they give tribunals great leeway in so doing.[766] For example, the Paris Court of Appeal decided to uphold the order recognizing and enforcing an award when the complaining party alleged that it had not received documents used by an expert because neither the tribunal nor the opposing party had relied on those documents.[767] Similarly, the Supreme Court of Austria rejected an alleged breach of due process, when a party claimed that the tribunal failed to investigate facts and refused certain evidence, because the party was still able to present its case.[768]

c. Narrow interpretation of "unable to present his case"

(i) Presence of parties and witnesses

42. A number of courts have interpreted the notion of being "unable to present his case" narrowly when parties have been unable to attend proceedings or hearings.[769]

43. For example, a Chinese court found that there was no breach of due process where a party, unable to attend the proceedings, sent its defences in a

---

[764] *Gas Natural Aprovisionamientos SDG S.A. v. Atlantic LNG Company* of *Trinidad and Tobago,* District Court, Southern District of New York, United States of America, 16 September 2008, 08 Civ. 1109 (DLC); Oberlandesgericht [OLG], Frankfurt, Germany, 27 August 2009, 26 SchH 03/09.

[765] *Inter-Arab Investment Guarantee Corporation v. Banque Arabe et Internationale d'Investissements,* Court of Appeal, Brussels, Belgium, 24 January 1997, XXII Y.B. COM. ARB. 643 (1997).

[766] *Société Unichips Finanziaria SPA et Société Unichips International BV v. Consorts Gesnouin,* Court of Appeal of Paris, France, 12 February 1993, 92-14017; Oberlandesgericht [OLG], Munich, Germany, 14 November 2011, 34, Sch 10/11; Bundesgerichtshof [BGH], Germany, 14 April 1988, III ZR 12/87; *Ministry* of *Defense & Support for the Armed Forces of Iran v. Cubic Defense Systems, Inc.,* District Court, Southern District of California, United States of America, 7 December 1998, 98-1165-B; *Austria C v. Vladimir Z,* Supreme Court, Austria, 31 March 2005, XXXI Y.B. COM. ARB. 583 (2006).

[767] *Société Unichips Finanziaria SPA et Société Unichips International BV v. Consorts Gesnouin,* Court of Appeal of Paris, France, 12 February 1993, 92-14017.

[768] *Austria C v. Dr. Vladimir* Z, Supreme Court, Austria, 31 March 2005, XXXI Y.B. COM. ARB. 583 (2006).

[769] *Ukraine Kryukovskiy Car Building Works v. Shenyang Changcheng Economic and Trade Company,* Shenyang Intermediate People's Court, China, 22 April 2003, Shen Min Zi No. 16; Oberlandesgericht [OLG], Düsseldorf, Germany, 15 December 2009, I-4 Sch 10/09; *Geotech Lizenz A.G. v. Evergreen Systems, Inc.,* District Court, Eastern District of New York, United States of America, 27 October 1988, CV 88-1406 (697 F. Supp 1248 (E.D.N.Y. 1988)).

letter.[770] As a further illustration, a German court found that there was no breach of due process despite the fact that the complaining party was unable to attend a hearing because the court reasoned that it could have sent a representative in its stead.[771] The United States Court of Appeals for the Fifth Circuit similarly found that there was no breach where a party alleged that it was unable to present its case because it could not be present due to a fear of being arrested. The Court noted that physical presence was not necessary to participate in a hearing and that the party could have sent a representative or participated remotely.[772] Likewise, the Supreme Court of Victoria in Australia held that even if a party itself did not present its own case, the requirements of article V (1)*(b)* have been met as long as a related entity has done so.[773]

44. United States courts have applied the same narrow interpretation where the presence of a party's representative is concerned.[774] For example, a United States court held that there was no violation when the tribunal refused to adjourn the proceedings when the Chief Executive Officer of one of the parties was medically unfit to attend.[775]

45. In addition, in a series of decisions, United States courts have held that the inability to cross-examine or present witnesses does not constitute a breach of a party's ability to present its case.[776]

---

770 *Ukraine Kryukovskiy Car Building Works v. Shenyang Changcheng Economic and Trade Company,* Shenyang Intermediate People's Court, China, 22 April 2003, Shen Min Zi No. 16.

771 Oberlandesgericht [OLG], Karlsruhe, Germany, 27 March 2006, 9 Sch 02/05.

772 *Consorcio Rive S.A. de C.V. (Mexico) v. Briggs of Cancun, Inc. (United States),* Court of Appeals, Fifth Circuit, United States of America, 26 November 2003, 01-30553.

773 *Altain Khuder LLC v. IMC Mining Inc.,* Supreme Court of Victoria, Australia, 28 January 2011, 3827 of 2010.

774 *Jiangsu Changlong Chemicals Co. (China) v. Burlington Bio-Medical & Scientific Corp. (United States),* District Court, Eastern District of New York, United States of America, 22 November 2005, CV 05-2082; *Budejovicky Budvar, N.P. v. Czech Beer Importers, Inc.,* District Court, District of Connecticut, 10 July 2006, 1246 (JBA).

775 *China National Building Material Investment Co. Ltd. v. BNK International LLC,* District Court, Western District of Texas, Austin Division, United States of America, 3 December 2009, A-09-CA-488-SS.

776 *Generica Ltd. v. Pharma Basics, Inc.,* Court of Appeals, Seventh Circuit, United States of America, 29 September 1997, 96-4004; *Parsons & Whittemore Overseas Co. v. Société Générale de L'Industrie du Papier (RAKTA),* Court of Appeals, Second Circuit, United States of America, 23 December 1974, 74-1642, 74-1676; *Sonera Holdings BV. v. Cukurova Holding A.S.,* District Court, Southern District of New York, United States of America, 10 September 2012, 11 Civ. 8909 (DLC); *Agility Public Warehousing CO. K.S.C., Professional Contract Administrators, Inc. v. Supreme Foodservice GMBH,* Court of Appeals, Second Circuit, United States of America, 6 September 2012, 11-5201-CV; *Phoenix Aktiengesellschaft v. Ecoplas, Inc.,* Court of Appeals, Second Circuit, United States of America, 10 December 2004, 03-9000; *Dalmine S.p.A. v. M. & M. Sheet Metal Forming Machinery A.G.,* Court of Cassation, Italy, 23 April 1997, 10229, XXIV Y.B. COM. ARB. 709 (1999).

(ii) Language of the arbitration

46. Arguments that the language of the proceeding affected a party's ability to present its case have generally failed.[777]

47. Most courts consider the context of the language used in the arbitration in assessing whether or not there is a breach of due process. For example, the Spanish Supreme Court did not find a breach of due process when a party complained that the proceedings were conducted in English, holding that English was the common language in international commercial transactions.[778] A German Court found that there was no breach when the proceedings and correspondence were in Russian and the respondent could not understand Russian because the burden was on the respondent to find a translator or interpreter and it should have done so.[779]

48. Some courts take into consideration the arbitration agreement[780] or the applicable procedural rules[781] to determine the language chosen by the parties and have been reluctant to refuse enforcement when parties have previously agreed to the language of an arbitration even if that later poses difficulties. For example, the Supreme Court of Colombia upheld recognition and enforcement of an award when the complaining party was unable to afford the costs of translators or interpreters and could not understand the language of the arbitration.[782]

C. Procedural hurdles to showing a breach of article V (1)*(b)*

a. Outcome determinative requirement

49. It is not uncommon for courts to require parties opposing enforcement under article V (1)*(b)* to prove not only a breach of due process, but also that the outcome of the case would have been different had the alleged breach not occurred.[783]

---

777 *Kastrup Trae-Aluvinduet A/S (Denmark) v. Aluwood Concepts Ltd. (Ireland),* High Court, Ireland, 13 November 2009, 2009 169 MCA, XXXV Y.B. COM. ARB. 404 (2009).

778 *Precious Stones Shipping Limited (Thailand) v. Querqus Alimentaria S.L. (Spain),* Supreme Court, Spain, 28 November 2000, 2658 of 1999, XXXII Y.B. COM. ARB. 540 (2007).

779 Oberlandesgericht [OLG], Celle, Germany, 2 October 2001, 8 Sch 3/01.

780 *Petrotesting Colombia S.A. & Southeast Investment Corporation v. Ross Energy S.A.,* Supreme Court of Justice, Colombia, 27 July 2011, 11001-0203-000-2007-01956-00; *K (Ukraine) v. F AG (Austria),* Supreme Court, Austria, 23 October 2007, XXXIII Y.B. COM. ARB. 354 (2008).

781 Oberlandesgericht [OLG], Munich, Germany, 22 June 2009, 34 Sch 26/08.

782 *Petrotesting Colombia S.A. & Southeast Investment Corporation v. Ross Energy S.A.,* Supreme Court of Justice, Colombia, 27 July 2011, 11001-0203-000-2007-01956-00.

783 *Firm P v. Firm F,* Oberlandesgericht [OLG], Hamburg, Germany, 3 April 1975, II Y.B. COM. ARB. 241 (1977); *German (F.R.) charterer v. Romanian shipowner,*

50. In a recent German decision, a higher regional court found that there was no basis for rejecting enforcement on the grounds of a violation of the right to be heard under article V (1)*(b)*, as the alleged failure to properly inform the buyer of the constitution of the arbitral tribunal was not relevant because it had failed to show that it would have raised any additional defences had it been properly informed of such constitution.[784] The court followed the same reasoning in relation to the alleged failure to duly summon the buyer to the oral hearing. As stated by the higher regional court, violations of the right to be heard would only form the basis for rejecting enforcement if such violations had in fact prevented the affected party from raising its claims and defences. It concluded that in this case, the buyer knew of the arbitration proceedings and could thus have raised its defences, but failed to do so.[785]

b. Waiver

51. Violation of due process, under article V (1)*(b)*, may, as a general matter, be waived, subject to limitations.

52. A number of courts have considered that parties ought to object promptly to any violation of due process, rather than waiting until the enforcement stage to raise the issue for the first time. Courts have not found a violation of due process under article V (1)*(b)* where parties have waited until after the arbitration to raise a due process issue for the first time.[786] For example, in the face of a party's objection at the enforcement stage that one of the arbitrator's had given an opinion in a related case, the Paris Court of

---

Bundesgerichtshof [BGH], Germany, 15 May 1986, XII Y.B. COM. ARB. 489 (1987); *Seller v. Buyer,* Bundesgerichtshof [BGH], Germany, 26 April 1990, XXI Y.B. COM. ARB. 532 (1996); *Manufacturer (Slovenia) v. Exclusive Distributor (Germany)*, Oberlandesgericht [OLG], Schleswig, Germany, 24 June 1999, 16 SchH 01/99; *Buyer v. Seller,* Oberlandesgericht [OLG], Frankfurt, Germany, 27 August 2009, 26 SchH 03/09, XXXV Y.B. COM. ARB. 377 (2010); *Apex Tech Investment Ltd. (China) v. Chuang's Development (China) Ltd.,* Court of Appeal, Hong Kong, 15 March 1996, CACV000231/1995; *Polytek Engineering Company Limited v. Hebei Import & Export Corporation*, High Court of the Hong Kong Special Administrative Region, Court of Appeal, Hong Kong, 16 January 1998, 116 of 1997; Oberlandesgericht [OLG], Frankfurt, Germany, 18 October 2007, 26 Sch 1/07.

784 Oberlandesgericht [OLG], Frankfurt, Germany, 18 October 2007, 26 Sch 1/07.

785 Oberlandesgericht [OLG], Frankfurt, Germany, 18 October 2007, 26 Sch 1/07.

786 *AO Techsnabexport v. Globe Nuclear Services and Supply GNSS Lmt.*, Court of Appeals, Fourth Circuit, United States of America, 15 December 2010, 09-2064; Hanseatisches Oberlandesgericht [OLG], Germany, 26 January 1989, 6 U 71/88; *Standard Elec. Corp. v. Bridas Sociedad Anonima Petrolera, Indus. Y Commercial*, District Court, Southern District of New York, United States of America, 24 August 1990, 90 Civ. 0720 (KC); Oberlandesgericht [OLG], Hamm, Germany, 2 November 1983, 20 U 57/83; *Consultant company (United Kingdom) v. Painting contractors (Germany)*, Oberlandesgericht [OLG], Munich, Germany, 28 November 2005, XXXI Y.B. COM. ARB. 722 (2006); Oberlandesgericht [OLG], Karlsruhe, Germany, 27 March 2006, 9 Sch 02/05, XXXII Y.B. COM. ARB. 342 (2007); *Shenzhen Nan Da Industrial and Trade United Co. Ltd. v. FM International Ltd.*, High Court, Supreme Court, Hong Kong, 2 March 1992, MP 12492.

Appeal found that the party should have objected to the arbitrator's appointment at the time of the arbitral proceedings.[787] A German court similarly refused to find a breach when a party claimed that it had not been timely informed of the opposing party's counterclaims because it failed to object promptly at the time of the arbitral proceedings.[788] As stated by an Indian court, "if the Defendant after receipt of the interim award failed to contest the matter, the blame cannot be laid at the door of the arbitrators for no fault of theirs."[789]

53. Even though Article V (1)*(b)* does not mention the possibility of advance waivers, German courts have accepted limited waivers of certain procedures or deadlines,[790] but not complete waivers of all due process requirements.[791]

---

[787] *Compagnie Française d'études et de construction Technip (Technip) v. Entreprise nationale des engrais et des produits phyosanitaires (Asmidal),* Court of Appeal of Paris, France, 2 April 1998, 97/6929.

[788] Hanseatisches Oberlandesgericht [OLG], Germany, 26 January 1989, 6 U 71/88.

[789] *Glencore Grain Rotterdam B.V. v. Shivnath Rai Harnarain*, High Court, Delhi, India, 27 November 2008.

[790] *K Trading Company (Syria) v. Bayerischen Motoren Werke AG (Germany),* Bayerisches Oberstes Landesgericht [BayObLG], Germany, 23 September 2004, 4Z Sch 05-04, XXX Y.B. COM. ARB. 568 (2005).

[791] *Danish Buyer v. German (F.R.) Seller,* Oberlandesgericht, Koln, Germany, 10 June 1976, IV Y.B. COM. ARB. 256 (1979).

Article V (1)*(c)*

1. Recognition and enforcement of the award may be refused, at the request of the party against whom it is invoked, only if that party furnishes to the competent authority where the recognition and enforcement is sought, proof that:

[…]

c) The award deals with a difference not contemplated by or not falling within the terms of the submission to arbitration, or it contains decisions on matters beyond the scope of the submission to arbitration, provided that, if the decisions on matters submitted to arbitration can be separated from those not so submitted, that part of the award which contains decisions on matters submitted to arbitration may be recognized and enforced;

Travaux préparatoires

The *travaux préparatoires* on article V (1)*(c)* as adopted in 1958 are contained in the following documents:

Draft Convention on the Recognition and Enforcement of Foreign Arbitral Awards and comments by Governments and Organizations:

Report of the Committee on the Enforcement of International Arbitral Awards: E/2704 and Annex.

Comments by Governments and Organizations on the Draft Convention on the Recognition and Enforcement of Foreign Arbitral Awards: E/2822, Annexes I-II; E/2822/Add.4; E/2822/Add.5; E/2822/Corr.1; E/CONF.26/3; E/CONF.26/3/Add.1.

Comments on the Draft Convention on the Recognition and Enforcement of Foreign Arbitral Awards: Note by the Secretary General: E/CONF.26/2.

United Nations Conference on International Commercial Arbitration:

Amendments to the Draft Convention Submitted by Governmental Delegations: E/CONF.26/L.17; E/CONF.26/L.31; E/CONF.26/L.32; E/CONF.26/L.34.

Comparison of Drafts Relating to Articles III, IV and V of the Draft Convention: E/CONF.26/L.33; E/CONF.26/L.33/Rev.1.

Further Amendments to the Draft Convention Submitted by Governmental Delegations: E/CONF.26/L.40.

Text of Articles III, IV and V of the Draft Convention Proposed by Working Party III: E/CONF.26/L.43.

Text of Articles Adopted by the Conference: E/CONF.26/L.48.

Text of the Convention on the Recognition and Enforcement of Foreign Arbitral Awards as Provisionally Approved by the Drafting Committee: E/CONF.26/L.61; E/CONF.26/8.

Final Act and Convention on the Recognition and Enforcement of Foreign Arbitral Awards: E/CONF.26/8/Rev.1.

Summary records:

Summary Records of the Eleventh, Twelfth, Thirteenth, Fourteenth, and Seventeenth Meetings of the United Nations Conference on International Commercial Arbitration: E/CONF.26/SR.11; E/CONF.26/SR.12; E/CONF.26/SR.13; E/CONF.26/SR.14; E/CONF.26/SR.17.

Summary Records of the First and Sixth Meetings of the Committee on Enforcement of International Arbitral Awards: E/AC.42/SR.1; E/AC.42/SR.6.

Committee on the Enforcement of International Arbitral Awards:

Enforcement of International Arbitral Awards: statement submitted by the International Chamber of Commerce, a non-governmental organization having consultative status in category A: E/C.2/373.

Report of the Committee on the Enforcement of International Arbitral Awards: E/AC.42/4.

(Available on the Internet at http://www.uncitral.org)

(For the *travaux préparatoires*, case law and bibliographical references, see also on the Internet at http://newyorkconvention1958.org)

Introduction

1. Article V (1)*(c)* of the New York Convention allows the competent authorities in Contracting States to refuse recognition and enforcement of an arbitral award, or part of that award, where the award contains decisions on matters "beyond the scope of the submission to arbitration".

2. Article V (1)*(c)* finds its roots in article 2*(c)* of the 1927 Geneva Convention.[792] The language at the outset of article V (1)*(c)*, providing a ground for refusal of recognition or enforcement of awards exceeding the scope of the arbitration agreement, is largely unchanged from its counterpart in the 1927 Geneva Convention. The New York Convention, however, limits the scope of article V (1)*(c)* by omitting language found in article 2 of the 1927 Geneva Convention which permitted enforcing authorities to delay, or create conditions in relation to, the enforcement of awards, where the award did not cover all the questions submitted to the arbitral tribunal.[793]

3. The drafters of the New York Convention further built on the 1927 Geneva Convention by explicitly allowing for severability of the part of the award dealing with a difference not contemplated by or not falling within the terms of the submission to arbitration, or containing decisions on matters beyond the scope of the submission to arbitration, in order to permit recognition and enforcement of the part of the award containing decisions on matters submitted to arbitration. Although there is generally little discussion of article V (1)*(c)* in the *travaux préparatoires*, the inclusion of the provision allowing for partial recognition and enforcement was the subject of some debate. The *travaux préparatoires* show that various concerns were raised over the form and substance of this principle, including concerns that severability of arbitral awards would in practice "open the door to a review

---

[792] Article 2(*c*) of the 1927 Geneva Convention states: "Even if the conditions laid down in Article 1 hereof are fulfilled, recognition and enforcement of the award shall be refused if the Court is satisfied: [...] (c) That the award does not deal with the differences contemplated by or falling within the terms of the submission to arbitration or that it contains decisions on matters beyond the scope of the submission to arbitration."

[793] Article 2 of the 1927 Geneva Convention states in relevant part: "If the award has not covered all the questions submitted to the arbitral tribunal, the competent authority of the country where recognition or enforcement of the award is sought can, if it think fit, postpone such recognition or enforcement or grant it subject to such guarantee as that authority may decide".

as to substance",[794] which the drafters of the New York Convention sought to prevent. Courts have since uncompromisingly asserted that article V (1)*(c)* does not permit an enforcing authority to reconsider the merits of a dispute.[795]

4. Another concern raised at the time of drafting the provision that allows for partial recognition and enforcement was that "an arbitral award constitutes an organic whole, the spirit of which may be violated if it is split up into component parts."[796] That concern was not shared, and recent English case law, for example, has observed that "[i]mmediate enforcement of discrete parts of the award would go with the grain of the award, not undermine it or second guess it."[797] Ultimately the interest of facilitating enforcement of awards prevailed and the provision allowing partial enforcement of awards has since been applied broadly.

Analysis

A. General principles

a. Meaning of "submission to arbitration"

5. Article V (1)*(c)* provides that courts may refuse to recognize or enforce an award if it addresses disputes outside of the terms of the "submission to arbitration".

6. Courts and commentators agree that an arbitration agreement[798] constitutes a "submission to arbitration" within the meaning of article V (1)*(c)*. Consequently, where an arbitral tribunal has rendered an award which decides matters beyond the scope of the arbitration agreement, there is a ground for refusing to enforce an award under article V (1)*(c)*.[799]

---

[794] *Travaux préparatoires*, United Nations Conference on International Commercial Arbitration, Report by the Secretary-General - Recognition and Enforcement of Foreign Arbitral Awards, E/2822, p. 23.

[795] See the chapter of the Guide on article V (1)(*c*), paras. 43-45.

[796] *Travaux préparatoires*, United Nations Conference on International Commercial Arbitration, Report by the Secretary-General —Corrigendum—Recognition and Enforcement of Foreign Arbitral Awards, E/2822/Corr. 1, p. 1.

[797] *IPCO (Nigeria) Ltd. v. Nigerian National Petroleum Corp.*, High Court of Justice, England and Wales, 17 April 2008, [2008] EWHC 797 (Comm), para. 103.

[798] An arbitration agreement could take the form of either an arbitral clause in a contract or a separate arbitration agreement: for a further discussion about the form of the arbitration agreement, see the chapter of the Guide on article II, paras. 36-57.

[799] FOUCHARD GAILLARD GOLDMAN ON INTERNATIONAL COMMERCIAL ARBITRATION 987-88, para. 1700 (E. Gaillard, J. Savage eds., 1999); Christian Borris, Rudolf Hennecke, *Commentary to Article V (1)(c)*, in NEW YORK CONVENTION ON THE RECOGNITION AND ENFORCEMENT OF FOREIGN ARBITRAL AWARDS OF 10 JUNE 1958—COMMENTARY 309, 311,

7. Courts have also held that the term "submission to arbitration" can include an arbitration agreement modified, amended or supplemented by an arbitral institution's terms of reference agreed to by the arbitrators and disputing parties. Terms of reference may indeed supplement or modify the arbitration agreement. For example, a German court of appeal held that the parties had concluded a new arbitration agreement by signing ICC Terms of Reference.[800] Similarly, a decision by the English House of Lords stated that "[i]n the present case one is dealing with an ICC arbitration agreement. In such a case the terms of reference which under article 18 of the ICC rules are invariably settled may, of course, amend or supplement the terms of the arbitration agreement."[801]

8. Authors and courts have also considered whether article V (1)*(c)* provides grounds for refusing to recognize or enforce where the arbitrator's decision goes beyond the parties' pleadings or prayers for relief to render an award *ultra petita*. Though some authors have argued that article V (1)*(c)* provides a second, separate ground for refusal to enforce an award rendered *ultra petita*,[802] courts have rejected challenges to recognition or enforcement under article V (1)*(c)* based on the fact that the arbitrators had exceeded their authority by deciding on issues or granting forms of relief beyond those pleaded by the parties. As one United States court observed, "[u]nder the New York Convention, we examine whether the award exceeds the scope of the [arbitration agreement], not whether the award exceeds the scope of the parties' pleadings".[803] This interpretation of article V (1)*(c)* which

---

paras. 201-02 (R. Wolff ed., 2012); Paolo Michele Patocchi & Cesare Jermini, *Article 194*, in INTERNATIONAL ARBITRATION IN SWITZERLAND: AN INTRODUCTION TO AND A COMMENTARY ON ARTICLES 176-194 OF THE SWISS PRIVATE INTERNATIONAL LAW STATUTE 661, para. 95 (S.V. Berti et al. eds., 2000); Ulrich Haas, *The New York Convention on recognition and enforcement of foreign arbitral awards of 1958*, in PRACTITIONER'S HANDBOOK ON INTERNATIONAL ARBITRATION 499, paras. 39-40 (F.-B. Weigand ed., 2002); *Parsons & Whittemore Overseas Co. v. Société Générale de l'Industrie du Papier (RAKTA)*, Court of Appeals, Second Circuit, United States of America, 23 December 1974, 508 F.2d 969 , 976, para. 11.

[800] *Seller v. Buyer*, Oberlandesgericht [OLG] Stuttgart, Germany, 6 December 2001, 1 Sch 12/01, XXIV Y.B. COM. ARB. 742 (2004).

[801] *Lesotho Highlands Development Authority v. Impreglio SpA et al.*, House of Lords, England and Wales, 30 June 2005, [2005] UKHL 43, para. 21.

[802] JEAN FRANÇOIS POUDRET, SEBASTIEN BESSON, COMPARATIVE LAW OF INTERNATIONAL ARBITRATION 836-37, para. 913 (2007); Stefan Michael Kröll, *Commentary on the German Arbitration Law (10th Book of the German Code of Civil Procedure)*, in ARBITRATION IN GERMANY: THE MODEL LAW IN PRACTICE 541-42, para. 84 (K. H. Böckstiegel, S. Kröll, P. Nacimiento eds., 2007); Mercédeh Azeredo da Silveira & Laurent Levy, *Transgression of the Arbitrators' Authority: Article V (1)(c) of the New York Convention*, in ENFORCEMENT OF ARBITRATION AGREEMENTS AND INTERNATIONAL ARBITRAL AWARDS: THE NEW YORK CONVENTION IN PRACTICE 639, 650-53 (E. Gaillard, D. Di Pietro eds., 2008).

[803] *Ministry of Defense of the Islamic Republic of Iran v. Gould, Inc.; Gould Marketing, Inc.; Hoffman Export Corporation; Gould International, Inc.*, Court of Appeals, Ninth Circuit, United States of America, 30 June 1992, 969 F.2d 764; see also *The Ministry of Defense and*

distinguishes the parties' pleadings or prayers for relief from the "submission to arbitration" referred to in article V (1)*(c)*, is consistent with a narrow interpretation of the grounds for refusal to recognize or enforce an award.

9. A United States District Court rejected a challenge to an award in which the tribunal had ordered relief that neither party had requested, including conditional divestiture of a party's shares and an anti-suit injunction, in connection with an arbitration agreement which specifically empowered the tribunal to "grant any remedy or relief that they deem just and equitable." The court considered that "while an arbitrator may not award relief expressly forbidden by the [arbitration agreement], an arbitrator may award relief not sought by either party, so long as the relief lies within the broad discretion conferred by the [United States Federal Arbitration Act]."[804]

10. The United States Court of Appeals for the Second Circuit found that explicit authority in an arbitration agreement to award costs was not necessary under the ICC Rules of Arbitration.[805] The United States Court of Appeals for the Ninth Circuit later stated more broadly that "[s]ince we find the arbiters' authority to reach the main decision was within the scope of the letter agreement, it follows the arbiters also had the authority to award costs and fees for obtaining the arbitral decision."[806]

11. With respect to the award of interest, the Hamburg Court of Appeal rejected a challenge to enforcement under article V (1)*(c)*, made on the basis that the arbitral tribunal had awarded more interest than had been claimed, considering that an "arbitral tribunal can in its discretion and on its own initiative award interest and compound interest for the time until the rendition of the award and for the time after the rendition of the award."[807]

b. Article V (1)(c) only concerns issues "beyond" the scope

12. Leading commentators agree that article V (1)*(c)* does not apply to awards which fail to address all the issues submitted to the arbitral tribunal

---

Support for the Armed Forces of the Islamic Republic of Iran v. Cubic Defense Systems, Inc., District Court, Southern District of California, United States of America, 8 December 1998, Civ. Case No. 98-1165-B.

[804] *Telenor Mobile Communications AS v. Storm LLC*, District Court, Southern District of New York, United States of America, 2 November 2007, 524 F. Supp. 2d 332.

[805] *Parsons & Whittemore Overseas Co. v. Société Générale de l'Industrie du Papier (RAKTA)*, Court of Appeals, Second Circuit, United States of America, 23 December 1974, 508 F.2d 969.

[806] *Mgmt. & Tech. Consultants S.A. v. Parsons-Jurden Int'l Corp.*, Court of Appeals, Ninth Circuit, United States of America, 8 July 1987, 820 F.2d 1531.

[807] *Shipowner v. Time Charterer*, Oberlandesgericht [OLG] Hamburg, Germany, 30 July 1998, 6 Sch 3/98, XXV Y.B. COM. ARB. 641 (2000).

for resolution.[808] Though there are no reported cases addressing whether article V (1)*(c)* applies to awards rendered *infra petita*, the view that such awards do not provide grounds for refusal of recognition or enforcement is consistent with the text and spirit of the Convention.

13. First, the pleadings and requests for relief submitted by the parties to the arbitral tribunal do not constitute a "submission to arbitration" within the meaning of article V (1)*(c)* and therefore cannot provide the basis for a challenge to recognition or enforcement of an award under article V (1)*(c)*, regardless of whether the award extends beyond the pleadings or requests for relief, or fails to address all of the issues raised therein.

14. Second, the text of article V (1)*(c)* only provides grounds for refusing to recognize or enforce awards that decide on issues which go "beyond" the parties' agreement to arbitrate. Nothing in the language of article V (1)*(c)* grants enforcing authorities the discretion to refuse or otherwise limit the recognition or enforcement of an award which has failed to address all issues submitted by the parties, but which is otherwise enforceable as to the issues addressed.

15. As recorded in the *travaux préparatoires* of the New York Convention, the omission of language in the 1927 Geneva Convention allowing postponement of recognition or enforcement, or granting enforcement subject to a guarantee, of any award that "has not covered all the questions submitted to the arbitral tribunal", was a "significant change" from the wording of the 1927 Geneva Convention.[809] The omission is particularly notable given that article V (1)*(c)* contains very similar language to article 2*(b)* of the 1927 Geneva Convention.[810]

c. *Interpretation of "matters"*

16. Article V (1)*(c)* provides grounds for refusing to recognize or enforce awards that decide on "matters" which are outside the scope of the arbitration agreement. "Matters" has broadly been defined in two ways: first, as the subject matter over which the arbitral tribunal has jurisdiction pursuant

---

808 JEAN-FRANÇOIS POUDRET, SEBASTIEN BESSON, COMPARATIVE LAW OF INTERNATIONAL ARBITRATION 836-37, para. 914 (2007); FOUCHARD GAILLARD GOLDMAN ON INTERNATIONAL COMMERCIAL ARBITRATION 987-88, para. 1700 (E. Gaillard, J. Savage eds., 1999); Stefan Michael Kröll, *Commentary on the German Arbitration Law* (*10th Book* of *the German Code* of *Civil Procedure*), in ARBITRATION IN GERMANY: THE MODEL LAW IN PRACTICE 541-42, para. 84 (K. H. Böckstiegel, S. M. Kröll, P. Nacimiento eds., 2007).

809 *Travaux préparatoires*, United Nations Conference on International Commercial Arbitration, Comments by Governments on the Draft Convention on the Recognition and Enforcement of Foreign Arbitral Awards, E/2822/Add. 4, p. 6.

810 ALBERT JAN VAN DEN BERG, THE NEW YORK ARBITRATION CONVENTION OF 1958: TOWARDS A UNIFORM JUDICIAL INTERPRETATION 320 (1981).

to the arbitration agreement; and second, in some jurisdictions, as the personal jurisdiction over one of the parties addressed in the award. In relation to the latter interpretation, it is notable that in any event, article V (1)*(a)* directly addresses consent of the parties.[811]

(i) Subject matter jurisdiction

17. Courts and commentators have consistently considered that "matters" refers to the subject matter that is encompassed by the arbitration agreement and thus subject to the jurisdiction of the arbitral tribunal that issued the award in question.[812]

18. For example, pursuant to article V (1)*(c)*, the Trento Court of Appeal in Italy refused to enforce part of an award which granted damages in connection with "technical" disputes. The arbitration clause provided that the local arbitral tribunal issuing the award only had jurisdiction over "non-technical" disputes, and any "technical" disputes were to be resolved by an international arbitral tribunal under the ICC Arbitration Rules.[813]

19. Parties have also successfully challenged enforcement of awards under article V (1)*(c)* on the grounds that an award was based on an underlying contract which was not within the subject matter of the arbitration agreement. Although an arbitration agreement may extend to contracts which are not explicitly included within its scope, such extension is by no means automatic, and depends on the intention of the parties.[814]

(ii) Personal jurisdiction

20. Parties have brought successful challenges to enforcement of arbitral awards under article V (1)*(c)* in several jurisdictions on the grounds that the

---

[811] See the chapter of the Guide on article V (1)(c), paras. 5-11.

[812] GARY B. BORN, INTERNATIONAL COMMERCIAL ARBITRATION 3544 (2014); ALAN REDFERN, MARTIN HUNTER ET AL., REDFERN & HUNTER ON INTERNATIONAL ARBITRATION 645-47 (2009); FOUCHARD GAILLARD GOLDMAN ON INTERNATIONAL COMMERCIAL ARBITRATION 986-87, para. 1700 (E. Gaillard, J. Savage eds., 1999); *Parsons & Whittemore Overseas Co. v. Société Générale de l'Industrie du Papier (RAKTA)*, Court of Appeals, Second Circuit, United States of America, 23 December 1974, 508 F.2d 969, 977, para. 13.

[813] *General Organization of Commerce and Industrialization of Cereals of the Arab Republic of Syria v. S.p.a. SIMER (Società delle Industrie Meccaniche di Rovereto)*, Court of Appeal of Trento, Civil Section, Italy, 14 January 1981, VIII Y.B. COM. ARB. 386 (1983).

[814] See GARY B. BORN, INTERNATIONAL COMMERCIAL ARBITRATION 1369-72 (2014); BERNARD HANOTIAU, COMPLEX ARBITRATIONS: MULTIPARTY, MULTICONTRACT, MULTI-ISSUE AND CLASS ACTIONS (2005), Chapter III. See also *York Airconditioning & Refrigeration Inc. v. Lam Kwai Hung T/A North Sea A/C Elect Eng. Co.*, High Court, Supreme Court of Hong Kong, Hong Kong, 16 December 1994, [1995] 1 HKC 287; and *Four Seasons Hotels And Resorts B.V. et al. v. Consorcio Barr, S.A.*, District Court, Southern District of Florida, United States of America, 12 May 2009, Case No. 04-20673-CIV-MOORE/ISIMONTON.

arbitral award addressed a party that was not bound by the arbitration agreement. Several courts have therefore considered that *ratione personae* is also a "matter" within the meaning of article V (1)*(c)* and can therefore constitute a valid basis for an article V (1)*(c)* challenge to recognition or enforcement of an award.

21. For example, some Chinese courts have refused to enforce arbitral awards under article V (1)*(c)* on the grounds that the awards dealt with parties that were not bound by the arbitration agreement.[815] In one case, the Supreme People's Court overturned a lower court's decision denying recognition of an award pursuant to article V (1)*(c)* and decided to enforce the award.[816] A United States District Court denied enforcement of part of an arbitral award under article V (1)*(c)* on the basis that the arbitral tribunal had "exceeded its authority when it purported to bind a non-signatory who was not expressly covered by the arbitration agreement."[817]

22. In a multiparty context, where disputes under two separate contracts were joined in one arbitration, and where both contracts were not signed by the same parties, the Federal Arbitrazh Court of the Russian Federation refused to enforce an award which determined responsibilities between two parties who were not both signatories to the same arbitration agreement, and as such had not together agreed to arbitrate their disputes.[818] Similarly, a Russian Federal Arbitrazh Court refused enforcement under article V (1)*(c)* on the grounds that no valid arbitration agreement existed, though this decision was ultimately overturned by the Highest Arbitrazh Court based on the facts.[819]

23. The Court of Appeal of England and Wales considered a challenge to enforcement under article V (1)*(c)* on the basis that the award addressed parties who were not bound by the arbitration agreement. The court

---

815 *Gerald Metals Inc. v. Wuhu Smelter & Refinery Co., Ltd. and Wuhu Hengxin Copper (Group) Inc.*, Supreme People's Court, China, 12 November 2003, [2003] Min Si Ta Zi No. 12; *First Investment Corp. (Marshall Island) v. Fujian Mawei Shipbuilding Corp. and Fujian Shipbuilding Corp.*, Supreme People's Court, China, 27 February 2008, [2007] Min Si Ta Zi No. 35, XXXV Y.B. COM. ARB. 349 (2010); *Hemofarm DD, MAG International Trade Holding DD, Suram Media Ltd. v. Jinan Yongning Pharmaceutical Co. Ltd.*, Supreme People's Court, China, 2 June 2008, [2008] Min Si Ta Zi No. 11; *Aoetker Germany v. Sinotrans Nanjing Co., Ltd.*, Supreme People's Court, China, 11 September 2001, [2000] Jiao Ta Zi No. 11.

816 *Aoetker Germany v. Sinotrans Nanjing Co., Ltd.*, Supreme People's Court, China, 11 September 2001, [2000] Jiao Ta Zi No. 11.

817 *FIAT S.p.A. v. The Ministry of Finance and Planning of the Republic of Suriname, Suriname Rice Export Company N.V. et al. v. Alvaro N. Sardi,* District Court, Southern District of New York, United States of America, 12 October 1989, 1989 WL 122891, 4, para. 5.

818 *O&Y Investments Ltd. v. OAO Bummash,* Federal Arbitrazh Court, Northwestern District, Russian Federation, 12 October 2005, F09-2110/05-S6, XXXIII Y.B. COM. ARB. 687 (2008).

819 *HiPP GmbH & Co. Export KG v. ZAO SIVMA*, Highest Arbitrazh Court, Russian Federation, 14 June 2011, 1787/11.

ultimately rejected this challenge because the arbitral award, though mentioning other parties who were not bound by the arbitration agreement, did not make any award in their favour or any determination with respect to the rights of those parties.[820]

24. Though some courts have considered that challenges to personal jurisdiction may fall under article V (1)*(c)*, these challenges may alternatively be deemed to constitute disputes in relation to consent and the existence of a valid arbitration agreement, which fall more squarely under article V (1)*(a)*. Indeed, some commentators consider that only the subject matter jurisdiction of the arbitral tribunal is a "matter" within the meaning of article V (1)*(c)*, as opposed to the arbitral tribunal's jurisdiction over a particular party.[821]

d. Scope of the arbitration agreement versus scope of the underlying contract

25. The language of article V (1)*(c)* is clear that recognition or enforcement of an award may be refused if it addresses issues which exceed the scope of the parties' agreement to arbitrate. Following a narrow interpretation of article V (1)*(c)*, courts have consistently distinguished between examining the scope of the arbitration agreement itself and the scope of the underlying contract.

26. Courts have thus rejected challenges under article V (1)*(c)* brought by parties on the basis that an award has somehow exceeded limits imposed by the scope of the underlying contract, rather than the arbitration agreement. As stated in an often-cited decision by the United States Court of Appeals for the Second Circuit, "[a]lthough the Convention recognizes that an award

---

[820] *Deutsche Schachtbau-und Tiefbohrgesellschaft mbH v. R'as al-Khaimah National Oil Co.*, Court of Appeal, England and Wales, 24 March 1987, 3 W.L.R. [1986 D No. 2196] [1987 R No. 273].

[821] GARY B. BORN, INTERNATIONAL COMMERCIAL ARBITRATION 3544-45 (2014); ALAN REDFERN, J. MARTIN HUNTER ET AL., REDFERN & HUNTER ON INTERNATIONAL ARBITRATION 645, para. 11.76 (2009) (referring to The Arab Republic of Egypt v. Southern Pacific Properties, Court of Appeal of Paris, France, 12 July 1984, 23 ILM (1984)); Paolo Michele Patocchi & Cesare Jermini, *Article 194*, in INTERNATIONAL ARBITRATION IN SWITZERLAND: AN INTRODUCTION TO AND A COMMENTARY ON ARTICLES 176-194 OF THE SWISS PRIVATE INTERNATIONAL LAW STATUTE 660-61, para. 94 (S.V. Berti et al. eds., 2000); Stefan Michael Kröll, *Commentary on the German Arbitration Law (10th Book of the German Code of Civil Procedure)*, in ARBITRATION IN GERMANY: THE MODEL LAW IN PRACTICE 541, para. 83 (K.H. Böckstiegel, S. Kröll, P. Nacimiento eds., 2007); Mercédeh Azeredo da Silveira & Laurent Levy, *Transgression of the Arbitrators' Authority: Article V (1)(c) of the New York Convention*, in ENFORCEMENT OF ARBITRATION AGREEMENTS AND INTERNATIONAL ARBITRAL AWARDS: THE NEW YORK CONVENTION IN PRACTICE 639, 639-40 (E. Gaillard, D. di Pietro eds., 2008). But see JEAN FRANÇOIS POUDRET, SEBASTIEN BESSON, COMPARATIVE LAW OF INTERNATIONAL ARBITRATION 836-37, para. 913 (2007).

may not be enforced where predicated on a subject matter outside the arbitrator's jurisdiction, it does not sanction second-guessing the arbitrator's construction of the parties' agreement".[822]

27. One United States District Court found that an award for consequential damages was within the submission to arbitrate even though consequential damages were explicitly precluded by the terms of the underlying contract, in circumstances where consequential damages were included in the terms of reference and a reasoned award by the arbitral tribunal justified their application.[823]

28. In another example, a party challenged enforcement of an arbitral award before the Svea Court of Appeal in Sweden, claiming that the award determined disputes relating to a particular product that was not in existence at the time the underlying contract was entered into, and thus could not be within the scope of the arbitration agreement contained within the contract. Considering the challenge to enforcement pursuant to Section 54(3) of the Swedish Arbitration Act, which mirrors article V (1)*(c)*, the court found that the issue of whether the product was included in the subject matter of the relevant contract could not be resolved without an interpretation of the contract, which would go to the merits of the arbitral award, and therefore could not be considered by the court.[824]

B. Partial recognition of an award

29. In keeping with the pro-enforcement bias of the New York Convention, article V (1)*(c)* provides "that part of the award which contains decisions on matters submitted to arbitration may be recognized and enforced", provided that matters properly within the scope of the arbitration agreement "can be separated from those not so submitted."

30. The limited discussion in the *travaux préparatoires* on this issue could be understood as suggesting that severability would be appropriate in cases where the matters in the award going beyond the scope of the agreement were "secondary" in nature or which constituted, as one delegate

[822] *Parsons & Whittemore Overseas Co. v. Société Générale de l'Industrie du Papier (RAKTA)*, Court of Appeals, Second Circuit, United States of America, 23 December 1974, 508 F.2d 969.

[823] *Fertilizer Corp. of India v. IDI Mgmt. Inc.*, District Court, Southern District of Ohio, United States of America, 9 June 1981, 517 F. Supp. 948.

[824] *American Pacific Corp. v. Sydsvensk Produktutveckling AB*, Svea Court of Appeal, Sweden, 21 March 2001, Ö 4859-00, XXVII Y.B. COM. ARB. 551 (2002).

put it, "a small detail" in the context of the rest of the award.[825] In practice, its application is much broader.[826]

31. A United States District Court partially enforced an award that covered multiple contracts, after finding that one of the contracts was not within the scope of the arbitration agreement. The court enforced the part of the award dealing with the contracts that were covered by the arbitration agreement.[827]

32. Courts have also applied article V (1)*(c)* in the context of multiparty arbitrations to exclude from enforcement portions of an award which address a party not bound by the arbitration agreement, but enforce the award with respect to the remaining parties. This was the case in a challenge to enforcement brought under article V (1)*(c)* before the Supreme People's Court of China, which found that one of the respondents named in the award was not a party to the arbitration agreement. The court recognized only the portion of the award that dealt specifically and exclusively with the liability of the other respondent, who was a party to the arbitration agreement.[828] Similarly, following a challenge brought under article V (1)*(c)*, a United States District Court declined to enforce part of an arbitral award which was made against a non-signatory to the arbitration agreement, but enforced the remainder of the award against another respondent who was a party to the arbitration agreement.[829]

33. The severability provision of article V (1)*(c)*, permitting the part of an award to be recognized and enforced where it does address issues within the scope of the submission to arbitration, is consistent with the aim of the Convention to facilitate the enforcement of arbitral awards.[830] Some authors have gone so far as to suggest, in the same spirit, that despite the use of the

---

[825] *Travaux préparatoires*, United Nations Conference on International Commercial Arbitration, Summary Records of the Seventeenth Meeting, E/CONF.26/SR.17, p. 9. See also Albert Jan van den Berg, *The New York Convention* of *1958*: *An Overview,* in ENFORCEMENT OF ARBITRATION AGREEMENTS AND INTERNATIONAL ARBITRAL AWARDS: THE NEW YORK CONVENTION IN PRACTICE 59-60 (E. Gaillard, D. di Pietro eds., 2008).

[826] Mercédeh Azeredo da Silveira & Laurent Levy, *Transgression* of *the Arbitrators' Authority: Article V (1)(c) of the New York Convention*, in ENFORCEMENT OF ARBITRATION AGREEMENTS AND INTERNATIONAL ARBITRAL AWARDS: THE NEW YORK CONVENTION IN PRACTICE 639, 676 (E. Gaillard, D. di Pietro eds., 2008).

[827] *Four Seasons Hotels And Resorts B.V. et al. v. Consorcio Barr, S.A.*, District Court, Southern District of Florida, United States of America, 12 May 2009, 1:04-cv-20673-KMM.

[828] *Gerald Metals Inc. v. Wuhu Smelter & Refinery Co., Ltd. and Wuhu Hengxin Copper (Group) Inc.*, Supreme People's Court, China, 12 November 2003, [2003] Min Si Ta Zi No. 12.

[829] *FIAT S.p.A. v. The Ministry of Finance and Planning of the Republic of Suriname, Suriname Rice Export Company N.V. et al. v. Alvaro N. Sardi*, District Court, Southern District of New York, United States of America, 12 October 1989, 1989 WL 122891.

[830] See Christian Borris, Rudolf Hennecke, *Commentary to Article V (1)(c)*, in NEW YORK CONVENTION ON THE RECOGNITION AND ENFORCEMENT OF FOREIGN ARBITRAL AWARDS OF 10 JUNE 1958—COMMENTARY 309, 328, para. 259 (R. Wolff ed., 2012).

word "may" in article V (1)*(c)*, in light of the Convention's pro-enforcement bias, courts "must" recognize those parts of an award which are recognizable.[831]

C. Relationship with other articles in the Convention

a. Article V (1)(a)

34. Article V (1)*(a)* provides that courts may refuse recognition or enforcement of arbitral awards which are not based on a valid arbitration agreement.[832] Article V (1)*(a)* is similar in nature to article V (1)*(c)* in that both articles concern whether an arbitral award has been rendered on the basis of a valid arbitration agreement. Thus both articles V (1)*(a)* and V (1)*(c)* may be engaged by challenges regarding the validity of an arbitration agreement.[833]

35. At the same time, the provisions serve distinct purposes. Where article V (1)*(a)* concerns the existence of a valid arbitration agreement which is binding on all the parties addressed by an award, article V (1)*(c)* assumes the existence of a valid arbitration agreement between the parties and is concerned instead with whether an award has gone beyond the scope of the subject matter the parties intended to submit to arbitration.

36. However, this distinction is not always clearly made in practice. As noted above, courts in several jurisdictions have addressed the issue of whether a party has consented to be bound by an arbitration agreement as one falling under article V (1)*(c)* rather than V (1)*(a)*. In practice, it is uncontroversial that a party's lack of consent to arbitrate provides grounds for challenging recognition or enforcement of an award, regardless of which sub-paragraph of article V is invoked. However, addressing whether a party has consented to arbitrate under article V (1)*(a)* is ultimately consistent with the distinct purposes articles V (1)*(a)* and V (1)*(c)* that were given by the drafters of the Convention.

---

[831] GARY B. BORN, INTERNATIONAL COMMERCIAL ARBITRATION 3444 (2014); Nicola Christine Port, Scott Ethan Bowers, Bethany Davis Noll, *Article V (1)(c)*, in RECOGNITION AND ENFORCEMENT OF FOREIGN ARBITRAL AWARDS: A GLOBAL COMMENTARY ON THE NEW YORK CONVENTION 257, 276 (H. Kronke, P. Nacimiento et al. eds., 2010).

[832] See the chapter of the Guide on article V (1)(*a*).

[833] *Astro Nusantara International BV et al. v. PT Ayunda Prima Mitra et al.*, Court of First Instance, High Court of the Hong Kong Special Administrative Region, Hong Kong, 21 March 2012, HCCT 45/2010, para. 19.

b. *Extended application of the partial enforcement principle established by article V (1)(c)*

37. Article V (1)*(c)* is the only article in the Convention which expressly states that courts may partially enforce an award when there are grounds for refusing to recognize or enforce some aspects of the award.[834] Courts have referred to the principle of partial enforcement expressed in article V (1)*(c)* to partially enforce awards in connection with challenges brought under other provisions of the Convention. For example, some courts have partially recognized or enforced awards which would otherwise be refused enforcement on public policy grounds.[835]

38. Further, where an application to set aside the arbitral award was pending before a court at the seat of the arbitration, the Court of Appeal of England and Wales considered that the partial enforcement provisions of article V (1)*(c)* could be applied to enforce the parts of the award that were not subject to challenge.[836]

D. Procedural aspects

a. *Standing*

39. Article V (1) provides that it is the party against whom the award is invoked that may raise a challenge with respect to the grounds for refusal set forth in article V (1).

40. Courts have consistently confirmed this in relation to article V (1)*(c)*.[837] For example, the United States Court of Appeals for the Fifth

---

[834] Article V (1)(*c*) provides that where grounds for refusal of recognizing or enforcing an award exist with respect to only part of an arbitral award, "that part of the award which contains decisions on matters submitted to arbitration may be recognized and enforced", provided that matters properly within the scope of the arbitral agreement "can be separated from those not so submitted." See the chapter of the Guide on article V (1)(*c*), paras.29-33.

[835] See, e.g., *J. J. Agro Industries (P) Ltd. v. Texuna International Ltd.*, High Court, Supreme Court of Hong Kong, Hong Kong, 12 August 1992, HCMP000751/1992; *Buyer (Austria) v. Seller (Serbia and Montenegro)*, Supreme Court, Austria, 26 January 2005, 3 Ob 221/04b. See also GARY B. BORN, INTERNATIONAL COMMERCIAL ARBITRATION 3445-46 (2014).

[836] *Nigeria (NNPC) v. IPCO (Nigeria) Ltd.*, Court of Appeal, England and Wales, 21 October 2008, [2008] EWCA Civ 1157. See also *IPCO (Nigeria) Ltd. v. Nigerian National Petroleum Corp.*, High Court of Justice, England and Wales, 17 April 2008, [2008] EWHC 797 (Comm).

[837] *Ernesto Francisco v. Stolt Achievement MT; Stolt Achievement, Inc.; Stolt-Nielsen Transportation Group, Ltd.; Stolt Parcel Tankers, Inc.*, Court of Appeals, Fifth Circuit, United States of America, 4 June 2002, 293 F.3d 270; *Odfjell SE v. OAO PO Sevmash*, Highest Arbitrazh Court, Russian Federation, 26 May 2011 VAS-4369/11; *Not indicated v. Not indicated*, Hanseatisches Oberlandesgericht [OLG] Bremen, Germany, 30 September 1999, (2) Sch 04/99, XXXI Y.B. COM. ARB. 640 (2006).

Circuit denied a party's attempt to raise a challenge under article V (1)*(c)* to oppose an order compelling arbitration, that is, before the arbitral proceedings had even taken place.[838] The court noted that the provision could only be invoked by a party opposing enforcement of an award, which was not possible in circumstances where no award had been issued, and also unlikely where the party raising the challenge was the claimant in the would-be arbitration, and thus not the party who would be in a position to challenge any resulting arbitral award absent any counterclaims.[839]

b. Standard of review

41. Though the language of article V (1)*(c)* does not explicitly impose any particular standard of review, any decision by the arbitral tribunal as to its own subject matter jurisdiction and the scope of the submission to arbitration cannot be binding on the enforcing court, as this would render article V (1)*(c)* otiose. Accordingly, a Swiss court specified that it was not bound by the arbitral tribunal's decisions with respect to the scope of the submission to arbitration, nor by that of authorities in other States, though following its own determination of the issue, the court ultimately rejected the challenge to enforcement.[840]

42. Similarly, though noting that United States Federal Arbitration Act has established a general "presumption that an arbitral body has acted within its powers", the United States Court of Appeals for the Ninth Circuit clarified that it would "review *de novo* a contention that the subject matter of the arbitration lies outside the scope of a contract."[841]

43. However, courts have consistently held that article V (1)*(c)* must be construed narrowly, and as such, does not permit under any circumstances that an enforcing court review the merits of a dispute, as this would run contrary to the spirit and purpose of the Convention.[842]

44. In this vein, courts have resisted attempts, advanced as challenges under article V (1)*(c)*, by parties to reopen an examination on the merits. For

---

[838] *Ernesto Francisco v. Stolt Achievement MT; Stolt Achievement, Inc.; Stolt-Nielsen Transportation Group, Ltd.; Stolt Parcel Tankers, Inc.*, Court of Appeals, Fifth Circuit, United States of America, 4 June 2002, 293 F.3d 270.

[839] *Id.*

[840] Debt Collection and Bankruptcy Chamber of the Court of Appeal, Switzerland, 16 September 2002, 14.2002.00042.

[841] *Mgmt. & Tech. Consultants S.A. v. Parsons-Jurden Int'l Corp.*, Court of Appeals, Ninth Circuit, United States of America, 8 July 1987, 820 F.2d 1531.

[842] *Lesotho Highlands Development Authority v. Impreglio SpA et al.*, House of Lords, England and Wales, 30 June 2005, [2005] UKHL 43. See also *Kersa Holding Co. Luxembourg v. Infancourtage, Famajuk Investment and Isny*, Superior Court of Justice, Luxemburg, 24 November 1993, XXI Y.B. COM. ARB. 617 (1996).

example, the Spanish Supreme Court was faced with a challenge by a party claiming that the arbitral tribunal had not taken into account all relevant factors presented to the arbitral tribunal, which would have led to a different result. The court considered that the challenge failed under its own terms as the challenging party did not suggest that the decision was outside the scope of the arbitration agreement, but rather that it disagreed with the "basis and reasons for the decision". The court concluded that such a challenge "undoubtedly falls without the scope of [...] Article V (1)*(c)* of the New York Convention".[843]

45. Similarly, a United States District Court found that a party's argument that the arbitral tribunal had impermissibly acted as amiable compositeur was "a not especially elegant masque that [sought] to conceal the fatal weakness" of that party's case on the merits, noting that the court was "forbidden under the Convention to reconsider factual findings of the arbitral panel."[844]

c. *Waiver/preclusion*

46. The language of article V (1)*(c)* does not explicitly impose any requirements that the challenges invoked under article V (1)*(c)* must be raised at any particular time during the arbitral procedure or thereafter.

47. In practice, some courts have held that a failure to raise appropriate objections during the arbitral proceedings would impair a party's ability to raise a challenge under article V (1)*(c)* during enforcement proceedings. For example, the Paris Court of Appeal rejected a challenge to enforcement in which a party argued that the arbitral tribunal had disregarded the "submission to arbitration" by refusing to hold a third hearing following the submission of an expert report. The arbitral award noted that this decision was taken with the agreement of the parties, and the party opposing enforcement had not reserved it rights at the time of the decision or following receipt of letters confirming the decision. The court concluded that the party had therefore "impliedly but unequivocally waived their right to a third hearing", and as such its objection under article V (1)*(c)* should be dismissed.[845]

---

[843] *Saroc S.p.A. v. Sahece, S.A.*, Supreme Court, Spain, 4 March 2003, XXXII Y.B. COM. ARB. 571 (2007).

[844] *Standard Elec. Corp. v. Bridas Sociedad Anonima Petrolera, Industrial y Comercial*, District Court, Southern District of New York, United States of America, 24 August 1990, 745 F. Supp. 172.

[845] *Société Unichips Finanziaria SpA and Société Unichips International Bv Beslotene Venootschap v. François Gesnouin and Michèle Gesnouin*, Court of Appeal of Paris, France, 12 February 1993, XIX Y.B. COM. ARB. 658 (1994).

48. Similarly, though without specific reference to waiver or preclusion, the Moscow Arbitrazh Court, in rejecting a challenge to enforcement under article V (1)*(c)* (and other provisions), took into account the fact that the party did not object to examination of the case by the tribunal, filed a statement of defence recognizing jurisdiction of the tribunal and filed counterclaims for offset.[846] A United States District Court also rejected a challenge under article V (1)*(c)*, finding that where the challenging party had requested, agreed to submit and briefed the question whether certain matters should be decided by the arbitrators, and the arbitrators had made a determination on that basis, the party could not later claim that the issue was outside the scope of submission.[847]

[846] *Ansell S.A. v. OOO MedBusinessService-2000*, Moscow Arbitrazh Court, Russian Federation, 15 April 2010, A40-24208/10-63-209.

[847] *Halcot Navigation Limited Partnership v. Stolt-Nielsen transportation Group, BV and Anthony Radcliffe Steamship Co. Ltd*, District Court, Southern District of New York, United States of America, 11 June 2007, 491 F. Supp. 2d 413.

Article V (1)*(d)*

1. Recognition and enforcement of the award may be refused, at the request of the party against whom it is invoked, only if that party furnishes to the competent authority where the recognition and enforcement is sought, proof that:

[…]

d) The composition of the arbitral authority or the arbitral procedure was not in accordance with the agreement of the parties, or, failing such agreement, was not in accordance with the law of the country where the arbitration took place.

Travaux préparatoires

The *travaux préparatoires* on article V (1)*(d)* as adopted in 1958 are contained in the following documents:

Draft Convention on the Recognition and Enforcement of Foreign Arbitral Awards and comments by Governments and Organizations:

Report of the Committee on the Enforcement of International Arbitral Awards: E/2704 and Annex.

Comments by Governments and Organizations on the Draft Convention on the Recognition and Enforcement of Foreign Arbitral Awards: E/2822, Annexes I-II; E/2822/Add.2; E/2822/Add.4; E/CONF.26/3; E/CONF.26/3/Add.1.

Activities of Inter-Governmental and Non-Governmental Organizations in the Field of International Commercial Arbitration: Consolidated Report by the Secretary-General: E/CONF.26/4.

Comments on the Draft Convention on the Recognition and Enforcement of Foreign Arbitral Awards: Note by the Secretary General: E/CONF.26/2.

United Nations Conference on International Commercial Arbitration:

Amendments to the Draft Convention Submitted by Governmental Delegations: E/CONF.26/L.15; E/CONF.26/L.15/Rev.1; E/CONF.26/L.17; E/CONF.26/L.32; E/CONF.26/L.34.

Comparison of Drafts Relating to Articles III, IV and V of the Draft Convention: E/CONF.26/L.33/Rev.1.

Further Amendments to the Draft Convention Submitted by Governmental Delegations: E/CONF.26/L.39; E/CONF.26/L.40.

Text of Articles III, IV and V of the Draft Convention Proposed by Working Party III: E/CONF.26/L.43.

Amendments by Governmental Delegations to the Drafts Submitted by the Working Parties and Further Suggested Drafts: E/CONF.26/L.45.

Text of Articles Adopted by the Conference: E/CONF.26/L.48.

Text of the Convention on the Recognition and Enforcement of Foreign Arbitral Awards as Provisionally Approved by the Drafting Committee: E/CONF.26/L.61; E/CONF.26/8.

Final Act and Convention on the Recognition and Enforcement of Foreign Arbitral Awards: E/CONF.26/8/Rev.1.

Summary records:

Summary Records of the Second, Fourth, Eleventh, Thirteenth, Fourteenth, and Seventeenth Meetings of the United Nations Conference on International Commercial Arbitration: E/CONF.26/SR.2; E/CONF.26/SR.4; E/CONF.26/SR.11; E/CONF.26/SR.13; E/CONF.26/SR.14; E/CONF.26/SR.17.

Summary Records of the Fourth, Fifth, Seventh and Eighth Meetings of the Committee on Enforcement of International Arbitral Awards: E/AC.42/SR.4; E/AC.42/SR.5; E/AC.42/SR.7; E/AC.42/SR.8.

Committee on the Enforcement of International Arbitral Awards:

Enforcement of International Arbitral Awards: statement submitted by the International Chamber of Commerce, a non-governmental organization having consultative status in category A: E/C.2/373.

Comments received from Governments regarding the Draft Convention on the Enforcement of International Arbitral Awards: E/AC.42/1.

Report of the Committee on the Enforcement of International Arbitral Awards: E/AC.42/4.

(Available on the Internet at http://www.uncitral.org)
(For the *travaux préparatoires*, case law and bibliographical references, see also on the Internet at http://newyorkconvention1958.org)

Introduction

1. Article V (1)*(d)* of the Convention sets out the fourth enumerated defence to the recognition and enforcement of a foreign arbitral award. It enables the courts of a Contracting State to refuse recognition and enforcement where the constitution of the arbitral tribunal or the arbitral procedure was not in accordance with the agreement of the parties or, in the absence of an agreement, with the law of the country where the arbitration took place.

2. Procedural irregularities under article V (1)*(d)* have to be raised and proven by the party challenging the recognition and enforcement of an award,[848] and cannot be raised by a court of its own motion.[849]

3. Under article V (1)*(d)* the drafters of the Convention gave priority to the parties' agreement concerning the composition of the tribunal and the arbitral procedure. The law of the country where the arbitration took place

[848] See, e.g., Oberlandesgericht [OLG] Schleswig, Germany, 24 June 1999, 16 SChH 01/99; *DMT S.A. v. Chaozhou City Huayi Packing Materials Co., Ltd. Chaoan County Huaye Packing Materials Co., Ltd.*, Supreme People's Court, China, 12 October 2010, [2010] Min Si Ta Zi No. 51; *Conceria G. De Maio & F. snc v. EMAG AG*, Court of Cassation, Italy, 20 January 1995, XXI Y.B. COM. ARB. 602 (1996); *Deiulemar Compagnia di Navigazione, S.p.A. v. Transocean Coal Company, Inc. and others*, District Court, Southern District of New York, United States of America, 30 November 2004, 03 Civ. 2038 (RCC), XXX Y.B. COM. ARB. 990 (2005).

[849] FOUCHARD GAILLARD GOLDMAN ON INTERNATIONAL COMMERCIAL ARBITRATION 983, para. 1694 (E. Gaillard, J. Savage eds., 1999); GARY B. BORN, INTERNATIONAL COMMERCIAL ARBITRATION 2731 (2009).

plays only a subsidiary role in the event that the parties have not reached an express or implied agreement on the procedural point at issue.[850]

4. Article V (1)*(d)* may be regarded as an important step forward compared to the 1927 Geneva Convention, under which an award had to comply with the parties' agreement and, cumulatively, the law governing the arbitral procedure, in order to gain recognition and enforcement.[851] The novelty of the New York Convention lies in the supremacy given to the parties under article V (1)*(d)* to agree on the composition of the tribunal and the procedure.[852] This is consistent with the limited power of review of awards by enforcing courts under article V (1) of the Convention,[853] and reduces the risk that the recognition and enforcement of awards will be refused based on grounds of procedural irregularities in national laws.

5. Although article V (1)*(d)* moves beyond the text of the 1927 Geneva Convention, it is not as liberal as certain arbitration statutes, which attach even less importance than the New York Convention to the law of the country where the arbitration took place at the recognition and enforcement stage.[854] As explained in the chapter on article VII,[855] the Convention sets only a "ceiling", or the maximum level of control, which courts of the Contracting States may exert over foreign arbitral awards. A court will not breach the New York Convention by applying more liberal rules than article V (1)*(d)*, in accordance with article VII (1).

---

850 *Report of the Secretary-General: Study on the Application and Interpretation of the Convention on the Recognition and Enforcement* of *Foreign Arbitral Awards* (New York, 1958), A/CN.9/168, in X YEARBOOK OF THE UNITED NATIONS COMMISSION ON INTERNATIONAL TRADE LAW 106 (1979).

851 See article 1(*c*) of the 1927 Geneva Convention, which provided that the party seeking recognition and enforcement had to demonstrate "[t]hat the award has been made by the Arbitral Tribunal provided for in the submission to arbitration or constituted in the manner agreed upon by the parties and in conformity with the law governing the arbitration procedure."

852 *Polimaster Ltd. and NA&SE Trading Co. Ltd. v. Rae Systems, Inc.*, District Court, Northern District of California, United States of America, 23 January 2009, C 05-1887; *Joseph Müller A. G. v. Sigval Bergesen*, Federal Tribunal, Switzerland, 26 February 1982; *Encyclopedia Universalis S.A. v. Encyclopedia Britannica, Inc.*, Court of Appeals, Second Circuit, United States of America, 31 March 2005, 04-0288-CV.

853 *Travaux préparatoires*, United Nations Conference on International Commercial Arbitration, Comments on Draft Convention on the Recognition and Enforcement of Foreign Arbitral Awards, Note by the Secretary-General, E/CONF.26/2, pp. 5-6.

854 For instance, article 1520 of the French Code of Civil Procedure provides that an award should not be recognized where "*the arbitral tribunal was not properly constituted*". Under this provision, as well as the equivalent provision of the former French Code of Civil Procedure, the composition of the arbitral tribunal is measured against the will of the parties. Where the alleged irregularity resulted solely from a violation of the law of the place of the arbitration, recognition and enforcement would not be refused unless that law had been chosen by the parties to govern their procedure. FOUCHARD GAILLARD GOLDMAN ON INTERNATIONAL COMMERCIAL ARBITRATION 989, para. 1701 (E. Gaillard, J. Savage eds., 1999).

855 See the chapter of the Guide on article VII, para. 2.

6. In the vast majority of reported cases, parties have been unsuccessful in proving the grounds for non-enforcement under article V (1)*(d)*. It rarely occurs that the composition of a tribunal deviates from the parties' agreement or the applicable rules. Further, courts have taken into account the wide discretion vested in arbitral tribunals to organize and control the arbitral proceedings.[856]

7. Courts are usually not formalistic in their approach to article V (1)*(d)* and as a result have applied it in a restrictive manner.[857] This is consistent with the general discretion of courts to refuse challenges under article V (1) of the Convention, which provides that a court "may" refuse recognition and enforcement.[858]

8. Article V (1)*(d)* has some interaction and overlap with article V (2)*(b)* of the Convention, which provides that a court may refuse to recognize or enforce an award if the award "would be contrary to the public policy of that country." It is not unusual for parties to raise both provisions in their attempt to challenge recognition and enforcement. However, a defence based on article V (1)*(d)* must be raised by "the party against whom [the award] is invoked", whereas courts may raise *sua sponte* possible grounds based on article V (2)*(b)*. In practice, most courts have considered that the grounds for non-enforcement under each provision are distinct and have analysed them separately.[859]

---

[856] See, e.g., *K Trading Company v. Bayerischen Motoren Werke AG*, Bayerisches Oberstes Landesgericht [BayObLG], Germany, 23 September 2004, 4 Z Sch 05/04; *Industrial Risk Insurers v. M.A.N. Gutehoffnungshutte GmbH*, Court of Appeals, Eleventh Circuit, United States of America, 22 May 1998, 94-2982, 94-2530. See also Martin Platte, *Multi-party Arbitration: Legal Issues Arising out of Joinder and Consolidation*, in ENFORCEMENT OF ARBITRATION AGREEMENTS AND INTERNATIONAL ARBITRAL AWARDS: THE NEW YORK CONVENTION IN PRACTICE 481, 491 (E. Gaillard, D. Di Pietro eds., 2008); ALBERT JAN VAN DEN BERG, THE NEW YORK ARBITRATION CONVENTION OF 1958: TOWARDS A UNIFORM JUDICIAL INTERPRETATION 323 (1994).

[857] See, e.g., *Al Haddad Bros. Enterprises Inc. v. M/S "Agapi" and Diakan Love S.A.*, District Court, District of Delaware, United States of America, 9 May 1986, 635 F. Supp. 205; *China Nanhai Oil Joint Service Corporation Shenzen Branch v. Gee Tai Holdings Co. Ltd.*, High Court, Supreme Court of Hong Kong, Hong Kong, 13 July 1994, 1992 No. MP 2411.

[858] Sigvard Jarvin, *Irregularity in the Composition of the Arbitral Tribunal and the Procedure*, in ENFORCEMENT OF ARBITRATION AGREEMENTS AND INTERNATIONAL ARBITRAL AWARDS: THE NEW YORK CONVENTION IN PRACTICE 729, 734 (E. Gaillard, D. Di Pietro eds., 2008).

[859] See, e.g., Oberlandesgericht [OLG] Schleswig, Germany, 24 June 1999, 16 SChH 01/99; Bundesgerichtshof [BGH], Germany, 14 April 1988, III ZR 12/87; *Goldtron Limited v. Media Most B.V.*, Court of First Instance of Amsterdam, Netherlands, 27 August 2002, XXVIII Y.B. COM. ARB. 814 (2003); *Eddie Javor v. Fusion-Crete, Inc. and others*, Supreme Court of British Columbia, Canada, 6 March 2003, L022829, XXIX Y.B. COM. ARB. 596 (2004).

Analysis

General principles

A. Prevalence of party autonomy

9. Article V (1)*(d)* expressly affirms the supremacy of the parties' agreement concerning the composition of the tribunal and arbitral procedure, and that the law of the place of arbitration should apply only "failing such agreement." [860] Courts have consistently recognized that the grounds enumerated in article V (1)*(d)* must be measured, in the first instance, against the agreement of the parties.[861]

10. Article V (1)*(d)* is silent as to the form of the parties' agreement. Such an agreement includes an oral agreement or one in writing, and can be express or implied.[862]

11. Article V (1)*(d)* does not stipulate any minimum requirements for the content of the parties' agreement. The parties can agree on a national procedural law or institutional rules to govern these matters,[863] or can agree on their own rules independent of any system.[864]

---

[860] *Travaux préparatoires*, Draft Convention on the Recognition and Enforcement of Foreign Arbitral Awards and Comments by Governments and Organizations, Report by the Secretary-General, Recognition and Enforcement of Foreign Arbitral Awards, E/2822, Annex II, pp. 18-19; FOUCHARD GAILLARD GOLDMAN ON INTERNATIONAL COMMERCIAL ARBITRATION 454, para. 756 (E. Gaillard, J. Savage eds., 1999).

[861] See, e.g., *Polimaster Ltd., NA&SE Trading Co., Limited v. RAE Systems, Inc.*, Court of Appeals, Ninth Circuit, United States of America, 28 September 2010, 08-15708, 09-15369; *Rederi Aktiebolaget Sally v. S.r.l. Termarea*, Court of Appeal of Florence, Italy, 13 April 1978, IV Y.B. COM. ARB. 294 (1979); *Deiulemar Compagnia di Navigazione, S.p.A. v. Transocean Coal Company, Inc. and others*, District Court, Southern District of New York, United States of America, 30 November 2004, 03 Civ. 2038 (RCC), XXX Y.B. COM. ARB. 990 (2005); Hanseatisches Oberlandesgericht [OLG] Bremen, Germany, 30 September 1999, (2) Sch 04/99.

[862] See Sigvard Jarvin, *Irregularity in the Composition of the Arbitral Tribunal and the Procedure*, in ENFORCEMENT OF ARBITRATION AGREEMENTS AND INTERNATIONAL ARBITRAL AWARDS: THE NEW YORK CONVENTION IN PRACTICE 729, 730 (E. Gaillard, D. Di Pietro eds., 2008); GARY B. BORN, INTERNATIONAL COMMERCIAL ARBITRATION 2771 (2009).

[863] See, e.g., *Joseph Müller A,G, v. Sigval Bergesen*, Federal Tribunal, Switzerland, 26 February 1982; Hanseatisches Oberlandesgericht [OLG] Bremen, Germany, 30 September 1999, (2) Sch 04/99; *Mechanised Construction* of *Pakistan Ltd. v. American Construction Machinery & Equipment Corporation (ACME)*, Court of Appeals, Second Circuit, United States of America, 14 September 1987, 828 F.2d 117, XV Y.B. COM. ARB. 539 (1990); *Pactrans Air & Sea, Inc. v. China National Chartering Corp., et al.*, Northern District Court of Florida, United States of America, 29 May 2010, 3:06-cv-00369-RS-EMT.

[864] See, e.g., *Encyclopedia Universalis S.A. v. Encyclopedia Britannica, Inc.*, Court of Appeals, Second Circuit, United States of America, 31 March 2005, 04-0288-CV; *Société Européenne d'Etudes et d'Entreprises (S.E.E.E.) v. Federal Republic of Yugoslavia*, Court of Appeal of Rouen, France, 13 November 1984, 982/82.

12. Under the Convention, the choice of a place of arbitration by the parties is not to be construed as an agreement to adopt the procedural rules of that jurisdiction. Article V (1)*(d)* itself distinguishes between situations in which procedural rules apply as a result of the agreement of the parties and, as explained below, situations in which they apply as a function of the place of the arbitration.[865]

13. Accordingly, courts have rejected arguments that the composition of the tribunal or the procedure did not comply with the law of the place of the arbitration where the parties had agreed on other procedural rules. For instance, a German court enforced an award rendered in Turkey where the parties had agreed to the rules of the Arbitral Commission of the Istanbul Chamber of Commerce and Industry, and rejected a party's argument that the procedure was not in accordance with the requirements of the Turkish Code of Civil Procedure.[866]

14. Even where the composition of the tribunal or the procedure was valid under the procedural rules of the country where the arbitration took place, courts have denied recognition and enforcement under article V (1)*(d)* where those elements deviated from the parties' agreement. In a 1978 decision, for instance, the Court of Appeal of Florence refused to enforce an award rendered in England by only two arbitrators, who had declined to appoint a third arbitrator on the basis of the 1950 English Arbitration Act, pursuant to which a clause providing for a three-member tribunal was deemed to take effect as if it provided for an umpire. According to the Court of Appeal, since the parties had in fact agreed on a three-member tribunal, their agreement was to be given precedence over the requirements of English procedural law.[867]

B. Subsidiary role of the law of the country where the arbitration took place

15. Recognition and enforcement may be refused under article V (1)*(d)* if, "failing" an express or implied agreement between the parties, the composition of the tribunal or the procedure did not accord with the "law of the country where the arbitration took place". The place of arbitration may result from the choice made by the parties, or by an arbitral institution or the arbitral tribunal. A court that rules on an application for recognition and enforcement in reference to the procedural law of the country where the

[865] FOUCHARD GAILLARD GOLDMAN ON INTERNATIONAL COMMERCIAL ARBITRATION 990, para. 1702 (E. Gaillard, J. Savage eds., 1999).

[866] Hanseatisches Oberlandesgericht [OLG] Bremen, Germany, 30 September 1999, (2) Sch 04/99.

[867] *Rederi Aktiebolaget Sally v. S.r.l. Termarea*, Court of Appeal of Florence, Italy, 13 April 1978, IV Y.B. COM. ARB. 294 (1979).

arbitration took place, without first ascertaining the existence of a party agreement, will thus violate the Convention.[868]

16. Courts have assessed challenges under article V (1)*(d)* by reference to the provisions of the place of the arbitration in very few cases. This may be explained by the circumstances that typically give rise to situations covered by article V (1)*(d)*. As one commentator notes, where the parties have not agreed on how the arbitral tribunal should be constituted, this will be determined either by an arbitral institution or a court, which will likely follow the requirements of the law where the arbitration takes place.[869]

17. In one reported case where procedural rules of the country where the arbitration took place were applied, a United States court held that, because there was no agreement between the parties concerning the arbitral procedure, the allegation that the arbitrator had improperly refused to hear oral evidence that was pertinent and material to the dispute had to be assessed with reference to the arbitration procedure of the United States, where the arbitration took place.[870] The court found that the arbitrator's decision to decide the matter based solely on documentary evidence did not constitute misconduct under the rules of the place of arbitration, and enforced the award.

18. Article V (1)*(d)* places no express limitation on the autonomy of the parties to agree on the composition of the arbitral tribunal or the arbitral procedure.

19. However, the question whether parties' agreement should be limited by the mandatory rules of the seat has been raised by commentators. One commentator has suggested that a failure to comply with the parties' agreement should not constitute a ground for refusal under article V (1)*(d)*, where such failure is justified by the obligation to comply with the mandatory rules of the place of the arbitration.[871] Other authors have argued that it should be assumed that the parties' intention was to be bound by an agreement that is valid at the place of arbitration, and that the reference to

---

868 *Rederi Aktiebolaget Sally v. S.r.l. Termarea*, Court of Appeal of Florence, Italy, 13 April 1978, IV Y.B. COM. ARB. 294 (1979).

869 Sigvard Jarvin, *Irregularity in the Composition of the Arbitral Tribunal and the Procedure*, in ENFORCEMENT OF ARBITRATION AGREEMENTS AND INTERNATIONAL ARBITRAL AWARDS: THE NEW YORK CONVENTION IN PRACTICE 729, 740 (E. Gaillard, D. Di Pietro eds., 2008).

870 *InterCarbon Bermuda, Ltd. v. Caltex Trading and Transport Corporation*, District Court, Southern District of New York, United States of America, 12 January 1993, 91 Civ. 4631 (MJL), XIX Y.B. COM. ARB. 802 (1994).

871 JÖRG GENTINETTA, DIE LEX FORI INTERNATIONALER HANDESSCHEIDSGERICHTE 302 (1973).

"agreement of the parties" must therefore be understood within the limits of the mandatory rules of the forum.[872]

20. These interpretations do not seem to accord with the intention of the drafters of the Convention which, as shown in the explicit terms of article V (1)*(d)*, was to ensure that the parties' agreement should prevail over the provisions—mandatory or not—of the law of the seat. In this respect, the wording of article V (1)*(d)* departed from the 1927 Geneva Convention, in which the law of the country where the arbitration took place retained paramount importance.[873]

21. The secondary role of the procedural rules where the arbitration took place was confirmed in a 1979 Report on the Convention by the United Nations Secretary General, which stated that the "priority given to the parties' wishes" under article V (1)*(d)* "is merely limited by the public policy ground under paragraph 2*(b)*."[874] The Swiss Federal Tribunal affirmed this view in a 1982 case, where it considered that "by virtue of the agreement of the parties, even the mandatory rules of procedure of a State also can be declared inapplicable and they can be substituted with the parties' own rules."[875]

Application

A. The requirement that the composition of the arbitral tribunal accord with the governing rules

22. Article V (1)*(d)* provides that the composition of the arbitral authority must have been in accordance with the agreement of the parties, or in the absence of an agreement, the law of the country where the arbitration

---

[872] JEAN-FRANÇOIS POUDRET, SEBASTIEN BESSON, COMPARATIVE LAW OF INTERNATIONAL ARBITRATION 839-40 (2007).

[873] See article 1(*c*) of the 1927 Geneva Convention, which provided that the party seeking recognition and enforcement had to demonstrate "[t]hat the award has been made by the Arbitral Tribunal provided for in the submission to arbitration or constituted in the manner agreed upon by the parties and in conformity with the law governing the arbitration procedure".

[874] Report of the Secretary-General: Study on the Application and Interpretation of the Convention on the Recognition and Enforcement of Foreign Arbitral Awards (New York, 1958), A/CN.9/168, in X YEARBOOK OF THE UNITED NATIONS COMMISSION ON INTERNATIONAL TRADE LAW 106 (1979). Another commentator has noted that any potential conflict between the rules chosen by the parties and the mandatory rules of the forum is counterbalanced under the Convention by the public policy provision of article V (2)(*b*), as well as the due process requirement of article V (1)(*b*). Patricia Nacimiento, *Article V (1)(d)*, in RECOGNITION AND ENFORCEMENT OF FOREIGN ARBITRAL AWARDS: A GLOBAL COMMENTARY ON THE NEW YORK CONVENTION 281, 286 (H. Kronke, P. Nacimiento et al. eds., 2010).

[875] *Joseph Müller A. G. v. Sigval Bergesen*, Federal Supreme Court, Switzerland, 26 February 1982; see also Hanseatisches Oberlandesgericht [OLG] Bremen, Germany, 30 September 1999, (2) Sch 04/99.

took place, failing which recognition and enforcement of the award may be refused.

23. The standard of proof for showing that the constitution of the arbitral tribunal was irregular is high.[876] In the words of one United States court, the burden is "substantial because the public policy in favour of international arbitration is strong."[877]

24. Courts may require a showing that the alleged irregularity would have resulted in a different award had the procedural rule been observed. For example, a German court rejected the argument of a party that a three-member tribunal had been appointed by the wrong authority, since that party had failed to demonstrate that a different appointment procedure would have led to a different ruling.[878]

25. Furthermore, even where it has been established that the composition of the tribunal is irregular, courts may consider that the parties' subsequent behaviour results in a mutually agreed modification to the applicable procedure. For instance, a German court considered that, where both parties had appointed arbitrators who were not members of the institution specified in their agreement, the parties had tacitly modified their agreement. The court consequently rejected the challenge to enforcement based on article V (1)*(d)*.[879]

26. Courts have sometimes interpreted article V (1)*(d)* restrictively and have enforced awards where the composition of the tribunal deviated from the parties' agreement.

---

[876] See, e.g., *Conceria G. De Maio & F. snc v. EMAG AG,* Court of Cassation, Italy, 20 January 1995, XXI Y.B. COM. ARB. 602 (1996); *Transocean Shipping Agency P. Ltd. v. Black Sea Shipping & Ors.*, Supreme Court, India, 14 January 1998; *Polimaster Ltd., NA&SE Trading Co., Limited v. RAE Systems, Inc.*, Court of Appeals, Ninth Circuit, United States of America, 28 September 2010, 08-15708, 09-15369; *Encyclopedia Universalis S.A. v. Encyclopedia Britannica,* Inc., Court of Appeals, Second Circuit, United States of America, 31 March 2005, 04-0288-CV; *Karaha Bodas Co. (Cayman Islands) v. Perusahaan Pertambangan Minyak Dan Gas Bumi Negara (Indonesia)*, Court of Appeals, Fifth Circuit, United States of America, 23 March 2004, 02-20042, 03-20602.

[877] *Polimaster Ltd., NA&SE Trading Co., Limited v. RAE Systems, Inc.*, Court of Appeals, Ninth Circuit, United States of America, 28 September 2010, 08-15708, 09-15369.

[878] *Creditor under the award v. Debitor under the award*, Oberlandesgericht [OLG] Karlsruhe, Germany, 14 September 2007, 9 Sch 02/07.

[879] Oberlandesgericht [OLG] Dresden, Germany, 20 February 2001, 11 SchH 02/00.

27. For instance, the Hong Kong Supreme Court enforced an award rendered in China, even though its members were selected from a different list of arbitrators than provided in the parties' agreement.[880]

28. Courts have rejected challenges under article V (1)*(d)* where the parties choose institutional rules to govern their procedure that provide for flexibility concerning the manner in which the tribunal is to be composed.[881] On the other hand, a German court refused recognition and enforcement where an award was rendered by two, instead of three arbitrators, as expressly required by the rules of the International Arbitration Court of the Belarusian Chamber of Commerce that the parties had agreed would govern their arbitration.[882]

29. Courts have exercised the residual discretion they enjoy under article V (1) and have rejected challenges based on an irregular composition of the tribunal where it is clear that a party had previously intended to frustrate the arbitral procedure. For instance, the Supreme Court of Spain enforced an award rendered by a sole arbitrator appointed by one of the parties, where the party opposing enforcement had refused to appoint a co-arbitrator.[883] Similarly, a United States court enforced an award rendered by one of the party appointees as a sole arbitrator where the other party chose not to participate in the arbitration.[884]

30. In the few cases where courts have refused to enforce awards pursuant to article V (1)*(d)*, the manner in which the tribunal was constituted materially deviated from the parties' agreement.

31. For example, a United States court refused enforcement in a case where the parties had agreed that they would each appoint a co-arbitrator, who would appoint a president if they failed to reach a decision, and where

[880] *China Nanhai Oil Joint Service Corporation Shenzen Branch v. Gee Tai Holdings Co. Ltd.*, High Court, Supreme Court of Hong Kong, Hong Kong, 13 July 1994, 1992 No. MP 2411.

[881] See, e.g., *Shaheen Natural Resources Company Inc. v. Société Nationale pour la Recherche, la Production and others*, Court of Appeals, Second Circuit, United States of America, 15 November 1983, 733 F. Supp. 2d 260, X Y.B. COM. ARB. 540 (1985).

[882] *E20, Supplier (United States) v. State enterprise (Belarus)*, Bundesgerichthof [BGH], Germany, 21 May 2007, III ZB 14/07, XXXIV Y.B. COM. ARB. 504 (2009).

[883] *X v. Naviera Y S.A.*, Supreme Court, Spain, 3 June 1982, XI Y.B. COM. ARB. 527 (1986).

[884] *Al Haddad Bros. Enterprises Inc. v. M/S "Agapi" and Diakan Love S.A.*, District Court, District of Delaware, United States of America, 9 May 1986, 635 F. Supp. 205. See also *China Nanhai Oil Joint Service Corporation Shenzen Branch v. Gee Tai Holdings Co. Ltd.*, High Court, Supreme Court of Hong Kong, Hong Kong, 13 July 1994, 1992 No. MP 2411; *Conceria G. De Maio & F. snc v. EMAG AG*, Court of Cassation, Italy, 20 January 1995, XXI Y.B. COM. ARB. 602 (1996).

one of the arbitrators had failed to even contact the other before requesting the appointing authority to appoint the third arbitrator.[885]

32. An Italian court upheld a challenge where the parties' agreement that the tribunal should constitute a specific number of arbitrators was not followed, and noted that the composition of the tribunal would also have been invalid according to the laws of the place of the arbitration.[886]

33. Certain authors have considered that courts may refuse enforcement under article V (1)*(d)* based on the alleged bias of an arbitrator.[887] This may also constitute a ground for refusal under article V (2)*(b)* where it is contrary to public policy.[888]

34. The standard of proof for arbitrator bias under article V (1)*(d)* is particularly high. For example, a United States court held that the mere fact that the tribunal President and the counsel of one of the parties both served on the same board of directors and were members of the same organization was insufficient to justify a refusal, where the party bringing the challenge had provided no evidence that they had otherwise communicated with each other.[889] A Hong Kong court has equally affirmed this high burden of proof, finding that the party opposing enforcement had failed to prove its allegation that the tribunal's deliberations had been affected by the alleged bias of one member.[890]

---

[885] *Encyclopedia Universalis S.A. v. Encyclopedia Britannica, Inc.*, Court of Appeals, Second Circuit, United States of America, 31 March 2005, 04-0288-CV.

[886] *Rederi Aktiebolaget Sally v. S.r.l. Termarea*, Court of Appeal of Florence, Italy, 13 April 1978, IV Y.B. COM. ARB. 294 (1979).

[887] Christian Borris, Rudolf Henneke, Article V (1)(*d*), in NEW YORK CONVENTION ON THE RECOGNITION AND ENFORCEMENT OF FOREIGN ARBITRAL AWARDS OF 10 JUNE 1958—COMMENTARY 329, 339 (R. Wolff ed., 2012);

[888] See the chapter of the Guide on article V (2)(*b*), paras. 59-61.

[889] *HSN Capital LLC v. Productora y Comercializador de Television, S.A. de C.V.*, District Court, Middle District of Florida, Tampa Division, United States of America, 5 July 2006, 8:05-cv-1769-T-30TBM. See also *Nicor International Corporation v. El Paso Corporation*, District Court, Southern District of Florida, United States of America, 24 November 2003, 02-21769, where the court decided that the parties opposing enforcement had failed to prove that a sole arbitrator's previous representations or nationality influenced his decision-making; *Shaanxi Provincial Medical Health Products I/E Corporation v. Olpesa, S.A.*, Supreme Court, Spain, 7 October 2003, 112/2002, XXX Y.B. COM. ARB. 617 (2005).

[890] *Logy Enterprises Ltd. v. Haikou City Bonded Area Wansen Products Trading Co.*, Court of Appeal, Hong Kong, 22 May 1997, No. 65 (Civil).

B. The requirement that the arbitral procedure accord with the governing rules

a. Criteria for procedural irregularities

35. The recognition and enforcement of an award may be refused under article V (1)*(d)* where the arbitral procedure was not in accordance with the agreement of the parties or, "failing such agreement", with the law of the country where the arbitration took place.

36. The term "arbitral procedure" encompasses the period beginning with the filing of an action and ending when the award is rendered.[891] The application of the law by a tribunal, on the other hand, goes to the actual merits of a dispute and therefore falls outside the scope of review at the recognition and enforcement stage.[892]

37. The burden of proof for an alleged procedural irregularity is on the party opposing recognition and enforcement. The evidence must be provided[893] and it must be clear.[894]

38. As with the composition of the tribunal, the threshold of proof for showing an irregular arbitral procedure under article V (1)*(d)* is high. One United States court observed that the Convention does not "permit reviewing courts to police every procedural ruling made by the arbitrator and to set aside the award if any violation of the [...] procedures is found. Such an interpretation would directly conflict with the 'pro-enforcement bias' of the Convention and its intention to remove obstacles to confirmation of arbitral awards."[895]

---

[891] Christian Borris, Rudolf Henneke, *Article V (1)(d),* in NEW YORK CONVENTION ON THE RECOGNITION AND ENFORCEMENT OF FOREIGN ARBITRAL AWARDS OF 10 JUNE 1958—COMMENTARY 329, 344 (R. Wolff ed., 2012); Patricia Nacimiento, *Article V (1)(d),* in RECOGNITION AND ENFORCEMENT OF FOREIGN ARBITRAL AWARDS: A GLOBAL COMMENTARY ON THE NEW YORK CONVENTION 281, 292 (H. Kronke, P. Nacimiento et al. eds., 2010).

[892] *Vigel S.p.A. v. China National Machine Tool Corporation*, Court of Cassation, Italy, 8 April 2004, XXXI Y.B. COM. ARB. 802 (2006). See also *Venture Global Engineering, LLC v. Satyam Computer Services, Ltd.,* Court of Appeals, Sixth Circuit, United States of America, 15 May 2007, 062056, XXXIII Y.B. COM. ARB. 970 (2008).

[893] *Grow Biz International Inc. v. D.L.T. Holdings Inc., and Debbie Tanton*, Supreme Court of the Province of Prince Edward Island, Canada, 23 March 2001, GSC-17431, XXX Y.B. COM. ARB. 450 (2005).

[894] See, e.g., *Manufacturer v. Exclusive distributor*, Oberlandesgericht [OLG] Schleswig, Germany, 24 June 1999, 16 SchH 01/99.

[895] *Compagnie des Bauxites de Guinée v. Hammermills Inc.*, District Court, District of Columbia, United States of America, 29 May 1992, 90-0169, XVIII Y.B. COM. ARB. 566 (1993).

39. Article V (1)*(d)* is silent as to what types of procedural irregularities should lead to a refusal to recognize and enforce. Most courts require a substantial defect in the arbitral procedure and/or a causal nexus between the defect and the award. A range of approaches have been adopted for determining these criteria.[896]

40. One approach is to ascertain whether the alleged irregularity substantially prejudiced one of the parties.

41. In one case, an English court enforced an award where the tribunal applied a revised set of procedural rules that had superseded those provided for in the parties' agreement, holding the party opposing enforcement had not suffered sufficient prejudice to justify a refusal.[897] In another case where the arbitration was held at a different place than the agreed place of arbitration and a party had refused to participate, an English court held that the different location did not affect the fairness of the proceedings or prejudice that party. The court reasoned that the wording of the arbitration agreement had not made it clear that the parties regarded the venue as critically important.[898] The courts of the United States have similarly considered that the "appropriate standard of review would be to set aside an award based on a procedural violation only if such violation caused substantial prejudice to the complaining party."[899]

42. Another approach is to require a party opposing enforcement to prove that the outcome of the case would have been different had the alleged irregularity not occurred. As noted above, this approach has also been followed in challenges based on the composition of the tribunal.[900]

---

[896] Christian Borris, Rudolf Henneke, *Article V (1)(d)*, in NEW YORK CONVENTION ON THE RECOGNITION AND ENFORCEMENT OF FOREIGN ARBITRAL AWARDS OF 10 JUNE 1958—COMMENTARY 329, 344 (R. Wolff ed., 2012); Patricia Nacimiento, *Article V (1)(d)*, in RECOGNITION AND ENFORCEMENT OF FOREIGN ARBITRAL AWARDS: A GLOBAL COMMENTARY ON THE NEW YORK CONVENTION 281, 292-93 (H. Kronke, P. Nacimiento et al. eds., 2010).

[897] *China Agrobusiness Development Corporation v. Balli Trading*, High Court of Justice, Queen's Bench Division, England and Wales, 20 January 1997, XXIV Y.B. COM. ARB. 732 (1999).

[898] *Tongyuan International trading Group v. Uni-Clam Limited*, High Court of Justice, England and Wales, 19 January 2001, 2000 Folio No 1143.

[899] *Compagnie des Bauxites de Guinée v. Hammermills Inc.*, District Court, District of Columbia, United States of America, 29 May 1992, 90-0169, XVIII Y.B. COM. ARB. 566 (1993). See also *P.T. Reasuransi Umum Indonesia v. Evanston Insurance Company, Utica Mutual Insurance Company and others*, District Court, Southern District of New York, United States of America, 21 December 1992, 92 Civ. 4623 (MGC), XIX Y.B. COM. ARB. 788 (1994).

[900] See, e.g., *Creditor under the award v. Debitor under the award*, Oberlandesgericht [OLG] Karlsruhe, Germany, 14 September 2007, 9 Sch 02/07, where the court required that the party arguing that a three-member tribunal had been appointed by the wrong authority was

43. For example, in a 2004 decision, a German court enforced an award that was rendered five months after the time limit set in the parties' agreement. The Court found that the party opposing enforcement had not proven that the tribunal would have decided differently had the tribunal respected the time limit.[901] Other German courts have followed this approach.[902]

44. The distinction between the varying approaches may be more apparent than real, and in many cases may lead to the same outcome particularly since not all courts distinguish between them and/or refer to them simultaneously.[903] Of the few decisions where a foreign award has been refused enforcement pursuant to the second alternative of article V (1)*(d)*, the party opposing enforcement brought evidence of fundamental or unjustifiable procedural defects that one could consider would have met the criteria of both approaches. For instance, in a 1968 case, a Swiss court refused to issue an enforcement order on the grounds that the arbitral tribunal had not complied with the agreement of the parties that "all disputes should be settled in one and the same arbitral proceedings" and instead conducted the arbitration in two stages.[904] In a 2001 case, the Italian Supreme Court enforced a first award but not a second award made with respect to the same dispute. The Court held that the second award was contrary to the parties' agreement that contemplated only one arbitration, depending on which party commenced arbitration first.[905]

b. Tribunal's discretion to organize and control the arbitral proceedings

45. In assessing challenges to recognition and enforcement under article V (1)*(d)*, courts have recognized the broad discretion of arbitral tribunals to organize and control the arbitral proceedings.

---

required to demonstrate that a different appointment procedure would have led to a different ruling.

[901] *K Trading Company v. Bayerischen Motoren Werke AG*, Bayerisches Oberstes Landesgericht [BayObLG], Germany, 23 September 2004, 4 Z Sch 05/04.

[902] *Exclusive distributor v. Manufacturer*, Oberlandesgericht [OLG] Munich, Germany, 22 June 2009, 34 Sch 26/08; SpA Ghezzi v. Jacob Boss Söhne, Bundesgerichtshof [BGH], Germany, 14 April 1988, XV Y.B. COM. ARB. 450 (1990).

[903] Christian Borris, Rudolf Henneke, *Article V (1)(d),* in NEW YORK CONVENTION ON THE RECOGNITION AND ENFORCEMENT OF FOREIGN ARBITRAL AWARDS OF 10 JUNE 1958—COMMENTARY 329, 347 (R. Wolff ed., 2012); Patricia Nacimiento, *Article V (1)(d),* in RECOGNITION AND ENFORCEMENT OF FOREIGN ARBITRAL AWARDS: A GLOBAL COMMENTARY ON THE NEW YORK CONVENTION 281, 298 (H. Kronke, P. Nacimiento et al. eds., 2010).

[904] *Firm in Hamburg (buyer) v. Corporation (A.G.) in Basel (seller),* Court of Appeal of the Canton of Basel-Stadt, Switzerland, 6 September 1968, I Y.B. COM. ARB. 200 (1976).

[905] *Tema Frugoli SpA, in liquidation v. Hubei Space Quarry Industry Co. Ltd*, Court of Cassation, Italy, 7 February 2001, XXXII Y.B. COM. ARB. 390 (2001).

46. For instance, a United States court rejected an argument that the tribunal had deviated from the parties' agreement by consolidating claims arising out of two separate contracts. In the Court's view, the decision to consolidate the claims was within the tribunal's discretion, and this decision was reached after a careful interpretation of the parties' contract.[906] In another decision, a United States court held that there was no deviation from the rules of the American Arbitration Association agreed to by the parties where the tribunal had considered a belatedly submitted technical report, adding that "[a]rbitration proceedings are not constrained by formal rules of procedure or evidence."[907]

47. Courts have similarly held that a tribunal's adjudication of a case based on documentary evidence without an oral hearing does not justify a refusal under article V (1)*(d)*. A German court reached this decision where the provisions of the 1996 English Arbitration Act agreed to by the parties granted discretion to the tribunal to schedule an oral hearing.[908] A United States court held that a tribunal's decision of an issue of contract interpretation based solely on documentary evidence was not fundamentally unfair where the parties had not agreed on the applicable procedure. In this instance, the tribunal assessed the issue by reference to the laws of the United States, where the arbitration had taken place.[909]

c. *Failure to state reasons*

48. Certain national laws expressly require an arbitral tribunal to provide the reasons for its final decision.[910] The same is true of certain

---

[906] *Karaha Bodas Co. (Cayman Islands) v. Perusahaan Pertambangan Minyak Dan Gas Bumi Negara (Indonesia)*, Court of Appeals, Fifth Circuit, United States of America, 23 March 2004, 02-20042, 03-20602.

[907] *Industrial Risk Insurers v. M.A.N. Gutehoffnungshutte GmbH*, Court of Appeals, Eleventh Circuit, United States of America, 22 May 1998, 94-2982, 94-2530. See also *Compagnie des Bauxites de Guinée v. Hammermills Inc.*, District Court, District of Columbia, United States of America, 29 May 1992, 90-0169, XVIII Y.B. COM. ARB. 566 (1993), concerning the tribunal's application of the ICC Arbitration Rules; *China National Metal Products Import/Export Company v. Apex Digital, Inc.*, Court of Appeals, Ninth Circuit, United States of America, 16 August 2004, 03-55231, XXX Y.B. COM. ARB. 908 (2005), concerning the tribunal's application of the CIETAC Rules.

[908] Hanseatisches Oberlandesgericht [OLG] Hamburg, Germany, 30 July 1998, 6 Sch 3/98. See also Hanseatisches Oberlandesgericht [OLG] Bremen, Germany, 30 September 1999, (2) Sch 04/99.

[909] *InterCarbon Bermuda, Ltd. v. Caltex Trading and Transport Corporation,* District Court, Southern District of New York, United States of America, 12 January 1993, 91 Civ. 4631 (MJL), XIX Y.B. COM. ARB. 802 (1994).

[910] For instance, the laws of Australia, Belgium, England, France, Germany, Italy, Ireland, the Netherlands and Switzerland all expressly require arbitrators to state the reasons for their decision in their award.

institutional rules that the parties may choose to govern their dispute.[911] If the parties' agreement, or the agreed upon arbitration rules or national law, require the award to contain reasons, the failure to provide reasons may be a ground for refusal under article V (1)*(d)* .[912] Courts have observed the limited scope of review of arbitral awards at the enforcement stage when examining these types of challenges.[913]

49. Where an arbitration agreement or award falls within the field of application of both the New York Convention and the 1961 European Convention on International Commercial Arbitration, the requirement to state reasons will be assessed in light of the provisions of the European Convention. Article VIII of the European Convention provides that the parties to an arbitration shall be presumed to have agreed that reasons shall be given for the award unless they expressly declare otherwise, or have assented to an arbitral procedure under which it is not customary to give reasons, provided that neither party requests before the end of the hearing or the making of the award that reasons be given.[914]

50. In a case concerning an application for enforcement that was subject to both the New York Convention and the European Convention, the Italian Court of Cassation decided that enforcement should be denied where the presumption under Article VIII had not been rebutted because one party seeking enforcement had expressly requested during the arbitral proceeding that reasons be given for the award. This was notwithstanding the fact that the Arbitration Rules of the Sugar Association of London, which the parties agreed would govern the arbitral procedure, did not require that reasons for an award be provided.[915]

---

[911] For instance, Article 31(2) of the UNCITRAL Model Law on International Commercial Arbitration presumes that, in the absence of any indication to the contrary, the parties' intention is that the arbitrators should state the grounds for their awards.

[912] See however *Food Services of America, Inc. v. Pan Pacific Specialties Ltd.*, Supreme Court of British Columbia, Canada, 24 March 1997, A970243, XXIX Y.B. COM. ARB. 581 (2004), where the court held that an arbitrator's failure to state reasons, as required by the rules of the American Arbitration Association agreed upon by the parties, was not considered part of the arbitral procedure.

[913] Oberlandesgericht [OLG] Bremen, Germany, 30 September 1999, (2) Sch 04/99. See also *Inter-Arab Investment Guarantee Corp. v. Banque Arabe et Internationale d'Investissements*, Court of Appeal of Brussels, Belgium, XXII. Y.B. COM. ARB. 643 (1997).

[914] European Convention on International Commercial Arbitration, Geneva, 21 April 1961, Article VIII: "The parties shall be presumed to have agreed that reasons shall be given for the award unless they (a) either expressly declare that reasons shall not be given; or (b) have assented to an arbitral procedure under which it is not customary to give reasons for awards, provided that in this case neither party requests before the end of the hearing, or if there has not been a hearing then before the making of the award, that reasons be given."

[915] *Fratelli Damiano s.n.c. v. August Tropfer & Co.*, Court of Cassation, Italy, 8 February 1982, 722, IX Y.B. COM. ARB. 418 (1984).

C. Procedural issues in raising a challenge based on article V (1)*(d)*

51. The question has arisen whether a party may be estopped from raising the defence to enforcement under article V (1)*(d)*, where it has failed to do so before the arbitral tribunal. A number of courts have held that a complaint concerning the composition of the tribunal or the arbitral procedure will not be entertained at the enforcement stage if it existed at the time of the arbitral proceedings and could have been raised before the tribunal.

52. A German court has held that, even where it was shown that the tribunal was irregularly composed, the party raising the challenge was precluded from relying on article V (1)*(d)* because it had been aware of the defect but nonetheless participated in the arbitration without raising any objection.[916] The courts of China[917] and Italy[918] have also held that a party that has failed to raise an irregularity during the arbitral proceeding, although it could have done so, has waived its right to do so at the enforcement stage.

53. A refusal to uphold a challenge under article V (1)*(d)* that could have been raised during the proceedings has been linked by some courts to the principle of good faith. The Supreme Court of Hong Kong has considered that "there is indeed a duty of good faith which in the circumstances of this case required the defendant to bring [...] its objections to the formation of this particular arbitral tribunal. Its failure to do so and its obvious policy of keeping this point up its sleeve to be pulled out only if the arbitration was lost, is not one that I find consistent with the obligation of good faith nor with any notions of justice and fair play."[919]

54. Courts have similarly considered that a party will be barred from invoking a defence under article V (1)*(d)* based on an irregular procedure at the exequatur stage if it failed to object to the irregular arbitral proceedings during the course of the arbitration. In *Chrome Resources S.A. v. Leopold Lazarus Ltd.*, the Swiss Federal Tribunal rejected a challenge that the arbitral tribunal had consulted an expert in the absence of the parties, finding that the party's attempt to raise this objection at the enforcement stage was in bad

---

[916] *Manufacturer v. Supplier, in liquidation*, Oberlandesgericht [OLG] Munich, Germany, 15 March 2006, 34 Sch 06/05.

[917] *DMT S.A. v. Chaozhou City Huayi Packing Materials Co., Ltd. Chaoan County Huaye Packing Materials Co., Ltd.*, Supreme People's Court, China, 12 October 2010, [2010] Min Si Ta Zi No. 51.

[918] *Conceria G. De Maio & F. snc v. EMAG AG*, Court of Cassation, Italy, 20 January 1995, XXI Y.B. COM. ARB. 602 (1996)

[919] *China Nanhai Oil Joint Service Corporation Shenzen Branch v. Gee Tai Holdings Co. Ltd.*, High Court, Supreme Court of Hong Kong, Hong Kong, 13 July 1994, 1992 No. MP 2411. See also *X AG v. Y AS*, Federal Tribunal, Switzerland, 4 October 2010, 4A 124/2010, XXXVI Y.B. COM. ARB. 340 (2011).

faith and constituted an abuse of rights.[920] Courts in England,[921] Germany,[922] Greece,[923] and the United States[924] have similarly barred a party from asserting any defect of the arbitral procedure at a later stage if it had the opportunity to raise a reservation in a timely manner during the arbitral proceedings.

55. The same result has been reached in cases where the party opposing enforcement has alleged that the arbitral procedure was irregular, but at the same time chose not to participate in the proceedings. In a 1995 decision, a Singapore court held in a case where a party chose deliberately not to participate in an arbitration, that it had waived its rights to criticize the way in which the arbitration proceeding had been conducted.[925] Similarly, an English court decided that "in view of the fact that the sellers chose to take no part in the proceedings, it is impossible [...] to submit that any failure to comply with the agreement of the parties as to venue had any prejudicial effect as far as [the party] is concerned."[926] A German court has also considered that the participation of a party in an arbitration without raising any objection may be construed as an implicit agreement with the procedural rules applied by the tribunal.[927]

---

920 *Chrome Resources S.A. v. Léopard Lazarus Ltd.*, Federal Tribunal, Switzerland, 8 February 1978, XI Y.B. COM. ARB. 538 (1986).

921 *China Agrobusiness Development Corporation v. Balli Trading,* High Court of Justice, Queen's Bench Division, England and Wales, 20 January 1997, XXIV Y.B. COM. ARB. 732 (1999).

922 *Manufacturer v. Exclusive distributor*, Oberlandesgericht [OLG] Schleswig, Germany, 24 June 1999, 16 SchH 01/99.

923 *Greek Company v. FR German Company*, Court of Appeal of Athens, Greece, 4458, 1984, XIV Y.B. COM. ARB. 638 (1989).

924 *Shaheen Natural Resources Company Inc. v. Société Nationale pour la Recherche, la Production and others,* Court of Appeals, Second Circuit, United States of America, 15 November 1983, 733 F. Supp. 2d 260, X Y.B. COM. ARB. 540 (1985); *Imperial Ethiopian Government v. Baruch Foster Corporation*, Court of Appeals, Fifth Circuit, United States of America, 19 July 1976, 535 F.2d 334, II Y.B. COM. ARB. 251 (1977); *Karaha Bodas Co. (Cayman Islands) v. Perusahaan Pertambangan Minyak Dan Gas Bumi Negara (Indonesia)*, Court of Appeals, Fifth Circuit, United States of America, 23 March 2004, 02-20042, 03-20602.

925 *Hainan Machinery Import and Export Corporation v. Donald & McArthy Pte Ltd*, High Court, Singapore, 29 September 1995, 1056 of 1994, XXII Y.B. COM. ARB. 771 (1997).

926 *Tongyuan International Trading Group v. Uni-Clam Limited*, High Court of Justice, England and Wales, 19 January 2001, 2000 Folio No 1143.

927 *Manufacturer v. Supplier, in liquidation*, Oberlandesgericht [OLG] Munich, Germany, 15 March 2006, 34 Sch 06/05.

Article V (1)*(e)*

1. Recognition and enforcement of the award may be refused, at the request of the party against whom it is invoked, only if that party furnishes to the competent authority where the recognition and enforcement is sought, proof that:

e) The award has not yet become binding on the parties, or has been set aside or suspended by a competent authority of the country in which, or under the law of which, that award was made.

Travaux préparatoires

The *travaux préparatoires* on article V (1)*(e)* as adopted in 1958 are contained in the following documents:

Draft Convention on the Recognition and Enforcement of Foreign Arbitral Awards and comments by Governments and Organizations:

Report of the Committee on the Enforcement of International Arbitral Awards: E/2704 and Annex.

Comments by Governments and Organizations on the Draft Convention on the Recognition and Enforcement of Foreign Arbitral Awards: E/2822, Annexes I-II; E/2822/Add.2; E/2822/Add.5; E/CONF.26/3/Add.1.

Activities of Inter-Governmental and Non-Governmental Organizations in the Field of International Commercial Arbitration: Consolidated Report by the Secretary-General: E/CONF.26/4.

Comments on the Draft Convention on the Recognition and Enforcement of Foreign Arbitral Awards: Note by the Secretary General: E/CONF.26/2.

United Nations Conference on International Commercial Arbitration:

Amendments to the Draft Convention Submitted by Governmental Delegations: E/CONF.26/L.8;

E/CONF.26/L.15; E/CONF.26/L.15 Rev.1; E/CONF.26/L.16; E/CONF.26/L.17; E/CONF.26/L.24; E/CONF.26/L.30; E/CONF.26/L.34; E/CONF.26/L.35.

Comparison of Drafts Relating to Articles III, IV and V of the Draft Convention: E/CONF.26/L.33/Rev.1.

Further Amendments to the Draft Convention Submitted by Governmental Delegations: E/CONF.26/L.39; E/CONF.26/L.40.

Text of Articles III, IV and V of the Draft Convention Proposed by Working Party III: E/CONF.26/L.43.

Text of Articles Adopted by the Conference: E/CONF.26/L.48.

Text of the Convention on the Recognition and Enforcement of Foreign Arbitral Awards as Provisionally Approved by the Drafting Committee: E/ CONF.26/L.61; E/CONF.26/8.

New text of Articles I (3), V (1)*(a), (b),* and *(e)* Adopted by the Conference at its 23rd meeting: E/CONF.26/L.63.

Final Act and Convention on the Recognition and Enforcement of Foreign Arbitral Awards: E/CONF.26/8/Rev.1.

Summary records:

Summary Records of the Eleventh, Twelfth, Thirteenth, Fourteenth, Seventeenth, Twenty-Third and Twenty-Fourth Meetings of the United Nations Conference on International Commercial Arbitration: E/CONF.26/SR.11; E/CONF.26/SR.12; E/CONF.26/SR.13; E/CONF.26/SR.14; E/CONF.26/SR.17; E/CONF.26/SR.23; E/CONF.26/SR.24.

Summary Records of the Fifth, and Sixth Meetings of the Committee on Enforcement of International Arbitral Awards: E/AC.42/SR.5; E/AC.42/SR.6.

Committee on the Enforcement of International Arbitral Awards:

Enforcement of International Arbitral Awards: statement submitted by the International Chamber of Commerce, a non-governmental organization having consultative status in category A: E/C.2/373.

Comments received from Governments regarding the Draft Convention on the Enforcement of International Arbitral Awards: E/AC.42/1.

Report of the Committee on the Enforcement of International Arbitral Awards: E/AC.42/4.

(Available on the Internet at http://www.uncitral.org)
(For the *travaux préparatoires*, case law and bibliographical references, see also on the Internet at http://newyorkconvention1958.org)

Introduction

1. Article V (l)*(e)* allows national courts to refuse the recognition or enforcement of an award if the party opposing enforcement establishes that the award (i) has not yet become binding on the parties or (ii) has been set aside or suspended. Article V (1)*(e)* further requires that the setting aside or suspension of the award be ordered by a competent authority of the country in which, or under the law of which, the award was made.

2. Under the 1927 Geneva Convention, a party seeking enforcement or recognition of an award had to prove, among other conditions, that the award had become "final" in the country in which it was made. The 1927 Geneva Convention specified that the award would not be final if the award were still "open to opposition, appeal or *pourvoi en cassation*" or if it was "proved that any proceedings for the purpose of contesting the validity of the award [were] pending".[928] In practice, establishing the finality of the award could only be achieved by obtaining a leave of enforcement in the courts of the country of the seat of the arbitration. This required the party seeking enforcement to effectively obtain two decisions of exequatur, one at the country where the award was issued and one at the place of enforcement, thus generating more costs and delaying proceedings.[929] In addition, the requirement that the award be final in the country in which the award was rendered made it particularly easy for a party to obstruct or delay the enforcement by simply instituting proceedings for contesting the award's validity in the courts of the country where the award was issued.[930]

---

[928] See article 1(*d*) of the 1927 Geneva Convention.

[929] See *Travaux préparatoires*, Comments on Draft Convention on the Recognition and Enforcement of Foreign Arbitral Awards, E/CONF.26/SR.11, pp. 5-6. See also ALBERT JAN VAN DEN BERG, THE NEW YORK ARBITRATION CONVENTION OF 1958: TOWARDS A UNIFORM JUDICIAL INTERPRETATION 333 (1981); FOUCHARD GAILLARD GOLDMAN ON INTERNATIONAL COMMERCIAL ARBITRATION 971, para. 1677 (E. Gaillard, J. Savage eds., 1999); Nadia Darwazeh, *Article V (1)(e),* in RECOGNITION AND ENFORCEMENT OF FOREIGN ARBITRAL AWARDS: A GLOBAL COMMENTARY ON THE NEW YORK CONVENTION 301, 302, 304 (H. Kronke, P. Nacimiento et al. eds., 2010); Christoph Liebscher, *Article V (1)(e),* in NEW YORK CONVENTION ON THE RECOGNITION AND ENFORCEMENT OF FOREIGN ARBITRAL AWARDS OF 10 JUNE 1958—COMMENTARY 356, 356, paras. 353-56 (R. Wolff ed., 2012).

[930] ALBERT JAN VAN DEN BERG, THE NEW YORK ARBITRATION CONVENTION OF 1958: TOWARDS A UNIFORM JUDICIAL INTERPRETATION 333 (1981).

3. Article V (1)*(e)* of the New York Convention was drafted with a view to remedy these shortcomings. The drafters of the New York Convention abandoned the requirement of finality of the award, thereby putting an end to the mechanism of *double exequatur*, while providing that the non-binding nature of the award could still constitute a valid ground for refusing recognition and enforcement.[931] The Chairman of the Working Party in charge of drafting article V (1)*(e)* explained this decision as follows: "The text of paragraph 1 *(e)* of [article V] was drafted with the aim of making the Convention acceptable to those States which considered an arbitral award to be enforceable only if it fulfilled certain formal requirements which alone made the award binding on the parties. The Working Party agreed that an award should not be enforced if under the applicable arbitral rules it was still subject to an appeal which had a suspensive effect, but at the same time felt that it would be unrealistic to delay the enforcement of an award until all the time limits provided for by the statutes of limitations had expired or until all possible means of recourse, including those which normally did not have a suspensive effect, have been exhausted and the award has become 'final'."[932]

4. Courts from various countries have consistently referred to the abrogation of *double exequatur* as one of the major innovations of the New York Convention. For example, the English High Court of Justice held that "[i]t is common ground that the intention of the New York Convention was to make enforcement of a Convention award more straightforward, and in particular to remove the previous necessity for a *double exequatur*—i.e., the need, before a Convention award could be enforced in any other jurisdiction, for it to be shown that it has first been rendered enforceable in the jurisdiction whose law governs the arbitration [...]."[933] Likewise, the Swiss Federal Tribunal held that "the authors of the Convention wanted to exclude the requirement of exequatur in the award's country of origin, as well as any other proceedings to confirm that the award is enforceable in that country [...]."[934] Numerous other courts have similarly confirmed this principle.[935]

---

931 Nadia Darwazeh, *Article V (1)(e)*, in RECOGNITION AND ENFORCEMENT OF FOREIGN ARBITRAL AWARDS: A GLOBAL COMMENTARY ON THE NEW YORK CONVENTION 301, 306-07 (H. Kronke, P. Nacimiento et al. eds., 2010); ICCA'S GUIDE TO THE INTERPRETATION OF THE 1958 NEW YORK CONVENTION: A HANDBOOK FOR JUDGES 110 (P. Sanders ed., 2011).

932 *Travaux préparatoires*, Comments on Draft Convention on the Recognition and Enforcement of Foreign Arbitral Awards, E/CONF.26/SR.17, p. 3.

933 *Dowans Holding S.A. v. Tanzania Electric Supply Co. Ltd.*, High Court of Justice, England and Wales, 27 July 2011, 2010 Folio 1539.

934 *Y v. X*, Swiss Federal Tribunal, Switzerland, 3 January 2006, 5P.292/2005.

935 See, e.g., *SPP (Middle East) Ltd. v. The Arab Republic of Egypt,* President of the District Court of Amsterdam, Netherlands, 12 July 1984, X Y.B. COM. ARB. (1985) (stating that "the drafters of the Convention chose the word 'binding' in order to abolish the requirement of the *double exequatur* which was the result of the word 'final' in the Geneva Convention of 1927)"; *German (F.R.) party v. Dutch party*, President of Rechtbank, The

Analysis

A. The "binding" nature of an award

a. When does an award become binding?

5. The question of when an award becomes binding gave rise to a number of discussions among members of the Working Party in charge of drafting article V (1)*(e)*. Some delegates' view was that it should mean that the award is no longer open to ordinary, as opposed to extraordinary, means of recourse.[936] This distinction, being unknown in a number of legal systems, was eventually not retained. The drafters of the Convention decided not to define the term "binding" in the Convention itself, leaving it to the courts to decide the conditions under which an award should be considered as such.

6. Some courts have assessed the binding nature of the award by reference to the law of the country in which the award was rendered.[937] For instance, in a case where a party opposed enforcement on the ground that the award had not been duly delivered to it, and hence was allegedly not binding, a Swiss court decided that "[t]he issue whether an arbitral award has become binding on the parties, for instance by rendition, oral communication, written statement or communication to the parties or by expiry of the time limit for a legal means [of appeal] is governed in first instance by the law applicable to

---

Hague, Netherlands, 26 April 1973, IV Y.B. COM. ARB. 305 (1979) (stating that "[a]n important improvement of the New York Convention for the Execution of Foreign Arbitral Awards of 1927 is the fact that the *double exequatur* 'leave for enforcement' is abolished"); *Joseph Müller AG v. Bergesen und Obergericht (II. Zivilkammer) des Kantons Zürich*, Court of First Instance, Switzerland, 26 February 1982 (holding that "the aim of the New York Convention it to avoid the double exequatur"); *Company X SA v. Y Federation*, Swiss Federal Tribunal, Switzerland, 9 December 2008, 4A_403/2008 (holding that "the New York Convention sought to prevent "double enforcement"). See also *Palm and Vegetable Oils SDN. BHD. v. Algemene Oliehandel International B.V.*, President of Rechtbank, Court of First Instance of Utrecht, Netherlands, 22 November 1984, XI Y.B. COM. ARB. (1986) (ruling that "in view of the legislative history of the Convention, the latter implies that for obtaining a leave for enforcement abroad, i.e., the Netherlands, it is not required that in the country of origin, i.e., England, a definitive leave for enforcement be given"); Court of Appeal of the Republic and Canton of Ticino, Switzerland, 22 August 2012, 14.2012.102; Obergericht des Kantons Zürich, Switzerland, 8 December 1980, II.ZK.Nr. 8 A/80 (stating that "the New York Convention sought to avoid 'double exequatur'").

[936] *Travaux préparatoires*, Comments on Draft Convention on the Recognition and Enforcement of Foreign Arbitral Awards, E/CONF.26/SR.11-14, SR17. See also ALBERT JAN VAN DEN BERG, THE NEW YORK ARBITRATION CONVENTION OF 1958: TOWARDS A UNIFORM JUDICIAL INTERPRETATION 334-36 (1981).

[937] For a description of this approach, see FOUCHARD GAILLARD GOLDMAN ON INTERNATIONAL COMMERCIAL ARBITRATION 974-75, paras. 1681-83 (E. Gaillard, J. Savage eds., 1999); Nadia Darwazeh, *Article V (1)(e)*, in RECOGNITION AND ENFORCEMENT OF FOREIGN ARBITRAL AWARDS: A GLOBAL COMMENTARY ON THE NEW YORK CONVENTION 301, 312-13. (H. Kronke, P. Nacimiento et al. eds., 2010).

the arbitration". In that case, the court considered that the party opposing enforcement had not proved that the alleged difficulties in the delivery of the award resulted in it being non-binding under Swiss law, and therefore rejected the party's request that enforcement be denied.[938] In *Compagnie de Saint-Gobain-Pont-à-Mousson*, where the party opposing enforcement had argued that the award had not become binding on the parties in the country of the seat, the Court of Appeal of Paris noted that the courts of the seat themselves, namely Indian courts, had declared that the award was binding, and on that ground granted the request for enforcement.[939] Courts in Germany,[940] Italy,[941] the United States,[942] and Switzerland[943] have similarly referred to the law of the country where the arbitration took place as being the law applicable to determining the binding nature of the award.

7. Under a second approach, sometimes referred to as an "autonomous approach", courts have relied on their own interpretation of what a binding award under article V (1)*(e)* should be. In the majority of cases, courts following this approach have ruled that an award shall be considered as binding if it is no longer open to ordinary means of recourse, namely those where the substance of the award is reviewed, even if extraordinary means of recourse are still available, including actions to set aside.[944] For example,

---

[938] *Italian Party v. Swiss Company*, Court of First Instance, Zurich, Switzerland, 14 February 2003, XXIX Y.B. COM. ARB. (2004).

[939] *Compagnie de Saint-Gobain—Pont-à-Mousson v. The Fertilizer Corporation of India Limited*, Paris Court of Appeal, France, 10 May 1971.

[940] Oberlandesgericht [OLG] Düsseldorf, Germany, 19 January 2005, I-26 Sch 5/03 (dismissing the request for recognition of an award on the ground that the claims decided in the award had been set-off under Romanian law, the law of the seat of the arbitration); *Seller v. Buyer*, Oberlandesgericht [OLG] Celle, Germany, 6 October 2005, 8 Sch 06/05 (holding that whether an award is binding is to be determined pursuant to the law of the arbitration, in this case Russian law, and that the Russian law requirement that each party receive a copy of the arbitral award signed by the arbitrators for the award to be binding was met in this case).

[941] *Carters (Merchants) Ltd. v. Francesco Ferraro*, Corte di Appello di Napoli, Italy, 20 February 1975, IV Y.B. COM. ARB. (1979) (referring to the law applicable at the seat of the arbitration, namely English law, to rule on the binding nature of the award).

[942] *Pactrans Air & Sea, Inc. v. China National Chartering Corp., et al.*, District Court, Northern District of Florida, United States of America, 29 March 2010, 3:06-cv-369/RS-EMT (in a case where the seat of the arbitration was China, holding that the award was binding on the ground that, under Chinese arbitration law, "the legal effects of the award letter begin on the day it is written").

[943] *Denysiana S.A. v. Jassica S.A.*, Swiss Federal Tribunal, Switzerland, 14 March 1984 (in a case where the seat of the arbitration was Paris, stating that "the party opposing the enforcement must prove that the award has not yet become binding or set aside or suspended, pursuant to the law governing the arbitration", namely French law).

[944] For a description of this second approach, see FOUCHARD GAILLARD GOLDMAN ON INTERNATIONAL COMMERCIAL ARBITRATION 972, para. 1679 (E. Gaillard, J. Savage eds., 1999); Nadia Darwazeh, *Article V (1)(e)*, in RECOGNITION AND ENFORCEMENT OF FOREIGN ARBITRAL AWARDS: A GLOBAL COMMENTARY ON THE NEW YORK CONVENTION 301, 311-312 (H. Kronke, P. Nacimiento et al. eds., 2010); Christoph Liebscher, *Article V (1)(e)*, in NEW YORK CONVENTION ON THE RECOGNITION AND ENFORCEMENT OF FOREIGN ARBITRAL AWARDS OF 10 JUNE 1958—COMMENTARY 356, 360, paras. 361, 364 (R. Wolff ed., 2012).

the Swiss Federal Tribunal ruled that foreign arbitral awards are binding on parties under article V (1)*(e)* when they "can no longer be appealed by ordinary means."[945] Likewise, in a case where the place of the arbitration was London, a Dutch court held that because "no ordinary means of recourse [could] be made against the arbitral award in question", the award had "become binding on the parties within the meaning of the Convention."[946] In Hong Kong, courts have ruled that an award is "binding" when it is "no longer open to an appeal on the merits."[947]

8. These approaches to assessing the binding nature of an award are not necessarily mutually exclusive, and in a number of instances, courts have applied them in combination.[948] For example, in a case where the place of the arbitration was Paris, and after declaring that an award should be considered as binding "if it is no longer open to an appeal on the merits", the High Court of Hong Kong referred to both the arbitration rules and the provisions of the French arbitration law to determine whether the award could be subject to an appeal on the merits.[949] In other cases, national courts refrained from applying the requirements of the law of the seat when these requirements would have led to a result contrary to the purpose of the New

---

945 *Company X SA v. State Y*, Swiss Federal Tribunal, Switzerland, 9 December 2008, 4A_403/2008. See also *Y v. X*, Swiss Federal Tribunal, Switzerland, 3 January 2006, 5P.292/2005 (stating that an award can be considered as binding under art. V (1)*(e)* when "an ordinary appeal against the award is no longer possible"); *X v. Y*, Swiss Federal Tribunal, Switzerland, 21 February 2005, 5P.353/2004 (stating that the binding nature of an award shall be recognised as soon as the award becomes "*res judicata* and can no longer be appealed"); *X v. Y*, Cour de Justice de Genève, 1ère section, Switzerland, 23 September 2004 (ruling that an award is binding as soon as the award has *res judicata* effect and is not subject to ordinary recourse).

946 *Palm and Vegetable Oils SDN. BHD. v. Algemene Oliehandel International B.V.*, President of Rechtbank of Utrecht, Netherlands, 22 November 1984. See also *SPP (Middle East) Ltd. v. The Arab Republic* of *Egypt*, President of the District Court of Amsterdam, Netherlands, 12 July 1984, X Y.B. COM. ARB. (1985) (ruling that "an arbitral award is not binding if it is open to appeal on the merits before a judge or an appeal arbitral tribunal").

947 *Société Nationale d'Opérations Pétrolières de la Côte d'Ivoire—Holding v. Keen Lloyd Resources Limited*, High Court of the Hong Kong Special Administrative Region, Court of First Instance, Hong Kong, 20 December 2001, 55 of 2011, XXIX Y.B. COM. ARB. (2004). See *also Diag Human SE v. Czech Republic*, High Court, Queen's Bench Division, United Kingdom, 22 May 2014 (stating that "if an award is subject to 'ordinary' recourse, it will not be binding").

948 See Christoph Liebscher, *Article V (1)(e)*, in NEW YORK CONVENTION ON THE RECOGNITION AND ENFORCEMENT OF FOREIGN ARBITRAL AWARDS OF 10 JUNE 1958—COMMENTARY 356, 362, paras. 364-65 (R. Wolff ed., 2012); FOUCHARD GAILLARD GOLDMAN ON INTERNATIONAL COMMERCIAL ARBITRATION 975, para. 1683 (E. Gaillard, J. Savage eds., 1999).

949 *Société Nationale d'Opérations Pétrolières de la Côte d'Ivoire—Holding v. Keen Lloyd Resources Limited,* High Court of the Hong Kong Special Administrative Region, Court of First Instance, Hong Kong, 20 December 2001, 55 of 2011, XXIX Y.B. COM. ARB. (2004).

York Convention, for instance a requirement that the award be granted a national exequatur to become binding.[950]

9. In line with these decisions, for the purposes of assessing the binding nature of an award under the Convention, some commentators have distinguished between, on the one hand, the principles which were clearly intended to apply under the Convention and, on the other hand, the residual grounds found in the law of the country where the award was rendered which the party opposing enforcement is likely to invoke.[951]

10. The first of these principles is that the binding nature of the award does not depend on whether the award is enforceable in the country where it was issued. National courts have repeatedly recalled that this requirement would amount to reinstating the mechanism of *double exequatur*; and they have systematically rejected arguments that an award would not be binding on the parties on the ground that it had not been enforced at the place of the arbitration. In *AB Götaverken v. General National Maritime Transport Company (GMTC), Libya and others*, for example, the Swedish Supreme Court expressly stated that, for an award to be binding under article (V) (1)*(e)*, the party relying on the award does not need to "prove that the award is enforceable according to the authorities of the country in which it was rendered."[952] A Spanish court likewise expressly stated that "the binding character of the award may not be made to depend on an exequatur by the courts of the State of rendition."[953]

---

[950] See chapter of the Guide on article V (1)*(e)*, para. 11.

[951] See FOUCHARD GAILLARD GOLDMAN ON INTERNATIONAL COMMERCIAL ARBITRATION 976, para. 1684 (E. Gaillard, J. Savage eds., 1999); Christoph Liebscher, *Article V (1)(e)*, in NEW YORK CONVENTION ON THE RECOGNITION AND ENFORCEMENT OF FOREIGN ARBITRAL AWARDS of 10 June 1958—COMMENTARY 356, 360, para. 360 (R. Wolff ed., 2012).

[952] *AB Götaverken v. General National Maritime Transport Company (GMTC), Libya and others*, Supreme Court, Sweden, 13 August 1979, SO 1462. See also *German (F.R.) party v. Dutch party,* President of Rechtbank, The Hague, Netherlands, 26 April 1973, IV Y.B. COM. ARB. 305 (1979).

[953] *Antilles Cement Corporation v. Transficem,* Supreme Court, Civil Chamber, First Section, Spain, 20 July 2004, XXXI Y.B. COM. ARB. (2006). For the same solution, see also *Joseph Müller AG v. Bergesen und Obergericht (II. Zivilkammer) des Kantons Zürich*, Court of First Instance, Switzerland, 26 February 1982 (stating that "[t]he requirement of a declaration of enforcement in the country of the arbitral award's origin would go squarely against the New York Convention's aim of avoiding the double exequatur"); Swiss Federal Tribunal, Switzerland, 8 December 2003, 4P.173/2003/ech.; *Company X SA v. Y Federation*, Swiss Federal Tribunal, Switzerland, 9 December 2008, 4A_403/2008; *X v. Y*, Swiss Federal Tribunal, Switzerland, 21 February 2005, 5P.353/2004 (stating that "a foreign arbitral award does not have to be enforceable in its country of origin; it merely has to be binding on the parties, and its binding nature must have been recognised as soon as the award becomes *res judicata* and can no longer be appealed").

11. The second principle is that the fact that an action to set aside the award still lies in the jurisdiction of the seat does not lead that award to be non-binding for the purposes of the Convention.[954] This principle has been continuously affirmed by national courts, for instance in the Netherlands,[955] Germany,[956] France,[957] the United States,[958] the United Kingdom[959] and Switzerland.[960]

12. Furthermore, regardless of the approach followed, courts assessing the binding nature of an award have often paid particular attention to the parties' intention resulting from the arbitration agreement or the arbitration rules. The Belgium Cour de cassation, for instance, stated that the binding nature of the award should be determined "by referring, successively and one in the absence of the other, to the arbitration agreement, the law that it

---

954 FOUCHARD GAILLARD GOLDMAN ON INTERNATIONAL COMMERCIAL ARBITRATION 976, para. 1684(E. Gaillard, J. Savage eds., 1999); Christoph Liebscher, *Article V (1)(e),* in NEW YORK CONVENTION ON THE RECOGNITION AND ENFORCEMENT OF FOREIGN ARBITRAL AWARDS OF 10 JUNE 1958—COMMENTARY 356, 358, para. 357 (R. Wolff ed., 2012); ALBERT JAN VAN DEN BERG, THE NEW YORK ARBITRATION CONVENTION OF 1958: TOWARDS A UNIFORM JUDICIAL INTERPRETATION 350 (1981).

955 *SPP (Middle East) Ltd. v. The Arab Republic of Egypt*, President of the District Court of Amsterdam, Netherlands, 12 July 1984, X Y.B. COM. ARB. (1985) (ruling that "the mere initiation of an action for setting aside [...] does not have as consequence that the arbitral award must be considered as not binding").

956 *Film distributor v. Film producer,* Bayerisches Oberstes Landesgericht [BayObLG], Germany, 22 November 2002, 4 Z Sch 13/02 (granting a request for enforcement of the award despite annulment proceedings having been commenced by the Respondent at the seat of the arbitration); *Seller v. Buyer*, Bundesgerichtshof [BGH], III ZB 06/02, Germany, 30 January 2003 (stating that "[t]he mere fact that the defendant states that it filed an 'appeal' from the decision of the Russian arbitral tribunal does not mean that there is a ground for refusal pursuant to Art. V (1)(e)"); *Supplier v. Carrier*, Oberlandesgericht [OLG] Celle, Germany, 20 November 2003, 8 Sch 02/03 (stating that the pending action for annulment in Sweden had no impact on the recognition of the award); Oberlandesgericht [OLG] München, Germany, 23 February 2007, 34 Sch 31/06 (stating that the possibility of having the award annulled at the seat does not hinder the recognition of the arbitral award).

957 *S.A. Recam Sonofadex v. S.N.C. Cantieri Rizzardi de Gianfranco Rizzardi*, Court of Appeal of Orleans, France, 5 October 2000 (stating that the recognition and enforcement of an award can only be rejected if the award has been effectively suspended by a competent authority of the country in which the award was rendered; initiating setting aside proceedings is not sufficient).

958 *Fertilizer Corporation* of *India et al. v. IDI Management, Inc.,* District Court, Southern District of Ohio, United States of America, 9 June 1981, C-1-79-570.

959 *IPCO (Nigeria) Ltd. v. NNPC (Nigeria)*, High Court of Justice, England and Wales, 27 April 2005, 2004 1031 (stating that the application of article V (1)(*e*) is not triggered automatically by a challenge being brought before a court in the country of origin); *Continental Transfer Technique Ltd. v. Federal Government of Nigeria*, High Court of Justice, England and Wales, 30 March 2010, 2008 Folio 1280 (stating that article V (1)(*e*) only applies where the award "has been set aside or suspended" and noting that "the fact that there is an application to set aside an award does not mean that the award has been set aside").

960 *Company X SA v. Y Federation*, Swiss Federal Tribunal, 9 December 2008, 4A_403/2008 (ruling that the mere fact that an action for setting aside an award is admissible or has been filed in the country in which the award was made does not make the award any less binding).

designates for such purpose, and last, the law of the country in which the award was rendered."[961] In *Joseph Müller*, a Swiss court ruled that whether an award has become binding on the parties is a question to be determined according to "in the first place [...] the agreement of the parties and, failing such agreement, subsidiarily [...] the law of the country where the arbitration takes place."[962] In the same vein, a Spanish court ruled that "the binding nature of the award must be examined under the rules governing the arbitration [...] rather than under the norms of the State where the arbitration took place or where the award was rendered." The court went on to state that "pursuant to [the ICC] Rules, the binding character of the award ensues from the submission to ICC arbitration and the valid waiver of any means of recourse implied in the submission to [ICC] institutional arbitration," and on that basis, decided that the award was binding.[963]

b. *Burden of proving that an award has become binding*

13. One of the main innovations of the New York Convention was to transfer the burden of proof from the party seeking enforcement to the party opposing it.[964] As with the other grounds for refusing recognition and enforcement listed under article V, this principle applies to article V (1)*(e)*.

---

[961] *Inter-Arab Investment Guarantee Corporation v. Banque Arabe et Internationale d'Investissements*, Cour de cassation, Belgium, 5 June 1998, XXIV Y.B. COM. ARB. (1999).

[962] *Joseph Müller AG v. Bergesen und Obergericht (II. Zivilkammer) des Kantons Zürich*, Court of First Instance, Switzerland, 26 February 1982. See also *X v.Y*, Swiss Federal Tribunal, Switzerland, 21 February 2005, 5P.353/2004 (stating that the binding nature of an award "must have been recognised as soon as the award becomes *res judicata* and can no longer be appealed" and ruling that, in the case at hand, the award was final and binding pursuant to the provisions of the contract entered into between the parties); *X v. Y*, Cour de Justice de Genève, 1ère section, Switzerland, 23 September 2004 (ruling that an award is binding as soon as the award has *res judicata* effect and is not subject to ordinary recourse, and that in this case the award was binding pursuant to the provisions of the agreement entered into between the parties).

[963] *Antilles Cement Corporation v. Transficem*, Supreme Court, Civil Chamber, First Section, Spain, 20 July 2004, XXXI Y.B. COM. ARB. (2006). See also *AB Götaverken v. General National Maritime Transport Company (GMTC), Libya and others,* Supreme Court, Sweden, 13 August 1979, SO 1462 (after noting that "[a] case in which a foreign award is not binding is when its merits are open to appeal to a higher jurisdiction", decided that the award was binding because the arbitration clause provided that the award would be "finally binding and enforceable," and because the ICC Rules applicable in this case provided that the arbitral award shall be final); *Dowans Holding S.A. v. Tanzania Electric Supply Co. Ltd.*, High Court of Justice, England and Wales, 27 July 2011, 2010 Folio 1539 (after holding that "the binding effect of an award depends upon whether it is or remains subject to ordinary recourse", referred to the arbitration agreement and the ICC Rules, which stated that "[t]he decision of the arbitration shall be final and binding upon the Parties, and shall not be subject to appeal", to conclude that the award was binding on the parties); *International Trading and Industrial Investment Company v. Dyncorp Aerospace Technology*, District Court for the District of Columbia, United States of America, 21 January 2011, Civil Action No. 09-791 (RBW) (referring to the ICC Rules to conclude that the award was binding on the parties).

[964] See the introduction to the chapter of the Guide on article V.

14. A party seeking to enforce an arbitral award is not required to establish that the award is binding; rather, it falls on the party opposing enforcement to establish that the award is not binding. This principle has been repeatedly affirmed by national courts. A Swiss court stated for instance that "[i]t is [...] the party opposing enforcement that must prove, pursuant to article V (1)*(e)* of the Convention, that the arbitral award is not yet binding or has been set aside."[965] Likewise, an Italian court ruled that "[the party seeking enforcement] has not to prove that the award is binding, but [the party opposing enforcement] has to prove that the binding force is lacking [...]."[966] Commentators of the Convention also confirm this interpretation.[967]

c. *Binding nature of partial and interim awards*

15. In a number of reported cases, parties have relied on article V (1)*(e)* to challenge the binding nature of partial or interim arbitral awards. While some national courts have upheld such challenges and refused to enforce interim or partial awards under this provision,[968] others have considered

---

965 *Italian Party v. Swiss Company*, Court of First Instance, Zurich, Switzerland, 14 February 2003, XXIX Y.B. COM. ARB. (2004). See also *Denysiana S.A. v. Jassica S.A.*, Swiss Federal Tribunal, Switzerland, 14 March 1984 (stating that "the party opposing the enforcement must prove that the award has not yet become binding or set aside or suspended").

966 *Carters (Merchants) Ltd. v. Francesco Ferraro*, Corte di Appello di Napoli, Italy, 20 February 1975, IV Y.B. COM. ARB. (1979). See also *C.C.M. Sulzer v. Société Maghrébienne de Génie Civil (SOMAGEC) et al.*, Court of Appeal of Paris, France, 17 February 1987, 864787 (stating that pursuant to article V (1)(*e*), it is for the party opposing the enforcement to demonstrate that the award has not yet become binding on the parties); *Antilles Cement Corporation v. Transficem*, Supreme Court, Civil Chamber, First Section, Spain, 20 July 2004, XXXI Y.B. COM. ARB. (2006); *Diag Human SE v. Czech Republic*, High Court, Queen's Bench Division, United Kingdom, 22 May 2014 (stating that the burden of proof is "firmly" on the party resisting opposing enforcement).

967 Nadia Darwazeh, *Article V (1)(e)*, in RECOGNITION AND ENFORCEMENT OF FOREIGN ARBITRAL AWARDS: A GLOBAL COMMENTARY ON THE NEW YORK CONVENTION 301, 305, 310 (H. Kronke, P. Nacimiento et al. eds., 2010); ALBERT JAN VAN DEN BERG, THE NEW YORK ARBITRATION CONVENTION OF 1958: TOWARDS A UNIFORM JUDICIAL INTERPRETATION 338 (1981); FOUCHARD GAILLARD GOLDMAN ON INTERNATIONAL COMMERCIAL ARBITRATION 968, para. 1673 (E. Gaillard, J. Savage eds., 1999); Christoph Liebscher, *Article V (1)(e)*, in NEW YORK CONVENTION ON THE RECOGNITION AND ENFORCEMENT OF FOREIGN ARBITRAL AWARDS OF 10 JUNE 1958—COMMENTARY 356, paras. 353-56 (R. Wolff ed., 2012).

968 *Merck & Co. Inc. v. Merck Frosst Canada Inc., Frosst Laboratories Inc. v. Tecnoquímicas S.A.*, Supreme Court of Justice, Colombia, 24 March 1999, XXVI Y.B. COM. ARB. (2001); *Living Consulting Group AB (Sweden) v. OOO Sokotel (Russian Federation)*, Presidium of the Highest Arbitrazh Court, Russian Federation, 5 October 2010, A56-63115/2009; *Hall Steel Company (United States) v. Metalloyd Ltd. (United Kingdom)*, District Court, Eastern District of Michigan, Southern Division, United States of America, 7 June 2007, 05-70743, XXXIII Y.B. COM. ARB. (2008). For further developments on the conditions under which procedural orders and interim and partial awards are enforceable under the Convention, see the chapter of the Guide on article I.

that, in certain circumstances, interim and partial awards could be considered binding within the meaning of article V (1)*(e)*.[969]

16. In some cases, courts have distinguished between awards relating to jurisdictional and procedural issues, and awards relating to the merits of a dispute, and have excluded that the former category of awards be considered as binding. For instance, the Colombian Supreme Court of Justice refused to enforce an interim award on jurisdiction on the ground that it was "clear that according to the Convention, 'arbitral awards' are those which materially end the arbitration by defining the disputes submitted in the request for arbitration, not those which arise out of the arbitration itself", such as an interim award on the jurisdiction of the arbitral tribunal.[970] A Russian court similarly stated that article V (l)*(e)* was not applicable to "interlocutory awards, including decisions of arbitrators on procedural matters (collection of arbitration costs, determination of jurisdiction, and security measures)" but only to "arbitral awards related to the procedural examination of the dispute on the merits and rendered at the end of the arbitral proceedings."[971]

17. Other courts looked to whether the partial or interim award finally settled a discrete claim on the merits, or could still be revised by the arbitral tribunal at a later stage of the arbitration, and excluded that the latter category of awards be considered as binding. For example, in a case where a party sought to enforce an "Interim Arbitration Order and Award", the Supreme Court of Queensland held that the award referred to under Article V (l)*(e)* is a type of award which "has determined some or all of the issues submitted to the arbitrator for determination rather than an interlocutory order of an arbitrator." The court further held that "[a]n interlocutory order which may be rescinded, suspended, varied or reopened by the tribunal which pronounced it" was not enforceable under the Convention.[972] Likewise, a United States District Court held that notwithstanding the absence of an award that finally disposes of all the claims that were submitted to arbitration, an award that "finally and definitely disposes of a separate independent claim" could be considered as binding. As a result, the

---

[969] *Resort Condominiums International Inc. v. Ray Bolwell and Resort Condominiums, Pty. Ltd.*, Supreme Court of Queensland, Australia, 29 October 1993, XX Y.B. COM. ARB. (1995). See also *Misr Foreign Trade Co. v. R.D. Harboties (Mercantile)*, Court of Cassation, Egypt, 22 January 2008, 2010/64.

[970] *Merck & Co. Inc. v. Merck Frosst Canada Inc., Frosst Laboratories Inc. v. Tecnoquímicas S.A.*, Supreme Court of Justice, Colombia, 24 March 1999, XXVI Y.B. COM. ARB. (2001).

[971] *Living Consulting Group AB (Sweden) v. OOO Sokotel (Russian Federation)*, Presidium of the Highest Arbitrazh Court, Russian Federation, 5 October 2010, A56-63115/2009 (denying enforcement of an interim award ordering one of the parties to reimburse the advance on arbitration costs to the other party).

[972] *Resort Condominiums International Inc. v. Ray Bolwell and Resort Condominiums, Pty. Ltd.*, Supreme Court of Queensland, Australia, 29 October 1993, XX Y.B. COM. ARB. (1995).

court upheld the enforcement of an interim award directing the parties to continue performing under the contract until the arbitrator had decided the underlying contractual issue.[973]

d. Doctrine of merger

18. While the practice of courts leaves no doubt that obtaining a leave of enforcement at the place of the arbitration is not necessary for an award to be enforced under the Convention,[974] some parties have argued that, *a contrario*, if a leave of enforcement has been issued by the courts at the seat of arbitration and the award has been merged into a judgment, such an award could no longer be considered as binding under article V (1)*(e)*.

19. This interpretation has been rejected by courts, in line with the opinion of a commentator of the Convention, who pointed that it would run contrary to the Convention's purpose of facilitating enforcement.[975] For example, in a case where the party opposing enforcement argued that the award had been merged into a judgment in the United Kingdom, and therefore could no longer be enforced under the Convention, an Australian court held that, even if a judgment had been entered into in the United Kingdom, the award would not be considered as having merged in this judgment for the purpose of enforcement in Australia.[976] Similarly, a German court held that, although an award had been merged into the judgment of an English court, this merger did not imply that the award should be considered as having been absorbed by the judgment in Germany, the purpose of the Convention being to facilitate enforcement of foreign arbitral awards.[977] German courts have however specified that, while the merger of an award into a judgment does not deprive the award of its binding nature under article V (1)*(e)* for the purposes of enforcement abroad, only the

---

[973] *Island Creek Coal Sales Company v. City of Gainesville*, Florida, Court of Appeals, Sixth Circuit, United States of America, March 15, 1984, 729 F.2d 1046.

[974] See the chapter of the Guide on article V (1)(*e*), para. 11.

[975] ALBERT JAN VAN DEN BERG, THE NEW YORK ARBITRATION CONVENTION OF 1958: TOWARDS A UNIFORM JUDICIAL INTERPRETATION 346-48 (1981). See also Christoph Liebscher, *Article V(1)(e)*, in NEW YORK CONVENTION ON THE RECOGNITION AND ENFORCEMENT OF FOREIGN ARBITRAL AWARDS OF 10 JUNE 1958— COMMENTARY 356, 378, paras. 413-14 (R. Wolff ed., 2012).

[976] *Brali v. Hyundai Corp.*, Supreme Court of New South Wales, Commercial Division, Australia, 17 October 1988.

[977] *German (F. R.) buyer v. English seller*, Hanseatisches Oberlandesgericht [OLG] Hamburg, Germany, 27 July 1978, IV Y.B. COM. ARB. (1979). See also *COSID Inc. Steel Authority of India Ltd.*, High Court of Delhi, India, 12 July 1985, XI Y.B. COM. ARB. (1986) (holding that the merger of an award into a judgment under Section 26 of the English Arbitration Act is no bar to the enforcement of the award in India).

award itself, not the judgment absorbing the award, can be enforced under the Convention.[978]

B. What is a "competent authority" of the country "in which, or under the law of which", the award was made?

20. Under article V (1)*(e)*, a court may refuse recognition or enforcement of an award if the party opposing enforcement proves that the award has been set aside or suspended by a "competent authority" in "the country in which" the award was made or "under the law of which" the award was made.

a. Meaning of "competent authority"

21. While article V (l)*(e)* does not define the terms "competent authority", there is little doubt that these terms refer to the court or courts having jurisdiction to suspend and/or set aside awards in each country.[979] A court from the Cayman Islands also envisaged that in a certain country, this power could be entrusted to a special tribunal or a "special executive arm of government."[980]

b. The country "in which" or "under the law of which" the award was made

22. The terms "in which [...] that award was made" are understood to refer to the country of the place of the arbitration.[981] In a case where the place of the arbitration was Singapore, for instance, a United States District Court stated, by reference to article V (1)*(e)*, that "clearly, Singapore was the country in which the award was made."[982]

---

[978] Bundesgerichtshof [BGH], Germany, 1 September 2009, XXXV Y.B. COM. ARB. (2010).

[979] *Resort Condominiums International Inc. v. Ray Bolwell and Resort Condominiums, Pty. Ltd.*, Supreme Court of Queensland, Australia, 29 October 1993, XX Y.B. COM. ARB. (1995) (stating that the reference to "competent authority" in article V (1)(*e*) "means a Court and not the arbitrator"). See also the developments and references cited in the chapter of the Guide on article VI.

[980] *The Republic of Gabon v. Swiss Oil Corporation*, Grand Court, Cayman Islands, 17 June 1988, XIV Y.B. COM. ARB. (1989).

[981] Nadia Darwazeh, *Article V (1)(e)*, in RECOGNITION AND ENFORCEMENT OF FOREIGN ARBITRAL AWARDS: A GLOBAL COMMENTARY ON THE NEW YORK CONVENTION 301, 319 (H. Kronke, P. Nacimiento et al. eds., 2010); Christoph Liebscher, *Article V (1)(e)*, in NEW YORK CONVENTION ON THE RECOGNITION AND ENFORCEMENT OF FOREIGN ARBITRAL AWARDS OF 10 JUNE 1958—COMMENTARY 356, 374, para. 404 (R. Wolff ed., 2012).

[982] *Steel Corporation of the Philippines v. International Steel Services, Inc.*, District Court for the Western District of Pennsylvania, United States of America, 31 July 2006, Civil Action No. 06-386. See also *International Trading and Industrial Investment Company v.*

23. Although the Convention does not provide guidance as to the meaning of the expression "under the law of which", with very few exceptions, courts have generally rejected arguments that these terms referred to the law applicable to the merits. Courts have decided that it referred instead to the procedural law governing the arbitration, in the rare situation where the parties have selected a law to govern the arbitration that is different from the law of the place of arbitration. In *Steel Corporation of the Philippines v. International Steel Services*, a United States District Court held that this expression "refers to the theoretical case that on the basis of an agreement of the parties the award is governed by an arbitration law which is different from the arbitration law of the country in which the award was made". In this case the place of the arbitration was Singapore, but the arbitration clause specified that "[t]he validity, performance and enforcement of this contract shall be governed by Philippine law". The respondent contended that the award had been made under the law of the Philippines and that, because it had filed a petition to vacate the award in the Philippines courts, the award should not be recognized under article V (1)*(e)*. The court held that "while it would be rare for the parties to choose a procedural law different from the arbitral situs, if they do, the selection must be clear", which it considered was not the case here.[983] In *Karaha Bodas*, the High Court of Hong Kong similarly stated that the reference to the law under which the award was made "undoubtedly refers to the law which governed

---

Dyncorp Aerospace Technology, District Court for the District of Columbia, United States of America, 21 January 2011, Civil Action No. 09-791 (RBW).

[983] *Steel Corporation of the Philippines v. International Steel Services, Inc.*, District Court for the Western District of Pennsylvania, United States of America, 31 July 2006, Civil Action No. 06-386, affirmed by *Steel Corporation of the Philippines v. International Steel Services, Inc.*, Court of Appeals for the Third Circuit, United States of America, 19 November 2009, Nos. 08-1853 and 08-2568. See also *Coutinho Caro & Co. USA, Inc. v. Marcus Trading, Inc. and others,* District Court, District of Connecticut, United States of America, 14 March 2000, Civil Action Nos. 3:95cv2362, 3:96cv2218, 3:96cv2219 (ruling that "the phrase 'under the law of which' the award was made refers to the theoretical case that on the basis of an agreement of the parties the award is governed by an arbitration law which is different from the arbitration law of the country in which the award was made*"); International Standard Electric Corp. v. Bridas Sociedad Anonima Petrolera, Industrial y Comercial,* District Court, Southern District of New York, United States of America, 24 August 1990, 90 Civ. 0720 (KC); *Belize Social Development Ltd. (Belize) v. Government of Belize,* Court of Appeals, D.C. Circuit, United States of America, 13 January 2012, 10-7167 (stating that the phrase "under the law of which" refers to "the procedural law governing the arbitration, not the substantive law governing the Agreement"); *M&C Corp. v. Erwin Behr GmbH & co.*, Court of Appeals, Sixth Circuit, United States of America, 3 July 1996, 95-1390; *International Trading and Industrial Investment Company v. Dyncorp Aerospace Technology et al.*, 21 January 2011, District Court, District of Columbia, United States of America, 09-791 (RBW); *Four Seasons Hotels and Resorts, B.V., et al. v. Consorcio Barr, S.A.*, District Court, Southern District of Florida Miami Division, United States of America, 4 June 2003, 02-23249 (stating that a competent authority is "a court of the country that supplied the procedural law used in the arbitration" and not the substantive law); *The Commercial Company for Investment v. Bell Rover Shipping Limited,* Court of Appeal of Cairo, Egypt, 19 March 1997, 68/113.

the procedural law of the arbitration, not the substantive law of the contract."[984]

24. In contrast with the solution stated above, in previous decisions the Indian Supreme Court considered that the expression "under the law of which" could designate the law applicable to the arbitration agreement or to the merits of the case. In most recent decisions, however, the Indian Supreme Court revised this case law. In the *Balco* case, the Indian Supreme Court ruled that the expression "under the law of which" referred to the procedural law of the arbitration in the case that it was different from the law of the seat of the arbitration, and not to the substantive law governing the underlying contract.[985]

25. The same interpretation is shared by the commentators of the Convention.[986]

26. As a result, an award can in practice only be denied enforcement under the Convention if it has been set aside or suspended by the competent courts of the place of the arbitration, or as the case may be, competent courts in the country of the law chosen by the parties to govern the arbitration. If the award has been set aside or suspended in any other country, this does not constitute a valid ground for denying enforcement. For example, a United States court refused to dismiss the enforcement of an award on the ground that the Belize courts had ordered that its enforcement be suspended "in any jurisdiction outside of Belize", while the place of the arbitration was England and the applicable procedural law was English law.[987] A number of courts

---

[984] *Karaha Bodas Company LLC v. Perusahaan Pertambangan Minyak Dan Gas Bumi Negara - Pertamina*, Court of First Instance, High Court of the Hong Kong Special Administrative Region, Hong Kong, 27 March 2003, [2003] HKCU 288.

[985] *Bharat Aluminum Co. v. Kaiser Aluminum Technical Service, Inc.*, Supreme Court, India, 6 September 2012, Civil Appeal No. 7019 of 2005. The Supreme Court added that the position adopted by Indian courts in the past, on the basis of which awards were set aside by Indian courts even when the seat of the arbitration was located abroad, amounted to ignoring "the spirit underlying the New York Convention which embodies a consensus evolved to encourage consensual resolution of complicated, intricate and in many cases very sensitive International Commercial Disputes".

[986] Nadia Darwazeh, *Article V (1)(e),* in RECOGNITION AND ENFORCEMENT OF FOREIGN ARBITRAL AWARDS: A GLOBAL COMMENTARY ON THE NEW YORK CONVENTION 301, 320-23 (H. Kronke, P. Nacimiento et al. eds., 2010); ALBERT JAN VAN DEN BERG, THE NEW YORK ARBITRATION CONVENTION OF 1958: TOWARDS A UNIFORM JUDICIAL INTERPRETATION 350 (1981); Christoph Liebscher, *Article V (1)(e),* in NEW YORK CONVENTION ON THE RECOGNITION AND ENFORCEMENT OF FOREIGN ARBITRAL AWARDS OF 10 JUNE 1958—COMMENTARY 356, 376, para. 409 (R. Wolff ed., 2012).

[987] *Belize Social Development Ltd. (Belize) v. Government of Belize,* Court of Appeals, D.C. Circuit, United States of America, 13 January 2012, 10-7167. See also *Continental Transfert Technique Limited v. Federal Government of Nigeria*, District Court for the District of Columbia, United States of America, 23 March 2010, Civil Action No. 08-2026 (PLF) (in a case where the seat of the arbitration was in the United Kingdom, ruling that an *ex parte* order issued by the courts of Nigeria and temporarily barring the Claimant "from seeking or

have held that, in practice, this provision amounts to granting the courts of the place of the arbitration exclusive jurisdiction to rule on requests for the setting aside or suspension of an arbitral award.[988]

C. Award set aside or suspended

27. Article V (1)*(e)* allows national courts to refuse recognition or enforcement if it is established that, in the courts of the country in which, or under the law of which, the award was made, the award has been set aside or suspended.

28. As pointed out in the commentary on the chapeau of article V, the use of the term "may" in the chapeau of article V (1) indicates that national courts have the possibility to refuse enforcement of an award on the grounds listed in this article, but they are not obliged to do so.[989] Furthermore, as discussed in the chapter of the Guide on article VII, a court will not breach the Convention by enforcing an arbitral award pursuant to more favourable provisions found in its domestic laws, in accordance with article VII (1). Accordingly, a number of courts have accepted to enforce awards suspended or set aside at the seat of the arbitration, either on the basis of the use of the

---

continuing to [seek] the recognition and enforcement of the Final Award [...] pending the hearing and determination" does not constitute a valid ground for refusing the enforcement of the award under article V (1)*(e)*).

[988] This has been repeatedly stated by the Court of Appeal of Cairo, for instance in *Brothers for Import, Export and Supply Company (Egypt) v. Hano Acorporish (Republic of Korea)*, Court of Appeal of Cairo, Egypt, 2 July 2008, 23/125 (stating that only the Courts of the country where the award was issued have jurisdiction to rule on requests for setting aside); *The Commercial Company for Investment v. Bell Rover Shipping Limited*, Court of Appeal of Cairo, Egypt, 19 March 1997, 68/113 (stating that only the Courts of the country where the award was issued have jurisdiction to rule on requests for the suspension of the enforcement of the arbitral award or its setting aside); *Cairo for Real Estate Company v. Abdel Rahman Hassan Sharbatly*, Court of Appeal of Cairo, Egypt, 26 February 2003, 23/119 (stating that only the Courts of the place of the arbitration have jurisdiction to rule on requests for setting aside). See also *Karaha Bodas Co. (Cayman Islands) v. Perusahaan Pertambangan Minyak Dan Gas Bumi Negara (Indonesia)*, Court of Appeals, Fifth Circuit, United States of America, 23 March 2004, 02-20042, 03-20602. See also ICCA'S GUIDE TO THE INTERPRETATION OF THE 1958 NEW YORK CONVENTION: A HANDBOOK FOR JUDGES 102 (P. Sanders ed., 2011).

[989] See the introduction to the chapter of the Guide on article V (1). See also Nadia Darwazeh, *Article V (1)(e)*, in RECOGNITION AND ENFORCEMENT OF FOREIGN ARBITRAL AWARDS: A GLOBAL COMMENTARY ON THE NEW YORK CONVENTION 301, 307-09 (H. Kronke, P. Nacimiento et al. eds., 2010); Christoph Liebscher, *Article V (1)(e)*, in NEW YORK CONVENTION ON THE RECOGNITION AND ENFORCEMENT OF FOREIGN ARBITRAL AWARDS OF 10 JUNE 1958—COMMENTARY 356, 356, para. 351 (R. Wolff ed., 2012). Some authors have however questioned this interpretation, relying on the French version of the text of the Convention. See, on this debate, Philippe Fouchard, *La portée internationale de l'annulation de la sentence arbitrale dans son pays d'origine,* 1997 REV ARB 344; Jan Paulsson, *Enforcing Arbitral Awards Notwithstanding a Local Standard Annulment* (LSA), 9(1) ICC BULL. 17 (1998).

term "may" in article V (1), or on the basis of a more favourable provision in the domestic law than article V (1)*(e)* in accordance with article VII (1).[990]

a. Award set aside

29. According to a commentator, this ground for refusal "seldom occurs and is almost never successful",[991] in a number of instances, national courts have rejected this ground for denying enforcement by applying national laws more favourable to enforcement than article V (1)*(e)* of the Convention.[992] On the other hand, the Convention does not obligate courts to enforce awards that have been set aside at the place of arbitration, and in some cases, courts have denied enforcement pursuant to article V (1)*(e)* on this ground.[993]

30. In cases where this ground for denying enforcement has been applied, courts have held that the award must have been effectively set aside for it to be denied enforcement, and that the mere initiation of setting aside proceedings does not constitute a valid ground.[994] A Russian court decided that if the award had effectively been set aside, however, this would

---

[990] See, e.g., *Société Bargues Agro Industrie SA v. Société Young Pecan Company*, Court of Appeal of Paris, France, 10 June 2004, 2003/09894; *Chromalloy Aeroservices v. Arab Republic* of *Egypt*, District Court, District of Columbia, United States of America, 31 July 1996, 94-2339; *Nigerian National Petroleum Corporation v. IPCO (Nigeria) Ltd.*, Court of Appeal, England and Wales, 21 October 2008, A3/2008/1037.PTA+(A); *Buyer (Poland) v. Seller (Poland)*, Hanseatisches Oberlandesgericht [OLG] Hamburg, Germany, 24 January 2003, 11 Sch 06/01 and see the decisions cited in the chapter of the Guide on article VII (1).

[991] ALBERT JAN VAN DEN BERG, THE NEW YORK ARBITRATION CONVENTION OF 1958: TOWARDS A UNIFORM JUDICIAL INTERPRETATION 332 (1981).

[992] See in particular the practice of the courts of France: *Société Pabalk Ticaret Sirketi v. Société Anonyme Norsolor*, Court of Cassation, France, 83-11.355, 9 October 1984, 1985 REV. ARB. 431, with English translation in 24 ILM 360 (1985); *Bargues Agro Industrie S.A. v. Young Pecan Company,* Court of Appeal of Paris, France, 10 June 2004, 2006 REV. ARB.; Société *PT Putrabali Adyamulia v.* Société *Rena Holding et* Société *Moguntia Est Epices*, Court of Appeal of Paris, France, 31 March 2005, 2006 REV. ARB. 665, *affirmed by Société PT Putrabali Adyamulia v. Rena Holding Société Moguntia Est Epices*, Court of Cassation, France, 05-18053, 29 June 2007, 2007 REV. ARB.; *Direction Générale de l'Aviation Civile de l'Emirat de Dubaï v. Société International Bechtel Co.*, Court of Appeal of Paris, France, 29 September 2005, 2006 REV. ARB.; *Société S.A. Lesbats et Fils v. Volker le Docteur Grub*, Court of Appeal of Paris, France, 18 January 2007, 05/10887.

[993] See in particular the practice of the courts of the United States and Germany: *Baker Marine Ltd. v. Chevron Limited, Chevron Corp., Inc. and others v. Danos and Curole Marine Contractors, Inc.*, Court of Appeals, Second Circuit, United States of America, 12 August 1999, 97-9615 and 97-9617 (refusing to enforce an award on the ground that it was annulled by the Nigerian courts of the seat); *TermoRio S.A. E.S.P. (Colombia) v. Electranta S.P. (Colombia),* Court of Appeals, D.C. Circuit, United States of America, 25 May 2007, 06-7058 (refusing to enforce an award annulled by the courts of the seat, namely Colombian courts); Oberlandesgericht [OLG] Rostock, Germany, 28 October 1999, 1 Sch 03/99 (denying enforcement of an award set aside at the seat of the arbitration, namely Moscow).

[994] See the chapter of the Guide on article V (1)(e), para. 12.

constitute a sufficient ground for denying enforcement; whether or not the decision setting aside the award is subject to appeal is irrelevant.[995]

b. Award suspended

31. Article V (1)*(e)* of the Convention also allows parties to challenge the enforcement of an award if the award has been "suspended". The Convention does not provide guidance as to the definition of the term "suspended"; nevertheless, with very few exceptions,[996] the majority of courts agree that this refers to a formal suspension resulting from a court decision. The Swiss Federal Tribunal, for instance, held that this rule covers a situation in which a court, "noticing that a fault is likely to impact the award, prevents its enforcement until such time as the issue is settled substantively by the court examining the action to set aside the award". In that case, a court decision dismissing the claimant's request to wind up the respondent was found not to call into question the validity of the award or to formally suspend its enforcement.[997]

32. Likewise, it is understood that the automatic suspension resulting from the initiation of an action to set aside the award in the court of the originating jurisdiction does not meet the requirement of article V (1)*(e)*. As noted by some commentators, if the term "suspension" were to refer to the automatic suspension of an award in the originating jurisdiction pending an action to set aside, this would defeat the whole system of the Convention, as it would suffice that the party opposing enforcement could initiate an application to set aside the award at the place of arbitration so that the award be refused enforcement everywhere.[998] In Switzerland, for instance, a party challenged the enforcement pursuant to article V (1)*(e)* on grounds that the initiation of setting aside proceedings at the courts of the place of arbitration

---

995 *Ciments Français (France) v. OAO Holding Company Siberian Cement (Russian Federation), OOO Financial Industrial Association Sibconcord (Russian Federation), Istanbul Çimento Yatırımları (Turkey)*, Federal Arbitrazh Court for the West-Siberian District, Russian Federation, 5 December 2011, A27-781/2011.

996 See, e.g., *Creighton Limited v. The Government of the State of Qatar (Ministry of Public Works)*, District Court, District of Columbia, United States of America, 22 March 1995, 94-1035 RMU, XXI Y.B. COM. ARB. (1996) (refusing to enforce an award on the ground that the initiation of annulment proceedings in France had, at the time, the effect of automatically suspending it).

997 Swiss Federal Tribunal, Switzerland, 21 March 2000, 5P.371/1999.

998 ALBERT JAN VAN DEN BERG, THE NEW YORK ARBITRATION CONVENTION OF 1958: TOWARDS A UNIFORM JUDICIAL INTERPRETATION 352 (1981). See also Nadia Darwazeh, *Article V (1)(e)*, in RECOGNITION AND ENFORCEMENT OF FOREIGN ARBITRAL AWARDS: A GLOBAL COMMENTARY ON THE NEW YORK CONVENTION 301, 341-42 (H. Kronke, P. Nacimiento et al. eds., 2010); FOUCHARD GAILLARD GOLDMAN ON INTERNATIONAL COMMERCIAL ARBITRATION 980-81, para. 1690 (E. Gaillard, J. Savage eds., 1999); Christoph Liebscher, *Article V (1)(e)*, in NEW YORK CONVENTION ON THE RECOGNITION AND ENFORCEMENT OF FOREIGN ARBITRAL AWARDS OF 10 JUNE 1958—COMMENTARY 356, 372, paras. 395-96 (R. Wolff ed., 2012).

in France automatically suspended the effects of the award. The Swiss Federal Tribunal held that the correct interpretation of the Convention should be that the suspension of the award in the originating jurisdiction would only constitute a ground for challenge if it were granted by a judicial decision, but not when it simply arises from an action brought against the award.[999] In *AB Götaverken*, the Swedish Supreme Court confirmed that the reference to a "suspended" award under article V (1)*(e)* refers to "a situation where, after specific consideration of the matter, the foreign authority orders the setting aside of a binding and enforceable award or the suspension of its enforcement". As a result, the court rejected the respondent's contention that enforcement should be denied on the ground that a recourse to set aside had been initiated in France, the country where the award was issued.[1000] The same principle led a United States court to deny the enforcement of an award. After confirming that "article V (1)*(e)* of the Convention require[s] a 'competent authority' to suspend the award, not just a statutory stay", the court held that, in that case, the stay ordered by the Argentinian courts was not merely an "automatic" stay resulting from the initiation of setting aside proceedings or a "pre-ordered" formality, and on that basis dismissed the request to enforce the award.[1001]

---

[999] *Company X S.A. v. Y Federation,* Swiss Federal Tribunal, Switzerland, 9 December 2008, 4A_403/2008.

[1000] *AB Götaverken v. General National Maritime Transport Company (GMTC), Libya and others*, Supreme Court, Sweden, 13 August 1979, SO 1462. See also *The Republic* of *Gabon v. Swiss Oil Corporation,* Grand Court, Cayman Islands, 17 June 1988, XIV Y.B. COM. ARB. (1989) (ruling that the automatic suspension of the effect of the award due to the initiation of a recourse to set aside the award under French law does not amount to "a competent authority [acting] consciously to stay the [award]" and therefore is not a ground to refuse enforcement under art. V (1)*(e)*); *S.A. Recam Sonofadex v. S.N.C. Cantieri Rizzardi de Gianfranco Rizzardi*, Court of Appeal of Orleans, France, 5 October 2000 (stating that the suspensive effect of setting aside proceedings initiated at the seat of the arbitration, namely Italy, does not amount to an effective suspension required by article V (1)*(e)* and cannot serve as a valid ground to reject the recognition and enforcement of the Award).

[1001] *EDF International S.A. v. YPF S.A.,* District Court for the District of Delaware, United States of America, 20 November 2008, Civil Action No. 08-167-JJF.

Article V (2)*(a)*

2. Recognition and enforcement of an arbitral award may also be refused if the competent authority in the country where recognition and enforcement is sought finds that: […] *(a)* The subject matter of the difference is not capable of settlement by arbitration under the law of that country […].

Travaux préparatoires

The *travaux préparatoires* on article V (2)*(a)* as adopted in 1958 are contained in the following documents:

Draft Convention on the Recognition and Enforcement of Foreign Arbitral Awards and comments by Governments and Organizations:

Report of the Committee on the Enforcement of International Arbitral Awards: E/2704 and Annex.

Comments by Governments and Organizations on the Draft Convention on the Recognition and Enforcement of Foreign Arbitral Awards: E/2822, Annexes I-II; E/2822/Add.2; E/2822/Add.5; E/CONF.26/3/Add.1.

Comments on the Draft Convention on the Recognition and Enforcement of Foreign Arbitral Awards: Note by the Secretary General: E/CONF.26/2.

United Nations Conference on International Commercial Arbitration:

Amendments to the Draft Convention Submitted by Governmental Delegations: E/CONF.26/L.17; E/CONF.26/L.32.

Comparison of Drafts Relating to Articles III, IV and V of the Draft Convention: E/CONF.26/L.33/Rev.1.

Further Amendments to the Draft Convention Submitted by Governmental Delegations: E/CONF.26/L.38.

Text of Articles III, IV and V of the Draft Convention Proposed by Working Party III: E/CONF.26/L.43.

Text of Articles Adopted by the Conference: E/CONF.26/L.48.

Text of the Convention on the Recognition and Enforcement of Foreign Arbitral Awards as Provisionally Approved by the Drafting Committee: E/CONF.26/L.61; E/CONF.26/8.

Final Act and Convention on the Recognition and Enforcement of Foreign Arbitral Awards: E/CONF.26/8/Rev.1.

Summary records:

Summary Records of the Eleventh, Thirteenth, Fourteenth, Seventeenth, and Twenty-First Meetings of the United Nations Conference on International Commercial Arbitration: E/CONF.26/SR.11; E/CONF.26/SR.13; E/CONF.26/SR.14; E/CONF.26/SR.17; E/CONF.26/SR.21.

Summary Records of the Fifth, and Seventh Meetings of the Committee on Enforcement of International Arbitral Awards: E/AC.42/SR.5; E/AC.42/ SR.7.

Committee on the Enforcement of International Arbitral Awards:

Enforcement of International Arbitral Awards: statement submitted by the International Chamber of Commerce, a non-governmental organization having consultative status in category A: E/C.2/373.

Report of the Committee on the Enforcement of International Arbitral Awards: E/AC.42/4.

(Available on the Internet at http://www.uncitral.org)
(For the *travaux préparatoires*, case law and bibliographical references, see also on the Internet at http://newyorkconvention1958.org)

Introduction

1. Article V (2)*(a)* of the New York Convention enables the courts of a Contracting State to refuse recognition and enforcement of an award if they find that the subject matter of the difference which led to the award is not

capable of settlement by arbitration under the law of the country where recognition and enforcement is sought.

2. Article 1*(b)* of the 1927 Geneva Convention conditioned recognition and enforcement on a positive showing that the subject matter of the award was capable of settlement by arbitration under the law of the country where the award was relied upon.[1002] By contrast, the New York Convention simply provides, in article V (2)*(a)*, that recognition and enforcement "may" be refused if the subject matter of a difference is not capable of settlement by arbitration. This departure from the text of the 1927 Geneva Convention underlines the pro-enforcement policy of the New York Convention.

3. The New York Convention also refers to the question whether the subject matter of a dispute is "capable of settlement by arbitration" in relation to the recognition of an arbitration agreement, under article II (1).[1003] As noted by commentators, the meaning of the phrase "capable of settlement by arbitration" in article II (1) and article V (2)*(a)* should be understood in the same manner.[1004]

4. The ground for refusal under article V (2)*(a)* may be raised by a court *ex officio.*[1005] Nonetheless, certain courts have considered that the party opposing recognition and enforcement retains the ultimate burden to prove that the subject matter of the underlying dispute is not capable of settlement by arbitration.[1006]

[1002] Article 1(b) of the 1927 Geneva Convention refers to the "subject matter of the award" being "capable of settlement by arbitration". The change to "subject matter of the difference" in the New York Convention has not given rise to any controversy or discussion.

[1003] Pursuant to article II (1), courts of the Contracting States shall recognize an agreement in writing under which the parties have undertaken to submit to arbitration all "differences" in respect of a legal relationship, concerning a subject which is "capable of settlement by arbitration." See the chapter of the Guide on article II.

[1004] Jan Paulsson, *Arbitrability, Still Through a Glass Darkly*, in ARBITRATION IN THE NEXT DECADE 95, 96 (ICC PUB. NO, 612E, 1999); ALBERT JAN VAN DEN BERG, THE NEW YORK CONVENTION OF 1958: TOWARDS A UNIFORM JUDICIAL INTERPRETATION 359 (1981); David Quinke, *Article V (2)(a)*, in THE NEW YORK CONVENTION ON THE RECOGNITION AND ENFORCEMENT OF FOREIGN ARBITRAL AWARDS OF 10 JUNE 1958—COMMENTARY 380, 383, para. 427 (R. Wolff ed., 2012). This chapter addresses decisions of national courts that analyse the ground to refuse recognition and enforcement of an arbitral award under article V (2)*(a)*. For cases interpreting the words "capable of settlement by arbitration" under article II (1), see the chapter of the Guide on article II.

[1005] FOUCHARD GAILLARD GOLDMAN ON INTERNATIONAL COMMERCIAL ARBITRATION 983, para. 169 (E. Gaillard, J. Savage eds., 1999) 3; ALBERT JAN VAN DEN BERG, THE NEW YORK CONVENTION OF 1958: TOWARDS A UNIFORM JUDICIAL INTERPRETATION 359 (1981).

[1006] *Italian Party v. Swiss Company*, Court of Appeal of Zurich, Switzerland, 17 July 2003, XXIX Y.B. COM. ARB. 819 (2004); *English Company X v. Spanish Company Y*, Supreme Court, Spain, 10 February 1984, X Y.B. COM. ARB. 493 (1985).

5. During the deliberations on article V (2)*(a)*, the French delegation questioned whether article V (2)*(a)* would allow national courts to apply local laws as a basis for refusing to recognize and enforce foreign arbitral awards.[1007] The practice of courts in the Contracting States has allayed these concerns. The question of whether the subject matter of a difference resulting in an arbitral award is capable of settlement by arbitration has been raised in a relatively small number of cases, and courts of the Contracting States have exercised their discretion to refuse recognition and enforcement pursuant to article V (2)*(a)* in only a handful of instances.

Analysis

A. Concept

6. Article V (2)*(a)* of the Convention provides that a court "may" refuse recognition and enforcement if the "subject matter of the difference" is "not capable of settlement by arbitration". The Convention does not define the phrases "subject matter of the difference" and "capable of settlement by arbitration". The *travaux préparatoires* to the Convention do not address the wording of article V (2)*(a)*.

7. It is generally accepted that article V (2)*(a)* allows national courts to refuse to recognize and enforce an arbitral award where there is a legal impediment to the resolution of the subject matter of the underlying dispute by arbitration, i.e., where the underlying dispute is not "arbitrable".[1008] In the context of article V (2)*(a)*, arbitrability is to be understood to mean whether a subject matter can be resolved through arbitration, or is reserved for resolution by courts.[1009] It should not be understood to mean whether a dispute falls within the scope of an arbitration agreement.[1010]

[1007] *Travaux préparatoires*, United Nations Conference on International Commercial Arbitration, Summary Record of the Eleventh Meeting E/CONF.26/SR.11, p. 7.

[1008] See GARY B. BORN, INTERNATIONAL COMMERCIAL ARBITRATION 948 (2014); W. LAURENCE CRAIG, WILLIAM W. PARK, JAN PAULSSON, INTERNATIONAL CHAMBER OF COMMERCE ARBITRATION 60 (2000). During the drafting of the Convention, the Society of Comparative Legislation proposed to replace the language "not capable of settlement by arbitration" by "not arbitrable". The proposal was not discussed further, nor was it taken up by the Drafting Committee. *Travaux préparatoires*, Recognition and Enforcement of Foreign Arbitral Awards, Report by the Secretary-General, Annex II, Comments by Non-Governmental Organizations, E/2822, p. 22.

[1009] W. LAURENCE CRAIG, WILLIAM W. PARK, JAN PAULSSON, INTERNATIONAL CHAMBER OF COMMERCE ARBITRATION 60 (2000); GARY B. BORN, INTERNATIONAL COMMERCIAL ARBITRATION 944, fn. 3 (2014); Albert Jan van den Berg, *Consolidated Commentary Cases Reported in Volumes XXII (1997) - XXVII (2002)*, XXVIII Y.B. COM. ARB. 666 (2003), para. 519; ICCA'S GUIDE TO THE INTERPRETATION OF THE 1958 NEW YORK CONVENTION: A HANDBOOK FOR JUDGES 104 (P. Sanders ed., 2011).

[1010] See in particular the terminology used by the United States Supreme Court in First *Options* of *Chicago, Inc. v. Manuel Kaplan, et ux. and MK Investments, Inc.*, Supreme Court,

8. "Arbitrability" is not a concept that is unique to the New York Convention. Rather, arbitrability forms part of a wider range of tools, such as the mandatory rules of the forum, which override party autonomy and enable a national court to protect the core interests of the legal order to which it belongs.

9. The drafters of the Convention rejected a proposal by the French delegation that article V (2)*(a)* be deleted on the grounds that it unduly attributed international importance to domestic rules, and that it would be sufficient that an award comply with international public policy under what is now article V (2)*(b)*.[1011] Instead, the final text of the Convention followed the approach of the 1927 Geneva Convention, which treated public policy ground (article 1(e)) and arbitrability ground (article 1*(b)*) in separate subsections, and maintained article V (2)*(a)* and article V (2)*(b)* as distinct grounds.

10. Furthermore, while the ground for refusal set forth at article V (2)*(a)* may sometimes coincide with that at article V (2)*(b)*, in other cases it does not. For instance, certain family law issues which also touch upon financial matters, such as the resolution of financial arrangements between spouses, are in some jurisdictions not capable of settlement by arbitration,[1012] while allowed in others to be settled by arbitration[1013] without falling under the concept of international public policy.

United States of America, 22 May 1995, 514 United States 938. This broader understanding of arbitrability is not generally used in international practice; see, e.g., in the context of negotiation of UNCITRAL Model Law on Arbitration, HOWARD M. HOLTZMANN AND JOSEPH E. NEUHAUS, A GUIDE TO THE UNCITRAL MODEL LAW ON INTERNATIONAL COMMERCIAL ARBITRATION—LEGISLATIVE HISTORY AND COMMENTARY 135 et seq. (1989).

[1011] *Travaux préparatoires*, United Nations Conference on International Commercial Arbitration, Summary Record of the Eleventh Meeting E/CONF.26/SR.11, p. 7. The later, tri-state proposal of France, the Netherlands and the Federal Republic of Germany also contemplated the deletion of what is now article V (2)(a): *Travaux préparatoires*, United Nations Conference on International Commercial Arbitration, Summary Record of the Fourteenth Meeting E/CONF.26/SR.14, p. 2. The Greek delegation proposed a re-wording "*in such a way that the fact that a foreign award was incompatible with fundamental principles* of *law (ordre public) would be sufficient grounds for refusing recognition". Travaux préparatoires*, Recognition and Enforcement of Foreign Arbitral Awards, Report by the Secretary-General, Annex I Comments by Governments, E/2822/Add. 2, p. 2.

[1012] See, e.g., Article 806 of the Italian Code of Civil Procedure, which allows parties to elect for dispute settlement through arbitration apart from disputes concerning, *inter alia*, "issues of personal status and marital separation"; Article 2060 of the French Civil Code, which provides inter alia that "[o]ne may not enter into arbitration agreements in matters [...] relating to divorce and judicial separation". Although this text does not apply to international arbitration, it nevertheless reveals the importance that the French legislature attaches to these issues.

[1013] See, e.g., Article 177 of the Swiss Private International Law Statute, under which "[a]ny dispute of financial interest may be the subject of an arbitration", i.e., any dispute which can be assessed in monetary terms, is capable of settlement by arbitration.

11. In line with the approach of the New York Convention to differentiate arbitrability and public policy, courts of the Contracting States have consistently addressed the grounds in articles V (2)*(a)* and V (2)*(b)* separately, without questioning whether they refer to the same concept.[1014]

12. It has been suggested that the fact that a particular matter is not capable of settlement by arbitration under a national law should not necessarily entail that it will not give rise to an enforceable award under the New York Convention. In *Parsons*, a United States Appeals court considered that "it may well be that the special considerations and policies" underlying international arbitration "call for a narrower view of non-arbitrability in the international than the domestic context".[1015] A number of commentators have also considered that the Convention's pro-enforcement policy requires courts to apply an international, rather than a domestic, notion of which subject matters are to be capable of settlement by arbitration.[1016]

[1014] See, e.g., *Parsons & Whittemore Overseas Co. v. Société Générale de L'Industrie du Papier (RAKTA)*, Court of Appeals, Second Circuit, United States of America, 23 December 1974, 508 F.2d 969, 975; *Angel v. Bernardo Alfageme, S.A.*, Supreme Court, Civil Chamber, First Section, Spain, 20 March 2001, XXXI Y.B. COM. ARB. 821 (2006); *Hemofarm DD, MAG International Trade Holding DD, Suram Media Ltd. v. Jinan Yongning Pharmaceutical Co. Ltd.*, Supreme People's Court, China, 2 June 2008, Min Si Ta Zi No. 11; Javor v. Francoeur, Supreme Court of British Columbia, Canada, 6 March 2003, BCSC 2003 350; *Bobbie Brooks Inc. v. Lanificio Walter Banci s.a.s.*, Court of Appeal, Florence, Italy, 8 October 1977, IV Y.B. COM. ARB. 289 (1979); KM v. JSC, Supreme Court, Lithuania, 21 February 2011, XXXVIII Y.B. COM. ARB. 414 (2013); *Drummond Ltd. v. Ferrovias en Liquidación, Ferrocariles Nacionales de Colombia S.A. (FENOCO)*, Supreme Court of Justice, Colombia, 19 December 2011, 11001-0203-000-2008-01760-00.

[1015] *Parsons & Whittemore Overseas Co. v. Société Générale de L'Industrie du Papier (RAKTA),* Court of Appeals, Second Circuit, United States of America, 23 December 1974, 508 F.2d 969, 975. The Court of Appeal found that there was no special national interest in the judicial, rather than arbitral, resolution of a breach of contract claim that would justify a refusal to recognize and enforce the ensuing award pursuant to article V (2)(a), and that it need not reach any distinction between the domestic and international arbitrability of the award. In a different context, courts in the United States have also confirmed that disputes involving issues of American antitrust law, which are normally subject to the jurisdiction of domestic courts, are capable of settlement by arbitration within the meaning of article II of the Convention. See, e.g., *Mitsubishi Motors Corp v. Soler Chrysler-Plymouth*, Supreme Court, United States of America, 20 December 1983, 473 United States 614, XI Y.B COM. ARB. 555 (1986), where the Supreme Court affirmed that it is "necessary for national courts to subordinate domestic notions of arbitrability to the international policy favouring commercial arbitration".

[1016] FOUCHARD GAILLARD GOLDMAN ON INTERNATIONAL COMMERCIAL ARBITRATION 995, para. 1707 (E. Gaillard, J. Savage eds., 1999); W. LAURENCE CRAIG, WILLIAM W. PARK, JAN PAULSSON, INTERNATIONAL CHAMBER OF COMMERCE ARBITRATION 62-63 (2000); GARY B. BORN, INTERNATIONAL COMMERCIAL ARBITRATION 3697-98 (2014); ALBERT JAN VAN DEN BERG, THE NEW YORK ARBITRATION CONVENTION OF 1958: TOWARDS A UNIFORM JUDICIAL INTERPRETATION 152-53 (1981); ICCA'S GUIDE TO THE INTERPRETATION OF THE 1958 NEW YORK CONVENTION: A HANDBOOK FOR JUDGES 105 (P. Sanders ed., 2011); David Quinke, *Article V (2)(a),* in THE NEW YORK CONVENTION ON THE RECOGNITION AND ENFORCEMENT OF FOREIGN ARBITRAL AWARDS OF 10 JUNE 1958—COMMENTARY 380, 388-89, paras. 438-40 (R. Wolff ed., 2012).

B. Application

13. Article V (2)*(a)* provides that a court may refuse to recognize and enforce an award where the subject matter of the dispute which gave rise to the award is not capable of settlement by arbitration.

14. The Convention does not identify the types of subject matters that are capable of settlement by arbitration. The wording of article V (2)*(a)* specifically directs the enforcing court to determine whether the subject matter of the dispute is capable of settlement by arbitration "under the law of that country" where recognition and enforcement is sought. In accordance with this wording, courts of the Contracting States have consistently applied their national laws to assess whether a dispute is capable of settlement by arbitration, and not the law of the country where the arbitration took place or any other law.[1017]

15. Courts applying article V (2)*(a)* have adopted different approaches to delineate which disputes are capable of settlement by arbitration under their laws. For instance, the Supreme Court of Lithuania, when deciding whether a dispute arising out of a contract between a basketball player and a local club was capable of settlement by arbitration, considered whether the dispute fell within the scope of Article 11(1) of the Commercial Arbitration Law of the Republic of Lithuania, which provides that certain disputes, such as employment and labor disputes, cannot be submitted to arbitration.[1018] Courts in other jurisdictions have applied article V (2)*(a)* by reference to similar provisions in their national laws.[1019]

[1017] See, e.g., *Société O.A.O. NPO Saturn v. Société Unimpex Entreprises*, Court of Appeal of Paris, France, October 2009, 07/17049; *Bankruptcy estate* of *Kommandiittiyhtiö Finexim O. Ivanoff (Finexim) v. Ferromet Aussenhandelsunternehmen,* Supreme Court, Finland, 27 February 1989, S88/310; *ED & F Man (Hong Kong) Co., Ltd. v. China National Sugar & Wines Group Corp.*, Supreme People's Court, China, 1 July 2003, Min Si Ta Zi No. 3; *Aloe Vera* of *America, Inc. v. Asianic Food (S) Pte Ltd. and Another*, Supreme Court of Singapore, High Court, Singapore, 10 May 2006, OS 762/2004, RA 327/2005, XXXII Y.B. COM. ARB. 489 (2007); *Construction Company Z v. State X*, Kammergericht [KG] Berlin, Germany, 11 June 2009, 20 Sch 04/07.

[1018] *KM v. JSC*, Supreme Court, Lithuania, 21 February 2011, XXXVIII Y.B. COM. ARB. 414 (2013).

[1019] See, e.g., *Quaglia v. Daros*, Court of Genoa, Italy, 30 April 1980, referring to Article 806 of the Italian Code of Civil Procedure, which provides as a default rule that parties may submit their disputes to arbitration, with the exception of disputes concerning issues of personal status and marital separation, and disputes concerning labour and social security issues; *Hemofarm DD, MAG International Trade Holding DD, Suram Media Ltd. v. Jinan Yongning Pharmaceutical Co. Ltd.*, Supreme People's Court, China, 2 June 2008, Min Si Ta Zi No. 11, referring to Article 2 of the Arbitration Law of China, which provides that only disputes between citizens, legal persons and other organisations concerning contractual and commercial matters are capable of settlement by arbitration.

16. Courts of Contracting States which do not specifically define in their legislation which disputes are arbitrable have adopted a different approach. In one reported case, the Supreme Court of Singapore determined whether the underlying difference, which concerned whether a person was the "alter ego of a company", was capable of settlement by arbitration by considering whether it touched on an element of public interest. The Court held that that there was no special public interest in such a dispute and dismissed the appeal of the order by a lower court granting the award enforcement.[1020]

17. In the United States, courts have resolved challenges to recognition and enforcement based on article V (2)*(a)* by reference to the implied legislative intent of entering into the New York Convention, namely to promote the use of international arbitration.[1021]

18. Regardless of the approach followed, courts of the Contracting States have set very few limits on the types of disputes that are capable of settlement by arbitration in the application of article V (2)*(a)*. This reflects the trend of reserving only a small category of disputes solely to the jurisdiction of courts and the growing confidence of most jurisdictions in arbitration. In the words of one United States Court, "the incapable of settlement by arbitration exception has been narrowly construed in light of the strong judicial interest in encouraging the use of arbitration".[1022]

19. The types of disputes which have been analysed in the limited case law on article V (2)*(a)* may be separated into two broad categories, namely those that concern commercial matters, and those types of non-commercial disputes which courts have, in exceptional circumstances, considered incapable of settlement by arbitration under their national laws.

[1020] *Aloe Vera* of *America, Inc. v. Asianic Food (S) Pte Ltd. and Another*, Supreme Court of Singapore, High Court, Singapore, 10 May 2006, OS 762/2004, RA 327/2005, XXXII Y.B. COM. ARB. 489 (2007).

[1021] *Mitsubishi Motors Corp v. Soler Chrysler-Plymouth*, Supreme Court, United States of America, 20 December 1983, 473 United States 614, XI Y.B COM. ARB 555 (1986); *McDermott International Inc. v. Underwriters at Lloyd's*, United States District Court, E.D. Louisiana, May 29 1996, Civ.A. No. 91—841; *Saudi Iron And Steel Co. v. Stemcor USA Inc*, United States District Court, Southern District of New York, 17 October 1997, 97 CIV. 5976 (DLC), XXIII Y.B. 1082 COM. ARB. (1998); *Parsons & Whittemore Overseas Co. v.* Société *Générale de L'Industrie du Papier (RAKTA)*, Court of Appeals, Second Circuit, United States of America, 23 December 1974, 508 F.2d 969, 975; *Shaheen Natural Resources Company Inc. v.* Société *Nationale pour la Recherche, la Production and others*, United States District Court, Southern District of New York, 585 F. Supp. 57; United States Court of Appeals, Second Circuit, 15 November 1983, 733 F. Supp. 2d 260, X Y.B. COM. ARB. 540 (1985); *VRG Linhas Aereas S.A. v. Matlin Patterson Global Opportunities Partners II L.P*, United States Court of Appeals, Second Circuit, Docket No. 12-593-cv, 3 June 2013.

[1022] *Saudi Iron And Steel Co. v. Stemcor USA Inc,* United States District Court, Southern District of New York, 16 October 1997, No. 97 CIV. 5976 (DLC), XXIII Y.B. 1082 COM. ARB. (1998).

a. Commercial disputes

20. There is broad agreement among courts of the Contracting States that a dispute whose subject matter is of a commercial nature is capable of being settled by arbitration, and an arbitral award that results from a commercial difference should not be refused enforcement pursuant to article V (2)*(a)*.

21. Courts in Germany,[1023] Switzerland,[1024] Italy,[1025] Spain,[1026] Colombia,[1027] the United States[1028] and Singapore[1029] have all expressly held that a difference arising out of a commercial matter should not be refused enforcement pursuant to article V (2)*(a)*.

22. Breach of contract claims are the most frequently reported example of differences found to be commercial in nature and, therefore, capable of settlement by arbitration. For instance, an Italian Court of Appeal found that a dispute concerning a product quality issue was capable of settlement by arbitration.[1030] Courts in Spain[1031] and China[1032] have reached similar

---

[1023] Oberlandesgericht [OLG] Hamm, Germany, 2 November 1983, 20 U 57/83; Oberlandesgericht [OLG] München, Germany, 23 February 2007, 34 Sch 31/06.

[1024] *Italian party v. Swiss company*, High Court of Zurich, Switzerland, 17 July 2003, XXIX Y.B. COM. ARB. 819 (2004).

[1025] *Società La Naviera Grancebaco S.A. v. Ditta Italgrani*, Court of Naples, Italy, 30 June 1976, IV Y.B. COM. ARB. 277 (1979); *Renault Jacquinet v. Sicea*, Court of Appeal, Milan, Italy, 3 May 1977, IV Y.B. COM. ARB. 284 (1979); *Bobbie Brooks Inc. v. Lanificio Walter Banci s.a.s.*, Court of Appeal, Florence, Italy, 8 October 1977, IV Y.B. COM. ARB. 289 (1979); *Efxinos Shipping Co. Ltd. v. Rawi Shipping Lines Ltd.*, Court of Appeal, Genoa, Italy, 2 May 1980, VIII Y.B. COM. ARB. 381 (1983).

[1026] *English Company X v. Spanish Company Y*, Supreme Court, Spain, 10 February 1984, X Y.B. COM. ARB. 493 (1985); *Thyssen Haniel Logistic International GmbH v. Barna Consignataria S.L.*, Supreme Court, Spain, 14 July 1998, XXVI Y.B. COM. ARB. 851 (2001); *Angel v. Bernardo Alfageme, S.A.*, Supreme Court, Civil Chamber, First Section, Spain, 20 March 2001, XXXI Y.B. COM. ARB. 821 (2006).

[1027] *Sunward Overseas S.A. v. Servicios Marítimos Limitada Semar (Ltda.)*, Supreme Court of Justice, Colombia, 20 November 1992, XX Y.B. COM. ARB. 651 (1995); *Drummond Ltd. v. Ferrovias en Liquidación, Ferrocariles Nacionales de Colombia S.A. (FENOCO)*, Supreme Court of Justice, Colombia, 19 December 2011, 11001-0203-000-2008-01760-00.

[1028] *Seven Seas Shipping Ltd. v. Tondo Limitada,* District Court, Southern District of New York, United States of America, 25 June 1999, 99 CIV. 1164 (DLC), XXV Y.B. COM. ARB. 641 (2000); *Stellar Lines, S.A. v. Euroleader Shipping and Trading Corp.*, District Court, Southern District of New York, United States of America, 16 August 1999, 99 CIV. 4073 (DLC), XXV Y.B. COM. ARB. 641 (2000).

[1029] *Aloe Vera of America, Inc. v. Asianic Food (S) Pte Ltd. and Another*, Supreme Court of Singapore, High Court, Singapore, 10 May 2006, OS 762/2004, RA 327/2005, XXXII Y.B. COM. ARB. 489 (2007).

[1030] *Renault Jacquinet v. Sicea*, Court of Appeal, Milan, (Sez. I), Italy, 3 May 1977, IV Y.B. COM. ARB. 284 (1979). See also *Bobbie Brooks Inc. v. Lanificio Walter Banci s.a.s.*, Court of Appeal, Florence, Italy, 8 October 1977, IV Y.B. COM. ARB. 289 (1979).

[1031] *Angel v. Bernardo Alfageme, S.A.*, Supreme Court, Civil Chamber, First Section, Spain, 20 March 2001, XXXI Y.B. COM. ARB. 821 (2006).

conclusions when deciding applications to enforce arbitral awards deciding differences arising out of sale of goods contracts.

23. Courts have found other types of contractual disputes capable of settlement by arbitration. For instance, the Supreme Court of Colombia held that a dispute concerning the performance of a contract for the transportation of coal was capable of settlement by arbitration.[1033] Courts in the United States,[1034] Colombia,[1035] Italy,[1036] and Spain[1037] have also consistently held that differences arising out of charter parties were capable of settlement by arbitration within the meaning of article V (2)*(a)*.

24. In another case, a Swiss court held that an award rendered in a dispute arising under a licence agreement concerning monetary claims can be subject to arbitration under Swiss law, and found that enforcement should not be denied under article V (2)*(a)*.[1038] Disputes arising under services contracts have also been held to be of a commercial nature, and therefore capable of settlement by arbitration within the meaning of article V (2)*(a)*.[1039]

b. Non-commercial disputes

25. Different categories of non-commercial disputes have been analysed in the case law on article V (2)*(a)*. As discussed above, the wording of article

[1032] *English Company X v. Spanish Company Y*, Supreme Court, Spain, 10 February 1984, X Y.B. COM. ARB. 493 (1985); *ED & F Man (Hong Kong) Co., Ltd. v. China National Sugar & Wines Group Corp.*, Supreme People's Court, China, 01 July 2003, Min Si Ta Zi No. 3.

[1033] *Drummond Ltd. v. Ferrovias en Liquidación, Ferrocariles Nacionales de Colombia S.A. (FENOCO)*, Supreme Court of Justice, Colombia, 19 December 2011, 11001-0203-000-2008-01760-00.

[1034] *Seven Seas Shipping Ltd. v. Tondo Limitada*, District Court, Southern District of New York, United States of America, 25 June 1999, 99 CIV. 1164 (DLC), XXV Y.B. COM. ARB. 641 (2000); *Stellar Lines, S.A. v. Euroleader Shipping and Trading Corp.*, District Court, Southern District of New York, United States of America, 16 August 1999, 99 CIV 4073 (DLC), XXV Y.B. COM. ARB. 641 (2000).

[1035] *Sunward Overseas S.A. v. Servicios Marítimos Limitada Semar (Ltda.)*, Supreme Court of Justice, Colombia, 20 November 1992, XX Y.B. COM. ARB. 651 (1995).

[1036] *Società La Naviera Grancebaco S.A. v. Ditta Italgrani*, Court of Naples, Italy, 30 June 1976, IV Y.B. COM. ARB. 277 (1979); *Efxinos Shipping Co. Ltd. v. Rawi Shipping Lines Ltd.*, Court of Appeal, Genoa, Italy, 2 May 1980, VIII Y.B. COM. ARB. 381 (1983).

[1037] *Thyssen Haniel Logistic International GmbH v. Barna Consignataria S.L.*, Supreme Court, Spain, 14 July 1998, XXVI Y.B. COM. ARB. 851 (2001).

[1038] *Italian party v. Swiss company*, High Court of Zurich, Switzerland, 17 July 2003, XXIX Y.B. COM. ARB. 819 (2004).

[1039] See, e.g., *Parsons & Whittemore Overseas Co. v. Société Générale de L'Industrie du Papier (RAKTA)*, Court of Appeals, Second Circuit, United States of America, 23 December 1974, 508 F.2d 969, 975; Oberlandesgericht [OLG] München, Germany, 23 February 2007, 34 Sch 31/06.

V (2)*(a)* directs national courts to determine the arbitrability of a particular dispute in accordance with their national law.

26. Concerning employment and labor disputes, the laws of some jurisdictions allow such disputes to be submitted to arbitration, while others do not.[1040] In the only reported case on article V (2)*(a)* that concerns an employment law dispute,[1041] the Supreme Court of Lithuania reversed an order of a lower court that refused recognition and enforcement of an award that had decided a dispute involving a local sports club, on the ground that it was an employment dispute that was incapable of settlement by arbitration under Lithuanian law. The Supreme Court reasoned that professional sports agreements are underpinned by the principle of freedom of contract and that there was no impediment to submitting disputes arising under those contracts to arbitration.[1042]

27. At this time, there are no reported cases analysing whether an arbitral award that decides matters of competition law should be refused recognition and enforcement pursuant to article V (2)*(a)*. In a different context, the United States Supreme Court held in the 1983 Mitsubishi Motors decision that statutory antitrust claims arising out of an "international transaction" was validly subject to the New York Convention, and that an agreement to arbitrate those claims should be enforced under article II. In reaching its decision, the Supreme Court noted that at the time of acceding to the Convention, the United States Congress did not expressly exclude any matters from the scope of the Convention's application, and that "[t]he utility of the Convention in promoting the process of international commercial arbitration depends upon the willingness of national courts to let go of matters they normally would think of as their own."[1043]

[1040] For instance, the United States legislature has favoured the arbitration of many types of labour disputes. See § 1 of the United States Federal Arbitration Act, which excludes from the Act's coverage agreements arising from only a limited range of employment relations involving "contracts of employment of seamen, railroad employees, or any other class of workers engaged in foreign or interstate commerce." Switzerland has also taken a liberal stance on the arbitration of labour and employment disputes. See Alexandra Johnson, Isabelle Wildhaber, *Arbitrating Labor Disputes in Switzerland*, 27(6) J. INT'L ARB. 631-55 (2010). In other jurisdictions such as Germany, an arbitration agreement between an employer and individual employees regarding the employment contract is invalid. JEAN-FRANCOIS POUDRET, SEBASTIEN BESSON, COMPARATIVE LAW OF INTERNATIONAL ARBITRATION 313 (2007).

[1041] The arbitrability of employment and labour disputes has more often arisen at the pre-award stage. See the chapter of the Guide on article II.

[1042] *KM v. JSC*, Supreme Court, Lithuania, 21 February 2011, XXXVIII Y.B. COM. ARB. 414 (2013). The Supreme Court referred the case back to the Court of Appeal to decide the separate ground of whether the award was contrary to public policy and should be refused recognition and enforcement under article V (2)(b).

[1043] *Mitsubishi Motors Corp v. Soler Chrysler-Plymouth*, Supreme Court, United States of America, 20 December 1983, 473 United States 614, XI Y.B COM. ARB 555 (1986).

28. It is generally accepted that the authority to commence and administer bankruptcy proceedings rests solely with national courts.[1044] Different conclusions have been reached concerning whether bankruptcy law related disputes are capable of settlement by arbitration under article V (2)*(a)*. For instance, the Supreme Court of Finland held that claims concerning debts of an insolvent company were capable of settlement by arbitration.[1045] In a different context, the Court of Appeal of Lithuania held that a dispute between two companies was not capable of settlement by arbitration because the legal status of their relationship had changed after one company had entered into insolvency. The Court concluded that the arbitration agreement in the original contract could not be relied on, and refused enforcement pursuant to article V (2)*(a)*.[1046]

29. In one reported case concerning issues of succession, the Supreme People's Court of China refused to recognize and enforce an award involving a wife's inheritance of her deceased husband's share in a company. The Court referred to Article 3 of the Arbitration Law of the People's Republic of China, which provides that matters of succession cannot be submitted to arbitration.[1047] Although there are no further reported cases on the issue at the time, it is noteworthy that the laws of some of the Contracting States, such as Switzerland,[1048] do not prohibit the settlement by arbitration of disputes relating to monetary issues between heirs.

[1044] See Gabrielle Kaufmann-Kohler, Laurent Lévy, *International Commercial Arbitration, Insolvency and International Arbitration*, in THE CHALLENGES OF INSOLVENCY LAW REFORM IN THE 21ST CENTURY 257, 262-63 (H. Peter, N. Jeandin, J. Kilborn eds., 2006); Fernando Mantilla-Serrano, *International Arbitration and Insolvency Proceedings*, 11 ARB. INT'L 51, 65 (1995) (quoting from unpublished award: "only those issues that have a direct connection with the insolvency proceedings, that is the issues that arise out of the application of rules particular to those proceedings" are nonarbitrable); ADAM SAMUEL, JURISDICTIONAL PROBLEMS IN INTERNATIONAL COMMERCIAL ARBITRATION: A STUDY OF BELGIAN, DUTCH, ENGLISH, FRENCH, SWEDISH, SWISS, UNITED STATES AND WEST GERMAN LAW 143 (1989) ("an arbitrator cannot officially declare someone bankrupt").

[1045] *Bankruptcy estate* of *Kommandiittiyhtiö Finexim O. Ivanoff (Finexim) v. Ferromet Aussenhandelsunternehmen*, Supreme Court, Finland, 27 February 1989, S88/310.

[1046] *Shipping Services A/S v. RAB Sevnaučflot, Fishery Group*, Court of Appeal, Lithuania, 13 May 2011, 2-1545/2011.

[1047] *Wu Chunying v. Zhang Guiwen*, Supreme People's Court, China, 2 September 2009, Min Si Ta Zi No. 33.

[1048] Article 177 of the Swiss Private International Law Statute, under which "[a]ny dispute of financial interest may be the subject of an arbitration", i.e., any dispute which can be assessed in monetary terms, is capable of settlement by arbitration.

Article V (2)*(b)*

2. Recognition and enforcement of an arbitral award may also be refused if the competent authority in the country where recognition and enforcement is sought finds that: […] (b) The recognition or enforcement of the award would be contrary to the public policy of that country.

TRAVAUX PRÉPARATOIRES

The *travaux préparatoires* on article V(2)*(b)* as adopted in 1958 are contained in the following documents:

Draft Convention on the Recognition and Enforcement of Foreign Arbitral Awards and comments by Governments and Organizations:

Report of the Committee on the Enforcement of International Arbitral Awards: E/2704 and Annex.

Comments by Governments and Organizations on the Draft Convention on the Recognition and Enforcement of Foreign Arbitral Awards: E/2822, Annexes I-II; E/2822/Add.1; E/2822/Add.4; E/CONF.26/3; E/CONF.26/3/Add.1.

Activities of Inter-Governmental and Non-Governmental Organizations in the Field of International Commercial Arbitration: Consolidated Report by the Secretary-General: E/CONF.26/4.

Comments on the Draft Convention on the Recognition and Enforcement of Foreign Arbitral Awards: Note by the Secretary General: E/CONF.26/2.

United Nations Conference on International Commercial Arbitration:

Amendments to the Draft Convention Submitted by Governmental Delegations: E/CONF.26/L.8; E/CONF.26/L.15; E/CONF.26/L.15/Rev.1;

E/CONF.26/L.17; E/CONF.26/L.31; E/CONF.26/L.34; E/CONF.26/L.35.

Comparison of Drafts Relating to Articles III, IV and V of the Draft Convention: E/CONF.26/L.33/Rev.1.

Further Amendments to the Draft Convention Submitted by Governmental Delegations: E/CONF.26/L.40.

Text of Articles III, IV and V of the Draft Convention Proposed by Working Party III: E/CONF.26/L.43.

Text of Articles Adopted by the Conference: E/CONF.26/L.48.

Text of the Convention on the Recognition and Enforcement of Foreign Arbitral Awards as Provisionally Approved by the Drafting Committee: E/CONF.26/L.61; E/CONF.26/8.

Final Act and Convention on the Recognition and Enforcement of Foreign Arbitral Awards: E/CONF.26/8/Rev.1.

Summary records:

Summary Records of the Second, Seventh, Eleventh, Thirteenth, Fourteenth, Seventeenth, Twenty-first, and Twenty-fourth Meetings of the United Nations Conference on International Commercial Arbitration: E/CONF.26/SR.2; E/CONF.26/SR.7; E/CONF.26/SR.11; E/CONF.26/SR.13; E/CONF.26/SR.14; E/CONF.26/SR.17; E/CONF.26/SR.21; E/CONF.26/SR.24.

Summary Records of the First, Second, Fifth, and Seventh Meetings of the Committee on Enforcement of International Arbitral Awards: E/AC.42/SR.1; E/AC.42/SR.2; E/AC.42/SR.5; E/AC.42/SR.7.

Committee on the Enforcement of International Arbitral Awards:

Enforcement of International Arbitral Awards: statement submitted by the International Chamber of Commerce, a non-governmental organization having consultative status in category A: E/C.2/373.

Comments received from Governments regarding the Draft Convention on the Enforcement of International Arbitral Awards: E/AC.42/1.

Report of the Committee on the Enforcement of International Arbitral Awards: E/AC.42/4.

(Available on the Internet at http://www.uncitral.org)

(For the *travaux préparatoires*, case law and bibliographical references, see also on the Internet at http://newyorkconvention1958.org)

Introduction

1. Article V (2)*(b)* of the New York Convention enables the courts of a Contracting State to refuse recognition and enforcement of an award when they find that such recognition or enforcement would be contrary to its public policy.

2. Public policy is not a concept unique to the New York Convention. Rather, public policy forms part of a wider range of tools, such as the mandatory rules of the forum that override private autonomy, that allow a court to protect the integrity of the legal order to which it belongs. It is, therefore, impossible to sever the concept of public policy in the sense of article V (2)*(b)* of the New York Convention from the concept of public policy as is understood in international law.

3. Nor did the New York Convention first introduce public policy as a ground for refusing the recognition and enforcement of awards. Article 1(e) of the 1927 Geneva Convention required that, in order for recognition and enforcement to be granted, it had to be positively demonstrated that such "recognition or enforcement of the award [was] not contrary to the public policy or to the principles of law of the country in which it is sought to be relied upon". The New York Convention simply provides, in article V (2)*(b)*, that recognition may be refused on the basis of public policy.[1049] In addition, the omission in the New York Convention of any reference to an award being contrary to "principles of law"[1050] is notable and underscores the strong pro-enforcement bias of the Convention.[1051]

[1049] See ANTON G. MAURER, THE PUBLIC POLICY EXCEPTION UNDER THE NEW YORK CONVENTION: HISTORY, INTERPRETATION AND APPLICATION 61 (2012); Bernard Hanotiau, Olivier Caprasse, *Public Policy in International Commercial Arbitration*, in ENFORCEMENT OF ARBITRATION AGREEMENTS AND INTERNATIONAL ARBITRAL AWARDS: THE NEW YORK CONVENTION IN PRACTICE 787, 802 (E. Gaillard, D. Di Pietro eds., 2008).

[1050] For various comments on this phrase which was eventually omitted, see *Travaux préparatoires*, Report of the Committee on the Enforcement of International Arbitral Awards,

Analysis

A. Concept

a. The public policy exception under the Convention

4. Although different jurisdictions define public policy differently, case law tends to refer to a public policy basis for refusing recognition and enforcement of an award under article V (2)*(b)* of the New York Convention when the core values of a legal system have been deviated from. Invoking the public policy exception is a safety valve to be used in those exceptional circumstances when it would be impossible for a legal system to recognize an award and enforce it without abandoning the very fundaments on which it is based.[1052]

5. In the words of the often-quoted judgment of the Second Circuit of the United States Court of Appeals in Parsons, "[e]nforcement of foreign arbitral awards may be denied on [the basis of public policy] only where enforcement would violate the forum state's most basic notions of morality

---

E/AC.42/4/Rev.1, p. 13; Report by the Secretary-General, Recognition and Enforcement of Foreign Arbitral Awards, E/2822, Annex II, pp. 20-21 and 23; Recognition and Enforcement of Foreign Arbitral Awards: Comments by Governments on the draft Convention on the Recognition and Enforcement of Foreign Arbitral Awards E/2822/Add.4, p. 2; Recognition and Enforcement of Foreign Arbitral Awards: Comments by Governments on the draft Convention on the Recognition and Enforcement of Foreign Arbitral Awards, E/CONF.26/3, p. 3; Activities of Inter-Governmental and Non-Governmental Organizations in the Field of International Commercial Arbitration: Consolidated Report by the Secretary-General, E/CONF.26/4, p. 29; Comments on draft Convention on the Recognition and Enforcement of Foreign Arbitral Awards, E/CONF.26/2, pp. 6-7; Yugoslavia: amendment to Articles III and IV of the draft Convention, E/CONF. 26/L.35; Federal Republic of Germany: amendment to Articles III and IV of the draft Convention, E/CONF. 26/L.34; Summary Record of the Sixth Meeting, E/AC.42/SR.6, p. 11; Summary Record of the Seventh Meeting, E/AC.42/SR. 7; Comments of the representative of the Peruvian Government, Mr. Maurtua: Summary Record of the Fourteenth Meeting, E/CONF.26/SR.14, pp. 9; Summary Record of the Seventeenth Meeting, E/CONF.26/SR.17, pp. 15-16. See also Joel R. Junker, *The Public Policy Defense to Recognition and Enforcement* of *Foreign Arbitral Awards*, 1977 CAL. W. INT'L L.J. 228, 229-30.

[1051] *See Parsons & Whittemore Overseas v. Société Générale de L'Industrie du Papier (RAKTA)*, Court of Appeals, Second Circuit, United States of America, 508 F.2d 969, 973 (1974).

[1052] For the exceptional nature of the defence, see the Comments of the Netherlands Government, *Travaux préparatoires*, Recognition and Enforcement of Foreign Arbitral Awards: Comments by Governments on the draft Convention on the Recognition and Enforcement of Foreign Arbitral Awards E/2822/Add.4, p. 2. See also the Comments of the representative of the French Government, Mr. Holleaux, *Travaux préparatoires*, Summary Record of the Eleventh Meeting, E/CONF.26/SR.11, p. 7. See also Jan Paulsson, *The New York Convention in International Practice—Problems* of *Assimilation*, ASA Special Series No. 9, 100, 113 (1996).

and justice".[1053] Several jurisdictions outside the United States have relied on this passage when assessing the public policy exception.[1054]

6. Similarly, the Federal Court of Australia has recently decided that "it is only those aspects of public policy that go to the fundamental, core questions of morality and justice in [the] jurisdiction [where enforcement is sought] which enliven this particular statutory exception to enforcement".[1055] In the same vein, the Hong Kong Court of Final Appeal defined an award that violates public policy as an award that is "so fundamentally offensive to [the enforcement jurisdiction]'s notions of justice that, despite it being party to the Convention, it cannot reasonably be expected to overlook the objection".[1056]

7. The Swiss courts have also defined the public policy exception under the Convention by reference to the concept of justice. In a seminal

---

[1053] *Parsons & Whittemore Overseas v. Société Générale de L'Industrie du Papier (RAKTA),* Court of Appeals, Second Circuit, United States of America, 508 F.2d 969, 974 (1974). Dealing with the argument of the party opposing enforcement that its actions had been dictated by the severance of diplomatic relations between the United States and Egypt, the Second Circuit of the United States Court of Appeals stated that "[t]o read the public policy defence as a parochial device protective of national political interests would seriously undermine the Convention's utility. This provision was not meant to enshrine the vagaries of international politics under the rubric of 'public policy'". See also *National Oil Corp. v. Libyan Sun Oil Co.,* District Court, District of Delaware, United States of America, 15 March 1990, 733 F. Supp. 800, XVI Y.B. COM. ARB. 651 (1991) (concerning an award whose recognition and enforcement was alleged to violate the United States sanctions against Libya). See also *Ameropa A.G. v. Havi Ocean Co. LLC,* District Court, Southern District of New York, United States of America, 16 February 2011, 2011 WL 570130 (concerning an award whose recognition and enforcement was alleged to violate the United States sanctions against Iran). See also Linda Silberman, *The New York Convention After Fifty Years: Some Reflections on the Role* of *National Law*, 2009-2010 GA. J. INT'L & COMP. L. 25, 35.

[1054] See, e.g., *BCB Holdings Limited and The Belize Bank Limited v. The Attorney General* of *Belize*, Caribbean Court of Justice, Appellate Jurisdiction, 26 July 2013, [2013] CCJ 5 (AJ); *Traxys Europe S.A. v. Balaji Coke Industry Pvt Ltd.,* Federal Court, Australia, 23 March 2012, [2012] FCA 276; *Uganda Telecom Ltd. v. Hi-Tech Telecom Pty Ltd.*, Federal Court, Australia, 22 February 2011, [2011] FCA 131; *Petrotesting Colombia S.A. & Southeast Investment Corporation v. Ross Energy S.A.,* Supreme Court of Justice, Colombia, 27 July 2011; *Hebei Import & Export Corp. v. Polytek Engineering Co. Ltd.,* Court of Final Appeal, Hong Kong, 9 February 1999, [1999] 2 HKC 205; *Renusagar Power Co. Ltd. v. General Electric Company & anor.*, Supreme Court, India, 7 October 1993, 1994 AIR 860; *Brostrom Tankers AB v. Factorias Vulcano S.A.*, High Court, Dublin, Ireland, 19 May 2004, XXX Y.B. COM. ARB. 591 (2005).

[1055] *Traxys Europe S.A. v. Balaji Coke Industry Pvt Ltd.*, Federal Court, Australia, 23 March 2012, [2012] FCA 276.

[1056] *Hebei Import & Export Corp. v. Polytek Engineering Co. Ltd.*, Court of Final Appeal, Hong Kong, 9 February 1999, [1999] 2 HKC 205. For a similar definition, see *Karaha Bodas Company LLC v. Perusahaan Pertambangan Minyak Dan Gas Bumi Negara and P.T. PLN (Persero),* Alberta Court of Queen's Bench, Canada, 9 December 2004, 2004 ABQB 918. For an insistence on the "essential" nature of the legal principles that public policy seeks to protect, see *Soc. Des Ciments d'Abijan v. Soc. Burkinabè des Ciments et Matériaux*, Court of First Instance, Ouagadougou, Burkina Faso, 13 June 2001.

judgment regarding the definition of public policy, albeit in the context of an action to set aside, the Swiss Federal Tribunal held that an award contravenes public policy "if it disregards essential and widely recognized values which, according to the conceptions prevailing in Switzerland, should form the basis of any legal order".[1057] In more recent decisions, the Swiss Federal Tribunal has defined an award which is contrary to public policy as an award which violates the Swiss concepts of justice in an "intolerable manner".[1058]

8. The French courts have taken a similar approach. For example, the Court of Appeal of Paris defined international public policy as "the body of rules and values whose violation the French legal order cannot tolerate even in situations of international character".[1059]

9. The German courts have considered that an award contravenes public policy when it violates a norm which affects the basis of German public and economic life or irreconcilably contradicts the German perception of justice.[1060] The Supreme Court of Cyprus also interpreted public policy exception under the Convention to mean the fundamental principles which a society recognizes, at a given time, as governing transactions as well as other manifestations of the life of its members, and on which the legal order to which the enforcement court belongs is based.[1061]

10. There have been occasions where courts considered that public policy is not a concept that lends itself to a precise definition. The Court of Appeal of England and Wales held that the public policy exception under the

---

1057 *X S.p.A. v. Y S.r.l.*, Federal Tribunal, Switzerland, 8 March 2006, Arrêts du Tribunal Fédéral (2006) 132 III 389; Paolo Michele Patocchi, *The 1958 New York Convention: The Swiss Practice*, 1996 ASA BULL. 145, 188-96. For a similar definition, see *Kersa Holding Co. Luxembourg v. Infancourtage Famajuk Investment & Isny*, Superior Court of Justice, Luxembourg, 24 November 1993, XXI Y.B. COM. ARB. 617 (1996).

1058 See, e.g., Federal Tribunal, Switzerland, 10 October 2011, Decision 5A_427/2011; Federal Tribunal, Switzerland, 28 July 2010, Decision 4A_233/2010. For a similar definition, see Supreme Court, Austria, Case 3Ob221/04b, 26 January 2005, XXX Y.B. COM. ARB. 421 (2005): it is for the Austrian courts to decide "whether the arbitral award is irreconcilable with the fundamental principles of the Austrian legal system because it is based on a foreign legal principle which is totally irreconcilable with the domestic legal system".

1059 *Agence pour la sécurité de la navigation aérienne en Afrique et à Madagascar v. M. N'DOYE Issakha*, Court of Appeal of Paris, France, 16 October 1997.

1060 See, e.g., Oberlandesgericht [OLG] München, Germany, 34 Sch 019/05, 28 November 2005; Oberlandesgericht [OLG] Düsseldorf, Germany, VI Sch (Kart) 1/02, 21 July 2004; Hanseatisches Oberlandesgericht [OLG] Bremen, Germany, (2) Sch 04/99, 30 September 1999; Bundesgerichtshof [BGH] Germany, III ZR 269/88, 18 January 1990.

1061 *The Attorney General* of *the Republic* of *Kenya v. Bank für Arbeit und Wirtschaft AG*, Supreme Court, Cyprus, 28 April 1999, XXV Y.B. COM. ARB. 641 (2000). See also for a similar definition, Court of Cassation, Greece, Case No. 1665/2009, 30 June 2009, XXXVI Y.B. COM. ARB. 284 (2011); *Misr Insurance Co. v. Alexandria Shipping Agencies Co.*, Court of Cassation, Egypt, 23 December 1991; *BCB Holdings Limited and The Belize Bank Limited v. The Attorney General* of *Belize*, Caribbean Court of Justice, Appellate Jurisdiction, 26 July 2013, [2013] CCJ 5(AJ).

New York Convention encompasses cases where "the enforcement of the award would be clearly injurious to the public good or, possibly, enforcement would be wholly offensive to the ordinary reasonable and fully informed member of the public on whose behalf the powers of the state are exercised".[1062] At the same time, the Court of Appeal acknowledged that "[c]onsiderations of public policy can never be exhaustively defined, but they should be approached with extreme caution".[1063]

11. Some jurisdictions have emphasized the relationship between public policy and national interest or national sovereignty. For example, when reviewing the compatibility of awards with public policy under the New York Convention, the Brazilian Superior Court of Justice has indicated that "the issue [before it] does not have a public policy character and that it does not relate to the concept of national sovereignty".[1064] Similarly, the Indian courts have held that an award is contrary to public policy if its enforcement would be contrary to "the interests of India".[1065]

12. The Russian courts have taken the following view. The Highest Arbitrazh Court of the Russian Federation has relied on the concept of public policy to deny recognition and enforcement of awards that produce results contrary to the "universally recognized moral and ethical rules or threaten the citizens' life and health or the security of the State".[1066]

b. International—transnational public policy

13. It is widely accepted that public policy within the meaning of article V (2)*(b)* of the New York Convention refers to the public policy of the forum

---

[1062] *Deutsche Schachtbau-und Tiefbohrgesellschaft m.b.H. v. Shell International Petroleum Co. Ltd.*, Court of Appeal, England and Wales, 24 March 1987, [1990] 1 A.C. 295.

[1063] *Id.*

[1064] See *Grain Partners S.p.A. v. Cooperativa dos Produtores Trabalhadores Rurais de Sorriso Ltda.*, Superior Court of Justice, Brazil, 18 October 2006.

[1065] See *Renusagar Power Co. Ltd. v. General Electric Company & anor.*, Supreme Court, India, 7 October 1993, 1994 AIR 860; *Penn Racquet Sports v. Mayor International Ltd.*, High Court of Delhi, India, 11 January 2011; *Shri Lal Mahal Ltd. v. Progetto Grano S.p.A.*, Supreme Court, India, 3 July 2013. See also for a national-interest-based analysis of public policy, *Petrotesting Colombia S.A. & Southeast Investment Corp. v. Ross Energy S.A.*, Supreme Court of Justice, Colombia, 27 July 2011. The Indonesian courts are also reported to have taken a similar approach by which national interest is considered part of Indonesian public policy: see Fifi Junita, *Refusing Enforcement* of *Foreign Arbitral Awards Under Article V (2)(b)* of *the New York Convention: The Indonesian Perspective*, 2009 CONTEMP. ASIA ARB. J. 301, 320.

[1066] See *Ansell S.A. v. OOO MedBusinessService-2000*, Highest Arbitrazh Court, Russian Federation, Ruling No. VAS-8786/10, 3 August 2010. See also Patricia Nacimiento, Alexey Barnashov, *Recognition and Enforcement* of *Arbitral Awards in Russian Federation*, 27(3) J. INT'L ARB. 295, 300-01 (2010).

State.[1067] Indeed, article V (2)*(b)* explicitly refers to "the public policy of that country", in reference to the country where recognition and enforcement is sought.[1068] However, in relation to the assessment of the international or domestic character of public policy, most jurisdictions recognize that a mere violation of domestic law is unlikely to amount to a ground to refuse recognition or enforcement on the basis of public policy.[1069]

14. In relation to the question whether there is a universal or transnational character to the concept of public policy, different jurisdictions have taken different approaches. The Supreme Court of India has held that providing a transnational definition of the concept of public policy is unworkable and accepted the principle that public policy in article V (2)*(b)* of the New York Convention should be taken to mean the public policy of the enforcement forum.[1070] In contrast, the Italian courts have stated that public policy refers to "a body of universal principles shared by nations of the same civilization, aiming at the protection of fundamental human rights, often embodied in international declarations or conventions".[1071]

15. The Highest Arbitrazh Court of the Russian Federation has often referred to public policy as constituting "universally recognized moral and

---

[1067] See, e.g., *Traxys Europe S.A. v. Balaji Coke Industry Pvt Ltd.,* Federal Court, Australia, 23 March 2012, [2012] FCA 276; *IPCO (Nigeria) Ltd. v. Nigerian National Petroleum Corp.*, High Court of Justice, England and Wales, 27 April 2005, [2005] EWHC 726; *Gao Haiyan & anor v. Keeneye Holdings Ltd. & anor,* Court of Appeal, Hong Kong, CACV 79/2011, 2 December 2011; *Renusagar Power Co. Ltd. v. General Electric Company & anor.*, Supreme Court, India, 7 October 1993, 1994 AIR 860; *Brostrom Tankers AB v. Factorias Vulcano S.A.*, High Court, Dublin, Ireland, 19 May 2004, XXX Y.B. COM. ARB. 591 (2005); *A v. B & Cia Ltda. & ors*, Supreme Court of Justice, Portugal, 9 November 2003, XXXII Y.B. COM. ARB. 474 (2007); Federal Tribunal, Switzerland, 10 October 2011, Decision 5A_427/2011; *Agility Public Warehousing CO. K.S.C., Professional Contract Administrators, Inc. v. Supreme Foodservice GmbH*, Court of Appeals, Second Circuit, United States of America, 6 September 2012, 11-5201-cv. See also ANTON G. MAURER, THE PUBLIC POLICY EXCEPTION UNDER THE NEW YORK CONVENTION: HISTORY, INTERPRETATION AND APPLICATION 54 (2012).

[1068] See *BCB Holdings Limited and The Belize Bank Limited v. The Attorney General* of *Belize, Caribbean* Court of Justice, Appellate Jurisdiction, 26 July 2013, [2013] CCJ 5 (AJ).

[1069] See, e.g., *Traxys Europe S.A. v. Balaji Coke Industry Pvt Ltd.,* Federal Court, Australia, 23 March 2012, [2012] FCA 276; *Petrotesting Colombia S.A. & Southeast Investment Corporation v. Ross Energy S.A.*, Supreme Court of Justice, Colombia, 27 July 2011; *Agence pour la sécurité de la navigation aérienne en Afrique et à Madagascar v. M. N'DOYE Issakha*, Court of Appeal of Paris, France, 16 October 1997; K.*M. v. UAB A. Sabonio Žalgirio krepšinio centras*, Court of Cassation, Lithuania, 4 November 2011.

[1070] See *Renusagar Power Co. Ltd. v. General Electric Company & anor.*, Supreme Court, India, 7 October 1993, 1994 AIR 860. See also *Hebei Import & Export Corp. v. Polytek Engineering Co. Ltd.*, Court of Final Appeal, Hong Kong, 9 February 1999, [1999] 2 HKC 205, agreeing with the conclusion reached by the Supreme Court of India.

[1071] *Allsop Automatic Inc. v. Tecnoski snc*, Court of Appeal of Milan, Italy, 4 December 1992, XXII Y.B. COM. ARB. 725.

ethical rules"[1072] or "fundamental and universal legal principles of highest imperative nature, of particular social and public significance, and forming the basis of the economic, political and legal system of the State".[1073]

16. In Switzerland, a 2006 decision of the Federal Tribunal concluded that "an award is incompatible with public policy if it disregards essential and widely recognized values which, according to the conceptions prevailing in Switzerland, should form the basis of any legal order".[1074]

c. *Mandatory rules as public policy*

17. As public policy is generally interpreted to mean those fundamental rules of the State where recognition and enforcement of an award is sought from which no derogation can be allowed, the question arises as to whether the forum's mandatory rules should be considered as part of its public policy, and consequently an exception to recognition and enforcement of an award under the New York Convention.[1075]

18. It is not disputed that certain mandatory rules meet the standard of the public policy defence to recognition and enforcement of awards.[1076] However, different views have been expressed as to whether specific sets of mandatory rules do rise to that standard in the context of recognition and enforcement of foreign awards in fields such as of competition law, bankruptcy, employment and consumer protection, interest rates, foreign exchange regulations, export prohibitions and futures contracts.

19. For example, in the field of competition law, the Court of Justice of the European Union (CJEU) held that article 101 of the Treaty on the Functioning of the European Union (TFEU), which renders automatically void certain anti-competitive agreements or decisions, constitutes "a fundamental provision which is essential for the accomplishment of the tasks entrusted to the [Union] and, in particular, for the functioning of the internal market". The CJEU held that for this reason it should be regarded as a matter of public policy within the meaning of article V (2)*(b)* of the New York

---

[1072] *Ansell S.A. v. OOO MedBusinessService-2000*, Highest Arbitrazh Court, Russian Federation, Ruling No. VAS-8786/10, 3 August 2010.

[1073] Presidium of the Highest Arbitrazh Court, Russian Federation, Information Letter No. 156 of 26 February 2013.

[1074] *X S.p.A. v. Y S.r.l.*, Federal Tribunal, Switzerland, 8 March 2006, Arrêts du Tribunal Fédéral (2006) 132 III 389, 395.

[1075] Bernard Hanotiau, Olivier Caprasse, *Public Policy in International Commercial Arbitration*, in ENFORCEMENT OF ARBITRATION AGREEMENTS AND INTERNATIONAL ARBITRAL AWARDS: THE NEW YORK CONVENTION IN PRACTICE 787, 791-94 (E. Gaillard, D. Di Pietro eds., 2008).

[1076] See Luke Villiers, *Breaking in the "Unruly Horse": The Status* of *Mandatory Rules* of *Law as a Public Policy Basis for the Non-Enforcement* of *Arbitral Awards*, 2011 AUSTL. INT'L L.J. 155, 179-80 (2011).

Convention.[1077] It has thus imposed on the courts of the EU Member States the obligation to refuse recognition and enforcement to all awards which conflict with article 101 TFEU.[1078]

20. In proceedings to set aside an award handed down in Switzerland regarding a dispute between two Italian companies, the Federal Tribunal acknowledged the existence of other economic systems based on a planned economy and favoring State intervention in the economy. It concluded though that "no one would consider labeling them immoral or contrary to fundamental legal principles simply because they do not follow the Swiss model.[1079] The Federal Tribunal thus held that "the provisions of competition law do not form part of the essential and widely-recognized values, which, according to the prevailing position in Switzerland, should form the basis of any legal order".[1080]

21. These decisions highlight the fact that Article V (2)*(b)* refers to the public policy of the country where recognition and enforcement is sought. It does not require a New York Convention signatory to uphold the public policy of another State. As Switzerland has not acceded to the European Union, it is not required to consider that Article 101 TFEU forms part of Swiss public policy.

22. The United States Supreme Court held that claims arising out of the Sherman Antitrust Act are arbitrable but that public policy can be used to ensure that the legitimate interest in the antitrust issues had been appropriately addressed, leaving the issue to be decided on an *ad hoc* basis.[1081]

23. In the field of insolvency, the French courts have held that the principle according to which individual actions brought by creditors against the estate of the bankrupt are stayed during bankruptcy to be part of public

---

1077 *Eco Swiss China Time Ltd. v. Benetton International NV*, Court of Justice of the European Union, 1 June 1999, Case C-126/97, [1999] ECR I-3055, paras. 37-39.

1078 See, e.g., *SNF SAS v. Cytec Industries B.V.*, Court of Appeal of Paris, 23 March 2006, XXXII Y.B. COM. ARB. 282 (2008), where the French court accepted that EU competition law forms part of French public policy; Oberlandesgericht [OLG] Düsseldorf, Germany, VI Sch (Kart) 1/02, 21 July 2004, Court of Cassation, Greece, Case No. 1665/2009, 30 June 2009, XXXVI Y.B. COM. ARB. 284 (2011), and *Marketing Displays International Inc. v. VR Van Raalte Reclame B.V.*, Court of Appeal, The Hague, Netherlands, 24 March 2005, XXXI Y.B. COM. ARB. 808 (2006), where the German, Greek and Dutch courts respectively recognized that article 101 TFEU formed part of their public policy.

1079 *X S.p.A. v. Y S.r.l.*, Federal Tribunal, Switzerland, 8 March 2006, Arrêts du Tribunal Fédéral (2006) 132 III389.

1080 *Id.*

1081 *Mitsubishi Motors Corp v. Soler Chrysler-Plymouth*, Supreme Court, United States of America, 2 July 1985, 473 United States 614.

policy,[1082] while the German courts have not considered the arbitration of insolvency disputes to be contrary to public policy.[1083]

24. In the context of interest rates, while acknowledging that a mere incompatibility of a foreign award with domestic mandatory rules does not amount to a breach of public policy, several courts have refused to recognize and enforce awards, or the part of the award which was considered to be contrary to public policy,[1084] where they considered that the awarded interest was unreasonably high.[1085]

25. Other examples of domestic mandatory rules that have been considered to be a public policy matter under which recognition and enforcement can be refused, include foreign exchange regulations, with regard to which the German Federal Court of Justice held that an award conflicting with German foreign exchange regulations is contrary to public policy;[1086] export prohibitions, in relation to which the Indian courts have refused recognition of awards which conflict with an Indian ban on the export of hot rolled steel sheet coils due to a shortage in the domestic market;[1087] and offshore futures transactions, in relation to which the Chinese courts have refused recognition to an award on the basis that it conflicted with the Chinese mandatory rules forbidding futures contracts.[1088]

26. The criteria forming the basis of the determination as to whether mandatory national law constitutes public policy are often not specified by national courts. Commentators note that it is consistent with the letter and spirit of the New York Convention that, as a matter of principle, the mandatory rules of the enforcement forum should be considered as part of its

---

[1082] *Mandataires judiciaires Associés, in the person* of *Mrs. X as liquidators* of *Jean Lion et Cie S.A. v. International Company for Commercial Exchanges*, Court of Cassation, France, 6 May 2009, XXXV Y.B. COM. ARB. 353 (2010).

[1083] Oberlandesgericht [OLG] Karlsruhe, Germany, 9 Sch 02/09, 4 January 2012.

[1084] See J. J. *Agro Industries (P) Ltd. v. Texuna International Ltd.*, High Court, Hong Kong, 12 August 1992.

[1085] See Supreme Court, Austria, Case 3Ob221/04b, 26 January 2005, XXX Y.B. COM. ARB. 421 (2005). See to the same effect, *Laminoires-Trefileries-Cablerie de Lens S.A. v. Southwire Co. and Southwire International Corp.,* District Court, Northern District of Georgia, United States, 484 F. Supp. 1063 (1980); *Misr Foreign Trade Co. v. R.D. Harboties (Mercantile),* Court of Cassation, Egypt, 22 January 2008; *Belaja Rus v. Westintorg Corp.*, Court of Cassation, Lithuania, 10 November 2008.

[1086] See Bundesgerichtshof [BGH], Germany, II ZR 124/86, 15 June 1987. See also Susan Choi, *Judicial Enforcement* of *Arbitration Awards Under the ICSID and New York Conventions,* 1196 N.Y.U. J. INT'L L. & Pol. 175, 202-04 (1995).

[1087] See *COSID Inc. v. Steel Authority* of *India Ltd.,* High Court of Delhi, India, 12 July 1985, XI Y.B. COM. ARB. 502 (1986).

[1088] See *ED & F Man (Hong Kong) Co., Ltd. v. China National Sugar & Wines Group Corp.,* Supreme People's Court, China, 1 July 2003, [2003] Min Si Ta Zi No. 3. See also Lanfang Fei, *Public Policy as a Bar to Enforcement* of *International Arbitral Awards: A Review* of *the Chinese Approach,* 26(2) ARB. INT'L 301, 305-06 (2010).

public policy when they reflect that forum's fundamental concepts of morality and justice, from which no derogation can be allowed.[1089]

d. *Public policy and constitutional principles*

27. Constitutional principles may also interact with the public policy exception to the recognition and enforcement of foreign arbitral awards under the New York Convention.[1090]

B. Application

28. Public policy allows the courts of the Contracting Party where recognition and enforcement is sought to consider the merits of an award so as to satisfy themselves that there is nothing in the award that would infringe the fundamental values of that State. The enforcement court's assessment also extends to procedural matters, such that it might refuse to recognize or enforce an award where the procedure followed by the arbitral tribunal contradicts the understanding of basic procedural fairness in the State where recognition and enforcement is sought.[1091]

29. The Swiss Federal Tribunal distinguishes between substantive and procedural public policy (*ordre public matériel et ordre public procédural*).[1092] In its words: "[t]here is a difference between substantive and procedural public policy [...] procedural public policy guarantees parties the right to an independent judgment on their submissions and the facts submitted to the arbitral tribunal, in accordance with the applicable procedural law; substantive public policy is breached when fundamental and generally recognized principles are breached, leading to an untenable contradiction with the notion of justice, so that the decision appears incompatible with the values recognized in a state governed by the rule of law".[1093]

[1089] See FOUCHARD GAILLARD GOLDMAN ON INTERNATIONAL COMMERCIAL ARBITRATION 996 (E. Gaillard, J. Savage eds., 1996).

[1090] *BCB Holdings Limited and The Belize Bank Limited v. The Attorney General* of *Belize*, Caribbean Court of Justice, Appellate Jurisdiction, 26 July 2013, [2013] CCJ 5 (AJ).

[1091] See, e.g., *X S.p.A. v. Y S.r.l.,* Federal Tribunal, Switzerland, 8 March 2006, Arrêts du Tribunal Fédéral (2006) 132 III 389, 392.

[1092] For a similar distinction between substantive and procedural public policy (*ordre public quant à la procédure et ordre public quant au fond*), see *Soc. Excelsior Film TV v. Soc. UGC-PH*, Court of Cassation, France, 24 March 1998, 95-17.285.

[1093] *X S.p.A. v. Y S.r.l.*, Federal Tribunal, Switzerland, 8 March 2006, Arrêts du Tribunal Fédéral (2006) 132 III 389, 392.

a. Substantive public policy

30. Even though the defence of public policy allows courts to consider the merits of the award, the scope of such review is not unlimited. Courts have recognized that public policy does not furnish an opportunity to the party opposing recognition and enforcement to reargue the merits of the case or to allege that the case was wrongly decided.[1094]

31. In addition, most courts ascribe a narrow interpretation to public policy. It is thus not surprising that applications to refuse recognition and enforcement of a foreign arbitral award made under article V (2)*(b)* of the New York Convention have rarely been successful.[1095]

32. Such rare instances include cases where:

- The award conflicted with a previous judgment of the courts of the forum;[1096]

[1094] See, *e.g.*, *BCB Holdings Limited and The Belize Bank Limited v. The Attorney General* of *Belize*, Caribbean Court of Justice, Appellate Jurisdiction, 26 July 2013, [2013] CCJ 5 (AJ); *Karaha Bodas Company, L.L.C. v. Perusahaan Pertambangan Minyak Dan Gas Bumi Negara and P.T. PLN (Persero),* Alberta Court of Queen's Bench, Canada, 24 October 2007, 2007 ABQB 616; *Atecs Mannesmann GmbH v. Rodrimar S/A Transportes Equipamentos Industriais e Armazéns Gerais*, Superior Court of Justice, Brazil, 19 August 2009; *GRD Minproc Limited v. Shanghai Feilun Industrial Co.*, Supreme People's Court, China, 13 March 2009, [2008] Min Si Ta Zi No. 48; *Société I.A.I.G.C.- Inter-Arab Investment Guarantee Corporation v. Société B.A.I.I.- Banque arabe et internationale d'investissement S.A.,* Court of Appeal of Paris, France, 23 October 1997; Oberlandesgericht [OLG] München, Germany, 34 Sch 26/08, 22 June 2009, XXXV Y.B. COM. ARB. 371 (2010); Oberlandesgericht [OLG] Karlsruhe, Germany, 9 Sch 02/05, 27 March 2006; *Qinhuangdao Tongda Enterprise Development Company, et al. v. Million Basic Co. Ltd.*, High Court, Supreme Court of Hong Kong, 5 January 1993, XIX Y.B. COM. ARB. 675 (1994); *C.G. Impianti S.p.A. v. B.M.A.A.B. & Sons International Contracting Co. WLL,* Court of Appeal of Milan, Italy, 29 April 2009, XXXI Y.B. COM. ARB. 802 (2010); *Inter Maritime Management S.A. v. Russin & Vecchi*, Federal Tribunal, Switzerland, 9 January 1995, XXII Y.B. COM. ARB. 789 (1997); *Odfjell SE v. OAO PO Sevmash*, Highest Arbitrazh Court, Russian Federation, Ruling No. VAS-4369/11, 26 May 2011; Presidium of the Highest Arbitrazh Court, Russian Federation, Information Letter No. 156 of 26 February 2013; Supreme Court, Austria, Case 3Ob221/04b, 26 January 2005, XXX Y.B. COM. ARB. 421 (2005). See also William W. Park, *Private Adjudicators and the Public Interest: the Expanding Scope* of *International Arbitration*, 1986 BROOK. J. INT'L L. 629, 646-47.

[1095] See Pieter Sanders, *A Twenty Years' Review* of *the Convention on the Recognition and Enforcement* of *Foreign Arbitral Awards*, 1979 INT'L LAW 269, 270; Susan Choi, *Judicial Enforcement* of *Arbitration Awards Under the ICSID and New York Conventions*, 28 N.Y.U. J. INT'L & POL. 175, 206-07 (1995-1996).

[1096] See *Hemofarm DD, MAG International Trade Holding DD, Suram Media Ltd. v. Jinan Yongning Pharmaceutical Co. Ltd.*, Supreme People's Court, China, 2 June 2008, [2008] Min Si Ta Zi No. 11; *Ciments Français v. OAO Holding Company Siberian Cement, Istanbul Çimento Yatırımları*, Highest Arbitrazh Court, Russian Federation, No. VAS-17458/11, 27 August 2012.

- The award ordered the party opposing recognition and enforcement to pay interest at an amount considered excessive according to the standards of the *lex fori*;[1097]

- The parties to the arbitration settled secretly from the arbitral tribunal and the claimant in the arbitration failed to stop the arbitration so as to acquire an award condemning the respondent to pay twice the same debt;[1098]

- The award contravened mandatory rules of the forum in the area of competition law, consumer protection, foreign exchange regulation or bans on exports;[1099]

- The award was contrary to core constitutional values such as the separation of powers and sovereignty of Parliament;[1100]

- The award was contrary to the national interest of the forum State.[1101]

33. By contrast, without purporting to set out an exhaustive list of instances where applications made under article V (2)*(b)* of the New York Convention have been unsuccessful, courts have dismissed such applications on the merits where:

- It was alleged that the law applicable to the merits of the dispute was incorrectly applied by the arbitral tribunal;[1102]

1097 See Supreme Court, Austria, Case 3Ob221/04b, 26 January 2005, XXX Y.B. COM. ARB. 421 (2005); *Ahmed Mostapha Shawky v. Andersen Worldwide & Wahid El Din Abdel Ghaffar Megahed & Emad Hafez Raghed & Nabil Istanboly Akram Instanboly,* Court of Appeal of Cairo, Egypt, 23 May 2001; *Harbottle Co. Ltd. v. Egypt for Foreign Trade Co.*, Court of Cassation, Egypt, 21 May 1990, 815/52; *Belaja Rus v. Westintorg Corp.*, Court of Cassation, Lithuania, 10 November 2008, 3K-3-562/2008.

1098 See Bayerisches Oberstes Landgericht [BayObLG], Germany, 4 Z Sch 17/03, 20 November 2003.

1099 See Court of Cassation, Greece, Case No. 1665/2009, 30 June 2009, XXXVI Y.B. COM. ARB. 284 (2011); *SNF SAS v. Cytec Industries B.V.*, Court of Appeal of Paris, 23 March 2006, XXXII Y.B. COM. ARB. 282 (2008); *Elisa María Mostaza Claro v. Centro Móvil Milenium SL*, Court of Justice of the European Union, 26 October 2006, Case C-168/05, [2006] ECR I-10421; *Marketing Displays International Inc. v. VR Van Raalte Reclame B.V.*, Court of Appeal of The Hague, Netherlands, 24 March 2005, XXXI Y.B. COM. ARB. 808 (2006); Oberlandesgericht [OLG] Düsseldorf Germany, VI Sch (Kart) 1/02, 21 July 2004; *Eco Swiss China Time Ltd. v. Benetton International NV,* Court of Justice of the European Union, 1 June 1999, Case C-126/97, [1999] ECR I-3055; Bundesgerichtshof [BGH], Germany, II ZR 124/86, 15 June 1987; *COSID Inc. v. Steel Authority* of *India Ltd.*, High Court of Delhi, India, 12 July 1985, XI Y.B. COM. ARB. 502 (1986).

1100 See *BCB Holdings Limited and The Belize Bank Limited v. The Attorney General* of *Belize*, Caribbean Court of Justice, Appellate Jurisdiction, 26 July 2013, [2013] CCJ 5 (AJ).

1101 See *United World v. Krasny Yakor,* Federal Arbitrazh Court of the Volgo-Vyatsky Region, Russian Federation, Case No. A43-10716/02-27-10, 17 February 2003. See the chapter of the Guide on article V (2)(b).

- It was alleged that the recognition and enforcement of the award would violate the *exceptio non adimpleti contractus*;[1103]
- The benefit of domestic mandatory rules was sought by a sophisticated business person who should have been aware of the risks he/she had undertaken;[1104]
- The award debtor would have to obtain regulatory approval in order to perform an act necessary to comply with the award;[1105]
- The award included a substantial sum which appeared to represent an acceleration of future damages;[1106]
- It was alleged that the arbitration agreement was null and void because the parties submitted a non-foreign-related dispute to a foreign arbitration tribunal;[1107]
- The transaction in question was an offshore future transaction which violated the enforcement forum's mandatory rules;[1108]
- Compliance with the award was alleged to offend the law of the place of incorporation of the respondent company;[1109]
- The award concerned matters that were normally subject to the exclusive jurisdiction of the employment tribunals;[1110]
- The award granted compensation for legal costs;[1111]

1102 See Presidium of the Highest Arbitrazh Court, Russian Federation, Information Letter No. 156 of 26 February 2013; *Sei Societa Esplosivi S.p.A. v. L-3 Fuzing and Ordnance Systems, Inc.*, District Court, District of Delaware, United States of America, 17 February 2012, 11-149-RGA; *Penn Racquet Sports v. Mayor International Ltd.*, High Court of Delhi, India, 11 January 2011; *Odfjell SE v. OAO PO Sevmash*, Highest Arbitrazh Court, Russian Federation, 26 May 2011, Ruling No. VAS-4369/11; *Atecs Mannesmann GmbH v. Rodrimar S/A Transportes Equipamentos Industriais e Armazéns Gerais,* Superior Court of Justice, Brazil, 19 August 2009.

1103 See *Grain Partners S.p.A. v. Cooperativa dos Produtores Trabalhadores Rurais de Sorriso Ltda.*, Superior Court of Justice, Brazil, 18 October 2006.

1104 See *Bad Ass Coffee Company* of *Hawaii Inc. v. Bad Ass Enterprises Inc.*, Alberta Court of Queen's Bench, Canada, 2 July 2008, 2008 ABQB 404.

1105 See *Adamas Management & Services Inc. v. Aurado Energy Inc.*, New Brunswick Court of Queen's Bench, Canada, 28 July 2004, 2004 NBQB 342.

1106 See *Schreter v. Gasmac*, Ontario Court (General Division), Canada, 13 February 1992, 89 D.L.R. (4th) 365.

1107 See *Lifu Candy (Shanghai) Corporation v. Shanghai Lianfu Foodstuff Corporation*, Shanghai No. 2 Intermediate People's Court, China, 24 June 2009, [2008] Hu Er Zhong Min Wu (Shang) Chu Zi No. 19.

1108 See *ED & F Man (Hong Kong) Co., Ltd. v. China National Sugar & Wines Group Corp.,* Supreme People's Court, China, 1 July 2003, [2003] Min Si Ta Zi No. 3.

1109 See *Soinco SACI & anor. v. Novokuznetsk Aluminium Plant & Ors.*, Court of Appeal, England and Wales, 16 December 1997, [1998] CLC 730.

1110 See *Agence pour la sécurité de la navigation aérienne en Afrique et à Madagascar v. M. N'DOYE Issakha*, Court of Appeal of Paris, France, 16 October 1997.

1111 See Oberlandesgericht [OLG] München, Germany, 34 Sch 14/09, 1 September 2009.

- It was alleged that the arbitral tribunal awarded damages in an arbitrary fashion;[1112]
- It was alleged that the award debtor had no legal remedies against the decision of the sole arbitrator;[1113]
- It was alleged that the contractual penalty imposed by the arbitral tribunal rising to 40 per cent of the value of the main obligation under the contract was disproportionately high;[1114]
- It was alleged that the arbitral tribunal should have applied the Convention on the International Sale of Goods to the contract rather than the governing law chosen by the parties;[1115]
- Lump sum damages were prohibited under the law of the country where recognition and enforcement was sought but were allowed by the law applied to the dispute by the arbitral tribunal;[1116]
- The award granted compound interest which was allowed under the law of the seat of the arbitration;[1117]
- It was alleged that the award was contrary to EU competition law;[1118]
- The arbitrator had failed to expressly order one of the parties to pay certain taxes due in the United States;[1119]
- The party opposing enforcement failed to establish that the contractually stipulated penalties imposed by the tribunal was not reasonably related to the actual damages resulting from the breach;[1120]

[1112] See Oberlandesgericht [OLG] Frankfurt, Germany, 26 Sch 13/08, 16 October 2008.

[1113] See Oberlandesgericht [OLG] Frankfurt, Germany, 26 Sch 1/07, 18 October 2007.

[1114] See Oberlandesgericht [OLG] Celle, Germany, 8 Sch 06/05, 6 October 2005.

[1115] See Oberlandesgericht [OLG] Cologne, Germany, 9 Sch 13/99, 15 February 2000.

[1116] See Oberlandesgericht [OLG] Dresden, Germany, 11 Sch 06/98, 13 January 1999.

[1117] See Hanseatisches Oberlandesgericht [OLG], Germany, 6 U 71/88, 26 January 1989. For the view that the domestic prohibition of compound interest does not amount to public policy see *Inter Maritime Management S.A. v. Vecchi*, Federal Tribunal, Switzerland, 9 January 1995, XXII Y.B. COM. ARB. 789 (1997).

[1118] See *X S.p.A. v. Y S.r.l.*, Federal Tribunal, Switzerland, 8 March 2006, Arrêts du Tribunal Fédéral (2006) 132 III 389. For the opposite view, see *SNF SAS v. Cytec Industries B.V.*, Court of Appeal of Paris, 23 March 2006, XXXII Y.B. COM. ARB. 282 (2008); Oberlandesgericht [OLG] Düsseldorf, Germany, VI Sch (Kart) 1/02, 21 July 2004; Court of Cassation, Greece, Case No. 1665/2009, 30 June 2009, XXXVI Y.B. COM. ARB. 284 (2011); *Marketing Displays International Inc. v. VR Van Raalte Reclame B.V.*, Court of Appeal of The Hague, Netherlands, 24 March 2005, XXXI Y.B. COM. ARB. 808 (2006).

[1119] See *Subway International B.V. v. Panayota Bletas and John Bletas*, District Court, District of Connecticut, United States of America, 13 March 2012, 3:10-cv-01715 (JCH).

[1120] See *Chelsea Football Club Ltd. v. Adrian Mutu*, District Court, Southern District of Florida, United States of America, 13 February 2012, 1:10-cv-24028-FAM. See also Presidium of the Highest Arbitrazh Court, Russian Federation, Information Letter No. 156 of 26 February

- Compliance with the award resulting in the making of certain payments to the Iranian Government breached United States sanctions;[1121]
- The party opposing enforcement alleged that an order of specific performance breached public policy because an award of monetary damages would have been adequate and appropriate;[1122]
- The party opposing enforcement alleged that the award improperly imported and endorsed the conclusions of foreign prosecuting authorities;[1123]
- The award conflicted with judgments handed down by the courts of a foreign country;[1124]
- The party opposing enforcement alleged that its actions that resulted in the breach of the contract were justified as compliance with a change in its country's foreign policy;[1125]
- The tribunal calculated interest that would not be available under the law of the enforcement forum;[1126]
- The person seeking the enforcement was not a party to the arbitration but a successor to that party.[1127]

b. *Procedural public policy*

34. In applying article V (2)*(b)* of the New York Convention, courts review not only the substantive outcome of the award but also the procedure leading to the award.

2013; *Stena RoRo AB v. OAO Baltiysky Zavod*, Presidium of the Highest Arbitrazh Court, Russian Federation, 13 September 2011, Resolution No. 9899/09.

1121 See *The Ministry* of *Defense and Support for the Armed Forces of the Islamic Republic* of *Iran, as Successor in Interest to the Ministry* of *War* of *the Government* of *Iran v. Cubic Defense Systems, Inc*, Court of Appeals, Ninth Circuit, United States of America, 15 December 2011, 665 F.3d 1091. See also *Ameropa A.G. v. Havi Ocean Co. LLC*, District Court, Southern District of New York, United States of America, 16 February 2011, 2011 WL570130.

1122 See *NTT Docomo Inc. v. Ultra D.O.O.*, District Court, Southern District of New York, United States of America, 12 October 2010, 1:10-cv-03823-RMB -JCF.

1123 See *AO Techsnabexport v. Globe Nuclear Services and Supply Ltd.*, District Court, District of Maryland, United States of America 28 August 2009, AW-08-1521.

1124 See *Telenor Mobile Communications AS v. Storm LLC*, District Court, Southern District of New York, United States of America, 2 November 2007, 524 F. Supp. 2d 332.

1125 See *Parsons & Whittemore Overseas v. Société Générale de L'Industrie du Papier (RAKTA)*, Court of Appeals, Second Circuit, United States of America, 508 F.2d 969 (1974).

1126 See *Lugana Handelsgesellschaft mbH v. OAO Ryazan Metal Ceramics Instrumentation Plant*, Presidium of the Highest Arbitrazh Court, Russian Federation, 2 February 2010, Resolution No. 13211/09.

1127 See *Joy-Lud Distributors International Inc. v. OAO Moscow Refinery*, Presidium of the Highest Arbitrazh Court, Russian Federation, 22 January 2008, Ruling No. 5243/06.

35. Where the procedure followed in the arbitration suffered from serious irregularities, recognition and enforcement may be refused under article V (2)*(b)*. It is thus common for courts to review awards brought before them for recognition and enforcement for fraud, bribery or some other significant due process irregularity.[1128]

36. As with substantive public policy, applications to refuse recognition and enforcement on the basis of procedural public policy have rarely been successful. Courts have found a violation of public policy in cases where they considered that the right to be heard had been breached. For example, the Canadian courts have refused recognition and enforcement of an award where the tribunal had granted a remedy not requested by the parties on the basis that it violated the principle of *audiatur et altera pars*.[1129]

37. The same conclusion has been reached in a case in which the court found a failure of the arbitral tribunal to give reasons where the agreement of the parties contained stipulations to that effect. In such circumstances, the Canadian courts have refused to grant recognition and enforcement of an award on the basis that "recognition of the award would be contrary to public policy because [the award], contrary to the express wish of the parties, does not contain reasons. [...] What is at odds with fairness, equal treatment of the parties and consequently public policy, is not that an award lacks reasons but that it lacks reasons contrary to what the parties wanted. [...] in a democratic country one cannot imagine that the judiciary renders a decision without being able to verify if that decision is not arbitrary".[1130]

[1128] See, e.g., *Karaha Bodas Company, L.L.C. v. Perusahaan Pertambangan Minyak Dan Gas Bumi Negara and P.T. PLN (Persero)*, Alberta Court of Queen's Bench, Canada, 24 October 2007, 2007 ABQB 616; *Gater Assets Ltd. v. Nak Naftogaz Ukrainiy,* High Court of Justice, England and Wales, 15 February 2008, [2008] EWHC 237, [2008] 1 CLC 141; *Westacre Investments Inc. v. Jugoimport-SPDR Holding Ltd. & others*, Court of Appeal, England and Wales, 12 May 2000, [2000] 1 QB 288; *Karaha Bodas Co. LLC v. Perusahaan Pertambangan Minyak Dan Gas Bumi Negara (Petarmina),* Court of Appeal, Hong Kong, 9 October 2007; *Karaha Bodas Co. LLC v. Perusahaan Pertambangan Minyak Dan Gas Bumi Negara,* Court of Appeals, Fifth Circuit, United States of America, 23 March 2004, 364 F.3d 274;Oberlandesgericht [OLG] Düsseldorf, Germany, I-4 Sch 10/09, 15 December 2009; Oberlandesgericht [OLG] Frankfurt, Germany, 26 SchH 03/09, 27 August 2009; Oberlandesgericht [OLG] München, Germany, 34 Sch 019/05, 28 November 2005; *Drummond Ltd. v. Ferrovias en Liquidación, Ferrocariles Nacionales de Colombia S.A.*, Supreme Court of Justice, Colombia, 19 December 2011; *SAS C22 v. Soc. John K. King & Sons Ltd. Frontier Agriculture Ltd.*, Court of Appeal of Paris, France, 10 April 2008; *Cie de Saint-Gobain-Pont-à-Mousson v. The Fertilizer Corporation* of *India Ltd.*, Court of Appeal of Paris, 10 May 1971. See also Stephen M. Schwebel, Susan G. Lahne, *Public Policy and Arbitral Procedure*, in COMPARATIVE ARBITRATION PRACTICE AND PUBLIC POLICY IN ARBITRATION, ICCA CONGRESS SERIES No. 3, 205 (P. Sanders ed.,1987).

[1129] See *Louis Dreyfus S.A.S. v. Holding Tusculum B.V.*, Superior Court of Quebec, Canada, 12 December 2008, 2008 QCCS 5903.

[1130] *Smart Systems Technologies Inc. v. Domotique Secant Inc.*, Court of Appeal of Quebec, Canada, 11 March 2008, XXXIII Y.B. COM. ARB. 464 (2008). For circumstances

38. Courts have also found a breach of procedural public policy where arbitrators have acted in a manner that breaches the principles of independence and impartiality. For example, in a dispute involving two parallel arbitrations between the same parties, one of the arbitrators, who was sitting in both panels, provided false information to one tribunal about the other arbitration which had an impact on that tribunal's decision regarding its jurisdiction.[1131] In that case, the French Court of Cassation found that by acting in this manner, the arbitrator created an inequality between the parties which contravened the most basic requirements of due process.

39. In a Swiss case, the fact that counsel for one of the parties in contractual negotiations inserted a provision in the contract appointing himself as the sole arbitrator should a dispute arise between the parties, was held to violate public policy.[1132] The Swiss court found that "the behavior of arbitrator Dr. E. is so extreme, that it is hard to imagine that any free and democratic legal system could equate the award rendered by such an arbitrator to a sovereign State act and enforce it. [...] it is totally unacceptable that the person who draws up a contract must also, as an arbitrator, give a binding interpretation of it, particularly when he has been for years one of the parties' lawyer".[1133]

40. Another significant example of breach of procedural public policy, albeit in the context of an action to set aside, is that of the case where two parties to a tripartite contact and dispute were required to appoint one arbitrator. The French Court of Cassation considered that the principle of equality of the parties in the appointment of arbitrators was part of the French understanding of international public policy and could be waived only after a dispute had arisen. The court concluded that an award which was rendered by a three-member tribunal, one of whom was appointed, under protest and with all reservations, jointly by the two defendants, should be set aside.[1134]

41. An unusual example of a breach of procedural public policy is that of a case where the party opposing enforcement in Germany was a small

---

where the failure of the arbitrators to adhere to the agreement of the parties was considered to amount to a breach of public policy see also *Société Dubois & Vanderwalle S.A.R.L. v. Société Boots Frites BV,* Court of Appeal of Paris, France, 22 September 1995.

[1131] See *Soc. Excelsior Film TV v. Soc. UGC-PH,* Court of Cassation, France, 24 March 1998.

[1132] See District Court of Affoltern am Albis, Switzerland, 26 May 1994, XXIII Y.B. COM. ARB. 754, paras. 18-24 (1998).

[1133] *Id.*, paras. 21-22

[1134] See *Siemens A.G. v. BKMI Industrienlagen GmbH,* Court of Cassation, France, 7 January 1992, XVIII Y.B. COM. ARB. 140 (1993). See also Martin Platte, *Multi-Party Arbitration: Legal Issues Arising out* of *Joinder and Consolidation,* in ENFORCEMENT OF ARBITRATION AGREEMENTS AND INTERNATIONAL ARBITRAL AWARDS: THE NEW YORK CONVENTION IN PRACTICE 481, 491, 492-94 (E. Gaillard, D. Di Pietro eds., 2008).

franchisee that sold sandwiches and salads in a German provincial town but had been ordered by the arbitral tribunal to attend a hearing in New York. The German courts held that the location of such hearing placed an excessive burden on that party given its small size and refused recognition and enforcement on grounds of public policy.[1135]

c. *Relationship with article V (1)*

42. The public policy defence can be based on facts which may also give rise to a defence under article V (1) of the New York Convention. This is particularly so in cases in which the arbitration agreement is invalid[1136] or where there has been a violation of due process[1137] amounting to a breach of public policy.

43. For example, the Brazilian courts found that the fact that an arbitral tribunal had established its jurisdiction despite the failure of a party to sign the contract containing the arbitration agreement amounted to lack of consent to arbitrate and thus constituted a breach of public policy.[1138] Similarly, the German courts have refused recognition and enforcement on public policy grounds due to the arbitral tribunal's failure to examine whether the arbitration agreement was valid.[1139]

44. Some courts have taken the view that a proper characterization of the matter as one falling either under article V (1) or under article V (2)*(b)* is necessary. For example, the Highest Arbitrazh Court of the Russian Federation endorsed the practice of Russian lower courts according to which improper notice of the appointment of an arbitrator or of the arbitration proceedings as well as the inability of a party to present its case constitute an independent defence to recognition and enforcement of a foreign award pursuant to article V (1)*(b)* and that, in light of its exceptional nature, there is no need to apply the public policy defence contained in article V (2)*(b)* of the New York Convention.[1140]

1135 See Oberlandesgericht [OLG] Dresden, Germany, 11 Sch 08/07, 7 December 2007.

1136 See the chapter of the Guide on article V (2)(b), para. 36.

1137 See the chapter of the Guide on article V (2)(b), paras. 36, 38-39

1138 See, e.g., *Kanematsu USA Inc. v. Advanced Telecommunications Systems do Brasil Ltda.*, Superior Court of Justice, Brazil, 18 April 2012; *Indutech S.p.A. v. Algocentro Armazéns Gerais Ltda.*, Superior Court of Justice, Brazil, 17 December 2008; *Plexus Cotton Ltd. v. Santana Têxtil S/A*, Superior Court of Justice, Brazil, 15 February 2006.

1139 See Landgericht [LG] München, Germany, 20 June 1978, V Y.B. COM. ARB. 260 (1980).

1140 See Presidium of the Highest Arbitrazh Court, Russian Federation, Information Letter No. 156 of 26 February 2013, 10. See also ANTON G. MAURER, THE PUBLIC POLICY EXCEPTION UNDER THE NEW YORK CONVENTION: HISTORY, INTERPRETATION AND APPLICATION 67-70 (2012).

45. Other courts have simply acknowledged this duplication of grounds on which the same matter could be raised. For example, in the words of the Court of Final Appeal of Hong Kong, "[i]t has become fashionable to raise specific grounds in [...] Article V.1*(b)* [...], which are directed to procedural irregularities, as public policy grounds (Article V.2*(b)*). There is no reason why this course cannot be followed".[1141] Several courts have followed this approach. They simply address under article V (2) the allegations of procedural irregularities, without taking issue with the fact that they could also be properly brought under one of the grounds of article V (1).[1142]

46. Indeed, nothing in article V prevents a party from putting forward an argument under article V (2)*(b)* that could also properly be brought under one of the grounds of article V (1). To the contrary, there is some support in the *travaux préparatoires* for the proposition that parties wishing to argue that their procedural rights had been violated should be free do so on the basis of a violation of public policy.[1143] It should be noted that courts have generally taken a restrictive interpretation of public policy and implemented a high standard of proof in that respect, by comparison to the standard of proof under article V (1). One notable difference between the two paragraphs of article V is that article V (2)*(b)* allows a complaint to be examined by the court *ex officio*[1144] whereas a complaint under article V (1) can only be brought by the party seeking to oppose recognition and enforcement of an award.

[1141] See *Hebei Import & Export Corp. v. Polytek Engineering Co. Ltd.*, Court of Final Appeal, Hong Kong, 9 February 1999, [1999] 2 HKC 205.

[1142] See, *Inter-Arab Investment Guarantee Corporation v. Banque Arabe et Internationale d'Investissement,* Court of Appeal of Brussels, Belgium, 24 January 1997, XXII Y.B. COM. ARB. 643 (1997); Oberlandesgericht [OLG] Frankfurt, Germany, 26 Sch 03/09, 27 August 2009, XXXV Y.B. COM. ARB. 377; Oberlandesgericht [OLG] München, Germany, 34 Sch 26/08, 22 June 2009, XXXV Y.B. COM. ARB. 371 (2010); Kammergericht [KG] Berlin, Germany, 20 Sch 02/08, 17 April 2008; Oberlandesgericht [OLG] Frankfurt, Germany, 26 Sch 1/07, 18 October 2007; *Goldtron Ltd. v. Media Most B.V.*, Rechtbank, Amsterdam, Netherlands, 27 August 2002, XXVIII Y.B. COM. ARB. 814 (2003); *Shaanxi Provincial Helath Products I/E Corporation v. Olpesa S.A.*, Supreme Court, Spain, No. 112/2002, 7 October 2003, XXX Y.B. COM. ARB. 617 (2005); Federal Tribunal, Switzerland, 28 July 2010, Decision 4A_233/2010; *G. S.A. v. T. Ltd.,* Federal Tribunal, Switzerland, 12 January 1989, XV Y.B. COM. ARB. 509 (1990). See also Albert Jan van den Berg, *The New York Convention of 1958: An Overview*, in ENFORCEMENT OF ARBITRATION AGREEMENTS AND INTERNATIONAL ARBITRAL AWARDS: THE NEW YORK CONVENTION IN PRACTICE 39, 57-58 and 64 (E. Gaillard, D. Di Pietro eds., 2008); Herman Verbist, *Challenges on Grounds of Due Process Pursuant to Article V (1)(b) of the New York Convention*, in ENFORCEMENT OF ARBITRATION AGREEMENTS AND INTERNATIONAL ARBITRAL AWARDS: THE NEW YORK CONVENTION IN PRACTICE 679 (E. Gaillard, D. Di Pietro eds., 2008).

[1143] See *Travaux préparatoires*, Report of the Committee on the Enforcement of International Arbitral Awards, E/AC.42/4/Rev.1, p. 10; Comments of the Representative of the Egyptian Government, Mr. Osman: Summary Record of the Sixth Meeting, E/AC.42/SR.6, p. 4.

[1144] See the chapter of the Guide on article V (2)(b), paras. 53-61.

C. Procedural issues in raising the defence of article V (2)*(b)*

a. Estoppel and waiver

47. The question has arisen whether a party may be estopped from raising the defence of article V (2)*(b)* of the New York Convention where, to the extent possible, it has failed to do so before the arbitral tribunal.

48. In some instances, courts have held that failure of a party to raise a defect in procedure or on the merits of the award amounts to a waiver of its right to avail itself of this ground of complaint at the recognition and enforcement stage. One court however indicated that although a party may be precluded from raising complaints at the recognition and enforcement stage that it could have raised before the arbitral tribunal, this does not apply to complaints brought under article V (2)*(b)* of the New York Convention.[1145]

49. Certain courts have endorsed the proposition that a substantive complaint will not be entertained as a public policy complaint at the enforcement stage if it existed at the time of the arbitral proceedings and it could have been raised before the arbitral tribunal,[1146] or if it has been raised and rejected on the merits by the arbitral tribunal.[1147]

50. This conclusion is more commonly reached with regard to procedural irregularities. For example, in a case where it was alleged that the award was procured through fraud, the English courts held that it would not be appropriate to refuse recognition if the relevant evidence was available at the hearing before the arbitral tribunal or if the allegation has been raised with the tribunal and has been rejected.[1148] Other common law jurisdictions have also held that a party that failed to raise a procedural irregularity with the arbitral tribunal, while it could do so, has waived its right to do so at the enforcement stage.[1149]

[1145] Bayerisches Oberstes Landesgericht [BayObLG], Germany, 4 Z Sch 17/03, 20 November 2003.

[1146] See *Soinco SACI & anor. v. Novokuznetsk Aluminium Plant & Ors.*, Court of Appeal, England and Wales, 16 December 1997, [1998] CLC 730;Oberlandesgericht [OLG] Saarbrücken, Germany, 4 Sch 03/10, 30 May 2011; *Epis S.A. v. Roche Diagnostics GmbH*, District Court of Jerusalem, Israel, 23 November 2004, XXXI Y.B. COM. ARB. 786 (2006).

[1147] See Bundesgerichtshof [BGH] Germany, III ZR 269/88, 18 January 1990.

[1148] See *Westacre Investments Inc. v. Jugoimport-SDPR Holding Co. Ltd.*, Court of Appeal, England and Wales, 12 May 1999, [2000] QB 288; *Minmetals Germany GmbH v. Ferco Steel Ltd.*, High Court of Justice, Queen's Bench Division, Commercial Court, England and Wales, 20 January 1999, [1999] CLC 647; *Omnium de Traitement et de Valorisation S.A. v. Hilmarton Ltd.*, High Court of Justice, Queen's Bench Division, Commercial Court, England and Wales, 24 May 1999, [1999] 2 Lloyd's Rep. 222.

[1149] See, e.g., *Gao Haiyan & anor. v. Keeneye Holdings Ltd. & anor.*, Court of Appeal, Hong Kong, CACV 79/2011, 2 December 2011; *Karaha Bodas Co. LLC v. Perusahaan*

51. Similarly, civil law jurisdictions have considered that a party that has failed to seize the arbitral tribunal of a procedural irregularity should be barred from doing so at the enforcement stage.[1150] By contrast, where the party has lodged the complaint with the arbitral tribunal and reserved its rights, the French Court of Cassation held that that party ought to be permitted to raise the same complaint at the enforcement stage.[1151]

52. Certain courts have accepted that procedural irregularities may not be raised at the enforcement stage if the party opposing recognition and enforcement has failed to raise them in annulment proceedings brought before the courts of the seat of the arbitration.[1152] Given the rejection by the New York Convention of the *double exequatur* requirement,[1153] this line of case law seems somewhat at odds with the text and spirit of the Convention which enables a party to rely on an irregularity in the procedure before the arbitral tribunal in order to oppose recognition and enforcement under the New York Convention.

b. Ex officio review, burden of proof and standard of proof

53. Article V (2)*(b)* of the New York Convention provides that a foreign award may be refused recognition if the court where recognition and enforcement is sought "finds that" that the recognition and enforcement is contrary to the public policy of the forum where recognition and enforcement is sought. The question has thus arisen as to whether the courts can review an award on grounds of public policy *ex officio*, the identity of the party which bears the burden of proof, and the standard of proof to be met.

54. Regarding the ability of a court to review a foreign award on public policy grounds *ex officio*, there is a notable difference in wording between article V (1) and V (2) of the New York Convention. Article V (1) states that

Pertambangan Minyak Dan Gas Bumi Negara, Court of Appeals, Fifth Circuit, United States of America, 23 March 2004, 364 F.3d 274; *Europcar Italia S.p.A. v. Maiellano Tours Inc.*, Court of Appeals, Second Circuit, United States of America, 2 September 1998, 156 F.3d 310; *AAOT Foreign Economic Association (VO) Technostroyexport v. International Development & Trade Services Inc.*, Court of Appeals, Second Circuit, United States of America, 23 March 1998, 97-9075, XXIV Y.B. COM. ARB. 813 (1999).

[1150] See, e.g., *SAS C22 v. Soc. John K. King & Sons Limited Frontier Agriculture Ltd.*, Court of Appeal of Paris, France, 10 April 2008. See also Bundesgerichtshof [BGH], Germany, III ZR 12/87, 14 April 1988, where the German Federal Supreme Court held that there is no breach of public policy where a party fails to raise a procedural irregularity in a timely manner with the tribunal or the institution administering the arbitration. See also Bundesgerichtshof [BGH], Germany, VII ZR 163/68, 6 March 1969; *K.S. A.G. v. C.C. S.A.*, Execution and Bankruptcy Chamber of Tessin, Switzerland, 19 June 1990, XX Y.B. COM. ARB. 762 (1995); Oberlandesgericht [OLG] Hamm, Germany, 20 U 57/83, 2 November 1983.

[1151] See *Siemens A.G. v. BKMI Industrienlagen GmbH*, Court of Cassation, France, 7 January 1992, XVIII Y.B. COM. ARB. 140 (1993).

[1152] Oberlandesgericht [OLG] Frankfurt, Germany, 26 Sch 1/07, 18 October 2007.

[1153] See the chapter of the Guide on article V (1)(e).

recognition and enforcement of an award may be refused "at the request of the party against whom it is invoked". By contrast, article V (2)*(b)* provides that recognition and enforcement may be refused "if the competent authority in the country where recognition and enforcement is sought finds that [...] the recognition and enforcement of the award would be contrary to the public policy of that country".[1154]

55. On the basis of this difference of wording, certain courts have acknowledged that they can review an award for breach of public policy *ex officio.*[1155]

56. However, the ability to review an award for breach of public policy does not solely arise out of the difference in wording of paragraphs (1) and (2) of article V. It is also linked to the essence of public policy as a concept that allows the courts to reject a violation of it most fundamental norms of justice. The English courts have thus held that "the defence that enforcement would be contrary to public policy is stated without an express burden of proof [...]. This is no doubt because it must always be open to the court to take a point of public policy of its own motion".[1156]

57. Irrespective of whether a jurisdiction has the authority to review an award for breach of public policy *ex officio* or solely at the request of the party challenging recognition or enforcement, the burden of proof rests on this latter party.[1157]

[1154] During the negotiation of the Convention, the Netherlands Government pointed out that courts are allowed to proceed to an *ex officio* review of public policy: see *Travaux préparatoires*, Recognition and Enforcement of Foreign Arbitral Awards: Comments by Governments on the Draft Convention on the Recognition and Enforcement of Foreign Arbitral Awards, E/CONF.26/3/Add.1, p. 4. The same view was expressed by the Swedish Government: Summary Record of the Seventeenth Meeting, E/CONF.26/SR.17, p. 2. See also Albert Jan van den Berg, *The New York Convention of 1958: An Overview*, in ENFORCEMENT OF ARBITRATION AGREEMENTS AND INTERNATIONAL ARBITRAL AWARDS: THE NEW YORK CONVENTION IN PRACTICE 39, 56, 64 (E. Gaillard, D. Di Pietro eds. 2008).

[1155] See, e.g., *Hebei Import & Export Corp. v. Polytek Engineering Co. Ltd.*, Court of Final Appeal, Hong Kong, 9 February 1999, [1999] 2 HKC 205; Kammergericht [KG] Berlin, Germany, 20 Sch 4/07, 11 June 2009, XXXV Y.B. COM. ARB. 369 (2010); Oberlandesgericht [OLG] München, Germany, 17 December 2008, XXXV Y.B. COM. ARB. 359 (2010); *Efxinos Shipping Co. Ltd. v. Rawi Shipping Lines Ltd.*, Court of Appeal of Genoa, Italy, 2 May 1980, VIII Y.B. COM. ARB. 381 (1983); *Petrotesting Colombia S.A. & Southeast Investment Corp. v. Ross Energy S.A.*, Supreme Court of Justice, Colombia, 27 July 2011; *BCB Holdings Limited and The Belize Bank Limited v. The Attorney General of Belize*, Caribbean Court of Justice, Appellate Jurisdiction, 26 July 2013, [2013] CCJ 5 (AJ). See also ALBERT JAN VAN DEN BERG, THE NEW YORK ARBITRATION CONVENTION OF 1958: TOWARDS A UNIFORM JUDICIAL INTERPRETATION 299, 359 (1981).

[1156] *Gater Assets Ltd. v. Nak Naftogaz Ukrainiy*, Court of Appeal, England and Wales, 17 October 2007, [2007] EWCA Civ 988, [2007] 2 CLC 567.

[1157] See, e.g., Oberlandesgericht [OLG] Düsseldorf, Germany, VI Sch (Kart) 1/02, 21 July 2004; *Gater Assets Ltd. v. Nak Naftogaz Ukrainiy*, Court of Appeal, England and Wales,

58. The exceptional nature of the public policy defence explains the heightened standard of proof that courts normally require in order to refuse recognition and enforcement under article V (2)*(b)*. Thus the Canadian courts have requested that the party opposing recognition and enforcement should present compelling evidence.[1158] It is thus of no surprise that, while the enforcement courts recognize in principle that recognition of an award should be refused on the grounds of public policy in specific instances, such as for example bribery or fraud, parties alleging a breach of public policy more often than not fail on the facts.[1159]

59. In a case heard by the Court of Appeal of Hong Kong, it was held there was no proof of actual bias in a case where one of the arbitrators had had dinner with a person related to the respondent in the arbitration in the context of mediation, even though that would have been seen as bias in Hong Kong, because such dinners were normal course of business in the context of mediation at the place of the arbitration.[1160] The Court of Final Appeal of Hong Kong held that what is required is proof of actual bias and not of mere impartiality.[1161]

60. Although it is not clear whether other courts would have followed the reasoning of the courts of Hong Kong in assessing the existence of bias by reference to the standard existing at the place where the relevant facts took place, rather than the standard existing under their own law, several

---

17 October 2007, [2007] EWCA Civ 988, [2007] 2 CLC 567; *Hebei Import & Export Corp. v. Polytek Engineering Co. Ltd.,* Court of Final Appeal, Hong Kong, 9 February 1999, [1999] 2 HKC 205; *NTT Docomo Inc. v. Ultra D.O.O.*, District Court, Southern District of New York, United States of America, 12 October 2010; *Europcar Italia S.p.A. v. Maiellano Tours Inc.*, Court of Appeals, Second Circuit, United States of America, 2 September 1998, 156 F.3d 310; *Telenor Mobile Communications AS v. Storm LLC*, District Court, Southern District of New York, United States of America, 2 November 2007, 524 F. Supp. 2d 332; *Stawski Distributing Co., Inc. v. Zywiec Breweries plc,* District Court, Northern District of Illinois, United States of America, 29 September 2004, 02 C 8708.

[1158] See *Karaha Bodas Company, L.L.C. v. Perusahaan Pertambangan Minyak Dan Gas Bumi Negara and P.T. PLN (Persero)*, Alberta Court of Queen's Bench, Canada, 24 October 2007, 2007 ABQB 616.

[1159] See, e.g., *El Nasr Company for Fertilizers & Chemical Industries (SEMADCO) v. John Brown Deutsche*, Court of Cassation, Egypt, 10 January 2005; *Compagnie française d'études et de construction Technip (Technip) v. Entreprise nationale des engrais et des produits phytosanitaires (Asmidal),* Court of Appeal of Paris, France, 2 April 1998; *Soc. I.A.I.G.C.-Inter-Arab Investment Guarantee Corporation v. Soc. B.A.I.I. - Banque arabe et internationale d'investissement S.A.*, Court of Appeal of Paris, France, 23 October 1997; *Soc. Unichips Finanziaria S.p.A. & Soc. Unichips International B.V. v. Consorts Gesnouin,* Court of Appeal of Paris, France, 13 February 1993; Oberlandesgericht [OLG] München, Germany, 34 Sch 26/08, 22 June 2009, XXXV Y.B. COM. ARB. 371 (2010); Oberlandesgericht [OLG] Hamm, Germany, 25 Sch 09/08, 28 November 2008.

[1160] See *Gao Haiyan & anor. v. Keeneye Holdings Ltd. & anor.*, Court of Appeal, Hong Kong, CACV 79/2011, 2 December 2011.

[1161] See *Hebei Import & Export Corp. v. Polytek Engineering Co. Ltd.,* Court of Final Appeal, Hong Kong, 9 February 1999, [1999] 2 HKC 205.

courts have demanded that the party alleging fraud should present clear and convincing evidence to that effect, show that the fraud in question was not discoverable during the arbitration and that it was materially related to an issue in the arbitration. In other words, in cases of fraud or bias, where the public policy exception under the New York Convention is invoked, courts often require an additional fact to be proven, namely that the defect is such to influence the outcome of the arbitration.[1162]

61. This heightened standard of proof is compatible with the exceptional nature of the public policy defence as well as with the fact that article V (2)*(b)* provides a mere facility to the courts and not an obligation. Although courts may proceed to an *ex officio* review of the award for a breach of public policy, the fact that they place the burden of proof on the party opposing recognition and enforcement as well as the heightened standard of proof demonstrate an international consensus as to the pro-enforcement bias of the New York Convention and the conservative manner in which the public policy defence should be employed.

c. Consequences

62. The sanction for an award that is found to be contrary to public policy is that the courts of a Contracting State may refuse to grant recognition and enforcement. While that power is discretionary in the sense that the New York Convention does not require that recognition and enforcement be refused ("[r]ecognition and enforcement of an arbitral award may also be refused"), certain courts have decided that, where it is possible to sever the part of the award which is contrary to public policy, the rest of the award will be recognized and enforced.

63. The High Court of Hong Kong was faced with this issue in a case concerning an award which had been challenged on the ground of fraud and in particular that a witness had been kidnapped and forced to make a false affidavit. The High Court held that "[i]f an award contained an objectionable part it would be absurd if the remainder of the award was to fail as well".[1163] It thus allowed the enforcement of the award insofar as it related to the

[1162] See, e.g., *Westacre Investments Inc. v. Jugoimport-SPDR Holding Ltd. & others*, Court of Appeal, England and Wales, 12 May 2000, [2000] 1 QB 288; *Karaha Bodas Co. LLC v. Perusahaan Pertambangan Minyak Dan Gas Bumi Negara (Petarmina),* Court of Appeal, Hong Kong, 9 October 2007; *Karaha Bodas Co. LLC v. Perusahaan Pertambangan Minyak Dan Gas Bumi Negara*, Court of Appeals, Fifth Circuit, United States of America, 23 March 2004, 364 F.3d 274. German courts apply the same approach as to fraud, namely that it should be such to influence the outcome of the arbitration, also to due process violations: see Hanseatisches Oberlandesgericht [OLG] Bremen, Germany, (2) Sch 04/99, 30 September 1999; Bundesgerichtshof [BGH] Germany, III ZR 192/84, 15 May 1986.

[1163] *J. J. Agro Industries (P) Ltd. v. Texuna International Ltd.*, High Court, Hong Kong, 12 August 1992.

reimbursement of a deposit for the sale of undelivered goods, an issue which in its view would not be affected by the public policy challenge.

64. While article V (2)*(b)* of the New York Convention does not explicitly limit itself to the part of the award which is challenged under public policy, the High Court of Hong Kong considered that such an interpretation was appropriate and compatible with article V (1)*(c)*, which provides for the severability of the part of the award that "deals with a difference not contemplated by or falling within the terms of the submission to arbitration, or contains decisions on matters beyond the scope of the submission to arbitration".

65. Other examples of awards where the part contrary to public policy was severed and the recognition and enforcement was granted to the rest of the award include cases where the award ordered the payment of interest of such magnitude that was considered contrary to public policy. In those cases, the courts severed either the part of the award on interest as a whole[1164] or the part of the interest sum exceeding what would be considered appropriate in the enforcement State.[1165]

[1164] See *Laminoires-Trefileries-Cablerie de Lens S.A. v. Southwire Co. and Southwire International Corp.*, District Court, Northern District of Georgia, United States, 484 F. Supp. 1063 (1980); Oberster Gerichtshof, Austria, Case 3Ob221/04b, 26 January 2005, XXX Y.B. COM. ARB. 421 (2005).

[1165] See *Harbottle Co. Ltd. v. Egypt for Foreign Trade Co.*, Court of Cassation, Egypt, 21 May 1990.

Article VI

If an application for the setting aside or suspension of the award has been made to a competent authority referred to in article V(1)*(e)*, the authority before which the award is sought to be relied upon may, if it considers it proper, adjourn the decision on the enforcement of the award and may also, on the application of the party claiming enforcement of the award, order the other party to give suitable security.

Travaux préparatoires

The *travaux préparatoires* on article VI as adopted in 1958 are contained in the following documents:

Amendments to the Draft Convention Submitted by Governmental Delegations: E/CONF.26/L.34; E/CONF.26/L.16; E/CONF.26/L.44.

Summary Records of the 11th, 12th, 13th, 14th and 17th meetings of the United Nations Conference on International Commercial Arbitration.

(Available on the Internet at http://www.uncitral.org)
(For the *travaux préparatoires*, case law and bibliographical references, see also on the Internet at http://newyorkconvention1958.org)

Introduction

1. Article VI of the Convention addresses the situation where a party seeks to set aside an award in the country where it was issued, while the other party seeks to enforce it elsewhere.

2. In this context of parallel proceedings, article VI achieves a compromise between the two equally legitimate concerns of promoting the

enforceability of foreign arbitral awards and preserving judicial oversight over awards by granting courts of Contracting States the freedom to decide whether or not to adjourn enforcement proceedings.[1166]

3. Article VI was not included in the early drafts of the Convention and the issues it addresses were first considered during the United Nations Conference on International Commercial Arbitration convened for the preparation and adoption of the Convention. In turning their minds to these issues, the drafters of the Convention sought to ensure that a party wishing to frustrate the enforcement of an award could not circumvent the Convention by simply initiating proceedings to set aside or suspend the award, while at the same time limiting the risk that an enforced award would be subsequently set aside in the country in which it was made.

4. As explained by Mr. de Sydow, Chairman of Working Party No. 3 that drafted article VI: "[T]he Working Party recommended the adoption of that article in order to permit the enforcement authority to adjourn its decision if it was satisfied that an application for annulment of the award or for its suspension was made for a good reason in the country where the award was given. At the same time, to prevent an abuse of that provision by the losing party which may have started annulment proceedings without a valid reason purely to delay or frustrate the enforcement of the award, the enforcement authority should in such a case have the right either to enforce the award forthwith or to adjourn its enforcement only on the condition that the party opposing enforcement deposits a suitable security."[1167]

5. Article VI may be regarded as an important step forward compared to the 1927 Geneva Convention under which a foreign court was required to refuse enforcement upon the mere application to set aside the award in the country where it was issued.[1168] By contrast, article VI merely allows

---

1166 See FOUCHARD GAILLARD GOLDMAN ON INTERNATIONAL COMMERCIAL ARBITRATION 981 (E. Gaillard, J. Savage eds., 1996); Nicola C. Port, Jessica R. Simonoff et al., *Article VI*, in RECOGNITION AND ENFORCEMENT OF FOREIGN ARBITRAL AWARDS: A GLOBAL COMMENTARY ON THE NEW YORK CONVENTION 415, 416 (H. Kronke, P. Nacimiento et al. eds., 2010). See also *Continental Transfer Technique Ltd. v. Federal Government of Nigeria*, High Court of Justice, England and Wales, 30 March 2010, [2010] EWHC 780 (Comm); *IPCO v. Nigeria* (NNPC), High Court of Justice, England and Wales, 27 April 2005, [2005] EWHC 726 (Comm).

1167 *Travaux préparatoires*, United Nations Conference on International Commercial Arbitration, Summary Record of the Seventeenth Meeting, E/CONF.26/SR.17, p. 4.

1168 See article 1 of the 1927 Geneva Convention: "To obtain such recognition or enforcement, it shall, further, be necessary: [...] *(d)* That the award has become final in the country in which it has been made, in the sense that it will not be considered as such if it is open to opposition, appel or *pourvoi en cassation* (in the countries where such forms of procedure exist) or if it is proved that any proceedings for the purpose of contesting the validity of the award are pending; [...]." See also PHILIPPE FOUCHARD, L'ARBITRAGE COMMERCIAL INTERNATIONAL 535 (1965); ALBERT JAN VAN DEN BERG, THE NEW YORK ARBITRATION CONVENTION OF 1958: TOWARDS A UNIFORM JUDICIAL INTERPRETATION 353 (1981).

national courts to adjourn their decision on enforcement should they "consider it proper".[1169] The same principle is provided for, in substance, in article 36(2) of the UNCITRAL Model Law on International Commercial Arbitration.[1170]

6. Although article VI is often raised alongside article V (1)*(e)*, which provides that a court may refuse to recognize and enforce an award if it "has not yet become binding on the parties, or has been set aside or suspended by a competent authority of the country",[1171] it covers a different situation. By adjourning the enforcement proceedings, courts seek to preserve the status quo in order to enable the application to set aside or suspend the award to be made in the country where it was issued.[1172] In this sense, article VI may be regarded as "a corollary" to article V (1)*(e)* and as closing a "temporal gap" that exists when an action to set aside the award is pending before a competent authority.[1173]

7. It took a while for practitioners to avail themselves of the possibilities offered by article VI.[1174] Now, courts around the world have applied this provision with a view to promoting the objectives of the Convention by facilitating the recognition and enforcement of arbitral awards.

1169 The District Court of Columbia has provided the following definition of "adjourn" within the meaning of article VI of the Convention: "stay or dismiss without prejudice". See *Telcordia Technologies, Inc. v. Telkom SA, Limited*, District Court, District of Columbia, United States of America, 9 April 2004, 02-1990. See also *CP Construction Pioneers Baugesellschaft Anstalt v. The Government of the Republic Ghana, Ministry of Roads and Transport*, District Court, District of Columbia, United States of America, 12 August 2008, 1:04-01564 (LFO); *Continental Transfert Technique Lmt. v. Federal Government of Nigeria et al.*, District Court, District of Columbia, United States of America, 23 March 2010, 08-2026 (PLF).

1170 Article 36(2) of the UNCITRAL Model Law on International Commercial Arbitration provides that: "If an application for setting aside or suspension of an award has been made to a court referred to in paragraph (1) (a)(v) of this article, the court where recognition or enforcement is sought may, if it considers it proper, adjourn its decision and may also, on the application of the party claiming recognition or enforcement of the award, order the other party to provide appropriate security."

1171 For a more detailed analysis, see the chapter of the Guide on article V (1)*(e)*.

1172 *ESCO Corp v. Bradken Resources Pty Ltd*, Federal Court, Australia, 9 August 2011, NSD 876 of 2011.

1173 Christoph Liebscher, *Article VI*, in NEW YORK CONVENTION ON THE RECOGNITION AND ENFORCEMENT OF FOREIGN ARBITRAL AWARDS OF 10 JUNE 1958—COMMENTARY 438, 439 (R. Wolff ed., 2012); Michael H. Strub, *Resisting Enforcement* of *Foreign Arbitral Awards Under Article V (1)(e) and Article VI* of *the New York Convention: A Proposal for Effective Guidelines*, 68 TEX. L. REV. 1031, 1047 (1989-1990).

1174 See Pieter Sanders, *A Twenty Years' Review of the Convention on the Recognition and Enforcement of Foreign Arbitral Awards*, 13 INT'L LAW 269, 273 (1979).

Analysis

A. General principles

a. The requirement that an application for the setting aside or suspension of an award be pending

8. Article VI of the Convention requires that an application for the setting aside or suspension of an award "has been made" before a competent authority. In the absence of such an application, courts must refuse to adjourn the decision on the enforcement of the award.

9. Several courts have considered whether to adjourn enforcement proceedings pursuant to article VI in cases where it was not established that the pending application constituted an attempt to set aside or suspend the award. For example, the United States District Court for the Western District of Washington held that a damages claim in a second set of arbitral proceedings did not amount to an action to set aside or suspend the award within the meaning of article VI.[1175] In another case, the United States Court of Appeals for the Third Circuit dismissed a request for adjournment on the grounds that an action, initiated before the same arbitral tribunal, to remedy a harm that occurred after a first award was issued did not amount to an action to set aside or suspend the award.[1176] In a further case, the Supreme Court of New South Wales refused to grant an adjournment in a situation where the defendant had failed to establish that the application made before a competent authority in Sweden related to the setting aside or suspension of the award.[1177]

10. Courts also require the party opposing enforcement to demonstrate that an application to set aside or suspend an award is still pending. If the application has already been dismissed, courts will refuse to adjourn the decision on the enforcement of an award.[1178] By way of example, a French court denied adjournment on the ground that even though the party seeking adjournment had initiated proceedings to suspend the enforcement of the

[1175] *Korea Wheel Corporation v. JCA Corporation*, District Court, Western District of Washington at Seattle, United States of America, 16 December 2005, C05-1590C.

[1176] *Stephen and Mary Birch Foundation, Inc. v. Admart AG, Heller Werkstatt GesmbH and others*, Court of Appeals, Third Circuit, United States of America, 8 August 2006, 04-4014.

[1177] *Hallen v. Angledal*, Supreme Court of New South Wales, Australia, 10 June 1999, 50055 of 1999.

[1178] *S.A. Recam Sonofadex v. S.N.C. Cantieri Rizzardi de Gianfranco Rizzardi*, Court of Appeal of Orléans, France, 5 October 2000; Debt Collection and Bankruptcy Chamber of the Court of Appeal of the Republic and Canton of Ticino, Switzerland, 9 December 2010, 14.2010.98.

award in Italy, those proceedings had been dismissed by the Rome Court of Appeal.[1179]

b. The application for the setting aside or suspension of an award must be made to a "competent authority"

11. Article VI of the Convention provides that courts may adjourn the enforcement decision if the application to set aside or suspend the award has been made in front of a "competent authority." To determine whether this prerequisite has been satisfied, courts refer to the standards found in article V (1)*(e)* of the Convention.[1180]

12. As pointed out in the chapter of the Guide on article V (1)*(e)*, the country under the laws of which the award is made is often the same as the country in which the award is issued and thus, in practice, courts have mainly referred to the country in which the arbitration took place.[1181]

13. If the court is not satisfied that an application has been made before a "competent authority", within the meaning of articles V (1)*(e)* and VI, the request to adjourn proceedings will be denied. For example, the Luxembourg Court of Appeal dismissed a request for adjournment noting that there was no setting aside procedure pending in Belgium, the "court of the country of rendition".[1182] Similarly, the Court of First Instance of Rotterdam refused an adjournment request based on a setting aside application pending in the Belgian courts on the ground that Israeli courts had exclusive jurisdiction to hear a setting aside application of an award issued in Israel.[1183] The United States Court of Appeals for the District of Columbia held that where an arbitration occurred in London under the arbitration laws of England, the courts of England were the "competent authority with primary jurisdiction over the Final Award" and that, absent proceedings for the setting aside or

---

1179 *S.A. Recam Sonofadex v. S.N.C. Cantieri Rizzardi de Gianfranco Rizzardi*, Court of Appeal of Orleans, France, 5 October 2000.

1180 See, e.g., *Four Seasons Hotels and Resorts, B.V., et al. v. Consorcio Barr, S.A.*, District Court, Southern District of Florida, Miami Division, United States of America, 4 June 2003, 02-23249; *Belize Social Development Ltd. v. Government of Belize*, Court of Appeals, D.C. Circuit, United States of America, 13 January 2012, 10-7167; *The Commercial Company for Investment v. Bell Rover Shipping Limited*, Court of Appeal of Cairo, Egypt, 19 March 1997, 68/113.

1181 For a detailed analysis of the case law, see the chapter of the Guide on article V (1)*(e)*.

1182 *Kersa Holding Company Luxembourg v. Infancourtage, Famajuk Investment and Isny*, Superior Court of Justice, Luxembourg, 24 November 1993. See also *The Commercial Company for Investment v. Bell Rover Shipping Limited*, Court of Appeal of Cairo, Egypt, 19 March 1997.

1183 *Isaac Glecer v. Moses Israel Glecer and Estera Glecer-Nottman*, President of the District Court of Rotterdam, Netherlands, 24 November 1994, XXI Y.B. COM. ARB. 635 (1996).

suspension of the award in those courts, adjournment should be denied.[1184] In that case, the court recalled that enforcement may be adjourned "only if [...] an application for the setting aside or suspension of the award has been made to a competent authority."[1185]

14. In line with the principle that the party opposing enforcement of an arbitral award has the burden of proving that one or more of the defences under the Convention apply,[1186] the burden of proving that the authority to which the application was made is competent to hear the application lies with the party seeking the adjournment. On that basis, the Supreme Court of New South Wales in *Hallen v. Angledal* refused to adjourn its decision on enforcement as it did not "consider that the defendants have established that the necessary application has been made to competent authority in Sweden."[1187]

c. *Whether the party must request an adjournment and/or an order for security*

15. Pursuant to article VI of the Convention, the authority before which the award is sought to be relied upon may order that the party opposing enforcement give suitable security "on the application of the party claiming enforcement". The language of article VI allows the courts to order security only if the party seeking enforcement so requests.

16. In *Spier*, the United States District Court for the Southern District of New York first noted that it should not order security since "neither party [...] had briefed the question of security", but still requested the defendant to show cause as to the reasons why security in the full amount should not be required, even though neither party had addressed the issue.[1188] Since then, courts in the United States have consistently held that security should be

---

1184 *Belize Social Development Ltd. v. Government* of *Belize*, Court of Appeals, D.C. Circuit, United States of America, 13 January 2012, 10-7167.

1185 *Id.*

1186 See, e.g., *Encyclopaedia Universalis, S.A. v. Encyclopaedia Britannica, Inc.*, Court of Appeals, Second Circuit, United States of America, 31 March 2005, 403 F.3d 85. See also *Thai-Lao Lignite Co. Ltd. et al. v. Government of the Lao People's Democratic Republic*, District Court, Southern District of New York, United States of America, 3 August 2011, 10 Civ. 5256 (KMW); *Europcar Italia, S.p.A. v. Maiellano Tours*, Court of Appeals, Second Circuit, United States of America, 2 September 1998, 97-7224.

1187 *Hallen v. Angledal*, Supreme Court of New South Wales, Australia, 10 June 1999, 50055 of 1999. See also *Four Seasons Hotels and Resorts, B.V., et al. v. Consorcio Barr*, S.A., District Court, Southern District of Florida, Miami Division, United States of America, 4 June 2003, 02-23249.

1188 *Spier v. Calzaturificio Tecnica S.p.A ("Spier I")*, District Court, Southern District of New York, United States of America, 29 June 1987, 663 F. Supp. 871.

ordered "on the application of the plaintiff".[1189] In a recent case, the United States District Court for the Western District of Michigan recognized its power to order security under article VI, but refused to make such an order as the party opposing enforcement had failed to make the appropriate motion.[1190]

17. It is thus accepted that article VI requires that the party seeking enforcement must "affirmatively" apply for security.[1191]

18. Article VI does not however contain a similar requirement for courts adjourning proceedings. Courts may adjourn enforcement proceedings without any of the parties having applied for such an adjournment. For example, the Court of Appeal of England and Wales held that, even though neither party had requested an adjournment, "a court might conclude of its own motion that the determination of an application under s. 103(5) [which directly incorporates and whose wording is equivalent to article VI] would be an inappropriate use of court time and/or contrary to comity or likely to give rise to conflict of laws problem."[1192] In the United States, courts have held that they have "inherent power to control [their] docket", irrespective of article VI of the Convention, and to stay the enforcement proceedings.[1193]

19. Commentators have also noted that courts could, pursuant to article VI, decide *sua sponte* to adjourn enforcement proceedings.[1194]

[1189] *Skandia America Reinsurance Corporation v. Caja Nacional de Ahorro y Seguros*, District Court, Southern District of New York, United States of America, 21 May 1997, 96 Civ. 2301 (KMW), XXIII Y.B. COM. ARB. 956 (1998); *Consorcio Rive, S.A. de C.V. v. Briggs* of *Cancun, Inc., David Briggs Enterprises, Inc.*, District Court, Eastern District of Louisiana, United States of America, 26 January 2000, 99-2205, XXV Y.B. COM. ARB. 1115 (2000).

[1190] *Leonard Higgins v. SPX Corporation*, District Court, Western District of Michigan, United States of America, 18 April 2006, 2006 WL 1008677.

[1191] Nicola C. Port, Jessica R. Simonoff et al., *Article VI*, in RECOGNITION AND ENFORCEMENT OF FOREIGN ARBITRAL AWARDS: A GLOBAL COMMENTARY ON THE NEW YORK CONVENTION 415, 434 (H. Kronke, P. Nacimiento et al. eds., 2010).

[1192] *Yukos Oil Co. v. Dardana Ltd.*, Court of Appeal, England and Wales, 18 April 2002, [2002] EWCA Civ 543.

[1193] *Oriental Republic of Uruguay, et al. v. Chemical Overseas Holdings, Inc. et al.*, District Court, Southern District of New York, United States of America, 24 January 2006, 05 Civ. 6154 (WHP); *Belize Social Development Ltd. v. Government of Belize*, Court of Appeals, D.C. Circuit, United States of America, 13 January 2012, 10-7167; *Korea Wheel Corporation v. JCA Corporation*, District Court, Western District of Washington at Seattle, United States of America, 16 December 2005, C05-1590C.

[1194] See, e.g., Christoph Liebscher, *Article VI*, in NEW YORK CONVENTION ON THE RECOGNITION AND ENFORCEMENT OF FOREIGN ARBITRAL AWARDS OF 10 JUNE 1958—COMMENTARY 438, 440 (R. Wolff ed., 2012); Rena Rico, *Searching for Standards: Suspension of Enforcement Proceedings under Article VI of the New York Convention*, 1 ASIAN INT'L ARB. J. 69, 79 (2005).

d. *The discretionary power of the courts to adjourn the decision on enforcement or order security*

20. Under article VI of the Convention, a court of a Contracting State "may, if it considers it proper, adjourn" proceedings and "may also [...] order the other party to give suitable security". In light of the "permissive language" of article VI,[1195] courts have full discretion to adjourn enforcement proceedings or order the defendant to provide security. As noted by the Supreme Court of Hong Kong, use of the term "may" indicates that the application for adjournment is a matter of discretion.[1196]

21. The fact that courts were granted full discretion in that respect has been widely recognized throughout the world. The President of the First Instance Court of Paris acknowledged, in *Saint-Gobain*, that article VI of the Convention gives discretion to the enforcing judge to decide whether enforcement proceedings should be adjourned when an application to set aside or suspend an award has been made to a competent authority in the country where the award was issued. Similar rulings have been rendered in many countries, including Canada, Italy, Germany, Sweden and the United States of America.[1197] Australian courts have found that section 8(8) of the International Arbitration Act 1974 (which implements article VI of the Convention) gives them "wide discretion" or a "general discretion" to adjourn enforcement proceedings if they are satisfied that an application for the setting aside or suspension of an award had been brought before a competent authority of the country in which, or under the law of which, the award was rendered.[1198] Similarly, English courts consider that they have

---

[1195] See *Europcar Italia, S.p.A. v. Maiellano Tours*, Court of Appeals, Second Circuit, United States of America, 2 September 1998, 97-7224.

[1196] *Hebei Import & Export Corp v. Polytek Engineering Co. Ltd.*, High Court, Supreme Court of Hong Kong, Hong Kong, 1 November 1996, [1996] 3 HKC 725.

[1197] *Powerex Corp. v. Alcan Inc.*, Supreme Court of British Columbia, Canada, 10 July 2003, 2003 BCSC 1096; *Nuovo Pignone SpA v. Schlumberger S.A.*, Court of Appeal of Florence, Italy, 17 May 2005, XXXII Y.B. COM. ARB. 403 (2007); Oberlandesgericht [OLG] Schleswig, Germany, 16 June 2008, 16 Sch 02/07; *AB Götaverken v. General National Maritime Transport Company (GMTC), Libya and others*, Supreme Court, Sweden, 13 August 1979, VI Y.B. COM. ARB. 237 (1981); *Korea Wheel Corporation v. JCA Corporation*, District Court, Western District of Washington at Seattle, United States of America, 16 December 2005, C05-1590C; *China National Chartering Corp. et al. v. Pactrans Air & Sea Inc.*, District Court, Southern District of New York, United States of America, 13 November 2009, 06 Civ. 13107 (LAK); *DRC Inc. v. Republic of Honduras*, District Court, District of Columbia, United States of America, 28 March 2011, 10-0003 (PLF).

[1198] *ESCO Corp v. Bradken Resources Pty Ltd.*, Federal Court, Australia, 9 August 2011, [2011] FCA 905; *Hallen v. Angledal*, Supreme Court of New South Wales, Australia, 10 June 1999, 50055 of 1999.

"wide" discretion[1199] under article VI and are "unfettered when considering the exercise of [their] discretion".[1200]

22. The courts' discretionary power applies not only to the decision to adjourn enforcement proceedings but also to whether a defendant should provide security and the amount of that security.[1201]

23. Leading commentators agree that, on the basis of the permissive language used in article VI and the *travaux préparatoires*,[1202] the decision to stay enforcement proceedings and/or order security is discretionary.[1203]

B. The decision to grant or deny adjournment

a. The absence of a standard

24. The Convention does not provide any standard by which a court should decide whether to stay enforcement proceedings, thereby leaving courts in Contracting States to use their discretion.[1204]

[1199] *IPCO v. Nigeria (NNPC)*, High Court of Justice, England and Wales, 27 April 2005, [2005] EWHC 726 (Comm). See also *Dowans Holding S.A. v. Tanzania Electric Supply Co. Ltd.*, High Court of Justice, England and Wales, 27 July 2011, [2011] EWHC 1957 (Comm).

[1200] *Continental Transfer Technique Ltd. v. Federal Government* of *Nigeria*, High Court of Justice, England and Wales, 30 March 2010, [2010] EWHC 780 (Comm). In the United States, article VI has also been construed as granting "unfettered discretion" to adjourn pending the outcome of an application to set aside: see *Ukrvneshprom State Foreign Economic Enterprise v. Tradeway, Inc.*, District Court, Southern District of New York, United States of America, 11 March 1996, 95 Civ. 10279, XXII Y.B. COM. ARB. 958 (1997).

[1201] *Spier v. Calzaturificio Tecnica S.p.A*, District Court, Southern District of New York, United States of America, 29 June 1987, 663 F. Supp. 871; *Consorcio Rive, S.A. de C.V. v. Briggs* of *Cancun, Inc., David Briggs Enterprises, Inc.*, District Court, Eastern District of Louisiana, United States of America, 26 January 2000, 99-2205, XXV Y.B. COM. ARB. 1115 (2000); *Yukos Oil Co. v. Dardana Ltd.*, Court of Appeal, England and Wales, 18 April 2002, [2002] EWCA Civ 543; *IPCO v. Nigeria (NNPC)*, High Court of Justice, England and Wales, 27 April 2005, [2005] EWHC 726 (Comm); *The Republic of Gabon v. Swiss Oil Corporation*, Grand Court, Cayman Island, 17 June 1988, XIV Y.B. COM. ARB. 621 (1989).

[1202] See the chapter of the Guide on Article VI, para. 4. See also a proposal of the Dutch delegate to the Conference, providing that the "judge in the country of enforcement must be given complete latitude either to grant an exequatur immediately, if he considered that there was no reason to refuse it, or to await the outcome of proceedings for its annulment instituted in the country in which it had been made." *Travaux préparatoires*, United Nations Conference on International Commercial Arbitration, Summary Record of the Eleventh Meeting, E/CONF.26/SR.11, p. 5.

[1203] See, e.g., GARY B. BORN, INTERNATIONAL COMMERCIAL ARBITRATION 2873-2874 (2009); W. Michael Tupman, *Staying Enforcement of Arbitral Awards under the New York Convention*, 3 ARB.INT'L 209, 211 (1987); Christoph Liebscher, *Article VI*, in NEW YORK CONVENTION ON THE RECOGNITION AND ENFORCEMENT OF FOREIGN ARBITRAL AWARDS OF 10 JUNE 1958—COMMENTARY 438, 438 (R. Wolff ed., 2012); ALBERT JAN VAN DEN BERG, THE NEW YORK ARBITRATION CONVENTION OF 1958: TOWARDS A UNIFORM JUDICIAL INTERPRETATION 353, 358 (1981).

25. In the 1981 *Fertilizer Corporation of India* case, the United States District Court for the Southern District of Ohio noted that it had been unable to discover any standard on which to base an adjournment decision, other than to ascertain whether an application for the setting aside or suspension of the award had been brought before a competent authority of the country in which, or under the law of which, the award was made.[1205] Similarly, the English High Court of Justice held that the 1996 Arbitration Act did not furnish a threshold test in respect of the exercise of the court's wide discretion pursuant to section 103(5) (which implements article VI of the Convention).[1206]

26. It is widely recognized that discretion should be "rationally" exercised.[1207] As stated by the United States Court of Appeals for the Second Circuit, "where a parallel proceeding is ongoing in the originating country and there is a possibility that the award will be set aside, a district court may be acting improvidently by enforcing the award prior to the completion of the foreign proceedings."[1208]

27. In the absence of a recognized standard, certain jurisdictions had in the past adjourned enforcement proceedings on the sole basis that setting aside proceedings were pending before the competent authority, as defined in articles V (1)*(e)* and VI of the Convention. For example, in *Norsolor*, the Paris Court of Appeal suspended enforcement proceedings pending the outcome of an application to set aside the award before the Vienna Court of Appeal on the ground that, if the award were to be set aside in Vienna, the enforcement proceedings would be stripped of their object.[1209] In the United States, the District Court for the Southern District of New York also

---

1204 W. Michael Tupman, *Staying Enforcement of Arbitral Awards under the New York Convention*, 3 ARB. INT'L 209, 220 (1987); Nicola C. Port, Jessica R. Simonoff et al., *Article VI*, in RECOGNITION AND ENFORCEMENT OF FOREIGN ARBITRAL AWARDS: A GLOBAL COMMENTARY ON THE NEW YORK CONVENTION 415, 419 (H. Kronke, P. Nacimiento et al. eds., 2010).

1205 *Fertilizer Corp. of India (India) v. IDI Mgmt. Inc. (United States)*, District Court, Southern District of Ohio, United States of America, 9 June 1981, C-1-79-570.

1206 *IPCO v. Nigerian National Petroleum Corp.*, High Court of Justice, England and Wales, 17 April 2008, [2008] EWHC 797 (Comm).

1207 *Dowans Holding S.A. v. Tanzania Electric Supply Co. Ltd.*, High Court of Justice, England and Wales, 27 July 2011, [2011] EWHC 1957 (Comm); Rena Rico, *Searching for Standards: Suspension of Enforcement Proceedings under Article VI* of *the New York Convention*, 1 ASIAN INT'L ARB. J. 69, 79 (2005).

1208 *Europcar Italia, S.p.A. v. Maiellano Tours*, Court of Appeals, Second Circuit, United States of America, 2 September 1998, 97-7224.

1209 *Norsolor S. A. v. Pabalk Ticaret Limited Sirket*, Court of Appeal of Paris, France, 15 December 1981. See also *C.C.M. SULZER v. Société Maghrébienne de Génie Civil (SOMAGEC), Société des Anciens Etablissements Riad Sahyoun (S.A.E.R.S.) et M. Riad Sahyoun*, Court of Appeal of Paris, France, 17 February 1987, 86.4767. On the current position in France, see chapter of the Guide on article VI, para. 30.

adjourned enforcement proceedings in *Spier* by deference to the ruling of the competent authority.[1210]

28. However, the Convention does not provide that enforcement proceedings are to be automatically stayed when a setting aside application is brought.[1211] As suggested by the *travaux préparatoires*, in appropriate circumstances, an award may be enforced despite a pending application to set it aside.[1212]

29. In accordance with the discretionary power granted to courts of Contracting States under article VI, courts maintain the discretion to enforce an arbitral award even if setting aside proceedings are pending in the country where the award was issued. For example, courts in the United States have more recently held that they are not required to stay an action "merely because an action is pending in the originating country"[1213] and that they "should not automatically stay enforcement proceedings on the ground that parallel proceedings are pending in the originating country".[1214] Similarly, the Supreme Court of New South Wales has held that Australian courts should not stay an action to enforce an arbitration agreement merely because an action to set aside the award is pending before the competent authority.[1215] In the words of the Supreme Court of New South Wales, "more must be established than that".[1216]

30. Similarly, in recent years, French courts have repeatedly refused to adjourn enforcement proceedings under article VI of the Convention. In the 2004 *Bargues* case, the Paris Court of Appeal held that the potential setting aside of the award in the country where it is rendered does not impact the existence of the award in a way that would prevent its recognition and

---

[1210] *Spier v. Calzaturificio Tecnica S.p.A*, District Court, Southern District of New York, United States of America, 29 June 1987, 663 F. Supp. 871.

[1211] Rena Rico, *Searching for Standards: Suspension of Enforcement Proceedings under Article VI of the New York Convention*, 1 ASIAN INT'L ARB. J. 69, 77 (2005); W. Michael Tupman, *Staying Enforcement of Arbitral Awards under the New York Convention*, 3 ARB. INT'L 209, 221 (1987).

[1212] *Travaux préparatoires*, United Nations Conference on International Commercial Arbitration, Summary Record of the Seventeenth Meeting, E/CONF.26/SR.17, p. 4.

[1213] *Sarhank Group v. Oracle Corporation*, District Court, Southern District of New York, United States of America, 9 October 2002, 2002 WL 31268635, XXVIII Y.B. COM. ARB. 1043 (2003).

[1214] *MGM Productions Group, Inc. v. Aeroflot Russian Airlines*, District Court, Southern District of New York, United States of America, 14 May 2003, 573 F. Supp. 2d 772, XXVIII Y.B. COM. ARB.1271 (2003). See also *Alto Mar Girassol v. Lumbermens Mutual Casualty Company*, District Court, Northern District of Illinois Eastern Division, United States of America, 12 April 2005, 04 C 773.

[1215] *Hallen v. Angledal*, Supreme Court of New South Wales, Australia, 10 June 1999, 50055 of 1999.

[1216] *Id.*

enforcement in other national legal orders and, as a result, that article VI "is of no use in the context of the recognition and enforcement of an award".[1217]

b. *Various factors considered by courts*

31. Courts have been developing their own reasons in exercising their discretion and have considered a wide variety of factors when deciding whether to grant a request for adjournment. Those factors include the Convention's goal of facilitating the enforcement of arbitral awards and expediting dispute resolution, the likelihood of the party prevailing in the setting aside proceeding, the expected duration of the proceedings pending in the country where the award was issued, the potential hardship to parties, judicial efficiency and international comity.

32. Swedish and Australian courts have taken the view that the duration of annulment proceedings, as well as their chances of success, should be taken into account by a court deciding whether to adjourn enforcement proceedings under article VI. German and Dutch courts have assessed the chances of success of annulment proceedings and weighed the interests of the parties when considering whether an adjournment is appropriate. A similar approach was followed by the Grand Court of the Cayman Islands in *Republic of Gabon v. Swiss Oil Corporation*. In this case, the Grand Court considered the duration and the probability of success of the annulment proceedings pending before the Paris Court of Appeal. In light of the expected short duration of the French proceedings and the fact that the "serious grounds" advanced by the applicant suggested that the application was not "merely a delaying tactic", the Grand Court decided to adjourn the enforcement proceedings. It held that that adjournment would not cause "any very substantial further hardship on the plaintiff [i.e., the Republic of Gabon]" and that "if this court were to render its decision before that of the Paris Court in this instance it would run the risk of giving free rein to enforcement of an award which in a few days' time might no longer provide a valid basis for its action."[1218] Similarly, the English High Court in *IPCO* found the following considerations to be relevant: whether the application before the court in the country where the arbitration took place is bona fide and not simply a delaying tactic, whether the application before the court in that country has at least a real (i.e., realistic) prospect of success, the extent

[1217] *Société Bargues Agro Industries S.A. v. Société Young Pecan Company*, Court of Appeal of Paris, France, 10 June 2004, 2003/09894.

[1218] *The Republic of Gabon v. Swiss Oil Corporation*, Grand Court, Cayman Islands, 17 June 1988, XIV Y.B. COM. ARB. 621 (1989).

of the delay occasioned by the potential adjournment and any resulting prejudice.[1219]

33. In the United States, the Court of Appeals for the Second Circuit Court provided a non-exhaustive list of factors to be considered when deciding an adjournment request in *Europcar Italia SpA v. Maeillano Tours Inc.* These factors include the general objective of arbitration (i.e., the expeditious resolution of disputes and the avoidance of protracted and expensive litigation), the status of the foreign proceedings and the estimated time for resolving those proceedings, whether the award sought to be enforced would receive greater scrutiny in the foreign proceedings under a less deferential standard of review, the characteristics of the foreign proceedings, a weighing of the possible hardship caused to the parties, and any other circumstances that could shift the balance in favour of or against adjournment.[1220]

34. A similar multifactor approach was adopted in Canada by the Supreme Court of British Columbia in *Powerex Corp. v. Alcan Inc.*[1221] In this case, the Supreme Court initially adjourned the proceedings after consideration of various factors, including whether the setting aside application in the United States was frivolous, whether an adjournment would inordinately delay the proceedings, and whether it would not be more convenient and efficient for a court in the United States to decide questions of domestic law. When the court in the United States dismissed the application to set aside the award, the decision was appealed by Alcan, and Powerex renewed its request for recognition and enforcement of the award. The Supreme Court of British Columbia held that the party seeking an adjournment must meet the threshold test of establishing that there is a "serious issue to be tried." In weighing the balance of convenience and irreparable harm, the court noted that it should consider a number of factors, including the estimated time to complete the case in the originating jurisdiction, whether the party opposing enforcement is "merely delaying the inevitable," whether a court in the originating jurisdiction has already refused

[1219] *IPCO v. Nigeria (NNPC)*, High Court of Justice, England and Wales, 27 April 2005, [2005] EWHC 726 (Comm).

[1220] *Europcar Italia, S.p.A. v. Maiellano Tours Inc*, Court of Appeals, Second Circuit, United States of America, 2 September 1998, 97-7224. Subsequent decisions rendered in the United States applied these factors in determining whether or not enforcement proceedings should be adjourned: see, e.g., *MGM Productions Group, Inc. v. Aeroflot Russian Airlines*, District Court, Southern District of New York, United States of America, 14 May 2003, 573 F. Supp. 2d 772, XXVIII Y.B. COM. ARB. 127 (2003); *G. E. Transp. S.P.A. v. Republic of Albania*, District Court, District of Columbia, United States of America, 28 March 2011, 08-2042 (RMU); *DRC Inc. v. Republic of Honduras*, District Court, District of Columbia, United States of America, 10-0003(PLF).

[1221] *Powerex Corp. v. Alcan Inc.*, Supreme Court of British Columbia, Canada, 30 June 2004, 2004 BCSC 876. See also *Powerex Corp. v. Alcan Inc.*, Supreme Court of British Columbia, Canada, 10 July 2003, 2003 BCSC 1096.

to set aside the award, the availability of security and the possibility that the party opposing enforcement would hide or disperse its assets prior to enforcement, and the willingness of the party opposing enforcement to undertake diligent prosecution of the action in the originating jurisdiction.

c. *Whether there are any prevailing factors to be considered by courts*

35. Although courts tend to consider the same set of factors when deciding whether to adjourn enforcement proceedings, some of them are most commonly referred to and the decision to adjourn enforcement proceedings often depends in significant part on one or two of these factors.

36. Certain courts place significant weight on the estimated time required for annulment proceedings in the country where the award was issued. The Supreme Court of Victoria held that "the determinative factor is that the adjournment will be only for a relatively short time".[1222] Courts applying this factor have denied enforcement when the decision on the setting aside application was "years rather than days away",[1223] and granted it when the decision was expected within a matter of days or a couple of months.[1224]

37. Likelihood of success in the setting aside proceedings is also an important factor relied upon by courts in determining whether to stay enforcement proceedings.[1225]

38. In the United States, a survey of the relevant case law prior and subsequent to *Europcar* suggests that courts often grant or refuse adjournments depending primarily on their assessment of the chances of success of the setting aside proceedings in the country where the award was issued.[1226] A similar approach is found in other common law countries. In

---

1222 *Toyo Engineering Corp v. John Holland Pty Ltd.*, Supreme Court of Victoria, Australia, 20 December 2000, 7565 of 2000. See also *Powerex Corp. v. Alcan Inc.*, Supreme Court of British Columbia, Canada, 10 July 2003, 2003 BCSC 1096.

1223 *Far Eastern Shipping Co. v. AKP Sovcomflot*, High Court of Justice, Queen's Bench Division (Commercial Court), England and Wales, 14 November 1994, XXI Y.B. COM. ARB. 699 (1996).

1224 See *The Republic of Gabon v. Swiss Oil Corporation*, Grand Court, Cayman Islands, 17 June 1988, XIV Y.B. COM. ARB. 621 (1989); *Toyo Engineering Corp v. John Holland Pty Ltd.*, Supreme Court of Victoria, Australia, 20 December 2000, 7565 of 2000.

1225 GARY B. BORN, INTERNATIONAL COMMERCIAL ARBITRATION 2876 (2009); Christoph Liebscher, *Article VI*, in NEW YORK CONVENTION ON THE RECOGNITION AND ENFORCEMENT OF FOREIGN ARBITRAL AWARDS OF 10 JUNE 1958—COMMENTARY 438, 441 (R. Wolff ed. 2012).

1226 See *Fertilizer Corp. of India v. IDI Mgmt. Inc.*, District Court, Southern District of Ohio, United States of America, 9 June 1981, 517 F. Supp. 948; *Spier v. Calzaturificio Tecnica S.p.A*, District Court, Southern District of New York, United States of America, 29 June 1987, 663 F. Supp. 871; *Ukrvneshprom State Foreign Economic Enterprise v. Tradeway, Inc.*,

Powerex Corp v. Alcan Inc., the Supreme Court of British Columbia emphasized the "possibility of success" factor in determining whether enforcement proceedings should be adjourned. Similarly, the Court of Appeal of England and Wales noted that one of the most important factors is "the strength of the argument that the award is invalid".[1227]

39. A number of courts require that the party opposing enforcement provide evidence of a reasonable chance of success of the application to set aside the award. When courts find that the proceedings to set aside the award are frivolous and dilatory, they will enforce the award in the belief that the chances of obtaining a judgment to set aside the award are remote.[1228]

40. Among the courts that have adjourned enforcement proceedings, the Supreme Court of Hong Kong held in *Hebei* that the party opposing enforcement had the burden of showing that a bona fide application had been made in the Beijing court and that there were grounds on which the Beijing court could reasonably set aside the award. The party opposing enforcement did not, however, need to show that it was likely to succeed in the Beijing proceedings. On the facts of the case, the court adjourned the proceedings pending the outcome of the application before the Beijing court on the ground that there was *prima facie* evidence indicating that the setting aside application had some prospect of success.[1229] In *Powerex Corp v. Alcan Inc.*, the Supreme Court of British Columbia adjourned the enforcement proceedings on the ground that *inter alia* Alcan's action to set aside the award before the Oregon court was not frivolous and had an "arguable case which [was] not bound to fail".[1230] In *IPCO*, the English High Court of Justice adjourned enforcement proceedings on the ground that the setting aside application had a "realistic prospect of success".[1231] In *Toyo Engineering*, the Supreme Court of Victoria held that "it could not be stated with confidence that the impeachment application is unarguable" and, after

---

District Court, Southern District of New York, United States of America, 11 March 1996, 95 Civ. 10279, XXII Y.B. COM. ARB. 958 (1997).

1227 *Soleh Boneh International Ltd. v. Government of the Republic* of *Uganda and National Housing Corporation*, Court of Appeal, England and Wales, 12 March 1993, [1993] 2 Lloyd's Rep 208. See also *Inter-Arab Investment Guarantee Corporation v. Banque Arabe et Internationale d'Investissements*, Court of First Instance, Belgium, 25 January 1996; *Hallen v. Angledal*, Supreme Court of New South Wales, Australia, 10 June 1999, 50055 of 1999; *Dowans Holding S.A. v. Tanzania Electric Supply Co. Ltd.*, High Court of Justice, England and Wales, 27 July 2011, [2011] EWHC 1957 (Comm); Oberlandesgericht [OLG] Celle, Germany, 20 November 2003, 8 Sch 02/03.

1228 Rena Rico, *Searching for Standards: Suspension of Enforcement Proceedings under Article VI of the New York Convention*, 1 ASIAN INT'L ARB. J. 69, 74 (2005).

1229 *Hebei Import & Export Corp v. Polytek Engineering Co. Ltd.*, High Court in the Supreme Court of Hong Kong, Hong Kong, 1 November 1996, [1996] 3 HKC 725.

1230 *Powerex Corp. v. Alcan Inc.*, Supreme Court of British Columbia, Canada, 10 July 2003, 2003 BCSC 1096.

1231 *IPCO v. Nigeria (NNPC)*, High Court of Justice, England and Wales, 27 April 2005, [2005] EWHC 726 (Comm).

noting the short expected duration of the setting aside proceedings, decided to adjourn the enforcement proceedings.[1232]

41. While applying a similar approach, a number of courts have refused to adjourn enforcement proceedings. For example, in *Inter-Arab Investment Guarantee Corporation v. Banque Arabe et Internationale d'investissements*, the Brussels Court of First Instance refused to adjourn proceedings, holding that the party opposing enforcement had not proven the existence of a "reasonable possibility of annulment".[1233] Similarly, the Supreme Court of New South Wales refused to adjourn enforcement proceedings on the ground that the party opposing enforcement failed to provide "some evidence to show that there is a *prima facie* or reasonably arguable case" to set aside the award in the country where it was issued.[1234] In Germany, the Higher Regional Court of Celle refused to adjourn proceedings as it did not appear that the party opposing enforcement had a "prevailing interest" and the "prospects of success" of the application to set aside the award were "entirely uncertain".[1235] In England, the High Court of Justice denied adjournment in *Far Eastern Shipping* on the ground that the "proceedings upon which the defendants rely to justify their application for a stay afford no more than a remote and uncertain prospect of recovery at best."[1236]

42. A different approach has been adopted by some courts which have granted adjournments when the determination of the chances of success of a setting aside application involved issues of domestic law of the country where the application was pending. In *Construction Pioneers*, the United States District Court for the District of Columbia found that adjournment under article VI was proper as "for the court to decide this issue now, it would have to decide an intricate point of Ghana law that is more properly decided by a Ghana court." It held that "[i]f a final Ghanaian decision setting aside the Awards existed, the court would not be 'free as it sees fit to ignore [that] judgment'."[1237] This is based on the notion that domestic courts are

1232 *Toyo Engineering Corp v. John Holland Pty Ltd.*, Supreme Court of Victoria, Australia, 20 December 2000, 7565 of 2000.

1233 *Inter-Arab Investment Guarantee Corporation v. Banque Arabe et Internationale d'Investissements*, Court of First Instance, Belgium, 25 January 1996. This decision was upheld by the Brussels Court of Appeal: see *Inter-Arab Investment Guarantee Corporation v. Banque Arabe et Internationale d'Investissements*, Court of Appeal of Brussels, Belgium, 24 January 1997, XXII Y.B. COM. ARB. 643 (1997).

1234 *Hallen v. Angledal*, Supreme Court of New South Wales, Australia, 10 June 1999, 50055 of 1999.

1235 Oberlandesgericht [OLG] Celle, Germany, 20 November 2003, 8 Sch 02/03.

1236 *Far Eastern Shipping Co. v. AKP Sovcomflot*, High Court of Justice, Queen's Bench Division (Commercial Court), England and Wales, 14 November 1994, XXI Y.B. COM. ARB. 699 (1996).

1237 *CP Construction Pioneers Baugesellschaft Anstalt v. The Government of the Republic Ghana, Ministry of Roads and Transport*, District Court, District of Columbia, United States of America, 12 August 2008, 1:04-01564(LFO); *Spier v. Calzaturificio Tecnica S.p.A*, District Court, Southern District of New York, United States of America, 29 June 1987, 663 F.

"better situated" to resolve domestic legal issues.[1238] In the same vein, the United States District Court for the Southern District of New York stated that "the limited scope of review allowed under the Convention favors deference to proceedings in the originating country on the premise that a foreign court well versed in its own law is better suited to determine the validity of the award."[1239]

43. Certain commentators have argued that the appropriate standard for determining whether to adjourn enforcement proceedings under article VI of the Convention should not be the mere possibility or even the probability of inconsistent judgments, but rather a balancing of the potential harm to the parties.[1240] These commentators consider that the Convention refrains from stating that the operation of article VI depends upon the chances of success of the application to set aside the award and that, in light of the Convention's objective of facilitating and expediting the recognition and enforcement of foreign arbitral awards, the enforcing court retains independent discretion to either enforce or suspend enforcement of the award.

44. This approach has been endorsed in a number of decisions in which courts have balanced factors supporting adjournment against the Convention's main goal of facilitating and expediting the enforcement of foreign arbitral awards. In the words of the Federal Court of Australia, discretion must be weighed against the obligation of the Court to pay due regard to the objectives of the Act and "the spirit and intendment of the [Convention]".[1241] Similarly, United States courts have held that courts must exercise their discretion in determining whether to adjourn or stay the confirmation of an arbitral award "by balancing the Convention's policy in favor of confirming such award against the principle of international comity embraced by the Convention"[1242] and that the primary goal of the

---

Supp. 871; *Powerex Corp. v. Alcan Inc.*, Supreme Court of British Columbia, Canada, 30 June 2004, 2004 BCSC 876.

[1238] *Consorcio Rive, S.A. de C.V. v. Briggs of Cancun, Inc., David Briggs Enterprises, Inc.*, District Court, Eastern District of Louisiana, United States of America, 26 January 2000, 99-2205, XXV Y.B. COM. ARB. 1115 (2000). See also *IPCO v. Nigeria (NNPC)*, High Court of Justice, England and Wales, 27 April 2005, [2005] EWHC 726 (Comm).

[1239] *Sarhank Group v. Oracle Corporation*, District Court, Southern District of New York, United States of America, 9 October 2002, 2002 WL 31268635, XXVIII Y.B. COM. ARB. 1043 (2003).

[1240] GARY B. BORN, INTERNATIONAL COMMERCIAL ARBITRATION 2876 (2009); Christoph Liebscher, *Article VI*, in NEW YORK CONVENTION ON THE RECOGNITION AND ENFORCEMENT OF FOREIGN ARBITRAL AWARDS OF 10 JUNE 1958—COMMENTARY 438, 443 (R. Wolff ed., 2012); W. Michael Tupman, *Staying Enforcement of Arbitral Awards under the New York Convention*, 3 ARB. INT'L 209, 222 and 225 (1987).

[1241] *ESCO Corp v. Bradken Resources Pty Ltd.*, Federal Court, Australia, 9 August 2011, [2011] FCA 905.

[1242] *Jorf Lasfar Energy Company, S.C.A. v. AMCI Export Corporation*, District Court, Western District of Pennsylvania, United States of America, 22 December 2005, 05-0423; *Alto*

Convention to facilitate the recognition and enforcement of arbitral awards should weigh heavily on the district courts' determination.[1243] In *AB Götaverken v. General National Maritime Transport Co.*, the Supreme Court of Sweden refused to adjourn enforcement proceedings pending the outcome of the judicial proceedings in France, "[h]aving regard to the general aim of the New York Convention [...] to facilitate the enforcement of foreign arbitral awards."[1244] The President of the District Court of Amsterdam issued a similar ruling.[1245]

45. This approach has been followed by a number of decisions applying a multi-factor approach—such as *Europcar Italia SpA v. Maeillano Tours Inc* (and subsequent decisions in the United States which considered the same factors)[1246]—which invites courts to balance various factors in order to ascertain whether the rights of the parties are better preserved and protected through adjournment or enforcement.

C. The decision to order suitable security

46. A court that adjourns enforcement proceedings pursuant to article VI of the Convention "may also [...] order the other party to give suitable security". The Convention offers little guidance as to how this provision is to be applied, and instead provides the courts with a wide discretion to determine when to require security and in what amount and form.

47. The purpose of this provision is threefold. First, it seeks to avoid dissipation and concealment of assets pending the setting aside proceedings in the country where the award was rendered and thus guarantees that the award may be successfully enforced if the setting aside action is dismissed.[1247] Second, it provides an incentive to the party opposing

---

Mar Girassol v. Lumbermens Mutual Casualty Company, District Court, Northern District of Illinois Eastern Division, United States of America, 12 April 2005, 04 C 773.

[1243] *Europcar Italia, S.p.A. v. Maiellano Tours*, Court of Appeals, Second Circuit, United States of America, 2 September 1998, 97-7224.

[1244] *AB Götaverken v. General National Maritime Transport Company (GMTC), Libya and others*, Supreme Court, Sweden, 13 August 1979, VI Y.B. COM. ARB. 237 (1981).

[1245] *Southern Pacific Properties v. Arab Republic of Egypt*, President of the District Court of Amsterdam, Netherlands, 12 July 1984, X Y.B. COM. ARB. 487 (1985).

[1246] See, e.g., *China National Chartering Corp. et al. v. Pactrans Air & Sea Inc*, District Court, Southern District of New York, United States of America, 13 November 2009, 06 Civ. 13107 (LAK); *DRC Inc. v. Republic of Honduras*, District Court, District of Columbia, United States of America, 28 March 2011, 10-0003 (PLF); *Alto Mar Girassol v. Lumbermens Mutual Casualty Company*, District Court, Northern District of Illinois Eastern Division, United States of America, 12 April 2005, 04 C 773.

[1247] See *Soleh Boneh International Ltd. v. Government of the Republic of Uganda and National Housing Corporation*, Court of Appeal, England and Wales, 12 March 1993, [1993] 2 Lloyd's Rep 208; *Alto Mar Girassol v. Lumbermens Mutual Casualty Company*, District Court, Northern District of Illinois Eastern Division, United States of America, 12 April 2005, 04 C 773. See also GARY B. BORN, INTERNATIONAL COMMERCIAL ARBITRATION 2877 (2009).

enforcement to proceed with its application to set aside or suspend the award "as expeditiously as possible",[1248] thereby preventing delays.[1249] Third, it provides the party seeking to enforce the award with adequate assurances of prompt payment once the dispute is resolved.[1250]

a. Relationship between adjournment and security

48. Notwithstanding the discretionary power granted to courts to adjourn enforcement proceedings and order security, most courts only consider ordering the party opposing enforcement to post security in situations where they decide to adjourn enforcement proceedings. As a result, adjournment is sometimes considered as a pre-condition for the ordering of security.[1251]

49. Under article VI, only the party opposing enforcement can be ordered to provide security. In one reported case, a court decided that it was "justified that the claimants give security [...] for the case of anticipatory enforcement."[1252] Several years later, another court in the same jurisdiction held that the Convention offers no basis to order security from the party seeking enforcement.[1253] In 1993, a court in Germany held that pursuant to article VI of the Convention, a court may only order the party opposing enforcement to provide adequate security, but not the party seeking enforcement.[1254] Since then, it appears that courts have consistently refused to order the party seeking enforcement to provide security as a condition for enforcing the award.[1255]

1248 *Continental Transfert Technique Ltd. v. Federal Government of Nigeria*, High Court, England and Wales, 30 March 2010, [2010] EWHC 780 (Comm); *Soleh Boneh International Ltd. v. Government of the Republic of Uganda and National Housing Corporation*, Court of Appeal, England and Wales, 12 March 1993, [1993] 2 Lloyd's Rep 208.

1249 *Europcar Italia S.p.A. v. Alba Tours International Inc.*, Court of Justice of Ontario, Canada, 21 January 1997, CLOUT Case 366, XXVI Y.B. COM. ARB. 311 (2001).

1250 *Jorf Lasfar Energy Company, S.C.A. v. AMCI Export Corporation*, District Court, Western District of Pennsylvania, United States of America, 22 December 2005, 05-0423.

1251 *Gater Assets Ltd. v. Nak Naftogaz Ukrainiy*, Court of Appeal, England and Wales, 17 October 2007, [2007] EWCA Civ 988; *Yukos Oil Co. v. Dardana Ltd.*, Court of Appeal, England and Wales, 18 April 2002, [2002] EWCA Civ 543.

1252 *Henri Lièvremont and v. Adolphe Cominassi, Maatschappij voor Industriele Research en Ontwikkeling B.V.*, President of Rechtbank, Court of First Instance of Zutphen, Netherlands, 9 December 1981, VII Y.B. COM. ARB. 399 (1982).

1253 *Southern Pacific Properties v. Arab Republic of Egypt*, President of the District Court of Amsterdam, Netherlands, 12 July 1984, X Y.B. COM. ARB. 487 (1985).

1254 Oberlandesgericht [OLG] Frankfurt, Germany, 10 November 1993, 27 W 57/93. See also *Powerex Corp., formerly British Columbia Power Exchange Corporation v. Alcan Inc., formerly Alcan Aluminum Ltd.*, Court of Appeal of British Columbia, Canada, 4 October 2004, 2004 BCCA 504.

1255 See, e.g., *Gater Assets Ltd. v. Nak Naftogaz Ukrainiy*, Court of Appeal, England and Wales, 17 October 2007, [2007] EWCA Civ 988; *Yukos Oil Co. v. Dardana Ltd.*, Court of Appeal, England and Wales, 18 April 2002, [2002] EWCA Civ 543.

50. The fact that courts of Contracting States only consider whether to order security when contemplating adjournment does not mean that those courts should always order the party opposing enforcement to provide suitable security when an adjournment is granted.

51. In practice, courts often order security when adjourning proceedings. As stated by the Court of Appeal of England and Wales, security is the price to pay for adjournment and serves to protect the party seeking enforcement.[1256]

52. In *IPCO*, the English High Court of Justice held that it had jurisdiction, pursuant to section 103(5) of the 1996 Arbitration Act (implementing article VI of the Convention), to make adjournment of the decision on the enforcement of the award conditional upon the giving of security.[1257] In the United States, courts also require the party opposing enforcement to provide suitable security as a condition for granting an adjournment.[1258] In *Nedagro*, the United States District Court for the Southern District of New York refused to require the posting of security given that the defendant had already provided "suitable security" by attaching property in the amount due.[1259] In the Netherlands, the President of the District Court of Amsterdam denied a request for adjournment on the ground that the defendant "had not shown any readiness to give suitable security".[1260]

53. In cases where the courts have found adjournments to be conditional on the posting of security,[1261] courts have held that if the party opposing enforcement failed to provide the ordered security within the timeframe provided by the court, the court may decide to proceed with the

---

[1256] *Yukos Oil Co. v. Dardana Ltd*, Court of Appeal, England and Wales, 18 April 2002, [2002] EWCA Civ 543.

[1257] *IPCO v. Nigeria (NNPC)*, High Court of Justice, England and Wales, 27 April 2005, [2005] EWHC 726 (Comm).

[1258] See, e.g., *Alto Mar Girassol v. Lumbermens Mutual Casualty Company*, District Court, Northern District of Illinois, Eastern Division, United States of America, 12 April 2005, 04 C 773; *Nedagro B.V. v. Zao Konversbak*, District Court, Southern District of New York, United States of America, 21 January 2003, 02 Civ. 3946 (HB); *Skandia America Reinsurance Corporation v. Caja Nacional de Ahorro y Seguros*, District Court, Southern District of New York, United States of America, 21 May 1997, 96 Civ. 2301 (KMW), XXIII Y.B. COM. ARB. 956 (1998); *Consorcio Rive, S.A. de C.V., Briggs* of *Cancun, Inc., David Briggs Enterprises, Inc.*, District Court, Eastern District of Louisiana, United States of America, 26 January 2000, 99-2205, XXV Y.B. COM. ARB. 1115 (2000).

[1259] *Nedagro B.V. v. Zao Konversbak*, District Court, Southern District of New York, United States of America, 21 January 2003, 02 Civ. 3946 (HB).

[1260] *Southern Pacific Properties v. Arab Republic of Egypt*, President of the District Court of Amsterdam, Netherlands, 12 July 1984, X Y.B. COM. ARB. 487 (1985).

[1261] *Consorcio Rive, S.A. de C.V. v. Briggs of Cancun, Inc., David Briggs Enterprises, Inc.*, District Court, Eastern District of Louisiana, United States of America, 26 January 2000, 99-2205, XXV Y.B. COM. ARB. 1115 (2000).

enforcement.[1262] As stated by the United States District Court for the Southern District of New York in *Spier*: "[I]f a party such as [the defendant] fails to post security, then it would seem that the proper remedy would be to deny its application for an adjournment of the decision."[1263]

54. Courts in Australia and Canada have also ordered security when adjourning enforcement proceedings.[1264] In *Toyo*, the Supreme Court of Victoria held that the adjournment "will be subject to an undertaking by [the party opposing enforcement] that it will diligently prosecute its application in Singapore and, further, subject to a condition that suitable security be given by it for the unpaid amount of the award including interest to the adjourned date of the enforcement application."[1265]

55. This approach finds some support in the *travaux préparatoires* which state that adjournment may be granted "only on the condition that the party opposing enforcement deposits a suitable security."[1266] This view is shared by some commentators who consider that, in order to safeguard the rights of the party seeking enforcement, it should always be a condition of a stay that the party opposing enforcement provides security.[1267]

56. Still, in light of the permissive language of article VI, which provides that courts may, within the ambit of their discretion, decide whether or not to order security, a number of courts have, as is evidenced below, decided to adjourn enforcement proceedings without ordering security.

b. Factors considered by courts in deciding whether to order "suitable security"

57. In deciding whether to order that the party opposing enforcement give security, courts usually consider various factors, including the

---

[1262] *Ingaseosas International Co. v. Aconcagua Investing Ltd.*, Court of Appeals, Eleventh Circuit, United States of America, 5 July 2012, 11-10914; SKANDIA AMERICA REINSURANCE CORPORATION V. CAJA NACIONAL DE AHORRO Y SEGUROS, District Court, Southern District of New York, United States of America, 21 May 1997, 96 Civ. 2301 (KMW), XXIII Y.B. COM. ARB. 956 (1998).

[1263] *Martin Spier v. Calzaturifico Tecnica S.p.A.*, District Court, Southern District of New York, United States of America, 12 September 1988, 1988 WL 96839.

[1264] *Toyo Engineering Corp v. John Holland Pty Ltd.*, Supreme Court of Victoria, Australia, 20 December 2000, 7565 of 2000. See also *Powerex Corp. v. Alcan Inc.*, Supreme Court of British Columbia, Canada, 30 June 2004, 2004 BCSC 876.

[1265] *Toyo Engineering Corp v. John Holland Pty Ltd.*, Supreme Court of Victoria, Australia, 20 December 2000, 7565 of 2000.

[1266] *Travaux préparatoires*, United Nations Conference on International Commercial Arbitration, Summary Record of the Seventeenth Meeting, E/CONF.26/SR.17, p. 4.

[1267] GARY B. BORN, INTERNATIONAL COMMERCIAL ARBITRATION 2877 (2009); W. Michael Tupman, *Staying Enforcement of Arbitral Awards under the New York Convention*, 3 ARB. INT'L 209, 223 (1987).

likelihood of success of the petition to set aside or suspend the award, the likelihood that assets will still be available if enforcement is delayed, and the relative hardship caused to the parties by the order.

58. English courts take into account the likelihood that the award will be set aside in the country where it was issued and that assets will still be available if the court decides to adjourn the enforcement proceedings. In *Soleh Boneh*, the Court of Appeal of England and Wales held that two important factors must be considered: the strength of the argument that the award is invalid and the "ease or difficulty of enforcement of the award".[1268] As to the strength of the award, the court stated that "[i]f the award is manifestly invalid, there should be an adjournment and no order for security; if it is manifestly valid, there should either be an order for immediate enforcement, or else an order for substantial security." A similar approach was adopted in *APIS AS v. Fantazia.*[1269] In *IPCO*, the Court of Appeal overturned the lower court's decision ordering security on the basis that there was little risk of dissipation of assets and that the party opposing enforcement had a strong case in the setting aside proceedings.[1270]

59. Similarly, the High Court of Hong Kong considered the same factors in *Karaha Bodas Co. v. Perusahaan Minyak Dan Bumi Negara (Pertamina)*. After noting that the uncertain merits of Pertamina's case "appear [...] to weigh in favour of KBC's application for security", the High Court turned to the difficulty of enforcement and found that requiring Pertamina to pay a substantial amount in the short period of time remaining before the enforcement hearing in Hong Kong could have a "seriously adverse and unnecessarily unjust effect on Pertamina's position", while the absence of security would have "little adverse effect on KBC's position in the Hong Kong litigation" given Pertamina's substantial assets throughout the world. Accordingly, the High Court refused to order Pertamina to give security.[1271] In *Hebei*, the Supreme Court of Hong Kong dismissed the application to order security on the ground that the defendant was a "substantially local company with ample assets and that there was no reason to suppose that any risk existed for the plaintiff to be protected by an order of security."[1272]

[1268] *Soleh Boneh International Ltd. v. Government of the Republic* of *Uganda and National Housing Corporation*, Court of Appeal, England and Wales, 12 March 1993, [1993] 2 Lloyd's Rep 208.

[1269] *Apis AS v. Fantazia Kereskedelmi KFT*, High Court of Justice, England and Wales, 21 September 2000, [2001] 1 All ER (Comm).

[1270] *IPCO v. Nigeria (NNPC)*, High Court of Justice, England and Wales, 27 April 2005, [2005] EWHC 726 (Comm).

[1271] *Karaha Bodas Co. LLC v. Perusahaan Pertambangan Minyak Dan Gas Bumi Negara—Pertamina*, High Court of the Hong Kong Special Administrative Region, Hong Kong, 20 December 2002, XXVIII Y.B. COM. ARB. 752 (2003).

[1272] *Hebei Import & Export Corp v. Polytek Engineering Co. Ltd.*, High Court, Supreme Court of Hong Kong, Hong Kong, 1 November 1996, [1996] 3 HKC 725.

60. In the Cayman Islands, the Grand Court declined to order security in light of the "impracticability" of requiring the effective provision of security by the defendant within the short period of time remaining before the decision of the Paris Court of Appeal in the setting aside proceedings.[1273]

61. Courts in the United States do not assess the likelihood of the award being set aside when determining whether to order security, but rather focus on the effect a security order would have on the parties. In *Jorf*, the District Court for the Western District of Pennsylvania refused to order that the defendant give security on the ground that while there was no indication that the plaintiff had suffered financial hardship as a result of its inability to immediately enforce the award (notwithstanding that it had gone nearly a year without being able to access the money owed under the award), the security order would cause "real harm" to the defendant.[1274]

62. Certain courts in the United States have assessed whether a sovereign state or its instrumentalities could be ordered to give security. In 1997, the District Court for the Southern District of New York found that article VI of the Convention allowed it to require sovereigns to post pre-judgment security if they moved to set aside or suspend an arbitral award.[1275] In a recent decision, the District Court for the District of Columbia refused to require the Republic of Honduras "a sovereign state that presumably is solvent and will comply with legitimate orders issued by courts in this country or in Honduras" to post any security.[1276]

c. *Form and amount of the security*

63. Courts determine at their own discretion the amount and form of the security to be posted by the party opposing enforcement.

64. In most jurisdictions, courts order defendants to provide either a bank guarantee,[1277] a deposit of a given amount in an escrow account,[1278] a

---

1273 *The Republic of Gabon v. Swiss Oil Corporation*, Grand Court, Cayman Island, 17 June 1988, XIV Y.B. COM. ARB. 621 (1989).

1274 *Jorf Lasfar Energy Company, S.C.A. v. AMCI Export Corporation*, District Court, Western District of Pennsylvania, United States of America, 22 December 2005, 05-0423. See also *Alto Mar Girassol v. Lumbermens Mutual Casualty Company*, District Court, Northern District of Illinois Eastern Division, United States of America, 12 April 2005, 04 C 773.

1275 *Skandia America Reinsurance Corporation v. Caja Nacional de Ahorro y Seguros*, District Court, Southern District of New York, United States of America, 21 May 1997, 96 Civ. 2301 (KMW), XXIII Y.B. COM. ARB. 956 (1998).

1276 *DRC Inc. v. Republic of Honduras*, District Court, District of Columbia, United States of America, 28 March 2011, 10-0003 (PLF).

1277 *Apis AS v. Fantazia Kereskedelmi KFT*, High Court of Justice, England and Wales, 21 September 2000, [2001] 1 All ER (Comm).

1278 *The Republic of Gabon v. Swiss Oil Corporation*, Grand Court, Cayman Islands, 17 June 1988, XIV Y.B. COM. ARB. 621 (1989).

bond or other form of equally satisfactory security.[1279] As noted by a commentator, courts have expressed a preference for cash paid into escrow accounts or internationally recognized instruments of payment.[1280]

65. In *Spier*, the United States District Court for the Southern District of New York refused to allow the Italian party opposing enforcement to post a guarantee in an Italian Bank, holding that "the party seeking to enforce the award is entitled to security giving him a direct claim against either property or a guarantor resident in the country of enforcement", whereas the security suggested by the party opposing enforcement "could only be issued under and subject to Italian law" and would therefore be subject to "the inherent risk of further proceedings in Italy". The District Court therefore suggested that the party opposing enforcement either post a bond or issue "an irrevocable letter of credit from a bank located in New York".[1281]

66. In determining the amount of the security, courts have adopted different approaches which have taken into account the expected value of the award, the solvency of the party opposing enforcement, and the disincentive effect the security would have on a party considering dilatory tactics.[1282] Courts often order security in the amount of the entire award and require that any interest made on the security go to the party seeking enforcement so as to protect its economic interests.[1283]

67. In England, courts rarely grant security in the full amount of the award when the award is likely to be set aside by the competent authority in the country where it was issued.[1284] As stated by the Court of Appeal in *Soleh*, "if the award is manifestly valid, there should either be an order for immediate enforcement, or else an order for substantial security." Similarly,

---

1279 *Consorcio Rive, S.A. de C.V., Briggs of Cancun, Inc.*, David Briggs Enterprises, Inc., District Court, Eastern District of Louisiana, United States of America, 26 January 2000, 99-2205, XXV Y.B. COM. ARB. 1115 (2000).

1280 Nicola C. Port, Jessica R. Simonoff et al., *Article VI*, in RECOGNITION AND ENFORCEMENT OF FOREIGN ARBITRAL AWARDS: A GLOBAL COMMENTARY ON THE NEW YORK CONVENTION 415, 435 (H. Kronke, P. Nacimiento et al. eds., 2010).

1281 *I. Martin Spier v. Calzaturifico Tecnica S.p.A.*, District Court, Southern District of New York, United States of America, 12 September 1988, 1988 WL 96839.

1282 Nicola C. Port, Jessica R. Simonoff et al., *Article VI*, in RECOGNITION AND ENFORCEMENT OF FOREIGN ARBITRAL AWARDS: A GLOBAL COMMENTARY ON THE NEW YORK CONVENTION 415, 435 (H. Kronke, P. Nacimiento et al. eds, 2010).

1283 *Toyo Engineering Corp v. John Holland Pty Ltd.*, Supreme Court of Victoria, Australia, 20 December 2000, 7565 of 2000; *Alto Mar Girassol v. Lumbermens Mutual Casualty Company*, District Court, Northern District of Illinois Eastern Division, United States of America, 12 April 2005, 04 C 773; *Europcar Italia S.p.A. v. Alba Tours International Inc.*, Court of Justice of Ontario, Canada, 21 January 1997, CLOUT Case 366, XXVI Y.B. COM. ARB. 311 (2001).

1284 *Soleh Boneh International Ltd. v. Government of the Republic of Uganda and National Housing Corporation*, Court of Appeal, England and Wales, 12 March 1993, [1993] 2 Lloyd's Rep 208.

the Federal Court of Australia, referring to *Soleh*, ordered the party opposing enforcement to provide "substantial security".[1285] In *IPCO*, the English High Court of Justice ordered security in the amount of a percentage of the award and the immediate payment of the amount that was "indisputably due".[1286]

68. As to the timeframe for posting security, reported cases suggest that courts usually order the relevant party to post security within a 20-30 day period.[1287] This period may be longer depending on the form of the security.[1288]

1285 *ESCO Corp v. Bradken Resources Pty Ltd.*, Federal Court, Australia, 9 August 2011, NSD 876 of 2011.

1286 *IPCO v. Nigeria (NNPC)*, High Court of Justice, England and Wales, 27 April 2005, [2005] EWHC 726 (Comm).

1287 *Skandia America Reinsurance Corporation v. Caja Nacional de Ahorro y Seguros*, District Court, Southern District of New York, United States of America, 21 May 1997, 96 Civ. 2301 (KMW), XXIII Y.B. COM. ARB. 956 (1998); *Jorf Lasfar Energy Company, S.C.A. v. AMCI Export Corporation*, District Court, Western District of Pennsylvania, Unites States of America, 22 December 2005, 05-0423; *IPCO v. Nigeria (NNPC)*, High Court, England and Wales, 27 April 2005, [2005] EWHC 726 (Comm).

1288 See *Martin Spier v. Calzaturifico Tecnica S.p.A.*, District Court, Southern District of New York, United States of America, 12 September 1988, 1988 WL 96839: in this case, the Court directed the defendant to issue a letter of credit within ninety days.

Article VII

1. The provisions of the present Convention shall not affect the validity of multilateral or bilateral agreements concerning the recognition and enforcement of arbitral awards entered into by the Contracting States nor deprive any interested party of any right he may have to avail himself of an arbitral award in the manner and to the extent allowed by the law or the treaties of the country where such award is sought to be relied upon.

2. The Geneva Protocol on Arbitration Clauses of 1923 and the Geneva Convention on the Execution of Foreign Arbitral Awards of 1927 shall cease to have effect between Contracting States on their becoming bound and to the extent that they become bound, by this Convention.

Travaux préparatoires

The *travaux préparatoires* on article VII as adopted in 1958 are contained in the following documents:

Draft Convention on the Recognition and Enforcement of Foreign Arbitral Awards and comments by Governments and Organizations:

Report of the Committee on the Enforcement of International Arbitral Awards: E/2704 and annex.

Comments by Governments and Organizations on the Draft Convention on the Recognition and Enforcement of Foreign Arbitral Awards: E/2822, annexes I-II; E/2822/Add.1, annex I.

United Nations Conference on International Commercial Arbitration:

Amendments to the Draft Convention Submitted by Governmental Delegations: E/Conf. 26/7; E/Conf. 26/L.16; E/Conf. 26/L.44.

Summary records

Summary Records of the Eighteenth, Nineteenth and Twentieth Meetings of the United Nations Conference on International Commercial Arbitration: E/ CONF.26/SR.18; E/CONF.26/SR.19; E/CONF.26/SR.20.

Summary Record of the Eighth Meeting of the Committee on the Enforcement of International Arbitral Awards: E/AC.42/SR.8. See also E/AC.42/4/Rev.1.

(Available on the Internet at http://www.uncitral.org)

(For the *travaux préparatoires*, case law and bibliographical references, see also on the Internet at http://newyorkconvention1958.org)

Article VII (1)

Introduction

1. Article VII (1) governs the relationship of the New York Convention with other treaties and domestic law and is considered to be one of the cornerstones of the Convention.[1289] By stipulating that the Convention shall not affect the validity of other treaties concerning the recognition and enforcement of arbitral awards, and facilitating the application of rules on recognition and enforcement that may be more liberal than the Convention, article VII (1) ensures the Convention's compatibility with other international instruments as well as its durability, with the result that foreign arbitral awards are recognized and enforced to the greatest extent possible.

2. By virtue of article VII (1), Contracting States will not be in breach of the Convention by enforcing arbitral awards pursuant to provisions of domestic laws or treaties that are more favourable to enforcement. This reflects the notion that the New York Convention sets a "ceiling", or the maximum level of control, which national courts of the Contracting States may exert over the recognition and enforcement of arbitral awards.[1290]

[1289] One commentator has described this provision as "the treasure, the ingenious idea" of the New York Convention. See Philippe Fouchard, *Suggestions pour accroître l'efficacité internationale des sentences arbitrales*, 1998 REV. ARB. 653, 663.

[1290] See Philippe Fouchard, *La portée internationale de l'annulation de la sentence arbitrale dans le pays d'origine*, 1997 REV. ARB. 329; Emmanuel Gaillard, *Enforcement* of *Awards Set Aside in the Country* of *Origin: The French Experience*, in IMPROVING THE EFFICIENCY OF ARBITRATION AGREEMENTS AND AWARDS: 40 YEARS OF APPLICATION OF THE NEW YORK CONVENTION, ICCA CONGRESS SERIES No. 9, 505 (A.J. van den Berg ed., 1998); Emmanuel Gaillard, *The Urgency of Not Revising the New York Convention*, in 50

3. Article VII (1) was based on the text of article 5 of the 1927 Geneva Convention, which granted an interested party the right to avail itself of an arbitral award in the manner and to the extent allowed by the law or treaties of the State where the award was sought to be relied upon.[1291]

4. The drafters of the New York Convention built on article 5 of the 1927 Geneva Convention by adding the rule that the provisions of the Convention shall not affect the validity of multilateral or bilateral agreements concerning the recognition and enforcement of awards entered into by the Contracting States.[1292] This first part of article VII (1) has been referred to as "the compatibility provision". The second part of article VII (1), which allows an interested party to rely on a more favourable treaty or domestic law concerning recognition or enforcement instead of the Convention, has become widely known as the "more-favourable-right" provision.[1293]

5. While it may be useful for certain analytical purposes to bisect the paragraph into two parts, article VII (1), when read as a whole, enshrines the notion of "more favourable right". The first part of article VII (1) is merely a precursor to the second part, confirming that the validity of other treaties is not affected by the Convention, such that they can be relied upon by an interested party if more favourable. Thus, article VII (1) ensures that whenever the New York Convention proves to be less favourable than the provisions of another treaty or law of the country where recognition or enforcement is sought by a party seeking "to avail himself of an arbitral award", the more favourable rules shall prevail over the rules of the New York Convention.

YEARS OF THE NEW YORK CONVENTION: ICCA INTERNATIONAL ARBITRATION CONFERENCE, ICCA CONGRESS SERIES NO. 14, 689 (A.J. van den Berg ed., 2009).

1291 For the legislative history of article VII (1) of the New York Convention and article 5 of the 1927 Geneva Convention, see Gerald H. Pointon, *The Origins* of *Article VII.1* of *the New York Convention 1958*, in LIBER AMICORUM EN L'HONNEUR DE SERGE LAZAREFF 499 (L. Lévy, Y. Derains eds., 2011).

1292 *Travaux préparatoires*, Report of the Committee on the Enforcement of International Arbitral Awards, E/AC.42/4/Rev.1, p. 15.

1293 ALBERT JAN VAN DEN BERG, THE NEW YORK ARBITRATION CONVENTION OF 1958: TOWARDS A UNIFORM JUDICIAL INTERPRETATION 81 (1981); Emmanuel Gaillard, *The Relationship of the New York Convention with other Treaties and with Domestic Law*, in ENFORCEMENT OF ARBITRATION AGREEMENTS AND INTERNATIONAL ARBITRAL AWARDS: THE NEW YORK CONVENTION IN PRACTICE 69, 70 (E. Gaillard, D. Di Pietro eds., 2008).

Analysis

A. General principles

a. Meaning of "interested party"

6. Article VII (1) provides that, in addition to the New York Convention, any "interested party" shall not be deprived of the right to rely on a more favourable domestic law or treaty.

7. A Swiss court has confirmed that the term "interested party" refers only to the party seeking enforcement of an award, and not to the party opposing enforcement.[1294] In a case where an Italian party sought enforcement of an arbitral award against a Swiss party, the Zurich Court of First Instance rejected the argument of the Swiss party that it was, in application of article VII (1), entitled to rely on the more stringent conditions of the Swiss-Italian bilateral treaty on the Recognition and Enforcement of Judgments of 1933 to resist enforcement of the award. In the words of the Court, "the more-favourable-right principle does not provide the party opposing enforcement with further grounds for refusal than are listed in the Convention."

8. As leading commentators have noted, allowing a respondent to assert the more stringent conditions of another law or treaty would run counter to the pro-enforcement basis of the New York Convention.[1295]

9. According to the *travaux préparatoires* to the New York Convention, an "interested party" may also be a Contracting State. During the negotiation of the Convention, the State delegates considered that to expressly stipulate this eventuality would be superfluous, as it was self-evident from the text of article VII (1).[1296] At the date of this Guide, there is, however, no publicly available case law where a State has sought to rely on article VII (1).

[1294] *Italian party v. Swiss company*, Bezirksgericht, Zurich, Switzerland, 14 February 2003.

[1295] ALBERT JAN VAN DEN BERG, THE NEW YORK ARBITRATION CONVENTION OF 1958: TOWARDS A UNIFORM JUDICIAL INTERPRETATION 333-34 (1981); Emmanuel Gaillard, *The Relationship of the New York Convention with other Treaties and with Domestic Law*, in ENFORCEMENT OF ARBITRATION AGREEMENTS AND INTERNATIONAL ARBITRAL AWARDS: THE NEW YORK CONVENTION IN PRACTICE 69, 74-75 (E. Gaillard, D. Di Pietro eds., 2008).

[1296] *Travaux préparatoires*, Report of the Committee on the Enforcement of International Arbitral Awards, E/AC.42/4/Rev.1, p. 15.

b. Subject matter of more favourable right

10. Article VII (1) refers without restriction to "any right" allowed by the laws or the treaties of the country where such award is sought to be relied upon. The German Federal Court of Justice has confirmed that, in application of article VII (1), an enforcing court may take into account the domestic law's conflict-of-laws rules, which may result in the application of a foreign law more favourable to recognition and enforcement than the New York Convention.[1297]

c. Party request not necessary

11. Article VII (1) provides that the Convention shall not deprive any "interested party" from "availing" itself of an arbitral award.

12. Most courts have adopted the view that an interested party need not explicitly request recognition or enforcement on the basis of laws or treaties that are more favourable to enforcement.[1298] As a court will not be in breach of the New York Convention by applying more liberal rules on recognition and enforcement, it may rely on article VII (1) of its own motion. The French Court of Cassation, accordingly, has stated that "[t]he judge cannot refuse enforcement when its own national system permits it, and [...] he should, even *sua sponte*, research the matter if such is the case."[1299]

d. Multiple enforcement regimes permissible

13. In certain decisions, German courts have considered that a party seeking to rely on another treaty or domestic law by virtue of article VII (1) must rely on it in its entirety, to the exclusion of the New York Convention.[1300] According to these decisions, it would not be permissible

[1297] Bundesgerichtshof, Germany, III ZB 18/05, 21 September 2005, SchiedsVZ 2005, 306, where the application of German conflict-of-laws rules via article VII (1) of the Convention directed the Court to apply Dutch law, which contained more liberal formal requirements for an arbitration agreement than those under article II of the Convention.

[1298] *Société Pabalk Ticaret Sirketi v. Société Anonyme Norsolor*, Court of Cassation, France, 83-11.355, 9 October 1984, 1985 REV. ARB. 431, with English translation in 24 I.L.M. 360 (1985). German courts have adopted the same view. See Bundergerichtshof, Germany, III ZB 50/05, 23 February 2006, SchiedsVZ 2006, 161. The Swiss Federal Supreme Court has deviated from this view, without discussion. *Sudan Oil Seeds Co. Ltd. (U.K.) v. Tracomin S.A. (Switz.)* Federal Supreme Court, Switzerland, 5 November 1985, Arrêts du Tribunal Fédéral (1985) 111 Ib 253.

[1299] *Société Pabalk Ticaret Sirketi v. Société Anonyme Norsolor*, Court of Cassation, France, 83-11.355, 9 October 1984, 1985 REV. ARB.431, with English translation in 24 I.L.M. 360 (1985).

[1300] Bundesgerichtshof, Germany, III ZB 18/05, 21 September 2005; Bundesgerichtshof, Germany, III ZB 50/05, 23 February 2006; Bundesgerichtshof, Germany, III ZB 68/02, 25 September 2003. See also Albert Jan van den Berg, *The German Arbitration Act 1998 and the*

for a party to base a request for enforcement on the Convention and, at the same time, rely on the more liberal formal requirements for an arbitration agreement under German law.

14. A view advanced by a number of other German courts[1301] is that the pro-enforcement policy of the Convention would permit an interested party to select the more favourable rules and combine them with the provisions of the New York Convention.[1302] For instance, a Higher Regional Court has enforced an award pursuant to procedural requirements under German domestic law, which are more favourable than article IV of the Convention, while applying article V of the Convention in respect of possible grounds for refusal to enforce.[1303] A court in the United States of America has also granted enforcement to a foreign arbitral award by combining elements of the New York Convention and more favourable domestic law.[1304]

15. Furthermore, as described at para. 17 below, the Swiss Federal Supreme Court has held that where competing legal provisions concerning recognition and enforcement apply to the enforcement of an arbitral award, precedence should be given to "the provision that allows for making such recognition and enforcement easier," thus implicitly accepting a combined application of two systems.[1305]

B. Interaction of the Convention with other treaties

16. Certain arbitral awards or agreements may fall under the field of application of the New York Convention as well as the field of application of a multilateral or bilateral treaty. Article VII (1) provides the basic rule that the Convention shall not affect the validity of multilateral or bilateral treaties concerning the recognition and enforcement of arbitral awards entered into by the Contracting States to the Convention, and that an interested party may rely on those treaties if they are more favourable to enforcement than the Convention. This is in keeping with the broader objective of the New York

---

New York Convention 1958, in LAW OF INTERNATIONAL BUSINESS AND DISPUTE SETTLEMENT IN THE 21ST CENTURY—LIBER AMICORUM KARL-HEINZ BOCKSTIEGEL 783 (R. Briner et al. eds., 2001).

[1301] For instance, Oberlandesgericht[OLG] Celle, 8 Sch 06/06, 31 May 2007; Oberlandesgericht [OLG] Karlsruhe, 9 Sch 02/07, 14 September 2007; Oberlandesgericht [OLG] Köln, Germany, 9 Sch 01-03, 23 April 2004; Oberlandesgericht [OLG] München, Germany, 34 Sch 31/06, 23 February 2007.

[1302] JULIAN LEW, LOUKAS A. MISTELIS, COMPARATIVE INTERNATIONAL COMMERCIAL ARBITRATION 697-98 (2003); FOUCHARD GAILLARD GOLDMAN ON INTERNATIONAL COMMERCIAL ARBITRATION (E. Gaillard, J. Savage eds., 1999), 350.

[1303] Oberlandesgericht [OLG] Köln, Germany, 9 Sch 01-03, 23 April 2004.

[1304] *Chromalloy Aeroservices v. Arab Republic of Egypt*, District Court, District of Columbia, United States of America, 31 July 1996, 94-2339.

[1305] *Denysiana S.A. v. Jassica S.A.*, Federal Supreme Court, Switzerland, March 14, 1984, Arrêts du Tribunal Fédéral 110 Ib 191, 194.

Convention to provide for the recognition and enforcement of arbitral awards and agreements whenever possible, either on the basis of its own provisions or those of another instrument.

17. As the Swiss Federal Supreme Court has confirmed, article VII (1) thus derogates from the rules that normally govern the application of conflicting provisions of treaties, namely that a later legal rule prevails over a prior inconsistent legal rule ("*lex posterior derogat legi priori*") and that wherever two or more norms deal with the same subject matter, priority should be given to the norm that is more specific ("*lex specialis derogat legi generali*"). As the Court explained, the Convention replaces these rules with the principle of maximum effectiveness ("*règle d'efficacité maximale*") by providing that the instrument which prevails is neither the more recent nor the more specific, but instead that which is the more favourable to the enforcement of the foreign arbitral award. In the words of the Court, "[t]his solution corresponds to the so-called rule of maximum effectiveness [...]. According to this rule, in case of discrepancies between provisions in international conventions regarding the recognition and enforcement of arbitral awards, preference will be given to the provision allowing or making such recognition and enforcement easier, either because of more liberal substantive conditions or because of a simpler procedure. This rule is in conformity with the aim of bilateral or multilateral conventions in this matter, which is to facilitate, as much as possible, the recognition and enforcement of arbitral awards."[1306]

18. While the provisions of the New York Convention rarely compete with other international instruments concerning recognition and enforcement, where courts have been faced with such conflicts, they have typically resolved them under the more-favourable-right provision under article VII (1).

a. European Convention of 1961

19. The European Convention on International Commercial Arbitration (done in Geneva, 21 April 1961) is one of the few regional instruments containing more liberal rules governing the arbitral process than the New York Convention. It is the first international instrument to treat international arbitration as a whole, and consequently to provide rules governing all of its

[1306] *Id.* Courts in Spain have also endorsed that article VII (1) follows the principle of maximum effectiveness. See *Actival Internacional S.A. v. Conservas El Pilar S.A.*, Tribunal Supremo, Spain, 16 April 1996, 3868/1992; *Unión de Cooperativas Agrícolas Epis-Centre v. La Palentina S.A.*, Tribunal Supremo, Spain, 17 February 1998, 3587/1996, 2977/1996; *Delta Cereales España S.L. v. Barredo Hermanos S.A.*, Tribunal Supremo, Spain, 6 October 1998.

various stages. As of the date of this Guide, 32 States have signed the European Convention.[1307]

20. Under the European Convention, the recognition and enforcement of arbitral awards is considered only very indirectly.[1308] Accordingly, where an arbitration agreement or award falls within the field of application of both the European Convention and the New York Convention, courts have correctly considered that the provisions of the New York Convention concerning enforcement complement the provisions of the European Convention and that they need not apply the more-favourable-right provision at article VII (1). For instance, when considering an application for the enforcement of a foreign arbitral award, a Spanish court applied both instruments, noting that "the European Convention concerns the applicable law and the jurisdiction of judicial authorities and arbitrators, whereas the New York Convention concerns the recognition and enforcement of arbitral awards."[1309] German courts have affirmed the complementary nature of these instruments by reference to Section 1061(1) of the German Code of Civil Procedure, which provides that the stipulations of other treaties concerning the recognition and enforcement of arbitral awards will remain unaffected by the application of the New York Convention.[1310]

b. Panama Convention of 1975

21. The Inter-American Convention on International Commercial Arbitration (done in Panama, 30 January 1975) was modelled after the New

---

[1307] For the current status of the European Convention, see the United Nations Treaty Collection, http:// treaties.un.org/

[1308] Pursuant to its article I, the European Convention applies to "arbitration agreements concluded for the purpose of settling disputes from international trade between physical legal persons having, when concluded the agreement, their habitual place of residence or their seat in different Contracting States" and to "arbitral procedures and awards based on" such agreements. Its application thus differs from that of the New York Convention in two respects: (i) the European Convention applies only to disputes arising from international trade; and (ii) the European Convention requires that the parties to the arbitration agreement come from different Contracting States. The scope of application of the New York Convention contains neither of these two requirements and is thus broader.

[1309] *Nobulk Cargo Services Ltd. v. Compania Española de Laminación S.A.*, Tribunal Supremo, Spain, 27 February 1991. See also the same view expressed by French courts in *Société Européenne d'Etudes et d'Entreprises (S.E.E.E.) v. République Socialiste Fédérale de Yougoslavie*, Court of Appeal, Rouen, France, 13 November 1984, 982/82.

[1310] For instance, Oberlandesgericht [OLG] München, Germany, 34 Sch 019/08, 27 February 2009. In contrast, where a party opposing enforcement has alleged that an interested party may not rely on both the European Convention and the New York Convention in support of its request for enforcement, an Italian court has referred to the compatibility in the first clause of article VII (1) to support its finding that both instruments would apply. See *Arenco-BMD Maschinenfabrik GmbH v. Societá Ceramica Italiana Pozzi-Richard Ginori S.p.A.*, Corte di Appello, Milan, Italy, 16 March 1984.

York Convention and written to be fully compatible with it.[1311] The Panama Convention contains provisions concerning the recognition and enforcement of awards which are similar, but not identical, to those found in the New York Convention.[1312] At the date of this Guide, the Panama Convention is applicable in 19 countries, all of which are also Contracting Parties to the New York Convention.[1313]

22. According to a 2008 survey of decisions from Latin America, most Latin American States that are party to both instruments have relied exclusively on the New York Convention when recognizing and enforcing foreign arbitral awards.[1314]

23. The majority of reported cases expressly discussing the Panama Convention were rendered in the United States of America, whose Federal Arbitration Act contains provisions governing the relationship between the New York Convention and the Panama Convention. Section 305 of the Federal Arbitration Act provides that when both Conventions are applicable to an arbitral award or agreement, the Panama Convention shall apply if a majority of the parties to the arbitration agreement are citizens of a State or States that have ratified or acceded to the Panama Convention and are member States of the Organization of American States. At the same time, Section 302 of the Federal Arbitration Act mandates that certain provisions of the Federal Arbitration Act shall apply together with the provisions of the Panama Convention.[1315]

24. In practice, courts in the United States of America have applied the New York Convention and the Panama Convention as if they were identical. For instance, in a case before the United States District Court, when a party seeking to enforce an award relied on both the New York Convention and the Panama Convention, the Court limited its consideration to the New York

---

[1311] Albert Jan van den Berg, *The New York Convention 1958 and the Panama Convention of 1975: Redundancy or Compatibility?*, 5 ARB. INT'L 214 (1989).

[1312] For instance, unlike article II (3) of the New York Convention, the Panama Convention nowhere specifically requires the courts of a Contracting State to refer the parties to arbitration when seized of an action subject to an arbitration agreement falling under its field of application. While article 5 of the Panama Convention largely incorporates the grounds for refusal under article V of the New York Convention, the precise wording of these articles differs in several respects. Furthermore, unlike the New York Convention, the Panama Convention contains provisions governing other aspects of the arbitral process, such as the appointment of arbitrators (article 2), the conduct of the arbitral proceedings (article 3).

[1313] The current status of the Panama Convention is available online at: www.oas.org/juridico/english/ sigs/b-35.html.

[1314] Cristián Conejero Roos, *The New York Convention in Latin America: Lessons From Recent Court Decisions*, in 2009 THE ARBITRATION REVIEW OF THE AMERICAS 21.

[1315] United States Code, Title 9—Arbitration, § 302, which specifies: "Sections 202, 203, 204, 205, and 207 of this title shall apply to this chapter as if specifically set forth herein, except that for the purposes of this chapter 'the Convention' shall mean the Inter-American Convention."

Convention on the grounds that "codification of the Panama Convention incorporates by reference the relevant provisions of the New York Convention [...] making discussion of the Panama Convention unnecessary."[1316]

25. The effect of article VII (1) in cases where both the New York Convention and the Panama Convention apply has not been considered in reported case law. In specific cases, however, the Panama Convention may offer enhanced enforcement options compared to those of the New York Convention. For instance, Article 4 of the Panama Convention may, in certain cases, imply more favourable options for enforceability for arbitral awards than the New York Convention by equating final arbitral awards with final judicial judgments.[1317] Pursuant to the more-favourable-right provision of the New York Convention, a party seeking to enforce an award falling under both instruments could take advantage of such an option.

c. *Bilateral treaties*

26. In accordance with article VII (1), an interested party may base its request for enforcement on a bilateral agreement that specifically concerns the recognition and enforcement of foreign arbitral awards and agreements, as well as bilateral agreements that contain, *inter alia,* provisions on these issues.[1318] The conditions for recognition and enforcement under bilateral agreements may be more or less favourable than the New York Convention, depending on the circumstances surrounding the award.

27. As an illustration, German courts have applied more favourable provisions of bilateral treaties in accordance with article VII (1). In a case before the German Federal Court of Justice, an interested party was permitted to rely on the 1958 German-Belgian Treaty concerning the

---

[1316] *TermoRio S.A. E.S.P. v. Electrificadora del Atlantico S.A. E.S.P.*, District Court, District of Columbia, United States of America, 17 March 2006, 421 F. Supp. 2d 87, (D.D.C. 2006). See also *Productos Mercantiles E Industriales, S.A. v. Faberge USA Inc.*, United States Court of Appeals, Second Circuit, United States of America, 18 April 1994, 23 F.3d. 41, where the court noted, "The legislative history of the Inter-American Convention's implementing statute [...] clearly demonstrates that Congress intended the Inter-American Convention to reach the same results as those reached under the New York Convention."

[1317] Article 4 of the Panama Convention provides as follows: "An arbitral decision or award that is not appealable under the applicable law or procedural rules shall have the force of a final judicial judgment. Its execution or recognition may be ordered in the same manner as that of decisions handed down by national or foreign ordinary courts, in accordance with the procedural laws of the country where it is to be executed and the provisions of international treaties." This provision however mitigates the equality of treatment between arbitral awards and judicial judgements by stating that the recognition or enforcement of an award "may be ordered", in contrast to the imperative "shall" of article III of the New York Convention.

[1318] Franz Matscher, *Experience with Bilateral Treaties*, in IMPROVING THE EFFICIENCY OF ARBITRATION AGREEMENTS AND AWARDS: 40 YEARS OF APPLICATION OF THE NEW YORK CONVENTION, ICCA CONGRESS SERIES NO. 9, 452 (A.J. van den Berg ed., 1999).

Reciprocal Recognition and Enforcement of Judicial Decisions, Arbitral Awards and Official Documents in Civil and Commercial Matters, which provides that an award rendered in Belgium must be recognized and enforced in Germany when it has been declared enforceable in Belgium and does not violate German public policy.[1319]

28. Courts have also inquired whether an applicable bilateral treaty specifically excludes the application of the New York Convention, and in the event that it does not, have enforced awards pursuant to either the New York Convention, or more favourable domestic law provisions. For instance, in a 1997 decision —*Chromalloy*— the Paris Court of Appeal considered an argument advanced by Egypt that enforcement of an award should be denied, *inter alia,* because it violated Article 33 of the 1982 France-Egypt Convention on Judicial Cooperation (the "France-Egypt Convention").[1320] According to the Court, since the France-Egypt Convention expressly stipulates that the recognition and enforcement of awards should be granted in accordance with the provisions of the New York Convention, the States had implicitly consented to the application of any more favourable domestic law pursuant to article VII (1). Enforcing the award, the Court relied on the more limited grounds for refusal of enforcement under the then applicable Article 1502 of the French Code of Civil Procedure.[1321]

C. Interaction of the Convention with domestic law

29. Article VII (1) facilitates the recognition and enforcement of foreign arbitral awards by ensuring that Contracting States will not be in breach of the Convention by enforcing arbitral awards pursuant to more favourable provisions found in their domestic laws.

30. The domestic laws of Contracting States to the New York Convention take a variety of approaches to the recognition and enforcement of foreign arbitral awards. While the domestic arbitration law of some jurisdictions provides that recognition and enforcement is to take place

---

[1319] Bundesgerichtshof, Germany, III ZR 78/76, 9 March 1978. See also Bundesgerichtshof, Germany, III ZB 50/05, 23 February 2006, in which the Federal Supreme Court remanded a case back to the Oberlandesgericht [OLG] Karlsruhe, which, it considered, had erroneously examined a request to refuse enforcement to an arbitral award rendered in Minsk in light of the provisions of the New York Convention, instead of the more restricted grounds for non-enforcement of the 1958 Bilateral Treaty on General Issues of Commerce and Navigation between Germany and the former USSR, which continue to apply in respect of Belarus.

[1320] *République arabe d'Egypte v. Société Chromalloy Aero Services*, Court of Appeal of Paris, France, 14 January 1997.

[1321] For similar reasoning by German courts, see Bundesgerichtshof, Germany, XI ZR 349/89, 26 February 1991; Oberlandesgericht [OLG] Frankfurt, Germany, 6 U (Kart) 115/88, 29 June 1989; and by an Italian court see *Viceré Livio v. Prodexport*, Corte di Cassazione, 11 July 1992.

pursuant to the New York Convention,[1322] others contain specific provisions concerning recognition and enforcement.[1323] Other laws provide that a foreign award can be enforced if the court in the country where the award was rendered has entered a judgment on the award.[1324]

a. Domestic law more favourable than article II

31. Article VII (1) refers only to the enforcement of "arbitral awards" and not "arbitration agreements". As commentators have noted, the omission of arbitration agreements from the text of article VII (1) was unintentional[1325] and can be explained by the inclusion of the provisions concerning arbitration agreements in the New York Convention at a very late stage of its negotiation.[1326]

32. French courts have long considered that article VII (1) applies to the recognition and enforcement of arbitration agreements. Thus, in a series of decisions beginning in 1993, French courts have held that pursuant to article VII (1) of the Convention, arbitration agreements could be enforced under the more favourable provisions of French arbitration law, rather than the more stringent requirements of article II of the New York Convention.[1327]

33. As confirmation that article VII (1) also applies to arbitration agreements, at its thirty-ninth session, in 2006, UNCITRAL adopted a Recommendation regarding the interpretation of articles II (1) and VII (1) of

---

[1322] See, e.g., Switzerland, Private International Law Act, 1987, Article 194; Germany, Arbitration Act, 1998, Article 1061.

[1323] See, e.g., France, New Code of Civil Procedure, Articles 1504-1527; Netherlands, Code of Civil Procedure, Article 1076.

[1324] For instance, Italy, Code of Civil Procedure, Article 830; Colombia, Code of Civil Procedure, Decree Number 1400 and 2019 of 1970, Article 694(3).

[1325] ICCA'S GUIDE TO THE INTERPRETATION OF THE 1958 NEW YORK CONVENTION: A HANDBOOK FOR JUDGES 27 (P. Sanders ed., 2011); ALBERT JAN VAN DEN BERG, THE NEW YORK ARBITRATION CONVENTION OF 1958: TOWARDS A UNIFORM JUDICIAL INTERPRETATION 86-88 (1981).

[1326] *Travaux préparatoires*, United Nations Conference on International Commercial Arbitration, Summary Records of the Sixteenth Meeting, E/CONF.26/SR.16.

[1327] See *Bomar Oil N.V. v. Etap - L'Entreprise Tunisienne d'Activités Pétrolières*, Court of Cassation, France, 87-15.094, 9 November 1993, 1994 REV. ARB. 108; *American Bureau* of *Shipping (ABS) v. Copropriété maritime Jules Verne*, Court of Cassation, France, 03-12.034, 7 June 2006, 2006 REV. ARB. 945; *S.A. Groupama transports v.* Société *MS Regine Hans und Klaus Heinrich K.G.*, Court of Cassation, France, 05-21.818, 21 November 2006. The former Article 1443 of the French Code of Civil Procedure, in force from 1981, stipulated that an arbitration agreement shall be contained in the main convention or in a document to which the convention refers, without setting further requirements for the validity of an arbitration agreement in international arbitration matters. The current Article 1507 of the French Code of Civil Procedure applicable to international commercial arbitration provides that "[a]n arbitration agreement shall not be subject to any requirements as to its form." At the date of this Guide, there were no reported cases where a French court relied on this provision by virtue of article VII (1) of the Convention.

the New York Convention. The Recommendation clarifies that article VII (1) "should be applied to allow any interested party to avail itself of rights it may have, under the law or treaties of the country where an arbitration agreement is sought to be relied upon, to seek recognition of the validity of such an arbitration agreement."[1328]

34. Since the UNCITRAL Recommendation, courts from a number of Contracting States have, in the application of article VII (1), enforced arbitration agreements pursuant to any less stringent formal requirements under their domestic laws. For instance, in a recent decision the German Federal Court of Justice enforced an arbitral award involving two commercial parties in light of the theory of *kaufmännisches Bestätigungsschreiben*, which recognizes that commercial contracts, including arbitration agreements, may be concluded by the tacit acceptance of a confirmation letter between merchants.[1329] Dutch courts have similarly applied article VII (1) to enforce awards pursuant to a domestic law provision which stipulates that, upon request, a court shall deem effective an arbitration agreement which is not included in a contract signed by the parties or contained in an exchange of letters or telegrams, conditions which are otherwise required to be met by article II of the New York Convention.[1330]

35. The domestic laws of certain other national legal systems also contain fewer formal requirements for an arbitration agreement than the New York Convention. For example, Switzerland's international arbitration law

---

[1328] Recommendation regarding the interpretation of article II, paragraph 2, and article VII, paragraph 1, of the Convention on the Recognition and Enforcement of Foreign Arbitral Awards, done in New York, 10 June 1958 (2006), *Official Records of the General Assembly*, Sixty-first Session, Supplement No. 17 (A/61/17), paras. 177-181 and Annex II, available at www.uncitral.org/pdf/english/texts/arbitration/NY-conv/A2E.pdf. The *Travaux préparatoires* to the Recommendation are contained in *Official Records of the General Assembly*, Fifty-sixth Session, Supplement No. 17 (A/56/17), para. 313; Ibid., Fifty-seventh Session, Supplement No. 17 (A/57/17), para. 183; and in United Nations documents A/CN.9/468, paras. 88-106; A/CN.9/485, paras. 60-77; A/CN.9/487, paras. 42-63; A/CN.9/508, paras. 40-50; A/CN.9/592, paras. 82-88; A/CN.9/WG.II/WP.118, paras. 25-33; A/CN.9/607; and A/CN.9/609, and its addenda 1 to 6.

[1329] Bundesgerichtshof, Germany, III ZB 69/09, 30 September 2010, SchiedsVZ 2010, 332. See also Kammergericht Berlin, Germany, 20 Sch 09/09, 20 January 2011; Oberlandesgericht [OLG] Celle, Germany, 8 Sch 14/05, 14 December 2006. German courts enforced arbitration agreements pursuant to this notion even before the 2006 UNCITRAL Recommendation. See Oberlandesgericht [OLG] Köln, Germany, 16 W 43/92, 16 December 1992. The concept, as it relates to arbitration agreements, was codified in 1998 at Section 1031(2) of the new German Code of Civil Procedure, which is contained in the rules concerning domestic awards. The Oberlandesgericht [OLG] Frankfurt has considered that article VII (1) of the Convention, which refers to the laws that relate to the enforcement of foreign arbitral awards, would not necessarily lead to the application of Section 1031(2). See Oberlandesgericht [OLG] Frankfurt, Germany, 26 Sch 28/05, 26 June 2006.

[1330] *Claimant v. Ocean International Marketing B.V., et al.*, Rechtbank, Rotterdam, Netherlands, 29 July 2009, 194816/HA ZA 03-925.

provides that an arbitration agreement shall be valid if it is made "in writing, by telegram, telex, telecopier or any other means of communication which permits it to be evidenced by text."[1331] In a still broader manner, the United Kingdom Arbitration Act explicitly stipulates that the writing need not be signed by one of the parties and may result from a recording by one of the parties, or by a third party if authorized by parties to the agreement. A party seeking enforcement of an arbitral award could avail itself of these provisions pursuant to article VII (1) of the Convention.[1332]

b. *Domestic law more favourable than article IV*

36. Article IV of the New York Convention sets out the documents to be submitted by a petitioner to the enforcing court at the time of a request for recognition and/or enforcement, namely: a duly authenticated original award or duly certified copy thereof, the original agreement referred to in article II or a duly certified copy thereof and translations of these documents into the language of the country where the award is relied upon, where relevant.

37. Courts in Germany have consistently applied the more-favourable-right principle in article VII (1) to allow an interested party to rely on the less stringent requirements of German law, pursuant to which a party seeking enforcement of a foreign arbitral award in Germany need only supply the authenticated original arbitral award or a certified copy.[1333]

38. Likewise, German courts have referred to the more favourable provisions of their domestic law to dispense with the requirement under article IV (2) of the Convention that an interested party produce translations of the award and the original arbitration agreement.[1334] The same approach

---

[1331] Switzerland, Private International Law Act, 1987, Article 178(1).

[1332] United Kingdom, Arbitration Act 1996, c. 23, Section 5.

[1333] Germany, Code of Civil Procedure, Sections 1064(1) and (3). See, e.g., Oberlandesgericht [OLG] München, Germany, 34 Sch 14/09, 1 September 2009; Bundesgerichtshof, Germany, III ZB 68/02, 25 September 2003. See also Oberlandesgericht [OLG] München, 22 June 2009; Oberlandesgericht [OLG] München, 34 Sch 19/08, 27 February 2009; Oberlandesgericht [OLG] München, 34 Sch 18/08, 17 December 2008; Oberlandesgericht [OLG] Frankfurt, 17 October 2007; Oberlandesgericht [OLG] München, 23 February 2007; Oberlandesgericht [OLG] Celle, 14 December 2006; Kammergericht, 10 August 2006; Oberlandesgericht [OLG] München, 15 March 2006; Oberlandesgericht [OLG] München, 28 November 2005; Oberlandesgericht [OLG] Dresden, 7 November 2005; Oberlandesgericht [OLG] Dresden, 2 November 2005; Oberlandesgericht [OLG] Hamm, 27 September 2005; Bayerisches Oberstes Landesgericht, 11 August 2000. For a contrary opinion, see Oberlandesgericht [OLG] Rostock, Germany, 1 Sch 03/00, 22 November 2001, in which the court considered that Article VII (1) could not allow a party to dispense with the formal requirements for enforcement under the New York Convention.

[1334] For instance, Oberlandesgericht [OLG] Celle, Germany, 8 Sch 14/05, 14 December 2006; Kammergericht Berlin, 20 Sch 07/04, 10 August 2006. See also Oberlandesgericht [OLG] München, 28 November 2005; Oberlandesgericht [OLG] Hamm, 27 September 2005; Oberlandesgericht [OLG] Köln, 23 April 2004.

has been followed by courts in Switzerland, which apply the more favourable provision in Article 193(1) of the Swiss Private International Law Act.[1335]

c. *Domestic law more favourable than article V (1)(e)*

39. Pursuant to article VII (1) of the New York Convention, an interested party may seek the application of a national law if that is more favourable than the provisions of the Convention, including the grounds for refusal listed in article V. Among these grounds, article V (1)*(e)* provides that recognition and enforcement may be refused if the award "has been set aside or suspended by a competent authority of the country in which, or under the law of which, that award was made."

40. The legislative history of the Convention does not discuss the relationship between articles V (1)*(e)* and VII (1). In particular, there is no record that the State delegates or their governments contemplated whether an award that has been set aside or suspended could be enforced through the application of article VII (1).

41. The final text of the New York Convention does not prohibit a court in a Contracting State from recognizing or enforcing such an award, if it can be recognized or enforced pursuant to that State's domestic law or another treaty to which it is party. In application of the more-favourable-right provision under article VII (1), courts in certain Contracting States have thus consistently enforced awards that have been set aside or suspended.

42. For instance, in a series of decisions beginning in 1984, French courts have established a rule that a party opposing enforcement is precluded from relying on grounds for non-enforcement under article V (1)*(e)* of the Convention in light of the more limited grounds under French law.[1336] In the *Hilmarton* case of 1994, the Court of Cassation enforced an award rendered in Switzerland despite the fact that it had been set aside by the Swiss Federal Supreme Court and a new arbitral tribunal had been constituted to hear the dispute. The Court reasoned that "the award rendered in Switzerland is an international award which is not integrated in the legal system of that State,

---

[1335] Federal Supreme Court, Switzerland, 2 July 2012, Decision 5A_754/2011. Courts in the Netherlands have also enforced awards pursuant to Article 1076 of the Netherlands Civil Procedure Code, which is more favourable than article IV of the Convention: *Dubai Drydocks v. Bureau voor Scheeps- en Werktuigbouw [X] B.V.*, Rechtbank, Dordrecht, Netherlands, 30 June 2010, 79684/KG RK 09-85.

[1336] The former Article 1502 of the French Code of Civil Procedure, in force until 2011, provided an exhaustive list of the five grounds upon which recognition and enforcement could be refused in France. See *Société Pabalk Ticaret Sirketi v. Société Anonyme Norsolor*, Court of Cassation, France, 83-11.355, 9 October 1984, 1985 REV. ARB. 431, with English translation in 24 I.L.M. 360 (1985). Articles 1520 and 1525(4) of the French Code of Civil Procedure that is currently in force provide for the same grounds for refusal.

so that it remains in existence even if set aside and its recognition in France is not contrary to public policy."[1337]

43. French courts have followed this reasoning in a series of subsequent cases.[1338] In the 2007 *Putrabali* decision, for instance, the Court of Cassation affirmed that "[a]n international arbitral award, which is not anchored in any national legal order, is a decision of international justice whose validity must be ascertained with regard to the rules applicable in the country where its recognition and enforcement is sought. Under article VII [the interested party] [...] could invoke the French rules on international arbitration, which do not provide that the annulment of an award in the country of origin is a ground for refusing recognition and enforcement of an award rendered in a foreign country".[1339]

44. The same year, the Paris Court of Appeal found that the rule according to which the setting aside of an arbitral award in a foreign country does not affect the right of the interested party to request the enforcement of the award in France (since the arbitrator is not part of the national legal order of the country where the award was rendered) constitutes a "fundamental principle under French law."[1340]

45. In the 1996 *Chromalloy* decision, the United States District Court of Columbia took a similar view and allowed an application to enforce an award rendered in Egypt and subsequently annulled by a Court of Appeal in Egypt.[1341] The Court considered that in contrast to article V of the

---

1337 *Société OTV v. Société Hilmarton*, Court of Cassation, France, 10 June 1997. XX Y.B. COM. ARB. 663 (1995). The new tribunal ordered to be constituted by the Swiss Federal Supreme Court then rendered a conflicting second award ordering the respondent to pay a consulting fee under the contract at issue. The French Court of Cassation rejected a lower court ruling recognizing the second award and held that only the first award was recognized in France, ruling that the recognition in France of the first award, set aside outside France, necessarily prevented the recognition or enforcement in France of the second award.

1338 *Bargues Agro Industrie S.A. (France) v. Young Pecan Company (United States)*, Court of Appeal of Paris, France, 10 June 2004, 2004 REV. ARB. 733; *PT Putrabali Adyamulia v. S.A. Rena Holding*, Court of Appeal of Paris, France, 31 March 2005, 2006 REV. ARB. 665, affirmed by *PT Putrabali Adyamulia v. S.A. Rena Holding*, Court of Cassation, France, 05-18053, 29 June 2007, 2007 REV. ARB. 507; *Direction Générale de l'Aviation Civile de l'Emirat de Dubaï v. International Bechtel Co.*, Court of Appeal of Paris, France, 29 September 2005, 2006 REV. ARB. 695.

1339 *PT Putrabali Adyamulia v. S.A. Rena Holding*, Court of Cassation, France, 05-18053, 29 June 2007, 2007 REV. ARB. 507, *affirming PT Putrabali Adyamulia v. S.A. Rena Holding*, Court of Appeal of Paris, France, 31 March 2005, 2006 REV. ARB. 665.

1340 Court of Appeal of Paris, France, 18 January 2007, *Société S.A. Lesbats et Fils v. Volker le Docteur Grub*.

1341 *Chromalloy Aeroservices v. Arab Republic of Egypt*, District Court, District of Columbia, United States of America, 31 July 1996, 94-2339. See David W. Rivkin, *The Enforcement of Awards Nullified in the Country of Origin: The American Experience*, in IMPROVING THE EFFICIENCY OF ARBITRATION AGREEMENTS AND AWARDS: 40 YEARS OF APPLICATION OF THE NEW YORK CONVENTION, ICCA CONGRESS SERIES NO. 9, 528 (A.J. van

Convention, which sets out a "permissive standard" under which a court "may" refuse to enforce an award, article VII (1) "mandates that this Court must consider [the interested party's] claims under applicable U.S. law." The Court analysed whether the Egyptian Court's reasons for vacating the award were grounds that would have justified vacating a domestic award under Section 10 of the Federal Arbitration Act, Chapter 1. It held that, because the award would not have been vacated under Section 10, it should enforce the award in accordance with article VII (1) of the Convention.

46. Conversely, the New York Convention does not require courts in the Contracting States to recognize an award that has been set aside or suspended and they will not violate the Convention by refusing to do so.

47. Some courts have decided that the enforcement of an award should be refused if it has been set aside in the country where it was rendered. German courts, for instance, have adopted this position based on the previous version of the Code of Civil Procedure, which required the validity (*Rechtswirksamkeit*) of a foreign arbitral award as a precondition for its enforcement,[1342] as well as the new German Code of Civil Procedure, which provides that recognition and enforcement "shall be granted in accordance with [the New York Convention]", including the grounds for refusal under article V (1)*(e)*.[1343]

48. Similarly, courts in the United States of America have distinguished the 1996 *Chromalloy* decision and have declined to enforce awards that have been annulled or suspended.[1344] For instance, in the 1999 decision *Baker Marine*, the Court of Appeals for the Second Circuit refused to enforce two awards rendered in Nigeria and set aside by the Nigerian courts, rejecting the argument of the interested party that the awards were set aside for reasons that would not be recognized under United States law as valid grounds for

---

den Berg ed., 1998); See Emmanuel Gaillard, *The Relationship of the New York Convention with other Treaties and with Domestic Law*, in ENFORCEMENT OF ARBITRATION AGREEMENTS AND INTERNATIONAL ARBITRAL AWARDS: THE NEW YORK CONVENTION IN PRACTICE 69, 80-86 (E. Gaillard, D. Di Pietro eds., 2008); Georgios C. Petrochilos, *Enforcing Awards Annulled In Their State Of Origin Under The New York Convention*, 48 Int'l Comp. L.Q. 856 (1999).

1342 Oberlandesgericht [OLG] Rostock, Germany, 1 Sch 03/99, 28 October 1999. See Klaus Sachs, *The Enforcement of Awards Nullified in the Country of Origin: The German Experience*, in IMPROVING THE EFFICIENCY OF ARBITRATION AGREEMENTS AND AWARDS: 40 YEARS OF APPLICATION OF THE NEW YORK CONVENTION, ICCA CONGRESS SERIES NO. 9, 552 (A.J. van den Berg ed., 1998).

1343 Bundesgerichtshof, Germany, III ZB 14/07, 21 May 2007.

1344 *Baker Marine Ltd. v. Chevron Ltd.*, United States Court of Appeal, Second Circuit, United States of America, 12 August 1999, 191 F.3d 194; *TermoRio S.A. E.S.P. v. Electrificadora del Atlantico S.A. E.S.P.*, District Court, District of Columbia, United States of America, 17 March 2006, 421 F. Supp. 2d 87; *Martin Spier v. Calzaturificio Tecnica, S.p.A*, District Court, Southern District of New York, United States of America, 22 October 1999, 86 Civ. 3447.

vacating an award. The Court reasoned that the "mechanical application of domestic arbitral law to foreign awards under the Convention would seriously undermine finality and regularly produce conflicting judgments."[1345]

49. By contrast, a court's refusal to enforce an award that has been set aside or suspended could constitute a violation of the European Convention which, when applicable,[1346] expressly limits the grounds for refusal that are set out at article V of the New York Convention. In this relation, Article IX(2) of the European Convention provides that where a State is party to both the European Convention and the New York Convention, a court's discretion to refuse enforcement on the basis of an award having been set aside shall be limited to those cases where the award has been set aside for one of the limited reasons enumerated in its Article IX(1).[1347]

50. Pursuant to its obligation under the European Convention, the Austrian Supreme Court has enforced an award that had been set aside for violation of public policy in Slovenia, reasoning that "[p]ursuant to Article IX(1) of the European Convention, even the annulment of an award for public policy of the country of origin [...] is not one of the grounds for

---

1345 *Baker Marine Ltd. v. Chevron Ltd.*, United States Court of Appeal, Second Circuit, United States of America, 12 August 1999, 191 F.3d 194. The Court distinguished *Chromalloy* on the basis of the nationality of the interested party, who was not a United States citizen, and of a provision in the arbitration clause stating that the decision of the arbitrator "could not be subject to any appeal or other recourse".

1346 For the application of the European Convention, see the United Nations Treaty Collection, available at http://treaties.un.org

1347 Article IX(1) of the European Convention provides in full: "1. The setting aside in a Contracting State of an arbitral award covered by this Convention shall only constitute a ground for the refusal of recognition or enforcement in another Contracting State where such setting aside took place in a State in which, or under the law of which, the award has been made and for one of the following reasons: (a) the parties to the arbitration agreement were under the law applicable to them, under some incapacity or the said agreement is not valid under the law to which the parties have subjected it or, failing any indication thereon, under the law of the country where the award was made, or (b) the party requesting the setting aside of the award was not given proper notice of the appointment of the arbitrator or of the arbitration proceedings or was otherwise unable to present his case; or (c) the award deals with a difference not contemplated by or not falling within the terms of the submission to arbitration, or it contains decisions on matters beyond the scope of the submission to arbitration, provided that, if the decisions on matters submitted to arbitration can be separated from those not so submitted, that part of the award which contains decisions on matters submitted to arbitration need not be set aside; (d) the composition of the arbitral authority or the arbitral procedure was not in accordance with the agreement of the parties, or failing such agreement, with the provisions of Article IV of this Convention. 2. In relations between Contracting States that are also parties to the New York Convention on the Recognition and Enforcement of Foreign Arbitral Awards of 10th June 1958, paragraph 1 of this Article limits the application of Article V (1)*(e)* of the New York Convention solely to the cases of setting aside set out under paragraph 1 above."

refusal exhaustively listed [...] and is therefore not a ground for refusing enforcement in the enforcement state."[1348]

d. Domestic law more favourable than article VI

51. Article VI of the New York Convention provides that a court before which the enforcement of the award is sought "may", if it considers it proper, adjourn its decision on enforcement if the award is subject to an action for setting aside in the country in which, or under the law of which, it is made. In application of article VII (1) of the Convention, courts have applied domestic laws more favourable to recognition and enforcement than article VI in order to dispense with any suspensive effect of an action for setting aside.

52. For instance, in a 1999 decision, the Luxembourg Court of Appeal considered the argument of the party opposing enforcement that an award rendered in Switzerland had no *res judicata* effect in light of proceedings to set the award aside at the Swiss Federal Supreme Court and that pursuant to article VI of the New York Convention, enforcement proceedings in Luxembourg should be suspended pending this decision. Rejecting this argument, the Court noted that "the principle of *favor arbitrandum* [...] permeates the Convention" and in particular article VII (1), which is "aimed at making the enforcement of foreign awards possible in the highest number of cases." The Court reasoned that "according to the Convention the Luxembourg court can only deny enforcement on one of the grounds provided for in its national law." Since Article 1028(3) of the Luxembourg Code of Civil Procedure does not include the challenge of the award abroad among its grounds for refusal, it refused to suspend its decision and enforced the award.[1349]

53. French courts have also refused to suspend enforcement proceedings pending an action to set aside an award. In the 2004 *Bargues Agro* case, for instance, the Paris Court of Appeal refused to stay the enforcement of an award rendered in Belgium pending the conclusion of setting aside proceedings there, applying the more favourable provisions of French law.[1350] The Court noted that because the award was rendered in the context of an international arbitration, it was not anchored in the national legal order of Belgium and its potential setting aside could not prevent its recognition and enforcement in another Contracting State. The Court thus held that article VI of the Convention "is of no use in the context of the recognition

---

[1348] Supreme Court, Austria, 26 January 2005, 3Ob221/04b.

[1349] *Sovereign Participations International S.A. v. Chadmore Developments Ltd.*, Court of Appeal, Luxembourg, 28 January 1999.

[1350] *Société Bargues Agro Industries S.A. v. Société Young Pecan Company*, Court of Appeal of Paris, France, 10 June 2004.

and enforcement of an award under [the then applicable] Article 1502 of the Code of Civil Procedure."

e. Other more favourable domestic law practice

54. German courts have relied on article VII (1) of the New York Convention to apply the domestic law principle of preclusion, which provides that a party that has participated in an arbitration proceeding without objecting to a known defect before the arbitral tribunal will not, in general, be able to rely on that defect as a ground for refusal to recognize or enforce the award.[1351] German courts have interpreted Section 1044(2)(1) of the former Code of Civil Procedure as requiring the preclusion of objections against the award, for instance based on the invalidity of an arbitration agreement, if that ground could have been asserted in an action to set aside the award in the country where the award was made and a party had not availed itself of that possibility.

55. The German Code of Civil Procedure does not contain specific provisions setting out the grounds for refusal to recognize and enforce an award, but instead provides that "recognition and enforcement of foreign awards shall be granted in accordance with the New York Convention."[1352] There is a divergence of opinion among German courts on the question of whether the preclusion principle may be applied on the basis of the New York Convention only. Some courts have held that while the grounds for non-enforcement under article V of the New York Convention do not preclude defences in this manner, a German court may nonetheless apply this principle despite the fact that it finds no explicit expression in the current Civil Code of Procedure.[1353]

56. At the date of this Guide, the most recent decision of the German Federal Court of Justice on this issue has affirmed that the preclusion of defences should have limited applicability. According to the Court, it would not necessarily amount to bad faith for a party to raise a defect for the first time at the enforcement stage and such party would be precluded from doing

---

[1351] Oberlandesgericht [OLG] Düsseldorf, Germany, 8 November 1971; Bundesgerichtshof, Germany, III ZR 206/82, 10 May 1984. See also Albert Jan van den Berg, *The German Arbitration Act 1998 and the New York Convention 1958*, in LAW OF INTERNATIONAL BUSINESS AND DISPUTE SETTLEMENT IN THE 21ST CENTURY—LIBER AMICORUM KARL-HEINZ BOCKSTIEGEL 783 (R.G. Briner, Y.L. Fortier, P.K. Berger, J. Bredow eds., 2001).

[1352] Germany, Code of Civil Procedure, Section 1061.

[1353] For instance, Oberlandesgericht [OLG] Karlsruhe, Germany, 9 Sch 02/05, 27 March 2006; Oberlandesgericht [OLG] Karlsruhe, Germany, 9 Sch 02/09, 4 January 2012. Certain lower courts have deduced from the absence of such an explicit provision that no preclusion of defences may be applied under New York Convention. See, e.g., Bayerisches Oberstes Landesgericht, Germany, 4 Z Sch 50/99, 16 March 2000; Oberlandesgericht [OLG] Celle, Germany, 8 Sch 11/02, 4 September 2003.

so only where circumstances make the party's behaviour appear to be contrary to good faith and the principle of consistency with previous conduct ("*venire contra factum proprium*").[1354]

Article VII (2)

57. The New York Convention was conceived as a replacement for the 1923 Geneva Protocol on Arbitration Clauses and the 1927 Geneva Convention (together, the "Geneva Treaties"), which were considered too cumbersome a legal framework for the enforcement of arbitral awards in the context of the growth of international trade after the Second World War.

58. According to the *travaux préparatoires*, it was suggested that article VII (2) should expressly provide that the Geneva Treaties shall become extinct ("cease to have effect") between Contracting States "on their becoming bound by [the New York Convention]". The addendum, "to the extent they become bound", was introduced in the text to accommodate the Contracting States that would not become bound by the New York Convention in all their territories simultaneously and not to ensure the continued application of the Geneva Treaties.[1355] The *travaux préparatoires* further confirm that the replacement mandated by article VII (2) refers to the entirety of the Geneva Treaties: a proposal to limit their replacement to the degree that they were incompatible with the New York Convention was rejected during the drafting process.[1356]

59. The rules for recognition and enforcement under the New York Convention introduced a number of improvements to the regime provided by the Geneva Treaties.

60. First, the 1927 Geneva Convention, which applied to awards based on agreements covered by the 1923 Geneva Protocol, provided for the execution of a foreign award only if the party seeking to rely on it could demonstrate that the award was "final" in its country of origin.[1357] An interested party thus had to seek an exequatur (or leave for enforcement) in the country where the award was made before seeking enforcement in

---

1354 Bundesgerichtshof, Germany, III ZB 100/09, 16 December 2010.

1355 *Travaux préparatoires*, United Nations Conference on International Commercial Arbitration, Text of the Convention on the Recognition and Enforcement of Foreign Arbitral Awards as provisionally approved by the drafting Committee on 6 June 1958, E/CONF.26/L.61, pp. 3-4; *Travaux préparatoires*, United Nations Conference on International Commercial Arbitration, Summary Records of the Twenty-fourth Meeting, E/CONF.26/SR.24, p. 4. See also comments in Oberlandesgericht [OLG] Düsseldorf, 8 November 1971.

1356 *Travaux préparatoires*, United Nations Conference on International Commercial Arbitration, Summary Records of the Eighteenth Meeting, E/CONF.26/SR.18, p. 7.

1357 This notion was defined in article 1(d) of the 1927 Geneva Convention as an award that was not (i) open to any form of recourse or (ii) the subject of pending proceedings contesting its validity.

another country, thus giving rise to a requirement of *double exequatur*. The more liberal regime under the New York Convention does not require an award to be final, but only requires it to be "binding".

61. Second, in order for the 1923 Geneva Protocol and 1927 Geneva Convention to be applicable, the parties to the arbitration both had to be subject to the jurisdiction of the States parties to the respective treaties. The New York Convention, by contrast, only requires that the award be made in the territory of another Contracting State or in the enforcing State if the award is considered as non-domestic in the State where recognition and enforcement is sought.

62. Third, the burden of proof under the New York Convention is less onerous on the party seeking enforcement. Pursuant to article 1 of the 1927 Geneva Convention, an interested party was required to demonstrate the existence of a valid arbitration agreement, concerning an arbitral subject matter, that the arbitral proceedings had been conducted in accordance with the parties' agreement and also that the award had become final in the place of arbitration and was not contrary to the public policy of the recognizing State. Under the New York Convention, a party seeking enforcement need only supply to a court the original award (or a duly certified copy thereof) along with the original arbitration agreement (or a duly certified copy thereof), and a translation of those documents where they are not in the official language of the country where recognition and enforcement is sought. Under the New York Convention, it is up to the party opposing enforcement to prove the existence of one of the grounds for refusal enumerated in article V of the New York Convention.

63. Reported case law on article VII (2) confirms the principle that the Geneva Treaties shall cease to apply to the recognition and enforcement of foreign arbitral awards in Contracting States that have become bound by the New York Convention.[1358]

64. With very few exceptions, all States which had adhered to the Geneva Treaties have now become Parties to the New York Convention.[1359] Article VII (2) is therefore of limited practical relevance today.

[1358] For instance, *S.p.A. Nosegno e Morando v. Bohne Friedrich und Co-Import-Export*, Corte Di Cassazione, Italy, 20 January 1977; *Jassica S.A. v. Ditta Polojaz*, Corte di Appello, Trieste, Italy, 2 July 1982; Supreme Court, Austria, 21 February 1978; Oberlandesgericht [OLG] Düsseldorf, 8 November 1971; *Trefileries & Ateliers de Commercy (T.A.C.) v. Société Philipp Brothers France et Société Derby & Co. Limited*, Court of Appeal, Nancy, France, 5 December 1980; *Minister of Public Works of the Government of the State* of *Kuwait v. Sir Frederick Snow & Partners*, House of Lords, England, 1 March 1984, [1984] A.C. 426.

[1359] The status of former colonies that were Contracting States to the Geneva Treaties is not clear, as some of them have not made formal announcements regarding their status. See

Dirk Otto, *Article IV*, in RECOGNITION AND ENFORCEMENT OF ARBITRAL AWARDS: A GLOBAL COMMENTARY ON THE NEW YORK CONVENTION 143 (H. Kronke, P. Nacimiento et al. eds, 2010).

Article VIII

1. This Convention shall be open until 31 December 1958 for signature on behalf of any Member of the United Nations and also on behalf of any other State which is or hereafter becomes a member of any specialized agency of the United Nations, or which is or hereafter becomes a party to the Statute of the International Court of Justice, or any other State to which an invitation has been addressed by the General Assembly of the United Nations.

2. This Convention shall be ratified and the instrument of ratification shall be deposited with the Secretary-General of the United Nations.

Travaux préparatoires

The *travaux préparatoires* on article VIII as adopted in 1958 are contained in the following documents:

Draft Convention on the Recognition and Enforcement of Foreign Arbitral Awards and comments by Governments and Organizations:

Report of the Committee on the Enforcement of International Arbitral Awards: E/2704 and Annex.

Comments by Governments and Organizations on the Draft Convention on the Recognition and Enforcement of Foreign Arbitral Awards: E/2822, E/2822/Add.1, E/2822/Add.5, E/2822/Add.6

United Nations Conference on International Commercial Arbitration:

Amendments to the Draft Convention Submitted by Governmental Delegations: E/CONF. 26/4; E/CONF.26/7; E/CONF.26/L.51.

Text of the Convention on the Recognition and Enforcement of Foreign Arbitral Awards as Provisionally Approved by the Drafting Committee: E/CONF.26/L.61; E/CONF.26/8.

Summary records:

Summary Records of the Nineteenth, Twentieth, and Twenty-fourth Meeting of the United Nations Conference on International Commercial Arbitration: E/CONF.26/SR.19; E/CONF.26/SR.20, E/CONF.26/SR.24.

Summary Records of the Fourth and Eighth Meetings of the Committee on the Enforcement of International Arbitral Awards: E/AC.42/4; E/AC.42/4/Rev.1; E/AC.42/SR.8.

(Available on the Internet at http://www.uncitral.org)
(For the *travaux préparatoires*, case law and bibliographical references, see also on the Internet at http://newyorkconvention1958.org)

Analysis

1. Article VIII is part of the final provisions of the Convention. It sets out who may become a Party to the Convention and the procedure for becoming a party to the Convention. It also determines who acts as the depositary for the Convention.

Article VIII (1)

2. The Convention, which was concluded on 10 June 1958, was open for signature until 31 December 1958. Twenty-four States signed the Convention before this deadline.[1360] Article VIII (1) provides that any other States which did not sign the Convention before the deadline, have acceded, or shall then accede to the Convention in accordance with the provisions of article IX of the Convention.

3. The Convention is open for signature by any "Member of the United Nations".[1361] Article VIII (1) further provides that the Convention is open for signature by any other State which is or becomes a member of any specialized agency of the United Nations, or which is or becomes a party to the Statute of the International Court of Justice, or any other State to which the General Assembly of the United Nations addresses an invitation.

4. During the United Nations Conference on International Commercial Arbitration convened for the preparation and adoption of the Convention, a debate arose concerning the use of the term "State" in the definition of who

---

[1360] See information on the status of the Convention on the Internet at http://www.uncitral.org/uncitral/en/uncitral_texts/arbitration/NYConvention_status.html.

[1361] At the time of the adoption of the Convention in 1958, 82 States were members of the United Nations (see on the Internet: http://www.un.org/en/members/growth.shtml).

may become a Party to the Convention.[1362] According to some delegations, the term "State" could not be used because it had no uniform meaning.[1363] No "State" had been invited by the General Assembly to sign the Convention prior to 31 December 1958.

Article VIII (2)

A. Procedure for becoming a party

5. Article VIII (2) expressly provides for States to express their consent to be bound by the Convention by signature subject to ratification. This allows States to seek approval for the Convention at the domestic level and to enact any legislation necessary to implement the Convention domestically, prior to undertaking the legal obligations under the Convention at the international level.[1364]

6. The act by which a State expresses its consent to be bound by the Convention is distinct from the Convention's entry into force. Consent to be bound is the act whereby a State demonstrates its willingness to undertake the legal rights and obligations under the Convention through the deposit of an instrument of ratification (under article VIII (2)) or of accession (under article IX). On the other hand, entry into force is the moment the Convention becomes legally binding for a State; that is, the moment at which that State becomes Party to the Convention. That moment is defined under article XII.

B. Depositary

7. The Secretary-General of the United Nations is the depositary for the Convention.[1365] In practice, the Treaty Section of the United Nations Office of Legal Affairs carries out depositary functions on behalf of the Secretary-General.

[1362] Still, nowadays, the Secretary-General, as depositary, has stated on a number of occasions that it would fall outside his competence to determine whether a territory or entity falls within any "all States" formula. Pursuant to a general understanding adopted by the General Assembly on 14 December 1973, the Secretary-General will, in discharging his functions as depositary of a convention with the "all States" clause, follow the practice of the General Assembly and, whenever advisable, will request the opinion of the Assembly before receiving a signature or an instrument of ratification or accession (See *United Nations Juridical Yearbook*, 1973 (United Nations publication, Sales No. E.75.V.1), part two, chap. IV, sect. A.3 (at 79, note 9), *and ibid.*, 1974 (United Nations publication, Sales No. E.76.V.1), part two, chap. VI, sect. A.9 (at 157-159)).

[1363] E/2704, p. 15 and E/2822, p. 29; E/CONF.26/7, p. 1; E/CONF.26/SR.19, p. 2.

[1364] United Nations Treaty Handbook, para. 3.3.2.

[1365] The Secretary-General derives his authority as depository for multilateral treaties from: *(a)* Article 98 of the Charter of the United Nations; *(b)* provisions of the treaties themselves; *(c)* General Assembly resolution 24 (1) of 12 February 1946; and *(d)* League of Nations resolution of 18 April 1946 (see United Nations Treaty Handbook, para. 2.1).

Article IX

1. This Convention shall be open for accession to all States referred to in article VIII.

2. Accession shall be effected by the deposit of an instrument of accession with the Secretary-General of the United Nations.

Travaux préparatoires

The *travaux préparatoires* on article IX as adopted in 1958 are contained in the following documents:

Draft Convention on the Recognition and Enforcement of Foreign Arbitral Awards and comments by Governments and Organizations:

Report of the Committee on the Enforcement of International Arbitral Awards: E/2704 and Annex.

Comments by Governments and Organizations on the Draft Convention on the Recognition and Enforcement of Foreign Arbitral Awards: E/2822; E/2822/Add.1; E/2822/Add.4.

United Nations Conference on International Commercial Arbitration:

Amendments to the Draft Convention Submitted by Governmental Delegations: E/CONF. 26/7; E/CONF.26/L.57.

Text of the Convention on the Recognition and Enforcement of Foreign Arbitral Awards as Provisionally Approved by the Drafting Committee: E/CONF.26/L.61; E/CONF.26/8; E/CONF.26/8/Rev.1.

Summary records:

Summary Records of the Twentieth and Twenty-fourth Meetings of the United Nations Conference on International Commercial Arbitration: E/CONF.26/SR20; E/CONF.26/SR.24.

Summary Record of the Eighth Meeting of the Committee on the Enforcement of International Arbitral Awards: E/AC.42/SR.8.

(Available on the Internet at http://www.uncitral.org)
(For the *travaux préparatoires*, case law and bibliographical references, see also on the Internet at http://newyorkconvention1958.org)

Analysis

1. Article IX provides that the Convention is open for accession by all States that fall within the description provided at article VIII (1).[1366]

2. A State may generally express its consent to be bound by the Convention by depositing an instrument of accession with the depositary. Accession has the same legal effect as ratification. However, unlike ratification, which is preceded by signature to create binding legal obligations under international law, accession requires only one step, namely, the deposit of an instrument of accession. The Secretary-General, as depositary, treats instruments of ratification that have not been preceded by signature as instruments of accession, and the States concerned are advised accordingly. There is no mandated form for an instrument of accession, but it must include certain information.[1367]

[1366] See information on the status of the Convention on the Internet at http://www.uncitral.org/uncitral/en/uncitral_texts/arbitration/NYConvention_status.html.

[1367] See United Nations Treaty Handbook para. 3.3.5 and annex 5. The instrument of accession must include: (i) the title, date and place of conclusion of the treaty concerned; (ii) the full name and title of the person signing the instrument, i.e., Head of State, Head of Government or Minister for Foreign Affairs or any other person acting in such a position for the time being or with full powers for that purpose issued by one of the above authorities; (iii) an unambiguous expression of the intent of the Government, on behalf of the State, to consider itself bound by the treaty and to undertake faithfully to observe and implement its provisions; (iv) the date and place where the instrument was issued; and (v) the signature of the Head of State, Head of Government or Minister for Foreign Affairs (the official seal only is not adequate) or any other person acting in such a position for the time being or with full powers for that purpose issued by one of the above authorities.

Article X

1. Any State may, at the time of signature, ratification or accession, declare that this Convention shall extend to all or any of the territories for the international relations of which it is responsible. Such a declaration shall take effect when the Convention enters into force for the State concerned.

2. At any time thereafter any such extension shall be made by notification addressed to the Secretary-General of the United Nations and shall take effect as from the ninetieth day after the day of receipt by the Secretary-General of the United Nations of this notification, or as from the date of entry into force of the Convention for the State concerned, whichever is the later.

3. With respect to those territories to which this Convention is not extended at the time of signature, ratification or accession, each State concerned shall consider the possibility of taking the necessary steps in order to extend the application of this Convention to such territories, subject, where necessary for constitutional reasons, to the consent of the Governments of such territories.

Travaux préparatoires

The *travaux préparatoires* on article X as adopted in 1958 are contained in the following documents:

Draft Convention on the Recognition and Enforcement of Foreign Arbitral Awards and comments by Governments and Organizations:

Report of the Committee on the Enforcement of International Arbitral Awards: E/2704.

Comments by Governments and Organizations on the Draft Convention on the Recognition and Enforcement of Foreign Arbitral Awards: E/2822; E/2822/Add.1; E/2822/Add.6.

United Nations Conference on International Commercial Arbitration:

Amendments to the Draft Convention Submitted by Governmental Delegations: E/CONF.26/L.57; E/CONF. 26/L.61.

Text of the Convention on the Recognition and Enforcement of Foreign Arbitral Awards as Provisionally Approved by the Drafting Committee: E/CONF.26/8; E/CONF.26/8/Rev.1.

Summary records:

Summary Records of the Twentieth and Twenty-fourth Meetings of the United Nations Conference on International Commercial Arbitration: E/CONF.26/SR20; E/CONF.26/SR.24.

Summary Record of the Eighth Meeting of the Committee on the Enforcement of International Arbitral Awards: E/AC.42/SR.8.

(Available on the Internet at http://www.uncitral.org)
(For the *travaux préparatoires*, case law and bibliographical references, see also on the Internet at http://newyorkconvention1958.org)

Analysis

1. Article X addresses the question of the effect of the Convention in domestic territorial units. At the time the Convention was concluded, this had a specific meaning as a number of States had colonies or territories for which they were responsible.[1368]

2. Nowadays, such a provision mainly applies to federal States (dealt with under article XI of the Convention). To date, 10 countries have made declarations in relation to matters covered by article X.[1369]

[1368] See *Travaux préparatoires*, E/2704, annex p. 4, E/CONF/SR.20, pp. 2-5.

[1369] See information on the status of the Convention on the Internet at http://www.uncitral.org/uncitral/en/uncitral_texts/arbitration/NYConvention_status.html and United Nations Treaty Collection at https://treaties.un.org/.

Article XI

In the case of a federal or non-unitary State, the following provisions shall apply:

a) With respect to those articles of this Convention that come within the legislative jurisdiction of the federal authority, the obligations of the federal Government shall to this extent be the same as those of Contracting States which are not federal States;

b) With respect to those articles of this Convention that come within the legislative jurisdiction of constituent states or provinces which are not, under the constitutional system of the federation, bound to take legislative action, the federal Government shall bring such articles with a favourable recommendation to the notice of the appropriate authorities of constituent states or provinces at the earliest possible moment;

c) A federal State Party to this Convention shall, at the request of any other Contracting State transmitted through the Secretary-General of the United Nations, supply a statement of the law and practice of the federation and its constituent units in regard to any particular provision of this Convention, showing the extent to which effect has been given to that provision by legislative or other action.

Travaux préparatoires

The *travaux préparatoires* on article XI as adopted in 1958 are contained in the following documents:

Draft Convention on the Recognition and Enforcement of Foreign Arbitral Awards and comments by Governments and Organizations:

Report of the Committee on the Enforcement of International Arbitral Awards: E/2704.

Comments by Governments and Organizations on the Draft Convention on the Recognition and Enforcement of Foreign Arbitral Awards: E/2822; E/2822/Add.1; E/2822/Add.5; E/2822/Add.6.

United Nations Conference on International Commercial Arbitration:

Amendments to the Draft Convention Submitted by Governmental Delegations: E/CONF.26/4; E/CONF.26/L.57; E/CONF. 26/L.61. and Enforcement of Foreign Arbitral Awards as Provisionally Approved by the Drafting Committee: E/CONF.26/8; E/CONF.26/8/Rev.1.

Summary records:

Summary Records of the Twentieth and Twenty-fourth Meetings of the United Nations Conference on International Commercial Arbitration: E/CONF.26/SR20; E/CONF.26/SR.24.

Eighth Meeting of the Committee on the Enforcement of International Arbitral Awards: E/AC.42/SR.8.

(Available on the Internet at http://www.uncitral.org)
(For the *travaux préparatoires*, case law and bibliographical references, see also on the Internet at http://newyorkconvention1958.org)

Analysis

1. Article XI is of interest to relatively few States—namely, federal states where the central Government lacks treaty power to establish uniform law on matters covered by the Convention. It should be noted however that a State that has two or more territorial units is only entitled to make a declaration under article XI if different systems of law apply in those units in relation to matters dealt with in the Convention.

2. As shown in the *travaux préparatoires*, the text of article XI was the subject of lengthy debate. It has however not created any particular difficulty in practice. Similar provisions are commonly included in other international treaties.

3. In most of the Contracting States with a federal system (e.g., Austria, Germany, India, Switzerland, the United States) the enforcement of foreign arbitral awards is governed by federal legislation. In the United States, for instance, Congress implemented the Convention in 1970 by passing enabling legislation, making it the supreme law of the land that binds both the federal and state Governments. The Convention and its

implementing legislation were subsequently codified as Chapter 2 of Title 9 of the United States Code (i.e., Chapter 2 of the Federal Arbitration Act ("FAA")). As a result, United States courts are required to enforce all foreign arbitral awards, which are governed by the Convention, pursuant to Chapter 2 of the FAA. The United States Supreme Court has held that the Convention, as incorporated into federal law, is intended "to encourage the recognition and enforcement in international contracts and to unify the standards by which agreements to arbitrate are observed and arbitral awards are enforced in the signatory countries".[1370] This rationale is also expressed in a decision from the United States District Court for the District of Columbia, which noted that "[b]y acting at the federal level, Congress ensured that the enforcement of foreign arbitral awards in the United States would be governed by one set of 'uniform rules of procedure,' rather than a diversity of state ones as might have occurred pursuant to article XI".[1371] In *Sedco*, the Court of Appeals for the Fifth Circuit proclaimed that since its enactment, the Convention has been "the Supreme law of the land" and therefore, "[a]ny law or decision prior in time to this express undertaking must be construed as consistent with the Convention or set aside by it".[1372]

4. In a few Contracting States, the legislative power concerning the enforcement of foreign arbitral awards is divided between the federal and provincial levels. In Canada, the New York Convention has been implemented at the federal level through the United Nations Foreign Arbitral Awards Convention Act, which stipulates that the Convention applies only to "differences arising out of commercial legal relationships, whether contractual or not". The Commercial Arbitration Act codified the UNCITRAL Model Law on International Commercial Arbitration at the federal level. In the words of the Canadian Federal Court of Appeal, this Act applies only "in relation to matters where at least one of the parties to the arbitration is Her Majesty in right of Canada, a departmental corporation or a Crown corporation or in relation to maritime or admiralty matters".[1373] The Court further explained that "[l]egislation has also been enacted to implement the New York Convention and the Model Law in each province and territory (to the exception of Quebec), which applies to most civil matters, except those falling under the jurisdiction of the Federal State. As a

---

[1370] *Scherk v. Alberto-Culver Co.*, Supreme Court, United States of America, 17 June 1974, 417 United States 506.

[1371] *Commission Import Export S.A. v. Republic of the Congo and Caisse Congolaise d'Amortissement*, District Court, District of Columbia, United States of America, 11 July 2014, 13-7004.

[1372] *Sedco Inc Mobile Drilling Uni Sedco v. Petroleos Mexicanos Mexican National Oil Co.*, Court of Appeals, Fifth Circuit, United States of America, 12 August 1985, 767 F.2d 1140. See also *Murphy Oil USA Inc. v. SR International Business Insurance Company Ltd*, District Court, Western District of Arkansas, United States of America, 20 September 2007, 07-CV-1071.

[1373] Commercial Arbitration Act, R.S.C., 1985, c. 17 (2nd Supp.) Section 5(2).

result, commercial disputes in Canada may be subject to either federal or provincial jurisdiction, depending on the subject matter of the dispute". The Federal Court of Appeal specified that the enforcement of a foreign arbitral award in maritime matters falls under the jurisdiction of federal courts and reminded that "Parliament had jurisdiction to give the Convention the force of law in areas within its authority such as 'navigation and shipping'".[1374]

[1374] *Northern Sales Company Limited v. Compania Maritima Villa Nova S.A.*, Federal Court of Appeal, Winnipeg Manitoba, Canada, 20 November 1991, XVIII Y.B. Com. Arb. 363 (1993).

Article XII

1. This Convention shall come into force on the ninetieth day following the date of deposit of the third instrument of ratification or accession.

2. For each State ratifying or acceding to this Convention after the deposit of the third instrument of ratification or accession, this Convention shall enter into force on the ninetieth day after deposit by such State of its instrument of ratification or accession.

Travaux préparatoires

The *travaux préparatoires* on article XII as adopted in 1958 are contained in the following documents:

Draft Convention on the Recognition and Enforcement of Foreign Arbitral Awards and comments by Governments and Organizations:

Report of the Committee on the Enforcement of International Arbitral Awards: E/2704.

Comments by Governments and Organizations on the Draft Convention on the Recognition and Enforcement of Foreign Arbitral Awards: E/2822; E/2822/Add.1; E/2822/Add.6.

United Nations Conference on International Commercial Arbitration:

Amendments to the Draft Convention Submitted by Governmental Delegations: E/CONF.26/L.55.

Text of the Convention on the Recognition and Enforcement of Foreign Arbitral Awards as Provisionally Approved by the Drafting Committee: E/CONF. 26/L.61; E/CONF.26/8; E/CONF.26/8/Rev.1.

Summary records:

Summary Records of the Twentieth, Twenty-first and Twenty-fourth Meetings of the United Nations Conference on International Commercial Arbitration: E/CONF.26/SR20; E/CONF.26/SR.21; E/CONF.26/SR.24.

Summary Record of the Fourth Meeting of the Committee on the Enforcement of International Arbitral Awards: E/AC.42/SR.4.

(Available on the Internet at http://www.uncitral.org)
(For the *travaux préparatoires*, case law and bibliographical references, see also on the Internet at http://newyorkconvention1958.org)

Analysis

1. Article XII governs the date of entry into force of the New York Convention.

2. The Convention entered into force on 7 June 1959, ninety days following the deposit of the instrument of ratification by Egypt, Israel, Morocco and the Syrian Arab Republic. In accordance with article XII, Contracting States became bound by the Convention upon its entry into force on 7 June 1959 or ninety days after the deposit of any subsequent instrument of ratification or accession.[1375]

3. In addition to being relevant for the recognition and enforcement of arbitral awards under the Convention in the State concerned, the date on which the Convention becomes applicable in a given State may also be used as a point of reference when a State applies a reciprocity reservation.[1376]

4. A question often arises whether the Convention applies to the recognition and enforcement of arbitration agreements entered into, and arbitral awards rendered, before the adoption of the Convention by the State concerned.

5. As shown by the *travaux préparatoires*, that matter was discussed by the State delegations, and a proposal was made, but not adopted, that the Convention should only apply to arbitral awards rendered after the date of adoption of the Convention.[1377] Some States objected to this proposal on the

---

[1375] For issues relating to the date of entry into force of the convention, see Report on the survey relating to the legislative implementation of the Convention on the Recognition and Enforcement of Foreign Arbitral Awards (New York, 1958), Note by the Secretariat, A/CN.9/656, paras. 14-17.

[1376] For a more detailed discussion on the reciprocity reservation, see the chapter of the Guide on article I.

[1377] *Travaux préparatoires*, United Nations Conference on International Commercial Arbitration, Summary Records of the Twentieth Meeting, E/CONF.26/SR.20, p. 12, where the Delegation from Yugoslavia questioned whether the Convention would "apply to [foreign

basis that many arbitral awards would be denied the benefit of the Convention, which was intended to apply to as many awards as possible. As explained by Israel's representative, "[s]ince the purpose of the draft Convention was to make recognition and enforcement as easy as possible; it would be in accordance with sound legal practice for it to apply to awards made before the Convention's entry into force".[1378] The Swiss and French representatives further pointed out that "the Convention would apply only to unenforced awards which had not been brought before the courts. Such awards could not be many and there was no reason to exclude them. [...] The majority of such awards were voluntarily enforced and the draft Convention would therefore apply retroactively only to awards whose enforcement had been prevented by the bad faith of the losing party".[1379]

6. Since the Convention was adopted, very few States have formulated a reservation with regards to the retroactive application of the Convention.[1380]

7. In the majority of Contracting States, courts have considered that the Convention applies to (i) arbitration agreements signed before the Convention's entry into force in the enforcing State, and (ii) arbitral awards which pre-date the adoption of the Convention either by the State where the award was rendered or by the enforcing State.[1381]

8. First, courts have accepted to apply the Convention in situations where the contract containing the arbitration agreement had been signed before the Convention entered into force in the enforcing State.[1382] For instance, the Brazilian Superior Court of Justice held, without referring to

---

arbitral awards] which had become operative after entry force [of the Convention] or also to those which had become operative before". The drafting proposal to limit application of the convention to arbitral awards rendered after the coming into force of the Convention read: "This convention shall apply only to arbitral awards which acquired the force of *res judicata* and became final after the entry into force of the Convention" (see *Travaux préparatoires*, United Nations Conference on International Commercial Arbitration, Summary Records of the Twentieth Meeting, E/CONF.26/L.55).

1378 *Travaux préparatoires*, United Nations Conference on International Commercial Arbitration, Summary Records of the Twenty-first Meeting, E/CONF.26/SR.21, p. 2.

1379 *Travaux préparatoires*, United Nations Conference on International Commercial Arbitration, Summary Records of the Twenty-first Meeting, E/CONF.26/SR.21, pp. 2-3.

1380 See information on reservations under the New York convention on the Internet at http://www.uncitral. org/uncitral/en/uncitral_texts/arbitration/NYConvention_status.html.

1381 Albert Jan van den Berg, *Does the New York Arbitration Convention* of *1958 apply retroactively?: decision of the House of Lords in Government of Kuwait v. Sir Frederic Snow*, 1 ARB. INT'L 103 (1985).

1382 *Republic of Ecuador, Petroecuador (Ecuador) v. Chevron Texaco Corporation*, District Court, Southern District of New York, United States of America, 27 June 2005, 376 F. Supp. 2d 334, XXXI Y.B. COM. ARB. 1162 (2006); *Travel Automation Ltd. v. Abacus International Pvt. Ltd. and others*, High Court of Karachi, Pakistan, Suit No. 1318 of 2004, 14 February 2006, XXXII Y.B. COM. ARB. (2007).

article XII of the Convention, that the fact that the arbitration agreement was signed prior to the Arbitration Act implementing the Convention was immaterial because procedural laws, such as the Arbitration Act, had immediate effect under Brazilian law.[1383]

9. Second, with few exceptions,[1384] courts have applied the Convention when an arbitral award had been rendered in a State which had not yet acceded to the Convention. For instance, the English House of Lords applied the 1975 Arbitration Act implementing the New York Convention to an arbitral award rendered in Kuwait prior to Kuwait's accession to the Convention. Without referring to article XII, the House of Lords held that the relevant time to assess whether a State was a "contracting state" was the time of enforcement, and not the time the award was made.[1385] Similarly, a German court applied the New York Convention to enforce an arbitral award rendered in London one month prior to the United Kingdom's accession to the Convention. The Court held that the Convention, having a procedural character, applies retroactively.[1386] Courts have also applied the Convention when an award was rendered before the State in which enforcement is sought had acceded to the Convention. In the United States, for instance, the Court of Appeals for the Second Circuit held that the Convention should apply retroactively to an arbitral award rendered in Japan on 18 September 1970, even though the Convention only came into force in the United States on 20 December 1970.[1387]

10. In the same vein, certain courts have applied the Convention retroactively in accordance with their national legislation implementing the Convention. For instance, the Canadian Federal Court applied the Convention with respect to an award rendered one year prior to Canada's accession pursuant to section 4(2) of the United Nations Foreign Arbitral

---

[1383] *Spie Enertrans S.A. v. Inepar S.A. Industria e Construcoes*, Superior Court of Justice, Brazil, 3 October 2007, SEC 831.

[1384] See *Société Nationale pour la Recherche, le transport et la Commercialisation des Hydrocarbures (Sonatrach) v. Ford, Bacon and Davis Inc.*, Court of First Instance of Brussels, Belgium, 6 December 1988, XV Y.B. COM. ARB. 370 (1990). See also *Murmansk State Steamship Line v. Kano Oil Millers Ltd.*, Supreme Court, Nigeria, 11 December 1974, VII Y.B. COM. ARB. 349 (1982); *Commoditex S.A. v. Alexandria Commercial Co.*, Court of Justice of Geneva, Switzerland, 12 May 1967, I Y.B. COM. ARB. 199 (1976).

[1385] *Sir Frederic Snow & Partners and Others (United Kingdom) v. Minister Public Works of the Government of Kuwait*, House of Lords, England and Wales, 1 March 1984, X Y.B. COM. ARB. 508 (1985).

[1386] *German (F.R.) buyer v. English seller*, Hanseatisches Oberlandesgericht [OLG] Hamburg, Germany, 27 July 1978, IV Y.B. COM. ARB. 266 (1979). See also *German party v. Austrian party*, Oberster Gerichtshof Austria, 17 November 1965, I Y.B. COM. ARB. 182 (1976).

[1387] *Copal Co. Ltd. v. Fotochrome Inc.*, District Court, Eastern District of New York, United States of America, 4 June 1974 and *Copal Co. Ltd. v. Fotochrome Inc.*, Court of Appeals, Second Circuit, United States of America, 29 May 1975, I Y.B. COM. ARB. 202 (1976).

Awards Convention Act, which provides that the Convention is to apply to "arbitral awards and arbitration agreements whether made before or after the coming into force of this Act".[1388]

[1388] *Compania Maritima Villa Nova S.A. v. Northern Sales Co.*, Federal Court of Appeal, Canada, 20 November 1991.

Article XIII

1. Any Contracting State may denounce this Convention by a written notification to the Secretary-General of the United Nations. Denunciation shall take effect one year after the date of receipt of the notification by the Secretary-General.

2. Any State which has made a declaration or notification under article X may, at any time thereafter, by notification to the Secretary-General of the United Nations, declare that this Convention shall cease to extend to the territory concerned one year after the date of the receipt of the notification by the Secretary-General.

3. This Convention shall continue to be applicable to arbitral awards in respect of which recognition or enforcement proceedings have been instituted before the denunciation takes effect.

Travaux préparatoires

The *travaux préparatoires* on article XIII as adopted in 1958 are contained in the following documents:

Draft Convention on the Recognition and Enforcement of Foreign Arbitral Awards and comments by Governments and Organizations:

Report of the Committee on the Enforcement of International Arbitral Awards: E/2704.

Comments by Governments and Organizations on the Draft Convention on the Recognition and Enforcement of Foreign Arbitral Awards: E/2822; E/2822/Add.1.

United Nations Conference on International Commercial Arbitration:

Amendments to the Draft Convention Submitted by Governmental Delegations: E/CONF.26/L.57.

Text of the Convention on the Recognition and Enforcement of Foreign Arbitral Awards as Provisionally Approved by the Drafting Committee: E/CONF. 26/L.61; E/CONF.26/8; E/CONF.26/8/Rev.1.

Summary records

Summary Records of the Twentieth and Twenty-fourth Meetings of the United Nations Conference on International Commercial Arbitration: E/CONF.26/SR20; E/CONF.26/SR.24.

Summary Record of the Fourth Meeting of the Committee on the Enforcement of International Arbitral Awards: E/AC.42/SR.4.

(Available on the Internet at http:// www.uncitral.org)
(For the *travaux préparatoires*, case law and bibliographical references, see also on the Internet http://www.newyorkconvention1958.org)

Analysis

1. A Contracting State may denounce the Convention in accordance with the provisions of article XIII. To date, no Contracting State has withdrawn from or denounced the Convention.

Article XIV

A Contracting State shall not be entitled to avail itself of the present Convention against other Contracting States except to the extent that it is itself bound to apply the Convention.

Travaux préparatoires

The *travaux préparatoires* on article XIV as adopted in 1958 are contained in the following documents:

Draft Convention on the Recognition and Enforcement of Foreign Arbitral Awards and comments by Governments and Organizations:

Report of the Committee on the Enforcement of International Arbitral Awards: E/2704.

Comments by Governments and Organizations on the Draft Convention on the Recognition and Enforcement of Foreign Arbitral Awards: E/2822; E/2822/Add.1; E/2822/Add.4.

United Nations Conference on International Commercial Arbitration:

Amendments to the Draft Convention Submitted by Governmental Delegations: E/CONF.26/4; E/CONF.26/L.56; E/CONF.26/L.57.

Text of the Convention on the Recognition and Enforcement of Foreign Arbitral Awards as Provisionally Approved by the Drafting Committee: E/CONF.26/8; E/CONF.26/8/Rev.1.

Summary records:

Summary Records of the Twentieth, Twenty-first and Twenty-fourth Meetings of the United Nations Conference on International Commercial Arbitration: E/CONF.26/SR20; E/CONF.26/SR21; E/CONF.26/SR.24.

(Available on the Internet at http://www.uncitral.org)

(For the *travaux préparatoires*, case law and bibliographical references, see also on the Internet http://www.newyorkconvention1958.org)

Analysis

1. Pursuant to article XIV, a Contracting State may only require another Contracting State to apply the Convention to the extent that it is itself bound by it. Article XIV is a general reciprocity clause that applies to obligations between Contracting States under all provisions of the Convention. This distinguishes article XIV of the Convention from article I (3), which contains a specific reciprocity provision that may be invoked by private parties in the context of enforcement proceedings.[1389]

2. As reflected in the *travaux préparatoires*, article XIV was originally drafted in almost identical wording as a second paragraph of the then article X addressing the rights and duties of federal or non-unitary contracting states (now article XI).[1390] As drafted at the time, this proposed reciprocity provision did not meet unanimous approval, as some delegations wished to clarify that it would only apply to federal states.[1391] It was not until the United Nations Conference on International Commercial Arbitration convened for the preparation and adoption of the Convention that the representative for Norway proposed an amendment for a general reciprocity clause that would stand as a separate article.[1392] A majority of the delegates accepted this amendment on the very last day of the Conference.

3. Parties opposing enforcement of an arbitration agreement or an arbitral award have rarely invoked article XIV and its reciprocity requirement. Based on available case law at the time of this Guide,

---

[1389] Albert Jan van den Berg, *Consolidated Commentary Cases Reported in Volumes XXII (1997) - XXVII (2002)*, XXVIII Y.B. COM. ARB. 699 (2003), para. 914. See also Patricia Nacimiento, *Article XIV*, in RECOGNITION AND ENFORCEMENT OF FOREIGN ARBITRAL AWARDS: A GLOBAL COMMENTARY ON THE NEW YORK CONVENTION 541, 544 (H. Kronke, P. Nacimiento et al. eds., 2010).

[1390] *Travaux préparatoires*, Report of the Committee on the Enforcement of International Arbitral Awards, E/2704, E/AC.42/4/Rev.1, pp. 15-16, and E/2704, E/AC.42/4/Rev.1, Annex, p. 5.

[1391] See, e.g., the comments by Yugoslavia on article X, *Travaux préparatoires*, Comments by Governments on the draft Convention on the Recognition and Enforcement of Foreign Arbitral Awards, E/2822/Add.6, Annex, pp. 2-3.

[1392] *Travaux préparatoires*, Consideration of the draft Convention on the Recognition and Enforcement of Foreign Arbitral Awards (Item 4 of the Agenda), Norway: proposed amendment to the draft Convention, E.CONF.26/L.28; *Travaux préparatoires*, United Nations Conference on International Commercial Arbitration, Summary Records of the Twenty-Fourth Summary Meeting, E/CONF.26/SR.24, pp. 6-7.

enforcement of an arbitral award has never been denied on the basis of article XIV.[1393]

4. One example of an unsuccessful attempt to rely on article XIV's reciprocity requirement is found in *Fertilizer Corporation of India v. IDI Management Inc.*, a decision from the United States District Court for the Southern District of Ohio. An arbitral award was rendered in India against a United States corporation, which argued before the Court that it should not be enforced in the United States on grounds that India would not have enforced the award had it been rendered in the United States in its favour, and that therefore, "the reciprocity between India and the United States as required by the Convention [article XIV] was absent".[1394] The contesting party further argued that article XIV requires courts to determine the extent to which India applies the Convention and whether India treats awards rendered in India in favour of Indian parties in a similar manner. The Court rejected this argument and enforced the award, finding that the Convention's reciprocity requirement was satisfied in that case. It noted that article XIV gave "states a defensive right to take advantage of another state's reservations with regard to territorial, federal or other provisions". The Court added that, in any event, it was satisfied that Indian courts were not engaged in a "devious policy to subvert the Convention by denying non-Indians their just awards".

5. In another case, the United States Court of Appeals for the Fifth Circuit emphasized the importance of respecting the reciprocity undertaking in article XIV. The Court reasoned that the rights of United States citizens under the Convention in other countries depend on the extent to which the United States "implements the Convention within its own borders".[1395]

6. Leading commentators have confirmed that article XIV does not allow a Contracting State which has not made any reservation, to deny

---

[1393] See, e.g., *Union of India, and others v. Lief Hoegh & Co. and others*, High Court of Gujarat, India, 4 May 1982, AIR 1983 Guj 34; *Audi NSU Auto Union A.G. v. Overseas Motors, Inc.*, District Court, Eastern District of Michigan, Southern Division, United States of America, 9 August 1976, II Y.B. COM. ARB. 252 (1977); *M.A. Industries Inc. v. Maritime Battery Ltd.*, New Brunswick Court of Queen's Bench, Canada, 19 August 1991, XVIII Y.B. COM. ARB. 354 (1993); *Odin Shipping Co. (Pte) Ltd. v. Aguas Industriales de Tarragona*, Supreme Court, Spain, 4 October 1983, XI Y.B. COM. ARB. 528 (1986). See also with respect to the recognition and enforcement of an arbitration agreement: *McDermott International v. Lloyds Underwriters of London*, Court of Appeals, Fifth Circuit, United States of America, 14 February 1992, 91-841, XVIII Y.B. COM. ARB. 472 (1993); *Ken Acosta (United States), et al. v. Master Maintenance and Construction Inc., et al.*, Court of Appeals, Fifth Circuit, United States of America, 8 June 2006, 05-30126.

[1394] *Fertilizer Corporation of India v. IDI Management Inc.*, District Court, Southern District of Ohio, Western Division, United States of America, 9 June 1981, C-1-79-570.

[1395] *Beiser v. Weyler*, Court of Appeals, Fifth Circuit, United States of America, 19 March 2002, 01-20152.

enforcement of an award rendered in another Contracting State which has made reservations. Conversely, a State which formulated a reservation under article I (3) would not be permitted to invoke the Convention against another Contracting State which had ratified the Convention without making any reservation.[1396]

[1396] See Angela Kolbl, *Commentary on Article XIV*, in NEW YORK CONVENTION ON THE RECOGNITION AND ENFORCEMENT OF FOREIGN ARBITRAL AWARDS OF 10 JUNE 1958—COMMENTARY 529, 531 (R. Wolff ed., 2012); Patricia Nacimiento, *Article XIV*, in RECOGNITION AND ENFORCEMENT OF FOREIGN ARBITRAL AWARDS: A GLOBAL COMMENTARY ON THE NEW YORK CONVENTION 541, 544 (H. Kronke, P. Nacimiento et al. eds., 2010).

Article XV

The Secretary-General of the United Nations shall notify the States contemplated in article VIII of the following:

a) Signatures and ratifications in accordance with article VIII;

b) Accessions in accordance with article IX;

c) Declarations and notifications under articles I, X and XI;

d) The date upon which this Convention enters into force in accordance with article XII;

e) Denunciations and notifications in accordance with article XIII.

Travaux préparatoires

The *travaux préparatoires* on article XV as adopted in 1958 are contained in the following documents:

Draft Convention on the Recognition and Enforcement of Foreign Arbitral Awards and comments by Governments and Organizations:

Report of the Committee on the Enforcement of International Arbitral Awards: E/2704.

Comments by Governments and Organizations on the Draft Convention on the Recognition and Enforcement of Foreign Arbitral Awards: E/2822; E/2822/Add.1.

United Nations Conference on International Commercial Arbitration:

Amendments

Drafting Committee: E/CONF.26/8; E/CONF.26/8/Rev.1.

Summary records:

Summary Records of the Twenty-first and Twenty-fourth Meetings of the United Nations Conference on International

Commercial Arbitration: E/CONF.26/SR21; E/CONF.26/SR.24.

(Available on the Internet at http:// www.uncitral.org)
(For the *travaux préparatoires*, case law and bibliographical references, see also on the Internet http://www.newyorkconvention1958.org)

Analysis

Article XV contains a list of notifications to be made by the Secretary-General of the United Nations as depositary for the Convention. This article is consistent with the actions to be undertaken by depositaries under international treaties.

Article XVI

1. This Convention, of which the Chinese, English, French, Russian and Spanish texts shall be equally authentic, shall be deposited in the archives of the United Nations.

2. The Secretary-General of the United Nations shall transmit a certified copy of this Convention to the States contemplated in article VIII.

Travaux préparatoires

The *travaux préparatoires* on article XVI as adopted in 1958 are contained in the following documents:

Draft Convention on the Recognition and Enforcement of Foreign Arbitral Awards and comments by Governments and Organizations:

Report of the Committee on the Enforcement of International Arbitral Awards: E/2704.

Comments by Governments and Organizations on the Draft Convention on the Recognition and Enforcement of Foreign Arbitral Awards: E/2822; E/2822/Add.1.

United Nations Conference on International Commercial Arbitration:

Amendments to the Draft Convention Submitted by Governmental Delegations: E/CONF.26/L.57; E/CONF.26/L.61.

Text of the Convention on the Recognition and Enforcement of Foreign Arbitral Awards as Provisionally Approved by the Drafting Committee: E/CONF.26/8; E/CONF.26/8/Rev.1.

Summary records:

Summary Record of the Twenty-first Meeting of the United Nations Conference on International Commercial Arbitration: E/CONF.26/SR21.

(Available on the Internet at http://www.uncitral.org)
(For the *travaux préparatoires*, case law and bibliographical references, see also on the Internet http://www.newyorkconvention1958.org)

Analysis

1. Article XVI provides that Chinese, English, French, Russian and Spanish—the official languages of the United Nations at the time of the preparation of the Convention—are the authentic languages of the Convention and are to be considered equally authoritative. The Convention does not include provision on how to address situations of diverging language versions.

2. Although some commentators have identified potential differences between the authentic versions of the Convention,[1397] none of the reported cases have discussed the matter of divergent language versions.

3. In case an ambiguity would exist in one of the authentic language versions of the Convention, courts could normally apply the rules of interpretation provided in the Vienna Convention on the Law of Treaties of 1969. Pursuant to Articles 31 and 32 of the Vienna Convention, "[a] treaty shall be interpreted in good faith in accordance with the ordinary meaning to be given to the terms of the treaty in their context and in the light of its object and purpose" and "[r]ecourse may be had to supplementary means of interpretation, including the preparatory work of the treaty and the circumstances of its conclusion, in order to confirm the meaning resulting from the application of article 31".

4. In *Kahn Lucas Lancaster Inc. v. Lark International Ltd.*, the United States Court of Appeals for the Second Circuit relied on the versions of the Convention listed in article XVI to assist it in interpreting the meaning of article II (2). In addition to its textual analysis of the English-language version, the Court reviewed article II (2) in each of the four other languages deemed to be authentic (i.e., Chinese, French, Russian and Spanish).[1398] The Court concluded that like the English version, the French, Spanish and Chinese versions of article II (2) suggest that regardless of whether an agreement to arbitrate is found in an arbitration clause in a contract or as a

[1397] See, e.g., Dorothee Schramm, Elliott Geisinger et al., *Article XVI*, in RECOGNITION AND ENFORCEMENT OF FOREIGN ARBITRAL AWARDS: A GLOBAL COMMENTARY ON THE NEW YORK CONVENTION 555, 556 (H. Kronke, P. Nacimiento et al. eds., 2010).

[1398] *Kahn Lucas Lancaster Inc. v. Lark International Ltd.*, Court of Appeals, Second Circuit, United States of America, 29 July 1999, 97-9436, XXIV Y.B. COM. ARB. 900 (1999). On this issue, see the chapter of the Guide on article II.

separate arbitration agreement, it must be signed by the parties or contained in an exchange of letters. The Court stated that it was "reluctant to allow the seemingly contradictory Russian language version to dictate a different result. This is particularly so in light of the stated purposes of the Convention, one of which is to 'unify the standards by which agreements to arbitrate are observed and arbitral awards are enforced in the signatory countries.'" The Court's interpretation of article II (2) was confirmed by the drafting and legislative history of this provision.

ANNEX I
Convention on the Recognition and Enforcement of Foreign Arbitral Awards (New York, 10 June 1958)

Article I

1. This Convention shall apply to the recognition and enforcement of arbitral awards made in the territory of a State other than the State where the recognition and enforcement of such awards are sought, and arising out of differences between persons, whether physical or legal. It shall also apply to arbitral awards not considered as domestic awards in the State where their recognition and enforcement are sought.

2. The term "arbitral awards" shall include not only awards made by arbitrators appointed for each case but also those made by permanent arbitral bodies to which the parties have submitted.

3. When signing, ratifying or acceding to this Convention, or notifying extension under article X hereof, any State may on the basis of reciprocity declare that it will apply the Convention to the recognition and enforcement of awards made only in the territory of another Contracting State. It may also declare that it will apply the Convention only to differences arising out of legal relationships, whether contractual or not, which are considered as commercial under the national law of the State making such declaration.

Article II

1. Each Contracting State shall recognize an agreement in writing under which the parties undertake to submit to arbitration all or any differences which have arisen or which may arise between them in respect of a defined legal relationship, whether contractual or not, concerning a subject matter capable of settlement by arbitration.

2. The term "agreement in writing" shall include an arbitral clause in a contract or an arbitration agreement, signed by the parties or contained in an exchange of letters or telegrams.

3. The court of a Contracting State, when seized of an action in a matter in respect of which the parties have made an agreement within the meaning of this article, shall, at the request of one of the parties, refer the parties to

arbitration, unless it finds that the said agreement is null and void, inoperative or incapable of being performed.

Article III

Each Contracting State shall recognize arbitral awards as binding and enforce them in accordance with the rules of procedure of the territory where the award is relied upon, under the conditions laid down in the following articles. There shall not be imposed substantially more onerous conditions or higher fees or charges on the recognition or enforcement of arbitral awards to which this Convention applies than are imposed on the recognition or enforcement of domestic arbitral awards.

Article IV

1. To obtain the recognition and enforcement mentioned in the preceding article, the party applying for recognition and enforcement shall, at the time of the application, supply:

(a) The duly authenticated original award or a duly certified copy thereof;

(b) The original agreement referred to in article II or a duly certified copy thereof.

2. If the said award or agreement is not made in an official language of the country in which the award is relied upon, the party applying for recognition and enforcement of the award shall produce a translation of these documents into such language. The translation shall be certified by an official or sworn translator or by a diplomatic or consular agent.

Article V

1. Recognition and enforcement of the award may be refused, at the request of the party against whom it is invoked, only if that party furnishes to the competent authority where the recognition and enforcement is sought, proof that:

(a) The parties to the agreement referred to in article II were, under the law applicable to them, under some incapacity, or the said agreement is not valid under the law to which the parties have subjected it or, failing any indication thereon, under the law of the country where the award was made; or

(b) The party against whom the award is invoked was not given proper notice of the appointment of the arbitrator or of the arbitration proceedings or was otherwise unable to present his case; or

(c) The award deals with a difference not contemplated by or not falling within the terms of the submission to arbitration, or it contains decisions on matters beyond the scope of the submission to arbitration, provided that, if the decisions on matters submitted to arbitration can be separated from those not so submitted, that part of the award which contains decisions on matters submitted to arbitration may be recognized and enforced; or

(d) The composition of the arbitral authority or the arbitral procedure was not in accordance with the agreement of the parties, or, failing such agreement, was not in accordance with the law of the country where the arbitration took place; or

(e) The award has not yet become binding on the parties, or has been set aside or suspended by a competent authority of the country in which, or under the law of which, that award was made.

2. Recognition and enforcement of an arbitral award may also be refused if the competent authority in the country where recognition and enforcement is sought finds that:

(a) The subject matter of the difference is not capable of settlement by arbitration under the law of that country; or

(b) The recognition or enforcement of the award would be contrary to the public policy of that country.

Article VI

If an application for the setting aside or suspension of the award has been made to a competent authority referred to in article V (1) (e), the authority before which the award is sought to be relied upon may, if it considers it proper, adjourn the decision on the enforcement of the award and may also, on the application of the party claiming enforcement of the award, order the other party to give suitable security.

Article VII

1. The provisions of the present Convention shall not affect the validity of multilateral or bilateral agreements concerning the recognition and enforcement of arbitral awards entered into by the Contracting States nor deprive any interested party of any right he may have to avail himself of an arbitral award in the manner and to the extent allowed by the law or the treaties of the country where such award is sought to be relied upon.

2. The Geneva Protocol on Arbitration Clauses of 1923 and the Geneva Convention on the Execution of Foreign Arbitral Awards of 1927 shall cease to have effect between Contracting States on their becoming bound and to the extent that they become bound, by this Convention.

Article VIII

1. This Convention shall be open until 31 December 1958 for signature on behalf of any Member of the United Nations and also on behalf of any other State which is or hereafter becomes a member of any specialized agency of the United Nations, or which is or hereafter becomes a party to the Statute of the International Court of Justice, or any other State to which an invitation has been addressed by the General Assembly of the United Nations.

2. This Convention shall be ratified and the instrument of ratification shall be deposited with the Secretary-General of the United Nations.

Article IX

1. This Convention shall be open for accession to all States referred to in article VIII.

2. Accession shall be effected by the deposit of an instrument of accession with the Secretary-General of the United Nations.

Article X

1. Any State may, at the time of signature, ratification or accession, declare that this Convention shall extend to all or any of the territories for the international relations of which it is responsible. Such a declaration shall take effect when the Convention enters into force for the State concerned.

2. At any time thereafter any such extension shall be made by notification addressed to the Secretary-General of the United Nations and shall take effect as from the ninetieth day after the day of receipt by the Secretary-General of the United Nations of this notification, or as from the date of entry into force of the Convention for the State concerned, whichever is the later.

3. With respect to those territories to which this Convention is not extended at the time of signature, ratification or accession, each State concerned shall consider the possibility of taking the necessary steps in order to extend the application of this Convention to such territories, subject, where necessary for constitutional reasons, to the consent of the Governments of such territories.

Article XI

In the case of a federal or non-unitary State, the following provisions shall apply:

(a) With respect to those articles of this Convention that come within the legislative jurisdiction of the federal authority, the obligations of the federal Government shall to this extent be the same as those of Contracting States which are not federal States;

(b) With respect to those articles of this Convention that come within the legislative jurisdiction of constituent states or provinces which are not, under the constitutional system of the federation, bound to take legislative action, the federal Government shall bring such articles with a favourable recommendation to the notice of the appropriate authorities of constituent states or provinces at the earliest possible moment;

(c) A federal State Party to this Convention shall, at the request of any other Contracting State transmitted through the Secretary-General of the United Nations, supply a statement of the law and practice of the federation and its constituent units in regard to any particular provision of this Convention, showing the extent to which effect has been given to that provision by legislative or other action.

Article XII

1. This Convention shall come into force on the ninetieth day following the date of deposit of the third instrument of ratification or accession.

2. For each State ratifying or acceding to this Convention after the deposit of the third instrument of ratification or accession, this Convention shall enter into force on the ninetieth day after deposit by such State of its instrument of ratification or accession.

Article XIII

1. Any Contracting State may denounce this Convention by a written notification to the Secretary-General of the United Nations. Denunciation shall take effect one year after the date of receipt of the notification by the Secretary-General.

2. Any State which has made a declaration or notification under article X may, at any time thereafter, by notification to the Secretary-General of the United Nations, declare that this Convention shall cease to extend to the territory concerned one year after the date of the receipt of the notification by the Secretary-General.

3. This Convention shall continue to be applicable to arbitral awards in respect of which recognition or enforcement proceedings have been instituted before the denunciation takes effect.

Article XIV

A Contracting State shall not be entitled to avail itself of the present Convention against other Contracting States except to the extent that it is itself bound to apply the Convention.

Article XV

The Secretary-General of the United Nations shall notify the States contemplated in article VIII of the following:

(a) Signatures and ratifications in accordance with article VIII;

(b) Accessions in accordance with article IX;

(c) Declarations and notifications under articles I, X and XI;

(d) The date upon which this Convention enters into force in accordance with article XII;

(e) Denunciations and notifications in accordance with article XIII.

Article XVI

1. This Convention, of which the Chinese, English, French, Russian and Spanish texts shall be equally authentic, shall be deposited in the archives of the United Nations.

2. The Secretary-General of the United Nations shall transmit a certified copy of this Convention to the States contemplated in article VIII.

ANNEX II

External Resources
(Interactive Guide, Bibliography, Case Law, Jurisdiction Briefs, Travaux Préparatoires, General Index)

Interactive Guide

http://nyc1958.org/guide

Bibliography

http://nyc1958.org/library

Case Law

http://nyc1958.org/cases

Jurisdiction Briefs

http://nyc1958.org/jurisdictions

Travaux Préparatoires

http://nyc1958.org/travaux

General Index

http://nyc1958.org/index

To access external resources on newyorkconvention1958.org, scan the QR code above using a smartphone, tablet or webcam with an appropriate reader application.

1958 NEW YORK CONVENTION GUIDE

Editorial Board

Experts:
Professor Emmanuel Gaillard and Professor George A. Bermann

Emmanuel Gaillard founded and heads Shearman & Sterling's 100-lawyers International Arbitration practice.

Professor Gaillard is universally regarded as a leading authority and a star practitioner in the fields of commercial and investment treaty arbitration. Through his practice, extensive writing and teaching, he has contributed to the shaping of contemporary international arbitration law.

He has advised and represented States, State-owned entities and companies in hundreds of international arbitration proceedings. He also regularly acts as arbitrator and expert witness. He has been appointed by France on the ICSID Panel of Arbitrators. In 2010, he was appointed as an expert by UNCITRAL for the drafting of the UNCITRAL Secretariat Guide on the New York Convention.

He is a Member of the Governing Board of the International Council for Commercial Arbitration (ICCA) and the SIAC Court of Arbitration. He is also a former Member of the LCIA Court of Arbitration (2002-2007).

As a Professor of Law, he has taught, in particular, in France (University of Paris XII, Sciences Po School of Law), Switzerland (MIDS) and the United States (Harvard Law School, Yale School of Law).

Professor Gaillard has written extensively on all aspects of arbitration law, in French and in English. He is the main author of *Fouchard Gaillard Goldman On International Commercial Arbitration*, a leading treatise in the field. He also has authored the first published essay on the legal theory of international arbitration. The volume, originally published in French (*Aspects Philosophiques du droit de l'arbitrage international*), was subsequently published in English (*Legal Theory of International Arbitration*), with translations in Arabic, Chinese, Spanish, Hungarian, Lithuanian, Portuguese, Italian and Russian.

He chairs the International Arbitration Institute (IAI) and was the first President and a co-founder of the International Academy for Arbitration Law.

George A. Bermann is the Jean Monnet Professor of EU Law, Walter Gellhorn Professor of Law, and the director for the Center for International Commercial and Investment Arbitration (CICIA) at Columbia Law School.

A Columbia Law School faculty member since 1975, Bermann teaches courses in transnational dispute resolution (international arbitration and litigation), European Union law, administrative law, and WTO law.

He is an affiliated faculty member of the School of Law of Sciences Po in Paris and the MIDS Masters Program in International Dispute Settlement in Geneva. He is also a visiting professor at the Georgetown Law Center. At the Law School, he founded both the European Legal Studies Center and the *Columbia Journal of European Law*.

Bermann is an active international arbitrator in commercial and investment disputes; chief reporter of the ALI's Restatement of the U.S. Law of International Commercial Arbitration; co-author of the *UNCITRAL Guide to the New York Convention on the Recognition and Enforcement of Foreign Arbitral Awards*; chair of the Global Advisory Board of the New York International Arbitration Center (NYIAC); co-editor-in-chief of the *American Review of International Arbitration*; and founding member of the governing body of the ICC Court of Arbitration and a member of its standing committee.

He has been a visiting scholar at the European Commission Legal Service in Brussels; the French Conseil d'Etat; the Max Planck Institute for Foreign Public Law and International Law in Heidelberg, Germany; and Princeton University's Center for International Studies.

His published works include: "International Arbitration and Private International Law", Hague Academy of International Law; *Interpretation and Application of the New York Convention by National Courts*; "Mandatory Rules in International Arbitration"; *Transnational Litigation:*

Cases & Materials on European Union Law; and Introduction to French Law. Among his most recent articles are "*Yukos v. Russia*: Unanswered Questions" and "International Standards as a Choice of Law Option."

Bermann has a J.D. and a B.A. from Yale University and an LL.M. from Columbia Law School. He holds honorary degrees from the Universities of Fribourg in Switzerland and Versailles-St. Quentin in France.

Executive Director and Coordinator: Dr. Yas Banifatemi

Yas Banifatemi is a partner in Shearman & Sterling's International Arbitration Group and leads the firm's Public International Law Practice.

She advises and represents States, State-owned entities and companies on public international law and international arbitration matters. She has acted as counsel and arbitrator in arbitration cases under the ICSID, UNCITRAL, ICC, LCIA, SCC, CRCICA and Swiss Arbitration Rules, with particular focus on investment protection, oil & gas and general commercial matters.

She is a Vice-President of the ICC International Court of Arbitration, and a Member of the LCIA Court of Arbitration.

She was the Chair of the Georgian International Arbitration Center (GIAC) Commission for Final Revision of the GIAC Arbitration Rules, as well as a Member of the SCC Rules Revision Committee.

She has contributed to a number of task forces and working groups, including World Bank's Investment Across Borders (IAB), the ILA Study Group on the Soft Law Instruments in Foreign Investment Law, the ILA Study Group on the Use of Private Law Principles for the Development of International Law, the IBA Investment Treaty Sub-Committee, and the IBA Recognition and Enforcement of Arbitral Awards Sub-Committee. She is also a Member of the Advisory Board of Africa International Legal Awareness (AILA).

Banifatemi has written extensively on all aspects of commercial and investment arbitration. She was a Member of the Editorial Board of ICSID

Review and the Editorial Board of the Yearbook on International Investment Law and Policy.

She teaches international arbitration at Panthéon-Sorbonne (University of Paris I) and Yale Law School. A former Director of Studies at The Hague Academy of International Law in 2004, she was invited to teach a Course at the 2019 session of the Academy, focussing on the powers of the arbitrators.

She was a co-founder and former co-Secretary-General of the International Academy for Arbitration Law.

UNCITRAL Secretariat

Renaud Sorieul is the Director of the International Trade Law Division (ITLD) of the United Nations Office of Legal Affairs, which functions as the substantive secretariat for the United Nations Commission on International Trade Law (UNCITRAL). He is the eighth Secretary of UNCITRAL since the Commission was established by the General Assembly in 1966. He took up his duties on 1 October 2008.

Corinne Montineri is a Legal Officer at the International Trade Law Division (ITLD) of the United Nations Office of Legal Affairs, which functions as the substantive secretariat for the United Nations Commission on International Trade Law (UNCITRAL). She has been the Secretary of the UNCITRAL Working Group II (Arbitration and Conciliation) since January 2009.

Monica Canafoglia is a Legal Officer at the International Trade Law Division (ITLD) of the United Nations Office of Legal Affairs, which functions as the substantive secretariat for the United Nations Commission on International Trade Law (UNCITRAL). Her responsiblities include the management of the Case Law on UNCITRAL Texts (CLOUT) system.

Cyril Emery is a Legal Officer at the International Trade Law Division (ITLD) of the United Nations Office of Legal Affairs, which functions as the substantive secretariat for the United Nations Commission on International Trade Law (UNCITRAL). He was the Librarian in charge of the UNCITRAL Law Library between May 2010 and July 2016.

Research Assistants

Team Leaders

Benjamin Siino

Margaret Clare Ryan

Research Assistants

Chloé Vialard

Julie Esquenazi

Emmanuel Jacomy

Paschalis Paschalidis

Ilija Mitrev Penusliski

Lara Kroop

Rachel Laut

Dimitris Katsikis

Marija Sobat

Knowledge Management & Website Team

Jean-Marc Elsholz

Bénédicte Soubrane

Maximilien Lemaire

Acknowledgement of Contributions

The Guide is the result of the cooperation between Professor Emmanuel Gaillard and Professor George Bermann, their research teams, and the UNCITRAL Secretariat.

In addition to the research assistants, the Experts' research teams have included the following contributors:

> Mary Arutyunyan, Tasiana Auguste, Gueorgui Babitchev, Leyla Bahmany, Ketevan Betaneli, Ana Boksay, Michael Bode, Simon Cassell, Jessica Crow, Youssef Daoud, Elise Edson, Ross Galvin, Claudia Gross (UNCITRAL), Becky Hurt, Jasmine Jin, Umaer Khalil, Paavana Kumar, Anne Leleu (logo design), Jo En Low, André Marini, Marina Matousekova, Olivia McNee, Carter Nelson, Gustavo Moser, Jenna Narayan, Diana Nielsen, Shannon O'Neill, Wesley Pang, Arianna Rosato, Benjamin Ross, Julia Salasky (UNCITRAL), Jaber Esfandi Sarafraz, Rudolf Simone-Pont, Karen Siwek, Anna Tevini, Pierre Viguier, Zuzana Vysudilova, Elizabeth Zorrilla.

The Guide also greatly benefited from contributions by the following institutions and individual contributors:

> Arbitration Institute of the Stockholm Chamber of Commerce (SCC); Associação Brasileira de Estudantes de Arbitragem (ABEArb); Cairo Regional Centre for International Commercial Arbitration (CRCICA); Centre of Documentation of the Italian Supreme Court; Deutsche Gesellschaft für Internationale Zusammenarbeit (GIZ); Deutsche Institution fur Schiedsgerichtsbarkeit e.V (DIS); DSP Publishing; Federal Court of Australia; High Court of Australia; Incorporated Council of Law Reporting (ICLR); New York International Arbitration Center (NYIAC); Permanent Secretariat, OHADA (Organisation pour l'Harmonisation en Afrique du droit des affaires); Republica e Cantone Ticino; Supreme Court of South Australia; Supreme Court of Tasmania; The People's Court Press (Supreme People's Court of the People's Republic of China) (人民法院出版社); Tribunal de Justiça do Estado de Sao Paulo; Domenico Di Pietro (Freshfields Bruckhaus Deringer LLP); Anna-Maria Tamminen (Hannes Snellman Attorneys Ltd); Niki K. Kerameus (Kerameus & Partner); Justinas Jarusevicius (Motieka & Audzevicius); Professor Jie

(Jeanne) Huang, S.J.D., Associate Professor of Law, Director of Foreign Affairs Department at the Shanghai Institute of Foreign Trade School of Law; Professor Liza Chen, Dean of Law School, Shanghai Institute of Foreign Trade School of Law; Sophie Tkemaladze (MCIArb, ADR Advisor for the Judicial Independence and Legal Empowerment Project (JILEP) implemented by the East-West Management Institute, Georgia); Christoph Liebscher (Wolf Theiss, Vienna, Austria); Charles Poncet (ZPG Avocats); Deyan Draguiev (CMS Cameron McKenna LLP-Bulgaria Branch); Grant Herholdt (ENS (Edward Nathan Sonnenbergs) South Africa); Duarte Gorjao Henriques (BCH Advogados).